Emerging Issues and Trends in INNOVATION AND TECHNOLOGY MANAGEMENT

Emerging Issues and Trends in INNOVATION AND TECHNOLOGY MANAGEMENT

Editor

Alexander Brem
University of Stuttgart, Germany

 **World Scientific**

NEW JERSEY · LONDON · SINGAPORE · BEIJING · SHANGHAI · HONG KONG · TAIPEI · CHENNAI · TOKYO

Published by

World Scientific Publishing Co. Pte. Ltd.

5 Toh Tuck Link, Singapore 596224

USA office: 27 Warren Street, Suite 401-402, Hackensack, NJ 07601

UK office: 57 Shelton Street, Covent Garden, London WC2H 9HE

British Library Cataloguing-in-Publication Data
A catalogue record for this book is available from the British Library.

EMERGING ISSUES AND TRENDS IN INNOVATION AND TECHNOLOGY MANAGEMENT

ISBN 978-981-124-771-2 (hardcover)
ISBN 978-981-124-772-9 (ebook for institutions)
ISBN 978-981-124-773-6 (ebook for individuals)

For any available supplementary material, please visit
https://www.worldscientific.com/worldscibooks/10.1142/12570#t=suppl

Desk Editor: Sandhya Venkatesh

Typeset by Stallion Press
Email: enquiries@stallionpress.com

Printed in Singapore

Preface

Few readers might ponder if another book on technological innovation is necessary. Read on to know why this book is necessary.

First, many articles are accepted and published each day in different journals. These numbers keep on growing since several years, and there is no end in sight. From a researcher's perspective, it becomes even more important to use established databases to make sure to capture all relevant articles. From a practitioner's view, it is another story. How should an interested person find relevant research results for his or her business practice? And even if they find it, how do they know if it is relevant? The idea for this book took form in such a background. The book contains recently published papers from the International Journal of Innovation and Technology Management. The papers in the book are carefully selected from an editorial perspective, bearing relevance and rigor in mind. With this approach, I hope that readers will enjoy getting a pre-selected overview of recent development in the field of technology and innovation management.

Second, this publication also serves as a kind of yearbook. Readers can know about relevant and emerging topics and questions related to such topics might be answered.

I sincerely hope you enjoy reading the book. Readers can contact me or the authors of chapters to give feedback or ask questions.

Alexander Brem
Editor-in-Chief,
International Journal of Innovation and Technology Management
University of Stuttgart, Germany
alexander.brem@eni.uni-stuttgart.de

© 2021 World Scientific Publishing Company
https://doi.org/10.1142/9789811247729_fmatter

CONTENTS

Preface   v

Chapter 1 Lean Startup Method Hampers Breakthrough
Innovations and Company's Innovativeness   1
Zornitsa B. Yordanova

Chapter 2 Involving Lead Users in Innovation: A Structured
Summary of Research on the Lead User Method 21
Alexander Brem, Volker Bilgram and Adele Gutstein

Chapter 3 An Exploratory Analysis on the Contextual Factors
that Influence Disruptive Innovation: The Case of Uber 49
*Andrea Urbinati, Davide Chiaroni, Vittorio Chiesa,
Simone Franzò and Federico Frattini*

Chapter 4 Exploring the Success Factors of Mobile Business
Ecosystems   77
*Juha Winter, Sandro Battisti, Thommie Burström
and Sakari Luukkainen*

Chapter 5 Innovation and Performance: An Empirical Study of
Russian Industrial Companies   101
Arkady Trachuk and Natalia Linder

Chapter 6 Sharing Economy: A Systematic Literature Review 125
Nivedita Agarwal and R. Steinmetz

Chapter 7 Understanding the Role of Team Member Personal
Style in Project Performance: Does the Type of
Innovation Matter?   143
Zvi H. Aronson, Richard R. Reilly and Gary S. Lynn

Chapter 8 The New Manufacturing: In Search of the Origins of the
Next Generation Manufacturing Start-Ups   183
*Xavier Ferrás-Hernández, Albert Armisen-Morell,
Anna Sabata-Alberich, Elisenda Tarrats-Pons
and Núria Arimany-Serrat*

Chapter 9   Identifying Emerging Technologies with Smart Patent
               Indicators: The Example of Smart Houses   203
               Carsten C. Guderian

Chapter 10   Evaluating the Agile-Stage-Gate Hybrid Model:
               Experiences from Three SME Manufacturing Firms   229
               Kasper Edwards, Robert G. Cooper, Tomas Vedsmand
               and Giulia Nardelli

Chapter 11   An Expanded Model of Success Factors for NPD
               Performance   265
               Tor Guimaraes, Ketan Paranjape and Mike Walton

Chapter 12   Internet of Management Artifacts: Internet of Things
               Architecture for Business Model Renewal   297
               Clarissa Rocha, Clarissa Fernandes Narcizo
               and Enrico Gianotti

Chapter 13   Building Blocks of Successful Digital Transformation:
               Complementing Technology and Market Issues   317
               Ulrich Lichtenthaler

Chapter 14   Global Diffusion of Innovation during the Fourth
               Industrial Revolution: The Case of Additive
               Manufacturing or 3D Printing   333
               Harm-Jan Steenhuis, Xin Fang and Tolga Ulusemre

Chapter 15   Barriers to Information Technology Adoption Within
               Small and Medium Enterprises: A Systematic
               Literature Review   369
               Marieme Chouki, Mohamed Talea, Chafik Okar
               and Razane Chroqui

Chapter 16   Innovating with Strangers; Managing Knowledge
               Barriers Across Distances in Cross-Industry Innovation   413
               Hilda Bø Lyng and Eric Christian Brun

Chapter 1

Lean Startup Method Hampers Breakthrough Innovations and Company's Innovativeness

Zornitsa B. Yordanova

Industrial Business Department
University of National and World Economy, Bulgaria
zornitsayordanova@abv.bg

The Lean Startup Method (LSM) provides a systematic management of innovation processes within startups and even within well-established companies. Despite its wide use by a lot of innovative companies, this study claims that using the LSM compromises the development of breakthrough and radical innovations and also companies' innovativeness is hindered given that companies usually follow the method and its principles blindly, without fully understanding its advantages and disadvantages. The aim of this study is to make a critical analysis of the LSM with focus on the above two statements and to test the critical findings from the analysis with the help of innovation experts. The methods employed in the study are mainly statistical ones like Pearson correlation, linear regression and statistical mean. The results show that innovation experts generally do agree with the formulated critical points (CPs) in the research but still use the method because they had not been aware of these disadvantages before entering the research as respondents. Another finding is the negative correlation between commercializing breakthrough innovations and using customers in the innovation development process. The contribution of the paper for the readers is mainly related to the impact of customer utilization within the breakthrough innovation development process and how using the LSM might compromise companies' innovativeness in general.

Keywords: Lean startup method; breakthrough and radical innovations; company innovativeness; innovation barrier; innovation development methods.

1. Introduction

The Lean Startup Method (LSM) has recently attracted the interest of many entrepreneurs, startups, serial innovators and researchers. Originally, it was designed for IT startups, but it has been increasingly used in companies of any size

---

This chapter was originally published in *International Journal of Innovation and Technology Management*, Vol. 15, No. 2, March 2018, published by World Scientific Publishing, Singapore. Reprinted with permission.

and industry, especially for managing innovation projects [Mueller and Thoring (2012)]. A lot of well-established companies have also turned their expectations to the method as a tool for fostering and boosting their innovation projects, activity processes, performance and management. Since its formal establishment in 2011 by introducing the book "How today's entrepreneurs use continuous innovation to create radically successful businesses" by Ries [2011], the method has been implemented within a lot of companies, especially within startups.

Being on the top of the wave, the method has been constantly developed by introducing new and extended concepts for its applications, elements and benefits. The benefits of the method have already been proven and a positive feedback has been received by lots of companies, but still researchers avoid performing critical analyses on the concept of the LSM. The aim of this study is to make a critical analysis of the LSM in terms of its characteristics that could hamper the innovativeness of companies and compromise the creation of breakthrough/radical innovations. The reason for conducting this research is that a lot of startups and innovative companies follow blindly the principles of the Lean Startup as it promises success. The research emphasizes the potential risks for company's innovativeness and the process of breakthrough/radical innovation creation and expressly criticizes that "blindness" in application of the LSM. An assumption and a limitation in the research is the unification of both kinds of innovations: breakthrough and radical ones. Their differentiation is not under discussion in the scope of this paper and they are both considered as being absolutely new innovations that create new markets.

The research has been inspired by the extremely increasing use of the method by startups and even well-established companies in their innovation processes. The paper is structured as follows: Sec. 2 presents a literature review on the main objectives of the study: the LSM, breakthrough innovations and company innovativeness, which is then used as a basis for a critical analysis on the formulated hypothesis. The critical analysis generates critical points (CPs) with focus on the hypotheses and for the purpose of testing the CPs, they are reformulated into questions. These questions are used for creating a questionnaire for innovation experts and the answers are interpreted so as to support or reject the hypotheses. The respondents used are widely selected in terms of industries and countries as the only criteria for their participation in the research is their belonging to innovation development within companies stating in their innovation strategies that they pursue innovations. The results are analyzed with statistical methods like linear regression, statistical mean and Pearson correlation.

The results from the research could be in favor of innovators, startups, serial innovators, researchers and practitioners in innovations. The paper contributes first with the critical analysis and the concrete CPs of the LSM and second with the results from the spread of the questionnaire which aims at supporting the hypotheses.

2. Literature Review

The aim of the literature review is to clarify the main stakeholders in the forthcoming critical analysis of the LSM. Literature review covers the LSM itself (as an object of the critical analysis), the term of breakthrough innovation (or radical innovation) and the term of a company's innovativeness (or organizational innovativeness, firm-level innovativeness, team innovativeness or group innovativeness) — as they are both subjects of the critical analysis. The literature review will help and explicate the developed hypotheses and is then used as a base for conducting the critical analysis. The critical analysis itself is built on the extracted elements and characteristics of the main subjects in the research: LSM, breakthrough innovations and companies' innovativeness.

2.1. *Lean startup method*

The LSM's purpose is to build and manage a continuous feedback loop with customers during the product development cycles [Maurya (2012)]. The core principles of LSM are based on the lean manufacturing approach by Toyota, including customers' centricity and value, as well as continuous flow of innovation activity, continuous improvement and improvisation [Ohno (1988); Womack *et al.* (1991)]. The method makes use of experiments of the company's business model on iterative principle, doing this in short sprints with a focus on learning [Blank and Dorf (2012)].

The main elements and characteristics of the method provide inherent information about what should be the direction and main activities focused by companies that use the method for their innovation development. Minimum Viable Product (MVP) is a specific term in the LSM that represents a version of a product enabling the product commercialization without fulfilling all possible improvements, completion and perfection. Split Testing is another contribution of the LSM to the innovation theory and practice. It helps innovators to identify the best combination of products, prices, or features by introducing in the market a set of products with various features and giving customers the opportunity to select the best version on their own. Build–Measure–Learn (B–M–L) process is the core process in the method that follows the main steps each innovation should follow according to the LSM. "Build" stands for creating innovation; "measure" stands for making some metrics and for assessing the innovation alignment to these metrics; and "learn" stands for taking lessons learnt. The LSM advices innovation projects to plan launching a prototype of the developed innovation early in the market, even if the prototype is of low quality and not fully completed. This principle as well as all the characteristics and concepts within the method are applicable for any kind of industry or company of any size. According to the LSM, entrepreneurship is a kind of management and requires a specific management approach. The method substantially tries to provide a whole set of methods that might be used as a methodology for innovation development [Yordanova (2017)]. As far as many other innovation development concepts use and employ customers within the innovation process, in the LSM, the customer cooperation and participation in this process is essential. Even more, the customers' role is idolized. Suppliers are within the group of potential customers/users. Their feedback (also known as "customer feedback" in the method) is even more important than the one of potential customers, because they have group knowledge for the market and the customers. The differentiation from other methods is the systematic approach and the use of customers during innovation development. Validation process/validated learning/verification is another cornerstone of the LSM. It is a process of gathering customer feedback during each innovation stage and incorporating this customer feedback within the incrementing innovation. It is used for minimizing risks and maximizing efficiency and profit in innovation projects. For achieving the previous requirement, the process of validation involves potential customers/users/other stakeholders in the validation/ development process. Scalability is a widespread term when it comes to innovations. It requires a business consisting of repeatable sales and a marketing roadmap to be created [Cooper and Vlaskovits (2010)]. Scalability could be indicated if there is a prodigious growth in revenue with a slight increase in expenses/investments [Zwilling (2013)]. Scalability in the LSM is among the main targets and an expected result from applying the method. Decision-Based Design (DBD) concept as part of the method aims at finding the most profitable design based on the enterprise needs, by means of understanding the project's big picture, while simultaneously paying attention to engineering details in order to meet the technical requirements together with the economic rationality [Pease et al. (2014)]. The LSM emphasizes on problem–solution and product–market approach. According to the LSM, using Canvas is more efficient and flexible instead of creating and following business plans. Measurements play an important role and are among the basic concepts in the LSM. They are especially useful and applicable in tests and experiments that are part of the main process, proclaimed by LSM. A specific concept in the LSM is pivoting. It is an option that allows changing the current strategy and adoption of the innovation according to the test results. This flexibility of the method reminds the Agile method. However, the Agile is a method absolutely different from the LSM, they are often used in parallel at organizations, especially in software development. The Customer Development Process is a systematic approach to 'getting out of the building' and testing and validating each of those hypotheses to discover a repeatable, scalable business model [Blank (2014)]. Rapid iteration is a characteristic of the LSM as well as of the Agile and requires fast running through the main cycle of the LSM's B–M–L process– the faster and lighter the better [Nirwan and Dhewanto (2015)]. The LSM targets a repeatable solution — as the traditional innovation management postulates, the LSM also requires products to represent a repeatable solution. Similar to the repetitiveness of the solution, the method also employs the concept of continuous deployment. The process of continuous deployment represents shortening the process of the product development and the product release. By doing this, innovators continue to develop and improve their products but they are doing this with the customers' help and feedback. Innovation Accounting is a new term in innovation theory that the LSM especially contributed to. It helps entrepreneurs to define, measure, and communicate progress. It acts as the accountancy of the innovation process.

2.2. *Breakthrough innovations*

Depending on the level of novelty, innovations can be incremental (continuous) or breakthrough (discontinuous). Incremental innovations focus on improving existing products and services [Bessant (2003)]. In the current study, breakthrough innovations are considered to be the same as radical innovations even if some literature argues the differentiation between both terms. Generally, radical innovations are new products for new markets [Crawford and Di Benedetto (2002)] and breakthrough innovations are new products that create completely new markets and usually refer to revolutionary changes in companies, markets and industries. They provide substantially higher customer benefits compared to current products/ services in the industry [Urban *et al.* (1996); Christensen and Raynor (2003)]. Both terms are used in this study and their meaning is equivalent.

Breakthrough innovations are important for companies in order to sustain long-term competitiveness [Lettl *et al.* (2005)]. Usually, breakthrough innovations are not an accident, but a consequence of systematic and purposeful activities as part of a company's innovativeness.

2.3. *Company's innovativeness*

The term "Company's Innovativeness" is used in the literature to describe organizational innovativeness, firm-level innovativeness, team innovativeness or group innovativeness. These terms explain the capability of companies to reflect the turbulent economic environment characterized by radical changes in a short time, companies' ability to be adoptive by developing a unique strategy with high standards of innovation, proactivity, calculated risk-taking and learning through analyses of changes taking place in customers' preferences and competitors' behavior [Preda (2013)]. Innovativeness reflects the tendency of companies to promote and support new ideas, experimentation and creative processes [Lumpkin and Dess (1996)]. The company's innovativeness is not measured by its new products, services and processes. It is the company's ability to generate and develop innovations as a systematic process. The innovativeness of a company is part of its characteristics, competences and part of its performance [Yordanova and Blagoev (2015)]. Usually company's innovativeness is related also to its ability to participate in networks and partnerships so to be able to extend and improve innovations. In the context of the research, the LSM supposes companies use such partnerships and networks with customers so innovations can be incrementally developed and improved by their potential customers. The method also encourages partnerships with suppliers and partner organizations, but it has nothing in common with ordinary partnership in innovation development as it is in bio-medical sciences [Coccia (2014)].

3. Methodology and Formulation of Hypotheses

With no intention of criticism on purpose, two internal conflicts within the concept of LSM contradict and allude to a logical gap. These two contradictory points are formulated as the main hypotheses in the current research. The purpose is for these two hypotheses to disclose some weaknesses, strengths, opportunities and threats of the LSM when it comes to breakthrough innovations and company's innovativeness.

Hypothesis 1: User involvement in the process of developing innovations (based on LSM) compromises the development of breakthrough/radical innovations.

Hypothesis 2: Companies' innovativeness is compromised as companies follow the LSM and its principles blindly, without fully understanding its advantages and disadvantages.

The methodology aims at proving the exposed hypotheses by elicitation and then testing some weaknesses of the LSM. The hypotheses themselves are a consequence of the author's observation that the methodology is likely to be followed and used blindly by any kind of companies, both startups and already established companies, both trying to make radical and incremental innovations. From here comes the assumption that some of these companies do not fully understand the method.

Both hypotheses were the starting point of creating CPs as a result from the author's critical analysis on the LSM with focus on these aspects, exposed in the hypotheses. The critical analysis is based on the literature overview, author's professional expertise and some informal interviews with LSM experts. The formulated 13 CPs from this critical analysis are reformulated into questions and together with three additional questions were sent to innovation experts for an opinion. The selected respondents in the research are experts, involved in innovation development and innovation management in companies that either use or do not use LSM as the main or subsidiary method for innovation development. The experts are from companies that state in their companies' innovation strategies that they pursue innovation development. The selection of the experts was made with the support of LinkedIn and some professional groups within the professional social platform. The main criteria in the selection procedure was the job position of the experts which had to be "product development", "innovation development", "R&D" or "project

management" for entering in the shortlisted experts list. The questionnaire was sent
to 250 experts via mass mailing.

The first 13 questions to experts are related to the CPs (from the author's critical
analysis):

CP1 — Do you think attempts to decrease innovation cost could damage your
innovation process?

The question refers the statement of Boehm [2006] who said the innovation process is
connected primarily with value creation, not with cost-reduction.

CP2 — Do you think it is feasible to use one and the same methodology for innovation management for all your innovation projects: product, process, marketing or
organizational innovations?

Some researchers claim [Mueller and Thoring (2012)] that the LSM is not a method
for managing any kind of innovation projects and innovation products because it
focuses only on product development activities in the process of project management. Other researches point out that development of radical innovations requires
completely different managerial approaches than incremental innovations
[Leifer *et al.* (2000); McDermott (1999); McDermott (2002)].

CP3 — Do you think involving users in the innovation process could rather result in
incremental than breakthrough innovations?

Lynn *et al.* [1996] state that since user involvement competence is well suited for
incremental innovations, it is low performed in the process of market researching in
radical innovation projects.

CP4 — Do you think user validation process might be compromised by the principle
of social perception when it comes to breakthrough innovations?

The theory of social perception asserts that forming impressions and making inferences usually is based on stereotypes and not on facts [Snyder and Decker Tanke
(1977); Bruner (1957)], videlicet, users might be a help to the innovation process,
for validation purposes as the LSM proposes or for identifying particular needs, but
still radical innovations require an individual approach than a method.

CP5 — Do you think user validation process might be misleading because of the self-
perception theory?

The theory of self-perception explains the effects of cognitive dissonance. It states
that people without experience on something tend to react like they have already
experienced the situation, not having in mind the specifics of the proper situation
itself [Bem (1972); Festinger and Carlsmith (1959); Zanna and Cooper (1974)].

This theory directly compromises the validation process and user involvement in testing innovations, especially radical ones. The self-perception shows that potential users could react to the innovation according to their own experiences and not to assess the innovation itself as they would be able to do it if the product is already completed and targeted to them with explanation, marketing and need-orientation.

CP6 — Do you think functional fixedness might trouble developing of breakthrough innovation if the innovation product is launched with no proper targeting and marketing?

Functional fixedness is an explanation of people's inadaptability, because of their user experience and mindset of doing things the traditional way [Arnon and Kreitler (1984)]. It is considered to be one of the biggest barriers for creative thinking. This concept significantly increases the importance of proper implementation and of defining the innovation target group, correctly positioning innovations, commercializing activities and clear communicating with potential users about the purposes of the innovation and needs that it is going to satisfy. For all these, a complete product is necessary. If potential users are involved at earlier stages, the results could be unreliable.

CP7 — Do you think that bounded rationality is a reason for inappropriate user involvement in breakthrough innovation development?

Concept of bounded rationality is an element of decision-making process, which implies that rationality of individuals is limited by the information they have at the moment, the cognitive limitations of their mindset, narrow-minded perception, and the scant time for a decision [Simon (1972)]. By involving potential users in the first stages of innovation projects as part of the validation learning process, results might provoke a pivot of the innovation concept based on misunderstanding by these users of the innovation idea (because it is not fully developed and completed). This is valid especially for breakthrough innovations, which are generally hardly accepted and the commercialization phase is marketing fortified and well-targeted.

CP8 — Do you think locality and national–cultural specifics of potential users in validation learning could deviate the breakthrough innovation process?

Locality and national–cultural specifics in validation learning might drive the innovation project towards an absolutely different or even wrong direction. In a study of innovations developed by mountain bikers, the researchers Lüthje et al. [2005] found that user-innovators almost always utilize "local" information–information already in their possession or generated by themselves–both to determine the need for and to develop the solutions for their innovations. That "local" mindset of users could baulk the scalability of radical innovations.

CP9 — Do you think that consumer inability to accept newness harms breakthrough innovation acceptance and customers' involvement in the innovation process is rather a limiting factor than an advantage?

A research by Reinders *et al.* [2010] shows the inappropriateness of using validation learning of the LSM in the process of creating and commercializing radical innovations. The validation process might fail in many cases of radical innovation, because of consumer inability to accept newness.

CP10 — Do you think that MVP could bring big troubles in industries like medicine, pharmaceutics, children's goods, vehicle production, and food production?

CP11 — Do you think that breakthrough innovations result from creative and non-methodological processes rather than a result from using an innovation development methodology?

CP12 — Do you think that making assumptions based on assumptions is one of the strongest tools in the innovation process and could be harmed if all assumptions are validated with customers?

CP13 — Do you think Split testing and continuous deployment provide risk to convert breakthrough innovations into incremental innovations?

The experts are asked to answer also three additional questions:

Q1: Does your company use LSM as part of its innovation development and innovation management processes?
Q2: Has your company commercialized breakthrough innovations in the last 2 years?

Table 1.   Methodology approach for hypotheses testing.

Approach for testing:	Relevant to hypothesis #:	Method for testing:
General confirmation by searching for the central tendency of acceptance of the CPs by experts no matter if they use or not the LSM. This analysis shows how reasonable and relevant CPs are to innovation development according to respondents' opinion and how these experts accept the CPs. The results of this analysis are presented by searching for the statistical mean of all CPs answers.	H1 and H2	Statistical mean
Seek for a positive correlation between using LSM and user involvement in innovation development (Q1 and Q3). Such a correlation will be a starting point for considering that all companies using LSM involve users in the process of developing innovations.	H1	Pearson correlation analysis

(Continued)

Table 1. (Continued)

Approach for testing:	Relevant to hypothesis #:	Method for testing:
Seek for a negative correlation between using LSM and having commercialized breakthrough innovations in the last 2 years (Q1 and Q2). Such a negative correlation will provide a proof of inconsistency between using the LSM and creating successful breakthrough innovations.	H1 and H2	Pearson correlation analysis
CPs from 3 to 9 which focus on customer utilization in the innovation development process and reveal some critical elements of user involvement in that type of innovation development. The confirmation of these CPs by the respondents is considered as a confirmation of some disadvantages of the LSM and especially of user involvement in breakthrough innovation development. The statistical mean of these 7 answers is executed and it is used in a Linear Regression as a dependent variable. The statistical average mean of CP 3 to 9 is analyzed in relation to using the LSM (Q1) and involving users in innovation development (Q3). The analysis seeks for a correlation/dependency between awareness of these disadvantages, using LSM and involving users in the innovation process. If such awareness exists, these companies blindly follow the LSM.	H2	Linear Regression
Seeking for a correlation between Q3 (using customers in innovation development) and Q2 (breakthrough innovation performance). Existing positive correlation will deny the H1 and a strong negative correlation will confirm it.	H1	Pearson correlation analysis
Searching for a positive correlation between confirming CPs and using LSM. If such exists, it would mean that the experts confirm the CPs and still use LSM. Proving of this test would mean blindly following the LSM and compromising company's innovativeness. The test is executed by calculating the average statistical mean of all CPs and then using it for Pearson correlation analysis for the purposes of revealing the correlation between accepting CPs and using LSM.	H2	Pearson correlation analysis

Q3: Do you involve users in your company's innovation development?

The hypotheses are tested according to the described methodology in Table 1.

4. Results

In the phase of empirical research, 151 questionnaires were returned with answers (60% response rate). The volunteer experts' details are given as a summary in Appendix. The information includes companies' industry and expertise in innovation development and innovation management.

The results from the research are shown in the paper as they are described in the methodology. The tool used for the statistical analyses is SPSS, v.19. The interpretation of the results is in the discussion part of the study. The selected statistical methods of analysis were selected according to the desired objectives of the study and the relevance to the data (binomial data, number of respondents).

5. Discussion and Results Interpretation

The **first test** of the gathered data is about finding the statistical mean of each CPs answers. The results are presented in Table 2. The statistical mean explains how the proper CP is accepted by the respondents (the questions are "do you think" style with dichotomous scale "Y-1" and "N-0"). The results show that all tested CPs are accepted from more than 50% of the respondents which could be considered as general acceptance of the substantiality and validity of the formulated CPs. Even more, some of the CPs gathered acceptance from more than 70% of the respondents. These are: CPs 5, 6, 10 and 13. These four CPs refer to both hypotheses. The general acceptance of the CPs gives an assumption that the respondents would generally agree with the stated negative points of the LSM.

As user involvement in the innovation process is just one of the features of the LSM, the **second test** aims at proving if all the respondents using the LSM apply that feature of the concept. The results from this second test are presented in Table 3. The purpose of this test is to be a starting point of further analyses and a generalization that could summarize the statement that companies which use the LSM also use customers in their innovation processes. The results from the performed Pearson correlation analysis between using the concept of the LSM in general and involving customers in innovation processes is positive and significant. The Sig. 2-tailed level is 0.000 which shows that the test is significant and reliable. The correlation from the analysis is 0.548. It means that there is a positive correlation between using the LSM method and involving customers in the innovation processes. The results mean that 55% of the companies that involve customers in their innovation processes at least partially use the LSM. It also means that at least 55% of those companies who already use the LSM also involve customers in their innovation processes. The correlation is strong enough to generally conclude that companies implementing the LSM use customers in their innovation development and management. That generalization is important for the research as the focus and the cornerstone of the hypothesis is a criticism exactly of customer involvement in innovation development and innovation process by default as the LSM states.

The **third test** aims at analyzing the correlation between a company's appliance of the LSM (Q1) and its breakthrough innovation performance in the last two years. The result from the Pearson correlation in Table 4 is negative (-0.586). That test proves that using the LSM is in conflict and trouble breakthrough innovation performance and commercialization (H1).

The **fourth test** aims at searching for a correlation/dependency between awareness of the mentioned disadvantages related to user involvement in

Table 2.   General acceptance of the formulated CPs — Mean of CPs.

		CP1	CP2	CP3	CP4	CP5	CP6	CP7	CP8	CP9	CP10	CP11	CP12	CP13
N	Valid	151	151	151	151	151	151	151	151	151	151	151	151	151
	Missing	0	0	0	0	0	0	0	0	0	0	0	0	0
Mean		0.56	0.53	0.52	0.67	0.71	0.76	0.68	0.60	0.62	0.81	0.64	0.61	0.70
Std. Error of Mean		0.041	0.041	0.041	0.038	0.037	0.035	0.038	0.040	0.040	0.032	0.039	0.040	0.038
Std. Deviation		0.498	0.501	0.501	0.472	0.456	0.428	0.467	0.492	0.488	0.395	0.481	0.490	0.462
Variance		0.248	0.251	0.251	0.223	0.208	0.183	0.218	0.242	0.238	0.156	0.231	0.240	0.213

Statistics

Table 3. Pearson correlation analysis of using LSM and user involvement in innovation development (Q1 and Q3).

Correlations			
		Q1	Q3
Q1	Pearson Correlation	1	0.548**
	Sig. (2-tailed)		0.000
	N	151	151
Q3	Pearson Correlation	0.548**	1
	Sig. (2-tailed)	0.000	
	N	151	151

Note: **Correlation is significant at the 0.01 level (2-tailed).

Table 4. Pearson correlation between using the LSM (Q1) and commercializing breakthrough innovations (Q2).

Correlations			
		Q1	Q2
Q1	Pearson Correlation	1	−0.586**
	Sig. (2-tailed)		0.000
	N	151	151
Q2	Pearson Correlation	−0.586**	1
	Sig. (2-tailed)	0.000	
	N	151	151

Note: **Correlation is significant at the 0.01 level (2-tailed).

breakthrough innovation development (CP 3 to 9) in relation to using LSM (Q1) and involving users in the innovation process (Q3). The results are presented in Table 5. First, all CPs from 3 to 9 are generalized as one indexed-mean for each respondent (meanCust in the result section). The reason for that is the desired unification of the general acceptance and agreement with the statements that concern critics of using customers in breakthrough innovation process on a respondent level. The average result from each respondent's answers is used for analyzing the correlation with both factors: Q1 and Q3. Then a linear correlation analysis is performed. Its purpose is to analyze the dependency between confirming the criticism on customer utilization in breakthrough innovation process and how this confirmation refers to using the LSM and using customers within the innovation process. The results show a positive correlation between confirmations of CPs from

Table 5.   Linear regression — CPs from 3 to 9 in relation to breakthrough innovation performance (Q2) using LSM (Q1) and involving users in innovation development (Q3).

			Coefficients[a]			
		Unstandardized coefficients		Standardized coefficients		
Model		B	Std. Error	Beta	t	Sig.
1	(Constant)	0.557	0.030		18.850	0.000
	Q1	0.218	0.022	0.600	10.115	0.000
	Q2	−0.076	0.032	−0.199	−2.396	0.018
	Q3	0.044	0.030	0.118	1.472	0.143

[a]Dependent Variable: meanCust.

respondents and using the LSM (Q1). This concrete result confirms the H2 because respondents obviously accept the stated criticism of the LSM, but simultaneously use the method. The second part of these tests is about searching for a correlation between acceptances of CPs 3 to 9 and involving customers within the process of innovation development at the same time. Unfortunately, the results are not acceptable for making conclusions because of their low significance rate of 0.143. However, they showed positive correlation is too close to 0 and it is not reliable enough.

The **fifth test** aims at proving that user involvement in the innovation process troubles breakthrough innovation performance (Q2 to Q3). The results are presented in Table 6. The Pearson correlation analysis is used. The results show strong negative correlation (−0.803). It means that the more customers companies' involve in their innovation processes, the less breakthrough innovation they execute. This concrete test refers to the H1 and it could be considered as a proof, because of the ambiguity of the results.

Table 6.   Pearson correlation: User involvement in the innovation process troubles breakthrough innovation performance (Q2 to Q3).

	Correlations		
		Q2	Q3
Q2	Pearson Correlation	1	−0.803**
	Sig. (2-tailed)		0.000
	N	151	151
Q3	Pearson Correlation	−0.803**	1
	Sig. (2-tailed)	0.000	
	N	151	151

Note: **Correlation is significant at the 0.01 level (2-tailed).

Table 7.   Pearson correlation between confirming CPs and using LSM.

	Correlations		
		Mean	Q1
Mean	Pearson Correlation	1	0.493**
	Sig. (2-tailed)		0.000
	N	151	151
Q1	Pearson Correlation	0.493**	1
	Sig. (2-tailed)	0.000	
	N	151	151

Note: **Correlation is significant at the 0.01 level (2-tailed).

The final **sixth test** shows that there is a dependency between accepting the formulated CPs by the author and at the same time using the LSM. The results are presented in Table 7. The Pearson correlation demonstrates that between experts' confirmation of the formulated 13 CPs of the author and these experts' usage of the LSM there is a positive correlation. So the experts who tend to agree with the CPs actually use the method in their innovation development process. This test aims at providing arguments for proving the H2. The results are significant, as Sig. is equal to 0. The correlation itself is 0.493. That means that almost half of the experts had not been aware of the weaknesses of the LSM till entering the research or they are aware of them but could not affect the decision to use or not to use the method in their companies' innovation processes.

All the performed tests show arguments for accepting the stated hypotheses. As a result, the research and the performed analyses reach the following conclusions:

There are evidences proving that user's involvement in the process of developing innovations and using the LSM *per se* compromise the development of break-through/radical innovations.

During the research, several confirmations are also received that companies follow the LSM and its principles blindly, without fully understanding its advantages and disadvantages. That might seriously compromise their innovation process.

6. Conclusion

In conclusion, the following deductions could be made:

First, the LSM is not a panacea and should not be used in any kind of companies without an analysis of its appropriate utilization first.

The research provides enough evidence and proofs that there are some disadvantages of the main LSM elements and characteristics which should be taken into account while working with and/or relying on the method, as well as when using its tools.

The method also could hamper companies' innovativeness and also might compromise the breakthrough innovation process, especially if companies are not fully aware of the method's disadvantages and specifics. The research proves that actually experts and companies that took part in the research and use the LSM are not fully aware of the method's disadvantages.

Answering both hypotheses was the purpose of this research but not the only final goal of the study. Unequivocal proof is impossible. However, all the evaluation methods employed in this study prove some negative impacts of the LSM on the company's innovativeness and on the breakthrough innovation process. Answers of 151 innovation experts on innovation management also tipped the scales in favor of the hypotheses.

The study contributes with a deep critical analysis on the LSM and emphasizes the chance and the way how the method could hamper innovativeness of companies and their efforts to create breakthrough innovations. Around 13 CPs had been elicited and then assessed with different evaluation and statistical techniques. The final conclusion is that the LSM should be well investigated and understood by companies before implementing it within their innovation processes and operational activities during innovation development and management.

The author plans to continue to explore the LSM and its impact and application. The topic how the LSM affects innovation processes and innovation projects should be explored in depth. As a sequel of the research, the author intends to go further and evaluate how the LSM might affect each of the main perspectives of innovative products: functional, aesthetic, technological, and quality [Scott Swan Kotabe and Allred (2005)] and the interaction between the LSM and open innovation models.

References

Arnon, R. and Kreitler, Sh. (1984). Effects of meaning training on overcoming functional fixedness. *Current Psychological Research and Reviews*, **3**, 4: 11–24.

Bem, D. J. (1972). *Self-Perception Theory, Advances in Experimental Social Psychology*, Vol. 6. Academic Press Inc., USA, pp. 33–39.

Bessant, J. (2003). *High-Involvement Innovation: Building and Sustaining Competitive Advantage Through Continuous Change*, Wiley, Chichester, pp. 23–41. ISBN: 978-0-470-84707-7.

Blank, S. and Dorf, B. (2012). *The Startup Owner's Manual: The Step-by-Step Guide for Building a Great Company*. K&S Ranch Inc., pp. 19–28.

Blank, S. (2014). How Investors Make Better Decisions: The Investment Readiness Level, Available at: http://steveblank.com.

Boehm, B. W. (2006). *Value-Based Software Engineering: Overview and Agenda, Value-Based Software Engineering*. Springer, Berlin Heidelberg, pp. 3–14. doi: 10.1007/3-540-29263-2_1.

Bruner, J. S. (1957). On perceptual readiness. *Psychological Review*, **64**: 123–152.

Christensen, C. M. and Raynor, M. (2003). *The Innovator's Solution: Creating and Sustaining Successful Growth.* Harvard Business School Press, Boston, Massachusetts.

Coccia, M. (2014). Converging scientific fields and new technological paradigms as main drivers of the division of scientific labor in drug discovery process: The effects on strategic management of the R&D corporate change. *Technology Analysis & Strategic Management*, **26**, 7: 733–749. doi: 10.1080/09537325.2014.882501.

Cooper, B. and Vlaskovits, P. (2010). *The Entrepreneur's Guide to Customer Development: A Cheat Sheet to The Four Steps to the Epiphany.* Cooper-Vlaskovits, pp. 90–110.

Crawford, M. C. and Di Benedetto, A. (2002). *New Product Management*, 7th edition. McGraw Hill, Boston, pp. 9–13. ISBN-13:978-0072471632.

Festinger, L. and Carlsmith, J. M. (1959). Cognitive consequences of forced compliance. *Journal of Abnormal and Social Psychology*, **58**: 203–211.

Leifer, R., McDermott, C. M., O'Connor, G. C., Peters, L., Rice, M. and Veryzer, R. (2000). *Radical Innovation: How Mature Companies Can Outsmart Upstarts.* Harvard Business, School Press, Boston.

Lettl, C., Herstatt, C. and Gemuenden, H. G. (2005). Learning from users for radical innovation. *International Journal of Technology Management*, **33**, 1: 25–45.

Lumpkin, G. T. and Dess, G. (1996). Clarifying the entrepreneurial orientation construct and linking it to performance. *Academy of Management Review*, **21**, 1: 135172.

Lüthje, C., Herstatt, C. and Hippel, E. (2005). User-innovators and "local" information: The case of mountain biking. *Research Policy*, **34**, 6: 951–965.

Lynn, G. S., Morone, J. G. and Paulson, A. S. (1996). Marketing and discontinuous innovation: The probe and learn process. *California Management Review*, **38**, 3: 8–37.

Maurya, A. (2012). *Running Lean: Iterate from Plan A to a Plan That Works*, 2nd edition. O'Reilly Media, USA, pp. 4–10. ISBN-10: 1449305172.

McDermott, C. (1999). Managing radical product development in large manufacturing firms: A longitudinal study. *Journal of Operations Management*, **17**, 6: 631–644.

McDermott, C. and O'Connor, G. (2002). Managing radical innovation: An overview of emergent strategy issues. *The Journal of Product Innovation Management*, **19**: 424–438.

Müeller, R. and Thoring, K. (2012). *Leading Innovation through Design: Proceedings of the DMI 2012 International Research Conference.* University of Virginia, pp. 181–192.

Nirwan, M. D. and Dhewanto, W. (2015). Barriers in implementing the lean startup methodology in Indonesia — case study of B2B startup. *Procedia — Social and Behavioral Sciences*, **169**: 23–30. doi: 10.1016/j.sbspro.2015.01.282.

Ohno, T. (1988). *Toyota Production System: Beyond Large-Scale Production.* Productivity Press, Cambridge, pp. 23–70.

Pease, J. F., Dean, J. H. and Van Bossuyt, D. L. (2014). Lean design for the developing world: Making design decisions through the use of validated learning techniques in the developing, world. *Proceedings ASME 2014 International Mechanical Engineering Congress and Exposition*, Paper No. IMECE2014-36612, pp. V011T14A040, Montreal, Quebec, Canada, November 14–20, 2014.

Preda, G. (2013). The influence of entrepreneurial orientation and market-based organizational learning of the firm's strategic innovation capability. *Management & Marketing Challenges for the Knowledge Society*, **8**, 4: 607–622.

Reinders, M. J., Frambach, R. T. and Schoormans, J. P. L. (2010). Using product bundling to facilitate the adoption process of radical innovations. *Journal of Product Innovation Management*, **27**: 1127–1140. doi: 10.1111/j.1540-5885.2010.00775.x.

Ries, E. (2011). *The Lean Startup: How Today's Entrepreneurs Use Continuous Innovation to Create Radically Successful Businesses.* Crown Business, USA.

Scott Swan, Kotabe, M. and Allred, B. (2005). Exploring robust design capabilities, their role in creating global products, and their relationship to firm performance. *Journal of Product Innovation Management*, **22**, 2: 144–164. doi: 10.1111/j.0737-6782.2005.00111.x.

Simon, H. (1972). *Decision and Organization.* North — Holland publishing company, Amsterdam; Netherlands, pp. 161–164.

Snyder, M. and Decker, T. (1977). Social perception and interpersonal behavior: On the self-fulfilling nature of social stereotypes. *Journal of Personality and Social Psychology*, **35**, 9: 655–666.

Urban, B., Weinberg, D. and. Hauser, J. R. (1996). Premarket forecasting for really-new products. *Journal of Marketing*, **60**: 47–60.

Womack, J. P., Jones, D. T. and Roos, D. (1991). *The Machine that Changed the World: The Story of Lean Production, Harper Perennial.* HarperCollins, USA.

Yordanova, Z. B. (2017). Knowledge transfer from lean startup method to project management for boosting innovation projects' performance. *International Journal of Technological Learning Innovation and Development*, **9**, 4: 293–309. doi: 10.1504/IJTLID.2017.10010040.

Yordanova, Z. and Blagoev, D. (2015). Company innovative leadership model. *Economic Alternatives*, Issue 2, pp. 5–16.

Zanna, M. P. and Cooper, J. (1974). Dissonance and the pill: An attribution approach to studying the arousal properties of dissonance. *Journal of Personality and Social Psychology*, **29**, 5: 703–709.

Zwilling, M. (2013). 10 Tips For Building The Most Scalable Startup, Forbes, Entrepreneurs section, Sep 6, 2013, available at: https://www.forbes.com/sites/martinzwilling/2013/09/06/10-tips-for-building-the-most-scalable-startup/#3d8724475f28.

Appendix 1

Sectors and roles in innovation process	Average of Expertise (Y)
Banking & finance	**9**
IT expert	11
Market researcher	7
Product manager	5
Product specialist	5
Project manager	16
R&D expert	10
Startup founder	5
Beauty and healthcare	**7**
IT expert	1
Market researcher	5
Marketing manager	9
Product manager	19
Product specialist	10
R&D expert	3
Startup founder	6

Appendix 1. (*Continued*)

Sectors and roles in innovation process	Average of Expertise (Y)
Pharmacy	**9**
Engineer	2
IT expert	8
Market researcher	11
Product manager	11
Project manager	11
Startup founder	8
Tester	5
Food production	**8**
IT expert	7
Market researcher	9
Product manager	5
Project manager	4
R&D expert	14
Startup founder	10
Household products	**5**
IT expert	5
Market researcher	4
Product manager	5
Project manager	4
Startup founder	7
International commerce	**14**
Project manager	14
IT	**7**
IT expert	5
Market researcher	7
Product manager	8
Product specialist	9
Project manager	7
R&D expert	6
Startup founder	8
Tourism	**6**
IT expert	6
Market researcher	8
Product manager	7
Product specialist	3
Project manager	8
Startup founder	7
Trading with food	**9**
IT expert	7
Market researcher	12
Product manager	11
Product specialist	10
Project manager	7
R&D expert	9

Biography

Zornitsa B. Yordanova is a Chief Asst. Professor at the Industrial Business Department in University of National and World Economy, Bulgaria. She currently gives lectures in business innovations, innovation projects, investment projects and economics of enterprise. Zornitsa Yordanova has received her Ph.D. in the area of Business Innovations Management in 2015 from the University of National and World Economy, Sofia, Bulgaria. Her research interest includes innovation projects, user-lead innovation, innovation management, business management information systems. Her working experience is the banking and the IT sector. She is also a certified PMP® and CSM® in the area of project management and she is a practitioner in the field of business application software projects.

Chapter 2

Involving Lead Users in Innovation: A Structured Summary of Research on the Lead User Method[*]

Alexander Brem[†,‡,¶], Volker Bilgram[§,‖] and Adele Gutstein[†,**]

[†]*Friedrich-Alexander-Universität Erlangen-Nürnberg*
Chair of Technology Management
Fürther Str. 246c, 90429 Nürnberg, Germany

[‡]*University of Southern Denmark*
Mads Clausen Institute
Alsion 2, 6400 Sonderborg, Denmark

[§]*HYVE the Innovation Company*
Schellingstr. 45, 80799 München, Germany
[¶]*alexander.brem@fau.de*
[‖]*volker.bilgram@hyve.net*
[**]*adele.gutstein@gmail.com*

Research on the lead user method has been conducted for more than thirty years and has shown that the method is more likely to generate breakthrough innovation than traditional market research tools. Based on a systematic literature review, this paper shows a detailed view on the broad variety of research on lead user characteristics, lead user processes, lead user identification and application, and success factors. The main challenge of the lead user method as identified in literature is the resource issue regarding *time, manpower*, and *costs*. Also, internal *acceptance and the processing* of the method have been spotted in literature, as well as the intellectual property protection issue. From the starting point of the initial lead user method process introduced by Lüthje and Herstatt (2004), results are integrated into a revisited view on the lead user method process. In addition, concrete suggestions for corporate realization options are given. The article closes with limitations and future research suggestions.

Keywords: Lead user; user innovation; lead user method; user involvement; lead user workshop.

1. Introduction

Several studies investigated the impact of customers on new product development (NPD) and found that their involvement, particularly in the early and late stages of

---

[¶]Corresponding author.

This chapter was originally published in *International Journal of Innovation and Technology Management*, Vol. 15, No. 3, March 2018, published by World Scientific Publishing, Singapore. Reprinted with permission.

the NPD process, can enhance product success [Gruner and Homburg (2000)]. Additionally, lead users were found to be of special value to companies' innovation activities (e.g. Sänn [2017]). In comparison to ordinary customers, lead users are ahead of market trends and provide both need and solution information [von Hippel (1986); Urban and von Hippel (1988)]. One study revealed that intensified collaboration with lead users during the NPD process increases product variety and has a significant impact on NPD speed [Al-Zu'bi and Tsinopoulos (2012)].

The lead user method to systematically identify lead users and integrate them into companies' ideation processes was developed in the 1980s by Eric von Hippel [1986]. Since then, this method has been constantly advanced and several applications show that it can generate innovative ideas and concepts that may even lead to radically new products and services (e.g. Olson and Bakke [2001]; Lilien *et al.* [2002]; Herstatt *et al.* [2002]; Lüthje and Herstatt [2004]). Moreover, when applying the lead user approach, cross-functional teamwork and efficiency of the NPD process can improve [Olson and Bakke (2002)]. A study by Eisenberg [2011] showed that the lead user method leads to new products and services, strategic directions, markets, applications, and technology platforms. Furthermore, Lilien *et al.* [2002] found that the lead user method generates concepts of greater commercial potential than concepts developed by traditional idea generation techniques.

These findings show the high potential of the lead user method; however, surprisingly, companies rarely repeat the method or integrate it into their standard NPD processes. This phenomenon was already underlined by Reichwald and Piller [2009] and Diener and Piller [2010], who stated that only few companies periodically and systematically conduct lead user projects in practice. In the context of overall challenges and barriers to open innovation, Chesbrough and Brunswicker [2014] noted the organizational changes necessary to institutionalize open innovation methods and tools. This might also be the case for the application of the lead user method.

Against this background, this paper aims to show detailed insights into the current state of the lead user method and its success.

2. Literature Review Approach

To identify relevant literature for the underlying research, a systematic literature review was conducted following the methodological approach of Dahlander and Gann [2010]. Because literature in the field of lead user research is broad and reaches from a single analysis of its characteristics [Lüthje and Herstatt (2004); Morrison *et al.* (2004); Schreier and Prügl (2008)] to the diffusion of lead user innovations [Schreier *et al.* (2007)], this review focuses on literature on the lead user method itself. Therefore, step four in our review design explicitly emphasizes the "lead user method," "concept," and "process."

Table 1. Eight steps of systematic literature review.

Step 1:	Screening of literature by keyword search for "lead* user" in EBSCOhost Business Source Complete and ISI Web of Knowledge: 165 publications identified (03.12.2013)
Step 2:	Using limiters in title, keyword, and abstract, and limit search to journals (EBSCO) and articles and reviews (ISI Web of Knowledge): 107 publications remaining (03.12.2013)
Step 3:	Elimination of duplicates (24) and French papers (3): 80 publications remaining
Step 4:	Screening of abstracts of remaining publications for lead user method, concept, or process: 14 publications remaining
Step 5:	Full text review of publications regarding the lead user method in theory or studies and selection of final publications: seven publications remaining
Step 6:	Review of references of remaining publications to identify further publications on the lead user method that have to date not been included: three publications
Step 7:	Integration of further publications and handbooks of researchers known in the field of the lead user method but that have to date not been included in the literature review: three publications
Step 8:	Consolidation of relevant publications into the final literature basis for the review: 13 publications

The literature review process is presented in detail in Table 1. The EBSCOhost Business Source Complete and the ISI Web of Knowledge databases were used because they are considered most comprehensive for scholarly work in this field. With the aim of receiving a complete list of relevant studies, papers from the reference analysis and books and handbooks written by key researchers in the field of lead user research were identified and included. Moreover, other relevant publications were included that are related to the research subject.

3. Understanding Lead Users and the Lead User Method

3.1. *Lead users*

Research on lead users arose from research on sources of innovation, which revealed that users frequently play an important role in the development of new products. Innovations are often initiated through specific users' needs and requests [Utterback *et al.* (1975); von Hippel (1977); Biemans (1991)], a concept that is rooted in the market-pull concept [Brem and Voigt (2009)]. In some industries, individual users or user firms[a] rather than manufacturers were the initial developers of new products and processes [von Hippel (2005)]. In the semi-conductor industry, 67 percent of the innovations were user-driven [von Hippel (1977)]. However, the majority of innovations related to industrial products, such as CAD/CAM systems [Mantel and Meredith (1986)], scientific instruments [von Hippel (1976)], and medical equipment [Shaw (1985)], were initially developed by users. These examples show that users dominated the entire innovation process, from idea generation to prototyping and the building of the first devices [Lüthje and Herstatt (2004)]. In the consumer

---

[a] User firms are composed of one or a small number of leading-edge user(s) who develop, produce, and sell innovations and benefit from their use [Shah (2000)].

industry, 56% of commercially important innovations for skateboard, snowboarding, and windsurfing equipment were developed first by users or user firms [Shah (2000)]. These users benefitted from using the invention, participating in small companies, as well as producing and selling these innovations [Shah (2000)].

Other research investigated the share of innovative users among a user population. For instance, [Lüthje and Herstatt (2004)] found that 37% of users in the outdoor industry improved existing products or even invented new ones. Furthermore, large shares of innovative users can be found in the fields of library information systems [Morrison *et al.* (2000)], medical surgery equipment [Lüthje and Herstatt (2004)], Apache server security systems [Franke and von Hippel (2003)], and mountain-biking equipment [Lüthje *et al.* (2002)]. In conclusion, literature shows that innovative users are frequently initial developers of new products or processes, and that innovation activities are not limited to a small group of users.

At the same time, researchers found that user innovation is concentrated among lead users. Several studies, such as the previously mentioned ones on library information systems, medical surgery equipment, and even the Apache server security system, revealed that correlations between innovation by users and lead user status are highly significant [Morrison *et al.* (2000);[b] Lüthje *et al.* (2002); Franke and Shah (2003)].[c] In addition, Urban and von Hippel [1988] found that 87% of lead users engaged in innovation, in contrast to 1% of non-lead users. Further studies revealed that "lead userness" is significantly linked to the commercial attractiveness of lead user innovations [Morrison *et al.* (2000); Franke *et al.* (2006)]. Franke *et al.* [2006] found that a higher intensity of lead user characteristics leads to greater commercial attractiveness of the lead user innovation.

Because lead users are "rare subjects" [von Hippel *et al.* (2009)] and challenges exist in identifying them [Olson and Bakke (2001); Lüthje and Herstatt (2004)], further research investigated the characteristics of lead users to identify and differentiate them from more ordinary users. In line with the definition by von Hippel [1986], theoretical and empirical research confirmed that lead users are *ahead of the market, face new needs earlier than ordinary users,* and *benefit* greatly if they achieve a solution to these needs [Lüthje and Herstatt (2004)]. Users' *dissatisfaction* with existing products offered on the market and *product development activities or modifications* are additional lead user characteristics and reflect high benefit expectations [Urban and von Hippel (1988); Lüthje and Herstatt (2004)]. Lead users possess more *consumer knowledge* and *use experience* in the field of investigation than ordinary users [Schreier and Prügl (2008)]. They have a high internal *locus of*

---

[b] Morrison *et al.* [2004] found that being a lead user or not is not dichotomous. Instead, the degree of the leading-edge status (LES) is distributed in a unimodal manner. Therefore, the authors argue that talking about "lead users" and "others" dissipates valuable information. For the purpose of this paper, the terms "lead user" and "non-lead user/ordinary user" are further used, underlying the assumption that lead users have a high degree of LES and non-lead users have a low degree of LES.

[c] Schreier and Prügl [2008] provided a detailed overview of studies that reveal evidence of innovations by lead users.

control [Schreier and Prügl (2008)] and demonstrate stronger *domain-specific innovativeness* [Schreier *et al.* (2007)]. Furthermore, lead users *adopt* new products faster than non-lead users [Morrison *et al.* (2004); Schreier and Prügl (2008)]. Related to this point is the finding that lead users are *opinion leaders* and can help accelerate the diffusion process of new products [Schreier *et al.* (2007)].

Bilgram *et al.* [2008] proposed that, today, *online participation* is a pre-requisite of lead userness. Because lead users are characterized by being unsatisfied with an existing product and, therefore, strongly invest in obtaining solutions, the internet offers significant potential (e.g. social media such as blogs and communities). In particular, new forms of social media offer the potential for the integration of lead users [Ernst *et al.* (2013); Ernst and Brem (2017)]. This concept is emphasized by several empirical studies that showed that users with strong lead user characteristics enjoy sharing knowledge in online communities, communicate their needs and preferences concerning products, and exchange use experiences [Sawhney *et al.* (2005); Jeppesen and Frederiksen (2006); Jeppesen and Laursen (2009)]. Additionally, the existence of virtual lead user communities underlines the notion that lead users act and engage in the online environment [Mahr and Lievens (2012)]. Related to this point are findings that indicate that lead users are *intrinsically motivated* and freely *reveal product modifications* respective of their knowledge [Morrison *et al.* (2000); Franke and Shah (2003)].

3.2. *Lead user method*

The lead user method is a qualitative, process-oriented approach that aims at the systematic and active integration of lead users to develop new ideas and concepts for products and services [von Hippel (1986); Herstatt and von Hippel (1992)] and new strategic directions, markets, applications, and technology platforms [Eisenberg (2011)]. Regarding process classification, the lead user method is embedded in the early phase of NPD, when ideas are generated and concepts are developed [Khurana and Rosenthal (1997); Kim and Wilemon (2002)]. There is no consistent understanding of *the* lead user method in the reviewed literature. The method can be differentiated between two possibilities to profit from lead users [Reichwald and Piller (2009); Diener and Piller (2010)]. First, companies search for existing lead user innovations and transfer them into their company as described in the case of the rodeo kayak industry [Baldwin *et al.* (2006)]. This interpretation of the lead user method depends on the behavior of lead users and assumes that they have already created innovative solutions. From a company's point of view, this process is typically random and non-systematic [Diener and Piller (2010)]. Second, a company identifies lead users to systematically and actively integrate them into the innovation process by conducting a workshop to develop new ideas and concepts for a given problem, as was done in several cases in the existing literature (e.g. Urban and von Hippel [1988]; Herstatt and von Hippel [1992]; von Hippel *et al.* [1999]; Olson and

Bakke [2001]; Herstatt *et al.* [2002]). This approach is used in the underlying paper because it represents a more popular understanding of the method.

3.3. *Comparison of the lead user method with other user integration approaches*

The lead user method and traditional market research differ in several process, and result-related aspects and in their degree of innovativeness. Hence, traditional market research techniques often solely create incremental improvements [Herstatt *et al.* (2002); Lilien *et al.* (2002)]. This phenomenon is attributable to the fact that most customers are strongly constrained by their real-world experiences, preventing them from thinking freely about using familiar objects in a novel manner (functional fixedness) [Duncker (1945); Adamsons and Taylor (1954); Adamsons (1952); von Hippel (1986)]. In contrast, the lead user method does not focus on representative users but on lead users, who are innovative personalities, and often stem from analog industries. A different background and skill set enables lead users to break with certain fixations in a given area and adapt their knowledge to the new field or recombine it. Thus, lead users from analog markets are crucial to address functional fixedness and reapply knowledge in new fields of application. Lead userness is a domain-specific attribute rather than a general personality trait [Franke (2014)]. Hence, not every creative and innovative individual can or should be regarded as a lead user in every field. Furthermore, this method collects both need and solution information by involving lead users [Lilien *et al.* (2002); Eisenberg (2011)]. Perceiving needs long before the mass of consumers do so and being ahead of trends enable lead users to create more radical innovation. Therefore, the lead user method is more likely to generate breakthrough innovation than traditional market research [Herstatt *et al.* (2002); Lilien *et al.* (2002)].

Apart from the lead user approach, other methods were developed to integrate external knowledge into companies' innovation activities (open innovation), such as focus groups. Focus groups apply a group discussion technique in which one moderator and a group of eight to 10 representative customers discuss views and opinions about a predefined set of topics [Van Kleef *et al.* (2005)]. Within the NPD process, focus groups are applied to explore new concepts, identify new opportunities, and generate ideas [McQuarrie and McIntyre (1986)]. The rapid technological development of the internet enabled companies to virtually integrate customers. Toolkits,[d] online brainstorming, research communities, [Kröper *et al.* (2013)], and idea contests[e] are new tools for integrating users into the idea generation and concept

---

[d]Toolkits are web-based interfaces that enable users to design a novel product by trial-and-error experimentation and provide simulated feedback on the outcome. Toolkits exist in various fields and can focus on gaining access to either need or solution information [Franke and Piller (2004); Piller and Walcher (2006)].

[e]Idea contests are web-based competitions initialized by manufacturers who encourage users to use their skills and creativity to create innovative ideas and solutions for a particular contest challenge [Piller and Walcher (2006); Bullinger and Moeslein (2010)].

development of companies' NPDs [Schweitzer *et al.* (2012)]. These methods differ from the lead user method through the online (toolkits, research communities, idea contests) versus offline (focus groups, lead user concept) environment in which they occur [Schweitzer *et al.* (2012)]. The main difference between the lead user method and focus groups, toolkits, online brainstorming, research communities, and idea contests is the type of individuals who are integrated. When using focus groups or Web 2.0 tools, users, representative customers, or potential customers are typically integrated [Nambisan (2002)]. The lead user method explicitly focuses on lead users who differentiate themselves from ordinary users through certain characteristics, such as being ahead of the market, facing new needs sooner than ordinary users, and significantly benefitting if their idea succeeds [von Hippel (1986); Lüthje and Herstatt (2004)]. Hence, lead users are less focused on providing only need information, such as ordinary users, and are more focused on delivering solution information [Lilien *et al.* (2002); Eisenberg (2011)], combined with a need for an innovative solution and the ability to derive benefits from using the new solution for themselves. However, provision of solution-related information is not a distinct characteristic of lead users; any average user, that participates in crowd sourcing competitions and comes up with ideas or concrete concepts and the like, delivers solution-related information. Hence, ordinary users might also provide very concrete solution-oriented information if they are involved through toolkits, without being explicit lead users. Lead users develop the solution, whereby an ordinary user is focused on the input only.

Table 2 provides an overview of the mentioned methods in terms of their expected outcomes and the possibility to govern innovative activities (based on the categories of Pisano and Verganti [2008] and Keinz *et al.* [2012]). This differentiation shows that the lead user method is the main one that is specifically suitable for generating radical ideas. Online tools are potentially also a considerable source for such ideas, but the number of people that need to be integrated, as well as the corresponding

Table 2.   Comparison of lead user method with other relevant approaches.

Method	Number of external individuals involved	Expected outcome	Possibility to "govern" innovative activities	Possibility to do it online/offline	Innovation approach
Lead user method	Low	Radical and incremental ideas	Low	Offline	Searching
Traditional market research techniques	Low	Incremental ideas	High	Online, offline	Searching
Focus groups	Low	Incremental ideas	High	Offline	Searching
Online tools (e.g. toolkits, idea contests)	High	Radical and incremental ideas	Low	Online	Harvesting

resource input, is by far higher. For more risk-averse companies, both methods bear the danger of a low chance to regulate the innovative activities and behaviors on a strategic level. Such companies might be better off with focusing on the lead user method. Such an approach for radical innovation involves a lower investment in terms of personnel resources, and it is less visible to the public that the company is working on a radical new product — at least compared with other approaches like idea contests.

4. Application of the Lead User Method

4.1. *Process of the lead user method*

The lead user method proposal by von Hippel [1986] originated more than 30 years ago and has been constantly advanced. Several descriptions of the process can be found in literature, and the main process steps of these descriptions are consistent but their inherent aspects differ. The process as displayed in Fig. 1 is well established in literature, as it was used in many past applications (e.g. Herstatt and von Hippel [1992]; Thomke and Sonnack [1999]; Olson and Bakke [2001]; Herstatt *et al.* [2002]; von Hippel *et al.* [2007]).

4.1.1. *Phase* 1: *Project initiation*

A lead user project usually begins with the definition of the search field, which can be a market, product field, or service area, for which innovative ideas or concepts should be developed [Lüthje and Herstatt (2004)]. Thereafter, the goal of the project is specified, which determines the requirements that the solution should fulfill (e.g. degree of innovation, number of solution concepts) [Lüthje and Herstatt (2004); Reichwald and Piller (2009)]. In this context, considering general conditions such as budgets and development times that influence the accomplishment of the project,

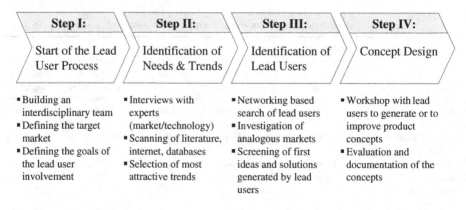

Fig. 1.   The lead user method process [Lüthje and Herstatt (2004, p. 561)].

are also important [Herstatt *et al.* (2007)]. Moreover, an interdisciplinary team with experienced employees from marketing, R&D, and manufacturing is built [von Hippel *et al.* (1999); Eisenberg (2011); Wagner and Piller (2011)].

4.1.2. *Phase 2: Identification of needs and trends*

The aim of this phase is to identify and understand critical market and technology trends in the field explored. Depending on the search field, economic, legal, and social developments should be considered [Lilien *et al.* (2002); Lüthje and Herstatt (2004)]. The identification of needs is also important because trends illustrate general and long-term developments and form the basis for the determination of potential (new) needs [Wagner and Piller (2011)]. Various secondary literature from internal and external sources, such as industry and technology reports, academic publications, databases, and the internet, can be used [Churchill *et al.* (2009); Eisenberg (2011)]. Moreover, interviews with experts (e.g. from inside/outside the company, of analogous markets) have proven to be of particular value [Lilien *et al.* (2002); Lüthje and Herstatt (2004)]. Thereafter, key trends are selected [Churchill *et al.* (2009)], which form the basis for the identification of lead users in the next step. A study from Keinz and Prügl [2010] showed that the amount of promising ideas could be five times higher if users are part of the search process, a finding that should be considered from a strategic perspective.

4.1.3. *Phase 3: Identification of lead users*

To identify lead users, the team first defines a set of attributes that distinguish lead users from ordinary users. The set of attributes combines lead user characteristics and, very importantly, the trends and needs determined in the previous step [Herstatt *et al.* (2002); Lüthje and Herstatt (2004)]. Several methods can be used to identify lead users. Identifying lead users not only from target markets but also from analogous markets is strongly suggested[f] because empirical research has shown that the novelty of solutions created by lead users from analogous domains is evaluated as being significantly higher than those of target market lead users [Lilien *et al.* (2002); Franke *et al.* (2013)]. After the identification of lead users, the best-suited users are selected and invited to a workshop.

Some researchers also proposed that solution concepts be compiled in this project stage [Churchill *et al.* (2009); Eisenberg (2011)]. Thus, insights from the literature review and interviews with experts and lead users are used to develop rough concepts, which are further developed in the subsequent lead user workshop. The question of developing preliminary concepts depends on the particular workshop goal, that is, whether it is an open process or whether solutions should be guided in a special direction [Wagner and Piller (2011)].

---

[f]An analogue market resembles the needs of the consumer and/or the technology used, but frequently belongs to a completely different industry [Reichwald and Piller (2007)].

4.1.4. *Phase 4: Concept design*

Participants are invited to a workshop in which preliminary concepts are further elaborated on or entire new solution concepts are developed to meet previously defined trends, needs, and requirements. The workshop duration depends on the complexity of the problem and lasts between one and three days [von Hippel *et al.* (1999); Lilien *et al.* (2002); Reichwald and Piller (2009)]. Ten to 20 individuals should attend the workshop and, of these individuals, 10 to 15 should be lead users [Lilien *et al.* (2002); Churchill *et al.* (2009)]. Little is known about the concrete process of a lead user workshop and the creativity methods particularly suitable for such workshops.[g] In lead user method applications, participants often worked in small groups, changed team compositions, and designed final concepts together [von Hippel *et al.* (1999)]. Churchill *et al.* [2009], as well as Wagner and Piller [2011], proposed a workshop structure in their handbooks that consisted of (1) introduction, (2) activation and processing, and (3) integration and discussion phases.

For some applications, at the end of the workshop, participants, the company, or an expert panel evaluated concepts concerning different factors, such as originality, problem solving capacity, the ability to be realized [Herstatt *et al.* (2002)], novelty and value [Hienerth *et al.* (2007)], or technical feasibility, market appeal, and management priorities [Lilien *et al.* (2002)].

Originally, von Hippel [1986] proposed that market acceptance tests be subsequently conducted to verify whether the solutions developed by lead users meet customer requirements. In some lead user applications, project teams followed this proposal [Urban and von Hippel (1988); Herstatt and von Hippel (1992)]. Market acceptance tests could be viewed as an extra process step, but were not inherently part of the method in recent process descriptions [Olson and Bakke (2001); Herstatt *et al.* (2002); Lüthje and Herstatt (2004); Hienerth *et al.* (2007)].

After the completion of workshops, the results are documented and the concepts are presented to decision makers and managers [Herstatt and von Hippel (1992)]. If concepts should be further processed, the standard development and evaluation process of the company is applied [Herstatt *et al.* (2002)]. At least one project team member should stay involved during subsequent commercialization activities to appropriately transfer knowledge [von Hippel *et al.* (1999); Churchill *et al.* (2009)].

4.2. *Application fields of the lead user method*

Table 3 provides a detailed overview of applications of the lead user method that were identified in literature.[h]

---

[g] Brem and Brem [2013] propose a concrete structure for such creativity workshops, and the appropriate combination of creativity techniques.

[h] As Eisenberg [2011] mentions, other companies like Cabot, Bell Atlantic (now Verizon) or Kellogg's are also successfully applying the lead user method. However, she only mentions the company and project name, as well as the level of the general outcome (product or service platform, business model, concepts, etc.). Despite further literature research no information could be identified how the lead user method was applied in these projects. Hence, these ones cannot be further included in our analysis.

Table 3.   Overview of lead user studies and their outcomes.

Industry/product field	Year	Company	Findings	Source
Information Systems/ PC-CAD	1986	University project	▪ Developed lead user concept was significantly preferred over competing PC-CAD systems ▪ Preference for lead user concept maintained even when it was priced higher than competing systems	Urban and von Hippel [1988]
Manufacturing/Pipe hangers	1980s	Hilti	▪ Developed lead user concept was judged to be very valuable by Hilti and a group of non-lead users ▪ Products developed on the basis of this concept created a new business unit, "technical assembly," and are today a key area of the Hilti product portfolio ▪ Improvement in teamwork ▪ Lead user method was significantly faster and cheaper than conventional marketing research methods typically used by Hilti	Herstatt and von Hippel [1992] Lüthje and Herstatt [2004]
Medical Products/Surgical drapes	1996	3M	▪ Generation of concepts for six new product lines where of three were finally developed ▪ Generation of radical new strategic direction for infection control that was finally implemented	von Hippel *et al.* [1999]
Information Systems/ Desktop-PC	1997	Cinet	▪ Generation of 30 ideas whereof 22 were added to products ▪ Implementation of ideas in next generation products was very practical and cost-effective ▪ Improvement in cross-functional teamwork and efficiency in the NPD process	Olson and Bakke [2001]
Information Systems/ Software Product	1997	Cinet	▪ Nine ideas created whereof seven were added to products ▪ Implementation of ideas in next generation products was very practical and cost-effective ▪ Improvement of cross-functional teamwork and efficiency in the NPD process	Olson and Bakke [2001]

(Continued)

Table 3. (Continued)

Industry/product field	Year	Company	Findings	Source
Medical Products/Surgical hygiene products	2000	Johnson & Johnson Medical	▪ Generation of four concepts where of three were rated outstanding regarding originality, problem solving capacity, and ability to be realized ▪ All four concepts included new products that were not part of the existing product program and were the world's first ▪ Resulted in the further development of the existing market offer, the expansion of their program, and the development of completely new product lines	Herstatt *et al.* [2002]
Information Systems	2000	Nortel Networks	▪ Generation of concrete applications for mobile tracking systems that allow the transfer of multiple forms of data ▪ Four concepts were ultimately released to the market	Herstatt *et al.* [2002]
Diverse (10)	2003–2006	Companies (10)	▪ Generation of an average of four concepts per workshop ▪ All generated concepts scored significantly higher than companies' internal projects in novelty, potential value, and realizability	Hienerth *et al.* [2007]
	2000	3M	▪ Ideas generated by the lead user method have greater commercial potential than non-lead user ideas because they: - are more original - have significantly higher market share - have greater potential to develop into an entire product line - are strategically more important - have projected annual sales in year five that are eight times higher ▪ Lead user ideas led to major product lines whereas non-lead user ideas only led to product improvements and extensions of existing products ▪ Lead user idea generation methods cost more in time and money than non-lead user idea generation methods	Lilien *et al.* [2002]

All empirical studies, except for Lilien *et al.* [2002], described the application of the lead user method and the positive outcomes, such as innovative concepts, that resulted from the workshops. The first application in 1986 [Urban and von Hippel (1988)] showed that the concept developed by lead users was preferred over existing PC-CAD systems and that the preference remained when it was priced higher than competing systems. Subsequent studies revealed similar findings. In the case of Johnson & Johnson Medical (J&J) [Herstatt *et al.* (2002)], four concepts were developed in the workshop, of which three were rated outstanding for originality, problem-solving capacity, and ability to be realized. Hienerth *et al.* [2007] conducted 10 lead user projects, and all of their generated concepts scored higher in novelty, potential value, and realizability than companies' internal projects.

In addition to the generation of innovative concepts, many lead user ideas were also realized and ultimately released to the market (e.g. Olson and Bakke [2001]; Lilien *et al.* [2002]; Herstatt *et al.* [2002]; Lüthje and Herstatt [2004]). Success reaches from simple product improvements to the development of completely new products and/or product lines, the creation of new business units, and the generation of radical new strategic directions. For example, the four concepts generated in J&J Medical's lead user project included new products that were the world's first and resulted in further development of the existing market offer, program expansion, and completely new product lines [Herstatt *et al.* (2002)]. Moreover, the lead user method can also improve (cross-functional) teamwork and the efficiency and speed of the NPD process [Olson and Bakke (2001)].

Lilien *et al.* [2002] conducted a study in which researchers investigated the efficiency of the lead user method relative to that of traditional methods that rely on only internal resources. They found that innovations generated by lead users are valued higher with respect to degree of innovation (breakthrough versus incremental), novelty and originality, realizability, turnover, market share, and strategic significance.

Despite the lead user method's success, only 3M and Nortel Networks conducted further lead user projects [von Hippel *et al.* (1999); Olson and Bakke (2004)]. Others did not integrate the method into their NPD given time and staff turnover or an engineering-based company culture that was not motivated to become customer focused [Olson and Bakke (2001)]. Further indicators might be high resource efforts, which were not directly identified but were regarded as significant challenges.

5. Success Factors of the Lead User Method

This final part focuses on the success factors when applying the lead user method.

5.1. *Success considerations*

Empirical research on the *success factors* for processing the lead user method is available but also scarce [Lüthje and Herstatt (2004)]. Rockart [1979, p. 85] defined success factors as "the limited number of areas in which results, if they are satisfactory, will ensure successful competitive performance for the organization. They are the few key areas where things must go right for the business to flourish." With regard to research on the lead user method, success factors are not considered at the company level but at the project level and primarily influence achieving the goal of the lead user project — the generation of innovative ideas and first concepts [Schreier et al. (2007)].

First, the lead user project depends heavily on the *project team*. A cross-disciplinary team consisting of individuals with technical and market-related experience is important. The members should be highly skilled, have profound knowledge of the firm, the innovation area, and the industry, be creative, and have good teamwork skills [Churchill et al. (2009); Eisenberg (2011)]. An interdisciplinary team has the advantage of a broader knowledge pool that facilitates the treatment of diverse knowledge and promotes company representatives' acceptance and in-depth understanding of subsequently developed solution concepts [Lüthje and Herstatt (2004); Wagner and Piller (2011)]. The *time* resource is also linked to the team. The team must have enough time to appropriately process the single steps and to accomplish successful workshop results [Eisenberg (2011)].

An in-depth understanding of the lead user method and *expertise* are also very important to identifying suitable trends and lead users, and to successfully master the project in the end [Churchill et al. (2009); Eisenberg (2011)]. Better than that concept, *management support* is fundamental [Churchill et al. (2009); Eisenberg (2011); Wagner and Piller (2011)], not only for the first goal but, most importantly, to achieve the long-term aim of bringing breakthrough innovations to the market. Active management backup is important for the credibility of the project and the acceptance of ideas and solutions, particularly when the method is conducted for the first time [Churchill et al. (2009)]. To further elaborate on the concepts generated in the workshop, management commitment and involvement as well as support from decision makers are crucial to advancing ideas through the subsequent NPD process [Wagner and Piller (2011)].

Furthermore, *measuring the final outcomes* of generated ideas and concepts regarding the degree of innovation, creation of new product categories, and changes in lines and/or financial results is crucial [Olson and Bakke (2004)]. This shortcut was also used in Cinet's lead user project and might have provided motivation to continue the method. In comparison, 3M measured outcome differences of lead user and non-lead user projects and continued to periodically use the lead user method given the positive findings in terms of the degree of innovation and higher levels of sales [Lilien et al. (2002)].

From the perspective of user-centric innovation, Hienerth et al. [2011] identified the following success factors: user-to-user interaction in a user-friendly manner, transparency regarding intellectual property, intrinsic (i.e. non-monetary) incentive systems (see also Raasch and von Hippel [2013]), offering entrepreneurial opportunities, integration into corporate strategy (see also Stieger *et al.* [2012]), ongoing communication and feedback, and strategies to overcome internal resistance.

5.2. *Role of lead user method realization*

In the literature to date, no distinction is made between the realization of the lead user method either internally or in cooperation with an intermediary. However, in most applications found, companies were supported by universities (e.g. Urban and von Hippel [1988]; Herstatt and von Hippel [1992]; Olson and Bakke [2001]; Herstatt *et al.* [2002]; Hienerth *et al.* [2007]) and seemed to adopt the purpose of research instead of simply being part of the regular innovation process. Typically, the division of tasks is unknown. For example, Hienerth *et al.* [2007] conducted 10 lead user projects with different companies, in which phases two and three were processed by the university.[i] Regarding these cases, the university arguably acted as an intermediary because it took over the complete process steps on behalf of a company.

As Eisenberg [2011] and Diener and Piller [2010] recently reported, lead user projects can also be accomplished by consultants or Open Innovation Accelerators (OIAs). However, no proper description of conducted projects could be found in the scientific literature, which is in line with the finding that sourcing knowledge for innovation has to date focused on direct industry–university links, whereas little is known about the role of consultants and private research organizations in innovation systems [Tether and Tajar (2008)]. Handbooks and descriptions of the lead user method solely aim at the processing within a company without the help of an intermediary. Except for 3M [von Hippel *et al.* (1999)], no evidence exists in the literature on companies that solely conducted lead user projects. When processing the method for the first time, Churchill *et al.* [2009] proposed that training and coaching be sought from consultants who have expertise and experience using the lead user method. Consequently, the lead user method can be realized in different ways — in cooperation with an intermediary such as consultants or universities, or internally. Within the group of intermediaries, the method can further be distinguished between the private sector, in which consultancies such as OIAs act, and the public sector to which academic institutions belong.

Lead user projects require time, and financial and human resources. The company's project team should be composed of three to six people, with one serving as project leader [von Hippel *et al.* (1999); Eisenberg (2011); Wagner and Piller (2011)]. Applications showed that project team members typically spend 15 to 20 h per week or 50% of their working time on a project [von Hippel *et al.* (1999); Lilien *et al.* (2002); Churchill *et al.* (2009)]. Regarding the total duration of a lead user project,

---

[i]This information is based on a personal communication with one of the authors of this paper.

the literature recommends four to six months. However, applications vary broadly between four and nine months.[j] Regarding the single process steps, von Hippel *et al.* [1999] suggested planning between four to six weeks for each project phase and Churchill *et al.* [2009] recommended four weeks for the first and second project phases and four to five weeks for phases three and four. No consensus was reached on the costs of the lead user method and how such costs compare to the costs of traditional market research methods. Churchill *et al.* [2009] estimated project expenses of $30.000–40.000 (excluding travel costs to distant customer or lead user sites). The Hilti project costs were about $51.000 and were half as expensive as the conventional marketing research method that the company normally used [Herstatt and von Hippel (1992)]. However, an investigation into five lead user projects conducted by 3M revealed that a successful lead user project costs an average of three times as much as a successful alternative idea-generation method ($100.000 versus $30.000) and requires 2.5 times more personnel resources [Lilien *et al.* (2002)].[k]

5.3. *Role of lead user identification*

The most frequently discussed instruments used to identify lead users are screening and pyramiding, which have both been used in previous applications of the lead user method. Through the rise of social media, the way to search for lead users also changed towards the use of online tools like netnography, broadcasting, crowdsourcing, etc.

The *screening approach* is based on screening a large number of potentially relevant users through a survey to test whether they indicated the previously defined set of lead user attributes [von Hippel *et al.* (2009)]. This approach was used during the first applications of the lead user method [Urban and von Hippel (1988); Herstatt and von Hippel (1992)], but has turned out to be expensive because of its low efficiency [von Hippel *et al.* (2008)].

Therefore, in subsequent lead user studies, *pyramiding/networking* has increasingly been used to identify lead users [von Hippel *et al.* (1999); Olson and Bakke (2001); Lilien *et al.* (2002)]. This approach begins with interviews of a small number of relevant people in the target market and works its way up the pyramid through recommendations. The approach is based on the notion that users with special interests, attributes, and needs know other people with similar or even better knowledge [von Hippel *et al.* (1999, 2009)]. This method has empirically proven to be particularly valuable for the identification of lead users in analogous markets. One-third of interviewees who provided a recommendation led researchers into an analogous domain that was previously unknown to them [Pötz and Prügl (2010)]. An

---

[j] von Hippel *et al.* [1999, p. 51], Lilien *et al.* [2002, p. 1044], and Wagner and Piller [2011, p. 11] recommended four to six months, Eisenberg [2011, p. 53] reported six to eight months, and the total duration of the Hilti lead user project was nine months [Herstatt and von Hippel (1992, p. 220)].

[k] Successful in this content means the implementation of one or more innovative workshop results in the market.

empirical study showed that pyramiding requires only an average of 30% of the screening effort and is, therefore, more time and cost efficient [von Hippel *et al.* (2009)].

Another approach applied in lead user projects is *broadcasting/signaling/crowdsourcing* [Hienerth *et al.* (2007); Brem and Bilgram (2015)]. The formulation of a problem is broadcast outside the company, such as in an online community, in the hope of contacting successful problem solvers [Lakhani (2006); Tietz *et al.* (2006)]. Innovative customers identify themselves by contributing solutions to a problem (self-selection) [Jeppesen and Laursen (2009)].

A different approach for utilizing online communities is *netnography* [Belz and Baumbach (2010, 2015)]. Based on a passive analysis of selected online communities (e.g. forums, blogs) heavy users and highly involved consumers are identified and evaluated by investigating the need information they share as well as the solutions they present. Analyzing the content users generate online as well as their relevance and centrality in the community allows to find potential lead users.

Both search strategies for innovative partners, netnography and crowdsourcing, offer a high potential for the identification of lead users. To identify the most appropriate approach, Table 4 offers a structured comparison of both approaches.

Self-selection instruments are assumed to outperform screening and pyramiding because users' motivation, capabilities, innovativeness, and application of product knowledge can be evaluated through the submissions of ideas and solutions even before they are invited to a workshop. In contrast, by using screening and pyramiding, assumptions about users' potential are assembled before the workshop takes place; however, the real capabilities can only be evaluated after the workshop [Piller and Walcher (2006)].

Reichwald and Piller [2009] state that every approach has different advantages and disadvantages. Therefore, a combination of methods seems to be useful. For this, social media will gain higher importance in future [Ernst and Brem (2017)].

6. Discussion and Conclusion

6.1. *Challenges*

The main challenge of the lead user method as identified in the literature is the resource issue regarding *time, manpower,* and *costs.* Typically, only relatively small budgets are planned for the "fuzzy front end" stage [Cooper (2001)]. Pötz *et al.* [2005] investigated 13 case studies and found that, in 10 cases, the significant effort related to personnel, time, and budget was explicitly considered a problem for conducting the lead user method. Despite success with the method in terms of product innovations, improvement of cross-functional teamwork, and NPD efficiency, Cinet did not continue to use the method because of time pressure and a lack of resources [Olson and Bakke (2001)]. Lilien *et al.* [2002] and Eisenberg [2011] also

Table 4.   Comparison of netnography and crowdsourcing-based lead user search Brem and Bilgram (2015, p. 5)].

	Netnography	Crowdsourcing
Primary goal of the method	• Understanding consumers • Gaining insights	• Collecting innovative ideas • Getting inspiration
Type of community	Permanent, user driven communities aiming for a conversational exchange	• (Mostly) temporary • company-led communities aiming for collaboration
Company role	Observer	Interactor, moderator
Type of interaction in the community	User-to-user conversations led by the community moderator	Company-to-user interaction in the following format: open call for ideas by firm — idea submission by user — feedback by firm — iterative refinements by user
Characteristics of community members	• Users who have common interests and needs • Users seeking specific solutions to their needs • Users who like to connect with like-minded people • High level of intrinsic motivation	• Skilled users attracted by the innovation challenge • Users with a passion for solving problems • Users with a need or passion for idea communication • Brand fans • Both intrinsic and extrinsic motivation
Indicators of lead userness	• Good articulation of advanced needs → future needs • Persistent search for solutions and trial-and-error experiments → high benefit from solution • Free sharing of self-designed solutions → creativity and knowledge • Constructive contributions to conversations → conversational skills • Empathic participation in conversations → social skills	• High-quality ideas → creativity, knowledge, and design skills • Strong articulation of advanced needs in idea description → future needs • Positive feedback and high evaluations of the idea(s) by the community → good fit with a relevant need • Constructive feedback for others' ideas → true interest in the topic and conversational skills
Assessment of lead userness	• Passive observation and analysis of consumer conversations and user-generated content • Profiling of users through data collection • Analysis of user statistics	• Evaluation of submitted ideas • Analysis of user comments • Analysis of user statistics and network centrality
Required resources	• Time range of two to six weeks • Main cost factor is time for analysis (manual reading)	• Time range of eight to 12 weeks (live phase four to eight weeks) • Main cost factor is recruiting participants, community management, and filtering ideas
Methodological advantages	• Unobtrusive analysis without bias through asking questions • Easy identification of the top 1% of active users • Availability of a long history of user activities in the community • Context-rich information, i.e. needs embedded in extensive real-life context	• Submitted ideas reveal real innovative behavior and skills of users • Self-selection mechanism saves time • The best ideas are a valid proxy for lead user potential and are easy to identify • High probability of finding concrete product ideas

consider the greater time and effort relative to alternative approaches as a key challenge. Related to those concerns is the challenge of not receiving adequate *management support*, which can undermine effectiveness and reduce the needed resources [Eisenberg (2011)].

Another challenge can be *acceptance*. Two cases showed that technical personnel were reluctant to accept ideas and concepts generated by inventors outside the company [Lüthje and Herstatt (2004)]. Because of this *not invented here syndrome* (NIH) [Katz and Allen (1982); Chesbrough and Brunswicker (2014); Antons and Piller (2015)], company representatives who are responsible for the subsequent stages of the NPD must participate in the workshop to prevent the NIH. Frequently, pessimistic professionals change their position into a positive attitude when working with lead users [Herstatt *et al.* (2007)].

Further challenges were found regarding the actual processing of the method. Concerning the *trend identification* phase, identifying experts and managing information can be challenging. For example, Cinet reported that finding, qualifying, and recruiting experts were viewed as difficult tasks [Olson and Bakke (2001)]. For Hilti and J&J, the variety of information sources and significant amount of approachable pieces of information resulted in information overload, and the team was uncertain as to how to evaluate in advance the sources that would lead to good results. Prioritizing and making decisions related to the trends that should be further examined were also judged as challenging by both companies [Lüthje and Herstatt (2004)]. J&J perceived a trade-off between an adequate search and the efficiency of this process step because some trends proved to be insignificant for lead user search [Lüthje and Herstatt (2004)].

In the *lead user identification* phase, finding the right people can be demanding [Eisenberg (2011)]. Cinet considered the effort to find, qualify, and recruit lead users as burdensome and, in the case of the desktop PC, lead users turned out to be not far enough ahead of market trends [Olson and Bakke (2001)]. The *intellectual property issue* can be a further challenge, particularly for industrial users who might already have developed solutions to a problem [Lüthje and Herstatt (2004)]. In the case of J&J, some potential lead users declined to cooperate because they did not want to freely reveal their knowledge, held patents, or were already cooperating with other manufacturers [Lüthje and Herstatt (2004)]. The intellectual property issue also depends on the workshop goal. J&J searched for a solution; yet, in most workshops, ideas arise from a group of lead users and are combined and further elaborated on to become concepts. Consequently, new intellectual property rights are not assigned to a specific user but to the company [Lilien *et al.* (2002)]. Moreover, lead users are often willing to freely reveal their knowledge and agree that generated concepts are the company's property [Harhoff *et al.* (2003)]. This phenomenon is underlined by the finding that the level of intellectual property protection for ideas generated by the lead user method is as strong as that for ideas created by non-lead user methods [Lilien *et al.* (2002)]. Finally, users must perceive their involvement as fair, as indicated by the prior research of Franke *et al.* [2014]: "potential contributors not only want a good deal, they also want a fair deal" (p. 1495).

As shown in this review, the lead user method follows a systematic process that provides access to knowledge and innovative ideas. Several applications have been conducted, reaching from the improvement of teamwork to the generation of completely new products, services, and strategic directions. Despite the success, only few companies regularly implemented the lead user method into their NPD processes, which might be related to the need for organizational changes that companies do not or cannot implement.

Finally, the question from the introduction of this paper remains unanswered: Why aren't there many more lead user workshops conducted in companies if the method has such high potential? Two basic approaches exist to addressing this question. First, one could question the merits of the lead user method as propagated by many user innovation researchers. Second, one could question the applicability and efficiency of the lead user method. As shown in previous sections, this method faces several challenges in theory and in practice that hinder its implementation. One explanation might be the fact that open and user innovation approaches in general — and repeated lead user projects in particular — call for several serious organizational changes to work effectively [Chesbrough and Brunswicker (2014); Keinz *et al.* (2012)]. Companies might perceive these changes as a loss of control and expertise [Hienert *et al.* (2011)].

6.2. *Research and managerial implications*

To overcome these challenges, the following implications might be derived to foster the applicability and the efficiency of the lead user method. From the starting point of the initial lead user method process introduced in Fig. 1 by Lüthje and Herstatt [2004], all results were integrated into a revisited view on the lead user method process. For this, we incorporated specific earlier research results [Herstatt *et al.* (2002); Herstatt and von Hippel (1992); Lilien *et al.* (2002); Lüthje and Herstatt (2004); Olson and Bakke (2001); Urban and von Hippel (1988); von Hippel *et al.* (1999)] as well as our implications derived in the last part of this paper. As a result, Fig. 2 shows a revisited lead user method process chart, which will be explained in the following.

The traditional lead user method view by [Lüthje and Herstatt (2004)] is extended with one more phase. This is the result from splitting their "concept design" phase into "ideation workshop" and "refinement", following earlier researchers who argue that market acceptance tests can be seen as an extra process step in the lead user method (e.g. Olson and Bakke [2001]; Herstatt *et al.* [2002]; Lüthje and Herstatt [2004]; Hienerth *et al.* [2007]). The rationale behind that is the idea of the original concept by von Hippel [1986], that market acceptance should be conducted as early as possible to investigate if customer requirements are met.

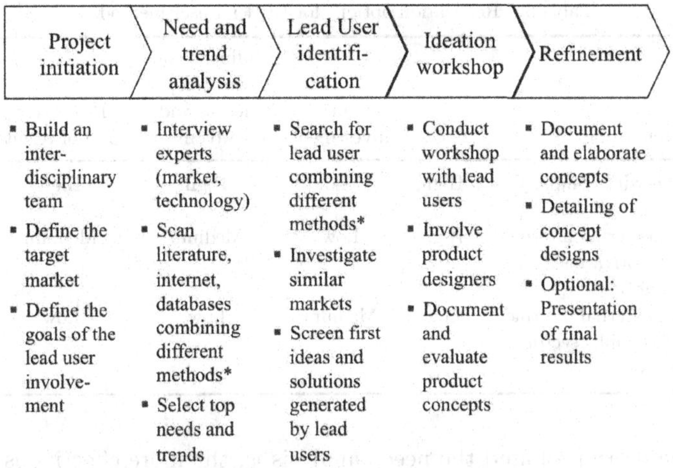

Project initiation	Need and trend analysis	Lead User identification	Ideation workshop	Refinement
• Build an interdisciplinary team	• Interview experts (market, technology)	• Search for lead user combining different methods*	• Conduct workshop with lead users	• Document and elaborate concepts
• Define the target market	• Scan literature, internet, databases combining different methods*	• Investigate similar markets	• Involve product designers	• Detailing of concept designs
• Define the goals of the lead user involvement	• Select top needs and trends	• Screen first ideas and solutions generated by lead users	• Document and evaluate product concepts	• Optional: Presentation of final results

Note: * Screening, Pyramiding, Signaling (Netnography, Crowdsourcing).

Fig. 2.   Lead user method process revisited (based on Lüthje and Herstatt [2004, p. 561]).

The phase "ideation workshop" is to emphasize the role of physical workshops as part of the lead user method. There not only lead users should be involved, but also (product) designers to support the lead users in visualizing their ideas. All results from the workshop need to be documented as well as evaluated based on criteria, which should be discussed and agreed upon with the users. The last phase of "refinement" emphasizes an extra stage to improve project documentation, which is supported by Olson and Bakke [2011], as the lead user method can fail due to changes in staff and poor transfer of knowledge. Here participants should have the opportunity to further elaborate on their earlier idea, which can be part of the second day of a lead user workshop, or in another setup like a project team meeting with end users afterwards. Optionally, there should be another opportunity to present the results to the other lead users, the clients and even to end customers for discussion. In some lead user methods this is already done through project teams who follow up on the ideas [Urban and von Hippel (1988); Herstatt and von Hippel (1992)]. Overall, the development of concepts can already be part of the "lead user identification" phase, depending on the goal of the workshop [Wagner and Piller (2011)]. The more detailed this early work is done, the more concrete the results of the lead user workshop will be.

The second major change to the original lead user method process is the integration of different methods in screening, pyramiding and signaling. Here, especially netnography and crowdsourcing, might play a key role as new (online) tools for an effective process. In the second phase of "need and trend analysis", these tools might be used, as well as in the "lead user identification". This is critical in terms of

Table 5.   Realization options for the lead user method.

Realization option	Costs	Time investment	Influence on workshop design and outcome	Protection level of results	Company learning
Direct realization with company employees	High	High	High	High	Low
Realization with external intermediary from the private sector (e.g. consultants)	High	Low	Medium	Medium	Low
Realization with external intermediary from the public sector (e.g. academics)	Low	Medium	Low	Low	High

efficiency: the more profound the needs analysis is, the more effective is the identification of appropriate users [Brem and Bilgram (2015)].

As discussed, the in-depth understanding of the lead user method is critical for the success of a lead user project [Churchill *et al.* (2009); Eisenberg (2011)]. In terms of organizational aspects, the role of an intermediary might help to overcome the challenges linked with the lead user method. Only a few companies have the practical experience to run a lead user workshop by themselves. Companies that do not have the Know-how and experience to apply the lead user method may consider using a service of an intermediary from the public or the private sector. Table 5 gives an overview when which approach might be taken.

Hence, the best realization for the lead user method depends on the prerequisites and the goals of the company. If the costs play a key role, a partner like a local university might be the best option, instead of an external consultancy. Usually motivated students are involved, and the researchers have an interest in publishing about the results and the workshop itself, so the costs are comparably low. However, the time investment is higher than working with consultants, who offer a full-service concept. If the workshop is done in-house, the influence in all phases is the highest. As soon as external people are involved, changes e.g. in the design of a workshop are more difficult because of different communication channels. With an in-house setup, it is easier to protect the results from getting known to outsiders, which is a key factor for intellectual property rights protection. Finally, companies may learn a lot about the method in an academic setup, rather than working with consultants, who want to keep their knowledge to get future engagements.

6.3. *Limitations and further research*

The main limitations of this study are the narrow focus of the literature review, the time of the research, and the challenge of involving all relevant papers. First, the limited focus on the mentioned databases needs to be noted. In the future, other databases such as Google Scholar or ProQuest could be used. Moreover, the literature review was conducted in December 2013; given the large number of journals and other publications in this field that are published each month, covering all relevant papers on a regular basis is very important. Hence, a regularly updated version of this analysis is recommended. A more important point concerns "radical or breakthrough innovations" and the method suggested greater effectiveness as opposed to "traditional market research". This effectiveness is used in the article as justification for the trouble with the much heavier resource use required by the method. However, there is little support in the literature for this specific greater effectiveness. The literature points out the lead users' role in new products. It is not much vocal on the lead user method as a means to radical innovation. Indeed, this literature makes little use of the radical incremental distinction. Hence, future research should focus on the lead user method effectiveness on radical new products concept generation. Finally, we focused on the term lead user and lead user workshops. However, given the emergence of the internet, many related terms and forms such as user innovation, online communities, crowdsourcing, user-centric innovation, and others have evolved and may be relevant. Therefore, we call for a consolidation of terms to streamline future research.

As the anonymous reviewers of this paper made interesting remarks on areas for further research, we would like to present the reviewer's following points:

- What new research findings on trend forecasting could be relevant for the lead user method? Are there new approaches to this time-consuming part of a lead user project? Which are the most interesting empirical studies that have been conducted in recent years?
- Considering the empirical studies on identification methods: What do we know about the efficiency and efficacy of alternative search methods? Which identification method is most suitable for different settings? Are there studies outside the narrow field of lead user research that exhibit relevant results on this matter?
- Has the lead user method become obsolete in times of online user communities and given the numerous ways to identify lead users and innovative solutions on the internet? Do we need a lead user method 2.0 suitable for the digital age?
- Are there key differences if the lead user method is used by academic institutions, specialized consultants, or directly by the company?
- What are contextual or situational factors under which the lead user method seems to be more or less promising? Taking the documented lead user studies: Can we reach a conclusion about industries, product/service fields, innovation tasks, companies etc. in which the lead user method has higher or lower odds of success?

We hope that, through this research, we develop the basis on which other researchers may continue.

References

Adamsons, R. E. (1952). Functional fixedness as related to problem solving: A repetition of three experiments. *Journal of Experimental Psychology*, **44**, 4: 288–291.

Adamsons, R. E. and Taylor, D. W. (1954). Functional fixedness as related to elapsed time and to set. *Journal of Experimental Psychology*, **47**, 2: 122–126.

Al-Zu'bi, Z. M. F. and Tsinopoulos, C. (2012). Suppliers versus lead users: Examining their relative impact on product variety. *Journal of Product Innovation Management*, **29**, 4: 667–680.

Antons, D. and Piller, F. T. (2015). Opening the black box of "not invented here": Attitudes, decision biases, and behavioral consequences. *The Academy of Management Perspectives*, **29**, 2: 193–217.

Baldwin, C., Hienerth, C. and von Hippel, E. (2006). How user innovations become commercial products: A theoretical investigation and case study. *Research Policy*, **35**, 9: 1291–1313.

Belz, F. M. and Baumbach, W. (2010). Netnography as a method of lead user identification. *Creativity and Innovation Management*, **19**, 3: 304–313.

Biemans, W. G. (1991). User and third-party involvement in developing medical equipment innovations. *Technovation*, **11**, 3: 163–182.

Bilgram, V., Brem, A. and Voigt, K. I. (2008). User-centric innovations in new product development — systematic identification of lead users harnessing interactive and collaborative online-tools. *International Journal of Innovation Management*, **12**, 3: 419–458.

Brem, A. and Voigt, K. I. (2009). Integration of market pull and technology push in the corporate front end and innovation management — Insights from the German software industry. *Technovation*, **29**, 5: 351–367.

Brem, A. and Bilgram, V. (2015). The search for innovative partners in co-creation: Identifying lead users in social media through netnography and crowdsourcing. *Journal of Engineering and Technology Management*, **37**, 40–51.

Brem, A. and Brem, S. (2013). *Kreativität und Innovation im Unternehmen: Methoden und Techniken zur strukturierten Sammlung und Generierung von Ideen*. Schäffer-Poeschel Verlag.

Chesbrough, H. and Brunsuicker, S. (2014). A fad or a phenomenon?: The adoption of open innovation practices in large firms. *Research-Technology Management*, **57**, 2: 16–25.

Churchill, J., von Hippel, E. and Sonnack, M. (2009). *Lead User Project Handbook: A Practical Guide for Lead User Project Teams*. Lead User Concepts, Inc., Cambridge and Minneapolis.

Cooper, R. G. (2001). *Winning at New Products: Accelerating the Process from Idea to Launch*, 3rd edn. Perseus Books, Massachusetts.

Dahlander, L. and Gann, D. M. (2010). How open is innovation. *Research Policy*, **39**, 6: 699–709.

Diener, K. and Piller, F. T. (2010). *The Market for Open Innovation — Increasing the Efficiency and Effectiveness of the Innovation Process*. Lulu Press, Inc., Raleigh.

Duncker, K. (1945). On problem solving. *Psychological Monographs*, **58**, 5: i–113.

Eisenberg, I. (2011). Lead-user research for breakthrough innovation. *Research Technology Management*, **54**, 1: 50–58.

Ernst, M. and Brem, A. (2017). Social media for identifying lead users? Insights into lead users' social media habits. *International Journal of Innovation and Technology Management*, **14**, 4: 1750022-1–1750022-21.

Ernst, M., Brem, A. and Voigt, K. I. (2013). Innovation management, lead-users, and social media — Introduction of a conceptual framework for integrating social media tools in lead-user management. *Social Media in Strategic Management*, eds. M. R. Olivas-Luján and T. Bondarouk (eds.), Advanced Series in Management, Vol. 11. Emerald, Bingley, pp. 169–195.

Franke, N., Keinz, P. and Klausberger, K. (2013). Does this sound like a fairdeal?: Antecedents and conseqvences of fairness expectations in the individual's decision to participate in firm innovation. *Organization Science*, **24**, 5: 1495–1516.

Franke, N. and Shah, S. (2003). How communities support innovative activities: An exploration of assistance and sharing among end-users. *Research Policy*, **32**, 1: 157–178.

Franke, N. and von Hippel, E. (2003). Finding commercially attractive user innovations: An exploration and test of "lead user" theory. MIT Sloan School of Management Working Paper 4402-03, pp. 1–31.

Franke, N. and Piller, F. (2004). Value creation by toolkits for user innovation and design: The case of the watch market. *Journal of Product Innovation Management*, **21**, 6: 401–415.

Franke, N., Poetz, M. K. and Schreier, M. (2013). Integrating problem solvers from analogous markets in new product ideation. *Management Science*, **60**, 4: 1063–1081.

Franke, N., von Hippel, E. and Schreier, M. (2006). Finding commercially attractive user innovations: A test of lead user theory. *Journal of Product Innovation Management*, **23**, 4: 301–315.

Gruner, K. E. and Homburg, C. (2000). Does customer interaction enhance new product success. *Journal of Business Research*, **49**, 1: 1–14.

Harhoff, D., Henkel, J. and von Hippel, E. (2003). Profiting from voluntary information spillovers: How users benefit by freely revealing their innovations. *Research Policy*, **32**, 10: 1753–1769.

Herstatt, C. and von Hippel, E. (1992). From experience: Developing new product concepts via the lead user method: A case study in a "low-tech" field. *Journal of Product Innovation Management*, **9**, 3: 213–221.

Herstatt, C., Lüthje, C. and Lettl, C. (2002). Innovationsfelder mit lead usern erschließen. *Harvard Business Manager*, **24**, 1: 60–68.

Hienerth, C., Keinz, P. and Lettl, C. (2011). Exploring the nature and implementation process of user-centric business models. *Long Range Planning*, **44**, 5–6: 344–374.

Hienerth, C., Pötz, M. and von Hippel, E. (2007). Exploring key characteristics of lead user workshop participants: Who contributes best to the generation of truly novel solutions? *Proceedings of the DRUID Summer Conference 2007 on Appropriability Proxionity, Routines and Innovation*. Copenhagen.

Jeppesen, L. B. and Frederiksen, L. (2006). Why do users contribute to firm-hosted user communities? The case of computer-controlled music instruments. *Organization Science*, **17**, 1: 45–63.

Jeppesen, L. B. and Laursen, K. (2009). The role of lead users in knowledge sharing. *Research Policy*, **38**, 10: 1582–1589.

Katz, R. and Allen, T. J. (1982). Investigating the not invented here (NIH) syndrome: A look at the performance, tenure, and communication patterns of 50 R&D project groups. *R&D Management*, **12**, 1: 7–20.

Keinz, P., Hienerth, C. and Lettl, C. (2012). Designing the organization for user innovation. *Journal of Organization Design*, **1**, 3: 20–36.

Keinz, P. and Prügl, R. (2010). A user community-based approach to leveraging technological competences: An exploratory case study of a technology start-up from MIT. *Creativity and Innovation Management*, **19**, 3: 269–289.

Khurana, A. and Rosenthal, S. R. (1997). Integrating the fuzzy front end of new product development. *MIT Sloan Management Review*, **38**, 2: 103–120.

Kim, J. and Wilemon, D. (2002). Focusing the fuzzy front-end in new product development. *R&D Management*, **32**, 4: 269–279.

Kröper, M., Bilgram, V. and Wehlig, R. (2013). Empowering members of a brand community to gain insights and create new products: The case of the Vorwerk Thermomix Research Community. *Strategy and Communication for Innovation*, eds. N. Pfeffermann, T. Minshall and L. Mortara. Springer Verlag, Berlin, pp. 415–426.

Lakhani, K. R. (2006). Broadcast search in problem solving: Attracting solutions from the periphery. In *Technology Management for the Global Future, 2006. PICMET 2006*, IEEE, Vol. 6, pp. 2450–2468.

Lilien, G., Morrison, P., Searls, K., Sonnack, M. and von Hippel, E. (2002). Performance assessment of the lead user idea-generation process for new product development. *Management Science*, **48**, 8: 1042–1059.

Lüthje, C., Herstatt, C. and von Hippel, E. (2002). The dominant role of "local" information in user innovation: The case of mountain biking. MIT Sloan School of Management Working Paper 4377-02, pp. 1–32.

Lüthje, C. (2004). Characteristics of innovating users in a consumer goods field. *Technovation*, **24**, 9: 683–695.

Lüthje, C. and Herstatt, C. (2004). The lead user method: An outline of empirical findings and issues for future research. *R&D Management*, **34**, 5: 553–568.

Mahr, D. and Lievens, A. (2012). Virtual lead user communities: Drivers of knowledge creation for innovation. *Research Policy*, **41**, 1: 167–177.

Mantel, S. J. and Meredith, J. R. (1986). The role of customer cooperation in the development, marketing, and implementation of innovations. *Proceedings of the Fourth International Conference on Product Innovation Management*, ed. H. Hübner. Elsevier, Amsterdam, pp. 27–36.

McQuarrie, E. F. and McIntyre, S. H. (1986). Focus groups and the development of new products by technologically driven companies: Some guidelines. *Journal of Product Innovation Management*, **3**, 1: 40–47.

Morrison, P. D., Roberts, J. H. and von Hippel, E. (2000). Determinants of user innovation and innovation sharing in a local market. *Management Science*, **46**, 12: 1513–1527.

Morrison, P. D., Roberts, J. H. and Midgley, D. F. (2004). The nature of lead users and measurement of leading edge status. *Research Policy*, **33**, 2: 351–362.

Nambisan, S. (2002). Designing virtual customer environments for new product development: Toward a theory. *Academy of Management Review*, **27**, 3: 392–413.

Olson, E. L. and Bakke, G. (2001). Implementing the lead user method in a high technology firm: A longitudinal study of intentions versus actions. *Journal of Product Innovation Management*, **18**, 6: 388–395.

Olson, E. L. and Bakke, G. (2004). Creating breakthrough innovations by implementing the lead user methodology. *Telektronikk*, **100**, 126–132.

Piller, F. T. and Walcher, D. (2006). Toolkits for idea competitions: A novel method to integrate users in new product development. *R&D Management*, **36**, 3: 307–318.

Pisano, G. P. and Verganti, R. (2008). Which kind of collaboration is right for you. *Harvard Business Review*, **86**, 12: 78–86.

Pötz, M. K., Steger, C., Mayer, I. and Schrampf, J. (2005). Evaluierung von Case Studies zur Lead User Methode. Available at http://www.iluma.at/ [accessed on 10 February 2013].

Pötz, M. K. and Prügl, R. (2010). Crossing domain-specific boundaries in search of innovation: Exploring the potential of pyramiding. *Journal of Product Innovation Management*, **27**, 6: 897–914.

Raasch, C. and von Hippel, E. (2013). Innovation process benefits: The journey as reward. *MIT Sloan Management Review*, **55**, 1: 33–39.

Reichwald, R. and Piller, F. T. (2009). *Interaktive Wertschöpfung: Open Innovation, Individualisierung und neue Formen der Arbeitsteilung.* Gabler Verlag, Wiesbaden

Rockart, J. F. (1979). Chief executives define their own data needs. *Harvard Business Review*, **57**, 2: 81–93.

Sänn, A. (2017). Lead user product development. *The Preference-Driven Lead User Method for New Product Development*, ed. A. Sänn. Springer Fachmedien, Wiesbaden, pp. 9–53.

Sawhney, M., Verona, G. and Prandelli, E. (2005). Collaborating to create: The Internet as a platform for customer engagement in product innovation. *Journal of Interactive Marketing*, **19**, 4: 4–17.

Schreier, M., Oberhauser, S. and Prügl, R. (2007). Lead users and the adoption and diffusion of new products: Insights from two extreme sports communities. *Marketing Letters*, **18**(1–2): 15–30.

Schreier, M. and Prügl, R. (2008). Extending lead-user theory: Antecedents and consequences of consumers' lead userness. *Journal of Product Innovation Management*, **25**, 4: 331–346.

Schweitzer, F. M., Buchinger, W., Gassmann, O. and Obrist, M. (2012). Crowdsourcing: Leveraging innovation through online idea competitions. *Research Technology Management*, **55**, 3: 32–38.

Shah, S. (2000). Sources and patterns of innovation in a consumer products field: Innovations in Sporting Equipment. MIT Sloan School of Management Research Paper No. 4105, pp. 1–27.

Shaw, B. (1985). The role of the interaction between the user and the manufacturer in medical equipment innovation. *R&D Management*, **15**, 4: 283–292.

Stieger, D., Matzler, K., Chatterjee, S. and Ladstätter, F. (2012). Democratizing strategy — how crowdsourcing can be used for strategy dialogues. *California Management Review*, **43**, 4: 1–26.

Tether, B. S. and Tajar, A. (2008). Beyond industry–university links: Sourcing knowledge for innovation from consultants, private research organisations and the public science-base. *Research Policy*, **37**(6–7): 1079–1095.

Tietz, R., Füller, J. and Herstatt, C. (2006). Signaling — an innovative approach to identify lead users in online communities. *Customer Interaction and Customer Integration*, eds. T. Blecker, G. Friedrich, L. Hvam and K. Edwards, International Mass Customization Meeting (IMCM06). Technical University Hamburg-Harburg, Hamburg, pp. 453–468.

Tsinopoulos, C. and Al-Zu'bi, Z. M. F. (2012). Clockspeed effectiveness of lead users and product experts. *International Journal of Operations & Production Management*, **32**, 9: 1097–1118.

Urban, G. L. and von Hippel, E. (1988). Lead user analyses for the development of new industrial products. *Management Science*, **5**, 5: 569–582.

Utterback, J. M., Allen, T. J., Hollomon, J. H. and Sirbu, M. A. (1975). The process of innovation in five industries in Europe and Japan. *IDEE Transactions of Engineering Management*, **23**, 1: 3–9.

Van Kleef, E., Van Trijp, H. C. M. and Luning, P. (2005). Consumer research in the early stages of new product development: A critical review of methods and techniques. *Food Quality and Preference*, **16**, 3: 181–201.

von Hippel, E. (1976). The dominant role of users in the scientific instrument innovation process. *Research Policy*, **5**, 3: 212–239.

von Hippel, E. (1977). Transferring process equipment innovations from user-innovators to equipment manufacturing firms. *R&D Management*, **8**, 1: 13–22.

von Hippel, E. (1986). Lead users: A source of novel product concepts. *Management Science*, **32**, 7: 791–805.

von Hippel, E., Thomke, S. and Sonnack, M. (1999). Creating breakthroughs at 3M. *Harvard Business Review*, **77**: 47–57.

von Hippel, E. (2005). Democratizing innovation: The evolving phenomenon of user innovation. *Journal für Betriebswirtschaft*, **55**, 1: 63–78.

von Hippel, E., Franke, N. and Prügl, R. (2008). "Pyramiding": Efficient identification of rare subjects. MIT Sloan School of Management Research Paper 4720-08, pp. 1–23.

von Hippel, E., Franke, N. and Prügl, R. (2009). Pyramiding: Efficient search for rare subjects. *Research Policy*, **38**, 9: 1397–1406.

Wagner, P. and Piller, F. T. (2011). *Mit der Lead-User-Methode zum Innovationserfolg.* Center for Leading Innovation and Cooperation, Leipzig.

Biography

Alexander Brem holds the Chair of Technology Management at Friedrich-Alexander–Universität Erlangen-Nürnberg (FAU) which is located at the Nuremberg Campus of Technology. Before joining FAU, Alexander Brem was Professor of Technology and Innovation Management and Head of SDU Innovation and Design Engineering at the Mads Clausen Institute, University of Southern Denmark (Sønderborg, Denmark).

Volker Bilgram is Managing Director at HYVE, an end-to-end innovation consulting company. He is also an associated researcher at the TIM Group, RWTH Aachen University, with a research focus on open innovation, co-creation and consumer empowerment.

Adele Gutstein is Head of Customer Service Europe at car2go, the world's largest carsharing provider. In her previous role she was working for product management at car2go, being responsible for rollouts of product enhancements and usability studies. Adele is also researching at the Chair of Technology Management at the FAU.

Chapter 3

An Exploratory Analysis on the Contextual Factors that Influence Disruptive Innovation: The Case of Uber

Andrea Urbinati*, Davide Chiaroni, Vittorio Chiesa,
Simone Franzò† and Federico Frattini

*Politecnico Di Milano, Department of Management
Economics and Industrial Engineering
Via R. Lambruschini, 4/b, Milan 20156, Italy
*andrea.urbinati@polimi.it
†simone.franzo@polimi.it*

In the last years, management scholars have looked into the phenomenon of disruptive innovation, mostly focusing on the characteristics that identify a disruptive innovation and on the managerial solutions that incumbent firms should adopt to respond to the threat of a disruptive innovation. However, studying the characteristics of the context in which a disruptive innovation unfolds remains an under-researched topic. To fill this gap, this exploratory study examines how the disruptive innovation phenomenon is influenced by a set of variables that shape the context in which it takes place. This is done through a historical analysis of Uber, a widely discussed example of disruptive innovation. The exploratory analysis suggests that the extant regulatory framework plays a key role in influencing the impact that Uber has had on the taxi industry. By doing so, the paper points to the importance — for future researchers — to study disruptive innovation by carefully placing it in the regulatory context in which it takes place, given the importance that this aspect plays in influencing the anatomy of the disruption phenomenon.

Keywords: Disruptive innovation; contextual factors; Uber; city.

1. Introduction

In the last years, management scholars have paid great attention to the concept of disruptive innovation, i.e. the process through which an innovation changes the rules of competition in a given industry, bringing newcomers and start-ups to the top ranks of that industry and disrupting the position of incumbents [e.g. Bower and Christensen (1995); Christensen and Bower (1996); Christensen (1997); Christensen

---

*Corresponding author.

This chapter was originally published in *International Journal of Innovation and Technology Management*, Vol. 15, No. 3, March 2018, published by World Scientific Publishing, Singapore. Reprinted with permission.

and Raynor (2003); Kostoff *et al.* (2004); Danneels (2004); Markides (2006)]. This literature has focused mostly on the characteristics of new product, service, or business model innovations that make them disruptive, and on the managerial and organizational approaches that incumbent firms can adopt to respond to the threat of disruptive innovation [e.g., Christensen and Overdorf (2000); Adner (2002); Kostoff *et al.* (2004); Birkinshaw and Gibson (2004); O'Reilly and Tushman (2004); O'Connor and DeMartino (2006)]. However, little attention has been paid to the contextual factors that influence the extent to which a given innovation disrupts the established position of incumbent firms. This aspect deserves particular attention, if we aim to develop a comprehensive theoretical understanding of the disruption phenomenon [Schumpeter (1934); Tushman and Anderson (1986)], which takes into account the impact that the characteristics of the market in which a disruptive innovation diffuses have on the extent to which this innovation has a disruptive effect.

In this paper, we refer to "external factors", "contextual factors" and "exogenous factors" as synonymous, to denote the characteristics of the external environment, which captures the industry-, country- and society-level conditions characterizing the context in which innovations take place and diffuse.

The importance of looking at external factors on the disruptive impact of an innovation can be explained considering anecdotic evidence showing that a number of innovations that have had a disruptive impact in some contexts (and, in particular, in some countries), have not had the same disruptive impact in other contexts, due to the presence of a different set of external factors. For instance, Yu and Hang [2010] point out the example of the disruptive impact of the hard disk drive, which changed the rule of competition in the US and not in Japan, because of the different regulatory framework, financing system and cultural factors between the two countries [see, also, Chesbrough (1999)]. In another case, the Personal Handphone Systems (PHSs) did not succeed in Japan, but were a clear example of disruptive innovation in China [Yu and Hang (2010)], and these differences can be explained due to the different economic conditions and entrepreneurial culture distinguishing the two countries.

Therefore, considering the two examples mentioned above and many others that can be found in the literature, we argue that the external environment plays a pivotal role in influencing the extent to which an innovation has a disruptive impact on the market. In particular, the examples above suggest that external factors such as the regulatory framework, economic conditions, and the entrepreneurial culture of a country may all have a strong impact to the extent to which an innovation has a disruptive impact on the market.

Starting from these premises, our exploratory study aims to fill the gap underlined above, by analyzing the case of Uber, a widely discussed example of disruptive innovation, and examining the role that a set of contextual factors have played in influencing the extent to which Uber has had a disruptive impact on the market.

Uber is a taxi-hailing company based in San Francisco, which launched its taxi-hailing service in June 2010. Uber is the first Unicorn tech-company in "The Billion Dollar Start-up Club" ranking released by the Wall Street Journal, i.e. the club of venture-backed private companies valued at least $1 billion by venture capital companies. In December 2016, the value of the company is about $69 billion (Source: "Bloomberg"), with its service currently available in 550 cities in 74 different countries (Source: "Uber"). The nature of Uber as a disruptive innovation has been discussed at length in existing literature, with controversial viewpoints. This stems for the lack of a general agreement on the definition of the concept of disruptive innovation, as noted by many scholars [such as Danneels (2004); Tellis (2006)], who argue that "what constitutes a real disruptive innovation deserves examination through different lenses, and it is crucial to discuss the definition in any further research on disruptive innovation, as well as clarification of some potential misunderstandings" [Yu and Hang (2010)]. On one hand, Uber is recognized as a disruptive innovation, highlighting its capability to exploit digital technology to threaten the traditional taxi industry [Isaac (2014); Gil (2014); Stuart (2014)]. Others provide support to this view emphasizing that Uber is a clear example of a low-end disruption, due to its ability to move upstream-market starting from downstream-market to attack taxis directly [Moazed and Johnson (2016)]. More-over, in a recent study of The Strategy Group [The Strategy Group (2016)], Uber has been identified as an excellent example of disruptive innovation on the basis of the range of new features — such as the double rating system, the electronic payment, or the use of taximeters based on GPS technology — it is able to offer compared with similar services. On the other hand, some scholars [e.g. McAlon (2015); Hill (2015); Christensen *et al.* (2015)] hold that Uber is not "genuinely" a disruptive innovation. They argue that Uber does not come from the low-end of a market, which incumbents have neglected, or created a market where none existed. Con-versely, they say that the company is more genuinely disruptive in its attack on the lower end of the limousine market. Moreover, as underlined by McAlon [2015]: "Uber just made a more convenient taxi system using your smartphone, going after the taxi companies' core business right from the start. While Uber does now serve people living in areas often overlooked by taxis, they moved more down-market than up-market — the opposite of a disruptive company like Netflix. Uber is innovative, sure, but not disruptive in the way Christensen used the word." Although the inner nature of Uber, we recognize that this innovation is disrupting the transportation and, in particular, the taxi industry to a different extent in different countries and in different cities around the world, as highlighted by MacMillan [2016] in a Wall Street Journal article, as well as in the two reports of The Financial Times published in 2014 and 2016, respectively titled "Disrupters bring destruction and opportunity" and "Uber's total funding nears $10 bn".

The observations above suggest that the extent to which an innovation has a disruptive impact on established industries, not only depends on its intrinsic features, but is also very likely to be dependent upon the characteristics of the context in which it diffuses. In other words, under the effect of different contextual factors, an innovation may have a higher or weaker disruptive impact into the market.

We provide hereafter a brief discussion of the differences between the business models of Uber and of traditional taxi service providers, as this will be useful to better understand the following analysis.

Uber has a peculiar business model. It cannot be considered as a taxi or a transportation company, since it does not own taxies and has no drivers as employees. Uber is a marketplace and plays the role of matchmaker, matching drivers with customers who access the service through a smartphone app. Uber holds 20% of the fare paid by customers and gives the remaining part to the drivers. The core activity of the company refers to the selection of drivers and the control of the quality of the service. Uber assigns to candidate drivers who pass the selection a smartphone application, which allows them to manage incoming customer requests. The Uber app is one of the core elements of its business model: it is available for smartphone devices and it uses GPS to display the map of all available Uber cars in the area. In addition, the app sends the requests from customers to the closest driver, and provide customers with the information about the estimated pick-up time. Moreover, the app handles electronic payments and, at the end of the service, it requires both customers and drivers to leave a rating. Uber offers five different levels of taxi-hailing service, depending on the different customers' needs (especially in terms of price and quality). In particular: (i) UberLux is the most expensive and luxurious service that the company offers, where drivers have "F-segment" luxury cars (such as Mercedes S-Class, Audi A8, BMW 7 Series); (ii) UberSuv panders to users who require more seats (up to six people). In this case, the service is provided by assigning to users a SUV or a MPV (Multi-Purpose Vehicle); (iii) UberBlack is the original service that Uber offers since the inception of the company. Drivers provide this service through the "E-segment" cars; (iv) UberTaxi allows users residing in cities where Uber signed agreements with local cab companies to request a taxi. Uber handles the transaction through its application by applying the same price of taxi service set by the local regulator; finally, (v) UberX (or UberPop) is the low-cost service and is based on the employment of non-professional drivers (differently from the other four services).

Several differences compared with the business model of traditional taxi service providers emerge, considering that Uber identifies simplicity as its main source of competitive advantage, instead of price. On one hand, it enables the provision of a high-quality service, e.g. by offering a portfolio of five different levels of taxi-hailing services, reducing uncertainty about waiting times, as well as on the typology of vehicle that will arrive at the customer's premises, and through a driver rating system. On the other hand, the ease of use stems from the possibility to leverage on a single app in most major cities or countries around the world (instead of a dedicated taxi phone line in each city or country) and on a simple ordering and payment process (which does not

Table 1.   The business model of traditional taxi service providers and Uber.

Characteristics of the business model	Uber	Traditional taxi service providers
Hiring procedures	Through app	Through flag/call center/app/dedicated taxi queue
Payment procedures	Cashless	Cash/credit card
Pricing structure	Flexible	Structured
Drivers/passengers rating	Available	Not available
Car	Self	Rented from taxi companies

require hailing, phoning, searching and cash payment). Finally, security is a third pillar which differentiates the business model of Uber from traditional taxi services, through (i) the rating system for drivers and customers, (ii) the tracking of each route and (iii) the price transparency (thanks to an accurate fare estimation before the trip).

Table 1 summarizes the main differences between the business models of traditional taxi service providers and Uber.

In this paper, we present and discuss the results of an exploratory historical analysis on the diffusion of Uber in different cities around the world, to highlight how the characteristics of the context in which it diffuses have influenced its disruptive impact on the transportation sector and, in particular, on the taxi industry. Our analysis is particularly useful to illuminate the impact that a set of contextual factors, which exist in different countries and cities, has on the disruptive nature of Uber. This represents an important contribution to our current understanding of the disruptive innovation phenomenon and to the development of a comprehensive theoretical understanding of the disruption phenomenon in its whole complexity and of a theory of disruptive innovation that is able to interpret and predict whether, why and how a new product, service, or business model will disrupt an established industry.

The paper is organized as follows. Section 2 provides an overview of the existing literature on the topics of disruptive innovation (Section 2.1) and on internal and contextual factors affecting disruptive innovation (Sections 2.2 and 2.3). Afterwards, Section 3 summarizes the methodological details, whereas Section 4 provides the results of the historical analysis. The main findings are discussed in Section 5. Finally, conclusions and avenues for future research are outlined in Section 6.

2. Literature Review

2.1. *Disruptive innovation*

In the last years, management scholars have paid special attention to the concept of disruptive innovation [Bower and Christensen (1995); Christensen and Bower (1996); Christensen (1997); Veryzer (1998); Adner (2002); Christensen and Raynor (2003); Kostoff *et al.* (2004); Danneels (2004); Markides (2006); Govindarajan and Kopalle (2006)]. Disruptive innovation describes the process through which a new product, service or business model deeply changes the nature of competition in a given industry, bringing new companies (newcomers or start-ups) to the top ranks of that industry and seriously challenging the position of incumbent firms. According to Bower and Christensen [1995] and Christensen [1997], many large, profitable companies fail to stay at the top of their industries when disruptive innovations, mainly launched by newcomers, enter established markets. This happens because disruptive innovations offer a very different value proposition compared to existing products, services and business models, characterized by a different set of performance attributes.

In particular: (i) disruptive innovations are typically simpler and cheaper than existing products, services or business models, with worse performance than existing products or services, but with a different value proposition; (ii) they generally promise lower margins, not greater profits, as they have typically lower prices; (iii) disruptive innovations are first commercialized in emerging and small market niches, given that the most profitable customers of established firms are reluctant to purchase disruptive innovations; and, finally, (iv) disruptive innovations are typically developed and launched by start-ups or newcomers, which are not perceived as a challenge to the market position of established firms [Bower and Christensen (1995); Christensen and Bower (1996); Christensen (1997); Christensen and Overdorf (2000); Christensen and Raynor (2003)].

Table 2 summarizes the main characteristics of disruptive innovations.

Following these seminal studies, scholars have identified different types of disruptive innovations [Danneels (2004); Markides (2006)], and tried to capture the disruptive nature of an innovation with "reliable and valid measures" [Govindarajan and Kopalle (2006)]. Moreover, literature has long inquired into the strategic and organizational approaches that incumbent firms should adopt to quickly identify disruptive innovations and successfully react to them, such as structural and contextual ambidextrous organizations, acquisitions of new small companies, spin-offs or spin-outs, exploitation of both managerial commitment and internal capabilities through the creation of dedicated teams [Suarez and Utterback (1995); Bower and Christensen (1995); Christensen and Bower (1996); Christensen (1997); Sull et al. (1997); Tripsas (1997); Christensen and Overdorf (2000); Adner (2002); Kostoff et al. (2004); Birkinshaw and Gibson (2004); O'Reilly and Tushman (2004); O'Connor and DeMartino (2006)].

Table 2. Main characteristics of disruptive innovations.

Performance	Cost	Target market	Innovator
Worse than existing products or services, but different value propositions	Lower cost to buy or use the innovation (lower profits for the innovator)	Initially a niche, then expands into the mainstream market	Start-ups/ newcomer

2.2. *Internal factors influencing disruptive innovation*

In addition to the characteristics that distinguish a disruptive innovation, and the managerial practices that should be used to deal with disruptive innovations, this stream of research points to the existence of a set of internal factors, which influence the extent to which this innovation will have a disruptive impact on the market. For instance, some scholars [e.g., Christensen (1997)] have pointed to the importance of the phenomenon of technology oversupply and of the existence of asymmetric incentives for existing and disruptive innovations in influencing the speed at which a disruptive innovation impacts the market. Furthermore, King and Tucci [2002] have highlighted the importance of the transformational capabilities of an organization in reorganizing and redirecting its efforts toward the pursuit of a disruptive innovation opportunity. Moreover, Myers [2002] and Denning [2005] have emphasized how a set of relationships with the network of technological suppliers and partners has a relevant impact on the commercialization of a disruptive innovation. Finally, Rothaermel [2001] has underlined how complementary technologies and assets have to be developed prior to, or together with, the development of potential disruptive innovations in order to influence their diffusion on the market.

Interestingly, these studies mostly focus on the role of internal factors on disruptive innovation, i.e. factors that refer to the characteristics of the firm involved in developing and launching the innovation on the market. Surprisingly, there is lack of extensive discussion about the role of external factors, which capture the industry-, country- and society-level conditions, characterizing the context in which disruptive innovations occur [see, e.g. Chesbrough (1999)]. This although economics of innovation and industrial economics research stresses the critical role played by this type of factors in shaping the outcome of innovation processes [Tushman and Anderson (1986); Romanelli and Tushman (1986); Artoni (2001); Aghion *et al.* (2005); Autio *et al.* (2014); Antonelli (2014)].

Accordingly, further theoretical and empirical research efforts are needed to shed light on the role of these external factors on disruptive innovations. We provide hereafter a brief overview on the contextual factors analyzed in the economics of innovation and industrial economics literature, and discuss in the following how a set of contextual factors stemming from these streams of research may influence the extent to which an innovation has a disruptive impact on the market.

2.3. *Contextual factors influencing disruptive innovation*

Several contextual factors have been studied in the fields of economics of innovation and industrial economics, which significantly influence the level of innovation activities and the outcome of innovation processes.

We provide in Table 3 a brief summary of these contextual factors.

The aforementioned contextual factors influence in a more or less significant extent the level of the innovation activity and the outcome of innovation processes in

Table 3.   Contextual factors in the fields of economics of innovation and industrial economics.

Contextual factor	Description
Market concentration	Market concentration indicates the number of firms operating in a given industry and the distribution of their market share [Schumpeter (1934, 1950); Hirschman (1945); Herfindahl (1950); Ross and Scherer (1990)]
Level of competition	Level of competition means the intensity of rivalry among existing competitors in a given industry [Porter (1979)]. It is usually driven by the numbers of competitors, industry growth, switching costs, capacity and exit barriers.
Level of price of productivity factors	Level of price of productivity factors indicates the weight that productivity factors (such as raw materials and labor) have on a firm's cost structure [Antonelli (2014)]
Growth of demand	Growth of demand indicates the amount of consumption required by the market for a certain product, given a determined level of price [Schmokler (1966); Antonelli (2014)]
Regulatory framework	Regulatory framework indicates the outcome of the public intervention of an administrative entity, which influences the spontaneous actions and decisions taken by economic actors [Philips (1971); Ross and Scherer (1990); Artoni (2001)]
Entry/exit barriers	Entry/exit barriers indicate the barriers present in a given industry deterring the entry or the exit of new or existing competitors [Porter (1979)]. Entry barriers are usually driven by economies of scale, availability of substitutive products or services, capital requirements, cost disadvantages, access to distribution channels and government policy. Exit barriers are usually driven by specialized assets and management's loyalty to a particular business.
Cultural factors	Cultural factors indicate the basic values, perceptions, desires and behaviors that a person learns by living in a given country and society [Chesbrough (1999); Yu and Hang (2010)]
Financing system	Financing system indicates the number of actions, tools and incentives allowed by public and private institutions for the growth of the industrial sector [Chesbrough (1999)]

a given industry [Porter (1979); Audretsch (1995); Chesbrough (1999); Artoni (2001); Antonelli (2014)].

However, we focused our attention in this paper on three particular contextual factors within the list identified above, choosing those for which information could be collected through the historical analysis of Uber, i.e. the market concentration, the regulatory framework and the availability of substitutive products or services. The other contextual factors, such as cultural factors or the financing system, although can be useful for understanding the disruptive impact of an innovation [Chesbrough (1999); Yu and Hang (2010)], are not in the focus of our analysis and are left to future research. This important aspect is further discussed in Section 3.

A more detailed description of the three external contextual factors on which we focus is provided hereafter:

- Market concentration captures the number of firms operating in a given industry and the distribution of their market share [Schumpeter (1934, 1950); Hirschman (1945); Herfindahl (1950)]. A market is defined as concentrated if the number of firms in the industry is low, or if more unequal is the distribution of market shares among the firms themselves. Some scholars have pointed to the existence of a correlation between industry concentration and the diffusion of innovation [Ross and Scherer (1990); Gayle (2001); Aghion *et al.* (2005); Yanbing (2007)]. In particular, they have underlined how different concentration levels in a given industry can positively or negatively influence the extent to which innovations diffuse into the markets. This suggests that this factor should have an impact on the disruptive innovation process as well.

- Regulatory framework captures the outcome of the public intervention of an administrative entity, which influences the spontaneous actions and decisions taken by economic actors [Phillips (1971); Ross and Scherer (1990); Artoni (2001)]. Thus, the regulatory framework can influence competition in a given industry, by shaping the competitive mechanisms, creating entry barriers for new entrants and influencing the scope of innovation activities [Rogge *et al.* (2011)]. Again, this explains why the characteristics of the regulatory framework are likely to have a key impact on the outcome of the disruptive innovation process.

- Availability of substitutive products or services in an industry [Porter (1979)] is a peculiar driver of entry barrier and captures the different ways through which customers have access to a similar function (e.g. transportation via taxis) with alternative products or services (e.g. other public transportation systems). Even in this case, a larger or smaller availability of substitutive products or services in a given industry influences the capability of firms to grow, innovate and diffuse their products or services into the market [Hitt *et al.* (1997); Garcia-Vega (2006)]. This is why this factor represents a further contextual element capable of shaping the disruptive innovation process.

Starting from the premises above, this paper addresses the following research question: *"How do the factors characterizing the context in which an innovation diffuses influence the extent to which it has a disruptive impact in the industry?"*

To answer to this research question, we have studied the case of Uber, which is particularly suited to the purposes of this exploratory research for a number of reasons. First, Uber is disrupting the transportation industry and, in particular, the taxi industry to a different extent in different countries and in different cities around the world [MacMillan (2016)]. This allows analyzing the impact that different external factors have on the disruptive innovation process in different contexts. Moreover, although the nature of Uber as a disruptive innovation has been questioned by some authors, as we have underlined above, it has a number of characteristics in common with disruptive innovations and for sure it is having an impact on incumbent players. In particular, as pointed out by several scholars [see, e.g. Isaac

(2014); Gil (2014); Stuart (2014); Moazed and Johnson (2016)], Uber offers a different value proposition compared to its competitors, characterized by a range of services that can satisfy any kind of customer's need [The Strategy Group (2016)]. Moreover, Uber has heterogeneous prices for its services, thus allowing specific services (such as UberX/UberPop) to have a low price-quality and to be aligned with the typical characteristics of a disruptive innovation [Isaac (2014); Gil (2014); Stuart (2014)]. Finally, other scholars argue that Uber is a typical example of a disruptive innovation having moved upstream-market starting from down-market to attack the taxi industry [see, e.g. Moazed and Johnson (2016)].

Accordingly, the paper aims to understand how a set of external contextual factors (i.e. the level of market concentration, the characteristics of the regulatory framework and the availability of substitutive products or services) influences the diffusion of Uber in different contexts. To understand how these factors characterizing the context in which Uber diffuses influence the extent to which it has a disruptive impact on the transportation sector and, in particular, on the taxi industry, the study has been conducted by using the city as a unit of analysis, due to the availability of more homogeneous and comparable information compared to those available at country-level. The empirical analysis has focused on four cities (i.e. San Francisco, New Delhi, London, and Milan) in which Uber has had different levels of disruptive impact and for which a significant set of comparable data is available.

Sections 3 and 4 provide more details about the methodology and the exploratory empirical analysis that we conducted to answer to the research question outlined above.

3. Methodology

3.1. *Choosing historical analysis*

This paper analyzes the diffusion of Uber in different cities by adopting a historical analysis methodology [Gottschalk (1969)]. Historical analysis is the process of "assembling, critically examining, and summarizing the records of the past" or, put it differently, "assembling, critically examining, and summarizing the chronological dimension of past events" [Chiesa and Frattini (2011)]. This methodology is suitable to analyze phenomena that occurred in the past and evolved over time, as it happens with Uber. In addition, historical analysis implies that information and data are gathered from multiple secondary sources, such as different magazines, reports, and newspapers, allowing cross-comparisons and triangulation of information. Moreover, information and data are assembled when the phenomena occurred for the first time, to avoid *post hoc* explanations and rationalizations.

3.2. *Procedure*

We collected and analyzed information on the diffusion of Uber gathered from published sources of information. In particular, the research has been conducted through a longitudinal analysis of articles published in the most relevant economic journals such as Bloomberg, Business Insider, Forbes, Il Sole 24 Ore, The Economist, The Financial Times, The Verge, The Wall Street Journal. In addition, publicly available reports, which have studied the evolutionary phases of Uber over time, have been analyzed as well. To search and identify valuable sources of information, we used LexisNexis, a web-based and professional full-text journal database. After having collected articles and reports, we conducted a content analysis [Weber (1990)] built around the key theoretical concepts underlying this research (i.e. Uber, disruptive innovation, external factors, contextual factors, exogenous factors, taxi service, taxi industry).

The analysis of secondary sources of information followed two specific steps:

1. In a first phase, each author conducted independently the content analysis and applied within-case and cross-case explanation procedures. To select and accept the sources of information, each author applied the control criteria for historical analysis suggested by Golder and Tellis [1993], which are (i) competence, (ii) objectivity, (iii) reliability, and (iv) corroboration. The guidelines of Golder and Tellis [1993] for historical analysis were rigorously followed because this methodology "implies a certain unavoidable level of uncertainty, which pushes the researcher to be confronted with complex and sometimes contradictory empirical evidence" [Chiesa and Frattini (2011)]. Accordingly, in order to avoid any issues resulting from the use of ambiguous and equivocal data, the same piece of information was accepted only if it was mentioned in at least three different documents.

2. Afterwards, each author contrasted his own interpretation of the phenomenon with the other authors, to reach a shared understanding and interpretation. Therefore, the authors finally triangulated all the accepted information and started to cluster them for easing the data analysis and the following inter-pretative discussion.

The analysis of secondary sources showed that the recurrent contextual factors were:

- Market concentration, which refers to the number of taxi drivers and their orga-nisational structure to operate within a greater taxi company or as single entities;
- Regulatory framework, which refers to the intervention of policy makers in favor or against the entry into the market of new entrants;
- Availability of substitutive products or services, which refers to the number of different substitutive products or services that consumers could use to satisfy their public transportation needs.

Moreover, we found in the city a reliable unit of analysis to answer to our research question, due to the availability of more homogeneous and comparable information compared to those available at country-level. In particular, the empirical analysis focused on four cities (i.e. San Francisco, New Delhi, London, and Milan) in which

Uber has had different levels of disruptive impact and for which a significant set of comparable and accepted data on our set of contextual factors is available.

Finally, a panel of experts in the field of disruptive innovation, economics of innovation, industrial economics and regulatory policies of public transportation services was involved to discuss and corroborate the findings ensuing from the historical analysis. This panel consisted in (i) one Professor of Strategy and Innovation Management of the School of Management of Politecnico di Milano (Italy), (ii) one Consultant active in the field of Digital Innovation, (iii) two managers working for Uber in Italy and (i) one manager of ATM (Azienda Trasporti Milanesi S.p.A.) company, which is responsible in one of our cities of our sample (i.e. Milan) for offering public transportation service.

With each expert, we conducted personal and direct face-to-face interviews at least twice to both discuss about our data and our empirical analysis. Overall, each meeting lasted on average an hour and half, for a total of over 15 hours of interviews. We triangulated all the information ensuing from the face-to-face interviews, and shared with our panel of experts, with the secondary sources of information we assembled for the historical analysis. In doing so, for each city, we first analyzed the role of each contextual factor in influencing the disruptive impact of Uber. Thereafter, to identify the communalities and differences amongst each city, a cross-case comparison between the four cities of our sample was undertaken. We continuously compared the results of the empirical evidence with the information ensuing from the literature review on the contextual factors in order to enrich, refine and modify the theoretical setting.

The main topics ensuing from the analysis of the historical information and discussed with the panel of experts concerned: (i) the nature of Uber as a disruptive innovation, (ii) the extent to which the characteristics of Uber have been influencing its disruptive impact and diffusion at worldwide level, and finally (iii) the extent to which the contextual factors have influenced the way through which Uber has disrupted the taxi industry in the cities considered in this study.

4. Empirical Analysis

4.1. *The birth and diffusion of Uber*

In March 2009, Travis Kalaninick and Garrett Camp founded Uber, a taxi-hailing company based in San Francisco. Uber launched its taxi-hailing service in San Francisco in June 2010 and the service is now available in more than 550 cities in 74 different countries. In addition, the value of the company is about $69 billion, with a potential level of annual revenues of about $5.5 billion in 2016 (Source: "Bloomberg").

The level of diffusion of Uber in different cities around the world, and therefore its impact on the local transportation and taxi industry, is quite heterogeneous. Fischer

[2015] shows how the weight of Uber in several US cities is quite different and rapidly changing over time. For example, in New York City, Uber had the 21% of market-share in 2015 against the 9% of 2014, while in Los Angeles it had the 49% of market-share in 2015 against the 23% of 2014, whereas it covered the 56% of the market in 2015 against the 27% of 2014 in Dallas. In Chicago Uber had the 25% of market-share in 2015 against the 8% of 2014, while in Washington D. C. it had the 49% of market-share in 2015 against the 20% of 2014. Furthermore, Uber had the 41% of the market in 2015 against the 8% of 2014 in Atlanta, whereas in Miami it had the 23% of market-share in 2015 against the 0% of 2014. The diffusion of Uber in other countries is smaller compared with the US. Moreover, a recent report of Palaniappan [2015], the Regional General Manager of Eastern Europe, Middle East & Africa at Uber, anticipated a consistent investment of about $250 million across MENA in order to make Uber available to more people in more cities. On the other hand, Reuters [2015] argued, without providing quantitative estimation, that Uber has experienced a lower expansion in several cities of Western Europe, such as Milan, Berlin, Paris, Bruxelles, as well as in several Australian cities, if compared to US.

This information suggests that an innovation like Uber can have very dissimilar impacts on an industry (i.e. the taxi industry), depending on the contest in which it diffuses. For this reason, the empirical analysis has been conducted in four different cities, i.e. San Francisco, New Delhi, London and Milan, in which Uber has shown different diffusion patterns and for which relevant information is publicly available. In particular, in San Francisco, New Delhi and London, Uber has spread very fast and with a strong impact on the taxi industry. For instance, in San Francisco Uber earned the 71% of market-share in the taxi industry in 2015, against the 58% of 2014 [Fischer (2015)]. Similarly, in New Delhi, despite the market-share of official the company is unknown, there are some evidences of the incredible diffusion and impact of Uber in the taxi industry. Indeed, as pointed out by Sharma Punit [2015], from February to November 2015, the company gained over the 5% of weekly registered users, trying to closing the gap with Ola Cab, the market leader of taxi services in India. Moreover, Uber announced on July 2015 that they will be investing more than $1 billion to strengthen their position in India, its potential biggest global market after US [Lien (2015)]. In 2016, however, the market share of Uber in the Indian market is around 5–10%. In London, as reported by the Department for Transport [Statistical Release 2015], the licensed vehicles that provide the taxi service accounted for a 35% of the all licensed vehicles in England, which are around 242.200. On the other hand, the number of drivers for Uber is growing in London, to arrive to more than 20.000 [Anastasio (2015)]. This trend implies an important presence of Uber in the taxi industry of London, which accounts for over the 20% of the market share. On the other hand, in Milan Uber's diffusion is very limited, with an estimated market share below 10%.

4.2. *The influence of the contextual factors on the disruptive impact of Uber*

The influence of the three contextual factors on the impact that Uber has on the local taxi industry in the four selected cities was qualitatively evaluated, due to the substantial lack of quantitative information in the analyzed secondary sources.

Accordingly,

- The level of market concentration is evaluated either "high" or "low" on the basis of the capacity of taxi drivers to organize themselves in a greater taxi company (high concentration) rather than operating as single entities (low concentration);
- The regulatory framework is evaluated either "open" or "closed" on the basis of the willingness of policy makers to enable the entry into the market of new entrants, even with alternative business models, such as Uber;
- The availability of substitutive products or services is evaluated either "high" or "low" on the basis of the number of different substitutive services within each city that consumers can use to satisfy their public transportation needs.

However, according to the scientific contributions dealing with the contextual factors above, which provide criteria with which measure and evaluate them, we tried to adopt a quantitative manner to differentiate in "high" or "low" the level of market concentration and the availability of substitutive products or services.

In particular, we differentiated the level of the market concentration in "high" or "low" on the basis of the number of taxi companies (and the number of required minimum fleet of vehicles for being considered as taxi companies when specified), the number of authorized permits and/or licenses available in our set of cities. Therefore, we associated a "high" level of market concentration to the cities mainly organized in taxi companies, and requiring a minimum number of vehicles to operate with this organizational structure, instead of being organized in taxis that provide the service in an autonomous way. The same procedure was adopted for the availability of substitutive products or services, differentiating them in "high" or "low" on the basis of the number of public transportation services available in our set of cities. Therefore, we associated a "high" availability of substitutive products or services to the cities that were able to offer at least more than two different typologies of public transportation service.

In these cases, we were able to provide a measure of the level of market concentration and of the availability of substitutive products or services following a "threshold" logic, which took into account measurable values.

As far as the case of the regulatory framework is concerned, we differentiated in "open" or "closed" on the basis of the content of the main taxi and transportation industry regulations, which highlighted a more or less favorable environment for local competition due to the entry of new potential players, sometimes with different characteristics and business models, such as in the case of Uber if compared with the taxi service.

In this case, we were able to provide a measure of the propensity or inclination of a particular regulatory framework to allow new entrants to take part in the local competition of taxi and transportation industry.

4.2.1. San francisco

Regulatory framework

Uber's legal problems in San Francisco started in October 2010, when Uber received a cease-and-desist notice from the Consumer Safety and Protection Division of CPUC (California Public Utilities Commission), followed by a $20.000 fine to unlicensed passenger carriers. Moreover, in December 2014, Uber received a complaint by the Superior Court of California (County of San Francisco), for a misrepresentation regarding background checks, an improper use of the app to measure distance for fare calculation and an unlawful operation at airports. Furthermore, the Public Commission of the State of California does not recognize Uber as a real taxi service, rather, as an Online Enabled Transportation Service (OETS). OETS, indeed, "use smartphone applications to carry out their operations and essentially act as taxi companies delivering service to customers who require it". Indeed, the Public Commission of the State of California observed how these OETS operate in a gray area of the existing regulation applying to the taxi industry due to the absence of a compliant taximeter that the law requires for taxis. In particular, OETS use the taximeter included in the smartphone applications (i.e. a GPS-based taximeter) and not the traditional meter required by the existing regulation. Moreover, the Public Commission of the State of California underlined further violations to existing regulations of OETS such as:

(1) Absence of an adequate insurance coverage;
(2) Absence of a license to deliver service;
(3) Non-compliance with the existing regulation on fees;
(4) Double rating system;
(5) Absence of control on criminal background of drivers;
(6) Absence of control of vehicles maintenance status.

However, San Francisco is recently moving toward a greater deregulation of the taxi industry in order to encourage competition and entry of new potential players. In particular, a CPUC's Consumer Safety and Protection Division act claims that OETS need to be regulated in order to guarantee the safety of customers/passengers.

Market concentration

The San Francisco Taxi Commission regulates the taxi service in San Francisco. On November 2007, there were 1431 authorized permits to operate, organized in 34 taxi companies, or "colour schemes". On May 2015, there were 1900 authorized permits to operate a taxi, and organized in 28 taxi companies. Taxi drivers do not operate as independent entities with a personal license, but they have to adhere to a "colour scheme". Moreover, license holders can operate directly as drivers or may lease their permits to a taxi company, who may lease them to other drivers. Currently, the top four "colour schemes" cover more than 60% of the market. However, San Francisco represents for Uber not only the city where the service was born, but it is, with its 16,000 drivers, the second largest city in United States for the number of active drivers, after Los Angeles (21,000 drivers). Moreover, if we compare the numbers of Uber active drivers in the city with those of "taxi -cab driver" there is a ratio of 2.29 in favor of the former. This suggests how Uber has a greater capillarity than the traditional taxi service.

Availability of substitutive products or services

The taxi service in San Francisco is basically standardized and the taxi offering is not diversified such as that of Uber. In addition to the taxi service, San Francisco inhabitants can use two public transportation systems as substitutive services, i.e. Bay Area Rapid Transfer (BART) and Municipal Railway (MUNI). BART enables connections between the city center and key locations of the Bay Area through five metro lines. On the other hand, MUNI is the public transportation system that allows traveling within the city center through 10 tram lines (three lines covered by the historic cable car), 17 trolleybus lines and 54 bus lines.

4.2.2. New Delhi

Regulatory framework

On December 2014, the New Delhi police filed a complaint against Uber for fraud and violation of government regulations, accusing the company of not carrying out checks on criminal records of its potential drivers. This temporarily banned Uber services. Nevertheless, Uber tried to improve service's safety by strengthening the drivers' selection system. In particular, Uber added an additional layer of screening represented by:

(1) An independent background checks on all driver partners plus vehicle documentation reviews;
(2) The deactivation of drivers' account with low users rating;
(3) An emergency button as part of its app, which allows users to contact the police.

Moreover, according to the "Terms and conditions for taxi-radio scheme in 2006" of the Transport Department Government of Delhi, other critical aspects of Uber not complying with this scheme refer to:

(a) Absence of a valid license to provide the taxi service;
(b) Absence of checks on the status and on seniority of cars;
(c) Absence of a regular taximeter;
(d) Other issues related to UberX drivers, such as the fact that they do not make driving tests or do not wear the regulatory uniform;
(e) Absence of control on criminal background of drivers.

Although the presence of such aspects, mostly related to single drivers, Uber is currently able to operate because it is assimilated to taxi aggregators, which are companies that do not own vehicles such as Uber, but aggregate taxis inside a brand. This particular category of actors is compliant with the New Delhi transportation regulation.

Market concentration

Currently, there are 53739 regulated taxis for a population of more than 16 million and the market is growing fast at 20–25% rate per year. The taxi industry is mainly characterized by two typologies of segments with different actors that provide the taxi service:

(1) "Regulated market", which includes three types of players:
   "Aggregators", operators as Uber that aggregate taxis inside their brand, without any direct control on the vehicles. This kind of operator covers about the 0.5% of the market share;

   "Affiliators", operators that aggregate taxis inside their brand and allow the presence of sheds for the maintenance and control of vehicles. This kind of operator covers about the 5% of market share;

   "Radio Cabs", real taxi companies that physically possess the vehicles with which the service is provided. This kind of operator covers about the 4.5% of market share;

(2) "Unorganized market", which includes independent operators who provide the service in many areas of the city, without being aggregated under companies or brand and representing about the 90% of the market share.
   The first three kinds of actors represent the regulated and organized market of taxis. In the regulated and organized market, these operators have a minimum fleet of 500 vehicles, as required by the existing law. One of them (i.e. "Radio Cabs") holds nearly the 70% of the regulated and organized market.

Availability of substitutive products or services

The taxi service in New Delhi is basically standardized and the taxi offering, if we consider the regulated market, is not diversified. However, in New Delhi inhabitants could also use only one alternative transportation service as a substitute, represented by the six metro lines of the city.

4.2.3. London

Regulatory framework

On July 2014, the local authority for transportation — the "Transport for London" (TfL) — proved the compliance of Uber with the existing Private Hire Vehicles

(PHV) Act of 1998, even though the presence of several provisions that Uber is not compliance with:

(a) Any private hire vehicles driver must apply to the Secretary of State for a London PHV operator's license;
(b) The vehicle must have a private-vehicle license to provide service;
(c) Uber does not allow inspecting and testing any vehicle to which a London PHV license relates;
(d) Vehicles have not a disc or plate, to which a London PHV license relates, which identifies that vehicle for which the license is in force;
(e) UberX app can be considered such as a taximeter, and no vehicle to which a London PHV license relates shall be equipped with a taximeter.

Market concentration
Currently the licensed vehicles that provide the taxi service in London are organized in 14 taxi companies. Out of these, five taxi companies cover the most part of the market.

Availability of substitutive products or services
The taxi service in London is basically standardized and the taxi offering, if we consider the regulated market, is not diversified such as that of Uber. However, taxis are not the only transportation systems, indeed there are many substitutive services:

(a) Eleven underground lines;
(b) The Docklands Light Railway (DLR), an automated light rail system serving the Dockland area of east London;
(c) The Tramlink, which is a light rail/tram system in South London;
(d) Twenty-six lines of bus, served by the red double-decker London bus.

4.2.4. Milan

Regulatory framework
On May 2015, Uber was completely blocked by the local court, because with its UberX/UberPop service, the company was performing unfair competition and infringing laws that regulate the taxi service, with particular reference to the role of Uber drivers, which were not qualified to offer the service and without any authorization to operate within the area.

In particular, the service did not conform to the provisions of the Law 21 of 15 January, 1992 and subsequent modifications and integrations. This law regulates the taxi and car hire with driver services in Italy and represents the main entry barrier into the Italian taxy industry. According to this law, UberX can be associated to the car hire with driver service, indeed drivers can refuse to provide the service for customers or negotiate directly with them the travel fare. Instead, taxis have to provide the race each time they are called and with tariffs in line with those set by the authority. However, although UberX is considered for its functionalities comparable to the car hire with driver service, it surely violates some aspects underlined in the law:

(1) UberX drivers are not registered to the Italian Chamber of Commerce for covering the role of drivers, therefore in accordance with the above-mentioned Law, they cannot provide the service;
(2) UberX does not have permission to operate within the Italian municipalities where it has decided to activate the service and does not possess any shed where to repair and maintain the vehicles;
(3) Cars used for UberX service do not respect the same regulation of car hire with driver services because they do not exhibit the related identification plates required;
(4) UberX drivers do not make back to the shed at the end of the race, but wait for the next call stationing on public land. The existing law allows this option only for drivers who take a regular taxi service and not for those taking a kind of car hire with driver service.

Therefore, differently from what happens in London, the diffusion of the service as a whole has been hampered by the local regulation.

Market concentration
Actually, in Milan there are 4855 licenses for the taxi service, with a density of 3.7 taxis per 1000 inhabitants, while in the airport area (which include the routes to Malpensa and Linate airports) the licenses are 5323 with 2.4 taxis per 1000 inhabitants. Thus, Milan is the first Italian city in terms of taxi density and the second, after Rome, for the number of licenses issued. However, it is far from cities as Paris that have in their metropolitan area 15500 licenses, with a density of 6.9 taxis per 1000 inhabitants. In addition, taxis are not organized in taxi companies, but operate independently.

Availability of substitutive products or services
The taxi service in Milan is basically standardized and the taxi offering is not diversified such as that of Uber. However, considering the transportation industry as a whole, consumers can use many substitutive services. Indeed, Milan is served by four metro lines, by 1503 buses and by 19 tramlines. These services are provided and managed by the ATM (Azienda Trasporti Milanesi S.p.A.) company, which also offers bike- and car-sharing services. In addition, there are also two main railway stations, which connect the city to the rest of the Lombardy through 14 suburban lines.

5. Discussion and Results

In this section, we present and discuss the results of our exploratory analysis on the level of diffusion of Uber in the four sampled cities. The aim of this analysis is to provide evidence of the influence of the three external contextual factors on the diffusion and disruptive impact of Uber in the taxi industry.

Market concentration in the analyzed four cities is rather different. In San Francisco, market concentration is high because taxi drivers must be aggregated within dedicated companies to regularly operate on the market. In London, considering the aggregation of taxis in a number of dedicated companies and the relative market share, the market ends up being highly concentrated. On the other hand, in Milan the largest part of taxi drivers operates independently, and the resulting market concentration is low. The same can be said for New Delhi, where the largest part of taxi drivers operate as single entities.

The regulatory framework in the analyzed metropolitan areas is also quite heterogeneous. In San Francisco, the regulatory framework enables the diffusion of Uber in the taxi industry. Although it seems that Uber operates illegally in the city, local authorities have been willing to change local laws to encourage a greater competition in the market, thus showing an open regulatory system regarding Uber diffusion in the market. The same can be said for New Delhi, in which a new regulation in favor of taxis aggregators is under development. Indeed, in these two cities there are several taxi operators, which act as taxi aggregators such as Uber. Similarly, in London the Uber service is completely considered legal. On the other hand, in Milan the existing laws banned the service, thus strongly hindering its whole diffusion in the city.

Focusing on the taxi industry, and in particular on the regulated-side of this market, the availability of substitutive products or services is generally low in all the four analyzed cities, given also the high standardization of such service. Considering the broader transportation service industry as a whole, it emerges that in Milan, San Francisco and London the availability of substitutive products or services is high, mainly because of the presence of several public transportation options. Instead, in New Delhi the availability of substitutive products or services is much lower, due to the presence of just one competitor, represented by a not well diffused system of metro lines.

Based on this evidence, and considering that in San Francisco, New Delhi and London, Uber has spread very fast and has had a strong impact on the taxi industry (whereas in Milan the diffusion of Uber is very limited), we can argue that the regulatory framework has the most relevant impact on the diffusion of Uber and on its disruptive impact. Indeed, only where the regulatory framework is very closed and severe, such as it happens in Milan, Uber has not had a real disruptive impact in the market and has not represented a serious threat to the established players of this industry.

The role of the other two contextual factors does not seem to be as important as it happens with the regulatory framework. For example, New Delhi shows a very different situation in terms of both market concentration and availability of substitutive products or services compared with San Francisco and London. However, the diffusion of Uber in the three cities can be compared and it has had a strong disruptive impact on incumbent players.

From the empirical evidence above, two critical aspects emerge on the influence that the contextual factors have on the disruptive impact of Uber in the four analyzed cities, with particular reference to the regulatory framework. First, local authorities can erect entry barriers in an established industry, through a new interpretation of the existing regulatory framework in the light of the emergence of an innovation. Therefore, players launching an innovation with a disruptive potential might find particularly complex to understand in advance how policy makers will interpret the existing regulatory framework once they have slipped into the market. In addition, empirical analysis shows that in some cases, as happened in San Francisco, the emergence of an innovation with disruptive potential can even enable an amendment of the existing regulatory framework, definitely more difficult to predict by the newcomer.

This is particularly interesting if compared with the traditional models of economics of innovation and industrial economics, such as the models of Porter [1979] on the contextual factors characterizing the external environment. In particular, the porterian models look into the structure and organization of the competitive arena in a static perspective, i.e. without considering the dynamism of the contextual factors in the light of the emergence of an innovation. Put it differently, the emergence of an innovation with disruptive potential requires the newcomer to look into the competitive arena and on its contextual factors in a dynamic perspective, trying to predict structural and organizational amendments in that arena. The Uber case shows that the regulatory framework in our sample of cities did not initially represent an entry barrier for the company, however the policy makers acted in favor or against the newcomer as soon as it slipped into the market, through a different interpretation of the existing regulatory framework or, in one case, its amendment.

6. Conclusions

The role of contextual factors in determining the impact that a disruptive innovation has in the market is an under-researched topic in the innovation management research. Starting from this premise, this paper represents a first exploratory attempt to understand whether and how a set of contextual factors influences the disruptive impact that an innovation has on the market. In particular, the paper analyzes the effects of three main contextual factors, i.e. market concentration, the characteristics of the regulatory framework and the availability of substitutive products or service, on the extent to which Uber is having a disruptive impact in the local taxi industry.

In particular, the paper explores, using a historical analysis methodology, the case of Uber, a taxi-hailing company based in San Francisco, which launched its taxi-hailing service in June 2010 and is disrupting the taxi industry to a different extent in different countries and in different cities around the world. The paper highlights the influence of the level of market concentration, the characteristics of the regulatory framework and the availability of substitutive products or services on the diffusion of Uber in four different cities (i.e. San Francisco, New Delhi, London, and Milan) in which Uber has experienced different levels of diffusion and disruptive impact.

The results of this paper offer interesting insights for disruptive innovation research. In particular, the empirical analysis illuminates the strong impact that the local regulatory framework has on the disruptive nature of Uber. Indeed, from our historical analysis it emerges that the regulatory framework represents the most important contextual factor significantly influencing the extent to which Uber service diffuses on the market. This stems, on one hand, from the fact that, through the regulatory framework, local authorities determine the height of the entry barriers in the industry and establish how many taxi operators, and how, have to compete. On the other hand, a disruptive innovation (i.e. Uber) often causes relevant changes in existing industries (i.e. in the taxi industry) which require a different interpretation or an amendment of existing regulations. The strong interplay between the disruptive innovation and the characteristics of the regulatory framework, which our analysis highlights as a very important aspect, is something that existing literature has not adequately considered. Accordingly, we encourage future theoretical and empirical studies to conceive the disruptive innovation embedded in the regulatory context in which it develops and unfolds over time, because this is fundamental to understand how the phenomenon takes place and impacts established market positions. Put it differently, we suggest researchers should consider how disruptive innovations not only create changes for customers and companies that develop and launch them, but also in the broader regulatory framework that significantly influence the extent to which they diffuse and have a disruptive impact in the market. In other words, if we do not fully consider how policy makers react to the emergence of a disruptive innovation, i.e. assuming a dynamic perspective in analyzing contextual factors, we will not be able to develop a comprehensive understanding of the disruptive innovation phenomenon in its complexity. This represents an important contribution to our current understanding of disruptive innovation, which will hopefully inform research aimed at developing a theory of disruptive innovation capable to interpret and predict whether and why a new product, service, or business model will disrupt an established industry.

Besides these theoretical implications, the exploratory analysis presented in this paper has a number of important limitations that require future research efforts to be filled. First, we have focused on three contextual factors that economics of innovation and diffusion of innovation research suggests as highly important for understanding the outcome of the innovation diffusion process. However, there might be other factors (e.g. innovation adoption behavior, cultural variables, level of technology-intensity, importance of complementary assets and economies of scale in capturing value from innovation) that should be studied to develop a theory of disruptive innovation with a strong external validity. Similarly, we have limited our attention to four cities in which Uber has experienced varied degrees of diffusion in the last years. To enhance the external validity of our analysis it would be useful to consider other geographical areas, which could unearth different contextual factors as important in influencing the diffusion and disruptive impact of an innovation like Uber. Moreover, it should be remembered that our analysis has focused on one particular example of disruptive innovation, Uber, which is a service or business model innovation. Future research is needed to understand whether the weight of different contextual factors changes if we consider disruptive product innovation. It is likely that, for instance, due to the higher fixed costs that product innovations entail, the importance of market concentration on the diffusion of this type of innovation will be higher. Finally, considered the exploratory nature of our study, we have adopted a qualitative methodology, which does not allow for statistical generalizations. Our aim was to enable analytical generalizations about the role of a set of external contextual factors on the diffusion and disruptive impact of Uber. Future confirmatory analyses are needed to test our ideas and contribute to develop a more robust theory of disruptive innovation, which properly accounts for the role of contextual factors on the outcome of this particular type of innovation diffusion process.

References

Adner, R. (2002). When are technologies disruptive? A demand-based view of the emergence of competition. *Strategic Management Journal*, **23**, 8: 667–688.

Aghion, P., Bloom, N., Blundell, R., Griffith, R. and Howitt, P. (2005). Competition and innovation: An inverted U-shape. *Quarterly Journal of Economics*, **120**, 2: 701–728.

Anastasio, P. (2015). Uber vince a Londra: La app non è un tassametro. Available at https://www.key4biz.it/uber-vince-a-londra-la-app-non-e-un-tassametro/137095/.

Antonelli, C. (2014). *The Economics of Innovation, New Technologies and Structural Change*. Routled, London.

Artoni, R. (2001). *Lezioni di Scienza delle Finanze*. Il Mulino, Bologna.

Audretsch, D. B. (1995). Innovation, growth and survival. *International Journal of Industrial Organization*, **13**, 4: 441–457.

Autio, E., Kenney, M., Mustar, P., Siegel, D. and Wright, M. (2014). Entrepreneurial innovation: The importance of context. *Research Policy*, **43**, 7: 1097–1108.

Birkinshaw, J. and Gibson, C. (2004). Building ambidexterity into an organization. *MIT Sloan Management Review*, **45**, 4: 47–55.

Bower, J. L. and Christensen, C. M. (1995). Disruptive technologies: Catching the wave. *Harvard Business Review*, **73**, 1: 43–53.

Chesbrough, H. W. (1999). The differing organizational impact of technological change: A comparative theory of institutional factors. *Industrial and Corporate Change*, **8**, 3: 447–485.

Chiesa, V. and Frattini, F. (2011). Commercializing technological innovation: Learning from failures in high-tech markets. *Journal of Product Innovation Management*, **28**: 437–454.

Christensen, C. M. (1997). *The Innovator's Dilemma: When New Technologies Cause Great Firms to Fail.* Harvard Business School Press, Boston.

Christensen, C. M. and Bower, J. L. (1996). Customer power, strategic investment, and the failure of leading firms. *Strategic Management Journal,* **17**, 3: 197–218.

Christensen, C. M. and Overdorf, M. (2000). Meeting the challenge of disruptive change. *Harvard Business Review,* **78**, 2: 66–76.

Christensen, C. M. and Raynor, M. (2003). *The Innovator's Solution: Creating and Sustaining Successful Growth.* Harvard Business School Press, Boston.

Christensen, C. M., Raynor, M. E. and McDonald, R. (2015). What is disruptive innovation? *Harvard Business Review,* **93**, 12: 44–53.

Danneels, E. (2004). Disruptive technology reconsidered: A critique and research agenda. *Journal of Product Innovation Management,* **21**: 246–258.

Denning, S. (2005). Why the best and brightest approaches don't solve the innovation dilemma. *Strategy & Leadership,* **33**, 1: 4–11.

Department for Transport — GOV.UK. (2015). Taxi and private hire vehicle statistics: England 2015. Statistical Release. Available at https://www.gov.uk/government/uploads/system/uploads/attachment_data/file/456733/taxi- private-hire-vehicles-statistics-2015.pdf.

Fischer, B. (2015). In Uber vs. taxi cab fight, expense reports offer telling barometer. Available at http://www.bizjournals.com/newyork/blog/techflash/2015/04/uber-taxi-expense-report-certify-study.html.

Garcia-Vega, M. (2006). Does technological diversification promote innovation?: An empirical analysis for European firms. *Research Policy,* **35**, 2: 230–246.

Gayle, P. G. (2001). Market concentration and innovation: New empirical evidence on the Schumpeterian hypothesis. University of Colorado at Boulder, unpublished paper.

Gil, E. (2014). Uber and disruption. Available at http://techcrunch.com/2014/01/19/uber-and-disruption/.

Golder, P. N. and Tellis, G. J. (1993). Pioneer advantage: Marketing logic or marketing legend? *Journal of Marketing Research,* **30**, 2: 158–170.

Gottschalk, L. R. (1969). *Understanding History: A Primer of Historical Method.* Knopf, New York.

Govindarajan, V. and Kopalle, P. K. (2006). Disruptiveness of innovations: Measurement and an assessment of reliability and validity. *Strategic Management Journal,* **27**: 189–199.

Herfindahl, O. C. (1950). Concentration in the U.S. steel industry. Ph.D. Dissertation, Columbia University, New York.

Hill, A. (2015). Uber is not 'genuinely disruptive', says Clayton Christensen. Available at http://www.ft.com/intl/cms/s/0/43c4dca2-8c55-11e5-8be4-3506bf20cc2b.html#axzz45-KyhMSHc.

Hirschman, A. O. (1945). *National Power and the Structure of Foreign Trade.* University of California Press, Berkeley.

Hitt, M. A., Hoskisson, R. E. and Kim, H. (1997). International diversification: Effects on innovation and firm performance in product-diversified firms. *Academy of Management Journal,* **40**, 4: 767–798.

Isaac, E. (2014). Disruptive innovation: Risk-shifting and precarity in the age of Uber. Berkeley Roundtable on the International Economy, Working Paper.

King, A. A. and Tucci, C. L. (2002). Incumbent entry into new market niches: The role of experience and managerial choice in the creation of dynamic capabilities. *Management Science,* **48**, 2: 171–186.

Kostoff, R. N., Boylan, R. and Simons, G. R. (2004). Disruptive technology roadmaps. *Technological Forecasting and Social Change,* **71**: 141–159.

Lien, T. (2015). Uber will spend $1 billion to grow presence in India. Available at http://www.latimes.com/business/technology/la-fi-tn-uber-india-billion-20150731-story.html.

MacMillan, D. (2016). Uber spends big on international expansion. Available at http://www.wsj.com/articles/uber-spends-big-on-international-expansion-1456960083.

Markides, C. (2006). Disruptive innovation: In need of better theory. *Journal of Product Innovation Management*, **23**: 19–25.

McAlon, N. (2015). The father of 'disruption' theory explains why Netflix is the perfect example and Uber isn't. Available at http://uk.businessinsider.com/the-father-of-disruption- theory-explains-why-netflix-is-the-perfect-example-and-uber-isnt-2015-11?r=US&IR=T.

Moazed, A. and Johnson, N. (2016). Why Clayton Christensen is wrong about Uber and disruptive innovation. Available at http://techcrunch.com/2016/02/27/why-clayton-christensen-is-wrong-about-uber-and-disruptive-innovation/.

Myers, D. R. (2002). A practitioner's view: Evolutionary stages of disruptive technologies. *IEEE Transactions on Engineering Management*, **49**, 4: 322–329.

O'Connor, G. C. and DeMartino, R. (2006). Organizing for radical innovation: An exploratory study of the structural aspect of RI management systems in large established firms. *Journal of Product Innovation Management*, **23**, 6: 475–497.

O'Reilly, C. A. and Tushman, M. L. (2004). The ambidextrous organization. *Harvard Business Review*, **82**, 4: 74–81.

Palaniappan, J. (2015). Uber: Innovation and investment in MENA. Available at https://newsroom.uber.com/uae/ubermena/.

Phillips, C. F. (1971). Review of industrial market structure and economic performance. *The Bell Journal of Economics and Management Science*, **2**, 2: 683–687.

Porter, M. (1979). How competitive forces shape strategy. *Harvard Business Review*, **57**, 2: 137–145.

Reuters (2015). Legal troubles — including 173 lawsuits in the US — threaten Uber's global push. Business Insider. Available at: http://www.businessinsider.com/r-legal-troubles-market-realities-threaten-ubers-global-push-2015-10?IR=T.

Rogge, K. S., Schleich, J., Haussmann, P., Roser, A. and Reitze, F. (2011). The role of the regulatory framework for innovation activities: The EU ETS and the German paper industry. *International Journal of Technology, Policy and Management*, **11**, 3–4: 250–273.

Romanelli, E. and Tushman, M. L. (1986). Inertia, environments and strategic choice: A quasi- experimental design for comparative-longitudinal research. *Management Science*, **32**: 608–621.

Ross, D. and Scherer, F. (1990). Industrial market structure and economic performance. University of Illinois at Urbana-Champaign's Academy for Entreprenencial Leadership Historical Research Reference in Entrepreneurship. Available at SSRN: https://ssm.com/abstract=1496716

Rothaermel, F. T. (2001). Incumbent's advantage through exploiting complementary assets via interfirm cooperation. *Strategic Management Journal*, **22**, 6–7: 687–699.

Schmokler, J. (1966). *Innovation and Economic Growth*. Harvard University Press, Cambridge, MA.

Schumpeter, J. A. (1934). *The Theory of Economic Development: An Inquiry into Profits, Capital, Credit, Interest and the Business Cycle*. Harvard University Press, Cambridge, MA.

Schumpeter, J. A. (1950). *Capitalism, Socialism and Democracy*, Paperback edition, Routledge, London.

Sharma Punit, I. (2015). The last three weeks could change India's taxi industry forever. Available at http://qz.com/554193/who-will-win-the-taxi-wars-in-india-home-grown-ola-or-world-leader-uber/.

Stuart, G. (2014). Can Chicago's taxi industry survive the rideshare revolution? Chicago Reader. Available at http://www.chicagoreader.com/chicago/ridesharechicago-uber-lyft-uberx-taxi-industry-cab-drivers-extinct/Content?oid=15165161.

Suarez, F. F. and Utterback, J. M. (1995). Dominant design and the survival of firms. *Strategic Management Journal*, **16**: 415–430.

Sull, D. N., Tedlow, R. S. and Rosenbloom, R. S. (1997). Managerial commitments and technological change in the U.S. tire industry. *Industrial and Corporate Change*, **6**: 461–501.

Tellis, G. J. (2006). Disruptive technology or visionary leadership? *Journal of Product Innovation Management*, **23**: 34–38.

The Strategy Group (2016). Excellent example of disruption — Uber. Available at http://www.thestrategygroup.com.au/pellentesque-commodo-aliquam-lorem/.

Tripsas, M. (1997). Unravelling the process of creative destruction: Complementary assets and incumbent survival in the typesetter industry. *Strategic Management Journal*, **18**: 119–142.

Tushman, M. L. and Anderson, P. (1986). Technological discontinuities and organisational environments. *Administrative Science Quarterly*, **31**, 3: 8–30.

Veryzer, R. (1998). Key factors affecting customer evaluation of discontinuous new products. *Journal of Product Innovation Management*, **15**: 136–150.

Weber, R. P. (1990). *Basic Content Analysis*. SAGE, Newbury Park, CA.

Yanbing, W. (2007). Firm size, market concentration and innovation: A survey. *Economic Research Journal*, **5**: 125–138.

Yu, D. and Hang, C. C. (2010). A reflective review of disruptive innovation theory. *International Journal of Management Reviews*, **12**, 4: 435–452.

Biography

Andrea Urbinati, Ph.D., is Assistant Professor of Strategy & Business Design at the School of Industrial Engineering of LIUC Università Cattaneo, Italy. His research interests are in the fields of circular economy, business model design, and digital technologies. He is Member of the Core Faculty and Director of the Center on Technological and Digital Innovation of LIUC Business School, the School of Management of LIUC Università Cattaneo. Andrea holds a Ph.D. in Management, Economics, and Industrial Engineering at the School of Management of Politecnico di Milano, Italy. He is also Member of the Extended Faculty of MIP, the Graduate School of Business of Politecnico di Milano, where he teaches in MBA, Executive MBA, and Flex EMBA courses. Andrea has more than seventy publications, as papers on international journals, book chapters, national and international conferences. Andrea is Associate Editor of the International Journal of Innovation and Technology Management, Member of the Editorial Board of Sustainability, Review Editor on the Editorial Board of Frontiers in Sustainability (specialty section on Circular Economy), and Ordinary Member of the International Society for Circular Economy (IS4CE).

Davide Chiaroni is Full Professor of Strategy & Marketing at Politecnico di Milano, where he obtained in 2007 his Ph.D. in Management, Economics and Industrial Engineering. His research interest is in the management of innovation, with a particular focus on energy, sustainability and smart ecosystems (grid, buildings, communities, cities). He is also among the most cited authors in the field of Circular Economy, where he studies the implications of the adoption of circular business models. The results of his research are documented by an intense scientific production. Davide Chiaroni is author of two books with international editors, one with an Italian publisher and more than 150 contributions on international and national journals, edited books, and conference proceedings..

Vittorio Chiesa is Full Professor at Politecnico di Milano — School of Management, where he is member of the Board. He teaches Strategy and Marketing and Energy and Sustainability Management in the MSc program in Management Engineering. He is responsible of the Technology Strategy area at MIP (the Graduate Business School of Politecnico di Milano) and Director of the Executive Master in Energy Management. His main research areas are in the fields of R&D management, strategic innovation, creation of start-ups in science-based industries. He is Director of the Energy & Strategy Group at the School of Management of Politecnico di Milano, which does research and consultancy in the field of energy management. He has been Visiting Researcher at London Business School. He is author of six books and more than 200 international publications. On the basis of his publications, he has been included in the list of the Top 60 World's Innovation Management Scholars in the period 1991–2010.

Simone Franzò is Assistant Professor at the School of Management of Politecnico di Milano, Italy. His research interest is in the management of innovation, with particular reference to Open Innovation — and Energy management, with particular reference to the assessment of new technologies and business models. He is also consultant and research fellow at the Energy & Strategy Group of Politecnico di Milano. Simone Franzò teaches Business Administration and Energy Management Lab in Bachelor and Master of Science programs in Management Engineering at Politecnico di Milano. He also teaches Energy Management courses in MBA, Executive MBA, and other Postgraduate courses at MIP, the Graduate School of Business of Politecnico di Milano. Simone Franzò is Member of the Core Faculty of the School of Management of the Politecnico di Milano.

Federico Frattini is Full Professor of Strategic Management and Innovation at the School of Management of Politecnico di Milano (Italy) and Honorary Researcher at the Lancaster University Management School (UK). At the School of Management of Politecnico di Milano, he is also Director of the MBA and Executive MBA

Programs, Coordinator of the Strategic Management Teaching Area, and Director of the ICT and Digital Learning Division. His research area is innovation and technology management. On these topics, he has written more than 200 books and papers published in conference proceedings and leading international journals such as Entrepreneurship Theory & Practice, Academy of Management Perspectives, California Management Review, Journal of Product Innovation Management, and many others. In 2013, he was nominated among the top 50 authors of innovation and technology management worldwide by IAMOT, the International Association for Management of Technology.

Chapter 4

Exploring the Success Factors of Mobile Business Ecosystems

Juha Winter

Aalto University, School of Science
P. O. Box 15400, FI-00076 Aalto, Finland
juha.winter@aalto.fi

Sandro Battisti*

Bruno Kessler Foundation
Center for Information and Communication Technology
Via Sommarive 18, 38123, Trento, Italy
s.battisti@fbk.eu

Thommie Burström

Hanken School of Economics
P. O. Box 479, FI-00101 Helsinki, Finland
thommie.burstrom@hanken.fi

Sakari Luukkainen

Aalto University, School of Science
P. O. Box 15400, FI-00076 Aalto, Finland
sakari.luukkainen@aalto.fi

Mobile business ecosystems are based on product innovations and complements created on platforms facilitating transactions between groups of users in a multi-sided market. The purpose of this research is to present a model of success factors (SF) of mobile ecosystems. This research establishes an empirical framework based on the Android ecosystem, which has been analyzed in-depth on firm and ecosystem level, identifying 16 success factors. The main theoretical contribution is a model that identifies SF of platforms, which are related to the identification of the role of users and complementors in increasing innovation success. The model advances research in innovation platforms.

Keywords: Innovation platforms; business ecosystems; success factors; two-sided market; Android.

---

*Corresponding author.

This chapter was originally published in *International Journal of Innovation and Technology Management*, Vol. 15, No. 3, March 2018, published by World Scientific Publishing, Singapore. Reprinted with permission.

1. Introduction

The deterioration of Nokia's market share in smartphones following its renewed strategy in 2011 illustrates a rare event in business history: an industry leader collapses in terms of market share and profitability in just a few years [Canalys (2014)]. Almost simultaneously, however, two new entrants to the smartphone market, Google Android and Apple, have asserted their dominance. Explaining this dramatic change in the market structure has to do with business ecosystems as explored by Iansiti and Levien [2004]. More specifically, this paper proposes that certain key characteristics or *success factors* (SF) of the competing business ecosystems, possessed by Google and Apple led to a chain of events that changed the smartphone industry landscape for good, and that the explicit identification of these SF deserves special attention.

Nevertheless, these SF are not easily identified. The literature discussing potential SF is scattered and in-depth holistic case descriptions are lacking in this field of research. What is clear is that the success behind mobile ecosystems is related to the *platform* construct. Gawer and Cusumano [2008] identified four *levers of platform leadership* as well as generic strategies for becoming a platform leader. Other platform researchers propose that management of competitive dynamics and pricing are significant SF [e.g. Rochet and Tirole (2003)]. Indeed, some researchers have also taken a very narrow perspective on the Android ecosystem, focusing on design aspects and user acceptance of technology [e.g. Bouwman *et al.* (2014)], as well as the creation of mobile ecosystems that enable users to control their experiences during the use of technology [e.g. Remneland-Wikhamn *et al.* (2011)]. Still, although both Gawer [2014] and Thomas *et al.* [2014] have tried to bridge various platform concepts, the views on SF are far from unified.

From this perspective, the main research gap is to explicitly identify and discuss SF of ecosystems and platforms in the mobile industry, in particular extending the research of Gawer and Cusumano [2014] and the work of Davis [2016] by analyzing the business dynamics inside the Android ecosystem.

This paper takes a normative approach in designing and presenting an analysis framework with the purpose of explicitly identifying SF of mobile business ecosystems based on both firm-level and ecosystem-level analysis, bringing together the various theoretical constructs in ecosystem and platform research. This conceptual model is the main contribution to the field of innovation and technology management. Thus, the research question is: *What are the SF of mobile business ecosystems, particularly in terms of engaging users and complementors?*

The paper is structured as follows: in Sec. 2, we review research related to key theoretical constructs as they relate to SF of ecosystems, then in Sec. 3, we present our research design that is subsequently applied to a case study in Sec. 4. This is followed by discussion of the results and the presentation of the model before conclusions and implications.

2. Theoretical Background

This section discusses the general characteristics of, and the relationship between, two related research streams; business ecosystems and platforms.

First, management scholars have studied the origins of competitive advantage of companies, in order to explain business performance [Rumelt *et al.* (1991)]. Dyer and Singh [1998] argued that competitive advantage could stem from *idiosyncratic interfirm linkages*, forming a *relational view*. Thus, four sources are defined: (i) *investments in relation-specific assets*, (ii) *substantial knowledge exchange*, (iii) *complementary resources/capabilities enabling the joint creation of new products, services, or technologies*, and (iv) *effective governance mechanisms resulting in lower transaction costs*. Although not explicitly mentioning ecosystems, the above findings are noticeably similar to those of, e.g. Williamson and De Meyer [2012] who identified the "six keys to ecosystem advantage" as follows: *structuring differentiated partner roles, enabling flexibility and co-learning, stimulating complementary partner investments, reducing transaction costs, pinpointing the added value*, and *engineering value capture mechanisms*. Based on the above, it is proposed in this paper that SF of ecosystems could well originate from *relationships between firms* and should therefore be further studied.

Thomas and Autio [2012; 2014] define a business ecosystem as a *"network of interconnected organizations, organized around a focal firm or a platform and incorporating both production and use side participants"*, having three common characteristics: a network of participants, a governance system, and a shared logic. The ecological analogy of *business ecosystem* has been analyzed from several different perspectives in innovation and management research, often describing the advances in information and communications technology (ICT). It has been mainly used to explain the competition and collaboration among organizations. From this point of view, the research is focused on exploring the perspective of creating value, in particular oriented to the creation of mobile business ecosystems. Furthermore, SF could stem from health measures of business ecosystems, as defined by Iansiti and Levien [2004] and quantitatively by Den Hartigh *et al.* [2006]. Additionally, Bosch [2009] outlines SF for operating systems (OS)-centric software ecosystems. A key point is to understand that in innovation ecosystems, innovation is performed through multi-partner innovation efforts, but such boundary conditions are understudied [Davis (2016, p. 33)]. This type of literature will therefore be used in a later stage of this paper in order to identify and discuss success factors.

Second, this study uses platform literature in order to identify success factors. Particularly, it draws on Gawer and Cusumano [2002, pp. 2–3] and defines platform as an evolving system made of interdependent pieces that can each be innovated upon. The general literature on platforms can be seen as being divided into four distinct streams of research: (1) *organizational platforms* (with dynamic capabilities as the key construct), (2) *product family platforms*, (3) *market intermediary platforms* (serving two or multi-sided markets), and (4) *platform ecosystems*, as discussed by Thomas *et al.* [2014]. This is compatible with and builds upon the typology of platforms by Gawer [2009], comprising *internal platforms, supply chain platforms, two-sided (or multi-sided) markets*, and *industry platforms*. In our study of ecosystem success factors, particularly the last two streams of research are of relevance and will be further discussed below.

Multiple researchers emphasize the importance of understanding the logic behind *two-sided markets* [Parker and Van Alstyne (2005); Rochet and Tirole (2003); Eisenmann *et al.* (2006)]. Within this line of research, it is further proposed that the issue of pricing [e.g. Hagiu (2006, 2009b)] is an important topic, and so is the subsidization of the two-sided markets whose transactions are facilitated by a platform [Armstrong (2006); Armstrong and Wright (2007); Hagiu and Spulber (2013)]. Moreover, Hagiu [2009a] and Rysman [2009] discuss that *multi-sided platforms* could be considered as a generalization of two-sided markets. Although case studies are common within this stream of literature, often using credit cards, computer OS, or business directories as examples (e.g. Rysman (2004)], relevant studies of mobile ecosystems are lacking.

Although being presented as two different concepts there is actually a strong resemblance between platform ecosystem studies and industry platform studies. *Platform ecosystems*, as presented by Thomas *et al.* [2014] roughly equate to industry platforms as discussed by Gawer and Cusumano [2008; 2014]. Both streams of research view the focal firm as a hub or a central point of control in technology-based business ecosystems. Contextually, the literature has focused on the information technology and Internet sectors, with extensive case studies on, e.g. Intel [Gawer and Henderson (2007)]. Still, these studies can work as inspiration for defining SF in mobile ecosystems.

A special issue to consider for ecosystem leaders in mobile ecosystems is the question of openness (cf. Eisenmann [2008]). Thomas *et al.* [2014] elaborate on this issues and present a model of *architectural leverage*, combining three distinct logics of leverage, namely *production, innovation,* and *transaction logic*, with *architectural openness* based on the degree of disaggregation of the industry value chain, also identifying situated types of platform variants within the model. The authors further argued that market intermediary platforms and platform ecosystems typically exhibit so-called *many-to-many architectures* where both supply and demand sides are open to participants. This seems compatible with Eisenmann's [2008] dimensions of platform openness, although he defines openness also in terms of two additional roles, the platform provider and sponsor.

Furthermore, Muegge [2013] made an attempt to integrate the theories of industrial platforms and business ecosystems, arguing that in a complex hierarchical system, they represent different but complementary layers of analysis. In a similar line of argumentation, Gawer [2014] observes the resemblances between roles such as being a *platform leader* and/or a *keystone firm*. Thus, both Muegge and Gawer communicate the importance of the possibility to use both the firm level and the ecosystem level as distinct levels of analysis.

Thomas *et al.* [2014] also identified different levels of analysis but did not explore the theory of platform concepts beyond the level of the firm. They did allude to, e.g. industry and ecosystem-level analysis and advocated further research from different analytical perspectives. Thus, it would appear that in management research, there is interest in multi-level analytical frameworks and more holistic exploration of the theory behind platforms and ecosystems. Furthermore, although Gawer's [2014] proposal may well be the most advanced integrative framework of platform concepts to date, she does not discuss the SF of platforms or ecosystems, nor the interaction of decisions related to different parts of the framework, such as platform scope (including possible envelopment) and openness. Also, as she acknowledges herself, the framework requires systematic empirical validation.

Finally, indeed some scholars have explored the level of analysis of software ecosystems and developer marketplaces with particular focus on those of Apple, Google, BlackBerry, and Microsoft [see, e.g. Campbell and Ahmed (2011); Idu *et al.* (2011); Tuunainen *et al.* (2011); Hyrynsalmi *et al.* (2012)]. In particular, the main contributions of these scholars have been in the area of application marketplaces and developer programs. However, these researchers have lacked a holistic understanding of the platforms and methods for capturing value inside the respective ecosystems of organizations. Therefore, in Secs. 2.1 and 2.2, the particularities of the firm-level and ecosystem-level analysis dimensions are discussed.

2.1. *Firm-level dimension*

Firm level forms the first and most granular part of our framework, since we look at the value creation and extraction of the platform leader or ecosystem orchestrator, being the central firm or *keystone* of its ecosystem, followed by a discussion of the firm's platform approach and governance. It is related to the breadth of business activities of companies, such as the product offering, development and commercialization, as well as the services delivered to specific customers, and the place where the business activity is carried out.

Various monetization models may be mixed and utilized by firms sometimes simultaneously. In our analysis framework, the method of value configuration analysis as defined by Stabell and Fjeldstad [1998] is applied for the purpose of identifying alternative means of value creation, serving as a generalization of traditional value chain analysis. In spite of this, our study considers the question of monetization reflecting on existing capabilities and assets, also considering historical developments. The theory of path dependence [David (1985); Arthur (1989)] supports our idea that the historical legacy of a firm mainly in terms of its previous business and related activities, capabilities, and assets has had an impact on more recent strategic decisions and choices the firm has made with regard to ecosystems and platforms.

The *four levers of platform leadership* [Gawer and Cusumano (2008)] and the descriptions of the roles of platform leaders and complementors form the basis for the study of the case company's platforms. We separate the analysis of how much the firm innovates and produces complements in-house from how the firm manages and incentives its external complementors. The latter point is also relevant in the analysis of ecosystems, where software ecosystems and particularly application marketplaces are examined. We also consider the strategic approaches taken by firms to become platform leaders, such as "coring", "tipping" [Gawer and Cusumano (2008)], expanding the scope of one's platform by incorporating some of the functionality of the platforms being used in an adjacent market.

The control paradigm of a platform may be either *proprietary* or *shared*, and this has profound implications especially on value capture and the management of complementary innovation. Eisenmann [2008] argued that both paradigms can be successful and examines factors that are favorable to each when designing new platforms. Shared platforms are prone to free rider problems that make it challenging to protect returns from infrastructure investments or to offer user subsidies. In contrast, proprietary platforms do not have such problems.

Regarding the effects of the number of complementors on the intensity of competition, Boudreau [2008] argued that having too many complementors can reduce a platform's ability to generate new innovation and profits for firms making complements on it, mainly due to crowding-out effects and substitution instead of market expansion. These effects would affect both the attractiveness of the platform negatively from end-user and complement producer perspective.

Differentiation through either vertical integration or exclusivity is often sought by platform providers to make themselves stand out from their rivals. Lee [2013], who has studied this phenomenon and its implications, contended that exclusive software is a key leverage for platform entrants, allowing them to differentiate and gain market traction more effectively. In terms of the overall market, however, exclusivity actually decreases the total market revenue as well as consumer welfare.

This research focuses mostly on technical and organizational concepts, comprising mainly analysis on firm level. While network effects and multi-sided markets do play a fundamental role also in platform theory, we discuss the related analysis dimensions under *ecosystem-level analysis*.

2.2. *Ecosystem-level dimension*

Iansiti and Levien [2004] have studied the characteristics of business ecosystems such as their structure and health. The three critical measures defined by them, *productivity, robustness*, and *niche creation*, are also applied in our analysis framework. Alternative health metrics have been suggested by Den Hartigh *et al.* [2006], divided into partner health and network health metrics. These metrics, as they argue, are better suited for measuring the health of business ecosystems on the company level and of more practical value to managers.

In our framework, the *software ecosystems* considered are OS-centric in the sense that the OS and its interfaces play a key role in defining what really constitutes the software ecosystem. They also set the technical boundaries for what kinds of complements can be produced on a particular platform. We use the following SF identified by Bosch [2009] specifically for OS-centric ecosystems for the evaluation of the case company's software ecosystems: (i) *minimal effort required by developers to build applications on top of the OS, thereby enabling both breadth and quality of the application offering*, (ii) *generic, evolving functionality and set of features provided by the OS that maintains attractiveness for developers*, and (iii) *the number of customers that use the OS and that are accessible to developers for monetization.*

Being a key component of a mobile software ecosystem, a mobile *application marketplace* is also a well-known example of a two-sided market, and thus relevant characteristics of two-sided markets are used in the case study to analyze them. Joining multiple platforms to make one's products available on more than one market, i.e. multi-homing, is a key phenomenon in mobile application stores as discussed by Hyrynsalmi *et al.* [2012].

The *openness* of a platform ecosystem is defined by Eisenmann *et al.* [2008] along four distinct dimensions, each of which corresponds to a certain role in a platform-mediated network: demand-side platform users, supply-side platform users, platform providers who operate the platform and interface directly with the customer, and platform sponsors who own the platform and decide who gets to participate. Many kinds of platforms can be analyzed using this set of dimensions of openness, not tied to a particular industry. However, specific to mobile application stores, Müller *et al.* [2011] identified a total of 12 distinct value network roles, namely *end user, network operator, payment broker, advertisement broker, marketplace, operating system developer, testing and verification party, signing partner, software developer, content provider, software distributor*, and *device manufacturer*. Our framework applies this extended list to evaluate the openness of the platforms and ecosystems.

3. Research Design

The research methodology is a case study, following an in-depth empirical inquiry of a contemporary phenomenon as proposed by Yin [2003]. We focused on analyzing a specific case in depth, aiming to identify relevant SF of the case and not to generalize the findings of the case. Our study is primarily based on a literature review of both academic (i.e. using the Scopus database and Google Scholar) and nonacademic literature, following the secondary data analysis method proposed by Heaton [2008]. Furthermore, while success could be defined in a number of ways, we considered SF that enable innovations to be diffused throughout the markets [e.g. Rogers (2003)].

The main motivation for the case selection is that the Android ecosystem is a very particular success case in the literature and in managerial practices. In particular, the justification for selecting this mobile business ecosystem for our case study is that in just six years between 2008 and 2014, it has been able to capture an unparalleled 80% share of the global smartphone market [Canalys (2014)].

Because the subject matter of the study is very topical and developing rapidly, receiving up-to-date information required the extensive utilization of nonacademic literature such as magazine articles and web pages related to the Android ecosystem, the collection of which was based on online sources published between June 2005 and December 2015. These literary sources were carefully selected based on their accurate descriptive nature, providing detailed evidence and insights about the subject matter so that we could apply the analysis framework created for this study. Moreover, we carried out the analysis without using any special software tools,

Table 1.   Analysis framework dimensions.

Levels	Dimensions	Metrics
Firm	**F1.** Firm scope and value creation	**F1.1.** Understanding the sources of revenue, also from a historical and path-dependent perspective [David (1985); Arthur (1989)]
		F1.2. Design of the monetization models and the value configuration of the firm [Stabell and Fjeldstad (1998)]
	F2. Platform approach and governance	**F2.1.** Extensibility and openness of platform architecture and technology [Gawer and Cusumano (2008); Gawer (2014)]
		F2.2. In-house versus external focus in complements [Gawer and Cusumano (2008)]
		F2.3. Managing and incentivizing complementors [Gawer and Cusumano (2008)]
		F2.4. Internal organization and propensity to advance the overall good of the ecosystem [Gawer and Cusumano (2008)]
		F2.5. Control paradigm/openness [Eisenmann (2008); Eisenmann *et al.* (2008)]
		F2.6. Vertical integration and exclusivity [Lee (2013)]
Ecosystem	**E1.** Ecosystem approach and governance	**E1.1.** Role of the firm in the ecosystem [Iansiti and Levien (2004)]
		E1.2. Ecosystem health metrics (e.g. productivity, robustness, niche creation) [Iansiti and Levien (2004); Den Hartigh *et al.* (2006)]
	E2. Software ecosystem and application marketplace	**E2.1.** Occurrence of SF for OS-centric software ecosystems [Bosch (2009)]
		E2.2. Openness along various roles in the value network: end users, developers, platform providers, platform sponsors [Müller *et al.* (2011)]
		E2.3. Occurrence of multi-homing [Hyrynsalmi *et al.* (2012)]

because we considered it unnecessary for the proper understanding of SF in business ecosystems.

We have created an analysis framework for the empirical part of this study. As recommended by Davis [2016], this paper moves beyond the dyad and instead studies complex boundary conditions. The main goal of our framework is to explore both *firm*-level (including internal and supply-chain platforms) and *ecosystem*-level (including industry platforms) SF of mobile business ecosystems as discussed in the previous section. When discussing platforms, we do not make a clear division between supply-chain platforms and industry platforms, as a certain degree of architectural openness exist in both cases.

Following the criteria presented above and in the theoretical background, we have synthesized a set of metrics representing the various dimensions of analysis that we utilize in this research, as presented in Table 1. For each metric, a unique identifier (e.g. F2.1) is assigned that is used later in this paper whenever referring to that particular metric. Furthermore, the key references pertaining to each metric are listed after the description.

4. Data Analysis and Propositions

This section serves the purpose of analyzing the SF of the Google Android ecosystem. We use a step-by-step approach where we first make an analysis on the firm level, followed by an analysis on the ecosystem level, according to the framework and the metrics presented in Table 1. Whenever appropriate, each paragraph is linked to a specific metric or metrics as per Table 1 that the evidence presented is linked to. This is denoted after each paragraph in parentheses.

4.1. *Firm-level analysis*

Google's advertising business model is by and large built on two programs: AdWords and AdSense. However, Google also provides services such as display advertising, Google Apps and Google Drive. Some of these services are subscription based and some are built on a freemium model. That is, customers can use, for example, search services free of charge as long as they can be targeted for ads and promotion. For sure, Google also sells some hardware such as Chromebooks and Nexus/Pixel products. Thus, Google's primary revenue model can be described as sales of search and display advertisements on the web and on mobile devices, which is complemented by sales of subscriptions for cloud-based apps and services. Nevertheless, the main source of income is still based on sales of advertisement, apps, and other services (metrics F1.1 and F1.2).

More importantly, Google is also renewing its business model. Google is using its close relationship with the Open Automotive Alliance (OAA) in order to establish itself in the automotive industry. This strategic move can be realized through close collaboration with already established manufacturers in the automotive industry. This type of strategic work shows some similarities with Google's previous strategy of connecting to the smart home and home entertainment ecosystem, the automotive ecosystem being yet another area of life where Google desires to be present. Google has also been testing a "self-driving car". The idea is to create a fully autonomous car navigating using sensors and highly accurate data. Just as in an airplane, the driver would have more of a supervising role (metric F1.2).

Cloud-based services have become a central part of the Google business model. The cloud-based marketplace labeled Google Play has well over one million applications and games in its catalogue in addition to other media content. The company has also introduced a virtual wallet service (Google Wallet). This service offers secure management of debit, credit, and reward cards. Google also offers a cloud based storage service directed towards consumers and small businesses (metric F1.2).

Google has reduced the amount of complexity by focusing on software and cloud services while supporting largely generic hardware. Through this strategy, people who access the Internet are likely to use Google services, or Google Network Members' websites, and consequently such use generates income for Google (metrics F1.1 and F1.2).

Google has, through its strategy, created a high brand value; the brand is obviously very appreciated by its customers. Google was ranked as the third most loved firm according to Sustainable Brands [2013] and reached a fifth place in relation to brand value [Forbes (2013)]. A high brand value, in turn, contributes to demand for the company's services, strengthening its ecosystem. Thus, we propose the following SF:

- **SF1.** If a platform-agnostic business model is used by a company, with independence regarding types of devices and hardware supported, then the likelihood of success of the company's business ecosystem is increased (metrics F1.1 and F1.2).
- **SF2.** If no burden of legacy in the form of a hardware business exists at a company, which enables a clear focus on cloud services, software, and content, then it increases the likelihood of success of the company's business ecosystem (metric F1.1).
- **SF3.** If a company and its services are loved by consumers, combined with a high level of brand equity, then it increases the likelihood of success of the company's business ecosystem (metric F1.1).

With more than a billion Android devices in use globally as of 2014 [Gartner (2014)], Google has reached a very competitive position such that the firm can make use of the swift growth in the smartphone industry and the huge number of connected devices running on Android. Although Google is not monetizing Android directly, it can still benefit from knowledge about customer preferences, their online activities, and patterns of usage. Through this knowledge, Google can build user profiles and have a high precision in targeted advertising (metric F1.1).

In terms of strategy, Google avoids vertical integration and physical domination in the smartphone industry. The Google strategy is to invite complementors and device manufacturers to innovate on top of the Google platform [Google (2014)]. The logic behind this strategy is simple. Google strives to promote the proliferation of Android and therefore encourages the creation of external devices and apps that are Android compatible (metrics F2.2, F2.3, and F2.6).

Android was acquired by Google in 2005, and gained customer acknowledgement after Google announcing the creation of the Open Handset Alliance (OHA), using this alliance as a way to promote Android. Through this action, Android was positioned as an open and comprehensive mobile software platform. The openness of the platform is further strengthened through the Android Open Source Platform project (AOSP), as argued by Pon *et al.* [2014], thus (metric F2.5).

The Google strategy has been to develop future versions of Android, and its core platform application programming interfaces (APIs), through a more closed development branch. Such development has usually also been done in collaboration with an original equipment manufacturer (OEM). This strategy can be seen as a deviation from the open source strategy. However, Google claims that it is in the best interest of all stakeholders since it allows for developers and OEMs to focus their development on readymade versions of the platform. This is not in line with the wishes of most OEMs, as they typically want to access the latest version of the platform. For the developers, however, this strategy fits well since they are interested in applying their solutions to a stable platform. Thus, we propose the following SF (metrics F2.1, F2.2, F2.3, F2.4, and F2.5):

- **SF4.** If a company gives more freedom to complementors with regard to developing service innovations on top of the company's technologies, then it increases the likelihood of success of the company's business ecosystem (metrics F2.2, F2.3, and F2.5).
- **SF5.** If a platform exposes enough APIs so that OEMs, accessory makers, and developers are able to create complementary products and apps with meaningful differentiation, then it increases the likelihood of success of the platform's business ecosystem (metrics F2.1 and F2.2).

Although Google is taking some steps to open up its core technologies also with Android, the fact remains that Google Mobile Services (GMS), Google Play Services, and a multitude of other Google's applications and services suite remain proprietary and protected by the company's intellectual property rights. These services and products will not be part of AOSP, that is, not part of open source [InfoWorld (2014)]. OEMs have also been forced to follow procedures such as the "GMS approval window". This measure has pushed OEMs to deliver products not older than nine months if they want to keep using the Google apps and services [DailyTech (2014)], thus (metric F2.5).

Taking this approach, Google performs a strategy of proprietary control in relation to Android platform key elements. These elements should be seen as critical for the platform. Furthermore, most device manufacturers do not create and ship products using only the AOSP code. Instead, they use the proprietary GMS suite licensed from Google. The behavior of relying on GMS can be explained by the fact that for example Google Play, Drive, Maps, and Gmail related APIs, central for application development, are also part of GMS. Consequently, application developers too have to decide on targeting the lean AOSP platform (with fewer APIs) or the more extensive GMS-equipped Android devices [InfoWorld (2014)]. The flipside for developers using the GMS solution is that it comes with multiple requirements giving Google increased control of Android based devices [InfoWorld (2014)]. Thus, we suggest the following success factor (metrics F2.3 and F2.5):

- **SF6.** If the software components of a platform that meaningfully differentiate it from the competition or otherwise create significant added value are kept closed source, then it increases the likelihood of success of the platform's business ecosystem (metric F2.5).

External software development has been a possibility to the general community since the Android platform was announced in November 2007. Software developers can access the Android platform's developer resources through a unique developer site. Developers can, without having to join a developer program, test their software and use the Android development tools free of charge. This is not the case with competing platforms such as Apple's iOS platform (metrics F2.1 and F2.3).

Google has nurtured Android applications development by announcing two Android Developer Challenges. The first challenge was announced in January 2008 and the second in May 2009. An impressive total of $10 million was awarded to developers. The first challenge was of significant importance in order to jump-start the creation of applications, and there were almost 2000 contributions from over 70 countries. The second challenge helped in creating a critical mass of applications so that the platform became big enough to attract developers without any further nurturing. Moreover, it is supported by the research of Battisti [2012; 2014] and Magnusson *et al.* [2016] on the social aspects of user involvement (metric F2.3).

Google sensibly implemented a similar revenue sharing model as Apple on the application marketplace. However, the publishing process was less rigid. Applying a method with a lack of rigorous pre-inspection before publication has a downside. Therefore, Android has had to deal with inappropriate software in a much bigger scale compared to competitors as iOS and Windows. However, in 2012 Google took measures and installed an in-house automated anti-virus program labeled "Bouncer". Installing that program resulted in a reduction of malicious apps with 40% [SC Magazine (2012)]. Furthermore, Google has also a reputation of allowing third-party application even if they should overlap with Google offerings, something that contrasts the policies of, e.g. Apple. Thus, we suggest the following SF (metrics F2.3, F2.5, and F2.6):

- **SF7.** If a platform is open with regard to end users, developers, platform providers, and platform sponsors alike, it enables a high degree of open innovation but possibly also major fragmentation, nevertheless increasing the likelihood of success of the platform's business ecosystem (metric F2.5).
- **SF8.** If a nonexclusive process of application development, verification, and publishing is applied on a platform, then it increases the likelihood of success of the platform's business ecosystem (metrics F2.3 and F2.6).
- **SF9.** If a platform has the most nonrestrictive policy for complementors, not limited by protective clauses against competition or substitution, then it increases the likelihood of success of the platform's business ecosystem (metrics F2.5 and F2.6).

The analysis above gives light to some critical firm-level success factors. Still, this picture of SF is incomplete. An ecosystem-level analysis is therefore performed in the following section.

4.2. *Ecosystem-level analysis*

In this section, we cover the ecosystem approach and governance of Android, Google's role in it, and the overall health of the ecosystem as well as the software ecosystem and application marketplace.

Google has built an ecosystem around Android where participation should be built on voluntary action. The idea of voluntarism is closely related to the idea of using open source code, as in AOSP, where anyone can change, use, and distribute the software to meet unique needs. Android product development teams typically focus on a limited number of devices and then integrate their hardware with the latest development version of the Android software so that new product launches can be secured, supporting the roll-out of the latest Android version [9 to 5 Google (2011)]. This strategy using so-called flagship devices has the benefit of also carrying the risk for the wider OEM community. This community can make follow-up device development that takes advantage of new features. Google managers claim that this strategy ensures co-evolution between the platform and the need for contemporary functional devices. Nevertheless, Google is not showing consistency in its Android strategy. They have been rotating partners for different releases, with varying terms of exclusivity. Thus, we suggest the following SF (metrics E1.1 and E2.1):

- **SF10.** If the OEMs benefit from having a state-of-the-art mobile OS platform, essentially royalty free and enjoying higher adoption rates than any competing platform, then it increases the likelihood of success of the platform's business ecosystem (metric E1.1).
- **SF11.** If generic, evolving functionality and a set of certain key features provided by the OS are available on the platform, then it increases the likelihood of success of the platform's business ecosystem (metric E2.1).

In June 2014, Google made an announcement; the program called "Android One" was presented. The program was targeted at the lower end of the smartphone market. In collaboration with suppliers and OEMs, Google had defined a reference platform for devices that would meet a certain minimum standard of technical specifications. These products would be able to support Google's mobile services in their entirety. Yet, the price would be kept at around 100 USD, then a modest price for such devices [BBC News (2014)]. The program would ultimately lead to improved performance of low-priced products and also improve the user experience of these products. Previously, the user experience of such products had been somewhat disappointing. In 2016, the program was extended to mid-range smartphones and new, developed markets such as Japan, totaling 21 countries [Google (2016)].

The Google management team is obviously aiming to secure a bigger chunk of the entry-level smartphone market, growing faster than any other handset segment. They are at the same time trying to unify the Android experience with standardized hardware and limit fragmentation by barring OEM skinning of the Android One product. Clearly, this initiative played a key role in reaching the large number of prospective smartphone users in emerging markets. The program allowed for reaching these users with Android and Google services in a controlled fashion. As a consequence, Google has also secured a fast-growing segment for its mobile advertising business. This step is vital in order to ensure future growth. With other smartphone OS providers such as Microsoft and other initiatives such as Firefox OS aiming to utilize the same opportunities in emerging markets, Google is seeking to secure its leading position by taking proactive steps. Thus, we propose the following SF (metrics E1.2 and E2.1):

- **SF12.** If mobile operators benefit from the transition to smartphones, driving up demand for mobile data plans, then it increases the likelihood of success of mobile business ecosystems enabling affordable smartphones (metric E1.2).
- **SF13.** If the number of customers that use the OS platform and that are accessible to developers is high compared to other platforms, then it increases the likelihood of success of the platform's business ecosystem (metric E2.1).

Using the definition of Iansiti and Levien [2004], Google can be defined as a *keystone* — a platform provider who enables and facilitates value creation for the whole of its ecosystem. In the Google ecosystem, website owners generate income by hosting Google's advertisements, and advertisers make use of Google's broad customer reach and effective high-converting, targeted ads. Some other stakeholders such as handset accessory makers appreciate the possibility to work with standard, well-defined interfaces without being dependent on any single OEM. The community of developers benefit from accessing the broad installed base of Android device owners, giving them the possibility to develop commercial or free apps. Developers additionally appreciate the open and nonrestrictive approach of Android in terms of app distribution (metrics E1.1 and E2.2).

Google has organized its business somewhat differently from rivals like Apple. As a matter of fact, Google earns only very limited revenue from selling small volumes of devices, and it does not charge for Android licenses. Unlike Apple, Google has refrained from utilizing proprietary interfaces on its devices and has not introduced such to Android either. Additionally, although multi-homing is a relatively rare phenomenon, the Android ecosystem appears to benefit from it more than, e.g. the Windows Phone ecosystem [Hyrynsalmi *et al.* (2012)]. Consequently, Google can be seen as benevolent, willing to provide possibilities for its ecosystem members to earn revenue and grow their business as they see fit. Thus, we propose the following SF (metrics E2.2 and E2.3):

- **SF14.** If accessory makers appreciate that they can work with standard, well-defined interfaces, then it increases the likelihood of success of mobile business ecosystems and platforms that support such standard interfaces (metric E2.2).
- **SF15.** If developers value the openness and nonrestrictive philosophy in application distribution, then it increases the likelihood of success of mobile business ecosystems that exhibit such policies (metrics E2.2 and E2.3).

There are also some health issues in the Android ecosystem that are of interest to discuss. For example, the Google Play marketplace offered just about 1.5 million Android applications in its catalogue as of January 2015 [AppBrain (2015)]. Such a vast offering of apps is clearly a sign of healthy diversity that we consider as an adequate proxy for niche creation, and also a sign of productivity. Actually, already in late 2012, Android managed to effectively close the gap in terms of available applications compared to iOS [see, e.g. Hyrynsalmi *et al.* (2012)]. This, in addition to additional indicators such as where applications are first published and how soon they migrate to other ecosystems, could provide additional insights on ecosystem health and success.

It is unfortunately very difficult to evaluate ecosystem robustness since there are no statistics illustrating the survival rates of developers. However, robustness might be questioned since a high proportion of developers only publish one application (58%). The situation also seems to be the same in the iOS ecosystem. This translates to higher churn than with large, professional developers. It should also be taken into account that from Android's fragmentation follows that the platform scores less satisfactorily in terms of *limited obsolescence* and *continuity of user experience and use cases*. These are metrics associated with the ecosystem health measure of robustness according to Iansiti and Levien [2004]. Thus, we suggest the following success factor:

- **SF16.** If an ecosystem is healthy, based on metrics of productivity, robustness, and niche creation, then it increases the likelihood of success of that ecosystem also in a mobile business context (metric E1.2).

5. Discussions and Findings

In order to present the main contribution of this research, a model that helps to analyze the SF of mobile ecosystems, we grouped the 16 factors into four findings, as presented as follows:

- **Finding 1.** Google's platform-agnostic business model, independent of devices and hardware and free of any burden of legacy, enables a clear focus on cloud services, software, and content, which in turn has enabled Google as well as its Android ecosystem partners to thrive (SF1 and SF2)

The first finding elaborates the notion that Google's firm scope, its historical legacy and current business and monetization model are beneficial to the Android ecosystem in the sense that they leave plenty of room and ways for ecosystem members to create value. Search advertising remains Google's key revenue source, and ultimately, any devices or platforms can serve to drive this revenue, not just Android. Unlike the orchestrators of some other mobile business ecosystems, Google does not attempt to capture the majority of the value created in the ecosystem, a behavior favored by physical and particularly value dominators, as described by Iansiti and Levien [2004]. Moreover, as the company lacks a burden of legacy and path dependency in its technology choices, it has been able to avoid being locked in to unfavorable technologies, also allowing its ecosystem partners more freedom to innovate and produce complements. This finding also appears to support the third hypothesis of Gawer [2014] stating that "*collaborative governance will increase complementors' incentives to innovate in platform-enhancing ways*", although whether all innovation in the Android ecosystem is platform-enhancing is subject to debate.

- **Finding 2.** While the Android platform has a generic, evolving set of functionality and exposes enough APIs so that various complementors are able to create products and apps with meaningful differentiation, the software components of the platform that meaningfully differentiate it from the competition or otherwise create significant added value are kept closed source (SF5, SF6, and SF11)

With the second finding, we emphasize the importance of having a sufficiently broad and evolving set of APIs that enable complementary innovation with potential for meaningful differentiation, a key prerequisite for a viable third-party application ecosystem. This is also in line with the observations of Bosch [2009] for OS-centric software ecosystems. At the same time, however, Android also has certain key components developed by Google that are kept closed source, and it would appear that the number of such components has increased rather than decreased as of late. This is to protect the substantial investments made by Google against free riders as described by, e.g. Eisenmann [2008], and to ensure that certain key features of the platform remain positive differentiators and are not simply copied by competing platform providers. Furthermore, it would appear that Google is also taking action in response to certain complementors-turned-competitors like Apple, who decisively replaced Google Maps with its own mapping software, or Facebook, who exploited Android APIs to create its own UI layer replacing the standard Android home screen, thus directly competing with Google for end-users' attention and advertising revenue. These two examples were also used by Gawer [2014] to justify her second hypothesis (*a number of platform complementors will turn into competitors over time even in platform ecosystems whose participants are largely complementary*) and fourth hypothesis (*emergence of competition from former complementors is likely to elicit a reaction from the platform leader, either closing its technical interface or enveloping the complementors-turned-competitors*).

- **Finding 3.** Android's appropriate balance of architectural openness, evident in mostly open and nonexclusive but also some closed policies, processes, and interfaces with regard to complementors such as device manufacturers, accessory makers, and application developers, content providers and publishers, platform providers such as alternative application store operators, and mobile operators, has enabled a high degree of innovation and added value in complements but also potentially severe fragmentation that is already evident in the various forked versions of Android available (SF3, SF4, SF7, SF8, SF9, SF14, and SF15)

The third finding emphasizes the partially shared, partially proprietary control paradigm and considerable openness of the Android platform and ecosystem with regard to the dimensions defined by Eisenmann *et al.* [2008] and Müller *et al.* [2011]. It would not be very meaningful to simply say to that Android is either "open" or "closed" as the matter is more complicated than that, depending on multiple dimensions of openness relating to the value network and ecosystem around the platform. Moreover, as argued by Müller *et al.* [2011], both relatively open and closed models have advantages and disadvantages.

Also, what works for the Android ecosystem may not be ideal for just any ecosystem, as is the case with, e.g. the considerably more closed iOS ecosystem where Apple as the sole device manufacturer and platform provider takes as much as 65% of the whole smartphone industry's profits, according to Canaccord Genuity analysts' statistics for the first quarter of 2014, cited by Fortune [2014]. The iOS ecosystem has low fragmentation, whereas with Android, the breadth of releases and forked variants of the platform in use is remarkable. The stricter testing and verification approach of iOS combined with a limited number of different hardware devices supported has contributed to an application catalogue where the number of low-quality applications is generally lower than with Android, the latter having 15% of its applications ranked as low quality according to AppBrain [2015].

Müller *et al.* [2011] argued that the iOS approach might lead to a better user experience and help prevent diseconomies of scale. On the other hand, they argued that the more open approach of Android would support a strategy aimed at becoming the largest application store provider, and it may lead to increased competition in both software and hardware, resulting in lower prices. Regardless of this, both platforms have broadly speaking an equal number of applications available, although Android enjoys a much larger share of the smartphone market than iOS, 80% versus 15% for 2013 [Canalys (2014)]. It would seem that Android's model of openness and governance works for a more distributed ecosystem with less vertical integration, whereas the iOS model works for a highly vertically integrated, centralized ecosystem where most roles in the value network are under proprietary control.

Again, this finding could be seen to support Gawer's [2014] third hypothesis but also her first hypothesis, "*as the platform interfaces become more open, more agents will be attracted into the platform ecosystem, and the platform leader will be able to access a larger set of potentially complementary innovative capabilities*". As evidenced by the fragmentation of the Android platform, however, extensive openness can also work against the platform despite spurring a higher degree of complementary innovation.

- **Finding 4.** The strong market position and healthy, established ecosystem of Android appeal to OEMs building devices on the platform, operators selling mobile broadband subscriptions and devices, developers and other complementors making complements for the devices, and ultimately consumers who enjoy an unrivalled variety in Android devices, accessories, and applications (SF10, SF12, SF13, and SF16)

The fourth finding highlights the importance of the Android ecosystem's health to its various members, particularly in terms of metrics such as productivity, robustness, and niche creation as defined by Iansiti and Levien [2004]. Furthermore, the large established user base of Android device owners, contributing to strong network effects, makes the ecosystem attractive to device OEMs and complementors such as application developers. Accounting for four fifths of the global smartphone market, Android is simply too large to be ignored by any party willing to address a major demographic of smartphone users. Furthermore, operators in many countries see affordable smartphones based on Android driving the transition from voice-centric feature phones to mobile broadband enabled smartphones, helping them sell more mobile data plans and at least partially offset the decline in traditional voice and text message revenue that, not coincidentally, is also related to the proliferation of smartphones and certain popular applications and services such as Skype and WhatsApp.

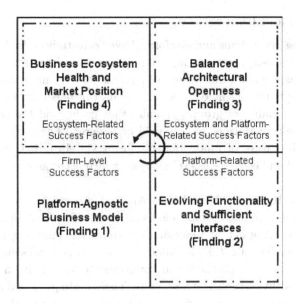

Fig. 1.   Ecosystem success factor model.

The above four findings together constitute the answer to the research question. To illustrate the relationship between these findings in the context of our multi-level analysis framework, we have crafted a model, as presented in Fig. 1.

Although the findings are derived from the case study, the model of SF itself is not specific to just Android. The basic notion of the model is that as the level of analysis becomes less granular, moving from firm-level analysis through platform analysis to ecosystem-level analysis not discretely but in a continuum as illustrated by the arched arrow, we eventually cover the whole breadth of success factors. Some of these may be attributed just as well to platform characteristics as to ecosystem characteristics, as is the case with Finding 3 that is enclosed both in the horizontal and the vertical dotted-line rectangles that group together ecosystem-related and platform-related SF respectively. The lower half of the diagram represents firm (and platform) level analysis (dimensions F1 and F2 in Table 1), whereas the upper half represents ecosystem level analysis (dimensions E1 and E2) with some aspects shared with platform-related analysis (dimension F2). Both points appear compatible with the thinking of Gawer [2014] whose classification of technological platforms is also a continuum where the last category, industry platform, takes the organizational form of an ecosystem. Similarly, Thomas *et al.* [2014] see platform ecosystems as the ultimate platform type that combines many-to-many architectural openness (as in Finding 3) with regard to three distinct logics of leverage: production, innovation, and transaction logic.

6. Conclusions and Implications

Although business ecosystems and platforms have been studied also in the context of the smartphone industry, few existing studies have considered firm-level as well as ecosystem-level aspects and dimensions of analysis jointly, integrating the different but related concepts into a single framework. Thus, this paper draws on Davis [2016] who recommends studies of group dynamics that go beyond the traditional dyad studies traditionally performed in this field of research. The proposed model contributes to the literature of innovation platforms via clustering the SF leveraged both on firm-level and ecosystem-level analysis, which is the key contribution of this study.

We identified 16 SF for the Google Android ecosystem, clustered into four findings pertaining to (i) the business model and focus of the ecosystem orchestrator, (ii) a generic, evolving set of functionality and APIs enabling the creation of differentiating complements, (iii) the balance of mostly open and some closed policies with regard to ecosystem partners and complementors, and (iv) a strong market position and a healthy, established ecosystem. These findings should help scholars of innovation management research as well as managers (particularly those that operate in the smartphone industry or adjacent industries such as consumer electronics or automotive infotainment) understand the key factors that have contributed to the rise and success of mobile business ecosystems. Especially, the key implication for managers could be summarized as: whether companies are seeking to join the Android ecosystem or perhaps replicate its success in a different industry context, they would do well to implement or enable the key SF in their companies.

Policy makers could enable the development of innovation platforms that create economic and social value. From this perspective, the contribution of our research for policy makers is a conceptual model with critical SF of mobile business ecosystems, which can be taken into consideration during the definition of initiatives for the development of innovations that can create economic and social impact for scaling up at the global level.

As for limitations, this research deals with the SF of the Android ecosystem. Furthermore, our perspective of analysis is that of qualitative research. Thus, to explore and validate the generalizability of the results, additional case studies would be needed, applying the same analysis framework as used in this paper. Such case studies on, e.g. the iOS ecosystem or the Windows Phone (now called Windows 10 Mobile) ecosystem would be suitable for further research, although the latter has all but lost its relevance. Another option could be to conduct case studies on emergent mobile ecosystems, attempting to identify SF that could contribute to the rise of new major mobile ecosystems, potentially disrupting the current duopoly of Android and iOS.

Additionally, further research could validate our model through quantitative analysis of data originating from firms in the Android ecosystem, as the measurement and analysis of ecosystem health (metric E1.2 in Table 1) in particular would benefit from quantitative data, as argued by Den Hartigh *et al.* [2006]. A potential new perspective to the research would be to study the social impact of scalable business platforms in the daily life of people.

References

AppBrain. (2015). Number of Android Applications. Available at http://www.appbrain.com/stats/number-of-android-apps. [accessed on 19 January 2015].

Armstrong, M. (2006). Competition in two-sided markets. *RAND Journal of Economics*, **37**, 3: 668–691.

Armstrong, M. and Wright, J. (2007). Two-sided markets, competitive bottlenecks and exclusive contracts. *Economic Theory*, **32**, 2: 353–380.

Arthur, W. (1989). Competing technologies, increasing returns, and lock-in by historical events. *The Economic Journal*, **99**, 394: 116–131.

Battisti, S. (2012). Social innovation: The process development of knowledge-intensive companies. *International Journal of Services Technology and Management*, **18**, 3/4: 224–244.

Battisti, S. (2014). Social innovation in living labs: The micro-level process model of public-private partnerships. *International Journal of Innovation and Regional Development*, **5**, 4/5: 328–348.

BBC News. (2014). Available at http://www.bbc.com/news/technology-29203249. [accessed on 30 September 2014].

Bosch, J. (2009). From software product lines to software ecosystems. In *Proceedings of the 13th International Conference on Software Product Lines (SPLC'09)*, San Francisco, CA, USA, 24–28 August 2009, pp. 111–119.

Boudreau, K. (2008). Too many complementors? Evidence on software developers. Working Paper. HEC-Paris/School of Management, pp. 1–33.

Bouwman, H., De Reuver, M., Hampe, F., Carlsson, C. and Walden, P. (2014). Mobile R&D Prototypes — What is Hampering Market Implementation. *International Journal of Innovation and Technology Management*, **11**, 01: 1440003.

Campbell, P. and Ahmed, F. (2011). An assessment of mobile OS-centric ecosystems. *Journal of Theoretical and Applied Electronic Commerce Research*, **6**, 2: 50–62.

Canalys. (2014). Android on 80% of smart phones shipped in 2013. Available at http://www.canalys.com/newsroom/android-80-smart-phones-shipped-2013. [accessed on 17 December 2014].

DailyTech. (2014). Available at http://www.dailytech.com/Report+Google+to+Force+OEMs+to+Provide+Recent+Android+Builds+or+Lose+Access+to+Google+Apps/article34311.htm. [accessed on 3 September 2014].

David, P. (1985). Clio and the economics of QWERTY. *American Economic Review*, **75**, 2: 332–337.

Davis, J. P. (2016). The group dynamics of interorganizational relationships: Collaborating with multiple partners in innovation ecosystems. *Administrative Science Quarterly*, **61**, 4: 621–661.

Den Hartigh, E., Tol, M. and Visscher, W. (2006). The health measurement of a business ecosystem. In *Proceedings of the European Network on Chaos and Complexity Research and Management (ECCON 2006) Annual Meeting*, Bergen aan Zee, The Netherlands, 20–21 October 2006.

Dyer, J. and Singh, H. (1998). The relational view: Cooperative strategy and sources of inter-organizational competitive advantage. *Academy of Management Review*, **23**, 4: 660–679.

Eisenmann, T. R. (2008). Managing proprietary and shared platforms. *California Management Review*, **50**, 4: 31–53.

Eisenmann, T., Parker, G. and Van Alstyne, M. (2006). Strategies for two-sided markets. *Harvard Business Review*, **84**, 10: 92–101.

Eisenmann, T., Parker, G. and Van Alstyne, M. (2008). Opening platforms: How, when and why? Harvard Business School, Working paper 09-30.

Forbes. (2013). Available at http://www.forbes.com/powerful-brands/list. [accessed on 25 August 2014].

Fortune. (2014). With 15.5% of smartphone sales in Q1, Apple took 65% of profits. Available at http://fortune.com/2014/05/09/with-15-5-of-smartphone-sales-in-q1-apple-took-65-of-profits. [accessed on 21 January 2015].

Gartner. (2014). Gartner says worldwide traditional PC, tablet, ultramobile and mobile phone shipments on pace to grow 7.6% in 2014. Available at http://www.gartner.com/newsroom/id/2645115. [accessed on 13 January 2015].

Gawer, A. (2009). Platform dynamics and strategies: From products to services. *Platforms, Markets and Innovation*, ed. A.Gawer. Edward Elgar, UK, pp. 45–76.

Gawer, A. (2014). Bridging differing perspectives on technological platforms: Toward an integrative framework. *Research Policy*, **43**: 1239–1249.

Gawer, A. and Cusumano, M. (2008). How companies become platform leaders. *MIT Sloan Management Review*, **49**, 2: 28–35.

Gawer, A. and Cusumano, M. (2014). Industry platforms and ecosystem innovation. *Journal of Product Innovation Management*, **31**: 417–433.

Gawer, A. and Henderson, R. (2007). Platform owner entry and innovation in complementary markets: Evidence from Intel. *Journal of Economics & Management Strategy*, **16**, 1: 1–34.

Google. (2014). Available at http://investor.google.com/pdf/20131231_google_10K.pdf. [accessed on 21 December 2016].

Google. (2016). Available at http://japan.googleblog.com/2016/07/android-one.html. [accessed on 21 December 2016].

Hagiu, A. (2006). Pricing and commitment by two-sided platforms. *RAND Journal of Economics*, **37**, 3: 720–737.

Hagiu, A. (2009a). Multi-sided platforms: From microfoundations to design and expansion strategies. Harvard Business School, Working paper.

Hagiu, A. (2009b). Two-sided platforms: Product variety and pricing structures. *Journal of Economics and Management Strategy*, **18**, 4: 1011–1043.

Hagiu, A. and Spulber, D. (2013). First-party content and coordination in two-sided markets. *Management Science*, **59**, 4: 933–949.

Heaton, J. (2008). Secondary analysis of qualitative data: An overview. *Historical Social Research/Historische Sozialforschung*, **33**, 3: 33–45.

Hyrynsalmi, S., Mäkilä, T., Järvi, A., Suominen, A., Seppänen, M. and Knuutila, T. (2012). App Store, Marketplace, Play! An analysis of multi-homing in mobile software ecosystems. In *Proceedings of the International Workshop on Software Ecosystems (IWSECO 2012)*, Boston, MA, USA, 18 June 2012.

Iansiti, M. and Levien, R. (2004). *The Keystone Advantage: What the New Dynamics of Business Ecosystems Mean for Strategy, Innovation, and Sustainability*. Harvard Business School Press, Boston, MA, USA.

Idu, A., van de Zande, T. and Jansen, S. (2011). Multi-homing in the Apple ecosystem: Why and how developers target multiple Apple app stores. In *Proceedings of the International Conference on Management of Emergent Digital EcoSystems (MEDES'11)*, San Francisco, CA, USA, 21–23 November 2011.

InfoWorld. (2014). Available at http://www.infoworld.com/d/mobile-technology/meet-aosp-the-other-android-while-you-stillcan-236070. [accessed on 17 June 2014].

Lee, R. (2013). Vertical integration and exclusivity in platform and two-sided markets. *American Economic Review*, **103**, 7: 2960–3000.

Magnusson, P. R., Wästlund, E. and Netz, J. (2016). Exploring users' appropriateness as a proxy for experts when screening new Product/service ideas. *Journal of Product Innovation Management*, **33**, 1: 4–18.

Muegge, S. (2013). Platforms, communities, and business ecosystems: Lessons learned about technology entrepreneurship in an interconnected world. *Technology Innovation Management Review*, **3**: 5–15.

Müller, R. M., Kijl, B. and Martens, J. K. (2011). A comparison of inter-organizational business models of mobile app stores: There is more than open vs. closed. *Journal of Theoretical and Applied Electronic Commerce Research*, **6**, 2: 63–76.

Parker, G. and Van Alstyne, M. (2005). Two-sided network effects: A theory of information product design. *Management Science*, **51**, 10: 1494–1504.

Pon, B., Seppälä, T. and Kenney, M. (2014). Android and the demise of operating system-based power: Firm strategy and platform control in the post-PC world. *Telecommunications Policy*, **38**, 11: 979–991.

Remneland-Wikhamn, B., Ljungberg, J., Bergquist, M. and Kuschel, J. (2011). Open innovation, generativity and the supplier as peer: The case of iPhone and Android. *International Journal of Innovation Management*, **15**, 1: 205–230.

Rochet, J.-C. and Tirole, J. (2003). Platform competition in two-sided markets. *Journal of the European Economic Association*, **1**, 4: 990–1029.

Rogers, E. M. (2003). *Diffusion of Innovations*, 5th ed., Free Press, New York.

Rumelt, R., Schendel, D. and Teece, D. (1991). Strategic management and economics. *Strategic Management Journal*, **12**: 5–29.

Rysman, M. (2004). Competition between networks: A study of the market for Yellow Pages. *Review of Economic Studies*, **71**, 2: 483–512.

Rysman, M. (2009). The economics of two-sided markets. *The Journal of Economic Perspectives*, **23**, 3: 125–143.

SC Magazine. (2012). Available at http://www.scmagazine.com.au/News/289242,google-employs-bouncer-to-cleanse-android-malware.aspx. [accessed on 3 September 2014].

Stabell, C. and Fjeldstad, Ø. (1998). Configuring value for competitive advantage: On chains, shops, and networks. *Strategic Management Journal*, **19**: 413–437.

Sustainable Brands (2013). Available at http://www.sustainablebrands.com/news_and_views/communications/disney-yahoo-googletop-list-100-companies-most-loved-consumers. [accessed on 25 August 2014].

Thomas, L. and Autio, E. (2012). Modeling the ecosystem: A meta-synthesis of ecosystem and related. In *Proceedings of the DRUID Society Conference 2012*, CBS, Copenhagen, Denmark, 19–21 June 2012.

Thomas, L. and Autio, E. (2014). The fifth facet: The ecosystem as an organizational field. In *Proceedings of the DRUID Society Conference 2014*, CBS, Copenhagen, Denmark, 16–18 June 2014.

Thomas, L., Autio, E. and Gann, D. (2014). Architectural leverage: Putting platforms in context. *The Academy of Management Perspectives*, **28**, 2: 198–219.

Tuunainen, V., Tuunanen, T. and Piispanen, J. (2011). Mobile service platforms: Comparing Nokia OVI and Apple App Store with the IISI[n] model. In *Proceedings of the 10th International Conference on Mobile Business*, Como, Italy, 20–21 June 2011, pp. 74–83.

Williamson, P. and De Meyer, A. (2012). Ecosystem advantage: How to successfully harness the power of partnerships. *California Management Review*, **55**, 1: 24–46.

Yin, R. (2003). *Case Study Research: Design and Methods*. Sage Publications, Thousand Oaks, CA, USA.

9to5Google. (2011). Available at http://9to5google.com/2011/09/07/shocker-android-has-been-developing-a-lead-device-for-two-years. [accessed on 20 December 2016].

Biography

Juha Winter received his MSEE degree from Helsinki University of Technology in 2005 and his predoctoral Lic.Sc. (Tech.) degree from Aalto University in 2014, in the field of networking business and technology management. He currently works for Strategy Analytics, a global market research and consulting company. He is also pursuing a full doctorate at the Aalto University School of Science. His professional experience comprises nearly 15 years mainly in large, multinational technology companies (Nokia Corporation, Robert Bosch GmbH) in various roles ranging from R&D to business analysis, strategic planning and management as well as business development and sales. His research interests are in the areas of business ecosystems, platforms, and multi-sided markets especially in a high-technology context.

Sandro Battisti holds a PhD in innovation management at Politecnico di Milano in Italy. He has around 20 years of experience in the management of innovation based on Information and Communication Technologies (ICT). He acts as Program Manager at Bruno Kessler Foundation (FBK) in Trento, Italy. He has considerable experience working at the international level in the Americas (Brazil and the US) and Europe (Italy, Finland, the UK, Germany and France). His research interests are focused on innovation platforms, technology-enabled innovation, and user engagement in social innovation.

Thommie Burström is working as Rettig Capital Assistant Professor at Hanken School of Economics in Helsinki, Finland. His academic interests are in projects, entrepreneurship, business ecosystems, and platform research. Thommie has previously published papers in, for example, the International Journal of Managing Projects in Business and International Journal of Management Research Review. He has lately participated as senior researcher and project manager in three different international platform research projects.

Sakari Luukkainen is a senior research scientist responsible at Aalto University for the Networking Business education and research, which combines business and technology studies in the telecommunications field. He has previous experience at the Technical Research Centre of Finland, where he directed the Multimedia Communications research group. He also has practical managerial experience in technology companies of the telecommunications industry.

Chapter 5

Innovation and Performance: An Empirical Study of Russian Industrial Companies[*]

Arkady Trachuk[†] and Natalia Linder[‡]

*Department of Management, The Financial University
Under the Government of the Russian Federation
15 Ulica Verhnjaja Maslovka, Moscow 127083
The Russian Federation*
[†]*ATrachuk@fa.ru*
[‡]*NVLinder@fa.ru*

The paper investigates the relationship between investment in research and development (R&D), innovation expenses, and productivity of manufacturing companies. These empirical results have shown that innovation investments (1) improve the performance of industrial companies with the elasticity of 0.09; (2) innovation investment has an impact on the performance of the company, and the extent of this impact depends on the value of R&D investment and has a range of elasticity ranging from 0.03 (for low volumes of R&D investment) to 0.16 in high volumes of R&D investment; (3) the relationship between innovation investment and the growth of performance is nonlinear in nature and has a strong positive relationship only after a critical mass of innovation investment has been reached; (4) a significant role in the relationship of innovation investment and productivity is played by the features of the industry in which the company operates (the companies that operate in high-tech industries not only invest more in R&D and innovation but also have a better performance due to research and development); (5) companies of low-tech industries have a negative elasticity of innovation investment and productivity, which is due to the influence of unprofitable innovation investments (appropriability effect), i.e. additional profits from the investment are not significant.

Keywords: Innovation; the CDM model; R&D investment; company productivity; unprofitable innovation investment.

---

[*]This paper was prepared on the basis of the results of the study "Ensuring the Controllability of Industrial Holdings and Stimulation of Innovative Development," which was held at the expense of budget financing within the public task of the Financial University, 2015.

[†]Corresponding author.

This chapter was originally published in *International Journal of Innovation and Technology Management*, Vol. 15, No. 3, March 2018, published by World Scientific Publishing, Singapore. Reprinted with permission.

1. Introduction

Innovation is of paramount importance for the growth and the competitiveness of any economy in the context of increasing global competition. However, there has been a decline in many sectors starting from 2014, which is associated primarily with the raw material orientation of Russian exports and the fall in commodity prices in the Russian economy. Thus, according to the Federal State Statistics Service of the Russian Federation,[a] the share of the raw materials sector in export amounted to 74.2% in 2014. The profitability of the raw materials sector in the period of economic growth from 2000 to 2013 was one of the highest, which created favorable conditions for the development of the "Dutch disease" effect in the Russian economy, when the growing raw materials sector suppressed all other sectors (due to the flow of investment and resources) and became dominant in the economy. Another source of economic growth in 2000–2013 was the domestic market, which accounted for approximately 60–70%.[b] Indeed, the growth of such sectors as food processing, real estate, trade, and entertainment was significant and stable. However, this type of growth did not mobilize the available human and technological potential because most of the technology in these segments had been borrowed and adapted from the world market. In addition, goods that are produced by these sectors are sold mainly in the country and have a low export potential, which allows defining them as sectors of non-tradable goods. According to the theory Vegh [2013, Chap. 4], the growth of the sectors of non-tradable goods is only possible with the growth of welfare of the population; at the same time, the Federal State Statistics Service of the Russian Federation has recorded a decline in real incomes since 2014.

Another component of the growth is the promotion of innovative and high-tech products to the domestic and the world markets. This growth component uses competitive advantages as well as scientific and technological potential of the economy to the maximum extent possible. In Russia, there are examples of similar projects in such industries as space, nuclear power engineering, software development, biotechnology, and crude oil refining. However, further development of sectors that are oriented to the global market and the international competition, as well as stimulation of innovative activity of industrial enterprises as an important source of economic growth, is necessary. In this regard, the study on the relationship between innovation and productivity of industrial companies is important.

The purpose of this study is to analyze the relationship between investment in research and development (R&D) and performance for manufacturing companies.

The peculiarity of this research, unlike the previous ones, is the inclusion into the analysis of both technological and non-technological (organizational and marketing) innovations aimed at creating uncopiable competitive advantages due to available patents and other intangible assets. In addition, we consider the influence of the

---

[a] http://www.gks.ru/bgd/regl/b15_58/Main.htm.

[b] http://www.gks.ru/bgd/regl/b15_58/Main.htm.

interfirm interaction factor on the effectiveness of innovation and the increase in the productivity of industrial companies operating in growing markets.

2. Theoretical and Empirical Studies

There are many studies that confirm the relationship between innovation investment and productivity [Griliches (1996); Pakes and Griliches (1984); Wakelin (2001)]. At the same time, some empirical studies confirm the relationship between investment in research and development and efficiency [Griliches (1996); Pakes and Griliches (1984); Wakelin (2001); Griffith *et al.* (2004)] while others confirm the relationship between the results of innovation, expressed in the number of patents [Hall *et al.* (1986)], the proceeds from the sale of new products [Janz *et al.* (2004)], or the creation of innovation [Parisi *et al.* (2006)] and efficiency. Despite the difference in the analyzed variables, all the studies confirm a positive relationship between innovation and the company's efficiency.

In addition, some researchers have focused their efforts on the study of sectoral differences (in particular, the paper [Griliches and Mairesse (1983)] shows that the relationship between innovation and efficiency is better pronounced in more high-tech companies (the elasticity of productivity in high-tech industries equals 0.20 while the one in other industries is 0.10)). This effect has been confirmed by the research panel data of different countries: Germany (1977–1989) [Harhoff (1998)], Japan (1995–1998) [Kwon and Inui (2003)], Taiwan (1994–2000) [Tsai and Wang (2004)] and others.

Innovative system literature review [Freeman and Barley (1989); Laursen and Salter (2006)] demonstrates that innovations are the result of interactions between companies and institutions that are managed both by market forces and the infrastructure created by the state. In this context, the key role is played not by "R&D inputs" but by the company's interfirm interaction as a determinant of innovative products in the concept of open innovation [Chesbrough (2003)]. In this regard, we have included the interfirm interaction of industrial companies in our analysis of factors.

However, these studies contain a number of limitations related to the endogeneity of the analysis. The first limitation is the fact that the company spending on research and development is not a constant value but depends substantially on the company forecast net cash flow [Griliches (1996); Crépon *et al.* (1998); Jefferson *et al.* (2006)]. The second limitation is the difficulty of measuring the accumulated knowledge of the company and the effectiveness of its transfer within the company, which contributes to the creation of innovation [Zucker *et al.* (2007); Ramani *et al.* (2008); Czarnitzki *et al.* (2009)]. In order to overcome these limitations, the CDM approach has been developed [Crépon *et al.* (1998)], which is based on the association of the investment decisions of the company in research and development and the results of innovation and operational efficiency of the company. The CDM structural model was suggested by Crépon, Duguet, and Mairesse in their 1998 work "Research, Innovation, and Productivity:

An Econometric Analysis at the Firm Level." The CDM model assesses three groups of relationships that connect innovations and productivity. The first group of relationships is described by two equations that explain the propensity of companies to invest in innovation activities. The second part of the model shows the relationship between different types of innovation (product, process, organizational, and marketing) and the value of innovation spending. The third dependency is designed to assess the relationship of innovation to other determinants of productivity.

The original model includes four equations. Equation (1) of the binary choice predicts the likelihood of investment of the company into research and development. If the latent variable (g_i) exceeds a certain threshold (t), which can be interpreted as a selection criterion, the company takes a positive decision about investments in research and development:

$$g_i = \begin{cases} 1 & \text{if } g_i^* = x_{1i}b_i + u_{1i} > t \\ 0 & \text{if } g_i^* = x_{1i}b_i + u_{1i} \geq 1, \end{cases} \tag{1}$$

where g_i is the observed binary variable, which equals 1 if the companies decide to invest in innovation and 0 for the rest of the companies;

g_i^* is the latent (unobservable) endogenous variable, which predicts the company's decision to invest in R&D;

x_{1i} is the independent variable that explains the probability of the decision of a company to invest in innovation;

b_i are parameters of the model; and

u_i are random terms.

Random errors of the model are assumed to be normally distributed.

Equation (2) describes the latent variable of the volumes of investments in research and development, which the authors [Crépon et al. (1998)] have proposed to calculate as the logarithm of investment in research and development per employee engaged in innovation:

$$\boldsymbol{w}_i = \begin{cases} \boldsymbol{w}_i^* = x_{2i}b_2 + u_{2i}, & \text{if } g_i = 1 \\ 0 & \text{if } g_i = 0, \end{cases} \tag{2}$$

where $\boldsymbol{w}_i^*$ is the unobservable variable, which estimates the amount of investments into employees training;

x_{2i} are factors that explain the dependence of the intensity of R&D investment, which will be selected further;

b_2 are parameters of the model; and

u_{2i} are random terms.

If the option "do not invest" is chosen in the first equation, $\boldsymbol{w}_i^*$ is assumed to be zero.

Equation (3) shows the dependence of the results of innovation and innovative inputs. According to Crépon et al., an innovative result has two indicators: the number of patents and the sale of innovative products (the logarithm of sales of new products per employee):

$$k_i^* = \overline{w*}_i \alpha_t + x_{3i} b_3 + u_{3i},\tag{3}$$

where k_i^* are the results of innovative activities;

$\overline{w*}_i$ is the average expenditure on R&D per employee, which is obtained as the result of the first model (the choice of "invest/do not invest");

x_{3i} are the independent variables that affect the level of innovation costs, the selection of which will be shown later;

α_t and b_3 are the vectors of parameters;

and u_{3i} is the remainder.

Equation (4) shows the dependence of the performance of the company (expressed as the logarithm of revenue from sales per employee) on the results of innovation activities. Equation (4) has been derived from the production function of Cobb–Douglas:

$$q_\iota = a_k k_i^* x_{4i} b_4 + u_{4\iota},\tag{4}$$

where q_ι is the performance of the company;

x_{4i} is the vector of exogenous variables;

a_k and b_4 are parameters of the model;

and $u_{4\iota}$ is the random term.

In the framework of the CDM approach as formulated by researchers, it is possible to analyze the relationship of innovation and productivity, which allows combining several different studies of innovative activity of a company in one model; moreover, the development of structural econometric models for the analysis of innovation and productivity and the use of Heckman's censored regression[c] for the analysis are also possible, which allow not only assessing the likelihood of the adoption of a decision to invest in innovation by the companies and determining the volume of these investments but also analyzing the companies that have not formally made any innovation investment.

Further empirical research concerned the study of the influence of various factors on the innovative activity: the company size [Lööf and Heshmati (2002)], the establishment of innovative networks and platforms by companies [Ponds *et al.* (2010)], the volume of investments allocated for research and development [Tone and Sahoo (2003); Trachuk and Linder (2016)], the availability of export activities

---

[c] Censored regression is a regression with a dependent variable that is observed with restricting (censoring) of possible values. In this case, the model can be censored from one side only (from below or from above) or from both sides. Heckmann's censored regression divides the model into two components: a binary choice model for participation and a linear model for the intensity of participation; the factors of these two models may be different.

[Wagner (1996); Love and Roper (2002); Liu and Buck (2007); Bratti and Felice (2012); Siedschlag *et al.* (2010)], inter-firm cooperation [Tether (2002); Savona and Steinmueller (2013)], and direct foreign investment (for example, the research [Criscuolo *et al.* (2010); Siedschlag and Zhang (2014)] show that foreign-owned companies and exporters are more active in the field of innovation).

It should be noted that a number of follow-up studies have also changed the very structure of the model. For example, [Mairesse and Robin (2009); Hall *et al.* (2010)] used the number of designed new products and the results of process innovation as the results of innovation activity. Also, studies have used a different measure of the company effectiveness: profit [Jefferson *et al.* (2006)], revenue from sales [Janz *et al.* (2004)], and productivity growth dynamics [Lööf and Heshmati (2006); Heshmati (2009)], which was measured as sales revenue per employee.

Thus, all the studies confirm a stable relationship between the expenditure on research and development, innovation effectiveness, and efficiency of a company. In addition, studies of different industries and countries [Janz *et al.* (2004); Griffith *et al.* (2006); Lööf and Heshmati (2006); Mairesse and Robin (2009); Musolesi and Huiban (2010); Hall (2011)] give comparable results of the most significant factors in the CDM model: the company size, the availability of export activities, inter-firm cooperation, and investment in technological innovation activities. However, all the above studies have used the data of foreign companies and are built on Community Innovation Surveys (CIS) data. This approach has not been used for the data of Russian industrial companies; however, it is clear that the revealed dependencies will differ in terms of specifics of the operation of companies on the Russian market.

This has determined the relevance of our study.

The analysis of the reference literature allows making the following hypotheses:

Hypothesis 1. There is a stable positive correlation between the innovation activity and the efficiency of Russian manufacturing companies; at the same time, the marginal efficiency of investment in research and development will be significantly different from companies in various industries (low-, medium-, or high-tech companies);

Hypothesis 2. The most significant factors in the CDM model for the Russian companies will be similar to the factors identified in international studies: the company size, the export activity, the amount of direct foreign investment, the presence of inter-firm cooperation, the investment of a company in its current activity, and the cost of technological, organizational, and marketing innovations. However, the strength of the influence of factors (according to the modulus) will vary considerably both from the values obtained for companies in other countries and by the sectors of the Russian manufacturing industry (low-, medium-, or high-tech companies).

3. Research Methodology

The empirical part of our study included two stages. During the first stage (the qualitative stage of the study), a form for the analysis of innovative activity of Russian industrial companies was compiled on the basis of theoretical and methodological research and in-depth interviews with representatives of seven industrial companies; this form consisted of four sections:

(1) General information about the company: the name, the scope of business activities, the membership in a group of companies, the origin of the capital of the company, the number of employees, and the implementation of business activities in foreign markets;
(2) Features of innovative activity of the company: the availability of research and development divisions in the company, the use of the "open innovation" model by the company, the partners that are the most important in order to create innovation, and the innovation activity factors (respondents were asked to rate 38 factors (the Likert scale was used (from 1 — the factor has no impact to 5 — the factor has a very strong impact). These data were used to select the factors that have a significant influence on innovation activity according to the respondents as reflected in Table 2;
(3) The use of indicators to assess the effectiveness of innovative activity: the growth of new product sales, revenues from sales of new products in total sales, the number of new products that appear in an average year, the cost of introduction of new technologies, the number of patents, and profits from the sale of new products. Moreover, the "Other" option (Table 1) has also been provided for;
(4) Information on the innovative activity of companies in Russia is integrated on the basis of the official statistical reports, harmonized in full with the statistical research system, developed in the countries of the European Union, where key data are collected by the harmonized questionnaire of the European Community Innovation Survey 2006. As a part of the research, we have asked the respondents to provide the relevant statistical report forms.

The second stage (the quantitative stage) consisted of the following steps:

(1) Compilation of a sample of manufacturing companies and the datasets for analysis in the retrospective period of 2012–2014;
(2) Construction of an econometric model based on the CDM approach; assessment of the adequacy of the resulting model; and selection of relevant factors;
(3) Analysis of the obtained results and research hypotheses.

Hereinafter, the methodology will be reviewed in accordance with the dedicated research steps.

Table 1.   Descriptive statistics of companies.

Characteristics of companies	Quantity	%
Areas of activity of companies		
B2C market	395	57
B2B market	76	11
B2C B2B market	222	32
Industry		
the high-tech sector:	153	22
manufacture of pharmaceutical products	55	36
the manufacture of medical devices	41	27
the manufacture of electronic and radio components	34	22
other	23	15
the medium-tech sector:	297	43
iron and steel manufacture	62	21
the manufacture of chemical products	95	32
the manufacture of machinery and equipment	42	14
other	98	33
the low-tech sector:	243	35
the manufacture of food products	58	24
publishing and printing	44	18
textile industry	15	6
other	126	52
Capital of companies		
Russian	464	67
foreign	76	11
mixed	153	22
Number of Personnel, people		
1000–4999	298	43
5000–10 000	236	34
More than 10 000	159	23

3.1. *Compilation of a sample*

For the analysis, major industrial companies of over 1000 employees have been selected whose data were analyzed for the period of 2012–2014. In order to improve its homogeneity, the analysis was conducted only among the processing industry companies (we have excluded extractive sector companies as well as power generation and distribution and gas and water companies from the sample), which were in turn then divided into high-tech, medium-tech and low-tech companies. The division was made according to the recommendations of the statistical survey regulations. High-tech companies included the companies engaged in the following types of activities: the manufacture of pharmaceutical products, the manufacture of office machinery and computers, electronic components, and equipment for radio, television, and communication, the manufacture of medical devices, aircraft, and spacecraft. Medium-tech companies included the companies engaged in the following types of activities: chemical industry, the manufacture of machinery and equipment, the manufacture of electrical machinery and equipment, the manufacture of automobiles, the manufacture of oil products, rubber, and plastic products, iron and steel production, and the manufacture of fabricated metal products. Low-tech companies included the companies engaged in the following types of activities: the manufacture of foodstuffs, tobacco products, textiles, clothing, wood processing and the manufacture of wood products, pulp, paper, paperboard, publishing and printing, and processing of secondary raw materials.

The size of the study sample was 693 manufacturing companies, of which 153 companies were in the high-tech sector; 297, in the medium-tech sector; and 243, in the low-tech sector. The sample included companies from six regions of the Russian Federation (the City of Moscow, Moscow region, the City of St. Petersburg, Leningrad region, and the Cities of Omsk and Yekaterinburg). Most of the surveyed companies were located in the City of Moscow (24%), Moscow region (28%), and the City of St. Petersburg (17%). However, as a result of discarding the surveys that have not been completely filled out or have been completed incorrectly, the sample consisted of 678 companies (the most common reason for discarding was the absent of statistical research forms). Sampling was done randomly.

Also, small companies were excluded from the sample due to lack of statistical data, provided by the small companies during the statistical research, that is necessary for the implementation of this study. Table 1 presents descriptive statistics of companies included in the sample for the study.

For the purposes of compilation of the universal set and subsequent verification of financial data on the companies included in the sample, we have used financial reporting databases of the Russian companies databases. The data have been selected for the 2012–2014 period.

Table 2 presents descriptive statistics of companies included in the sample for the study.

3.2. *Construction of an econometric model*

We have used a CDM model that consists of five equations (5)–(9):

Equation (5) estimates the likelihood of companies investing in research and development:

$$\text{RD\_doing}_{it} = \begin{cases} 1 & \text{if } \text{RD\_doing}^*_{it} = x_{1it}b_{it} + u_{1it} > t \\ 0 & \text{if } \text{RD\_doing}^*_{it} = x_{1it}b_{it} + u_{1it} \le t. \end{cases} \tag{5}$$

Explained variable RD_doing is set to 1 if the ith company at the time t makes a decision about investing in research and development; otherwise, it will be set to 0.

Equation (6) estimates the volume of investments in research and development per employee:

$$\text{RD}_{it} = \begin{cases} \text{RD}^*_{it} = x_{2it}b_{2t} + u_{2it}, & \text{if } \text{RD\_doing}_{it} = 1 \\ 0 & \text{if } \text{RD\_doing}_{it} = 0. \end{cases} \tag{6}$$

Table 2.   Average values of the variables of innovation activities (2012–2014).

Indicator		2012	2013	2014
1		2	3	4
High-tech manufacturing sector companies				
1	Companies that invest in R&D, %	34.5	36.1	36.7
2	Companies that profit from new product sales	74.8	77.6	77.9
3	The share of patents obtained in 2012–2014 in the total number of patents of companies, %	10.3	11.4	10.4
4	The share of organizations with research and development divisions, %	47.8	48.1	48.2
5	The share of exporters, %	44.3	42.1	43.7
6	Total level of innovation activity of organizations	31.3	30.4	31.2
7	The share of companies with a cooperation agreement for innovation	19.5	24.7	29.3
Medium-tech manufacturing sector companies				
1	Companies that invest in R&D, %	36.4	36.9	36.3
2	Companies that profit from new product sales	69.8	71.2	70.3
3	The share of patents obtained in 2012–2014 in the total number of patents of companies, %	9.3	9.2	10.3
4	The share of organizations with research and development divisions, %	36.8	37.1	37.3
5	The share of exporters, %	43.3	44.1	47.7
6	Total level of innovation activity of organizations	19.3	19.3	19.5
7	The share of companies with a cooperation agreement for innovation	23.2	24.1	22.3
Low-tech manufacturing sector companies				
1	Companies that invest in R&D, %	21.4	26.9	35.4
2	Companies that profit from new product sales	71.8	70.2	71.3
3	The share of patents obtained in 2012–2014 in the total number of patents of companies, %	2.3	2.2	2.3
4	The share of organizations with research and development divisions, %	16.8	15.1	15.3
5	The share of exporters, %	38.3	37.1	39.7
6	Total level of innovation activity of organizations	6.2	7.6	7.6
7	The share of companies with a cooperation agreement for innovation	16.9	28.1	28.3

The following have been estimated as independent variables:

- the existence of patents in the company (a dummy variable, which is equal to 1, if the company has patents, and to 0 otherwise);
- company size (measured as the logarithm of the number of employees);
- the company's performance in the last year (measured as the logarithm of the revenue from sales per employee). This indicator reflects the impact of the dynamics of performance indicators on the efficiency of innovation activities;
- availability of export earnings (a dummy variable, which is equal to 1 if the company operates only in the domestic market and to 0 if the company is an exporter) since we believe exporters to be more likely to innovate;
- the size of investments of the company into its current activity (measured as the logarithm of the total of the second section of the balance sheet, net of deferred tax assets); this figure is related to the financial possibilities of the company, which also affects its innovation activities;

- the intensity of innovation investment (calculated as the share of expenditure on technological, organizational, and marketing innovations in the total sale revenue);
- income (a dummy variable, which is equal to 1 if the company has a positive profit and to 0 otherwise);
- the label of the industry sector, which allows analyzing specific properties in the high-, medium-, and low-tech sector.

Equations (7) and (8) reflect the impact of innovation activities. Based on the survey results, we have used the following as performance indicators: the profit from the sales of new products and the number of patents obtained by the company is

$$P_{\text{new}}\text{pr}_{it} = \text{RD}_{1\iota t}\alpha_{r1t} + x_{3it}b_{3t} + u_{3it}, \tag{7}$$

$$\text{Patents}_{it} = \text{RD}_{2it}\alpha_{r2t} + x_{4it}b_{4t} + u_{4it}. \tag{8}$$

Both performance equations depend on a latent variable (the value of investments in research and development). This allows including the companies that have not formally invested in research and development into our analysis.

The dependent variable in (7) indicates whether the company has received profits from the sales of new products over three years (2012–2014). For the analysis, Eq. (7) has used a probit model. The dependent variable in (8) represents the ratio of the number of patents obtained by the company for the same three years (2012–2014) to the total number of patents obtained by the same company. Factors that have been measured in the model (7) and (8) are as follows:

- the predicted volume of R&D investment (expressed as the logarithm of the volume of R&D investment per employee);
- company size (measured as the logarithm of the number of employees);
- the size of investments of the company into its current activity (measured as the logarithm of the volume of current investments); this figure is related to the financial possibilities of the company, which also affects its innovation activities;
- availability of export earnings (a dummy variable, which is equal to 1 if the company operates only on the domestic market and to 0 if the company is an exporter);
- availability of cooperation with companies within its group if the company is integrated (a dummy variable, which is equal to 1, if the company cooperates with partners in the company, and to 0 otherwise);
- the intensity of innovation investment (calculated as the share of expenditure on technological, organizational, and marketing innovations in the total sale revenue);
- availability of an external inter-firm cooperation (a dummy variable, which is equal to 1, if the company cooperates with partners in the innovation process, and to 0 otherwise); in this case, we highlight and analyze the following types of cooperation:

— cooperation with consumers;

— cooperation with suppliers;

— cooperation with competitors;

— cooperation with consulting media companies;

— cooperation with universities and other of higher educational institutions;

— cooperation with scientific organizations;

- availability of own business units engaged in research and development (a dummy variable, which is equal to 1, if the company has its own business units, and to 0 otherwise);
- the cost of training of employees engaged in innovation activities (measured as the logarithm of the training costs per employee engaged in innovative activities);
- the cost of purchasing new technologies (measured as the logarithm of the amount of expenditures for the purchase of new technology).

All the variables in Eqs. (7) and (8) have been taken as the average of three years (2012–2014). The averaging of these indicators is due to the presence of gaps in the database and to the possible measurement errors as well as due to the existing time lag between R&D investment of the companies and the results of innovation activities.

Equation (9) shows the dependence of productivity (expressed as the logarithm of the ratio of revenues from sales to the number of employees) on latent variables: profit from the sales of innovative products $P_{\text{new}}\text{pr}_{it}$ and the number of patents Patents_{it}. Because performance depends not only on the impact of innovation but also on the company's investments in current activities, manpower used by the company, and so forth, we have added variables that demonstrate the impact of other factors:

$$Q_t = a_{NPt}P_{\text{new}}\text{pr}_{it} + a_{P}t\text{Patents}_{it} + a_{R3t}\text{RD}_{it} + x_{5it}b_{5t} + u_{5ti}. \tag{9}$$

The following indicators have been analyzed as factors:

- company size (measured as the logarithm of the number of employees);
- the size of investments of the company into its current activity (measured as the logarithm of the total of the second section of the balance sheet, net of deferred tax assets); this figure is related to the financial possibilities of the company, which also affects its innovation activities;
- the logarithm of the predicted value of R&D investment per employee;
- the logarithm of the predicted amount of profit from the sale of new products;
- the logarithm of the predicted number of patents obtained by the company as compared to the total number of patents obtained by the company;
- the logarithm of the number of employees engaged in innovation activities;
- the intensity of innovation investment (the logarithm of the share of expenditure on technological, organizational, and marketing innovations in the total sale revenue).

In order to test our hypotheses, we have calculated the models (5)–(9) for the companies of three manufacturing sectors: high-, medium-, and low-tech companies.

4. Results

Table 3 presents the results of the mathematical expectation of the number of companies that make decisions about investments in research and development. We have used a two-stage Heckman's model for the analysis of models (5) and (6). The dummy variable for assessing the company's decision to invest in R&D (5) has been defined for the three-year period from 2012 to 2014. The evaluation has been performed with the use of the probit model. The second equation (model 6) is intended only for the companies that decide to invest in R&D. The dependent variable is the logarithm of the average cost of R&D per employee for three years from 2012 to 2014.

The resulting model as a whole is significant since the value of the pseudo R-squared is equal to 0.245–0.367, which is acceptable for a model built on the basis of surveys.

The results indicate that the factors that influence the company's decision to invest in R&D from an administrative point of view are the availability of the company's assets (profits) and experience of the investment in fixed assets, the implementation of innovation activities, patenting, and the use of patents to create products, as well as the experience of the company in the foreign markets.

Predicted volume of R&D investment per employee varies greatly depending on the characteristics of the industry. The largest investments per employee are seen in high-tech companies and in exporters in the medium-tech sector. At the same time, the high-tech sectors are characterized by the practical independence of the volume of R&D investment regardless of whether the company is an exporter or not and is about the same for both companies that operate in the domestic market and exporters. However, the volumes of R&D investment in the low-tech companies are significantly higher for the companies that are not exporters (companies that operate in the domestic market) than for exporters. In the medium-tech sector, there is an inverse relationship: the volume of R&D investment is significantly higher for exporters.

Table 4 demonstrates the marginal effects for the determinants of innovation performance expressed as the profit from the sale of new products.

The resulting model as a whole is significant because the R-squared value is equal to 0.734–0.813.

The calculation results show that decisions of companies to invest into R&D have a positive relationship with the profit from the sale of new products by the companies; this relationship is the most significant in the medium-tech sector. A positive correlation can be observed between investment in fixed assets, acquisition of new technologies, and availability of the export business activities of the company.

Table 3.   Marginal effects for the probability of decisions on investment in research and development.

Characteristics of the manufacturing industry	High-tech industry		Medium-tech industry		Low-tech industry	
Dependent variables	Decision of innovation investment	Investments in employee training	Decision of innovation investment	Investments in employees training	Decision of innovation investment	Investments in employees training
Method of analysis	Censored regression (Heckman's model, the first equation)	Censored regression (Heckman's model, the second equation)	Censored regression (Heckman's model, the first equation)	Censored regression (Heckman's model, the second equation)	Censored regression (Heckman's model, the first equation)	Censored regression (Heckman's model, the second equation)
Company size (log average number)	0.087*** (0.007)	—	0.142*** (0.024)	—	0.145*** (0.011)	—
Availability of export earnings (1: yes, 0: no)	0.193*** (0.041)	0.219 (0.139)	0.492*** (0.071)	0.374*** (0.298)	0.158* (0.030)	0.076*** (0.122)
Investments in current activity (the logarithm of results of the second section of the balance sheet net of deferred tax assets)	0.284*** (0.051)	0.297 (0.023)	0.311*** (0.049)	0.304* (0.037)	0.249*** (0.021)	0.264*** (0.012)
Availability of profit (1: yes, 0: no)	0.134*** (0.012)	0.276*** (0.037)	0.164*** (0.021)	0.473*** (0.043)	0.317*** (0.032)	0.374*** (0.022)

(Continued)

Table 3. *(Continued)*

Characteristics of the manufacturing industry	High-tech industry		Medium-tech industry		Low-tech industry	
Dependent variables	Decision of innovation investment	Investments in employee training	Decision of innovation investment	Investments in employees training	Decision of innovation investment	Investments in employees training
The intensity of innovation investment (the logarithm of the share of expenditure on technological, organizational, and marketing innovations in the total sale revenue)	0.451*** (0.019)	0.427**** (0.012)	0.462** (0.115)	0.317** (0.107)	0.268** (0.134)	0.171** (0.017)
Availability of patents (1: yes, 0: no)	0.402*** (0.043)	0.219*** (0.043)	0.316*** (0.043)	0.275*** (0.048)	0.219*** (0.043)	0.0061*** (0.00006)
Availability of own divisions engaged in R&D (1: yes, 0: no)	0.234*** (0.009)	0.115*** (0.009)	0.221*** (0.009)	0.324*** (0.00003)	0.126*** (0.009)	0.186*** (0.00038)
Number of observations	149		291		238	
F-statistics (at the significance point of 6.7032e-11)	9.009278		8.99107		9.12098	
Pseudo − R-squared (%)	36.7		24.53		25.28	

Notes: (1) Presented numbers have marginal effect values. (2) The statistical significance of the coefficients: *** — $p \leq 0.001$; ** — $p \leq 0.01$; * — $p \leq 0.05$. (3) the values in parentheses indicate robust standard errors.

Table 4.   Results of innovation: The profit from sales of new products (estimated elasticities).

Characteristics of the manufacturing industry	High-tech industry	Medium-tech industry	Low-tech industry
Method of analysis	OLS	OLS	OLS
The logarithm of the projected R&D expenditure per employee	0.172**	0.285***	0.126***
	(0.002)	(0.007)	(0.004)
Company size (log average number)	0.029	0.171***	0.142***
	(0.043)	(0.031)	(0.061)
Availability of export activity (1: yes, 0: no)	0.267***	0.238***	0.163**
	(0.037)	(0.0236)	(0.016)
Investments into current activity (the logarithm of investments into current assets)	0.227**	0.257**	0.329**
	(0.018)	(0.014)	(0.0031)
The acquisition of new technologies (the logarithm of the costs of acquisition of new technology)	0.729*	0.483*	0.441**
	(0.0049)	(0.012)	(0.065)
Education and training of employees engaged in innovation activities (the logarithm of the training costs per 1 employee who is engaged in innovative activities)	−0.326	−0.211	−0.158**
	(0.127)	(0.114)	(0.0013)
The intensity of innovation investment (the logarithm of the share of expenditure on technological, organizational, and marketing innovations in the total sale revenue)	−0.389*	−0.650*	−0.321*
	(0.047)	(0.086)	(0.064)
Cooperation with enterprises within the company (1: yes, 0: no)	0.521*	0.221*	0.337*
	(0.043)	(0.0128)	(0.0127)
Cooperation with customers (1: yes, 0: no)	0.385*	0.518**	0.419*
	(0.0086)	(0.0165)	(0.112)
Cooperation with suppliers (1: yes, 0: no)	0.210**	0.412*	0.431
	(0.0045)	(0.108)	(0.121)
Cooperation with competitors (1: yes, 0: no)	0.397**	0.1278	0.217
	(0.0076)	(0.0053)	(0.0190)
Cooperation with consulting media companies (1: yes, 0: no)	0.196**	0.529**	0.652
	(0.006)	(0.0072)	(0.005)
Collaboration with universities etc. Higher education institutions (1: yes, 0: no)	0.154**	0.042*	0.064
	(0.0079)	(0.0038)	(0.0021)
Cooperation with scientific organizations (1: yes, 0: no)	0.196	0.159	0.129
	(0.117)	(0.108)	(0.097)
Number of observations	149	291	238
F-statistics (at the significance point of 6.3208e-11)	7.5548	8.11307	8.8797
R-squared (%)	78.271	73.363	81.293

Notes: (1) Presented numbers have marginal effect values. (2) The statistical significance of the coefficients: *** — $p \leq 0.001$; ** — $p \leq 0.01$; * — $p \leq 0.05$. (3) the values in parentheses indicate robust standard errors.

Company size also has a positive correlation with the results of innovation; but its effect in high-tech industries is relatively weak. In low-tech sectors, the likelihood of higher efficiency of innovative activity is observed in companies with a higher level of investment into fixed assets.

Manufacturing companies have a higher performance indicators of innovation in collaboration with other companies within their groups if the company is integrated (in high- and medium-tech sectors); with suppliers (in high- and medium-tech sector); with customers (in medium- and low-tech sectors); with universities (in the group of companies of the medium-tech sector only); with research and development organizations (in medium-tech sectors); and with consulting companies (in medium and low-tech sectors).

Table 5 demonstrates the results of calculations of the probit model for the efficiency of innovation activities expressed in the number of patents.

Table 5.   Estimates of the elasticity coefficients in the model of innovation: The number of patents.

Characteristics of the industry	High-tech industry	Medium-tech industry	Low-tech industry
Method of analysis	OLS	OLS	OLS
The logarithm of the projected R&D expenditure per employee	0.562***	0.414***	0.254***
	(0.012)	(0.028)	(0.017)
Company size (log average number)	0.221**	0.361***	0.318
	(0.011)	(0.014)	(0.0009)
Availability of export activity (1: yes, 0: no)	0.319	0.334***	0.217
	(0.061)	(0.039)	(0.031)
Investments into current activity (the logarithm of investments into current assets)	0.269*	0.198**	0.248**
	(0.0140)	(0.0034)	(0.0216)
The acquisition of new technologies (the logarithm of the costs of acquisition of new technology)	0.055	0.043	0.113
	(0.104)	(0.103)	(0.086)
Education and training of employees engaged in innovation activities (the logarithm of the training costs per 1 employee who is engaged in innovative activities)	0.214	0.315	0.274
	(0.097)	(0.108)	(0.075)
The intensity of innovation investment (the logarithm of the share of expenditure on technological, organizational, and marketing innovations in the total sale revenue)	0.497	0.526	0.423
	(0.106)	(0.072)	(0.0061)
Cooperation with enterprises within the company (1: yes, 0: no)	0.092**	0.049*	0.073*
	(0.0052)	(0.007)	(0.004)
Cooperation with customers (1: yes, 0: no)	−0.274**	−0.150*	−0.135*
	(0.0013)	(0.086)	(0.0019)
Cooperation with suppliers (1: yes, 0: no)	−0.239*	−0.174	−0.148
	(0.047)	(0.004)	(0.006)
Cooperation with competitors (1: yes, 0: no)	−0.071*	−0.007**	−0.125
	(0.043)	(0.0165)	(0.016)
Cooperation with consulting media companies (1: yes, 0: no)	0.184*	0.141*	0.231**
	(0.0086)	(0.108)	(0.119)
Collaboration with universities etc. Higher education institutions (1: yes, 0: no)	0.110**	0.142	0.026*
	(0.0045)	(0.0053)	(0.0062)
Cooperation with scientific organizations (1: yes, 0: no)	−0.177**	−0.151*	−0.127*
	(0.0076)	(0.0041)	(0.0069)
Number of observations	149	291	238
F-statistics (at the significance point of 7.4468e-11)	8.998301	9.56028	9.08299
R-squared (%)	81.382	82.259	72.173

Notes: (1) Presented numbers have marginal effect values. (2) The statistical significance of the coefficients: *** — $p \leq 0.001$; ** — $p \leq 0.01$; * — $p \leq 0.05$. (3) the values in parentheses indicate robust standard errors.

The resulting model as a whole is significant because the R-squared value is equal to 0.722–0.823.

It is estimated that the largest impact on the number of patents is demonstrated by the following indicators: the intensity of innovation investment activities, the amount of investment into fixed assets (in high-tech manufacturing industries).

In all three sectors, there is a positive relationship between the number of patents and the costs of the preparation and training of employees. The strength of its impact in medium- and low-tech sectors is higher than it is in high-tech companies.

The indicators of cooperation with companies within the same group, consulting companies, and research and development organizations have a positive correlation with the amount of patents obtained by the company. However, a negative relationship of cooperation with customers, suppliers, and competitors on the one hand, and the number of patents on the other was unexpected.

Table 6 demonstrates the marginal effects of performance of companies of the three manufacturing sectors.

Table 6.   Performance of companies (elasticity of coefficients).

Characteristics of the industry	High-tech companies	Medium-tech companies	Low-tech companies
Method of analysis (LSM — the least squares method)	LSM	LSM	LSM
Company size (log average number)	0.021**	0.018**	0.029***
	(0.011)	(0.0015)	(0.017)
Indicator of export activity (1: yes, 0: no)	0.099***	0.120***	0.134***
	(0.027)	(0.032)	(0.015)
The logarithm of the projected R&D expenditure per employee	0.11***	0.07**	−0.12 **
	(0.003)	(0.0028)	(0.132)
The intensity of innovation investment (the logarithm of the share of expenditure on technological, organizational, and marketing innovations in the total sale revenue)	0.160	0.06	0.03
	(0.106)	(0.072)	(0.0061)
Logarithm of the predicted amount of profit from the sale of new products	0.180***	0.351***	0.021***
	(0.0276)	(0.014)	(0.084)
Logarithm of the predicted number of patents obtained by the company	0.344***	0.262***	0.192***
	(0.027)	(0.032)	(0.015)
Investments into current activity (the logarithm of investments into current assets)	0.283***	0.215**	0.113**
	(0.024)	(0.031)	(0.028)
Logarithm of the number of employees engaged in innovation activities	0.214***	0.208***	0.114***
	(0.0276)	(0.014)	(0.084)
Number of observations	149	291	238
F-statistics (at the significance point of 7.51543e-11)	9.3761	8.7821	9.00397
R-squared (%)	72.462	79.852	71.497

Notes: (1) Presented numbers have marginal effect values. (2) The statistical significance of the coefficients: *** — $p \leq 0.001$; ** — $p \leq 0.01$; * — $p \leq 0.05$. (3) the values in parentheses indicate robust standard errors.

The resulting model as a whole is significant because the R-squared value is equal to 0.715–0.799.

Calculations in the table indicate that the low-tech sector is characterized by the appropriability effect (the elasticity of expenditures on innovation and the share of R&D costs are negatively correlated with the performance of the company), i.e. additional profits from the investment are not significant. This effect may further lead to an under-investment trap because the majority of firms in this sector do not see an incentive to implement major investment projects due to their incomplete margins.

However, the companies of the sector would be wrong to stop investments in innovation because not all industries of this segment are in stagnation; for example, in the industry of pulp and paper manufacture, the manufacture of packaging paper grows; in the food industry, innovation investment allows companies to produce goods at a lower price, which will increase their productivity.

In the high- and medium-tech sector, the impact of innovation and R&D expenditures are positively related to the performance of industrial companies; in this case, the strongest correlation between the results of innovation and productivity is observed for patents in the high-tech sector (the elasticity of productivity with respect to the number of patents is 0.344) and for profit from sales of new products in the medium-tech sector (0.351).

The obtained empirical results have demonstrated that the marginal effect of R&D investment and productivity in high-tech industries is 0.11; in the medium-tech sector, the elasticity is 0.07; while the low-tech sector is characterized by the appropriability effect. Thus, R&D investment increases the productivity of industrial companies of the manufacturing industry with an average elasticity of 0.09.

The relationship between the intensity of innovation investment and the productivity has a range of elasticity from 0.03 (for low-tech sectors with lower levels of "intensity" of innovative investments) to 0.16 (in high-tech industries, which are characterized by the highest volumes of R&D investment).

The intensity of innovation investment, which is calculated as the ratio of the share of technological, organizational, and marketing innovations expenditures in the total sale revenues, is characterized by approximately equal values in medium- and low-tech industries; however, the estimated elasticity of productivity from the innovation investment in high- and middle-tech companies is significantly higher. This suggests that the relationship between R&D investment, innovation results, and the growth of performance are nonlinear in nature and have a strong positive relationship only after a critical mass of innovation investment has been reached.

Finally, our results indicate that a significant impact on the relationship between R&D investment and the productivity is demonstrated by the diversity of sectoral differences in the same industry. According to calculations, high-tech companies are characterized by larger volumes of R&D investment and innovation; however, their elasticity and performance for all types of innovative investments are also higher due to research and development.

5. Conclusion and Further Research

This paper analyzes the relationship between the R&D investment of companies, their innovation effectiveness, and productivity for Russian manufacturing companies. To this end, we have used an econometric model of simultaneous equations (CDM), which has been calculated on the basis of statistical and financial data of processing industry companies. The results are shown for the three sectors of the manufacturing industry: high-, medium-, and low-tech industries.

The results of our study demonstrate that two out of three manufacturing sectors under consideration are characterized by a stable positive relationship between the R&D investment, the innovation effectiveness, and the performance of companies (this relationship has not been confirmed for the low-tech sectors of the manufacturing industry). The industry-average innovation investments increases the productivity with the elasticity of 0.09 (this value is obtained as the average weighted value of the marginal effects of investments in R&D and labor productivity in high- and medium-technology industries). Profits from sales of new products in all sectors of the manufacturing industry are of the greatest importance for the performance of companies. Availability of patents in the organization has a much less pronounced impact on performance.

Cooperation indicators are significant enough for the performance expressed as the profit from the sale of new products and patents. The greatest marginal effect is the cooperation of companies with other companies within their groups if these companies are integrated (in high- and medium-tech sectors); with suppliers (in high- and medium-tech sector); with customers (in medium- and low-tech sectors); with universities (in the group of companies of the medium-tech sector only); with research and development organizations (in medium-tech sectors); and with consulting companies (in medium and low-tech sectors). Patenting activity is characterized by a negative impact of cooperation with customers, suppliers, and competitors of the company.

The conducted empirical analysis demonstrates a nonlinear relationship between the amount of R&D investment, the innovation effectiveness, and the growth of productivity. These results demonstrate that innovation investment on the average increases the productivity of industrial companies with the elasticity of 0.09; the impact of innovation investment on the performance of companies depends on the "intensity" of R&D investment and has a range of elasticity from 0.03 (for low volumes of R&D investment) to 0.16 (for high volumes of investments); the relationship between innovation investment and the growth of performance is nonlinear in nature and has a strong positive relationship only after the critical mass of innovation investment has been reached; a significant role in the relationship of R&D investment and productivity is played by the characteristics of industries in which the company operates (the companies that operate in high-tech industries not only invest more in R&D and innovation but also are characterized by better indicators of performance due to research and development while the companies that operate in low-tech industries have a negative elasticity of innovation investment and productivity due to the influence of the appropriability effect, i.e. additional profits from the investment are not significant).

A sustained positive correlation between the "intensity" of R&D investment, the innovation investment, and the growth of productivity can occur only after a critical mass of innovation investment has been reached.

Our study has also indicated a significant impact of the sectoral diversity on the relationship between the amounts of R&D investment, innovation expenditures, and performance. According to the calculations, high-tech companies have a large R&D investment per employee; however, the performance flexibility for all the types of innovative investments in these companies is also higher due to the results of research and development.

The study is the first description of the relationship of innovation and productivity that has been implemented on the basis of the data obtained from Russian manufacturing companies.

More reliable results can be obtained subject to further research and, above all, to the expansion of the sample of manufacturing companies through the inclusion of small and medium-sized businesses in the analysis.

However, our results can also be considered by manufacturing companies in the course of development of an innovative strategy. In particular, the resulting conclusion on the nonlinear effects of innovation investment and business performance is important.

Understanding nonlinear effects allow using a variety of tools in order to achieve the objectives of the companies with both high and low volumes of R&D investment as well as accounting for the characteristics of the industry in which the company operates.

Given that the relationship between spending on innovation and productivity is stronger in high-tech sectors, an industrial policy based on stimulating the expansion of high-tech sectors could become an alternative way to increase productivity in times of an economic crisis and the need to support industrial companies.

Later, in our opinion, one should expand the list of surveyed companies and determinants of innovation performance and see whether there are differences in the factors that affect innovation depending on the industry. Then, in case of identification of various factors that are responsible for the characteristics of operation of a company in the industry, they should be included in the analysis. Moreover, one should produce a regional analysis of the dependence of innovation investment and productivity, which would allow for a more accurate consideration of the marginal effects of innovation investment and for their consideration when determining a regional industrial policy.

References

Bratti, M. and Felice, G. (2012). Are exporters more likely to introduce product innovations? *The World Economy*, **35**, 11: 1559–1598.

Chesbrough, H. (2003). *Open Innovation: The New Imperative for Creating and Profiting from Technology*, Harverd Business Press, Boston.

Criscuolo, C., Haskel, E. and Slaughter, M. (2010). Global engagement and the innovation activities of firms. *International Journal of Industrial Organization*, **28**, 2: 191–202.

Crépon, B., Duguet, E. and Mairesse, J. (1998). Research, innovation, and productivity: An econometric analysis at the firm level. *Economics of Innovation and New Technology*, **7**: 115–156.

Czarnitzki, D., Petr, H. and Julio, M. R. (2004). Evaluating the impact of R&D tax credits on innovation: A microeconometric study on canadian firms, Discussion Paper No. 04–77. Centre for European Economic Research, Mannheim, Germany.

Freeman, J. and Barley, S. R. (1989). The strategic analysis of interorganizational relations in biotechnology. *Strategic Management of Technological Innovations*, eds. R. Loveridge, M. Pitt and John Wiley, N.Y.

Griffith, R., Huergo, E., Mairesse, J. and Peters, B. (2006). Innovation and productivity across four european countries. *Oxford Review of Economic Policy*, **22**, 4: 483–498.

Griffith, R., Redding, S. and Reenen, J. V. (2004). R&D and absorptive capacity: From theory to data. *Scandinavian Journal of Economics*, **105**, 1: 99–118.

Griliches, Z. (1996). The discovery of the residual: A historical note. *Journal of Economic Literature*, **34**, 3: 1324–1330.

Griliches, Z. and Mairesse, J. (1983). Comparing productivity growth: An exploration of French and U.S. industrial and firm data. *European Economic Review*, **21**, 1–2: 89–119.

Hall, B. H., Mairesse, J. and Mohnen, P. (2010). Measuring the returns to R&D. *Handbook of the Economics of Innovation*, eds. B. H. Hall and N. Rosenberg, Vol. 2, Chap. 22, Elsevier, pp. 1033–1082.

Harhoff, D. (1998). R&D and productivity in German manufacturing firms. *Economics of Innovation and New Technology*, **6**, 1: 29–50.

Heshmati, A. (2009). A generalized knowledge production function. *The Icfai University Journal of Industrial Economics*, **VI**: 7–39.

Janz, N., Lööf, H. and Peters, B. (2004). Innovation and productivity in German and swedish manufacturing firms: Is there a common story?*Problems & Perspectives in Management*, **2**: 184–204.

Jefferson, G., Huamao, B., Xiaojing, G. and Xiaoyun, Y. (2006). R&D performance in Chinese industry. *Economics of Innovation and New Technology*, **15**: 345–366.

Kwon, H. and Inui, T. (2003). R&D and productivity growth in Japanese manufacturing firms. ERSI Discussion Paper Series 44, Economic and Social Research Institute.

Laursen, K. and Salter, A. (2006). Open for innovation: The role of openness in explaining innovative performance among UK manufacturing firms. *Strategic Management Journal*, **27**, 2: 131–150.

Liu, X. and Buck, T. (2007). Innovation performance and channels for international technology spillovers: Evidence from Chinese high-tech industries. *Research Policy*, **36**, 3: 355–366.

Lööf, H. and Heshmati, A. (2006). On the relationship between innovation and performance: A sensitivity analysis. *Economics of Innovation and New Technology*, **15**: 317–344.

Love, J. and Roper, S. (2002). Innovation and export performance: Evidence from UK and german manufacturing plants. *Research Policy*, **31**, 7: 1087–1102.

Mairesse, J. and Robin, S. (2009). Innovation and productivity: A firm-level analysis for French Manufacturing and Services using CIS3 and CIS4 data (1998–2000 and 2002–2004). Working paper.

Musolesi, A. and Huiban, J. (2010). Innovation and productivity in knowledge intensive business services. *Journal of Productivity Analysis*, **34**: 63–81.

Pakes, A. and Griliches, Z. (1984). Patents and R&D at the firm level: A first look. *R & D, Patents, and Productivity*, University of Chicago Press, US, pp. 55–72.

Parisi, M., Schiantarelli, F. and Sembenelli, A. (2006). Productivity, innovation creation and absorption, and R&D. Microevidence for Italy. *European Economic Review*, **50**: 2037–2061.

Ponds, R., Van Oort, F. and Frenken, K. (2010). Innovation, spillovers and university-industry collaboration: An extended knowledge production function approach. *Journal of Economic Geography*, **10**, 2: 231–255.

Ramani, S. V., El-Aroui Carrére, M.-A. and Carrére, M. (2008). On estimating a knowledge production function at the firm and sector level using patent statistics. *Research Policy*, **37**, 9: 1568–1570.

Savona, M. and Steinmueller, W. E. (2013). "Service output, innovation and productivity: A time-based conceptual framework. *Structural Change and Economic Dynamics*, **27**: 118–132.

Siedschlag, I., Zhang, X. and Cahill, B. (2010). The effects of the internationalisation of firms on innovation and productivity. ESRI Working Paper No. 363, Economic and Social Research Institute, Dublin, Ireland.

Siedschlag, I. and Zhang, X. (2014). Internationalisation of firms and their innovation and productivity. *Economics of Innovation and New Technology*, published online, 17 July 2014. Available at: http://dx.doi.org/10.1080/10438599.2014.918439.

Tether, B. S. and Tajar, A. (2008). The organisational-cooperation mode of innovation and its prominence amongst european service firms. *Research Policy*, **37**, 4: 720–739.

Tone, K. and Sahoo, B. K. (2003). Scale, indivisibilities and production function in data envelopment analysis. *International Journal of Production Economics*, **42**, 2: 165–192.

Trachuk, A. V. and Linder, N. V. (2016). Vliyanie ogranichenij likvidnostina vlozheniya promyshennyh kompanij v issledovaniya i razrabotki rezal'tativnost innovacionnoj deyatel'nosti. *Effective Crisis Management*, **1**: 80–89.

Tsai, K.-H. and Wang, J.-C. (2004). R&D productivity and the spillover effects of hightech industry on the traditional manufacturing sector: The case of Taiwan. *The World Economy*, **27**, 10: 1555–1570.

Vegh, C. A. (2013). *Open Economy Macroeconomics in Developing Countries* (MIT press).

Wagner, J. (1996). Export performance, human capital, and product innovation in Germany: A micro view. *Jahrbuch fur Wirtschaftswissenschaften*, **47**: 40–45.

Wakelin, K. (2001). Productivity growth and R&D expenditure in UK manufacturing firms. *Research Policy*, **30**: 1079–1090.

Zucker, L. G., Darby, M. R., Furner, J., Liu, R. C. and Ma, H. (2007). Minerva unbound: Knowledge stocks, knowledge flows and new knowledge production. *Research Policy*, **36**, 6: 850–863.

Biography

Arkady Trachuk is Doctor of Economics, Professor and Dean of the Faculty "Higher School of Management" of the Financial University under the Government of the Russian Federation. The head of the program Management Consulting, Digital innovation management. Areas of scientific interests: (1) strategy and management of company development;(2) economy of natural monopolies; (3) innovative company strategy; (4) innovation amplification and technological transfers;

(5) knowledge management; (6) transformation of companies' business models. Editor-in-Chief of the magazine *Strategic Decisions and Risk Management*.

Natalia Linder is a Candidate of Economics, Professor and Head of the Department of Management and Innovation of the Financial University under the Government of the Russian Federation. The head of the master's program Management of Innovations and Entrepreneurship, Business management. Areas of scientific interests: (1) innovation management; (2) strategy and development management; (3) sustainable development of the company; (4) transformation of business models of industrial and energy companies. Deputy Editor-in-Chief of the magazine *Strategic Decisions and Risk Management*.

Chapter 6

Sharing Economy: A Systematic Literature Review

Nivedita Agarwal*

*Schallershofer Strasse 68a
91056 Erlangen, Germany
nivedita.agarwal@yahoo.com*

Robert Steinmetz

*School of Business, Economics and Society
Friedrich-Alexander-University Erlangen-Nuremberg
LangeGasse 20, 90403, Nuremberg, Germany
Robert.Steinmetz@gmx.de*

The paper employs a Systematic Literature R eview approach to investigate the evolution of the term sharing economy and to identify the future potential research pathways. Analysis of the key publications reveals high emphasis on conceptual studies and qualitative methodologies within the academic literature on sharing economy. This study classifies the literature into five main categories of sustainability, participant behavior, regulatory framework, business models and conceptual studies. Highlighting the research gaps, this study also calls for further research on understanding the roles of other stakeholders such as government and municipalities, analyzing the influence of cultural background and exploring the possibilities for B2B businesses to engage in sharing economy.

Keywords: Sharing economy; sustainability; collaborative consumption; access-based consumption; peer-to-peer sharing.

1. Introduction

Over the last few years, the term "Sharing Economy" seems to have been getting increasing attention in our everyday lives. In fact, it has opened a new pathway to

---

*Corresponding author.

This chapter was originally published in *International Journal of Innovation and Technology Management*, Vol. 16, No. 6, August 2019, published by World Scientific Publishing, Singapore. Reprinted with permission.

deal with capitalism and modern consumerism, driven by the global financial and economic crises and paired with the urgent need for sustainable resource usage [Heinrichs and Grunenberg (2012); Hamari *et al.* (2016)]. In 2015, five sharing economy-related key sectors generated platform revenues of nearly four billion euros and transactions of over 28 billion euros, solely in Europe [PWC (2016)]. The rise of the sharing economy and the growth of people's interest in participating in it are emphasized by several sources [Hamari *et al.* (2016); Heinrichs and Grunenberg (2012)]. Academics have linked this rising attention to the financial crisis of 2008 [Habibi *et al.* (2017)]. However, in comparison to the business view, from an academic perspective the topic of sharing economy is still relatively new.

In academic literature, the term sharing economy is often referred to as an umbrella term for a variety of non-ownership forms of consumption activities such as "collaborative consumption" [Botsman and Rogers (2010)] and "access-based consumption" [Bardhi and Eckhardt (2012)]. To date, researchers have examined the concept of sharing economy from various perspectives, including motivations to participate [Hawlitschek *et al.* (2016); Hamari *et al.* (2016); Balck and Cracau (2015)] and sustainability [Heinrichs and Grunenberg (2012)], and from business model aspects [Richter *et al.* (2017); Cheng (2016)]. However, it still lacks a structured synthesis and a consensus on a single definition or a single shared meaning. Therefore, as the field is maturing, it explicitly requires consolidation of the knowledge gained so far and structured review to identify future research directions [Cheng (2016)]. Addressing this requirement, we conduct a Systematic Literature Review (SLR) on sharing economy to explore the current state of the art and define future research pathways. The review follows the three-stage process of conducting a systematic review given by Tranfield *et al.* [2003].

Literature review reveals high emphasis on conceptual studies and qualitative methodologies that were used to explore the topic of sharing economy. A bias on North American region is evident, as most of the studies have focused on cases from North America as compared to any other region. Based on the literature review, the study also attempts to offer a structure to the literature by categorizing it into five main categories and highlight the underexplored areas therein. The five main categories include conceptual studies and different aspects of sharing economy such as sustainability, participant behavior, regulatory framework and business models.

Following this introduction, the structure of the paper is organized as follows. First, the concept of sharing economy is discussed in detail. Following the background (Sec. 2), the methodology is illustrated with the different steps of SLR process (Sec. 3). Then the findings are illustrated (Sec. 4), followed by a discussion on the identified research categories (Sec. 5). Finally, implications for future research and limitations are presented (Sec. 6).

2. Background

The term sharing economy refers to the field of sharing resources in an efficient way. Given the continuing process of digitization, Web 2.0 and even social network growth, the idea of sharing has undergone a major development in the last few years [Richter *et al.* (2015)]. Due to the involvement of different business models, as well as product sections and markets, arriving at a common definition is not easy. Botsman and Rogers [2010] define the sharing economy as an economic model for sharing underutilized assets for monetary or non-monetary benefits. Focusing on Web 2.0, the sharing economy is also defined as "the peer-to-peer-based activity of obtaining, giving, or sharing the access to goods and services, coordinated through community-based online services" [Hamari *et al.* (2016), p. 2047]. In this context, Schor and Fitzmaurice [2015] also emphasize the importance of digital technology and platforms, including monetized or non-monetized exchange, as the basis for a new way of providing goods and services. A more comprehensive definition is given by Stephany [2015, p. 9] explaining that "The sharing economy is the value in taking underutilized assets and making them accessible online to a community, leading to a reduced need for ownership of those assets." This concept includes five main elements, namely:

- value creation,
- underutilized assets,
- online accessibility,
- community,
- reduced need for ownership.

Habibi *et al.* [2017] offer a broader view on sharing economy which includes several non-ownership forms of consumption activities such as "collaborative consumption" [Botsman and Rogers (2010)] and "access-based consumption" [Bardhi and Eckhardt (2012)]. However, both these activities are defined differently in the literature. On the one hand, Belk [2014b, p. 1597] defines "collaborative consumption" as "people coordinating acquisition and distribution of a resource for a fee or other compensation," whereby various sharing activities like couch surfing are excluded, because no compensation of the provider is involved. Additionally, gifting is excluded, as it involves a permanent transfer of ownership. According to this definition, collaborative consumption is seen as a "middle ground between sharing and marketplace exchange, with elements of both." The other definition of collaborative consumption as given by Hamari *et al.* [2016, p. 2050] is "it is a peer-to-peer-based activity of obtaining, giving, or sharing access to goods and services, coordinated through community-based online services." It includes activities such as "bartering, lending, renting, gifting and swapping" in different categories such as "product service systems", "redistribution markets" and "collaborative lifestyles" [Botsman and Rogers (2010, p. 12)]. On the other hand, "access-based consumption" is defined as "transactions that can be mediated but where no transfer of ownership takes place and differ from ownership and sharing" [Bardhi and Eckhardt (2012, p. 881)], focusing more on the role of mediation. While both these approaches share similar characteristics, they focus on different aspects of the term sharing economy.

Furthermore, there have also been some recent attempts to review the literature on sharing economy using multi-level perspectives [Görög (2018); Guimarães *et al.* (2018); Ter Huurne *et al.* (2017); Dillahunt *et al.* (2017); Cheng (2016)]. For example, Cheng [2016], using co-citation and content analysis, highlights the focus of sharing economy literature on business models, nature of sharing economy and sustainability development, specifically in the field of tourism and hospitality. Dillahunt *et al.* [2017] provide an SLR on sharing economy articles published in the Association for Computing Machinery Digital Library to understand the computer community contribution to the field of sharing economy, with a special focus on the human–computer interaction aspect. Görög [2018] analyzes 14 core definitions closely related to sharing economy and specifies their boundaries. Ter Huurne *et al.* [2017], focusing on how the trust of users in the sharing economy is influenced, offer a review of 45 articles to show various antecedents of creating trust amongst users in a sharing economy. And, Guimarães *et al.* [2018] discuss the thematic pattern and types of consumption activities studied in sharing economy literature.

3. Methodology

The SLR is conducted with two main goals. The first goal is to present a comprehensive contemplation of the research on sharing economy and establish structured categorization. The second goal is to identify the current research gaps and define future research directions.

A three-stage approach of conducting a Systematic Literature Review — *planning the review, conducting the review* and *reporting and dissemination* — suggested by Tranfield *et al.* [2003] is used to identify 26 papers on sharing economy. In the following subsection, the identification process is explained in detail.

3.1. *Search method and selection procedure*

Since "sharing economy" is considered as an umbrella term [Habibi *et al.* (2017)], the search for keywords was critical. Therefore, multiple papers were screened to identify the most commonly used terms in literature to describe the sharing economy. After screening multiple articles, eight terms were identified as keywords for the literature search: *sharing economy, collaborative consumption, collaborative economy, access-based consumption, circular economy, peer-to-peer (P2P) economy, peer-to-peer market* and *peer-to-peer production.*

The database used was Business Source Complete (BSC) as it covers the articles from more than 2100 active full-text journals and magazines and more than 840 active full-text journals indexed in Web of Science or Scopus [Business Source Complete (2018)]. The initial keywords search led to the result of 2659 publications. Only scholarly (peer-reviewed) and academic journals, published in English language, were considered. As the financial crisis of 2008 is deemed as a sharp turning point in the field of sharing economy [Del Rowe (2016)], the years of publication were restricted from 2008 to 2017. Based on these filters the search was narrowed down to 399 articles. After going through the titles, abstracts and given the availability of the full-text, 70 articles were selected for a full-text read. From these 70 articles, based on the relevance to the objective of the literature review, 20 articles (including one book) were finally identified as the most relevant articles on the topic. Using a forward and backward search apart from these 20 identified articles, six additional articles were identified. In conclusion, 25 publications in journals and one book were identified and selected for the review. Figure 1 shows a graphical illustration of the selection procedure.

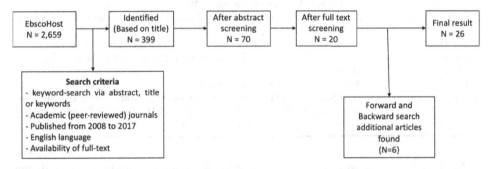

Fig. 1. Selection strategy and the final selection.

3.2. *Data extraction and analysis*

When extracting the data from the identified literature, the following information was retrieved: title, authors, publication year, keywords, journal name, research type, research method, research approach, thematic focus (research category), country of focus and country of origin. After the data extraction, the data of the publication was synthesized using descriptive analysis for further categorization in the key research focus areas.

4. Findings

4.1. *Descriptive analysis*

The publications considered for this SLR range from 2008 to 2017 and Fig. 2 shows how these publications are distributed over the selected time range.

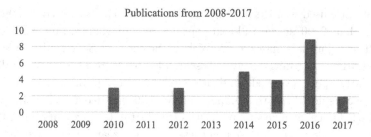

Fig. 2.   Distribution of publications from 2008 to 2017.

Table 1.   Distribution across journals and subject areas.

Subject areas	Relevant journal
Management Research	Business Horizons (1); Economics, Management & Financial Markets (1); Journal of Business Research (3); Mit Sloan Management Review (1); Strategy and Leadership (1)
Economics	Ecological Economics (1); Intereconomics (1)
Consumers	Journals of Consumer Affairs (1); Journal of Consumer Behaviour (2); Journal of Consumer Research (2)
Marketing	Journal of Marketing (1); Journal of Marketing Management (1); Journal of Services Marketing (1)
Regulation	Contemporary Economics Policy (1); Yale Journal on Regulation (1)
Technology	Journal of the Association for Information Science and Technology (1)
Environment	Organization & Environment (1)
Education	Journal of Entrepreneurship Education (1)
Other	Acta Scientiarum Polonorum, Oeconomica (1); Anthropologist (1); Business (Book) (1); Communications of the ACM (1); Research Papers of the Wroclaw University of Economics (1)

In 2010, two publications paved the way for sharing economy from an academic point of view. Belk [2010] made a distinction between various forms of sharing, while Botsman and Rogers [2010] focused on presenting a framework for collaborative consumption. Research was relatively thin until 2014, however 2016 was the year with the most publications (nine). These publications are distributed across various journals and subject areas. Table 1 shows the journals aligned with their respective subject areas in alphabetical order. Furthermore, the number of publications appearing in the specific journals is noted in brackets after the journal name. Most of the journals cover only one publication (with an exception of *Journal of Business Research* with three articles), which demonstrates that the research is still at a naive stage.

4.2. *Geographical focus*

Next, the articles were categorized by their country of origin (Fig. 3) and the country of focus (Fig. 4). The authors' residency was selected as an indicator of origin. The thematic focus or rather the countries, from where the data were collected, served as the indicators for the country of focus.

Figure 3 shows the distribution of the publications based on the country of origin. Research on sharing economy has been conducted across different countries and continents around the globe in varied capacities. As compared to the developing nations, majority of the articles are emerging from the countries of North American region (15).

In sync with Fig. 3 (country of focus), Fig. 4 shows a relatively high focus on USA with 20 articles, revealing that most of the examples of sharing economy are coming from this region. One reason of this geographical imbalance could be repetition of the cases studied and explored in the context of sharing economy.

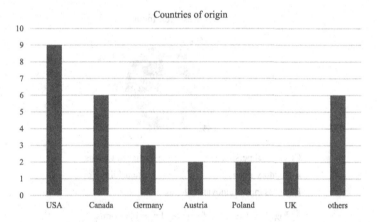

Others: Chile (1), China (1), Denmark (1), Finland (1), Italy (1) and New Zealand (1).

Fig. 3. Countries of origin of the publications.

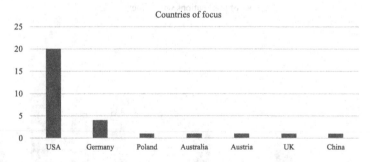

Fig. 4. Countries of focus of the publications.

4.3. *Research focus areas*

The identified articles can be categorized into five distinct categories based on the research focus. Figure 5 shows the distribution of publications across the five categories and Fig. 6 illustrates how the publications from each group are spread out over the years.

Figure 5 illustrates that most of the identified articles are conceptual papers. These articles offer various definitions and conceptualizations, as well as framings of the term sharing economy, and also other closely linked terms such as collaborative consumption. Six out of the 26 identified publications emphasize on the participant behavior. And the rest of the articles are equally distributed across regulation, sustainability and business model aspects of sharing economy.

Figure 6 shows how the different research focus areas have developed over the years. As with any new field of research, the initial focus of the articles is more on conceptualization of the topic and developing basic understanding of the topic.

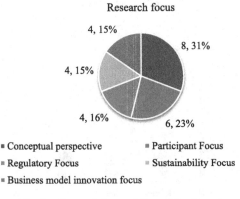

Fig. 5.   Research focus of the publications.

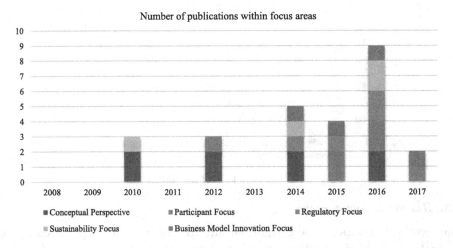

Fig. 6.   Numbers of publications within the focus areas.

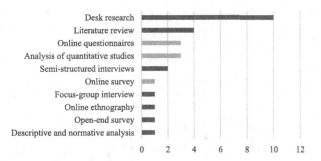

Blue lines stand for qualitative methods and orange lines for quantitative methods

Fig. 7.   Distribution based on the research methods.

Further research explorations were done on user's (or participant's) perspective and sustainability of the concept in the long run. Later part of the research, i.e., from 2014 onwards, focused on other areas like business models and associated regulatory frameworks to identify the opportunities and overcome the challenges of sharing economy.

Majority of the publications (20 articles) used qualitative research methods as compared to quantitative (six articles) ones. There was one article by Yang *et al.* [2017] which used a mixed approach of qualitative and quantitative methods and is counted in both the research methods. Figure 7 offers a detailed view on the specific research methods that were used across the identified articles.

5. Discussion

The review of the 26 articles revealed that literature covers the topic of sharing economy mainly from five different perspectives. Apart from the conceptual papers, the research also focuses on participant behavior, regulatory frameworks, sustainability aspect and business models of sharing economy. Figure 8 shows a graphical representation of these research categories. Next, each of these categories are explained in more detail.

5.1. *Conceptual perspective*

The conceptual perspective focuses on presenting frameworks of practices that fall under the term sharing economy. Research discusses the different concepts related to sharing economy and also sheds light on the embedded differences and similarities. For example, Belk [2010] distinguished between sharing in and sharing out, stating that "sharing in" is mainly within a family, whereas "sharing out" contains actions such as gift giving or commodity exchange with people outside a family. On the one hand, Botsman and Rogers [2010] dedicated a whole book to the phenomenon of *collaborative consumption*. They identified four principles, which are crucial for the

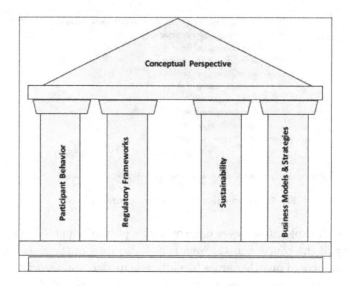

Fig. 8.   Graphical illustration of the research focus areas.

viability and functioning of a collaborative consumption system: *critical mass* (momentum), *idling capacity* (unused capacity), *belief in the commons* (public goods) and *trust between strangers*. Their detailed attempt to characterize collaborative consumption offered a basis for further conceptualizations and discussions on sharing economy as well. On the other hand, Belk [2014b] emphasized the similarities and differences of sharing and collaborative consumption. Belk [2014a] distinguished between sharing and pseudo-sharing activities, stating that pseudo-sharing is predominantly motivated by profit seeking, lacking the aspects of community and reciprocity. Similarly, Ert *et al.* [2016] focused on the distinction between collaborative consumption and conventional consumption. They defined collaborative consumption as a system, where consumers could be both users and providers and are also allowed to switch between the roles. For them, empowerment plays a big role in enabling consumers to directly collaborate with each other, distinguishing them from the conventional consumers. Authors from this research category also explored sharing systems in detail. Lamberton and Rose [2012] provided a framework for distinguishing between different sharing systems via intensity degrees of rivalry and exclusivity. Furthermore, Bardhi and Eckhardt [2012] investigated sharing systems with a focus on car-sharing models using examples like Zipcar. Linking the concept to access-based consumption, market mediation was identified as a major influencing factor in the sharing systems.

With the rise of companies like Airbnb and Uber, sharing economy gained more attention and popularity. Martin [2016, p. 153] presented a framework of common visions, stating that the sharing economy is: "(1) an economic opportunity, (2) a more sustainable form of consumption, (3) a pathway to a decentralized, equitable and sustainable economy, (4) creating unregulated marketplaces, (5) reinforcing the neoliberal paradigm and (6) an incoherent field of innovation."

5.2. *Participant behavior*

Research in this category focuses on participants' behaviors, motivations of users [Albinsson and Yasanthi Perera (2012); Hamari *et al.* (2016); Lawson *et al.* (2016)], satisfaction aspect Moehlmann [2015] and loyalty towards sharing systems [Moehlmann (2015); Yang *et al.* (2017)]. Furthermore, consumers' attitudes towards P2P renting have also been investigated [Philip *et al.* (2015)]. For example, Albinsson and Yasanthi Perera [2012] investigated the motivation of users participating in non-monetary marketplaces and sharing events including Really Really Free Markets (RRFM). Such markets are opened temporarily in public places so that people can share and take goods without the need to offer exchange or monetary compensation. Research revealed that participants in these sharing realms see these events as a chance to make political statements, to offer help or to educate public on sustainability. Participants enjoy the community aspect and consider this as a contribution towards social causes and anti-consumption. Hamari *et al.* [2016] further differentiated participants' motivations between intrinsic and extrinsic motivations. Enjoyment in the activity and supporting sustainability were identified as intrinsic motivators, whereas economic benefits and reputation were identified as extrinsic motivators.

Further attempts were made to classify participants based on their attitudes and motivations towards access and usage of short-term rentals. For example, Lawson *et al.* [2016] did a cluster analysis, classifying consumers into groups with various dispositions towards access-based consumption due to aspects like economic and ecologic consciousness, status seeking, brand loyalty, possessiveness and materialism. Their research suggested that consumers can be classified as "Fickle Floaters", "Premium Keepers", "Conscious Materialists" or "Change Seekers" [Lawson *et al.* (2016)] based on individual motivation.

Philip *et al.* [2015] examined consumer attitudes and motivations towards P2P renting. Apart from economic considerations, reciprocity and altruism were also identified as the reasons behind participation. Yang *et al.* [2017] focused on the loyalty aspect, and identified that in China confidence in service providers had a high impact on customers' loyalty. Moehlmann [2015] investigated the loyalty aspect in both business-to-consumer (B2C) (Car2go) and P2P (Airbnb) environments and found self-beneficial improvements as the prime motivator along with others like trust and cost-savings.

5.3. *Regulatory frameworks*

The challenge with sharing economy is that it does not fit into conventional regulatory standards. Especially, P2P practices like car-rentals are lacking guidelines on tax, insurance, product liability and employment. Furthermore, new challenges are emerging such as consumer protection and privacy issues [Katz (2015); Berke (2016)]. Research on this aspect of sharing economy is relatively new with the earliest ones being from 2014 on product liability of P2P car-rentals [Berke (2016)] and regulatory issues of short-term rental platforms and transportation network companies (TNCs) [Katz (2015)]. In a similar context, researchers have also explored the acceptance, governance and regulation within collaborative consumption [Hartl *et al.* (2016)] with a special focus on the hotel and taxi industry [Malhotra and Van Alstyne (2014)].

Berke [2016] performed a descriptive and normative analysis of product liability in sharing economy businesses, investigating whether companies in the sharing economy should be regulated via the strict product liability doctrine known from conventional businesses. He argued that strict product liability and regulation are not necessary as sharing economy itself has a self-regulation aspect which reduces risk and the implementation of strict regulations can hinder innovation by start-ups [Berke (2016)].

In contrast to this, Katz [2015] who examined regulatory issues and associated solutions of short-term rental platforms and TNCs, suggested to have tiered regulations, limited intermediary ability of platforms and involvement of third parties. She emphasized on inclusion of concepts like Big Data (anticipating privacy concerns), reputation systems (responsible private ordering) and the promotion of competition (improving consumers' choice) [Katz (2015)].

In a similar context, Malhotra and Van Alstyne [2014] also emphasized on the associated danger of not having regulatory structures, especially in the context of conflicts over tenement houses and private providers of ride-sharing not having purchase medallions. They also highlighted the necessity of fraud protection and reporting in sharing economy to overcome the threat of "secondary sharing becoming tertiary taking" (selling copies of Netflix movies). Hartl *et al.* [2016] also supported this argument and using a quantitative study showed that more people would participate in collaborative consumption communities if the goods and the access to the community are better controlled.

5.4. *Sustainability focus*

Researchers have primarily linked the concept of sharing economy and sustainability based on the aspects of sustainable consumption and capitalizing on underutilized assets. The most common sectors making use of idling capacity of goods are the automotive/transportation sector and the hospitality sector. In the automotive/transportation sector, private transit providers [e.g. car-sharing (B2C and P2P), ride-sharing and bike-sharing] can offer high sustainability impact where users can be motivated through economic and/or non-economic incentives [Cohen and Kietzmann (2014)].

Dabrowska and Gutkowska [2010] as well as Bachnik [2016] investigated how the sharing economy could support and foster sustainable consumption. Dabrowska and Gutkowska [2010] analyzed 1000 Polish consumers of sharing economy and identified that their willingness to support sustainable and collaborative consumption depends on the socio-demographic variables and their awareness towards collaborative consumption. However, Seegebarth *et al.* [2016] argued that collaborative consumption would have a bigger impact on sustainability only when it is practiced with an anti-consumption lifestyle that prevents people from using the money saved by participating in collaborative consumption for other harmful activities.

5.5. *Business models and strategies*

Sharing economy is characterized by heterogeneity, especially when it comes to the types of goods and business models involved in sharing economy. Main types of goods existing in the sharing economy include durable consumer goods, non-durable consumer goods, investment goods, intangibles and services. Research also identifies three main business models associated with sharing economy: B2C, consumer-to-consumer (C2C) and business-to-business (B2B) models. The B2C models are organized like the traditionally known business model, where the companies provide not only the platform to channel the demand, but also the supply of the goods and services for individuals. Given the similarity with the traditional business models, the B2C model is highly discussed in the literature [Hawlitschek *et al.* (2016)]. Sharing economy B2C companies use new technologies and are based on online platforms, but exclude a face-to-face interaction between businesses and consumers.

In the C2C model, or P2P sharing, within sharing economy, the goods are shared between co-equal individuals. The shared use is practiced among individuals either without a transfer of ownership (including co-using, lending and renting) or with a transfer of ownership (including giving away, swapping and reselling). Ert *et al.* [2016] highlight the increasing number of online P2P marketplaces. This either free of charge or fee-based trading system connecting strangers in P2P marketplaces involves asymmetric information and economic risks and hence requires reputation mechanisms to encourage trust among traders [Ert *et al.* (2016)].

B2B models can be a variation of the P2P model within sharing economy. However, this model of sharing is often excluded in the literature, since most of the definitions focus on private sharing. However, it is increasingly garnering attention as more companies decide to rent semi-finished goods or services instead of buying them.

Kathan *et al.* [2016] discuss four reasons why the sharing economy should be regarded as a serious new trend in the businesses. First, the sharing economy is thriving on the technology wave, as most of the businesses are presented via online platforms, giving the consumers instant access. Second, as already mentioned, a rising shift in consumer values occurs, with participants preferring access over ownership. Third, sharing economy businesses have the potential to increase sustainability, more likely than the conventional businesses. Fourth, sharing can pay off financially, since sharing access seems to be cheaper than bearing the costs of ownership individually. In line with Denning [2014], Matzler and Kathan [2015] suggest different strategies for conventional businesses to engage in sharing economy such as (1) by allowing sell/use rather than ownership, (2) by supporting customers in their attempts to resell assets, (3) by using the idling capacity, (4) by providing maintenance services, (5) by using collaborative consumption to reach new customers and finally, (6) by establishing totally new business models enabled by collaborative consumption.

Based on Belk [2010], Habibi *et al.* [2017] classify sharing economy practices into three categories namely sharing practice, dual-mode practice and pseudo-sharing practice, suggesting four strategies [community building, value perception focus, sustainability and the degree of (monetary) calculations] to implement or engage in sharing economy.

6. Future Perspectives

6.1. *Need for more quantitative studies and inclusion of other stakeholders*

Significant amount of researches are based on qualitative research methods and lack empirical and quantitative approaches. Furthermore, the review also reveals the lack of consensus on a single definition of sharing economy and higher focus on participant- or consumer-related aspects. Inclusion of other stakeholders such as governments and municipalities or businesses will facilitate a better understanding of the concept from different perspectives. This will also enable a robust and well-rounded definition of the term sharing economy. Usage of more quantitative and empirical research approaches will help in validating the different suggested frameworks, and also the strategies discussed in the literature. At a conceptual level, it would be also interesting to do a bibliometric analysis of the current literature to investigate the linkage between the related terms such as collaborative consumption, access-based consumption and sharing economy, among others, and understand whether they are just co-existing phenomena or emerging from one another.

6.2. *Increasing geographical focus and analyzing the impact of cultural background on consumer behavior*

On the one hand, in particular to the research on the participant's behavior, there is limited research on analyzing the impact of the economic conditions and cultural background. Differences in motivation, attitude and loyalty towards the sharing economy could be investigated, based on the participants' cultural backgrounds and countries of origin. Therefore, it would be interesting to investigate how the economic or educational background impacts the willingness to participate in a sharing system.

On the other hand, most of the studies are concentrated on the North American region and platforms like Airbnb and Uber that are leading the main discussions. Future research explorations are required to understand the participants and platforms from other sharing economy-active countries around the world.

6.3. *Defining robust regulatory frameworks*

Various attempts have been made to introduce regulations (e.g. reputation systems for online platforms) for sharing economy, however the research still fails to come up with a well-defined regulatory structure. Rather than presenting the regulatory frameworks ahead of time, research has only responded after the incidents appeared. Sharing system and the included stakeholders such as municipalities/governments/ businesses are lacking concrete solutions or suggestions to the practical issues they are currently struggling with. Since sharing economy is a relatively new phenomenon, it is questionable whether the conventional regulatory frameworks are suitable as a starting point to overcome the challenges of sharing economy or if it requires entirely new sets of rules and regulations. Especially, given the fact that participants appreciate governance and regulation, this research area definitely needs a deeper academic exploration.

6.4. *Analyzing the B2B model within sharing economy*

Researches on sharing economy with respect to business models have largely focused on B2C and C2C models. This is due to various reasons such as similarity between the conventional B2C business models and most of the definitions focusing on private sharing. However, as sharing economy is considered to be one of the strong emerging trends in business world, there is a need to explore different possibilities for the B2B businesses to engage in sharing economy.

6.5. *Analyzing the sustainability aspect of sharing economy*

Studies so far argue that there is a link between sharing economy and sustainability given its focus on using underutilized assets. However, this linkage is subject to debate and requires further exploration. Some researchers argue that sharing and collaborating do not consequently lead to sustainability. For example, using a P2P car-rental service liberates the participant from owning a car, but the actual utilization of the car is still producing negative effects on the environment and therefore is low in sustainability (CO_2). Bachnik [2016] and Cohen and Kietzmann [2014] state that using sharing practices instead of insisting on ownership leads to sustainability. Academic literature is missing the exploration of other supporting activities like spreading awareness and educating people about sustainability. Specifically, how higher sustainability can be achieved through the practices like access-based consumption or collaborative consumption? Anti-consumption as suggested by Seegebarth *et al.* [2016] might constitute a bigger impact on sustainability rather than just sharing and accessing.

Research shows that the sharing economy and collaborative consumption are important and have huge potential when supported and assisted in the right way (e.g. by local governments). To profit from the provided offers, people need to be educated and informed about the sharing economy and its potential. Furthermore, from a sustainable standpoint it seems to be necessary that people not only share the assets they possess, but also consume less in general. Therefore, the sustainability aspect needs a more detailed exploration along with an investigation on supporting awareness activities necessary to reach the full potential of sharing economy.

References

Albinsson, P. A. and Yasanthi Perera, B. (2012). Alternative marketplaces in the 21st century: Building community through sharing events. *Journal of Consumer Behaviour*, **11**, 4: 303–315.

Bachnik, K. (2016). Sustainable consumption through the sharing economy (Konsumpcja zrównoważona stymulowana gospodarką wspólnego użytkowania). *Prace Naukowe Uniwersytetu Ekonomicznego we Wrocławiu*, **423**: 36–44.

Balck, B. and Cracau, D. (2015). Empirical analysis of customer motives in the shareconomy: A cross-sectoral comparison. Working Paper No. (2/2015), Faculty of Economics and Management, Otto-von-Guericke-Universitäk Magdeburg, Germany.

Bardhi, F. and Eckhardt, G. M. (2012). Access-based consumption: The case of car sharing. *Journal of Consumer Research*, **39**, 4: 881–898.

Belk, R. (2010). Sharing. *Journal of Consumer Research*, **36**, 5: 715–734.

Belk, R. (2014a). Sharing versus pseudo-sharing in Web 2.0. *Anthropologist*, **18**, 1: 7–23.

Belk, R. (2014b). You are what you can access: Sharing and collaborative consumption online. *Journal of Business Research*, **67**, 8: 1595–1600.

Berke, D. (2016). Products liability in the sharing economy. *Yale Journal on Regulation*, **33**, 2: 603–653.

Botsman, R. and Rogers, R. (2010). *What's Mine is Yours: How Collaborative Consumption is Changing the Way We live*. Harper Collins, London.

Business Source Complete (2018). About the database. Available at: https://www.ebsco.com/products/research-databases/business-source-complete 13 [accessed on 20 June 2017].

Cheng, M. (2016). Sharing economy: A review and agenda for future research. *International Journal of Hospitality Management*, **57**: 60–70.

Cohen, B. and Kietzmann, J. (2014). Ride on! Mobility business models for the sharing economy. *Organization and Environment*, **27**, 3: 279–296.

Dabrowska, A. and Gutkowska, K. (2010). Collaborative consumption as a new trend of sustainable consumption. *Acta Scientiarum Polonorum, Oeconomica*, **17**, 2: 491–498.

Del Rowe, S. (2016). The rise of the sharing economy. *Customer Relationship Management*, 23–25.

Denning, S. (2014). An economy of access is opening for business: Five strategies for success. *Strategy & Leadership*, **42**, 4: 14–21.

Dillahunt, T. R., Wang, X., Wheeler, E., Cheng, H. F., Hecht, B. and Zhu, H. (2017). The sharing economy in computing: A systematic literature review. *Proceeding of the ACM Human-Computer Interaction*, **1**, CSCW: 38.

Ert, E., Fleischer, A. and Magen, N. (2016). Trust and reputation in the sharing economy: The role of personal photos on airbnb. *Tourism Management*, **55**: 62–73.

Ertz, M., Durif, M. and Arcand, M. (2016). Collaborative consumption: Conceptual Snapshot at a buzzword. *Journal of Entrepreneurship Education*, **19**, 2: 1–23.

Görög, G. (2018). The definitions of sharing economy: A systematic literature review. *Management*, **13**, 2: 175–189.

Guimarães, A., Franco, R. and de Souza, C. (2018). Sharing economy: A review of the recent literature. *European Review of Service Economics and Management*, **2**, 6: 77–96.

Habibi, M. R., Davidson, A. and Laroche, M. (2017). What managers should know about the sharing economy. *Business Horizons*, **60**, 1: 113–121.

Hamari, J., Sjöklint, M. and Ukkonen, A. (2016). The sharing economy: Why people participate in collaborative consumption. *Journal of the Association for Information Science and Technology*, **67**, 9: 2047–2059.

Hartl, B., Hofmann, E. and Kirchler, E. (2016). Do we need rules for "what's mine is yours"? Governance in collaborative consumption communities. *Journal of Business Research*, **69**, 8: 2756–2763.

Hawlitschek, F., Teubner, T. and Weinhardt, C. (2016). Trust in the sharing economy. *Die Unternehmung — Swiss Journal of Business Research and Practice*, **70**, 1: 26–44.

Heinrichs, H. and Grunenberg, H. (2012). Sharing economy: Auf dem Weg in eine neue Konsumkultur? *Berliner Journal Für Soziologie*, **17**, 1: 2–4.

Kathan, W., Matzler, K. and Veider, V. (2016). The sharing economy: Your business model's friend or foe? *Business Horizons*, **59**, 6: 663–672.

Katz, V. (2015). Regulating the sharing economy. *Berkeley Technology Law Journal*, **30**: 1067–1126.

Lamberton, C. P. and Rose, R. L. (2012). When is ours better than mine? A framework for understanding and altering participation in commercial sharing systems. *Journal of Marketing*, **76**, 4: 109–125.

Lawson, S. J., Gleim, M. R., Perren, R. and Hwang, J. (2016). Freedom from ownership: An exploration of access-based consumption. *Journal of Business Research*, **69**, 8: 2615–2623.

Malhotra, A. and Van Alstyne, M. (2014). The dark side of the sharing economy ... and how to lighten it. *Communications of the ACM*, **57**, 11: 24–27.

Martin, C. J. (2016). The sharing economy: A pathway to sustainability or a nightmarish form of neoliberal capitalism? *Ecological Economics*, **121**: 149–159.

Matzler, K. and Kathan, W. (2015). Adapting to the sharing economy. *Mit Sloan Management Review*, **56**, 2: 71–77.

Moehlmann, M. (2015). Collaborative consumption: Determinants of satisfaction and the likelihood of using a sharing economy option again. *Journal of Consumer Behaviour*, **14**, 3: 193–207.

Philip, H. E., Ozanne, L. K. and Ballantine, P. W. (2015). Examining temporary disposition and acquisition in peer-to-peer renting. *Journal of Marketing Management*, **31**, 11–12: 1310–1332.

PWC (2016). Future of the sharing economy in Europe 2016. Available at: http://www.pwc.co.uk/issues/megatrends/collisions/sharingeconomy/future-of-the-sharing-economy-in-europe-2016.html [accessed on 15 July 2017].

Richter, C., Kraus, S. and Syrjä, P. (2015). The shareconomy as a precursor for digital entrepreneurship business models. *International Journal of Entrepreneurship and Small Business*, **25**, 1: 18.

Richter, C., Kraus, S., Brem, A., Durst, S. and Giselbrecht, C. (2017). Digital entrepreneurship: Innovative business models for the sharing economy. *Creativity and Innovation Management*, **26**: 300–310.

Schor, J. B. and Fitzmaurice, C. J. (2015). Collaborating and connecting: The emergence of the sharing economy. In *Handbook of Research on Sustainable Consumption*, eds. L. A. Reisch and J. Thogersen, Edward Elgar, Cheltenham, pp. 410–425.

Seegebarth, B., Peyer, M., Balderjahn, I. and Wiedmann, K. P. (2016). The sustainability roots of anticonsumption lifestyles and initial insights regarding their effects on consumers' well-being. *Journal of Consumer Affairs*, **50**, 1: 68–99.

Stephany, A. (2015). *The Business of Sharing: Making it in the New Sharing Economy*. Palgrave Macmillan, Basingstoke, Hampstire.

Ter Huurne, M., Ronteltap, A., Corten, R. and Buskens, V. (2017). Antecedents of trust in the sharing economy: A systematic review. *Journal of Consumer Behaviour*, **16**, 6: 485–498.

Tranfield, D., Denyer, D. and Smart, P. (2003). Towards a methodology for developing evidence-informed management knowledge by means of systematic review. *British Journal of Management*, **14**: 207–222.

Yang, S., Song, Y., Chen, S. and Xia, X. (2017). Why are customers loyal in sharing-economy services? A relational benefits perspective. *Journal of Services Marketing*, **31**, 1: 48–62.

Biography

Nivedita Agarwal is an assistant professor at the Chair of Technology Management at the Friedrich-Alexander-Universität Erlangen-Nürnberg, Germany. Her research focuses on new product development, social entrepreneurship and constraint-based innovation especially in context of emerging markets. Her research highlights the role of innovation and entrepreneurship enabled by disruptive technologies in shaping the complex ecosystem at the BoP.

Robert Steinmetz is a student at the Friedrich-Alexander-Universität-Erlangen-Nürnberg. Associated with the business science faculty his focus topics are finance and sustainability management.

Chapter 7

Understanding the Role of Team Member Personal Style in Project Performance: Does the Type of Innovation Matter?

Zvi H. Aronson*, Richard R. Reilly[†] and Gary S. Lynn[‡]

School of Business, Stevens Institute of Technology
Hoboken, USA
*zvi.aronson@stevens.edu
[†]rreilly@stevens.edu
[‡]glynn@stevens.edu

Teams are progressively becoming primary in the way employees in organizations conduct work. We investigated the role of staff personal style in project performance for teams working on incremental and radical innovations. Regression results based on 149 teams suggest that, for employees, conscientiousness and agreeableness, predominantly, seem to be beneficial for new product development (NPD) performance. Slope tests promote our proposition that for speed, radical NPD might gain from extra open and stable staff. Further, exceedingly agreeable employees do not seem to provide support when new ideas are fostered, since it could be a precursor to group think and less successful innovation. We provide implications for selection and training of employees assigned to work in innovation teams.

Keywords: Project teams; innovation; personal style.

1. Introduction

When new product development (NPD) speed and success are critical, what can organizations establish? Of the many variables examined that affect how fast an idea moves from conception to a successful product in the marketplace, staff member characteristics play an important role [e.g. Chen *et al.* (2010)]. Staff members are the people who transform value ideas, concepts specifications into new products, and they are a key in facilitating NPD speed and success [Brown and Eisenhardt (1995)] we refer to as NPD performance. Scholars document the value of team member dedication and cooperation to increased NPD performance [e.g. Atuahene-Gima (2003); Hoegl *et al.* (2004); Keller (2001)]. Researchers [e.g. Aronson *et al.* (2006,

---

*Corresponding author.

This chapter was originally published in *International Journal of Innovation and Technology Management*, Vol. 16, No. 4, August 2018, published by World Scientific Publishing, Singapore. Reprinted with permission.

2008); Strang (2011)] center on the role of leader personal style in NPD performance. Yet, few scholars examine the role of staff member personal style in NPD performance, for teams working on different types of innovations. Personal style traits have considerable utility for predicting how people behave and perform in the workplace [e.g. Barrick et al. (2001)]. Can optimum personal style selection criteria be established for individuals assigned to work in innovation teams? How might the optimal team personal style profile change for NPD employees working on radical innovations?

Because teams developing innovations work in a context ripe with uncertainty, handling this uncertainty should place special demands on the staff of such teams. Researchers suggest that staff personal style effects ought to be examined in different kinds of teams, including cross-functional task teams in management and NPD teams [e.g. Reilly et al. (2002)]. To this end, we consider the role of staff member personal style in NPD performance for two different types of NPD teams: radical and incremental. (1) Radical NPD occurs when the market for the product is not clear and the technology used is new and uncertain; (2) Incremental NPD occurs when the markets are well-established and there are few questions about the technology.

In the following sections, we describe radical and incremental NPD teams, and the Five-Factor model (FFM) of personality we use as a framework for organizing the research on personal style traits. We then examine the role of staff member personal style in NPD performance. Unlike past research that mostly focuses on the leader's personal style, our research provides a theoretical rationale and hypotheses on the links between staff member personal style and NPD performance, and furthermore addresses the question of whether different staff member personal styles are needed depending on the type of innovation — radical or incremental, which has been called for [e.g. Barrick et al. (2001)].

2. Theoretical Background

Researchers have distinguished between two broad types of innovations that differ in the extent to which the innovation is similar to or different from existing practice. Radical innovation represents significant change for the firm, and often opens up new markets and potential applications. Radical innovations include products completely new to the firm, products based on new technologies and new ventures unrelated to existing businesses. Such major innovations require skills, abilities, and knowledge different from those required to master the old technologies. Incremental innovation, in contrast, introduces relatively minor changes to an existing product. Incremental innovations are related to the firm's current products and businesses, and generally take the form of product modifications, upgrades, and line extensions. These innovations build on existing know-how [e.g. Tushman and Anderson (1986)]. Because the nature of these innovations differ, the literature argues that teams performing these innovations be different [Barczak and Wilemon (1991)]. For example, Barczak and Wilemon note that teams responsible for radical innovation should be autonomous and separate from the existing organization. The more dissimilar the technology or markets from current practice, the greater should be the use of independent venture forms, they argue. NPD teams are accordingly assembled to implement their tasks outside the established organization structure. Indeed, high levels of autonomy are reported throughout the teams studied in an investigation by Gemünden *et al.* [2005]. Gemünden and colleagues' work implies that high levels of autonomy also pose severe challenges (e.g. access to complementary resources is more difficult for separated units than for embedded units) for these NPD teams. In contrast, routine and related new products are best suited to be carried out within the firm's existing divisions and units. These differences have implications for the way these teams are effectively staffed, and for the personal style traits their employees should possess. However, research on the optimal personal style traits the staff members should have in these respective teams is scarce. The research we identified focuses on the project leaders' personal style. To this end, we also examine the role of staff member personal style traits in NPD performance for teams developing radical and incremental innovations. We next describe the FFM of personality we use as a framework for organizing the research on personal style traits.

2.1. *Personal style as captured by the FFM*

In this research, we focus on the effect of personal style variables as captured by the FFM. The FFM represents the current orthodoxy in personal style assessment and is a simple, robust, and comprehensive way of understanding fundamental personal style differences [Barrick and Mount (1991); McCrae and Costa (1996)]. Although it has its critics, general consensus suggests that it adequately captures the content domain of personality [Wiggins (1996)].

Meta-analytic research [e.g. Barrick and Mount (1991); Hurtz and Donovan (2000); Tett *et al.* (1991); Salgado (1997)] suggests that personal style traits, as measured by the FFM, have considerable utility for predicting how people behave and perform in the workplace. Of particular interest is evidence [Tett *et al.* (1994); Day and Silverman (1989); Barrick and Mount (1991)] that specific personal style traits are related in predictable ways to performance in certain kinds of jobs. A meta-analysis by Judge *et al.* [2002] provides support for the relevance of the FFM as a framework for organizing personal style traits in research. The dimensions comprising the FFM are emotional stability, openness, conscientiousness, agreeableness, and extraversion (often termed the Big Five). Emotional Stability represents the extent to which an individual is calm, enthusiastic, poised, and secure. Openness represents the extent to which an individual is imaginative, sensitive, intellectual and polished. Conscientiousness represents the extent to which an individual is careful, thorough, achievement-oriented, responsible, organized, self-disciplined, and scrupulous. Agreeableness represents the extent to which an individual is good-natured, gentle, cooperative, forgiving, and hopeful. Extraversion represents the extent to which an individual is sociable, talkative, assertive, and active [e.g. Aronson *et al.* (2006, 2008); Barrick *et al.* (2001)].

Our central hypothesis, rooted in earlier work and detailed later, is that the effect of two personal style traits, conscientiousness and agreeableness will be most important in their influence on the performance of NPD teams [e.g. Barrick *et al.* (1998); Hough (1992); Kichuk and Wiesner (1997); Neuman and Wright (1999)]. Conscientiousness is related to performance outcomes across jobs [e.g. Barrick and Mount (1991); Barrick *et al.* (2001); Salgado (1997)]. Agreeableness is vital in team-based contexts [Aronoff and Wilson (1985); Costa and McCrae (1989)]. To test these initial hypotheses, we will scrutinize the beta weights when all staff personal style variables are entered into a multiple regression equation. Additionally, based on previous research [e.g. Driskell *et al.* (1988); Bouchard (1972); DeBiasio (1986); Tuckman (1967)], we posit that when considering the type of innovation the teams are working on, the relationship between staff personal style traits and NPD performance criteria will vary, as we elaborate below. To examine these final propositions, we will compare the slopes and intercepts of the regression lines for each of the staff personal style variables, detailed in the method section.

It is noteworthy that although a couple of our research propositions are stated for two categories of teams, incremental and radical, which we define below, it is important to recognize that the variables that distinguish between the two teams are continuous. Thus, a proposition that suggests a zero correlation between a personal style variable and NPD performance does not necessarily imply that the variable is completely unimportant, but rather that it is unlikely to distinguish successful from unsuccessful teams. As an example, a threshold level of creativity may be important for incremental NPD teams but may not differentiate success from failure. On the other hand, the level of creativity beyond the threshold level might have a significant relationship with performance outcomes in radical NPD teams.

2.2. Radical versus incremental NPD teams

Two major types of teams responsible for NPD have been identified: operating and innovating [Barczak and Wilemon (1989)]. Operating teams are concerned with maintaining competitive positions in existing businesses and, as a result, they usually focus on incremental innovation or small improvements to current products. Characteristics of these groups include operating in relatively stable environments, being rule and planning-oriented, and emphasizing current products. Innovating teams, in contrast, focus on developing a new business for the firm. They are more likely to focus on important new products for unfamiliar markets. These types of teams produce radical or discontinuous innovations. The development of radical innovations is associated with more challenges than the development of incremental ones [O'Connor and Veryzer (2001)]. Teams developing radical innovations are usually separated from the daily activities of the firm. Characteristics of innovating groups include operating in a dynamic environment, emphasizing initiative and risk taking and maintaining loose methods of control. These product development teams must choose an innovation strategy that is tailored to the degree of market and technology uncertainty [Ansoff (1965, 1988); Moriarty and Kosnik (1990)]. These two major types of NPD teams have been labeled Incremental and Radical [Lynn and Akgun (1998)]. In the current study, we focus on the effect of staff personal style on performance, in incremental and radical NPD teams.

Incremental innovation exists under highly certain environments, when a currently served market with mature technologies is targeted. Incremental innovations may include product changes or improvements, product line extensions, and "me too" products that are similar to the competition. A good example of incremental innovation is the double stuff Oreo cookie by Nabisco. Under such conditions, the appropriate innovation strategy focuses on being market-based and process-based. The customers are well defined and are typically well known, as is the technology required to produce the innovation. This type of innovation usually encounters fewer surprises than the more radical type.

Radical innovation, in contrast, exists when both market and technology uncertainties are high. Innovations of this type pose severe challenges for new product teams because the market is not well understood, and the product is still evolving and changing with the market. These types of innovations require focus on a learning-based strategy because experimenting is an essential component of the process. Product teams may try a product in the market to learn, improve it, and try it again [Lynn *et al.* (1996)]. For example, the early video cassette recorder (VCR) models were too expensive and limited and consequently, they failed in the marketplace. However, manufacturers continued to interact with users, learned from them, and accordingly improved the technical performance of the VCR, reduced its price, and successfully reintroduced the product to the market [Rosenbloom and Cusumano (1987)]. Scholars suggest that different personal styles are required depending upon the team's task. Because NPD teams differ with respect to typical tasks, scholars [e.g. Driskell *et al.* (1987); Bouchard (1972); DeBiasio (1986); Tuckman (1967)] would suggest that it is important to consider the role of staff personal style for different types of NPD teams.

2.3. *Personal style and product development teams*

Research on team member personal style has provided some interesting insights, but has left some unanswered questions in terms of the relationship with team outcomes, and the importance of personal style variables for diverse teams [Altman and Haythorn (1967); Burchfield (1997); Driskell and Salas (1992); Hogan and Hogan (1989); Oser *et al.* (1989); Morgan and Lassiter (1992); Schutz (1955)]. While these studies show significant relationships for some variables, the results are difficult to interpret and apply to NPD teams for two reasons. The first reason has to do with the inconsistency of the personal style framework used in the different research. Not all studies use the Five Factor Personal Style Framework. With some exceptions, the research is often marked by inconsistent constructs used to define personal style. A second problem with the past research is that many of the studies have been done with simulated teams and short-range tasks or projects, sometimes consisting of tasks less than an hour's length. As an example, a number of studies have investigated the relationship between team-member personal style and creativity as the team outcome [e.g. Bouchard (1969); DeBiasio (1986); George and Bettenhausen (1990); Strube et al. (1989)]. All of these studies were done in laboratory settings.

We identified a few studies that directly examined the role of personal style in NPD project outcomes, none of which included speed among the performance criteria, nor did these studies differentiate between various kinds of innovation teams. Most of the research we uncovered focused on the project leaders' personal style [e.g. Aronson et al. (2006, 2008); Strang (2011)]. One study examined relationships between the personality of an "Analyst", who evaluates product ideas at the fuzzy front end. The period between when the opportunity for NPD and when a serious effort is mounted on the development project is known [Smith and Reinertsen (1997)]. Another study [Stevens et al. (1999)] found significant differences between the number of decisions and the degree of success for different personality styles. Although this research does not directly bear on the issue of team performance outcomes, it provides evidence for the impact of personal style on NPD. Research [Kichuk and Wiesner (1997)] done with simulated NPD teams, found significant differences between successful and unsuccessful teams for average team member scores on extraversion, agreeableness, and neuroticism (instability).

Because we are dealing with teams, the role of personal style within a team can take two different forms. First, the average **level** of a particular personal style variable within the team may be related to team performance. Second, the degree of **heterogeneity** of a particular trait may play a role in team performance. The average level of a personal style trait is usually indicated by the mean of a variable. For a single variable, the variance or standard deviation would be an indicator of the degree of heterogeneity of the team. For multiple variables, a variety of distance measures such as Euclidian, Squared Euclidian or City Block metrics could be used to characterize the heterogeneity of a team. Our hypotheses are related to the average level of a particular personal style variable within an NPD team and NPD performance criteria, including speed and success. The speed criterion included the extent the NPD project was developed and launched faster than the major competitor for a similar product, was completed in less time than what was considered normal and customary for our industry, was launched on or ahead of the original schedule developed at initial project go-ahead and the extent top management was pleased with the time it took us from specs to full commercialization. The success criterion included the extent the project overall met or exceeded sales expectations, met or exceeded profit expectations, met or exceeded return on investment expectations, met or exceeded overall senior management's expectations, met or exceeded market share expectations, met or exceeded customer expectations. These performance criteria are frequently mentioned in the literature [e.g. Lynn *et al.* (2000)], are detailed in the methods section, and are important in the context of our investigation of NPD staff personal style and performance in project-based work for several reasons, described in the following sections.

2.3.1. *Conscientiousness*

We posit that the average level of NPD staff on conscientiousness should be important for NPD performance in several ways. In particular, conscientious staff tend to be reliable [Costa and McCrae (1992)], which should be important for NPD speed, where sticking to a certain schedule is important. Conscientious employees are inclined to be achievement-oriented, which ought to be essential for NPD, where setting high goals and working harder to achieve these goals may result in the development of a product faster than competitors for a similar product, thus meeting overall senior management expectations. Researchers [e.g. Keller (1997)] support the contention that conscientiousness should be predictive of NPD performance in general for scientists and engineers.

Scholars illustrate the value of team member conscientiousness for team performance outcomes across settings [e.g. Barrick *et al.* (1998); Guzzo *et al.* (1992); Neuman and Wright (1999); Schneider and Delaney (1972); Zander and Forward (1968)]. Studies on person–role congruence show that team effects occur as a result of the match between personal style characteristics and staff members' roles [Shaw and Harkey (1976)]. Because conscientiousness predicts performance outcomes across job categories and criteria [e.g. Barrick and Mount (1993)], investigators suggest that conscientious staff should be dedicated to implementing the multiple role requirements of teams. Accordingly, it is conceivable that conscientious NPD staff members will concentrate on fulfilling the needs of the team, possibly affecting the success of the NPD project, and the pace in which the NPD project is implemented.

Conscientious NPD members tend to be task-focused and self-disciplined as well, which ought to result in team member attention to goal accomplishment [LePine *et al.* (1997)]. The tendency to be task focused can reduce the likelihood of social loafing [e.g. Karau and Williams (1993)], which in turn could affect the extent the NPD project is developed and launched faster than the major competitor for a similar product and perhaps the extent market share expectations are met.

Researchers [e.g. Brown and Eisenhardt (1995); Gemünden *et al.* (2005); Imai *et al.* (1985)] report that for fast product development, staff members had relative freedom to work autonomously, making the conscientiousness of NPD staff members a valuable trait, when it comes to launching the project on or ahead of the initial schedule and perhaps meeting management expectations. Accordingly we propose that the level of NPD staff conscientiousness should be related (highest beta weights when all personal style variables are entered into a multiple regression equation) to NPD performance.

H1: *Staff member conscientiousness will be positively related to NPD performance.*

2.3.2. *Agreeableness*

The literature [e.g. Imai *et al.* (1985); Keller (1986)] illustrates the value of continuous communication among NPD project staff members. Constant communication increases the information flow among team members, making it easier for team members to understand each other's specialties and to coordinate. Because agreeable team members tend to be trusting and straightforward [Costa and McCrae (1989)], they should facilitate communication with others on the team, in pursuit of NPD team's objectives [Aronoff and Wilson (1985)].

Further, agreeable people tend to be sympathetic to others and willing to help, and believe that others will be equally helpful in return. Helpful staff members might inform each other about non-routine demands, allowing them to take steps to mitigate problems, contributing to completion of the NPD project on schedule. NPD project participants who voluntarily disseminate their functional expertise to fellow staff members further expose their associates to diverse information [Katz and Tushman (1981)]. Such increased information sharing should further help NPD staff members to catch downstream problems such as manufacturing difficulties or marketing mismatches, before they happen, when these problems are generally smaller and easier to fix [Brown and Eisenhardt (1995)], and perhaps also consume less project time. It is plausible that NPD staff who help each other out would not have to turn to their project managers for assistance, leaving the project managers free to carry out more important tasks, such as obtaining needed personnel and securing financial support, resulting in the NPD project achieving its goals, and meeting senior manager and customer expectations. Further, in the demanding project setting, in which resources and goals are uncertain and customer demands are evolving, the less time project participants consume complaining or finding fault with project colleagues, the more time these agreeable individuals can invest in more productive purposes, perhaps affecting the time it takes from specs to full commercialization (highest beta weights when all personal style variables are entered into a multiple regression equation). Based on the literature reviewed, we arrive at our second hypothesis.

H2: *Staff member agreeableness will be positively related to NPD project performance.*

2.3.3. *Extraversion*

In a team setting, scholars report that higher scores on extroversion should relate to higher levels of social activity [e.g. Barczak and Wilemon (1991)]. Interestingly, the research on the value of extraversion for team performance outcomes is mixed. Some scholars show that extraversion is related to group creative problem solving [e.g. Bouchard (1969)], effectiveness [e.g. Greer (1955)] and team viability [e.g. Barrick *et al.* (1998)]. Other researchers [e.g. Kirkman and Rosen (1999)] provide empirical evidence that a proactive personality, which is consistently associated with two of the FFM factors, one of which is extraversion [e.g. Bateman and Crant (1993); Crant and Bateman (2000)], is positively related to work group performance outcomes. Yet, other investigators [e.g. Gurnee (1937)] report a positive relationship between group members' extraversion and the number of errors that groups make. Still other researchers [e.g. Barry and Stewart (1997)] find a negative relationship between extraversion and task focus. Finally, additional assessments [e.g. Kichuk and Wiesner (1997)] using simulated NPD teams, show higher levels of extraversion in teams that succeeded in meeting their objectives. In sum, due to the inconsistent results in the literature on the value of staff member extraversion in team contexts, we do not provide a hypothesis for this personal style.

In the next section, we consider personal style traits that might be important for NPD performance criteria, speed or success, depending upon the type of innovation, radical or incremental. Figure 1 will guide the literature review leading to the remaining hypotheses.

2.3.4. *Openness*

Scholars [e.g. Driskell *et al.* (1987); Bouchard (1972); DeBiasio (1986); Tuckman (1967)] suggest that staff member openness should be more essential depending upon the type of NPD team. We argue that staff member openness should be valuable in

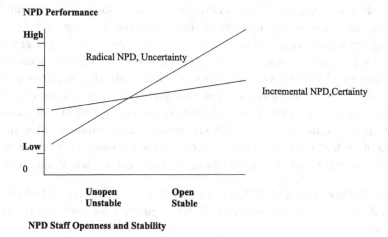

Fig. 1.   Theoretical effect of the type of NPD team on the relationship between NPD staff personal style and performance.[a]

---

[a]An example for NPD Staff Openness and Stability.

NPD teams involved in creative tasks, or tasks performed under conditions of high uncertainty, characteristic of radical innovation, and less important for groups performing routine mechanical or structured tasks [e.g. Driskell et al. (1988)], characteristic more of incremental innovation. Investigators illustrate that openness is positively related to novel solutions [McCrae (1987, 1996)], to "open communication" [e.g. Barry and Stewart (1997)], and is negatively correlated with conformity [e.g. Crutchfield (1955)].

Innovation is a process rife with uncertainty. Research shows that teams developing innovations deal with uncertainty internal to the firm and external to the firm. To handle this uncertainty, these teams must efficiently gather, process and disseminate information. In this vein, they can be viewed as information creating and processing systems. Open NPD staff can play a critical role in fostering this information. Open individuals are open to new ideas and information [Costa and McCrae (1992)], and open NPD staff should be open to new information whether it is from purchasing, vendor management, or the customer. Staff members who are open to new information, e.g. from the customer, could conceivably develop products that are perceived as new or different from existing products, or develop a completely new product that is acceptable in the market, at the pace of, or ahead of major competitors. These NPD teams need to obtain resources such as required talent, and larger budgets for the team [Brown and Eisenhardt (1995)], and open staff members could be more creative and resourceful when it comes to suggesting novel strategies for obtaining these resources, perhaps helping to reduce the time it takes to deliver the product to market.

Development teams, working on radical innovations, face severe challenges because the market is not well understood and the product is still evolving and changing with the market. These innovations require focus on a learning-based strategy because experimenting is an essential component of the process. Product teams may try a product in the market to learn, improve it, and try it again [Lynn et al. (1996); Rosenbloom and Cusumano (1987)]. NPD staff high in openness should be more successful on such trial and error research tasks that require maintaining flexibility and learning through experience, conceivably resulting in launching the NPD project at or ahead of schedule. Taken together, we propose that NPD staff openness will have a stronger positive effect on the NPD performance criterion speed, when the degree of uncertainty is high (The slopes and intercepts of the regression lines will be compared for each of the staff personal style variables), characteristic of radical innovation.

H3: *Staff member openness will be positively related to NPD speed when innovation is radical, but will not be related to NPD speed when innovation is incremental.*

2.3.5. Emotional stability

Teams with a higher aggregate level of emotional stability should contribute to a relaxed atmosphere and promote team cooperation. On the other hand, "unstable teams" are more likely to engage in disruptive behaviors, lose focus and have difficulty in cooperating [e.g. Watson and Tellegen (1985)], which could consume project time, plausibly affecting profit expectations. For teams that work on tasks over a long period of time, emotional stability can contribute to team viability [e.g. Haythorn (1953); Hough (1992)]. Unstable team members could be disruptive in meetings and have higher absenteeism, for example, both of which would slow progress. Additionally, emotional stability is paramount in team contexts, in terms of perceived self-efficacy for performing in self-managed teams and in terms of orientation toward job completion [e.g. Thoms *et al.* (1996)] as opposed to "nervousness tendencies" (i.e. instability).

Radical product innovation typically takes longer than incremental innovation, so teams must typically function together for longer periods of time — a condition that can make the favorability of the radical NPD staffs' moods and the emotional stability of the staff an important trait. The emotional stability of NPD staff members may be particularly important during radical NPD. Radical NPD encounters many more surprises than the incremental type, and the radical NPD staff members deal with conditions of high market and technology uncertainty. Having radical NPD staff members who are stable, and who do not waste time becoming frustrated when faced with the uncertainty, rapid change, and surprises involved with radical innovation could be particularly functional. Having team members with greater emotional stability might help buffer the radical NPD team from the stress associated with this uncertainty, thus enabling the team to continue functioning together over long periods of time, which can contribute to the completion of the radical NPD project on or ahead of its initial schedule. Emotional stability may be relatively unimportant for incremental NPD staff, who work under conditions that are more certain and routine.

H4: *Staff member emotional stability will be positively related to NPD speed when innovation is radical, but will not be related to NPD speed when innovation is incremental.*

2.3.6. *Agreeableness*

Researchers suggest that having a team high on agreeableness could be associated with team cohesiveness, which under some conditions might lead to successful performance [e.g. McCrae and Costa (1989)]. Yet, when teams are highly cohesive they could also be susceptible to "groupthink" [Janis (1972)]. Teams with more agreeable members tend to be less conflictual [McCrae and Costa (1989)]. Researchers suggest that conflict and deliberation which is task related (cognitive) can have more benefits, depending on the nature of the goals and degree of uncertainty facing the team [Amason (1996); Jehn (1995)]. When innovation is incremental, teams are given clear, detailed goals, less deliberation is necessary and team members are able to organize the issues and accomplish their tasks efficiently [Cohen and Bailey (1997)].

NPD staff members who are less agreeable could bring about task related conflict and deliberation which is not beneficial given that project goals are clear. When innovation is radical, teams should benefit more from staff members that are less agreeable, in that, these individuals can foster the needed task related conflict. In fact, an argument could be made that agreeable staff, who are less conflictual, might inhibit the development of breakthrough ideas. Thus, we propose that staff agreeableness will have a stronger positive effect on NPD success when innovation is incremental.

H5: *Staff member agreeableness will be positively related to NPD success when innovation is incremental, but will not be related to NPD success when innovation is radical*

3. Method

3.1. *Sample*

We selected a contact person for 149 NPD teams in a variety of technology-based companies in the northeastern U.S. to participate in this study. To avoid industry bias, we sampled a variety of industries including telecommunications, computers and electronics, fabricated metal products, information services, pharmaceuticals, chemical manufacturing, food manufacturing, and machinery manufacturing. In each company, the contact person chose NPD professionals as respondents, detailed below. Respondents were asked by the contact person to select a completed NPD project and respond to the survey within one week. In order to achieve a large sample of projects, we gathered data on NPD projects during 2008–2009, following a pilot study that was conducted earlier. Our high response rate (94%) was related to our use of participants in an executive management program, most of whom, worked in R&D organizations.

The typical radical innovations in our study can be categorized as falling into one (some times more) of the following: electronics and computing, telecommunications, advanced materials and chemicals, pharmaceuticals. These categories are comparable to those presented by Veryzer [1998]. Specific examples of radical innovations in our research include Telcom Interactive Television, computer operating system, an automated mail processing system, MRS (Materials Research Society) bulletin "link" paper, anti-HIV therapy drug. Among the projects we sampled, 37.6% of the projects the NPD teams worked on involved a new technology, 38.3% involved several new technologies, and 10% of the sample involved non-proven or non-existing technologies, which was consistent with what we expected to investigate at technology-based firms. Our operational definition for teams working on radical and incremental NPD appears below. The median NPD team size was 11 people, the average NPD team size was 23 people and the S.D. was 38. Most projects were from large companies: 69.6% of the projects were from companies with annual incomes over

500 million dollars, 26.8% of the projects were from companies employing 500–5000 workers, and 47.1% of the projects were from companies employing over 5000 people.

In each company, the contact person chose primarily product, senior engineering, technical and marketing managers as respondents. All these individuals were NPD team members. Participation in the study was voluntary, and the participants were assured that their responses would be kept confidential. Forty one percent of the respondents were product managers, 25% and 13% of the respondents were senior engineering or technical managers and the remainder were marketing managers, all of whom were project members. To test for differences in respondent type, one-way analyses of variance (ANOVAs) were performed with all of the major personal style constructs as dependent variables, and respondent type as the independent variable. No significant differences were found.

The respondents were instructed to choose teams who had completed an NPD project. Our sample included a range of successful and unsuccessful NPD projects, however our data were skewed toward successful projects. Some unsuccessful projects were undoubtedly not included because they were never completed. Such restriction in range tends to impact correlations more than regression weights [e.g. Aronson *et al.* (2006)], however, so we feel that this restriction did not seriously bias our results.

Further, to ensure a reasonably comparable level of familiarity with the NPD teams and their staff members across the sample, each respondent was asked to choose a team working on an NPD project with which he/she was intimately familiar with, and involved with throughout its development. Product development studies routinely use retrospective methods for reasons of feasibility [e.g. Meyer and Utterback (1995)]. To improve the accuracy of retrospective reports, respondents were asked by the contact person to select recent projects, to eliminate the elapsed time between the events of interest and the collection of data.

In the current sample, there was one informant per NPD team. Based on our study's empirical findings, we do not believe the respondents' retrospective assessment of the personal style of the NPD staff members, was dependent on the extent the team developing the new product met the performance criteria. Our results show there were differences in correlations between NPD staff personal style and the NPD speed and success criteria, depending on the type of NPD team. For example, the average openness of the staff was significantly associated with NPD speed for radical NPD teams only. The average agreeableness of the staff was significantly associated with NPD success for incremental NPD teams only. These findings support the argument that single respondents can provide good data.

What is more, Klein and Kozlowski [2000] note that while multilevel models are relevant to a majority of organizational phenomena it is not always essential that they be applied. One exception cited [Klein and Kozlowski (2000)] is when researching phenomena that have been previously unexplored as in the current case.

Finally, use of self-report data is a common practice in management research, and has led to the so-called "common method variance" problem. Reviews of other research and our own data would indicate that method variance is not a significant issue in the present study. Theoretically, there are several explanations why method variance should not substantially affect our results. First, self-report data is most problematic for topics which generate strong sentiments, such as attitudes [Cote and Buckley (1987)]. New product speed and success are much less emotionally laden subjects, and hence less likely to be distorted by self-reports. Second, social desirability bias often leads to response range compression [Podsakoff and Organ (1986)] which was not evident in our sample. Third, Lukas and Ferrell [2000] and Podsakoff and Organ [1986] found that managers rely on their own self-reports and provide reliable and objective data.

3.2. *Measures*

3.2.1. *Radical versus incremental innovation*

We were interested in teams developing radical innovations and teams developing incremental innovations. Based on the work of Lynn and Akgun [1998] described earlier, staff personal style was analyzed under high uncertainty (radical innovation) and low uncertainty (incremental innovation). A measure of radical versus incremental innovation was derived based on information provided by the respondents to two items representing market and technology uncertainty. Both items were rated on a scale ranging from 0 (strongly disagree) to 10 (strongly agree) and were as follows: "The technology required to develop this product (R and D) was totally new to our company", and "This product had to be sold to people or organizations outside our company's traditional customer base". The rationale for this measure is that teams working on incremental innovation operate under more certain environments, when a currently served market with mature technologies is targeted. On the other hand, teams working on radical innovation operate under more uncertain environments, when both market and technology uncertainties are high. We were interested in the role of staff personal style in NPD performance for two types of teams: NPD teams that develop radical innovations and operate under conditions of higher uncertainty and NPD teams that develop incremental innovations and operate under conditions of lower uncertainty. Accordingly we first took the average of the two items, and then dichotomized at the scale mid-point. Consequently, the 149 NPD teams yielded 75 incremental and 74 radical NPD teams.

It is worth mentioning that there might be alternative ways to operationalize teams working on radical versus incremental innovations. The rationale for our categorization of these teams is our concern with the differing uncertainty levels these teams face, and how this might relate to the optimal team personal style characteristics needed for success in NPD project-based work. Teams working on radical innovations operate under more uncertain environments, when both market and technology uncertainties are high. Our operationalization for each of these teams is derived from work by Lynn and Akgun [e.g. 1998] on incremental and radical teams, and Barczak and Wilemon [e.g. 1989] on operating and innovating teams. Lynn and Akgun mention that incremental innovation exists under highly certain environments, when a currently served market with mature technologies is targeted. Radical innovation, in contrast, exists when both market and technology uncertainties are high. Operating teams are concerned with maintaining competitive positions in existing businesses and, as a result, they usually focus on incremental innovation or small improvements to current products. Innovating teams, in contrast, focus on developing a new business for the firm. They are more likely to focus on important new products for unfamiliar markets. Lynn and Akgun characterize both these teams as incremental and radical, respectively. Other researchers [e.g. Aronson *et al.* (2006, 2008)] include the technology and the market as criteria to categorize various types of innovation teams.

3.2.2. *NPD project performance*

Our performance measure included two different criteria, NPD success and speed. The criteria were each assessed with items rated on a scale ranging from 0 (strongly disagree) to 10 (strongly agree) [Lynn *et al.* (2000)]. The following items were included in the success measure: this project (1) overall met or exceeded sales expectations, (2) met or exceeded profit expectations, (3) met or exceeded return on investment expectations, (4) met or exceeded overall senior management's expectations, (5) met or exceeded market share expectations, (6) met or exceeded customer expectations. Cronbach's alpha for the success measure was 0.96. We assessed NPD speed using the following items [Lynn *et al.* (2000)]: this project (1) was developed and launched faster than the major competitor for a similar product, (2) was completed in less time than what was considered normal and customary for our industry, (3) was launched on or ahead of the original schedule developed at initial project go-ahead, (4) top management was pleased with the time it took us from specs to full commercialization. Cronbach's alpha for the speed measure was 0.86.

In the current study, the performance measure included NPD speed and success. Although different terms such as time-to-market, cycle time, innovation speed, and speed-to-market have been used to portray NPD speed, it generally represents how quickly an idea moves from conception to a product in the marketplace, measuring firms' capabilities to move quickly through the NPD process [Chen *et al.* (2005)]. By developing products quickly, companies can achieve several important benefits. First, fast NPD can increase product profitability, margins, and market share. Firms are able to translate time into profits by satisfying their "impatient" customers, who are willing to pay a premium if they can get goods and services very quickly [Brown and Eisenhardt (1995)]. Second, companies with fast NPD have a greater chance to establish industry standards and may lock up distribution channels [Dumaine (1989)]. Third, a firm with the capability of developing products rapidly can quickly respond to market demands, improving the timeliness of its product entry and customer satisfaction. In the current study, in addition to NPD speed, we included an indicator of NPD success [e.g. Lynn *et al.* (2000)], capturing customer, profitability, market share and senior management expectations.

A recent survey suggested that NPD speed is the most important metric of innovation performance [Boston Consulting Group (2006)]. In addition, NPD speed is also a key component of time-based strategy and a pivotal way to achieve time advantage, either first-mover or fast-follower advantage [Stalk and Hout (1990)]. Shenhar colleagues [2005] viewed time advantage as a new generic competitive strategy, adding it to Porter's [1985] three generic strategies of cost leadership, differentiation, and focus. This strategy provides competitive advantage by enabling firms to adapt quickly to market needs in the dynamic and competitive business context [Eisenhardt and Tabrizi (1995)]. Further, through developing products quickly, companies learn to build new competencies to differentiate themselves from competitors [Wheelwright and Clark (1992)]. For example, they will be able to choose to be a market pioneer or to consciously adopt a fast follower strategy [Emmanuelides (1993)]. Because the first-mover advantage may not always lead to enduring market leadership [Tellis and Golder (2001)], companies with fast NPD may benefit from having more strategic alternatives than the slower innovators.

Some researchers and practitioners argue that there are potential trade-offs between NPD speed and other NPD performance indicators, such as speed-quality [Calantone and Di Benedetto (2000); Harter *et al.* (2000)] speed-cost [Gupta *et al.* (1992)], and speed-success [Griffin (2002)]. For example, Lukas *et al.* [2002] argue that a strict deadline might make NPD teams slip key processes, trim performance specifications, and/or reduce technological content, which typically undermine product quality. Lambert and Slater [1999] contend that fast NPD may make managers focus on schedules at the expense of more resources and product performance. While there may be pitfalls to fast product development, NPD speed is viewed as a primary indicator of firm innovation performance, and is essential for the success, survival, and renewal of firms in turbulent and uncertain environments [Eisenhardt and Tabrizi (1995); Kessler and Chakrabarti (1996)]. Consequently, in the current study, we included measures of NPD speed and NPD success as performance criteria [e.g. Lynn *et al.* (2000)], detailed earlier.

3.2.3. *Personal style*

As part of a survey designed to measure practices supportive of team learning, development speed, and new product success [Lynn *et al.* (2000); Aronson *et al.* (2006, 2008)] five single items were developed to assess team member personality (five-item measure of the Big Five). Building on past research [e.g. Costa and McCrae (1992); Lindner (1998); McCrae and Costa (1989); Tett *et al.* (1991)], each item of this measure of personality was designed to measure a single Big-Five trait (Appendix A). We obtained evidence to support the construct validity of this five-item measure of the Big Five as follows. In one study [Lindner (1998)], 193 students responded to the five-item measure of the Big Five, Goldberg's Adjective Checklist (1992) and the NEOFFI [Costa and McCrae (1992)], all of which measure the Big-Five personality traits. (Note that there was no overlap in items between the three personality measures). Correlations among similar constructs between the five-item measure of the Big Five and Goldberg's Adjective Checklist were 0.67, 0.61, 0.63, 0.55, 0.66 for extraversion, agreeableness, conscientiousness, neuroticism and openness to experience respectively, providing evidence of convergent validity.

The correlations among similar constructs between the five-item measure of the Big-Five personality traits and the NEO-FFI were 0.56, 0.56, 0.64, 0.55, 0.50, respectively. In both analyses, correlations across dissimilar constructs were much lower, providing evidence of discriminant validity. For comparative purposes, the convergent validities between the NEO-FFI and Goldberg's Adjective Checklist were very similar to the convergent validities reported above, 0.59, 0.61, 0.72, 0.64, 0.42, respectively for each of the five personally traits. These results resemble those reported by other researchers. For example, Goldberg [1992] reported correlations between similar personality dimensions from a set of 100 Big-Five markers and the NEO-PI (a Big-Five personality measure [Costa and McCrae (1985)] that ranged from 0.46 to 0.69 as evidence of the construct validity of those markers. Barrick and Mount [1993] reported correlations among similar personality dimensions from the personal characteristic inventory (PCI, a Big-Five personality measure), and the NEO-PI that ranged from 0.56 to 0.71 as evidence of the construct validity of the PCI. In summary, the rather high correlations of similar constructs of the five-item measure of the Big Five with those on the NEO-FFI and Goldberg's Adjective Checklist, and the low correlations between dissimilar constructs, which are similar to those reported by other researchers, provide evidence about the construct validity of the personality measure used in the current study.

It is worth mentioning that empirical evidence supporting the construct validity of this five-item measure of the Big Five was confirmed in the current study as well.

Table 2 provides evidence of discriminant validity between the five personality variables, with generally moderate correlations between staff personal style variables, which are comparable to correlations reported elsewhere for the FFM of personality [e.g. Barrick *et al.* (2002); Boudreau *et al.* (2001)]. Additionally, in the current research, staff personal style was differentially related to this study's performance criteria, NPD speed and NPD success, providing additional support that this measure can be a useful measure of the Big-Five traits.

We followed Cohen *et al.*'s [2003] guidelines for measuring multicollinearity. Cohen and colleagues discuss several multicollinearity indices that can provide useful information, but they argue that these indices do not substitute for basic checks of the data. First, Cohen and colleagues recommend to carefully examine the scatter plot matrix of the predictor variables, looking for outlier observations that may affect the relationship between each pair of independent variables (IVs). Cohen and colleagues add that outliers can greatly increase or decrease the magnitude of the relationship between variables, leading to values of multicollinearity indices that may be too high or too low. Additionally, Cohen and colleagues suggest to compare the results of a simple univariate regression analysis in which the outcome (e.g. NPD performance criteria, Y) is regressed separately on all of the predictor variables of interest (e.g. personal style variables, X). We followed Cohen and colleagues' suggestion and we compared the correlations (r) for each IV (xy) with its corresponding standard β in the regression equation. Large, unexpected changes in direction and magnitude of these coefficients would have suggested a substantial influence of multicollinearity. In our examination, we did not find large changes in direction and magnitude of these coefficients, which suggests that we did not have substantial influence of multicollinearity.

The NPD professionals in the current study rated the NPD team staff's personal style, using the five-item measure of the Big Five, on a scale from 1 to 5 (Appendix A). Justification for using observer ratings of personal style can be found in past research [Aronson (1998); Mount et al. (1994)]. Observers' assessments of other staff's personal style are at least as valid as self-assessments, because they are based on observations of these individuals, almost exclusively in the work environment. On the other hand, individuals (NPD staff members) see themselves in numerous situations, such as at home, at play, and at work. Consequently, self-ratings of personal style have less point-to-point correspondence between the predictor and the criterion. An operational definition of each of the FFM personal style variables was provided (e.g. "Extroversion–Introversion: the extent to which team members are sociable, talkative, assertive, active (Extroverted) versus retiring, sober, reserved, cautious (Introverted)". The responding NPD professionals were asked to distribute the percentage of NPD staff members into each of five categories ranging from high on one end of a bipolar scale (e.g. Highly Extraverted) to high on the other end (e.g. Highly Introverted). This procedure allowed to calculate the mean and standard deviation for the project team on each of the FFM personal style variables.

4. Results

The means and standard deviations for all staff personal style variables (e.g. Conscientiousness AVG, Agreeableness AVG, etc.) for incremental and radical NPD teams are presented in Table 1. No significant differences existed between the two types of NPD teams, with respect to all staff personal style variables. The intercorrelations between all five staff personal style variables for all NPD teams and NPD speed and success are reported in Table 2. As shown, for NPD speed, the magnitude of the correlations for staff conscientiousness, agreeableness and emotional stability were 0.27, 0.28 and 0.23 ($p < 0.01$, 2-tailed) respectively, and for openness and extraversion the correlations were 0.16 and 0.19 ($p < 0.05$, 2-tailed). For NPD success, the magnitude of the correlations for staff conscientiousness,

Table 1.   Means and standard deviations of all variables for incremental and radical NPD teams.

Variable	Incremental		Radical		
	M	SD	M	SD	t-Value
Speed	6.67	2.42	6.16	2.67	1.21
Success	6.74	2.90	5.79	2.80	2.02*
Extraversion AVG	3.54	0.63	3.58	0.70	−0.29
Agreeableness AVG	3.86	0.57	3.86	0.65	−0.02
Conscientiousness AVG	4.33	0.49	4.29	0.64	0.49
Stability AVG	4.14	0.66	4.20	0.65	−0.46
Openness AVG	4.00	0.67	4.10	0.59	−0.94

Note: *$p < .05$. Incremental: $n = 75$, radical: $n = 74$, AVG = average.

Table 2.   Correlations between staff personal style variables and NPD performance criteria.

Variable	1	2	3	4	5	6	NPD success
1. Extraversion AVG		0.40**	0.37**	0.21**	0.44**	0.19*	0.13
2. Agreeableness AVG			0.45**	0.58**	0.57**	0.28*	0.34**
3. Conscientiousness AVG				0.53**	0.59**	0.27**	0.31**
4. Stability AVG					0.51**	0.23**	0.23**
5. Openness AVG						0.16*	0.20*
6. NPD speed							0.56**

Note: *$p < 0.05$ (2-tailed), **$p < 0.01$ (2-tailed), AVG = average.

agreeableness and emotional stability were 0.31, 0.34, and 0.23 ($p < 0.01$, 2-tailed) respectively, and for openness and extraversion the correlations were 0.20 and 0.13 ($p < 0.05$; $p < 0.1$, 2-tailed). Table 2 provides evidence of discriminant validity between the five personal style variables. As shown, the personal style of the staff was differentially related to this study's NPD speed and success criteria, and the generally moderate correlations between staff personal style variables provide additional support that this measure can be a useful measure of the Big-Five traits.

The correlations between staff personal style variables and NPD speed for incremental and radical innovation teams are provided in Table 3. As hypothesized, the correlations with NPD speed were significantly higher when innovation was radical only for staff openness ($r = 0.32$, $p < 0.01$, 2-tailed) and emotional stability ($r = 0.36$, $p < 0.01$, 2-tailed), as the slope tests, detailed in the Hierarchical regression analysis, reveal below. The correlations between staff personal style variables and NPD success for incremental and radical innovation teams are provided in Table 4. As hypothesized, the correlations with NPD success were significantly higher when innovation was incremental only for staff agreeableness ($r = 0.53$, $p < 0.01$, 2-tailed) as illustrated in the slope tests described next.

Table 3.   Correlations between staff personal style and NPD **speed** for incremental and radical projects: F-test of slopes.

	Incremental	Radical	F-Test of slopes
Extraversion AVG	0.08	0.27*	1.36
Agreeableness AVG	0.20	0.33**	0.62
Conscientiousness AVG	0.12	0.37**	1.61
Stability AVG	0.08	0.36**	3.45+
Openness AVG	0.02	0.32**	4.52*

Notes: $*p < 0.05$ (2-tailed), $**p < 0.01$ (2-tailed), $+p < 0.10$ (2-tailed). Incremental: $n = 75$, radical: $n = 74$, AVG = average.

Table 4.   Correlations between staff personal style and NPD **success** for incremental and radical projects: F-Test of slopes.

	Incremental	Radical	F-Test of slopes
Extraversion AVG	0.21	0.10	1.24
Agreeableness AVG	0.53**	0.17	7.28*
Conscientiousness AVG	0.35**	0.26*	1.33
Stability AVG	0.33**	0.14	1.55
Openness AVG	0.24*	0.18	0.05

Note: $*p < 0.05$ (2-tailed), $**p < 0.01$ (2-tailed), AVG = average.

Hierarchical regression analyses were performed to test whether the regression lines for staff personal style and NPD speed and success were significantly different, for radical versus incremental innovation. A dummy variable was created to represent radical versus incremental innovation and cross-product terms were computed by multiplying this dummy variable by each of the five-factor personal style scores for each NPD type. The slopes and intercepts of the regression lines were compared for each of the staff personal style variables. For NPD speed (Table 3), the slope tests for staff openness showed a significant difference for radical versus incremental NPD supporting hypothesis 3, and a marginally significant difference for emotional stability, providing support for hypothesis 4. As hypothesized, for NPD speed, the slopes of the regression lines were significantly higher for staff openness when innovation was radical ($F = 4.52$, df $= 1, 145$, $p < 0.05$, 2-tailed). For NPD speed, the slopes of the regression lines were marginally higher for staff emotional stability when innovation was radical ($F = 3.45$, df $= 1, 145$, $p < 0.10$, 2 tailed). As hypothesized, for NPD success (Table 4), the slopes of the regression lines were significantly higher for staff agreeableness when innovation was incremental ($F = 7.28$, df $= 1,145$, $p < 0.05$, 2-tailed).

Finally, a multiple regression analysis was conducted using NPD speed and NPD success as the dependent variables to test which of the staff personal style variables was most important for the NPD performance criteria. Table 5 shows the beta

Table 5. Multiple regression: Beta weights and multiple correlations for staff personal style variables and NPD speed and success.

	β Speed	β Success
Extraversion AVG	0.08	−0.04
Agreeableness AVG	0.20+	0.32**
Conscientiousness AVG	0.21+	0.25*
Stability AVG	0.05	−0.04
Openness AVG	−0.14	−0.11
R	0.35	0.40
F-test of R^2	3.66**	5.08**

Note: $*p < 0.05$, $**p < 0.01$, $+p < 0.10$, AVG = average.

weights and multiple correlation, between all FFM personal style variables and the NPD performance criteria, speed and success. Conscientiousness and agreeableness had the highest beta weights. For example, for NPD success, the beta weight for staff conscientiousness and agreeableness were significant at the $p < 0.05$ and $p < 0.01$ levels correspondingly ($\beta = 0.25$ and 0.32 respectively), supporting hypotheses 1 and 2. Similar findings are reported in Table 5 for the NPD speed criterion. For NPD speed, the beta weights for staff conscientiousness and agreeableness were marginally significant at the $p < 0.10$ level ($\beta = 0.21$ and 0.20). Overall, for the NPD project performance criteria, staff personal style variables had a multiple correlation of $R = 0.35$ and 0.40 for the speed and success criteria respectively, indicating support for measuring staff personal style variables using the FFM model. Our findings are in line with recent meta-analytical research on personality and team performance [e.g. Peeters *et al.* (2006)]. Results illustrate the importance of considering personal style, in addition to functional expertise, when assigning employees to innovation teams [e.g. Atuahene-Gima (2003); Brown and Eisenhardt (1995); Chen *et al.* (2010); Hoegl *et al.* (2004); Keller (2001); Zirger and Hartley (1994)].

It is noteworthy that Cohen [e.g. 1988] mentions that judging whether a Pearson correlation coefficient r is strong, moderately strong or weak depends on the context in which the correlation has been computed. Within the behavioral sciences, and applied psychology, the criteria for evaluating the strength of the correlations were first introduced by Cohen [Cohen *et al.* (2003)]. These criteria, detailed below, are now widely used in behavioral sciences research, including individual differences studies, similar to the assessments we ran in the current research. According to the criteria [e.g. Cohen (1988)] often cited, a correlation $= \pm 0.50$ is considered a strong correlation in the behavioral sciences, a correlation of ± 0.30 is considered a moderate correlation, and a correlation of ± 0.10 is considered weak. Cohen's classification that a correlation of 0.50 is considered a strong correlation comes from the assertion that in applied social psychology and behavioral sciences, high correlations, e.g. 0.50 and above are achieved only when the correlations are measures of reliability. Cohen provides examples of correlations that are 0.82, which is classified as a strong correlation, and 0.32, which is classified as a moderately strong correlation between two variables. Yet, both these correlations are considered typical correlations in their respective contexts, e.g. in the behavioral sciences, note Cohen and colleagues. In our study for example, four of the five individual differences correlations for radical NPD speed reported in Table 3 are above 0.30; they are 0.33, 0.37, 0.36, 0.32, the final correlation is 0.27. The average correlation is 0.33 across all five personal style differences, which is above Cohen's benchmark of 0.30, for moderately strong correlations. In our study, three of the five individual differences correlations for incremental NPD success reported in Table 4 are above 0.30; they are 0.53, 0.35, 0.33, and the final two correlations are 0.24 and 0.21. The average correlation is 0.33 across all five personal style differences, which is above Cohen's benchmark of 0.30, for moderately strong correlations as well.

4.1. *Project management activities and the relevance of diverse team personality traits*

We conducted a series of *post-hoc* analyses, to identify team personality traits that have relevance to possible project management activities using additional limited qualitative data we had. For example, results (Table 6) illustrate that team conscientiousness was germane to several recording and filing behaviors (data gathering/information management), whether the NPD process was continuously analyzed, and to whether the team *followed* a clear plan — a roadmap with measurable milestones (project direction). These behaviors should help project members to be attentive to the plan and engender these members to work together toward project goals. Furthermore, team member agreeableness was pertinent to whether information captured on customers' needs and wants was shared (project member information sharing). Such info sharing can help NPD staff members to catch downstream problems such as manufacturing difficulties, before these happen, when the problems are generally smaller, easier to remedy and perhaps also consume less project time. Additionally, team member openness was relevant to whether market and technical information was organized and summarized in meaningful ways to reduce complexity (meaningful information was gathered), whether team members acknowledged conflict and worked to resolve issues on the team (conflict management) and to creative problem solving. These behaviors should help members encourage and handle new ideas that are necessary for innovations. These team personality traits and the remaining factors (stability and extraversion) were differentially related to project management activities including coordination/information and knowledge sharing, as hypothesized.

Table 6.   Qualitative information: Different project management activities and the relevance of diverse personality traits of team members.

Project members' activities	Team member personality				
Data gathering/information management	E	A	C	S	O
Action items resulting from team staff meetings were regularly recorded	√	√			
Technical quality prototype test results were proficiently recorded			√		
Overall, most information relating to this project was proficiently recorded			√		
Information collected by the team (e.g. test results) was coded and sorted to be understood easily by other team members	√	√			
A central file on this project was kept that included initial concepts, engineering specs, prototype protocols, and customer input/reaction to early concepts	√	√			
Project information was stored on a computer-based information system			√		
Past project reviews were filed with the **central** project file X	√	√			
During the project, the NPD process (from concept through launch) was continuously analyzed			√		
Project direction			√		
The overall business goals were clear			√		
The technical goals were clear			√		
The team had a clear understanding of target customers' needs and wants			√		
The team followed a clear plan — a roadmap with measurable milestones	√	√			
Conflict management					
Team members acknowledged conflict and worked to resolve issues on the team					√
Team members encouraged diverse perspectives and differing points of view from others on the team					√
Meaningful information was gathered					
Market information was summarized to reduce its complexity					√
Market information was organized in meaningful ways					√
Technical information was summarized to reduce its complexity					√
Technical information was organized in meaningful ways					√
Creative problem solving					
Team members practiced what-if analysis extensively to understand possible market and technical scenarios					√
Information captured on customers' needs and wants was *shared quickly* throughout the team	√				
Test results on this product were *shared quickly* throughout the team	√	√	√		
Teamwork behaviors: coordination/information and knowledge Sharing					
Team members *helped* others on the team by sharing knowledge and information	√	√	√		
Team members were working *together* toward a *unified goal*	√	√	√		
Team members would freely *share* information (technical, market, etc.) with others on the team	√	√	√		
Team members demonstrated interest and enthusiasm during team activities				√	√
Team members acknowledged the contributions made by others on the team	√			√	√

Note: A: agreeableness, C: conscientiousness, E: extraversion, S: stability, O: openness.

5. Discussion

In the current research, we centered on testing the effect of staff personal style on NPD project performance. As we hypothesized, in particular, two staff personal style variables appear to be most valuable in their influence on NPD performance. Agreeableness and conscientiousness have the highest correlations with NPD speed and success and the highest beta weights when all personal style variables are entered into a multiple regression equation. The present results for agreeableness and conscientiousness are consistent with earlier studies [e.g. Barrick *et al.* (1998); Hough (1992); Kichuk and Wiesner (1997); Neuman and Wright (1999)]. These findings are in line with recent meta-analytical research on personality and team performance [e.g. Peeters *et al.* (2006)].

Yet, our examination shows that when considering the type of innovation the teams are working on, the relationship between staff personal style variables and NPD performance criteria varies. The slope comparisons between incremental and radical innovation teams with speed as a dependent variable yielded a significant difference for openness and a marginally significant difference for stability. Openness is more highly correlated with speed when innovation is radical suggesting that having a team more apt to consider new ideas will speed up the process when new, breakthrough ideas are being developed. A more stable team may also contribute to speed when innovation is radical. Less stable team members might be disruptive in meetings and perhaps have higher absenteeism, for example, both of which would slow progress.

With success as the dependent variable a significant difference in slopes was found for staff agreeableness. Having team members who are agreeable does not appear to be important when new ideas are being developed. It could be that high levels of agreement lead to "groupthink" or failure to challenge ideas as frequently, conceivably leading to less successful innovation. Our findings add to the literature [e.g. Atuahene-Gima (2003); Brown and Eisenhardt (1995); Chen *et al.* (2010); Hoegl *et al.* (2004); Keller (2001); Zirger and Hartley (1994)] on the value of considering personal style, in addition to functional expertise, when assigning employees to innovation teams.

5.1. *Understanding the value of staff personal style for NPD performance*

Findings suggest that when it comes to NPD project performance, the level of staff conscientiousness tends to be important (Tables 2 and 5). Staffing NPD teams with conscientious employees might reduce the likelihood of social loafing, which could affect the extent the NPD project is developed and launched faster than the major competitor for a similar product, conceivably meeting market share and overall senior management's expectations. Other investigators' findings are consistent with this contention [e.g. Brown and Eisenhardt (1995); Gemünden *et al.* (2005)]. What is more, because conscientious individuals tend to be dedicated to implementing multiple role requirements of teams, NPD teams composed of conscientious staff members might conceivably concentrate on fulfilling the needs of the team, possibly affecting the success and the pace in which the NPD project is implemented. Scholars agree with this assertion and illustrate that conscientiousness predicts performance outcomes across job categories and criteria [e.g. Barrick and Mount (1993)]. Aligned with our findings, researchers [e.g. Keller (1997)] demonstrate that conscientiousness should be predictive of R&D performance in general for scientists and engineers.

Results also show that the level of NPD staff on agreeableness might be important for NPD project performance (Tables 2 and 5). Agreeable people are inclined to be sympathetic to others, willing to support, and believe that others will be helpful in return. Supportive staff members might inform each other about non-routine demands, allowing them to take steps to mitigate problems, contributing to completion of the NPD project on schedule. NPD project participants who disseminate their functional expertise to fellow staff members could expose their associates to diverse information. Such increased information sharing could further help NPD staff members to catch downstream problems such as manufacturing problems or marketing discrepancies, before they happen, when these challenges are generally easier to fix [Brown and Eisenhardt (1995); Katz and Tushman (1981)], and perhaps also consume less project time. It is plausible that NPD staff who support one another would not have to turn to their project managers for help, leaving the project managers free to complete more important tasks, such as obtaining personnel and financial support, resulting in the NPD project achieving its goals and satisfying customer expectations. Further, in the challenging project-based work context, in which resources and goals are uncertain and customer demands are changing, the less time project participants spend complaining or finding fault with project colleagues, the more time these agreeable individuals can devote to more productive purposes, perhaps affecting the time it takes from specs to full commercialization.

Interestingly, when considering the type of innovation the teams are working on, the relationship between staff personal style and NPD performance criteria might vary. Our examination shows when it comes to NPD speed, radical NPD teams might benefit from staff members that are more open (Table 3). It might be easier for open staff members to encourage and handle new ideas that are necessary for radical innovations. Radical NPD frequently involves a great deal of learning and improvising. The need to learn more about the markets and the technical issues necessary to successfully bring the product to market on time is likely to make the openness of the staff members a desirable personal style trait.

Open staff members may also play a role in fostering, processing and disseminating information necessary to handle the uncertainty facing radical NPD teams. Open individuals tend to be open to new ideas and information [Costa and McCrae (1992)] and open NPD staff could plausibly be open to new information whether it is from purchasing, vendor management, or the customer. NPD staff members who are open to new information from the consumer, could conceivably develop products that are perceived as new or, different to existing products, or develop a completely new product that is acceptable in the market, faster than key competitors. More open staff members might also be more creative when it comes to suggesting novel strategies for obtaining resources, such as needed talent, and larger budgets for the team [Brown and Eisenhardt (1995)], which in turn could conceivably help reduce the time it takes to complete the NPD project.

When innovations are radical, development teams face other severe challenges because the market is not well understood and the product is still evolving and changing with the market. Radical innovations require a focus on a learning-based strategy. Product teams try a product in the market to learn, improve it, and try it again [e.g. Lynn et al. (1996)]. Our results suggest that NPD staff high in openness might be more likely to be successful on, for example, "trial and error research tasks", among others, which, in turn, may involve maintaining flexibility and learning through experience, as well as other types of learning (e.g. observational learning), possibly resulting in launching the NPD project at or ahead of the original schedule.

Our examination also shows that the emotional stability of NPD staff members may be helpful during radical NPD (Table 3). Radical NPD encounters many more surprises than the incremental type. Having radical NPD staff who are more emotionally stable, and who do not waste time becoming frustrated as a result of the rapid change involved with radical innovation could be beneficial. Our results suggest that NPD teams comprised of more emotionally stable staff may be more likely to, for example, buffer the radical NPD team from the stress associated with the changes, perhaps helping the team to continue functioning together over long periods of time, which might facilitate the completion of the radical NPD project on schedule. Researchers [e.g. Watson and Tellegen (1985); Barrick et al. (1998)] illustrate that higher levels of team emotional stability should contribute to a relaxed atmosphere and to team viability, which is consistent with this contention. Emotional stability may be relatively insignificant in distinguishing between success and failure when it comes to the speed an incremental NPD project is completed, since the staff are working under conditions that are more certain. Although this argument might seem to depart from meta-analytical results [e.g. Salgado (1997, 2002)] that emotionally stable employees, including NPD employees, are likely to have higher levels of job performance, which could include completing NPD projects on schedule, these meta-analyses did not differentiate between, e.g. radical and incremental NPD teams. Similarly, notwithstanding the limitations of our study, we contend that a threshold level of staff emotional stability may be important for incremental NPD teams but may not differentiate success from failure, in terms of the speed the NPD project is completed. Yet, the level of staff emotional stability beyond the threshold level might have a significant relationship with the speed the radical NPD project is completed.

Finally, with success as the dependent variable, having team members who are high on agreeableness might not be helpful when new ideas are being developed

(Table 4). It could be that high levels of agreement lead to failure to challenge ideas as frequently, leading to less successful innovation. When innovation is incremental, teams are given clear, detailed objectives, less debate is necessary and team members are able to organize the issues and accomplish their tasks. NPD staff members who are less agreeable could plausibly bring about task related conflict and deliberation which may not be helpful, given that project goals are clear. On the other hand, radical innovation might benefit from staff members who are less agreeable, in that, these individuals could conceivably foster the needed task related conflict. In fact, more agreeable staff who tend to be less conflictual, might, for example, inhibit the development of breakthrough ideas necessary for radical NPD. Our assertion is in line with the views of other researchers [e.g. Amason (1996); Janis (1972); Jehn (1995); McCrae and Costa (1989)].

5.2. *Limitations and future research*

As always is the case, there are reasons to exercise care in generalizing from any one study. There are a few limitations that should be addressed in future research. First, in the current study single-source methodology was employed. Aviolo *et al.* [1991] note that, studies employing single-source methodology may be biased by artificially high intercorrelations because of an overall positive, or negative, response bias. Aviolo and colleagues emphasize, however, that simply assuming that single-source data are less valid than multi-source data is overly simplistic, advancing our argument presented in the method section. In addition, much of the research on the effect of single-source bias has been done with instruments that involve social perception. While it is not our intent to minimize the potential effects of response bias, the kinds of information sought in the present survey with respect to NPD speed and success tended to be more objective in nature than many surveys used in research in the social sciences. Implicit theories, cognitive schema [e.g. Aronson and Reilly (2006)], and other cognitive frameworks applied by respondents to social-perceptual stimuli may not apply to the same extent with our survey. Thus, responding to questions regarding NPD speed and NPD success should be based on more objective data. In addition, our data support the relative lack of response bias. Our results show that the personal style constructs are differentially related to the NPD performance criteria, speed and success. What is more, as we report in the results section, we tested for multicollinearity [Cohen *et al.* (2003)], and we did not find substantial influence of multicollinearity.

Yet, future research could obtain archival data for some variables such as NPD speed and success as objective measures. Further, data for a single NPD team could be gathered from multiple sources. Personal style measures could be provided by the NPD team staff, and NPD performance ratings could be provided by the customer or senior managers. Another variation of this approach is to obtain complete data from multiple sources so that the inter-rater reliability and response bias issues can be directly examined.

Second, the procedure used to gather data on the NPD staff personal style may have weakened the magnitude of some of the validities that we found. However, empirical evidence supporting the construct validity of this five-item measure of personal style traits has been provided [Lindner (1998)], supported in the current study (Table 2) and the discriminant validity results are comparable with results reported elsewhere for the FFM [e.g. Barrick *et al.* (2002); Boudreau *et al.* (2001)]. The validities obtained between NPD staff personal style and NPD project performance are similar to the validities reported in the literature [e.g. Peeters *et al.* (2006)].

Moreover, our study suggests the potential usefulness of this five-item personality measure for researching questions on NPD team personal style and performance relations. Most inventories assessing personal style are lengthy. The five-item personal style measure allowed us to gather data and conduct comparisons between specific NPD staff personal style traits, and NPD speed and success for teams working on different innovations. Gathering this data from busy NPD professionals would be challenging using lengthy personality inventories. By combining the five-item personal style measure with data on the criteria and type of innovation the NPD team is working on, we were able to substantiate the staff personal style NPD success and NPD speed link. In short, we were able to provide answers to some difficult theoretical questions because of our use of an alternative tool for personal style assessment.

Third, in the current study, there was limited statistical power, especially in the comparisons between slopes. Statistical power for each test was limited by two factors: one is the within-group sample sizes, and second is the operational definition for teams working on radical and incremental innovation used in the present study. We are aware that there are alternative ways to operationally define teams working on radical and incremental innovations. Yet, the rationale for our categorization of these teams was our concern with the differing uncertainty levels these teams face, and how this might relate to the optimal team personal style characteristics needed for success in NPD project-based work. Teams working on radical innovations operate under more uncertain environments, when both market and technology uncertainties are high. Our operationalization for each of these teams was derived from earlier work by Lynn and Akgun [e.g. 1998] on incremental and radical teams, and Barczak and Wilemon [e.g. 1989] on operating and innovating teams. Lynn and Akgun mention that incremental innovation exists under highly certain environments, when a currently served market with mature technologies is targeted. Radical innovation, in contrast, exists when both market and technology uncertainties are high. Operating teams are concerned with maintaining competitive positions in existing businesses and, as a result, they usually focus on incremental innovation or small improvements to current products. Innovating teams, in contrast, focus on developing a new business for the firm. They are more likely to focus on important new products for unfamiliar markets. Lynn and Akgun characterize both these teams as incremental and radical, respectively. Other researchers [e.g. Aronson et al. (2006, 2008)] include the technology and the market as criteria to categorize various types of innovation teams. Finally, future research conducted with larger samples, would allow the formation of more extreme groups leading to stronger findings for the comparisons of slopes.

Fourth, in this study, results show that conscientiousness and agreeableness are correlated with NPD performance criteria, speed and success. Future research could be designed to create empirical conditions for inferring causality [Cohen et al. (2003)], versus reciprocal causation or mutual causation by a third variable. Cohen and colleagues describe three conditions that need to hold to show that variable X (e.g. conscientiousness) may be a cause of another variable Y (e.g. NPD performance): 1. Relationship: X is correlated with Y; 2. Temporal precedence: X precedes Y in time; 3. Non-spuriousness: The $X-Y$ relationship holds even when the influences of other possible variables on this relationship are eliminated so that the effect can be said to have been isolated. In the current study, in terms of relationship (condition 1), there is a nonzero association between X and Y (e.g. conscientiousness and NPD performance). However, future research could establish temporal precedence (condition 2), by gathering data on staff personal style variables at time 1, and NPD performance data at time 2 using a longitudinal research design. Yet, it is noteworthy that Cohen and colleagues add that temporal precedence could be established on the basis of theory as well. Interestingly, several meta-analyses report that, for example, conscientiousness is related to performance outcomes across jobs [e.g. Barrick and Mount (1991); Barrick et al. (2001); Salgado (1997)]. Researchers also show that agreeableness is vital in team-based contexts [e.g. Aronoff and Wilson (1985); Costa and McCrae (1989)]. Finally, to establish non-spuriousness, these future longitudinal studies could be designed to remove the influence of possible extraneous factors that may affect the outcome variable, NPD performance. Taken together, future research designed in this way can strengthen the empirical conditions for inferring causality.

Fifth, future investigations might also explore narrow personality traits (e.g. autonomy, tough-mindedness, optimism, team-mindedness). Research suggests that there is incremental validity of narrow traits above and beyond the Big-Five traits [e.g. Dudley et al. (2006)]. Yet, interestingly, it seems that the degree to which the narrow traits contribute depends on the particular performance criterion and occupation in question. Upcoming studies could investigate the contribution of narrow personal style traits to performance for NPD professionals working in radical and incremental innovation teams.

Sixth, although other models of individual difference styles exist, such as Holland's Vocational Interests, recent meta-analyses reveal the overlap with the Big-Five Personal style factors [e.g. Larson et al. (2002)]. Larson and colleagues examine the overlap of the three most widely used measures of Holland's big six domains of vocational interest, namely the Self-directed Search [Holland (1985a)], the Strong Interest Inventory [Hansen and Campbell (1985); Harmon *et al.* (1994)], and the Vocational Preference Inventory [Holland (1985b)], with the Big-Five Personal Style Factors. Larson and colleagues show the similarity between Holland's Vocational Interests and the Big-Five Personal Style Factors respectively for artistic–openness to experience, enterprising–extraversion, social–extraversion, investigative–openness, and social–agreeableness.

Seventh, it is noteworthy that some personal styles might change throughout long term projects, by experience or over other lengthy periods of time. Although a couple of personality factors, such as agreeableness and conscientiousness, tend to increase over long periods of time between ages 20 and 60, little change occurs in other personal styles, such as openness-to-experience, a key personality style we centered on, among people over the ages of 20 [e.g. Whetten and Cameron (2016)]. In the current study, NPD project members' age was over 20 years. Nevertheless, future research might gather additional information on the duration of the long-term projects and collect more data on team members' personal style at project initiation as well as at the conclusion of the project, in order to control for possible changes in team member individual differences.

Eighth, future studies might examine other variables (e.g. values) that could mediate the relationship between staff personal style and NPD performance. For example, Open staff members are open to new ideas, emphasize the importance of seeking differing perspectives when solving problems, use non-traditional thinking to deal with traditional problems and are open to criticism. These behaviors are central to norms and values associated with an adaptive culture [Aronson and Lechler (2009); Kotter and Heskett (1992)], and in turn should influence NPD performance when uncertainty is high.

5.3. *Practical implications*

For organizations, the decision to develop innovations carries significant implications. One implication is for firms to consider measuring the personal style of their NPD professionals, in addition to considering their functional expertise. Once this is done, companies might use the personal style assessments to make selection decisions when assigning employees to NPD teams. For example, it makes sense that organizations establish threshold levels of conscientiousness for employees who are being considered to be a part of NPD teams. Additionally, minimum levels of agreeableness might be established as selection criteria for these individuals, detailed earlier. Our findings also show that depending on the type of innovation, certain personal style variables might be more important for NPD performance. The current study's results might imply that selecting NPD staff members who are high on openness and emotional stability can be important when innovation is radical, and could differentiate between successful and unsuccessful NPD projects when it comes to the speed the NPD project is completed. What is more, it seems that having NPD staff members who are high on agreeableness does not appear to be important when new ideas are being developed, since it could lead to failure to challenge ideas as frequently, leading to less successful innovation. These highly agreeable individuals could be counseled, as elaborated below, to recognize situations where challenging the status quo is beneficial even though it may be contrary to their highly agreeable nature. It is noteworthy that our sample for radical and incremental NPD showed no significant difference in means for any of the staff personal style variables, suggesting that there might be considerable room for improvement, by using personal style in addition to functional expertise to assign employees to different types of NPD teams.

A second type of application is developmental in nature. An understanding of the personal style characteristics of staff assigned to NPD teams should allow superior developmental planning and coaching of these employees. For example, highly open staff members could be selected to be a part of a radical NPD team, operating under conditions of uncertainty. Since radical NPD frequently involves a great deal of learning and improvising, the selected employees who are high on openness can be trained to use this asset to learn more about the markets and the technical issues necessary to successfully bring the product to market in a timely fashion. Given that NPD teams need to obtain resources such as necessary talent, and larger budgets for the team, open individuals could be guided to use their skill to suggest novel strategies for obtaining these resources, perhaps helping to reduce the time it takes to complete the NPD project. These highly open individuals can also be coached to use their strength on trial and error research tasks that require maintaining flexibility and learning through experience, conceivably resulting in successfully launching the radical NPD project at or ahead of schedule.

5.4. *Conclusion*

This study contributes to our knowledge of NPD staff, in that it demonstrates relationships between the Big-Five personal style traits and NPD performance, for teams developing radical and incremental innovations. The current study provides evidence that, for NPD staff members, threshold levels of conscientiousness and agreeableness can be important for NPD performance. Our data also suggest that considering the type of innovation, certain staff personal style variables may be more valuable than others, depending on the specific NPD performance criteria. For NPD speed, our findings suggest that radical NPD might benefit from more open and stable staff. Furthermore, having team members who are highly agreeable does not seem to be helpful when new ideas are being developed, since it could lead to groupthink, leading to less successful innovation. It is notable that our sample for radical and incremental NPD showed no significant difference in means for any of the staff personal style variables, suggesting that there might be considerable room for improvement, by using personal style in addition to functional expertise to assign employees to different types of NPD teams.

References

Altman, I. and Haythorn, W. W. (1967). The effects of social isolation and group composition on performance. *Human Relations*, **20**: 313–340.

Amason, A. C. (1996). Distinguishing the effects of functional and dysfunctional conflict on strategic decision making: Resolving a paradox for top management teams. *Academy of Management Journal*, **39**, 1: 123–148.

Ansoff, H. I. (1965). *Corporate Strategy*. McGraw-Hill, New York.

Ansoff, H. I. (1988). *The New Corporate Strategy*. John Wiley and Sons, New York.

Aronoff, J. and Wilson, J. P. (1985). *Personality in the Social Process*. Erlbaum, Hillsdale, NJ.

Aronson, Z. H. (1998). The validities of situationally framed personality ratings: An examination of self and peer ratings. Doctoral Dissertation, Stevens Institute of Technology, Hoboken, NJ.

Aronson, Z. H. and Lechler, T. (2009). Contributing beyond the call of duty: The role of culture in fostering citizenship and success in project-based work. *R&D Management*, **39**, 5: 461–480.

Aronson, Z. H. and Reilly, R. R. (2006). Personality validity: The role of schemas and motivated reasoning. *International Journal of Selection and Assessment*, **14**, 4: 372–380.

Aronson, Z. H., Reilly, R. R. and Lynn, G. S. (2006). The impact of leader personality on NPD teamwork and performance: The moderating role of uncertainty. *Journal of Engineering and Technology Management*, **23**: 221–247.

Aronson, Z. H., Reilly, R. R. and Lynn, G. S. (2008). The role of leader personality in new product development success: An examination of teams developing radical and incremental innovations. *International Journal of Technology Management*, **44**, 1/2: 5–27.

Atuahene-Gima, K. (2003). The effects of centrifugal and centripetal forces on product development speed and quality: How does problem solving matter? *Academy of Management Journal*, **46**, 3: 359.

Aviolo, B. J., Yammarino, F. J. and Bass, B. M. (1991). Identifying common methods variance with data collected from a single source: An unresolved sticky issue. *Journal of Management*, **17**: 571–587.

Barrick, M. R. and Mount, M. K. (1991). The Big Five personality dimensions and job performance: A meta-analysis. *Personnel Psychology*, **44**: 1–26.

Barrick, M. R. and Mount, M. K. (1993). Autonomy as a moderator of the relationship between the Big Five personality dimensions and job performance. *Journal of Psychology*, **78**: 111–118.

Barrick, M. R., Mount, M. K. and Judge, T. A. (2001). Personality and performance at the beginning of the new millennium: What do we know and where do we go next [Special issue]. *International Journal of Selection and Assessment*, **9**: 9–30.

Barrick, M. R., Stewart, G. L., Neubert, M. J. and Mount, M. K. (1998). Relating member ability and personality to work-team processes and team effectiveness. *Journal of Applied Psychology*, **83**, 3: 377–391.

Barrick, M. R., Stewart, G. L. and Piotrowski, M. (2002). Personality and job performance: Test of the mediating effects of motivation among sales representatives. *Journal of Applied Psychology*, **87**, 1: 43–51.

Barczak, G. and Wilemon, D. (1989). Leadership differences in new product development teams. *Journal of Product Innovation Management*, **6**: 259–267.

Barczak, G. and Wilemon, D. (1991). Communications patterns of new product development team leaders. *IEEE Transactions on Engineering Management*, **38**, 2: 101–109.

Barry, B. and Stewart, G. L. (1997). Composition, process, and performance in self-managed groups: The role of personality. *Journal of Applied Psychology*, **82**, 1: 62–78.

Bateman, T. S. and Crant, J. M. (1993). The proactive component of organizational behavior: A measure and correlates. *Journal of Organizational Behavior*, **14**: 103–118.

Boston Consulting Group (2006). The world's most innovative companies. Business Week Online, Special report — Innovation, April 24.

Bouchard, T. J., Jr. (1969). Personality, problem solving procedure, and performance in small groups. *Journal of Applied Psychology Monograph*, **53**: 1–29.

Bouchard, T. J., Jr. (1972). Training, motivation, and personality as determinants of the effectiveness of brainstorming groups and individuals. *Journal of Applied Psychology*, **56**: 324–331.

Boudreau, J. W., Boswell, W. R., Judge, T. A. and Bretz, Jr. R. D. (2001). Personality and cognitive ability as predictors of job search among employed managers. *Personnel Psychology*, **54**, 1: 25–50.

Brown, S. L. and Eisenhardt, K. M. (1995). Product development: Past research, present findings and future research. *Academy of Management Review*, **20**, 2: 343–378.

Burchfield, M. (1997). Personality composition as it relates to team performance. Doctoral Dissertation, Stevens Institute of Technology, Hoboken, NJ.

Calantone, R. J. and Di Benedetto, C. A. (2000). Performance and time to market: Accelerating cycle time with overlapping stages. *IEEE Transactions on Engineering Management*, **47**, 2: 232–244.

Chen, J., Damanpour, F. and Reilly, R. R. (2010). Understanding antecedents of new product development speed: A meta-analysis. *Journal of Operations Management*, **28**: 17–33.

Chen, J., Reilly, R. R. and Lynn, G. S. (2005). The impacts of speed-to-market on new product success: The moderating effects of uncertainty. *IEEE Transactions on Engineering Management*, **52**, 2: 199–212.

Cohen, J. (1988). *Statistical Power Analysis for the Behavioral Sciences* (2nd edn.). Erlbaum, Mahwah, NJ.

Cohen, S. G. and Bailey, D. E. (1997). What makes teams work? Group effectiveness research from the shop floor to the executive suite. *Journal of Management*, **23**, 3: 239–290.

Cohen, J., Cohen, P., West, S. G. and Aiken, L. (2003). Applied multiple regression/correlation analysis for the behavioral science. Lawrence Erlbaum Associates, Mahwah, NJ.

Costa, P. T. and McCrae, R. R. (1985). *The NEO-PI Personality Inventory*. Professional manual. Psychological Assessment Resources, Odessa, FL.

Costa, P. T. and McCrae, R. R. (1989). *The NEO-PI/NEO-FFI Manual Supplement*. Psychological Assessment Resources, Odessa, FL.

Costa, P. T. and McCrae, R. R. (1992). *Revised NEO Personality Inventory (NEO-PIR-I) and NEO Five-Factor-Inventory (NEO-FFI)*. Professional manual. Psychological Assessment Resources, Odessa, FL.

Cote, J. A. and Buckley, R. (1987). Estimating trait, method, and error variance: Generalizing across 70 construct validation studies. *Journal of Marketing Research*, **24**: 315–318.

Crant, J. M. and Bateman, T. S. (2000). Proactive behavior in organizations. *Journal of Management*, **26**: 435–465.

Crutchfield, R. S. (1955). Conformity and character. *American Psychologist*, **10**: 191–198.

Day, D. V. and Silverman, S. B. (1989). Personality and job performance: Evidence of incremental validity. *Personnel Psychology*, **42**: 25–36.

DeBiasio, A. R. (1986). Problem solving in triads composed of varying numbers of field-dependent and field-independent subjects. *Journal of Personality and Social Psychology*, **51**: 749–754.

Driskell, J. E., Hogan, R. and Salas, E. (1988). Personality and group performance. *Review of Personality and Social Psychology*, **14**: 91–112.

Driskell, J. E. and Salas, E. (1992). Collective behavior and team performance. *Human Factors*, **34**: 277–288.

Driskell, J. E., Salas, E. and Hogan, R. (1987). Taxonomy for composing effective naval teams. (Tech. Rep. No. TR87002). Naval Training Systems Center, Orlando, FL.

Dudley, N. M., Orvis, K. A., Lebiecki, J. E. and Cortina, J. M. (2006). Meta-analytic investigation of conscientiousness in the prediction of job performance: Examining the intercorrelations and the incremental validity of narrow traits. *Journal of Applied Psychology*, **91**, 1: 40–57.

Dumaine, B. (1989). How managers can succeed through SPEED. *Fortune*, **119**, 4: 54–59.

Eisenhardt, K. M. and Tabrizi, B. N. (1995). Accelerating adaptive processes: Product innovation in the global computer industry. *Administrative Science Quarterly*, **40**: 84–110.

Emmanuelides, P. A. (1993). Towards an integrative framework of performance in product development projects. *Journal of Engineering and Technology Management*, **10**, 4: 363–392.

Gemünden, H. G., Salomo, S. and Krieger, A. (2005). The influence of project autonomy on project success. *International Journal of Project Management*, **23**: 366–373.

George, J. M. and Bettenhausen, K. (1990). Understanding prosocial behavior, sales performance and turnover. *Journal of Applied Psychology*, **75**: 698–709.

Goldberg, L. R. (1992). The development of markers of the Big Five factor structure. *Psychological Assessment*, **4**: 26–42.

Greer, F. L. (1955). Small group effectiveness. Institute Report No. 6. Institute for Research on Human Relations, Philadelphia.

Griffin, A. (2002). Product development cycle time for business-to-business products. *Industrial Marketing Management*, **31**, 4: 291–304.

Gurnee, H. (1937). Maze learning in the collective situation. *Journal of Psychology*, **3**: 437–443.

Gupta, A. K., Brockhoff, K. and Weisenfeld, U. (1992). Making trade-offs in the new product development process: A German/US comparison. *Journal of Product Innovation Management*, **9**, 1: 11–18.

Guzzo, R. A., Yost, P. R., Campbell, R. J. and Shea, G. P. (1993). Potency in groups: Articulating a construct. *British Journal of Social Psychology*, **32**: 87–106.

Hansen, J. C. and Campbell, D. P. (1985). *Manual for the SVIB-SCII* (4th edn.). Stanford University Press, Stanford, CA.

Harmon, L. W., Hansen, J. C., Borgen, F. H. and Hammer, A. L. (1994). *Strong Interest Inventory: Applications and Technical Guide*. Stanford University Press, Stanford, CA.

Harter, D. E., Krishnan, M. S. and Slaughter, S. A. (2000). Effects of process maturity on quality, cycle time, and effort in software product development. *Management Science*, **46**, 4: 451–466.

Haythorn, W. (1953). The influence of individual members on the characteristics of small groups. *Journal of Abnormal and Social Psychology*, **48**: 276–284.

Hoegl, M., Weinkauf, K. and Gemuenden, H. G. (2004). Interteam coordination, project commitment, and teamwork in multiteam R&D projects: A longitudinal study. *Organization Science*, **15**, 1: 38–55.

Hogan, J. and Hogan, R. (1989). Noncognitive predictors of performance during explosive ordinance disposal training. *Military Psychology*, **1**: 117–133.

Holland, J. L. (1985a). *Self-Directed Search*. Psychological Assessment Resources, Odessa, FL.

Holland, J. L. (1985b). *Manual for the Vocational Preference Inventory*. Psychological Assessment Resources, Odessa FL.

Hough, L. M. (1992). "The Big Five" personality variables–construct confusion: Description versus prediction. *Human Performance*, **5**: 139–155.

Hurtz, G. M. and Donovan, J. J. (2000). Personality and job performance: The Big Five revisited. *Journal of Applied Psychology*, **85**: 869–879.

Imai, K., Ikujiro, N. and Takeuchi, H. (1985). Managing the new product development process: How Japanese companies learn and unlearn. *The Uneasy Alliance: Managing the Productivity-Technology Dilemma*, eds. K. B. Clark, R. H. Hayes and C. Lorenz, Harvard Business School Press, Boston, pp. 937–375.

Janis, I. L. (1972). *Groupthink*. Houghton Muffin, Boston.

Jehn, K. (1995). A multimethod examination of the benefits and detriments of intragroup conflict. *Administrative Science Quarterly*, **40**: 256–282.

Judge, T. A., Bono, E. J., Ilies, R. and Gerhardt, M. (2002). Personality and leadership: A qualitative and quantitative review. *Journal of Applied Psychology*, **87**, 4: 765–780.

Karau, S. J. and Williams, K. D. (1993). Social loafing: A meta-analytic review and theoretical integration. *Journal of Personality and Social Psychology*, **65**, 4: 681–706.

Katz, R. and Tushman, M. L. (1981). An investigation into the managerial roles and career paths of gatekeepers and project supervisors in a major R&D facility. *R&D Management*, **11**: 103–110.

Keller, R. T. (1986). Predictors of the performance of project groups in R&D organizations. *Academy of Management Journal*, **29**: 715–726.

Keller, R. T. (1997). Job involvement and organizational commitment as longitudinal predictors of job performance: A study of scientists and engineers. *Journal of Applied Psychology*, **82**: 539–545.

Keller, R. T. (2001). Cross-functional project groups in research and new product development: Diversity, communications, job stress, and outcomes. *Academy of Management Journal*, **44**, 3: 547–555.

Kessler, E. H. and Chakrabarti, A. K. (1996). Innovation speed: A conceptual model of context, antecedents and outcomes. *Academy Management Journal*, **21**, 4: 1143–1191.

Kichuk, S. L. and Wiesner, W. H. (1997). The Big Five personality factors and team performance: Implications for selecting successful product design teams. *Journal of Engineering and Technology Management*, **14**: 195–221.

Kirkman, B. L. and Rosen, B. (1999). Beyond self management: Antecedents and consequences of team empowerment. *Academy of Management Journal*, **42**: 58–74.

Klein, K. J. and Kozlowski, S. W. J. (2000). *Multilevel Theory, Research and Methods in Organizations*. Jossey-Bass, San Francisco.

Kotter, J. P. and Heskett, J. L. (1992). *Corporate Culture and Performance*. Free Press, New York.

Lambert, D. and Slater, S. F. (1999). Perspective: First, fast, and on time: The path to success or is it? *Journal of Product Innovation Management*, **16**, 5: 427–438.

Larson, L. M., Rottinghaus, P. J. and Borgen, F. H. (2002). Meta-analyses of Big Six Interests and Big Five Personality Factors. *Journal of Vocational Behavior*, **61**: 217–239.

LePine, J. A., Hollenbeck, J. R., Ilgen, D. R. and Hedlund, J. (1997). Effects of individual differences on the performance of hierarchical decision-making teams: Much more than g. *Journal of Applied Psychology*, **82**: 803–811.

Lindner, S. J. (1998). Generalizability and validity of behaviorally-based measurement of the Big-Five personality traits. Doctoral Dissertation, Stevens Institute of Technology, Hoboken, NJ.

Lukas, B. A. and Ferrell, O. C. (2000). The effect of market orientation on product innovation. *Journal of the Academy of Marketing Science*, **28**: 239–247.

Lukas, B. A., Menon, A. and Bell, S. J. (2002). Organizing for new product development speed and the implications for organizational stress. *Industrial Marketing Management*, **31**, 4: 349–355.

Lynn, G. S. and Akgun, A. E. (1998). Innovation strategies under uncertainty: A contingency approach for new product development. *Engineering Management Journal*, **10**, 3: 11–17.

Lynn, G. S., Morone, J. and Paulson, A. (1996). Marketing and discontinuous innovation: The probe and learn process. *California Management Review*, **38**, 3: 8–37.

Lynn, G. S., Reilly, R. R. and Akgun, A. E. (2000). Knowledge management in new product teams: Practices and outcomes. *IEEE Transactions on Engineering Management*, **47**: 221–231.

McCrae, R. R. (1987). Creativity, divergent thinking and openness to experience. *Journal of Personality and Social Psychology*, **52**: 1258–1265.

McCrae, R. R. (1996). Social consequences of experiential openness. *Psychological Bulletin*, **120**: 323–337.

McCrae, R. R. and Costa, P. T. (1996). Toward a new generation of personality theories: Theoretical contexts for the five-factor model. *The Five-factor Model of Personality*, ed. J. S. Wiggins, Guilford Press, New York, pp. 81–91.

McCrae, R. R. and Costa, P. T. Jr. (1989). A five-factor theory of personality. *Handbook of Personality Theory and Research*, eds. L. A. Pervin and O. P. John, Guilford Press, New York.

Meyer, M. H. and Utterback, J. M. (1995). Product development cycle time and commercial success. *IEEE Transactions on Engineering Management*, **42**: 297–304.

Moriarty, R. T. and Kosnik, T. J. (1990). High-tech concept, continuity, and change. *IEEE Engineering Management Review*, **3**: 25–35.

Morgan, B. B., Jr. and Lassiter, D. L. (1992). Team composition and staffing. *Teams: Their Training and Performance*, eds. R. W. Swezey and E. Salas, Ablex Publishing, Norwood, NJ, pp. 76–100.

Mount, M. K, Barrick, M. R. and Strauss, J. P. (1994). Validity of observer ratings of the Big Five personality factors. *Journal of Applied Psychology*, **79**, 2: 272–280.

Neuman, G. A. and Wright, J. (1999). Team effectiveness: Beyond skills and cognitive ability. *Journal of Applied Psychology*, **84**: 376–389.

O'Connor, G. C. and Veryzer, R. W. (2001). The nature of market visioning for technology-based radical innovation. *Journal of Product Innovation Management*, **18**: 231–246.

Oser, R. L., McCallum, G. A., Salas, E. and Morgan, B. B., Jr. (1989). Toward a definition of team work: An analysis of critical team behavior (NTSC Tech. Rep. No. 89–018). Naval Training Systems Center, Orlando, FL.

Peeters, M. A., Van Tuijl, H. F., Rutte, C. G. and Reymen, I. M. (2006). Personality and team performance: A meta-analysis. *European Journal of Personality*, **20**, 5: 377–396.

Podsakoff, P. M. and Organ, D. (1986). Self-reporting in organizational research: Problems and prospects. *Journal of Management*, **12**: 531–544.

Porter, M. E. (1985). *Competitive Advantage: Creating and Sustaining Superior Performance.* Free Press, New York, NY.

Reilly, R. R., Lynn, G. S. and Aronson, Z. H. (2002). The role of personality in new product development team performance. *Journal of Engineering and Technology Management*, **19**: 39–58.

Rosenbloom, R. S. and Cusumano, M. A. (1987). Technical pioneering and competitive advantage: The birth of the VCR industry. *California Management Review*, **29**, 4: 51–76.

Salgado, J. F. (1997). The five factor model of personality and job performance in the European community. *Journal of Applied Psychology*, **82**: 30–43.

Salgado, J. (2002). The Big Five personality dimensions and counterproductive behaviors. *International Journal of Selection and Assessment*, **10**, 1–2: 117–125.

Schneider, F. W. and Delaney, J. G. (1972). Effect of individual achievement motivation on group problem solving efficiency. *Journal of Social Psychology*, **86**: 291–298.

Schutz, W. D. (1955). What makes groups productive? *Human Relations*, **8**: 429–465.

Shaw, M. E. and Harkey, B. (1976). Some effects of congruency of member characteristics and group structure upon group behavior. *Journal of Personality and Social Psychology*, **34**: 412–418.

Shenhar, A. J., Dvir, D., Guth, W., Lechler, T., Panatakul, P., Poli, M. *et al.* (2005). Project strategy: The missing link. Paper presented at the *Academy of Management Annual Conference*, Hawaii.

Smith, P. G. and Reinertsen, D. G. (1997). *Developing Products in Half the Time: New Rules, New Tools* (2nd edn.). John Wiley and Sons, New York.

Stalk, G. J. and Hout, T. M. (1990). *Competing Against Time: How Time-based Competition is Reshaping Global Markets*. The Free Press, New York.

Stevens, G., Burley, J. and Divine, R. (1999). Creativity + business discipline = higher profits faster from new product development. *Journal of Product Innovation Management*, **16**, 5: 455–468.

Strang, D. K. (2011). Leadership substitutes and personality impact on time and quality in virtual new product development projects. *Project Management Journal*, **42**, 1: 73–90.

Strube, M. J., Keller, N. R., Oxenburg, J. and Lapido, D. (1989). Actual and perceived group performance as a function of group composition: The moderating role of type A and B behavior patterns. *Journal of Applied Social Psychology*, **19**: 140–158.

Tett, R. P., Jackson, D. N. and Rothstein, M. (1991). Personality measures as predictors of performance: A meta-analytic review. *Personnel Psychology*, **44**: 703–742.

Tett, R. P., Jackson, D. N., Rothstein, M. and Reddon, J. R. (1994). Meta-analysis of personality and job performance relations: A reply to Ones, Mount, Barrick, and Hunter. *Personnel Psychology*, **47**: 157–171.

Tellis, G. J. and Golder, P. N. (2001). *Will and Vision: How Latecomers Grow to Dominate Markets*. McGraw-Hill, New York.

Thoms, P., Moore, K. S. and Scott, K. S. (1996). The relationship between self efficacy for participating in self-managed work groups and the big five personality dimensions. *Journal of Organizational Behavior*, **17**: 349–362.

Tuckman, B. W. (1967). Group composition and group performance of structured and unstructured tasks. *Journal of Experimental Social Psychology*, **3**: 25–49.

Tushman, M. P. and Anderson, P. (1986). Technological discontinuities and organizational environments. *Administrative Science Quarterly*, **31**: 439–465.

Veryzer, R. W. J. (1998). Key factors affecting customer evaluation of discontinuous new products. *Journal of Product Innovation Management*, **15**: 136–150.

Watson, D. and Tellegen, A. (1985). Toward a consensual structure of mood. *Psychological Bulletin*, **98**: 219–235.

Wiggins, J. S. (1996). *The Five Factor Model of Personality*. Guilford Press, New York.

Wheelwright, S. C. and Clark, K. B. (1992). *Revolutionizing Product Development: Quantum Leaps in Speed, Efficiency Quality*. Free Press, New York.

Whetten, D. A. and Cameron, K. S. (2016). *Developing Management Skills* (9th edn.). Pearson, Upper Saddle River, NJ.

Zander, A. and Forward, J. (1968). Position in group, achievement orientation, and group aspirations. *Personality and Social Psychology*, **8**: 282–288.

Zirger, B. J. and Hartley, J. L. (1994). A conceptual model of product development cycle time. *Journal of Engineering and Technology Management*, **11**: 229–251.

Appendix A. Five-Item Measure of the Big-Five Personal Style Traits

(1) Conscientiousness: The extent to which NPD staff members are careful, thorough, responsible, organized, self-disciplined, scrupulous (Conscientious) versus irresponsible, disorganized, undisciplined, unscrupulous (Unconscientious).

Please place an "X" in the cells that best capture the distribution of your NPD staff members on conscientious:

Description	Highly conscientious	Somewhat conscientious	Neither conscientious nor unconscientious	Somewhat unconscientious	Highly unconscientious
% Must Total 100%	%(1)	___%(2)	—%(3)	___%(4)	—%(5)

(2) Agreeableness: The extent to which NPD staff members are good-natured, gentle, cooperative, forgiving, hopeful (Agreeable) versus irritable, ruthless, suspicious, uncooperative, inflexible (Disagreeable).

Please place an "X" in the cells that best capture the distribution of your NPD staff members on agreeableness:

Description	Highly agreeable	Somewhat agreeable	Neither agreeable nor disagreeable	Somewhat disagreeable	Highly disagreeable
% Must Total 100%	___%(1)	—%(2)	___%(3)	—%(4)	___%(5)

(3) Extroversion-Introversion: the extent to which NPD staff members are sociable, talkative, assertive, active (Extroverted) versus retiring, sober, reserved, cautious (Introverted).

Please place an "X" in the cells that best capture the distribution of your NPD staff members on extraversion:

Description	Highly extroverted	Somewhat extroverted	Neither extroverted nor introverted	Somewhat introverted	Highly introverted
% Must Total 100%	—%(1)	—%(2)	—%(3)	—%(4)	—%(5)

(4) Openness: The extent to which team members are imaginative, sensitive, intellectual, polished (Open) versus down to earth, insensitive, narrow, crude, simple (Unopen).

Please place an "X" in the cells that best capture the distribution of your NPD staff members on openness:

Description	Highly open	Somewhat open	Neither open nor unopen	Somewhat unopen	Highly unopen
% Must Total 100%	—%(1)	—%(2)	—%(3)	—%(4)	—%(5)

(5) Emotional stability: The extent to which team members are calm, enthusiastic, poised, secure (Stable) versus depressed, angry, emotional, insecure (Unstable).

Please place an "X" in the cells that best capture the distribution of your NPD staff members on emotional stability:

Description	Highly stable	Somewhat stable	Neither stable nor unstable	Somewhat unstable	Highly unstable
% Must Total 100%	—%(1)	—%(2)	—%(3)	—%(4)	—%(5)

Biography

Zvi H. Aronson is affiliate Associate Professor at the School of Business, Stevens Institute of Technology, USA. Dr. Aronson's interests center on the behavioral aspects of innovation and technology management. Zvi joined the Editorial Board of *IEEE Transactions on Engineering Management* in 2018. His research is focused on the behavioral features of project leader and team performance and on the role played by culture in project-based contexts. Implications are for identifying levers available to the project leader to alter culture and motivate workers and how they affect success in project-based work. Zvi's work appears in several journals including *R&D Management*, the *International Journal of Selection and Assessment*, *Project Management Journal*, the *Journal of Engineering and Technology Management*, *Journal of High Technology Management Research*, the *International Journal of Technology Management* and in several book chapters. A book to which Zvi contributed a chapter, on managing contextual performance, received the R. Wayne Pace Book of the Year Award from the Academy of Human Resource Management, USA. He received the best paper award from the *International Journal of Innovation and Technology Management*. Dr. Aronson spearheaded the Stevens' Institute Review Board for the protection of human subject in research. Zvi is the Heath

Lecture Series Lead. Prior to joining Stevens' faculty, he was employed at Bakara Ltd., Israel, where he conducted research in the areas of training and selection and provided software instruction to clients.

Richard R. Reilly is emeritus Professor at the School of Business, Stevens Institute of Technology, USA. He received his PhD from the University of Tennessee at Knoxville. Before joining Stevens, he was a Research Psychologist for Bell Laboratories, the Educational Testing Service and AT&T. He has developed and delivered courses in project and team leadership and recently headed a team that won a grant from the Project Management Institute for the human side of project management. He has over 60 publications related to organizational behavior and team performance. Recent publications include *Blockbusters: The Five Keys to Developing Great New Products*, HarperCollins, 2002; How to build a blockbuster (Boston, MA, *Harvard Business Review*, 2002). He is a Fellow of the American Psychological Association and the American Psychological Society. He is on the Editorial Board of Personnel Psychology.

Gary S. Lynn is a Full Professor at Stevens Institute of Technology. Dr. Lynn has authored or co-authored five books and over 60 refereed publications at the intersection of technology, marketing, entrepreneurship and new product development. Dr. Lynn has 10 years of industrial experience; he started, built and sold three companies. He was formerly a technical design and marketing specialist at the General Electric Company, where he designed components of aircraft engines, held a "Secret" security clearance, and developed and implemented commercialization plans for high-technology products including robotics, numerical and programmable controls, artificial vision systems and CAD/CAM equipment. Dr. Lynn was also Director of New Product and Market Development for the Guardian Products Division of Sunrise Medical where he conducted trade negotiations with the Minister of Economics in Taiwan and the Minister of Trade in the Philippines.

Chapter 8

The New Manufacturing: In Search of the Origins of the Next Generation Manufacturing Start-Ups

Xavier Ferrás-Hernández[*], Albert Armisen-Morell[†], Anna Sabata-Alberich[‡],
Elisenda Tarrats-Pons[§] and Núria Arimany-Serrat[¶]

University of Vic – Central University of Catalonia
C/Sagrada Familia 7, 08500, Vic (Barcelona, Spain)
[*]*xavier.ferras@uvic.cat*
[†]*albert.armisen@uvic.cat*
[‡]*anna.sabata@uvic.cat*
[§]*elisenda.tarrats@uvic.cat*
[¶]*nuria.arimany@uvic.cat*

Manufacturing is undergoing a deep model change due to the convergence of several forces: (a) the simultaneous emergence of new disruptive technologies, (b) the accelerated substitution of men by machines, (c) the restructuring of global competition, with the consolidation of some global manufacturing clusters, and (d) a new market dynamic dominated by a growing consumer power. Much has been said about how industries adapt to these forces (a widely known example is the so-called "industry 4.0" paradigm). Scholarly literature states that, in moments of accelerated technological change and industry effervescence, new technology-based firms play a critical role in reshaping the markets and reconfiguring competition. Yet, little has been said in the literature about the features of new manufacturing start-ups. Our aim is to explore the origins of the new technological firms that are emerging in the manufacturing industry. To do so, we have created a database of 184 manufacturing start-ups, incepted since 2013, and which have attracted some US $2.4 billion in total funding; of these firms, we have analyzed a set of 291 founders' profiles, looking for their backgrounds and previous experiences. Our findings suggest that promising new manufacturing technology-based firms are created mainly by teams formed by experienced managers and experts with solid scientific or technological backgrounds.

Keywords: Manufacturing; startups; entrepreneurship; high tech industries; innovation.

---

*Corresponding author.

This chapter was originally published in *International Journal of Innovation and Technology Management*, Vol. 16, No. 2, July 2018, published by World Scientific Publishing, Singapore. Reprinted with permission.

1. Introduction

The manufacturing industry has been at the heart of industrial capitalism of the twentieth century; it creates strong territorial value chains in multiple industries, such as chemical, pharmaceutical, automotive, electronics, and textiles, which have consolidated the middle class, supported democracies, and boosted economic development as well as the well-being of most advanced economies. Manufacturing has been the cornerstone of an economic model that has prevailed since Henry Ford invented the mass production paradigm; it is a vital source of economic and social progress, and comparatively generates high wages. It is an exporter of good management practices, and is the great engine of technological innovation in developed economies. Even today, in the US, manufacturing employees earn 20% more than the national average. Manufacturing accounts for 75% of private R&D investment, for 60% of jobs in R&D, and for most of the US patents, although it creates only 12% of US GDP. In addition, manufacturing activity generates a large number of positive externalities, since the accumulated know-how in the industry is the source of world class management practices and product design leadership [National Economic Council (2016)].

However, manufacturing today is in a process of deep transformation, driven by technological change, which is the origin of the rapid globalization and expansion of plant automation. This transformation is also due to the phenomenon of the internet, which democratizes information and gives the consumer a growing bargaining power. A swarm of new disruptive technologies, digital in nature, is invading the economy today, affecting strategies and structures of manufacturing. According to scholarly literature, when such a kind of phenomena happens, there is a window of opportunity created for entrepreneurs. Young and new technology-based firms (NTBFs) become the carriers of technological disruption. Much has been said about the new manufacturing paradigm, where supply chains gain new competences and configurations thanks to digitization, and about how incumbents adapt to the new rules of the game (in what has been called "digital transformation"). There is also a wide stream of engineering literature on the technologies that affect new manufacturing supply chains, yet few have been researched in terms of the features and origins of the next-generation NTBFs: who they are, where they come from, and who their founders are. Our aim is to shed light on these very questions.

2. Time for a Model Change

Manufacturing is changing rapidly due to the confluence of different factors originated by rapid technological change and the globalizing process of the markets. Among them, the emergence of disruptive technologies of exponentially increasing levels of performance, the intensive robotization of production lines, the reconfiguration of global competition (with the deployment of national strategies that affect manufacturing strategies and structures), and the necessary adaptation of manufacturing companies to increasingly dynamic markets.

The emergence of a set of technologies with disruptive potential that affect the entire value chain (advanced materials, 3D printing, internet of things, big data, artificial intelligence, or new energy techniques) is changing the whole strategy of global manufacturing. Critical disruptive technologies have arrived together, simultaneously, in a convergent way, and with mutual reinforcement to each other. At the base of all of them, lays a great transversal enabling technology: digitization, which fosters exponential growth for the rest of the technologies. As the old industrial value chains are digitized, they are subjected to Moore's famous law, according to which the computing power of electronic processors, and their memory storage capacity double every 2 years [Schaller (1997)]. This law of exponential growth in the performance of digitized processes (indeed, an empirical observation, not of course a natural law) underlies most of the emerging disruptive technologies that are being introduced into the manufacturing supply chains today. Digitization, the interconnection and permanent communication between devices (internet of things) enable the design and deployment of digitally "smart" data-driven factories. Big data enables the improvement of predictive processes in quality, maintenance, and production planning, as well as their mathematical optimization. The incorporation of ever increasing layers of artificial intelligence, fueled by cognitive computing, deep learning, and machine learning algorithms allows greater autonomy, reliability, and speed in decision-making, and permits a self-learning feedback that entails systematic improvement of productivity, effectiveness, and efficiency in the whole supply chain. The possibilities of part customization thanks to additive manufacturing (better known as "3D Printing") positively affect the speed and quality of prototypes created (accelerating innovation lifecycles), fostering drastic stock reduction (with a growing number of parts and components to be printed in any point, in real time, without the need for spare parts in the warehouses), and enabling personalization in the supply chain, moving ever closer to the final consumer (or even at the final point of sale). Additive manufacturing also makes the production of short or very short series economically efficient, enabling the production of high value parts at very low volumes, which was impossible or nonviable so far. On the other hand, product and process development can be simulated virtually through digital software before its physical implementation, reducing errors, costs, and time-to-market. The so-called "business digital transformation" is a phenomenon induced by numerous digitally disruptive technologies, affecting virtually all business processes, reconfiguring the supply chain and making it an efficient data-processing machine. Integrated, digitized, and increasingly intelligent supply chains become more dynamic, adaptive, and capable of combining the competitive advantages of mass and craft production at the same time, thereby offering greater flexibility, speed, and customization at a very low cost [Weller *et al.* (2015); McKinsey (2017)].

The extension of robotization, with the change in the nature of the work entailed, is also transforming the economic structure of manufacturing activities from the inside, and threatening millions of jobs. According to McKinsey [2017], in an analysis of 2,000 jobs across 800 occupations, 60% of current jobs may be affected, and out of that at least 30% of their constituent activities could be replaced by automatic electronic systems. Half of the work tasks (especially in manufacturing) can be automated by 2055. This transformation, beyond its impact on the nature of work on the demand side of the economy, or on the survival of capitalism itself, will mean profound changes in the dynamics of the manufacturing industry. Foxconn, the largest contract manufacturer in the world, maker of iPhones for Apple and Galaxy for Samsung, announced in 2016 the replacement of 60 000 employees by robots, as the start of a massive automation plan that can affect one million employees in Asia only. Automation thereby changes not only the cost structure of the industry, but also makes it independent of a location based on low labor costs. In a new global dynamics, manufacturing industries relocate to knowledge-intensive areas to accelerate their innovation cycles, or to distributed locations close to their end customers [Livesey (2012); McIvor (2013); Ellram et al. (2013); Bailey and De Propris (2014)]. Adidas's announcement of the company's intention to locate manufacturing to Germany again (using robots) is a clear evidence of this trend [The Guardian (2016)].

Responses and changes in the competitive positioning of different countries through specific policies are further forces that drive the reconfiguration of global manufacturing. After a time of massive offshoring towards emerging countries with high productive efficiency, the competitive landscape has mutated, due to at least three critical factors: (a) the increase in costs in China, (b) the new robotic manufacturing possibilities offered by the digital paradigm, and (c) the evidence of greater efficiency and speed of innovation processes in proximity to the so-called "innovation ecosystems", where the sources of R&D are located. In a world of limited jobs, nations are competing to attract and retain manufacturing plants. Knowing that manufacturing is a critical source of value and economic stability, advanced countries are beginning to adopt different competitive strategies in order to increase their productive bases, accelerate the process of concentrating manufacturing activities, and thereby generate industrial wealth within their territories. In the post-crisis world, three large productive mega-clusters are competing to lead global manufacturing [Deloitte (2016)]: the US, China and Germany. The US has lost six million manufacturing jobs during the crisis, and wants to regain industrial leadership, (with a declining manufacturing industry, an Obama administration that has been especially sensitive to technological development, and a Trump administration that has adopted strong protectionist measures in its early months). China, after two decades of very high growth, coming from a low base, is steadily advancing to become a major global industrial, scientific, and technological power [McKinsey (2015)]; and finally, in Europe, Germany, which surpasses the US in the main indicators of manufacturing production [Breznitz (2014)], has managed to integrate the new paradigm of digital industry in its traditional manufacturing culture, in what has come to be called "Industry 4.0," through a renewed and powerful technological policy [High Tech Strategy, German Federal Government (2014)].

Finally, it is necessary to consider the increasing nature of demand as a transforming force of manufacturing. Today, users have increasing levels of information and power; consumers are demanding increased customization, personalization and co-creation [Deloitte (2015)], without giving up immediate service and affordable cost. Technology development has been extended to the product level, transforming it from an inert object to a smart device, complemented with additional layers of high-value services. After-sales follow-up, constant interaction with the market and interpretation of the data that come from it, have become sources of strategic information flows for the design of the next generation of superior products.

3. Literature Review: New Firms and Technological Change

Among all the transformative forces that are reshaping manufacturing, we focus this research on technological change, which is the very basis of all the other driving forces like globalization or new market trends. The emergence of new technologies changes the competitive base of industries. The patterns that drive this change have been extensively studied in academic literature. Joseph Schumpeter [1942], pioneer economist in introducing the phenomenon of innovation in economic science, coined the term "waves of creative destruction". For Schumpeter, innovation was the phenomenon by which new technologies are introduced into the economy, technologies that destroy the previous competitive dynamics and create a new and superior order of things. The effect of technological change on the transformation of industries, and on the whole economy, has been further analyzed by Solow [1957], Abernathy and Utterback [1978], Elliott [1980], Abernathy and Clark [1985], Tushman and Anderson [1986], Foster [1986], Romer [1990], Tripsas [1997], and Chun *et al.* [2008] among others. Abernathy and Utterback [1978] draw the theoretical foundations of industrial innovation. Foster [1986] proposes his "S curve" model to explain the dynamics of technological innovation: all technology starts with an experimental phase, which requires investments and scientific/engineering effort without easily achieving an appreciable or sensible increase in its performance. During this phase, scientists are trying to understand the foundations of this technology. After this period, when researchers are able to understand, reproduce and scale up this technology, a rapid phase of expansion comes (especially accelerated if that technology awakes the market interest and is able to attract investment capital). Finally, all technologies inevitably reach their physical limit, and enter an asymptotic curve of exhaustion (increasing investments lead only to incremental improvements in the technology's performance). Romer [1990] explains the critical role of technological change in economic growth. The stock of human capital determines economic growth through the generation and introduction in the market of new technologies. Abernathy and Clark [1985] describe how new technologies have redefined markets, identifying four effects of introducing new technologies: regular innovations (when new technology does not change competition or existing markets); niche creation (when new technologies maintain the industry's competitive bases but create new market relations); radical innovations (when the competitive equilibrium is broken, but without altering the former configuration of markets); and the creation of new architectures (when a new technology reconfigures the competition and creates new market relationships). Teece *et al.* [1997] explain that technological change is based on the creation and exploitation of dynamic capacities within companies (bundles of skills, knowledge, and specific know-hows). For these authors, technology management must be a part of strategic management of companies. Tushman and Anderson [1986] have demonstrated that technology evolves through periods of stability interrupted by the emergence of breakthroughs, which in turn initiate competence-destroying or competence-enhancing cycles. Cycles generated by new emerging companies usually destroy the technological competencies that have sustained the former leaderships. Technological discontinuities generate the introduction of flows of new entrepreneurial opportunities that compete for the creation of new dominant architectures (designs) in product and business models, seizing the leadership from the incumbents. After phases of intense competition in product innovation, once a new dominant design emerges, a phase of process innovation takes place, seeking to manufacture with maximum efficiency, the product architecture that has already been widely accepted by the market [Abernathy and Utterback (1978)]. Christensen [1992, 1997, 2003] introduces the concept of "disruptive innovation" to characterize how new technologies, emerging from low-end positions, can lead to the obsolescence of large, leading businesses, captured in their established value chains. When a new technology emerges, it is not necessary for the new technology to surpass the benefits of the former, in order for the technological substitution effect to take place (changing the technological base that underpins the competitiveness of the industry). It is sufficient that the new technology surpasses the expectations of the old market, offering new benefits in other dimensions not explicitly expressed before (smaller size, greater mobility, greater convenience, and faster service).

The specific role of NTBFs in shifting the structure of industries has also been widely discussed in scientific literature. Technological discontinuities create windows of opportunity for the entry of new competitors into the industry [Tushman and Anderson (1986)]. When new technologies are competence destroying (rendering obsolete the skills of the incumbent players), new generations of NTBFs develop the winning dominant architectures. If new products and business models generate new value networks with customers (new relational models), these young NTBFs use that to take over from the old dominant players and assume new leadership of the industry [Christensen and Rosenbloom (1995)]. Baumol [2002] notes that while large companies tend to turn technological change processes into routines of simple adaptation to the environment, the real source of disruptive change is the individual entrepreneur, who brings breakthrough innovations. Spencer and Kirchhoff [2006] postulate that, while small technology-based companies invest only very little in R&D compared to the leaders, they play a decisive role in job creation, the creation of new patents, introduction of disruptive technologies in the market, and generation of new waves of creative destruction. These authors list the advantages of NTBFs over the old leaders in scenarios of rapid technological change: strategic flexibility, independence from established investors, and freedom from internal resistance to change.

There is also a great body of scholarly knowledge about disruptive technologies that transform the structure of the manufacturing industry, and even about their potential applications: additive manufacturing [Horn and Harrysson (2012); Wong and Hernandez (2012); Vaezi *et al.* (2013); Stampfl and Hatzenbichler (2014); Baumers *et al.* (2016)], artificial intelligence [Michalski *et al.* (2013); Renzi *et al.* (2014)], the Internet of things [Bi *et al.* (2014); Stankovic (2014)], and big data [Dubey *et al.* (2016)], among others. There is also an abundance of academic papers on Industry 4.0 [Lee *et al.* (2014, 2015); Brettel *et al.* (2014)].

However, all these papers belong to engineering and technical literature. We have found a research gap in management research journals, where there is a lack of knowledge about the manufacturing NTBFs that carry such breakthrough technologies. The aim of this research is to bridge part of this gap by shedding light on a key characteristic of the next generation of technology-based firms that are entering the manufacturing industry today: the composition of the founding team. There is a relevant body of research related to venture team structure and firm performance [Eisenhardt and Schoonhoven (1990); Delmar and Shane (2006); Beckman (2006); Eesley *et al.* (2014)]. While entrepreneurship research has usually focused on the figure of the "lone genius" or lead founder [Baron (2007)], new firms are generally created by teams, rather than by individuals [Cooper *et al.* (1989); Kamm *et al.* (1990); Lechler (2001)]. Similar backgrounds and experiences help entrepreneurs to achieve quick consensus and shared strategic decisions. But homogeneity in entrepreneurial teams potentially constrains strategic choices, and this lack of perspective can especially become a liability in turbulent environments [Klotz *et al.* (2014)]. Specific entrepreneurial experience improves the identification of opportunities [Ucbasaran *et al.* (2003)]. However, the mix of the team's industrial and entrepreneurial experience positively influences the firm's ability to succeed in the market. Heterogeneous teams (involving managers, technical specialists, and serial entrepreneurs) develop more innovative strategies [Beckman (2006)]. Heterogeneity (the mixed presence of diverse founders' profiles) has a positive impact on profitable firm creation, and this effect is greater when the team has more experience in the specific industry where the NTBF competes [Muñoz-Bullon *et al.* (2015); Vanaelst *et al.* (2006)]. Heterogeneity is also found to be related to superior levels of performance in terms of growth in university-based NTBFs [Visintin and Pittino (2014)].

Recent studies on the composition of founding teams in successful NTBFs have been carried out in the automotive industry [Ferràs-Hernández *et al.* (in press)], with the significant finding that few of the founding teams count experienced automotive managers in their ranks. It suggests that, in the case of a substitution in the industry's technological base, previous experience in the industry is not significant for NTBF success. Instead, the founders were mainly entrepreneurs with previous business creation experience (but not necessarily in the automotive sector), or scientists or engineers with deep knowledge of computing sciences (but without managerial experience). The low presence of experienced managers in successful founding teams seems to confirm the model change: the former mechanical machine (the car) is being converted into a computer.

4. Research Questions

After presenting the motivations and background that guide us, we now present the research questions that inspire our work. According to empirical evidence, the manufacturing sector is being transformed by technological change; and, according to literature, the carriers of this change are NTBFs with disruptive potential. Our work focuses on the analysis of these companies. Our interest is centered in knowing: (a) who are the new technology-based companies that are emerging in the manufacturing sector, (b) which is their origin (who are their founders), and (c) whether different founding profiles have an impact on the firms' performance. In particular, we are interested in knowing whether their founders have technological profiles (they come from scientific or technical backgrounds), whether they are entrepreneurs (have previous entrepreneurial experience) or whether they are professional managers (have previous experience in manufacturing). With the objective of analyzing the role of managerial experience, entrepreneurial experience, and scientific background of the founding teams, we developed an exploratory study of a representative set of venture-backed NTBFs operating today in the manufacturing industry.

5. Data Collection and Sample Characterization

To build our database, we used Crunchbase, one of the most complete NTBFs databases used today in research. Crunchbase is an international database of NTBFs, investors, and venture capital funds managed by the owners of Tech-Crunch, an internationally recognized blog on technological innovation. The database provides information on companies, operating sectors, product technologies, headquarters, the sequence of investments received, investors, founding teams, the date and quantity of initial public offerings (IPOs), among other things. We selected companies classified within the "manufacturing" sector, created since January 1, 2013, in Europe, the United States and China, whose total funding amount is more than US $1 000 000. We assume that, above this threshold, companies have technological capabilities and business models interesting enough to attract professional venture capital funds (beyond initial funding by "fools, friends, and family"). The data were extracted on December 23, 2016.

The initial sample was made up of a total of 184 companies. Around 69.6% of them were founded in the US, 25.5% in Europe, and 4.9% in China. Of the American companies, 35.9% are Californian (25% of the total sample). Figure 1 represents the territorial distribution of the companies.

The companies of the sample accumulate a total financing amount of US $2 383 906 237, with an average of US $12 956 M investment per company. Two of the companies (1.1%) have obtained a total financing of over US $500 M. Six of them (3.3%), obtained between US $100 M and US $500 M. The next six (3.3%) have raised total funding amounts between US $50 M and US $100 M. Thirty-three companies (17.9%) have obtained financing between US $10 M and US $50 M. Thirty companies more (16.3%) obtained between US $5 M and US $10 M; and finally 107 companies (58.15% of the total) have received funds for an amount between US $1 M and US $5 M. Figures 2 and 3 represent the companies' funding levels. Figure 4 shows the number of companies per product/technology.

Since the concept of manufacturing is very broad, and the companies of the sample presented widely dispersed typologies, technologies, and products, we segmented the scope of activity of companies into 27 fields, depending on the technology used and the product/market in which they operated. The most important fields present in the sample are related to additive manufacturing (32 companies, 17.4% of the total); hardware devices (21 companies, 11.4% of the total): basically manufacturers of sensors, systems, and electronic components; and manufacturing IT systems (21 companies, 11.4%): basically of information management systems related to the manufacturing process.

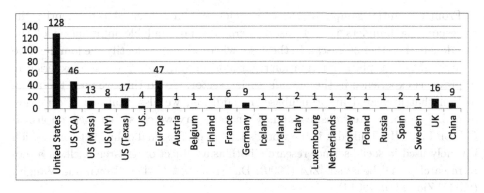

Fig. 1. Number of companies by headquarters' location.

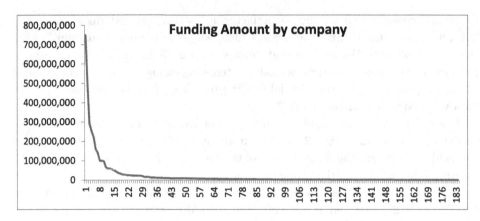

Fig. 2.   Funding amount by company.

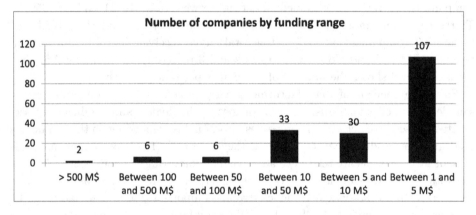

Fig. 3.   Number of companies by funding range.

From the initial sample of 184 companies, we have been able to identify the corresponding founders in 154 cases (there was no available information of the founders in the other 30 cases). In the cases where we could identify the founders, we have sought biographical information regarding training, entrepreneurial experience, or previous experience in the manufacturing sector. To do this, we used the information that appeared in Crunchbase. In addition, we also analyzed information available on corporate websites, and, when necessary we consulted their published CVs on LinkedIn. LinkedIn is the world's largest professional online network, which is widely used in social science research, both as a subject of research itself, or a tool to research social behavior [Zizi (2009); Davison *et al.* (2011); Brown and Vaughn (2011); Zide *et al.* (2014)].

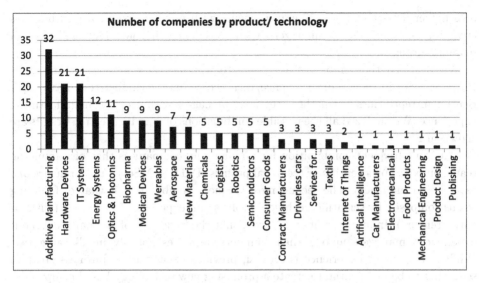

Fig. 4.   Number of companies by product/technology.

In 8 of the 154 cases, we did not find precise biographical information, so the final sample of companies whose founding teams could be characterized in detail was reduced to 146. Of those 146 companies, a total of 291 biographical profiles of founders were analyzed.

6. Results

Out the 291 entrepreneurs analyzed, we have found 64 individuals with PhD degrees (22% of the founders); 94 with Masters in Science (MSc) degrees (32.3%); 111 university graduates (38.1%), 114 (39.2%) founders with experience in business creation, who had founded a total amount of 212 companies before; and, finally, 204 founders (70.1%) that had previously been industrial managers in different manufacturing areas.

When we analyzed the founding teams of the companies of the sample, a total amount of 48 teams out of 146 companies were found with *at least* one PhD among their ranks (32.9%). Among those teams that do not have PhDs, there were 53 formed by *at least* one MSc (36.3%). That means that the founding teams that have *at least* one scientific or technological specialist reach 69.2%. Of the companies whose founding teams do not incorporate PhDs or MScs, 43 of them (29.5%) were funded by teams with *at least* one founder with university degree. Out of the total number of companies, 83 (56.8%) have some experienced entrepreneur among their founders. Finally, 126 out of the 146 companies (86.3%) analyzed have founding teams with *at least* one manager with previous experience in manufacturing. The companies analyzed have an average of 0.43 PhDs per company in their founding teams, 0.64 MScs,

0.76 university graduates, 0.77 entrepreneurs with previous experience in business creation, and 1.45 senior managers with experience in some technical field of manufacturing.

We classified the companies according to whether their founding teams have PhDs or MScs in their ranks ("science/tech" companies), whether they have experienced entrepreneurs or whether they have managers with previous manufacturing experience. We analyzed all the possible combinations of founding teams. Results are shown in Fig. 5.

The most frequent combination for an emerging company is that of a founding team composed by scientific or technical profiles (PhDs or MScs), entrepreneurs *and* experienced managers. The second most frequent combination is that of founding teams composed by scientific–technical profiles and experienced managers (without entrepreneurs). In any case, it is observed that the frequency of companies without experienced managers among their founders decreases notably in all categories. While management experience is critical, previous experience in business creation seems not to be as essential to create a promising new technology-based company in manufacturing. To explore the effect of the founding team composition on the firms' output, and given that we didn't dispose of their financial figures, we chose to analyze the number of appearances of the firms in the news, a variable which is available at Crunchbase, as a proxy for firms' "notoriety," or the degree of awareness raised by those firms. The main descriptors and their associated correlations are found in Table 1. We classified the companies in function of (5) whether they had technical specialists/scientists (i.e. those with an MSc or PhD), (6) serial entrepreneurs, or (7) experienced managers on the founding teams. The companies were compared to the (0) notoriety of the company measured in terms of number of

Founding teams with...				
PhDs or MScs	**Entrepreneurs**	**Experienced Managers**	**Companies**	**%**
NO	NO	NO	0	0
NO	NO	YES	16	11,0
NO	YES	NO	9	6,2
NO	YES	YES	20	13,7
YES	NO	NO	4	2,7
YES	NO	YES	43	29,5
YES	YES	NO	7	4,8
YES	YES	YES	47	32,2
		Total	**146**	

Fig. 5.   Companies classified according to their founders' profiles.

Table 1. Descriptive statistics and associated correlations.

	μ	sd	(0)	(1)	(2)	(3)	(4)	(5)	(6)	(7)
Dependent variable										
(0) Notoriety of the company	1.84	1.05		−0.08	0.04	0.00	−0.07	0.60	0.44	0.66
Control variables										
(1) Funding	15.36	1.37	−0.08		−0.06	0.12	−0.06	−0.11	−0.02	−0.10
(2) 2013	0.48	0.50	0.04	−0.06		−0.49	−0.25	0.06	0.13	−0.03
(3) 2014	0.21	0.41	0.00	0.12	−0.49		−0.13	0.03	−0.11	0.04
(4) 2015	0.06	0.24	−0.07	−0.06	−0.25	−0.13		−0.02	−0.03	0.01
Independent variables										
(5) Presence of technol-ogists/scientists	0.69	0.46	0.60	−0.11	0.06	0.03	−0.02		0.16	0.42
(6) Presence of serial entrepreneurs	0.57	0.50	0.44	−0.02	0.13	−0.11	−0.03	0.16		0.04
(7) Presence of experi-enced managers	0.86	0.35	0.66	−0.10	−0.03	0.04	0.01	0.42	0.04	

Table 2. Poisson regression for the control and full model.

Control variables	Control model		Full model	
Constant	−1.33*	(0.67)	−1.28	(0.75)
(1) Funding	0.06	(0.04)	0.07	(0.04)
(2) 2013	0.02	(0.15)	0.01	(0.15)
(3) 2014	0.00	(0.18)	0.02	(0.18)
(4) 2015	−0.12	(0.30)	−0.10	(0.30)
Independent variables				
(5) Presence of technologists/scientists			0.30*	(0.14)
(6) Presence of serial entrepreneurs			0.34**	(0.13)
(7) Presence of experienced managers			0.38	(0.21)
Parameters of the model				
Degrees of freedom	141		138	
Residual variance	78.87		64.34	
φ^2			14.53*	
Adjusted R^2	0.02		0.12	

Note: * Significative relation; ** Strong relation.

appearances in the news. Finally, two controls were considered: (1) the amount of funding, and the year in which they were founded, which ranged from 2013 to 2015 (2), (3), and (4). For data skewness reasons, log transformations were performed on the (1) funding.

As the dependent variable (i.e. notoriety of the company) is a count variable, there are two possible regression models we can adopt: Poisson or negative binomial regressions. Fitting our data set to both models showed that both Poisson and negative binomial regression led to similar fit, indicating that there was no need to account for over-dispersion. Therefore, the Poisson model was selected. Table 2 depicts the results of the Poisson regression with a control model and full model. The full model was significant above and beyond the control model ($\varphi^2 = 14.53^*$) with a proper predictive power (Adjusted R^2 of 0.12).

The presence of technical specialists/scientists or the presence of serial entrepreneurs was positively significant in our model in predicting the firm's appearance in the media. However, no significative correlations were found between the presence of experienced managers, and appearance of the company in the news.

7. Conclusions, Limitations, and Further Research

We have analyzed a sample of venture-backed manufacturing NTBFs. The most frequent composition of the founding teams combines solid scientific or technological background, business creation experience, and managerial experience in the industry. In any case, our findings indicate that venture capitalists (VC) prefer founding teams with a scientific/technological background and previous management experience in the industry to support manufacturing startups. Hundred and twenty-six out of 146 founding teams (86.3%) have experienced managers in their ranks. This confirms previous studies [Delmar and Shane (2006); Kotha and George (2012)], which find the role of previous managerial experience critical. The need for a "track record" with outside buyers and suppliers means that experience is necessary to enhance NTBFs' performance [Eisenhardt and Schoonhoven (1990); Stinchcombe and March (1965)]. Experienced founders raise more resources from their helpers [Kotha and George (2012)]. The lower proportion of previous entrepreneurs in the founding teams (83 out of 146 cases, 56.8%) could be explained as follows: given that companies have been selected by investors (probably with entrepreneurial experience of their own), we can suggest that these investors would be open to providing entrepreneurial guidance to the new venture rather than to providing specialist scientific/technical and managerial input. The positive effect of heterogeneity would be, in this case, provided by the investors. Further research should confirm this hypothesis.

When analyzing the notoriety of the company, we found significative correlations between the presence of entrepreneurs or the presence of technical specialists/scientists, and the firm's appearance in the news. It may suggest that, while the presence of an experienced manager is perceived by the investors as a necessary, or "hygienic" factor for a company's success, it is not sufficient for raising media awareness. Companies with entrepreneurs or technicians/scientists are more frequently in the news, which may indicate the creation of a higher degree of differentiation, or a higher level of expectations of these firms.

The high presence of experienced managers in manufacturing startups contrasts with similar studies performed recently in the automotive industry [Ferràs et al.

(2017)]. This divergence may suggest that, while the automotive industry is suffering a substitution in its technological base (the mechanical car being transformed into an electronic device) with a complete redesign of its value network, this level of industrial change is lower in our more heterogeneous sample of companies supplying advanced manufacturing solutions. Technological or scientific backgrounds are present in 101 out of 146 founding teams (69.2%). Entrepreneurial experience seems to be least essential (only 83 out of 146 (56.8%) founding teams count with previous entrepreneurs; while 101 teams (69.2%) have scientific/technical specialists, and 126 (86,3%) have experienced managers). In any case, we confirm the positive effect of founding teams' heterogeneity stated by Visintin and Pittino [2014], Muñoz-Bullon *et al.* [2015] and Vanaelst *et al.* [2006]. Further research should clarify whether the preeminence of founding teams with mixed profiles (mainly, scientific/technical specialists and experienced managers) in the ranks of emerging startups is a direct consequence of venture capital selection, or if this composition is motivated by previous reasons in the very origins of the NTBFs' creation. On the other hand, longitudinal studies must be performed in the future to confirm whether founding teams' heterogeneity is related to the true survival and long-term economic and financial success of those companies. Further research should also go in depth with the analysis of the possible differences between NTBFs founded in the US, Europe, or China.

A collateral result of this research is the evidence of the dominant presence of companies operating on 3D Printing technologies (additive manufacturing), which accounts for 17.4% of the total sample of firms. It could lead us to think that this technology is at the peak of its hype cycle. However, according to the consulting firm Gartner [2015, 2016], by 2015, this technology had surpassed the peak of over-expectations and the area of undervaluation ("trough of disillusionment") of its model emerging technologies analysis. In fact, by 2015, it was anticipated that additive manufacturing would reach its "productivity plateau" (consolidation zone) in a span of 2 to 5 years. In our research, 29 of the 32 companies dedicated to the additive manufacture of the sample (90.6%) accumulate more than one million dollars of financing. Fourteen of them (43.7%) exceed 5 million and 10 companies (31.2%) attracted funding amounts above 10 million. The funding levels of these companies exceed those expected for companies operating with embryonic technologies (early-stage phases), which seems to confirm Gartner's predictions of consolidation and extension of additive manufacturing as a mature technology. On the other hand, behind the segment of additive manufacturing companies, we find that the second and third most frequent categories are formed by hardware devices manufacturers (21 companies, 11.4% of the sample), and manufacturing information systems (21 companies, 11.4% of the sample).

The dominant profile of a next-generation manufacturing firm is thus that of an electronics-based company founded preferably by mixed teams, and composed of scientific/technical specialists, entrepreneurs, and experienced managers. The most frequent combination is the one that bears the highest heterogeneity among the venture team. Experienced managers may be a necessary condition for success, while entrepreneurs or technical/scientific profiles may constitute a differentiation factor in terms of market appraisal.

References

Abernathy, W. J. and Clark, K. B. (1985). Innovation: Mapping the winds of creative destruction. *Research Policy*, **14**, 1: 3–22.

Abernathy, W. J. and Utterback, J. M. (1978). Patterns of industrial innovation. *Technology Review*, **80**, 7: 40–47.

Bailey, D. and De Propris, L. (2014). Manufacturing reshoring and its limits: The UK automotive case. *Cambridge Journal of Regions, Economy and Society*, **7**, 3: 379–395.

Baron, R. A. (2007). Behavioral and cognitive factors in entrepreneurship: Entrepreneurs as the active element in new venture creation. *Strategic Entrepreneurship Journal*, **1**, 1–2: 167–182.

Baumers, M., Dickens, P., Tuck, C. and Hague, R. (2016). The cost of additive manufacturing: Machine productivity, economies of scale and technology-push. *Technological Forecasting and Social Change*, **102**: 193–201.

Baumol, W. J. (2002). Entrepreneurship, innovation and growth: The David-Goliath symbiosis. *The Journal of Entrepreneurial Finance*, **7**, 2: 1.

Beckman, C. M. (2006). The influence of founding team company affiliations on firm behavior. *Academy of Management Journal*, **49**, 4: 741–758.

Bi, Z., Da Xu, L. and Wang, C. (2014). Internet of things for enterprise systems of modern manufacturing. *IEEE Transactions on Industrial Informatics*, **10**, 2: 1537–1546.

Brettel, M., Friederichsen, N., Keller, M. and Rosenberg, M. (2014). How virtualization, decentralization and network building change the manufacturing landscape: An Industry 4.0 Perspective. *International Journal of Mechanical, Industrial Science and Engineering*, **8**, 1: 37–44.

Breznitz, D. (2014). *Why Germany Dominates the U.S. in Innovation*. Harvard Business Review. Available at https://hbr.org/2014/05/why-germany-dominates-the-u-s-in-innovation [accessed on 15 April 2015].

Brown, V. and Vaughn, E. (2011). The writing on the facebook wall: The use of social networking sites in hiring decisions. *Journal of Business and Psychology*, **26**: 219–225.

Christensen, C. M. (1992). Exploring the limits of the technology S-curve. Part I: Component technologies. *Production and Operations Management*, **1**, 4: 334–357.

Christensen, C. M. (1997). *The Innovator's Dilemma: When New Technologies Cause Great Firms to Fail*. 1st Edition, Harvard Business Review Press, Boston, MA.

Christensen, C. M. (2003). *The Innovator's Dilemma: The Revolutionary Book that will Change the Way You Do Business*. Harper Business Essentials, New York, p. 320.

Christensen, C. M. and Rosenbloom, R. S. (1995). Explaining the attacker's advantage: Technological paradigms, organizational dynamics, and the value network. *Research Policy*, **24**, 2: 233–257.

Chun, H., Kim, J. W., Morck, R. and Yeung, B. (2008). Creative destruction and firm-specific performance heterogeneity. *Journal of Financial Economics*, **89**, 1: 109–135.

Cooper, A. C., Woo, C. Y. and Dunkelberg, W. C. (1989). Entrepreneurship and the initial size of firms. *Journal of Business Venturing*, **4**, 5: 317–332.

Davison, H., Maraist, C. and Bing, M. (2011), Friend or Foe? the promise and pitfalls of using social networking sites for HR decisions. *Journal of Business and Psychology*, **28**, 2: 153–159.

Delmar, F. and Shane, S. (2006). Does experience matter? The effect of founding team experience on the survival and sales of newly founded ventures. *Strategic Organization*, **4**, 3: 215–247.

Deloitte (2015). *The Future of Manufacturing: Making things in a changing world*. Available at https://www2.deloitte.com/content/dam/Deloitte/za/Documents/manufacturing/ZA_Future_of_Manufacturing_2015.pdf [accessed on 15 April 2017].

Deloitte (2016). *Global Manufacturing Competitiveness Index*. from https://www2.deloitte.com/content/dam/Deloitte/global/Documents/Manufacturing/gx-global-mfg-competitiveness-index-2016.pdf [accessed on 15 April 2017].

Dubey, R., Gunasekaran, A., Childe, S. J., Wamba, S. F. and Papadopoulos, T. (2016). The impact of big data on world-class sustainable manufacturing. *The International Journal of Advanced Manufacturing Technology*, **84**, 1–4: 631–645.

Eesley, C. E., Hsu, D. H. and Roberts, E. B. (2014). The contingent effects of top management teams on venture performance: Aligning founding team composition with innovation strategy and commercialization environment. *Strategic Management Journal*, **35**, 12: 1798–1817.

Eisenhardt, K. M. and Schoonhoven, C. B. (1990). Organizational growth: Linking founding team, strategy, environment, and growth among US semiconductor ventures, 1978–1988. *Administrative Science Quarterly*, **1**, 504–529.

Elliott, J. E. (1980). Marx and Schumpeter on capitalism's creative destruction: A comparative restatement. *The Quarterly Journal of Economics*, **95**, 1: 45–68.

Ellram, L. M., Tate, W. L. and Petersen, K. J. (2013). Offshoring and reshoring: An update on the manufacturing location decision. *Journal of Supply Chain Management*, **49**, 2: 14–22.

Ferràs-Hernández, X., Tarrats-Pons, E. and Arimany-Serrat, N. (2017). Disruption in the automotive industry: A Cambrian moment. *Business Horizons*, **60**, 6: 855–863.

Foster, R. N. (1986). Working the S-curve: Assessing technological threats. *Research Management*, **29**, 4: 17–20.

Gartner (2015). *Gartner's 2015 Hype Cycle for Emerging Technologies*. Available at http://www.gartner.com/newsroom/id/3114217. [accessed on 15 April 2017].

Gartner (2016). *Gartner's 2016 Hype Cycle for Emerging Technologies*. Available at http://www.gartner.com/newsroom/id/3412017. [accessed on 15 April 2017].

German Federal Government (2014). *The New High-Tech Strategy: Innovations for Germany*. Available at https://www.bmbf.de/pub/HTS_Broschuere_eng.pdf. [accessed on 15 April 2017].

High Tech Strategy. German Federal Government (2014). Retrieved from https://www.bmbf.de/pub/HTS_Broschuere_eng.pdf on 16/07/2018.

Horn, T. J. and Harrysson, O. L. (2012). Overview of current additive manufacturing technologies and selected applications. *Science Progress*, **95**, 3: 255–282.

Kamm, J. B., Shuman, J. C., Seeger, J. A. and Nurick, A. J. (1990). Entrepreneurial teams in new venture creation: A research agenda. *Entrepreneurship Theory and Practice*, **14**, 4: 7–17.

Klotz, A. C., Hmieleski, K. M., Bradley, B. H. and Busenitz, L. W. (2014). New venture teams: A review of the literature and roadmap for future research. *Journal of Management*, **40**, 1: 226–255.

Kotha, R. and George, G. (2012). Friends, family, or fools: Entrepreneur experience and its implications for equity distribution and resource mobilization. *Journal of Business Venturing*, **27**, 5: 525–543.

Lechler, T. (2001). Social interaction: A determinant of entrepreneurial team venture success. *Small Business Economics*, **16**: 263–278.

Lee, J., Bagheri, B. and Kao, H. A. (2015). A cyber-physical systems architecture for industry 4.0-based manufacturing systems. *Manufacturing Letters*, **3**: 18–23.

Lee, J., Kao, H. A. and Yang, S. (2014). Service innovation and smart analytics for industry 4.0 and big data environment. *Procedia Cirp*, **16**: 3–8.

Livesey, F. (2012). The need for a new understanding of manufacturing and industrial policy in leading economies. *Innovations*, **7**, 3: 193–202.

McIvor, R. (2013). Understanding the manufacturing location decision: The case for the transaction cost and capability perspectives. *Journal of Supply Chain Management*, **49**, 2: 23–26.

McKinsey. (2017). *The Great re-make: Manufacturing for Modern Times*. Available at https://www.mckinsey.com/~/media/McKinsey/Business%20Functions/Operations/Our%20Insights/The%20great%20remake%20Manufacturing%20for%20modern%20times/The-great-remake-Manufacturing-for-modern-times-full-compenium-October-2017-final.ashx. [accessed on 01 Nov 2017].

McKinsey and Company (2015). *The China Effect on Global Innovation*. Available at http://www.mckinsey.com/~/media/McKinsey/Global%20Themes/Innovation/Gauging%20the%20strength%20of%20Chinese%20innovation/MGI%20China%20Effect_Full%20report_October_2015.ashx. [accessed on 15 April 2017].

McKinsey and Company (2017). *A Future that Works: Automation, Employment and Productivity*. Available at http://www.mckinsey.com/~/media/McKinsey/Global%20Themes/Digital%20Disruption/Harnessing%20automation%20for%20a%20future%20that%20works/MGI-A-future-that-works-Full-report.ashx. [accessed on April 15 2017].

Michalski, R. S., Carbonell, J. G. and Mitchell, T. M. (Eds.). (2013). *Machine Learning: An Artificial Intelligence Approach*. Springer Science and Business Media, Berlin, Heidelberg.

Muñoz-Bullon, F., Sanchez-Bueno, M. J. and Vos-Saz, A. (2015). Startup team contributions and new firm creation: The role of founding team experience. *Entrepreneurship and Regional Development*, **27**, 1–2: 80–105.

National Economic Council (2016). *Revitalizing American Manufacturing: The Obama Administration's Progress in Establishing a Foundation for Manufacturing Leadership*. Available at https://www.whitehouse.gov/sites/whitehouse.gov/files/images/NEC_Manufacturing_Report_October_2016.pdf. [acccessed on 15 April 2017].

Nikolaou, I. (2014). Social networking web sites in job search and employee recruitment. *International Journal of Selection and Assessment*, **22**, 2: 179–189.

Renzi, C., Leali, F., Cavazzuti, M. and Andrisano, A. O. (2014). A review on artificial intelligence applications to the optimal design of dedicated and reconfigurable manufacturing systems. *The International Journal of Advanced Manufacturing Technology*, **72**, 1–4: 403–418.

Romer, P. M. (1990). Endogenous technological change. *Journal of Political Economy*, **98**, 5, Part 2: S71–S102.

Schaller, R. R. (1997). Moore's law: Past, present and future. *IEEE Spectrum*, **34**, 6: 52–59.

Schumpeter, J. (1942). Creative destruction. *Capitalism, Socialism and Democracy*. Harper and Brothers, United States, pp. 82–85.

Solow, R. M. (1957). Technical change and the aggregate production function. *The Review of Economics and Statistics*, **39**, 3: 312–320.

Spencer, A. S. and Kirchhoff, B. A. (2006). Schumpeter and NTBFs: Towards a framework for how NTBFs cause creative destruction. *International Entrepreneurship and Management Journal*, **2**, 2: 145–156.

Stampfl, J. and Hatzenbichler, M. (2014). Additive manufacturing technologies. In *CIRP Encyclopedia of Production Engineering*, L. Laperrière and G. Reinhart (eds.), Springer Berlin Heidelberg, Berlin, Heidelberg, pp. 20–27.

Stankovic, J. A. (2014). Research directions for the internet of things. *IEEE Internet of Things Journal*, **1**, 1: 3–9.

Stinchcombe, A. L. and March, J. G. (1965). Social structure and organizations. *Handbook of Organizations*, **7**: 142–193.

Teece, D. J., Pisano, G. and Shuen, A. (1997). Dynamic capabilities and strategic management. *Strategic Management Journal*, **18**, 7: 509–533.

The Guardian. (2016). *Reboot: Adidas to make Shoes in Germany again. But using Robots.* Available at https://www.theguardian.com/world/2016/may/25/adidas-to-sell-robot-made-shoes-from-2017. [accessed on 15 April 2017].

Tripsas, M. (1997). Unraveling the process of creative destruction: Complementary assets and incumbent survival in the typesetter industry. *Strategic Management Journal*, **18**, S1: 119–142.

Tushman, M. L. and Anderson, P. (1986). Technological discontinuities and organizational environments. *Administrative Science Quarterly*, **31**, 3: 439–465.

Ucbasaran, D., Westhead, P., Wright, M. and Binks, M. (2003). Does entrepreneurial experience influence opportunity identification?. *The Journal of Private Equity*, **7**, 1: 7–14.

Vaezi, M., Seitz, H. and Yang, S. (2013). A review on 3D micro-additive manufacturing technologies. *The International Journal of Advanced Manufacturing Technology*, **67**, 5–8: 1721–1754.

Vanaelst, I., Clarysse, B., Wright, M., Lockett, A., Moray, N. and S'Jegers, R. (2006). Entrepreneurial team development in academic spinouts: An examination of team heterogeneity. *Entrepreneurship Theory and Practice*, **30**, 2: 249–271.

Visintin, F. and Pittino, D. (2014). Founding team composition and early performance of university — Based spin-off companies. *Technovation*, **34**, 1: 31–43.

Weller, C., Kleer, R. and Piller, F. T. (2015). Economic implications of 3D printing: Market structure models in light of additive manufacturing revisited. *International Journal of Production Economics*, **164**: 43–56.

Wong, K. V. and Hernandez, A. (2012). A review of additive manufacturing. *ISRN Mechanical Engineering*, **2012**.

Zide, J., Elman, B. and Shahani-Denning, C. (2014). LinkedIn and recruitment: How profiles differ across occupations. *Employee Relations*, **36**, 5: 583–604.

Zizi, P. (2009), The virtual geographies of social networks: A comparative analysis of facebook, linkedIn and a small world. *New Media Society*, **11**, 10: 199–222.

Biography

Xavier Ferrás-Hernández is PhD in Management Sciences, Telecommunication Engineer and MBA (ESADE Business School). He is Associate Professor and Dean at the Business and Communication School, University of Vic — Central University of Catalonia.

Albert Armisen-Morell is PhD in Management Sciences and Telecommunication Engineer. He is an Aggregated Professor at the Business and Communication School, University of Vic — Central University of Catalonia.

Anna Sabata-Alberich is PhD in Business Economics. She is Associate Professor at the Business and Communication School, University of Vic — Central University of Catalonia.

Elisenda Tarrats-Pons is PhD in Management Sciences. She is Aggregate Professor and Department Director at the Business and Communication School, University of Vic — Central University of Catalonia.

Núria Arimany-Serrat is PhD in Business Economics. She is Associate Professor, and Research Group Leader at the Business and Communication School, University of Vic — Central University of Catalonia.

Chapter 9

Identifying Emerging Technologies with Smart Patent Indicators: The Example of Smart Houses

Carsten C. Guderian*

*WHU-Otto Beisheim School of Management
Burgplatz 2, 56179 Vallendar, Germany
carsten.guderian@whu.edu*

Patent information plays a key role in technology intelligence. As granted patent rights provide temporary exclusivity to commercialize inventions, emerging technologies are marked by brisk increases in patenting, revealing patent-based information as sources for corporate technology intelligence. In this paper, I analyze one such emerging technology, smart houses, which refers to connected and centrally controlled everyday household solutions. I provide a detailed technology landscape study that tracks longitudinal patenting changes in the technology during the 18-year period from 2000 to 2017. Central to the analyses is the use of smart indicators and longitudinal annual data, allowing tracking changes over time. The analyses encompass general patenting trends in the technology of smart houses, including the detection of key players, pertinent technology class developments, and most relevant countries for the technology of smart houses. The case study results indicate that the use of smart indicators and longitudinal data supplements established patent indicators in technology intelligence by providing additional insights to the emergence of new technologies that cannot be detected by conventional measures.

Keywords: Emerging technologies; longitudinal data; patent analytics; smart houses; smart indicators; technological change; technological forecasting; technological foresight; technology intelligence.

1. Introduction

Identifying latest trends, pending technological change, and competitor strategies is an integral part of firms' routine intelligence activities [e.g. Ernst (1996); Gerybadze

*Carsten is also Data Analyst/Data Scientist at PatentSight GmbH in addition to his affiliation with WHU-Otto Beisheim School of Management.

This chapter was originally published in *International Journal of Innovation and Technology Management*, Vol. 16, No. 2, February 2019, published by World Scientific Publishing, Singapore. Reprinted with permission.

(1994); Martino (2003); Lichtenthaler (2004); Altuntas *et al.* (2015); Ernst (2017)]. Purposes for these intelligence activities include preventing competitors from advancing unnoticed, avoiding failure to maintain competitive business models, and crafting successful corporate strategies [Bower and Christensen (1995); Christensen (1997)]. Out of the variety of methods and sources used in technology intelligence and technological forecasting, patent data-based analytics has proven reliable and accurate [e.g. Campbell (1983); Ernst (1997); Altuntas *et al.* (2015); Mathew (2015)]. Reasons for this reliability include the timely availability of patents in a systematic, documented manner, also for firms that are not subject to publication requirements on their research and development efforts and outcomes [e.g. Pavitt (1985); Basberg (1987); Brockhoff (1992); Ernst (1996)].

Patent-based technology intelligence spans various fields of application, from technological change to trend analyses, firm performance ties, as well as industrial or national developments [e.g. Pavitt (1985); Basberg (1987); Wilson (1987a, 1987b); Ernst (1997)]. For all of these fields of application, various indicators that build on patent information were developed and empirically tested [e.g. Brockhoff (1992); Ernst (1996, 2001, 2003)]. The most common approaches to assign importance or value to patents are to analyze their (forward) citations [e.g. Campbell (1983); Ernst (1997); Daim *et al.* (2006); Nair and Mathew (2015)] or international scope and patent family sizes [Lanjouw *et al.* (1998); Harhoff *et al.* (2003); Fischer and Leidinger (2014)]. Other conventional measures span, for example, different types of citations, technology classes and their relatedness, and patent ages [e.g. Omland (2011)].

Prior use of patent information in technology intelligence predominantly relied on cross-sectional patent information, which does not allow tracking changes of patent indicator values over time and impedes both technology intelligence results as well as derivable strategic guidance. Most patent indicators are calculated based on filed or granted patent stocks, ignoring patents legal status. Only active patents are valid and enforceable. Contrastingly, recent patent indicators, called smart indicators, focus on qualitative patent information [e.g. Ernst and Omland (2011); Ernst (2017); Fankhauser *et al.* (2018)]. These new indicators allow identifying the development of emerging technologies during longer, pre-defined time periods, by incorporating information from multiple points in time and using indicators incorporating technological potential assessments. They are able to discern patenting activity or quantities from patenting quality or strength and account for patents' legal status.

To illustrate the effectiveness of longitudinal data and smart indicators in corporate technology intelligence, I present a unique case study on the technology of smart houses, for which the corresponding 24,264 patent families,[a] including 16,462 active patent families on December 31, 2017, were identified by the Swiss Federal Institute of Intellectual Property in cooperation with EconSight using International Patent Classification (IPC) and Cooperative Patent Classification (CPC) classes as

---

[a] The concept of patent families is defined in Sec. 2.2.

well as keywords. I cover the development of this technology during the 18-year time period from 2000 to 2017. The data is not limited to few countries or firms, but incorporates global data.

The results show that making use of smart indicators and longitudinal data allows to complement established patent indicators in technology intelligence by providing additional insights to the emergence of new technologies and patterns of change that are not detectable by conventional measures, e.g. indicators related to patenting activity like patent filings or forward citations. Focusing on smart patent indicators related to patent quality or patent strength allows decision-makers to identify general growth trends, to detect key players, i.e. those that own valuable portfolios, regardless of portfolio sizes, and to recognize overall developments of technologies [Fankhauser *et al.* (2018)]. Firms that are subject to brisk patent quantity or quality increases may be detected by use of longitudinal data, revealing their emphasis on technological trends. Regional focus of industries and inventive countries are also traceable. The analyses reveal that data quality is required as an important prerequisite to conduct meaningful technology intelligence by shifting analytical focus from detecting activity (patenting quantities) compared to impact (patenting quality).

This paper is structured as follows. Section 2 introduces patent analytics-based technology intelligence and provides an overview of patent-based indicators applied in technology intelligence. Advantages of using smart patent indicators and longitudinal rather than cross-sectional data in technology intelligence are introduced. Section 3 presents the domains and methods covered by the technology landscape analysis to detect emerging technologies in the area of smart houses. Section 4 depicts the results that Sec. 5 discusses further by drawing inferences for managerial purposes as well as future research.

2. Patent Analytics-Based Technology Intelligence

2.1. *Definition and introduction*

Lichtenthaler [2003] distinguished two schools of research to define corporate technology-related intelligence activities: technology forecasting and technology intelligence. Technology forecasting is "[to make] a conjecture about the future" [Martino (1993)]. It originated in military efforts to predict enemies' technological advancements and "studies the state of application of individual methods" [Organisation for Economic Co-operation and Development (1967); Lichtenthaler (2003)]. Technology intelligence refers to "the practice of analyzing competitors' technology" [Brockhoff (1991)]. It comprises the institutionalized collection of relevant data for managerial decision-making considering efficiency and effectiveness [Brockhoff (1991); Lichtenthaler (2003, 2004)]. However, Lichtenthaler [2003, 2004] suggested studying technology intelligence independent of how it is performed. Various methods and sources are employed in these technology intelligence and technological forecasting activities [e.g. Porter (2005); Cuhls (2008); Yoon and

Kim (2012)]. Patent analytics has proven most reliable and accurate for reasons such as the timely availability of patents in a systematic manner for all firms regardless of their sizes or publication requirements [e.g. Campbell (1983); Pavitt (1985); Basberg (1987); Brockhoff (1992); Ernst (1996, 1997); Altuntas et al. (2015); Mathew (2015)]. Firms conducting proficient patent analytics outperform firms who do not regularly apply patent analytics [Ernst et al. (2016)].

Corporate technology intelligence-related patent analytics spans various strategic purposes [Altuntas et al. (2015)].[b] These purposes range, e.g. from (I) the identification of new technologies to detect future technological change [e.g. Pavitt (1985); Basberg (1987); Brockhoff (1992)] to (II) trend analyses based on patents [e.g. Wilson (1987a); Ernst (1997); Yoon and Lee (2012); Gao et al. (2013)] and (III) competitor activity monitoring [e.g. Wilson (1987b); Ernst (1996, 1997)]. (I) Pavitt [1985] identified four areas where patent information can be used to trace innovative activities that lead to technological change, ranging from (i) trade and production effects to (ii) firm performances and industrial structures, (iii) technology fields and industrial sectors, to (iv) science proximity. Basberg [1987] reviewed the use of patent data to measure technological change, emphasizing on opportunities but particularly challenges to derive meaningful assertions. Brockhoff [1992] introduced measures of individual firms' patenting activities, patent portfolios for inter-firm comparisons, and matrix algebra for importance weightings for patents to predict technological change. (II) Ernst [1997] used patent data to describe the diffusion of CNC-technology along the stages of the technological lifecycle, showing that patents accordingly describe the trend. Gao et al. [2013] also conducted comparable lifecycle-related analyses. Yoon and Lee [2012] compared research and development inputs, i.e. expenditure, and output, i.e. patent application, data, fitting patent applications to technological S-curves to scrutinize latest technological trend and activities, also pertaining to sectoral differences in patenting. (III) Wilson [1987a, 1987b] valued patent analysis as an "aid to decision-making in such areas as acquisitions and divestitures, R&D planning and new product development," as it allows obtaining technological and competitive activity measures. Ernst [1996] depicted the relevance and identified potential use cases for patent analytics in corporate activities, relating technology intelligence to innovation management, research and development activities, and superior corporate performance. Analyzing trade patterns, Ernst [1997] showed that immediate market changes were caused by patenting activity, recommending to systematically and continuously monitoring patenting activity as part of corporate intelligence activities.

Technology intelligence and patent analytics using patent stock and citation data as measures of inventive activity were also linked to superior firm performance [e.g. Griliches et al. (1991); Ernst (2001); Hall et al. (2005); Ernst et al. (2016)] and

---

[b] Altuntas et al. [2015] provided a recent overview of patent-based technology intelligence, including related methods and strategic purposes.

national developments [e.g. Griliches (1990); Jaffe *et al.* (1993); Tijssen (2001); Criscuolo *et al.* (2005)]. Griliches *et al.* [1991] confirmed the importance of firms' technological investments for their future rates of return in the pharmaceutical industry. Ernst [2001] showed that international patenting activity is related to subsequent firm performance increases. Hall *et al.* [2005] measured patents' importance via their citations and found that market value is significantly increased by about three percent per citation, with self-citations being more valuable than external citations and unpredictable stronger affecting market value than predictable citations.[c] Ernst *et al.* [2016] showed that patent management is key to explain performance outcomes rather than the number of patents filed or patent portfolio sizes. On national level, Griliches [1990] used patent activity data to detect economic development. Jaffe *et al.* [1993], Tijssen [2001], and Criscuolo *et al.* [2005] relied on patents for cross-country comparisons and the identification of research and development patterns, e.g. via knowledge spillovers.

2.2. *Patent indicators and methods*

Various patent indicators were developed and empirically tested within technology intelligence-related patent analytics to achieve the previously stated purposes [e.g. Brockhoff (1992); Ernst (1995, 1996, 2003)]. Traditionally, counts of patenting activity or portfolio sizes, i.e. number of patents filed, applied, or granted, were benchmarked to competitors' figures or incumbent technologies [e.g. Comanor and Scherer (1969); Basberg (1987); Griliches (1990); Brockhoff *et al.* (1999)]. Brisk increases in patent counts in certain periods, firms, industries, countries or technologies proved indication of inventive activity [Ernst (1997, 2001)].

To augment the reliability of patent metrics, simple counts were combined with data mined from patents' texts [e.g. Brockhoff (1992); Ernst (1996, 2003); Yoon and Park (2004); Lee *et al.* (2009)]. Most commonly, importance and value to patents and their underlying technologies was assigned based on their number of forward citations [e.g. Campbell (1983); Griliches *et al.* (1991); Pavitt (1985); Ernst (1995, 1996); Nair and Mathew (2015)] and their international scopes in terms of family sizes [e.g. Ernst (1995, 1996); Lanjouw *et al.* (1998); Harhoff *et al.* (2003); Fischer and Leidinger (2014)]. Forward citations refer to references received by patents from future patents and are indicative of technologies' impacts on subsequent technologies. In terms of technology intelligence, the more citations certain technologies, that is their patents, receive, the more likely is that the underlying technology finds widespread application. Patent families are "a set of either patent applications or publications taken in multiple countries to protect a single invention by a common inventor(s) and then patented in more than one country" [European Patent Office (2017)]. Patent families refer to technologies' geographical scopes of protection.

---

[c] Patent citations originate from various sources, e.g. inventors, examiners, or appeals [Criscuolo and Verspagen (2008)].

Similar to citations, the more jurisdictions or geographical spheres are protected, the more likely is that the underlying technology finds global application. Other conventional measures span different types of citations, for example citations to non-patent literature as science proximity and self-citations as firms' concentrations on specific technologies, but also the number and relatedness of technology classes or patent ages [e.g. Ernst (1996); Harhoff *et al.* (2003); Harhoff and Reitzig (2004); Reitzig (2004); Omland (2011)].

The other alternative to these conventional measures in patent-based technology intelligence became multi-step processes using patent data characteristics as information sources. These approaches combined patent information with intelligence tools such as analogies, growth curves, and scenario planning [e.g. Daim *et al.* (2006); Lee *et al.* (2009); Yoon and Lee (2012); Lee *et al.* (2015)]. These approaches derived imprecise, subjective results, forfeiting the advantages of patents as objective data in technology intelligence.[d] As also identified by Yoon and Lee [2012], careful choices on where and how to apply patent analytics and which complementary data sources are chosen need to be made.

2.3. *Smart indicators and longitudinal data*

While most patent analysts relied on conventional patent indicators like patent counts, forward citations, and patent family sizes, several issues became important. Foremost, the established indicators introduced in Sec. 2.2 suffer from various distortions due to the heterogeneous global patent system [e.g. Pavitt (1985); Basberg (1987); Ernst and Omland (2011); Omland (2011)]. Reliable use of forward citations requires adjustments for issues such as patent ages, patent office practices like home biases in citations, and specific characteristics of technologies like varying marginal propensities to patent [e.g. Narin *et al.* (1997); McMillan *et al.* (2000); Criscuolo *et al.* (2005); De Rassenfosse *et al.* (2013)].

Conventional indicators become more appropriate to assess technological capabilities and opportunities when jointly measured [e.g. Fischer and Leidinger (2014)]. Patents deemed valuable from the technological perspective, i.e. due to high forward citations figures, are inoperable for its owners without active patent family members. This requires to account for patents' legal status instead of only looking at annual filing counts that do not reveal how many filed patents remain active for the point in time of interest [see also Fankhauser *et al.* (2018)]. Filing year trends are inferior to analyses that incorporate information which patents were active and legally enforceable at which point in time, which may be termed the reporting date. The geographical spheres where patent protection is sought needs to be considered, too, as often done when incorporating patent family sizes [e.g. Ernst (1995, 1996); Lanjouw *et al.* (1998); Harhoff *et al.* (2003); Fischer and Leidinger (2014)]. Markets where protection might

---

[d]For this reason, these hybrid technological forecasting and technology intelligence approaches are not focal to the subsequent deliberations.

be sought include domestic markets, sourcing markets, competitors' markets, customers' markets, or transit countries. Patents deemed valuable from the technological perspective, e.g. due to many subsequent citations, are less valuable to their owners if they are not protected in many geographical spheres. Similarly, low quality patents that are protected in many markets might waste financial resources required for patent maintenance. Due to substantial costs of filing and maintaining patents in each country, firms only seek to protect their inventions in various geographical spheres when it is economically promising or beneficial [e.g. Ernst (1995, 1996); Harhoff *et al.* (2003)]. Identifying and analyzing the quality of patents in patent portfolios is more important than identifying patenting activity, i.e. large patent portfolio quantities.

The recent rise in importance of intellectual property and particularly patents [e.g. Conley *et al.* (2013b); Ocean Tomo LLC (2015); Conley (2017)] led to the creation of patent analytics software and development of smart indicators [e.g. Allison *et al.* (2004); Ernst and Omland (2011); Thoma (2014); Baron *et al.* (2016); Ernst (2017); Fankhauser *et al.* (2018)].[e] Subsequently used in research, institutional, and corporate reports, Ernst and Omland [2011], for example, developed a set of indicators that incorporate patent quality and patent strength indication: Technology Relevance, Market Coverage, Competitive Impact, and Patent Asset Index. As depicted in Table 1, these measures are calculated at the patent family level.

Firms' patent portfolio sizes refer to firms' active patent stock, i.e. granted patents as well as patent applications, as the latter provide a certain level of protection [Ernst and Omland (2011); Stefan (2013)]. In contrast to patent counts that are often based on filed or granted patents, the portfolio size incorporates information whether these filed or granted patents remain active [Fankhauser *et al.* (2018)]. This is particularly valuable for longitudinal datasets, as decision-makers become able only to include those patent families in annual values that were active at these specific reporting dates. Scholars like Brem *et al.* [2016] and Fankhauser *et al.* [2018] already demonstrated the benefits of longitudinal patent data.

Technology Relevance refers to the number of forward citations, i.e. the number of citations patents received of a focal set[f] of patent families [Ernst and Omland (2011)]. The measure resembles the external view on the importance of the invention that is protected by its respective patent family. Technology Relevance comprises the subsequent use of the invention, with the interpretation that the technological value is higher for patent families that are cited more often by subsequent patent families. Underlying inventions of patents that cite a focal patent build on the invention protected by the focal patent. Instead of simplistic aggregations, adjustments for age, patent office's citation practices and technologies' peculiarities are

---

[e] For more information on various patent analytics software tools, refer to Stefan [2013] and Oldham and Kitsara [2016].

[f] The focal set is defined by the decision-maker and is usually customized to the desired analyses, e.g. covering the patent families of certain business units, firms, industries, or countries.

Table 1.   Smart patent indicators.

Measure	Definition and Explanation	Advantages	Disadvantages
Technology Relevance	• Defined as the weighted counts of worldwide patent citations received. Citations received corrected for age, technology field, and patent office practices	• Interpretable measure for patent value based on forward citations • Validated by scientific publications	• Might not reflect the ability to commercialize the underlying invention • Might not assess the value of young patents correctly
Market Coverage	• Defined as sum of the gross domestic product (GDP) of all countries in which the invention is patent-protected, relative to the GDP of the USA	• Measures geographical scope of protection incorporating relative market size importance • Approach allows cross-industry and cross-national comparisons	• Does not account for industry-, firm-, or business unit-specific importance of different markets
Competitive Impact	• Patent quality in terms of impact and scope of protection • Measured as a product of Technology Relevance and Market Coverage	• Requires high Technology Relevance and high Market Coverage to be assigned high Competitive Impact • Lowers patent value if these are unprotected in global markets and vice versa	• Does not indicate whether the patent family quality stems from Technology Relevance or Market Coverage
Patent Asset Index	• Sum of Competitive Impacts of all patents in a portfolio	• Depicts overall strength of a patent portfolio by accounting for impact, coverage, and portfolio size	• Does not account for portfolio size and resulting effects
Portfolio Size	• Sum of all active patent families owned by an entity	• Accounts legal status (active or not) compared to filing year or grant year patent counts	• Does not depict the quality or strength of a patent portfolio

Source: Own illustration, based on Ernst and Omland [2011].

made [Ernst and Omland (2011); Stefan (2013)]. Reasons for these sophistications are that patent citations are a function of time, propensities to cite focal art vary amongst national patent offices, and technologies are subject to different practices whether it is common to cite extensively or rarely [e.g. Ernst (2003); Hall *et al.* (2005); Omland (2011)].

Market Coverage refers to the sum of all countries where the focal set of patent families is active [Ernst and Omland (2011)]. The measure resembles the internal view on the importance of the invention that is protected by a patent family. It comprises the geographical scope of protection, with the interpretation that the value is higher for patent families with members in more countries. As patents are territorial rights, the respective inventions and its assigned patent families can only be enforced in the countries were protection had been sought for. As patents are protected in more countries, firms become able to operate in a larger geographical sphere. Instead of simply counting the number of countries with active protection, the countries are aggregated based on their market size in terms of their relative gross domestic products relative to the gross domestic product of the United States of America (USA) as the largest global economy [e.g. Ernst and Omland (2011); Stefan (2013)]. To account for patents' legal status, discounts to 70% for pending patents prior to grant are incorporated.

Competitive Impact refers to the multiplied product of Technology Relevance and Market Coverage [Ernst and Omland (2011)]. By combining corrected citation information and market size where patent families are protected, the measure integrates the two factors most established in prior research to indicate patent value [e.g. Campbell (1983); Griliches *et al.* (1991); Ernst (1995); Pavitt (1985); Ernst (1996); Lanjouw *et al.* (1998); Ernst (2003); Harhoff *et al.* (2003); Fischer and Leidinger (2014)]. Multiplying both indicators ensures that only patents with broad geographical scope and high forward citation figures score high in terms of Competitive Impact and are assigned high levels of patent quality [Ernst and Omland (2011); Stefan (2013); Fankhauser *et al.* (2018)]. For patent portfolios, Patent Asset Index is the sum of the Competitive Impact values assigned to all patent families of a focal set [Ernst and Omland (2011)]. For individual patent families, the Patent Asset Index value equals to the Competitive Impact. Comparable to established patent indicators like forward citations, patent counts, and family size indications, the smart indicators are employable for use cases such as benchmarking, merger and acquisition analyses, licensing, trend analyses, portfolio management, and R&D performance evaluations, as the measures allow comparisons across business-units, corporate portfolios or any other selected focal patent stocks [Buehler *et al.* (2017); Symrise (2017a, 2017b); Hofmann (2018)].

3. Method

I choose to investigate the technology of smart houses for two reasons. First, patent families exist for this technology for the entire investigation period since 2000. Thus, smart houses may be considered as an already established technology. Second, there has been an increase in patenting in this technology in recent years, particularly a duplication of the number of active and pending patents in the four years 2013 to 2017. Smart houses is an established but active technology with recent changes, thus ideal to test smart patent indicators [see also Shin *et al.* (2018)].

To analyze the technology of smart house technologies, the respective patent families belonging to this technology had to be identified. For this purpose, I relied on technology classifications provided by the Swiss Federal Institute of Intellectual Property and EconSight. Using searches incorporating the IPC and CPC schemes and keywords, the two institutions jointly categorized patents to technology fields [Swiss Federal Institute of Intellectual Property (2018)]. In their classification, smart houses are a subcategory of the technology area termed "Internet of Things", which also incorporates connected machines and smart city technologies. It encompasses all devices used in households and garages, including furniture, household appliances, etc. For devices to be considered smart, three criteria have to be fulfilled according to the Swiss Federal Institute of Intellectual Property and EconSight [2018] to include the respective patents in the technology: a device has to exist, it has to make interactions, and it needs to communicate. For illustration, consider these criteria for the capabilities of smart window blinds compared to those of regular, manually-operated window blinds. The blinds have to exist, i.e. be mantled to the wall and windows they cover (criterion 1). Moreover, they need to interact, i.e. close themselves when detecting sunlight or certain degrees of brightness during daylight or darkness at night (criterion 2). Whilst these two criteria qualify for basic sensors, the device turns smart if it also communicates, i.e. if the blinds can collect weather forecasts from internet sources or are connected to the heating system to switch heating on or off depending on the weather conditions outside (criterion 3).

Whilst the smartness of such devices stems from integrated sensors in the communicative devices, the main focus of this set of smart houses technology is on aspects related to digital features and data processing [Swiss Federal Institute of Intellectual Property (2018)]. The IPC and CPC classes of the technology of smart houses include the CPC classes G05B, H04L, Y02B, Y04S and IPC classes G05B and H04L [Swiss Federal Institute of Intellectual Property (2018)].[g] The search yields 24,264 patent families, which includes 16,462 active patent families on December 31, 2017.[h] These patent families constitute the sample used for the analyses. All analyses, whether longitudinal or cross-sectional, are based on these patent families.

For the analyses, I rely on the Business Intelligence analytics software provided by PatentSight GmbH. It is a German business analytics platform company providing insights into the global patent landscape for decision-makers since 2008 [Buehler *et al.* (2017); PatentSight (2017)].[i] The structure of the database interface allows querying for patents and conducting analyses based on filter and measure selection options. Via the software, users can trace annual patent data information for each year since 2000. These annual values are reported using the reporting date concept to account for the patent families' legal status. Instead of patents filed or granted, only those patent families active or pending at each point in time are considered, but not those that had ceased to exist, e.g. due to patent lapse or as they had been dropped [see also Fankhauser *et al.* (2018)]. Using the filter provided by the Swiss Federal Institute of Intellectual Property and EconSight, I select the patents belonging

---

[g] The exact search string used by the Swiss Federal Institute of Intellectual Property and EconSight is proprietary to these institutions.

[h] The analyses for Fig. 8 contained 16,466 active patent families as of December 31, 2017.

[i] Since 2018, the PatentSight GmbH is part of LexisNexis Legal & Professional, a division of the RELX Group.

to the technology of smart houses. For the individual analyses, I use the filter and measure selection as well as display options provided by the database interface.[j]

4. Results

Depicting the annual patent data values for the 18 years from 2000 to 2017, the technology of smart houses' growth becomes traceable (see Fig. 1), the field grew, both in terms of patent quantity as measured by the portfolio size and patent strength as measured by the Patent Asset Index. Steep increases are not detected, but fairly gradual increases become visible. Despite growing by 978.77% from 1,526 to 16,462 patent families for patent quantity (portfolio size) and from 5,659 to 38,380 in Patent Asset Index value for patent strength in the investigation period, the spread between patent strength and patent quantity gradually decreased from 3.71 to 2.33.[k] This means that the average patent quality in the technology has reduced, i.e. the growth in strength results from few patents only whilst many new patents are of low quality.

Choosing a different display option, the technology of smart houses is analyzed at a deeper level in terms of its top CPC Level 4 classes (see Fig. 2). The technology's

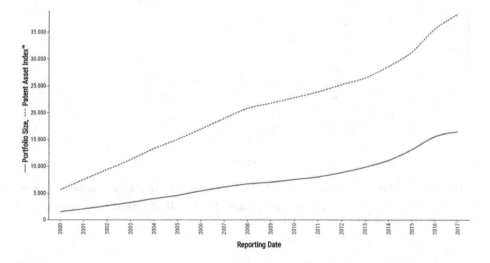

Source: Own illustration, Data December 31, 2017, PatentSight Business Intelligence Analytics Software.

Fig. 1. Smart houses technology development 2000–2017.

---

[j] The presented patent analytics are not subject to assumptions on firms' levels of knowledge on their patent portfolios and potential differences towards external portfolios or varying extends of patent analytics application between firms, as we analyze the technological field of smart houses based on externally available patent information.

[k] In 2000, the portfolio size was 1,526 and the Patent Asset Index was at 5,659. In 2017, the portfolio size was 16,462 and the Patent Asset Index was at 38,380.

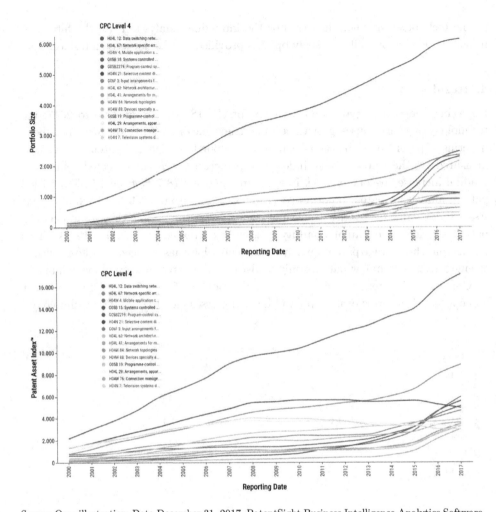

Source: Own illustration, Data December 31, 2017, PatentSight Business Intelligence Analytics Software.

Fig. 2.   Smart houses technology class development 2000–2017 (top 15 CPC Level 4 classes) in terms of patent quantity (top) and patent strength (bottom).

largest classes grew to diverging extends. The largest class, both in terms of patent quantity and patent strength, is H04L12 for "data switching networks interconnections of, or transfer of information". Throughout the years, it grew by 1023.54% from a portfolio size of 548 patent families to 6,157 patent families and a Patent Asset Index of 2,191 to 17,168. Among the other top ranked technology classes, it can be seen that some grew particularly in terms of patent strength as measured by Patent Asset Index, for example, CPC classes H04L67 or H04W4. Conversely, other technology classes grew particularly in terms of patent quantity as measured by portfolio size, for example, CPC classes G05B19 or G05B2219.

Exchanging the display filter from CPC Level 4 classes to owners, it is possible to detect the technology's key players (see Fig. 3). Large conglomerates like Samsung, LG Electronics, and Panasonic Corporation own the largest portfolios. Depending on ranking patent quantity, as measured by portfolio size, or patent strength, as measured by Patent Asset Index, the list of the key players pertains to different rank orders.

Switching from longitudinal to cross-sectional analytics, I take the key players and their data as of December 31, 2017. Identifying the key players that own at least one percent of the total Patent Asset Index in the technology of smart houses as in Fig. 4, it becomes visible that there is no one dominant player in this technology.

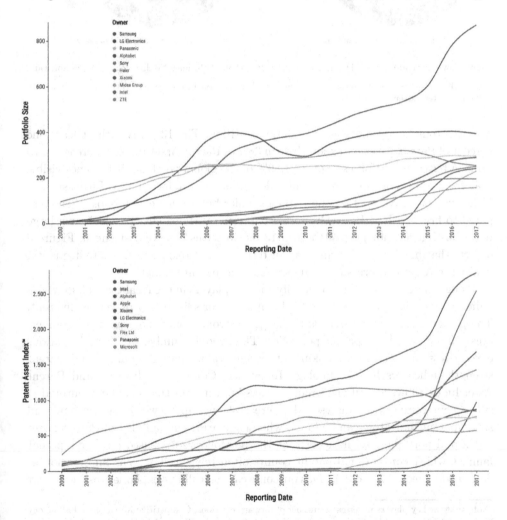

Source: Own illustration, Data December 31, 2017, PatentSight Business Intelligence Analytics Software.

Fig. 3. Key players in smart houses 2000–2017 (top 10 owners) in terms of patent quantity (top) and patent strength (bottom).

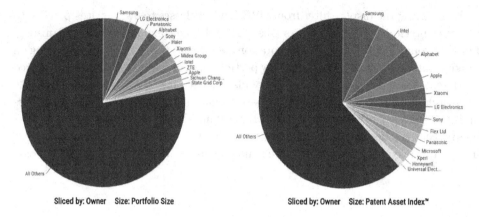

Source: Own illustration, Data December 31, 2017, PatentSight Business Intelligence Analytics Software.

Fig. 4.   Key players in smart houses on December 31, 2017 (top 14 owners in terms of patent quantity (left) and patent strength (right)).

The electronic conglomerates are relatively strong. The 13 firms with at least one percent of Patent Asset Index jointly own 38% of Patent Asset Index, whereas top 13 firms in terms of portfolio size own 21.89% of the global portfolio. It becomes visible that the two lists of top 13 firms differ depending on the focal index. Firms such as Honeywell or Universal Electronics own smaller but valuable portfolios when compared to firms such as Haier Group Corporation or Midea Group, which own large portfolios but are not part of the top 13 list in terms of patent strength. Figure 3 depicts that mainly Asian firms lead in terms of portfolio sizes, i.e. patent quality, whilst the American firms by tendency focus on patent strength.

Using different indicators to identify the key players in the focal technology yields indicator-specific results (see Fig. 5). Each indicator's list of key players is different. The portfolio size measure yields the large electronic conglomerates, as conglomerates usually have large patent portfolios. The average number of forward citations derives less known firms. Looking at patent value, patent quality, and patent strength indicators like Technology Relevance, Competitive Impact, and Patent Asset Index allows identifying smaller or less known firms that may be monitored in subsequent competition analyses. The greatest overlap between conventional and smart patent indicators can be found when comparing the rank list of Patent Asset Index and portfolio size, noticing that the portfolio size is based on active patent families whilst conventional patent counts often rely on filing year information as described in Secs. 2.2 and 2.3.[1] This outcome can logically be explained, as the patent

---

[1]Note that the key players in terms of number of forward citations, Competitive Impact and Technology Relevance (top row in Fig. 5) are average values for firms, typically resulting in lists with firms with smaller portfolios. By contrast, the Patent Asset Index and portfolio size are calculated based on all active patents of firms. The smart indicators support technology intelligence by showing these smaller yet important firms that market players have to watch out for.

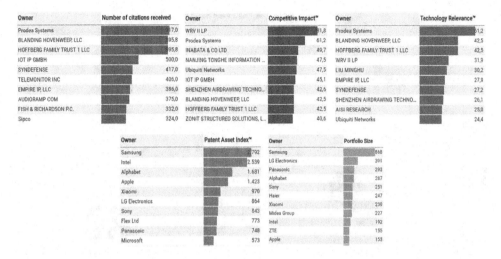

Source: Own illustration, Data December 31, 2017, PatentSight Business Intelligence Analytics Software.

Fig. 5.   Key players in smart houses on December 31, 2017 (smart patent indicators).

strength measure combines the patent quality and patent quantity measures, and the patent quantity takes its effect. Again, the results call to analyze measures beyond patent quantity to incorporate patent quality and other smart patent indicators not to miss important players with less massive portfolios. Another reason for this overlap between the mentioned smart and conventional patent indicators is due to the scale transformation that occurs when expressing cardinal-scaled indicators in rankings. As they become expressed on ordinal scales, information contained in cardinal-scaled indicators like the Patent Asset Index is not depicted, suggesting overlap but disregarding important information only detectable with cardinal-scaled indicators.

To identify the key players in specific industries, patents of firms and subsidiaries are jointly assessed. Patent assignees and patent owners are not necessarily the parent firms or holdings with their well-known corporate names, but may be small subsidiaries with completely different names or have undergone name changes.[m] Forfeiting the correct matching of only single subsidiaries may spoil the most sophisticated analytical procedures (see Fig. 6). Only the single subsidiary Nest Labs Inc.[n] with 135 active and inactive patent families was dropped from the portfolio of Alphabet Inc., the Google Inc. parent entity. Dropping Nest Labs Inc. from the

---

[m] To correctly identify firms' portfolios during the harmonization process, other patents such as reassignments to firms as well as patents from firms that had name changes have to be considered, too. Otherwise, portfolios may be incomplete.

[n] Nest Labs Inc. is an US producer of internet-connected smart house devices such as smoke detectors, thermostats, and security systems. For more information, please visit https://nest.com/.

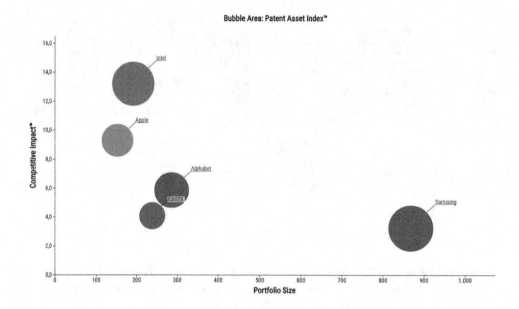

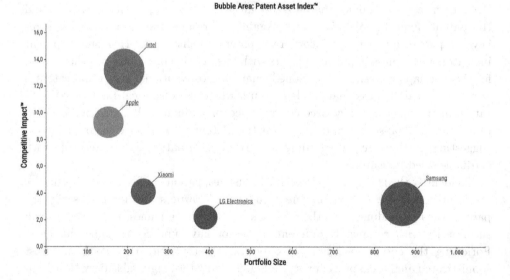

Source: Own illustration, Data December 31, 2017, PatentSight Business Intelligence Analytics Software.

Fig. 6.   Importance of data quality (top owner changes resulting from correct (top) versus incorrect (bottom) subsidiary information).

Alphabet Inc. portfolio discarded Alphabet Inc. from the list of top 5 firms in favor of LG Electronics.°

Returning to longitudinal analyses, it becomes possible to trace the geographical hubs of the smart houses technology. For this purpose, I identify the top countries where patents are active and their annual data points from 2000 to 2017 (see Fig. 7).

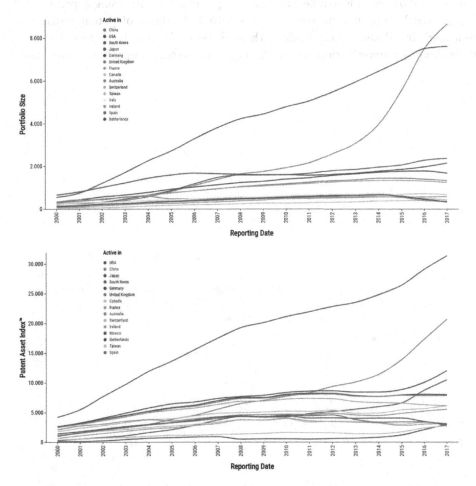

Source: Own illustration, Data December 31, 2017, PatentSight Business Intelligence Analytics Software.

Fig. 7.   Top active countries development in smart houses 2000–2017 (top 15 countries) in terms of patent quantity (top) and patent strength (bottom).

°Nest Labs, Inc. was acquired by Google, Inc. (Alphabet) with the purpose to gain expertise in smart houses. One reviewer pointed out that Google/Alphabet is not in top firms' list in smart houses for this reason. However, the analyses focus on what firms' control, not where firms' specific patents originated (i.e. internally or externally). Hence, this even reassures the reason why harmonized data is required for technology intelligence; omitting Nest Labs from Google's portfolio does not depict the knowledge base the firm controls in smart houses technology. Nonetheless, I thank the reviewer for making this important addition.

The number of active patent families rose particularly in the USA, Asian countries like China, Japan, and South Korea followed by European countries like France, Germany, and the United Kingdom. In 2016, China overtook the USA as the top country in terms of active patents in smart houses, after surpassing South Korea and Japan to become the world's second largest country in terms of smart house technology in 2007. South Korea became third largest country surpassing Japan in 2010, lagging the European countries to places 5 to 7. In terms of patent strength as measured by Patent Asset Index, the US portfolio has been more valuable throughout the investigation period. China rose to become runner-up in smart house

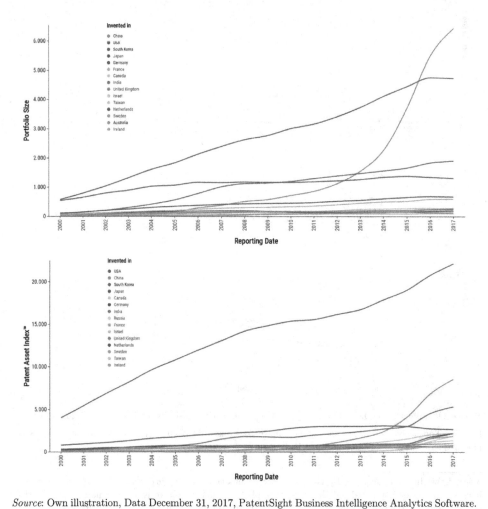

Source: Own illustration, Data December 31, 2017, PatentSight Business Intelligence Analytics Software.

Fig. 8.   Top inventor countries development in smart houses 2000–2017 (top 15 countries) in terms of patent quantity (top) and patent strength (bottom).

patent strength in 2011. Again, the Asian countries are in advance of the European countries particularly since 2015.

A comparable geographical analysis is conducted for the patents' countries of origin by analyzing inventor address data from 2000 to 2017, deriving a similar picture (see Fig. 8). In 2015, more patents were active that originated from China, i.e. were invented in China, for the first time with the US loosing leadership in this regard. Accounting for the patent strength, the USA has been the key player from 2000 to 2017, with China rising to become runner-up in 2014. In terms of portfolio size for active patents originating from the respective country, South Korea surpassed Japan in 2009, but only in 2015 in terms of Patent Asset Index.[P] Compared to the European countries, the number of active Canadian inventions in smart houses is relatively low, but these fewer patents outperform the European countries in terms of patent strength.

5. Discussion and Conclusion

Complementing conventional patent-based measures such as forward citations with smart indicators and analyses incorporating longitudinal rather than cross-sectional data improves patent-based technology intelligence, revealing additional insights on recent developments and pending technological change. Relying on the case study of smart houses, I analyze this technology and its corresponding 24,264 active and inactive patent families as identified by the Swiss Federal Institute of Intellectual Property over the 18-year period from 2000 to 2017. Using the smart patent indicators developed by Ernst and Omland [2011], I become able to detect the overall developments in this specific technology. I identify pivotal technology classes in smart houses and their annual as well as overall growth. Key players in terms of patenting activity, patenting quality, and patenting strength are identified.

The analyses, focusing on geographical hubs, key players, and technology class developments, smart indicators, complement conventional measures by discerning patent quantity and patent quality or patent strength information. Incorporating longitudinal data, China has most active patents in smart houses since 2016 and since 2015, it is the top inventor country in terms of patenting activity, but the US outperforms China and all other Asian, European, and North American countries. As expected, the large electronic conglomerates dominate the smart houses technology, but substantial patent portfolio differences may be detected. The list of key players is subject to differences when analyzing these firms, but the lists are highly indicator-dependent and indicator-specific. Additionally, the analyses show that it is important to integrate legal information, i.e. patents' status at each reporting date, and harmonize firms ensuring that all subordinate entities and their respective

---

[P]Note that both portfolio size and Patent Asset Index are smart patent indicators, as portfolio size contains only the active patents at each reporting date, contrasting prior research that is usually based on filing years and disregards patents' legal status.

patents are incorporated in analyses. Data quality prevents misinterpretations of patent data, yielding information that may be employed in various technology intelligence activities.

Smart indicators enhance prior patent-based technology intelligence approaches. The present case study yields several contributions to the literature in this regard. First, in contrast to conventional measures like patent filing, application, or grant counts, they incorporate information on patents' legal status; filing or grant counts to not contain information whether these patents remain active and enforceable or if they ceased to exist prior to the point in time of interest, e.g. as they lapsed or were dropped by their owners. Second, by discerning activity, i.e. patent quantities, from patent quality and patent strength, smart patent indicators provide insights beyond forward citation information or patent family sizes. As these smart indicators are data-based, they provide objective and replicable technology intelligence results, contrasting multi-sequential methodologies that are prone to subjective decisions.[q] The smart indicators further allow the identification of firms with smaller but important patent portfolios that are not detectable with conventional measures and approaches as they do not stand out in terms of patenting activity but may become disruptive even to currently non-competing firms, technologies, or industries due to the quality of their protected technological inventions [Bower and Christensen (1995); Christensen (1997); Funk and Owen-Smith (2017)]. Firms using smart patent indicators and patent analytics become able to detect potential threats prior to incurring impending losses or disadvantages, providing them with potentially vital advantages. In turn, the "smaller" firms may become future competitors or targets for licensing or merger and acquisition activities. Third, the smart patent indicators might also be employed in multi-sequential approaches that rely on patent information as information input sources to reduce arbitrariness in these technology intelligence results, complementing conventional measures and technology intelligence approaches.

The case study on the technology of smart houses provides important learnings and highlights improvement suggestions geared towards corporate managers and other decision-makers concerned with technology intelligence activities. Foremost, the selection and preparation of patent data prior to analytical procedures needs to be comprehensive and accurate to obtain meaningful technology intelligence results [see also Ernst and Omland (2011); Stefan (2013); Ernst (2017); Fankhauser *et al.* (2018)]. Efforts to assign patents to their actual owners should include accounting for complex corporate structures. Using only parent firm names is insuffient; patents owned by subsidiaries and subsidiaries' subsidiaries are also part of firms' portfolios

---

[q]Comparable technology intelligence results, i.e. relying on smart patent indicators and longitudinal patent data with correct ownership and legal status information, may be derived in other technologies, such as machine learning or robotics.

and need to find consideration when rating firms.[r] Data preparation requires patent information harmonization procedures such as corrections of misspellings, typographical errors, and spelling variations [e.g. Eurostat (2011); European Patent Office (2016)]. Failure to match patents to their owners, i.e. inaccurate patent ownership, impedes the detection of important players, technological classes, or geographical markets, potentially leading to sub-optimal decision-making. Other managerial implications include the benefits to move from patent activity analyses towards identifying patents and their underlying technologies and inventions that have the opportunity to outperform existing technologies, preventing competitor leapfrogging. This also involves looking at the development in technology classes, markets and key players over multiple points in time to detect above average changes.

The case study also opens an array of future research opportunities focused on employing longitudinal data and smart patent indicators in technology intelligence and patent analytics. One opportunity is to move from individual case studies, such as the present case of smart houses,. to empirical analyses on technologies that replaced incumbent technologies to enhance the validity of results. Another opportunity for scholars and practitioners is to collaborate on the development of other new indicators and indicator combinations, potentially even moving beyond the analyses of patent characteristics. Options could be to emphasize the consolidating or destabilizing nature of new technological inventions [e.g. Funk and Owen-Smith (2017)] as assessment criteria in the technology intelligence process or the incorporation of additional contingency factors, e.g. related to cross-industrial, cross-national, or cross-cultural differences. Relations to other intellectual property regimes like copyrights or trademarks and their integration in technology intelligence may be drawn [Conley *et al.* (2013a); Brem *et al.* (2017)]. Methodologically, factors from multiple levels of analyses might be integrated to understand the interplay of different levels or spheres of influence, such as multilevel modelling[s] using technology, corporate, industrial or country level data. Using inventor information, potential gender differences, e.g. concerning inventive output or inventive quality, may be assessed. Finally, incorporating kernel density estimates in addition to graphical analyses will augment future patent-based technology intelligence activities to extract additional information from smart patent indicators.

---

[r] In the present study, I analyze the technology of smart houses and the corresponding patent families that had been identified by the Swiss Federal Institute of Intellectual Property. Rating firms represented within this selection and their portfolio requires the correct assignment of patents to their ultimate entities regardless of the original identification filter, which was at the technology level.

[s] Multilevel modelling is sometimes also referred to as hierarchical linear modeling, HLM, or MLM.

Acknowledgments

The author thanks the Swiss Federal Institute of Intellectual Property (also referred to as the Swiss Patent Office), in particular Dr. Jochen Spuck and Markus Funk, EconSight, in particular Kai Gramke, as well as PatentSight GmbH, in particular Marco Richter, for the definition and patent families belonging to the technology of smart houses as well as access to the PatentSight Business Intelligence Analytics software. Furthermore, the author would like to thank Rahul Kapoor for supporting some of the analyses, as well as Marco Richter for his advice to use the corresponding database. Furthermore, the author thanks Prof. Dr. Holger Ernst (Chair of Technology and Innovation Management, WHU - Otto Beisheim School of Management) and Dr. Susann Grune, PatentSight GmbH, for valuable feedback. In addition, the author thanks the reviewers and editors for their excellent, helpful suggestions to improve this manuscript.

References

Allison, J. R., Lemley, M. A., Moore, K. A. and Trunkey, R. D. (2004). Valuable patents. *Georgetown Law Journal*, **92**, 3: 435–479.

Altuntas, S., Dereli, T. and Kusiak, A. (2015). Forecasting technology success based on patent data. *Technological Forecasting and Social Change*, **96**: 202–214.

Baron, J., Pohlmann, T. and Blind, K. (2016). Essential patents and standard dynamics. *Research Policy*, **45**, 9: 1762–1773.

Basberg, B. L. (1987). Patents and the measurement of technological change: A survey of the literature. *Research Policy*, **16**, 2–4: 131–141.

Bower, J. L. and Christensen, C. M. (1995). Disruptive technologies: Catching the wave. *Harvard Business Review*, **73**, 1: 43–53.

Brem, A., Nylund, P. A. and Hitchen, E. L. (2017). Open innovation and intellectual property rights: How do SMEs benefit from patents, industrial designs, trademarks and copyrights? *Management Decision*, **55**, 6: 1285–1306.

Brem, A., Nylund, P. A. and Schuster, G. (2016). Innovation and de facto standardization: The influence of dominant design on innovative performance, radical innovation, and process innovation. *Technovation*, **50–51**: 79–88.

Brockhoff, K. (1991). Competitor technology intelligence in German companies. *Industrial Marketing Management*, **20**, 2: 91–98.

Brockhoff, K. K. (1992). Instruments for patent data analyses in business firms. *Technovation*, **12**, 1: 41–59.

Brockhoff, K. K., Ernst, H. and Hundhausen, E. (1999). Gains and pains from licensing – Patent-portfolios as strategic weapons in the cardiac rhythm management industry. *Technovation*, **19**, 10: 605–614.

Buehler, B., Coublucq, D., Hariton, C., Langus, G. and Valletti, T. (2017). Recent developments at DG competition: 2016/2017. *Review of Industrial Organization*, **51**, 4: 397–422.

Campbell, R. S. (1983). Patent trends as a technological forecasting tool. *World Patent Information*, **5**, 3: 137–143.

Christensen, C. (1997). *The Innovator's Dilemma: When New Technologies Cause Great Firms to Fail.* Harvard Business School Press, Boston, USA.

Comanor, W. S. and Scherer, F. M. (1969). Patent statistics as a measure of technical change. *Journal of Political Economy*, **77**, 3: 392–398.

Conley, J. G. (2017). Innovation and intellectual property in the curriculum: Epistemology, pedagogy, and politics. *Technology & Innovation*, **19**, 2: 453–459.

Conley, J. G., Bican, P. M. and Ernst, H. (2013a). Value articulation: A framework for the strategic management of intellectual property. *California Management Review*, **55**, 4: 102–120.

Conley, J. G., Bican, P. M. and Wilkof, N. (2013b). WIPO study on patents and the public domain (II) — Impact of certain enterprise practices. *World Intellectual Property Organization White Paper*, pp. 1–70.

Criscuolo, P., Narula, R. and Verspagen, B. (2005). Role of home and host country innovation systems in R&D internationalisation: A patent citation analysis. *Economics of Innovation and New Technology*, **14**, 5: 417–433.

Criscuolo, P. and Verspagen, B. (2008). Does it matter where patent citations come from? Inventor vs. examiner citations in European patents. *Research Policy*, **37**, 10: 1892–1908.

Cuhls, K. (2008). *Methoden der Technikvorausschau – Eine Internationale Übersicht [Methods of Technological Foresight – An International Overview]*. Fraunhofer IRB Verlag, Stuttgart.

Daim, T. U., Rueda, G., Martin, H. and Gerdsri, P. (2006). Forecasting emerging technologies: Use of bibliometrics and patent analysis. *Technological Forecasting and Social Change*, **73**, 8: 981–1012.

De Rassenfosse, G., Dernis, H., Guellec, D., Picci, L. and van Pottelsberghe de la Potterie, B. (2013). The worldwide count of priority patents: A new indicator of inventive activity. *Research Policy*, **42**, 3: 720–737.

Ernst, H. (1995). Patenting strategies in the German mechanical engineering industry and their relationship to company performance. *Technovation*, **15**, 4: 225–236.

Ernst, H. (1996). *Patentinformationen für die strategische Planung von Forschung und Entwicklung [Patent Information for the Strategic Planning of Research and Development]*. Dissertation. DUV-Verlag, Wiesbaden, Germany.

Ernst, H. (1997). The use of patent data for technological forecasting: The diffusion of CNC-technology in the machine tool industry. *Small Business Economics*, **9**, 4: 361–381.

Ernst, H. (2001). Patent applications and subsequent changes of performance: Evidence from time-series cross-section analyses on the firm level. *Research Policy*, **30**, 1: 143–157.

Ernst, H. (2003). Patent information for strategic technology management. *World Patent Information*, **25**, 3: 233–242.

Ernst, H. (2017). Intellectual property as a management discipline. *Technology & Innovation*, **19**, 2: 481–492.

Ernst, H., Conley, J. G. and Omland, N. (2016). How to create commercial value from patents: The role of patent management. *R&D Management*, **46**, S2: 677–690.

Ernst, H. and Omland, N. (2011). The Patent Asset Index – A new approach to benchmark patent portfolios. *World Patent Information*, **33**, 1: 34–41.

European Patent Office (2016). *Name Harmonization Activities at the European Patent Office*. Available at http://www.wipo.int/edocs/mdocs/cws/en/cws_wk_ge_16/cws_wk_ge_16_epo.pdf, accessed 6 April 2018.

European Patent Office (2017). *Patent families*. Available at https://www.epo.org/searching-for-patents/helpful-resources/first-time-here/patent-families.html, accessed 14 November 2017.

Eurostat (2011). Patent Statistics at Eurostat: Methods for Regionalisation, Sector Allocation and Name Harmonisation. Publications Office of the European Union, Luxembourg.

Fankhauser, M., Moser, C. and Nyfelder, T. (2018). Patents as early indicators of technology and investment trends: Analyzing the microbiome space as a case study. *Frontiers in Bioengineering and Biotechnology*, **84**, 4: 1–7.

Fischer, T. and Leidinger, J. (2014). Testing patent value indicators on directly observed patent value — An empirical analysis of Ocean Tomo patent auctions. *Research Policy*, **43**, 3: 519–529.

Funk, R. J. and Owen-Smith, J. (2017). A dynamic network measure of technological change. *Management Science*, **63**, 3: 791–817.

Gao, L., Porter, A. L., Wang, J., Fang, S., Zhang, X., Ma, T., Wang, W. and Huang, L. (2013). Technology life cycle analysis method based on patent documents. *Technological Forecasting and Social Change*, **80**, 3: 398–407.

Gerybadze, A. (1994). Technology forecasting as a process of organisational intelligence. *R&D Management*, **24**, 2: 131–140.

Griliches, Z. (1990). Patent statistics as economic indicators: A survey. *Journal of Economic Literature*, **28**, 4: 1661–1707.

Griliches, Z., Hall, B. H. and Pakes, A. (1991). R&D, patents, and market value revisited: Is there a second (technological opportunity) factor? *Economics of Innovation and New Technology*, **1**, 3: 183–201.

Hall, B. H., Jaffe, A. and Trajtenberg, M. (2005). Market value and patent citations. *RAND Journal of Economics*, **36**, 1: 16–38.

Harhoff, D. and Reitzig, M. (2004). Determinants of opposition against EPO patent grants — The case of biotechnology and pharmaceuticals. *International Journal of Industrial Organization*, **22**, 4: 443–480.

Harhoff, D., Scherer, F. M. and Vopel, K. (2003). Citations, family size, opposition and the value of patent rights. *Research Policy*, **32**, 8: 1343–1363.

Hofmann, S. (2018). Gegenwind für Aromenhersteller Symrise [Headwind for Flavour Producer Symrise]. Handelsblatt, 14 March 2018. Available at http://www.handelsblatt.com/unternehmen/industrie/chemieindustrie-gegenwind-fuer-aromenhersteller-symrise/21071076-all.html, accessed 13 April 2018.

Jaffe, A. B., Trajtenberg, M. and Henderson, R. (1993). Geographic localization of knowledge spillovers as evidenced by patent citations. *The Quarterly Journal of Economics*, **108**, 3: 577–598.

Lanjouw, J. O., Pakes, A. and Putnam, J. (1998). How to count patents and value intellectual property: The uses of patent renewal and application data. *The Journal of Industrial Economics*, **46**, 4: 405–432.

Lee, C., Kang, B. and Shin, J. (2015). Novelty-focused patent mapping for technology opportunity analysis. *Technological Forecasting and Social Change*, **90**: 355–365.

Lee, S., Yoon, B. and Park, Y. (2009). An approach to discovering new technology opportunities: Keyword–based patent map approach. *Technovation*, **29**, 6: 481–497.

Lichtenthaler, E. (2003). Third generation management of technology intelligence processes. *R&D Management*, **33**, 4: 361–375.

Lichtenthaler, E. (2004). Technology intelligence processes in leading European and North American multinationals. *R&D Management*, **34**, 2: 121–135.

Martino, J. P. (2003). A review of selected recent advances in technological forecasting. *Technological Forecasting and Social Change*, **70**, 8: 719–733.

Mathew, M. (2015). Introduction to the special section on patent analytics. *International Journal of Innovation and Technology Management*, **12**, 3: 1502001.

McMillan, G. S., Narin, F. and Deeds, D. L. (2000). An analysis of the critical role of public science in innovation: The case of biotechnology. *Research Policy*, **29**, 1: 1–8.

Nair, S. S. and Mathew, M. (2015). The dynamics between forward citations and price of singleton patents. *International Journal of Innovation and Technology Management*, **12**, 03: 1540003.

Narin, F., Hamilton, K. S. and Olivastro, D. (1997). The increasing linkage between U.S. technology and public science. *Research Policy*, **26**, 3: 317–330.

Ocean Tomo LLC (2015). *Components of S&P 500 Market Value*. Available at http://www. oceantomo.com/intangible-asset-market-value-study/, accessed 14 March 2018.

Oldham, P. and Kitsara, I. (2016). *The WIPO Manual on Open Source Patent Analytics*. Available at https://wipo-analytics.github.io/, accessed 16 April 2018.

Omland, N. (2011). Valuing patents through indicators, In: *The Economic Valuation of Patents. Methods and Applications*, Munari, F. and Oriani, R., Edward Elgar Publishing, Cheltenham, UK, pp. 169–204.

Organisation for Economic Co-operation and Development (1967). Technological forecasting — What it is and what it does. *Management Review*, **56**, 8: 64–69.

PatentSight GmbH (2017). *About us. The Origin*. Available at https://www.patentsight. com/en-us/about-patentsight, accessed 14 March 2018.

Pavitt, K. (1985). Patent statistics as indicators of innovative activities: Possibilities and problems. *Scientometrics*, **7**, 1–2: 77–99.

Porter, A. L. (2005). QTIP: Quick technology intelligence processes. *Technological Forecasting and Social Change*, **72**, 9: 1070–1081.

Reitzig, M. (2004). Improving patent valuations for management purposes — Validating new indicators by analyzing application rationales. *Research Policy*, **33**, 6–7: 939–957.

Shin, J., Park, Y. and Lee, D. (2018). Who will be smart home users? An analysis of adoption and diffusion of smart homes. *Technological Forecasting and Social Change*, **134**: 246–253.

Stefan, I. (2013). Patent portfolio benchmarking in the logistics industry: Are Patents Relevant for Competitiveness in the Logistics Industry? Thesis, University of Gävle, Gävle, Sweden.

Swiss Federal Institute of Intellectual Property (2018). *Documentation to Technological Field Categorization of Patents*. Document 16-10377, Bern, Switzerland.

Symrise AG (2017a). Sharing Values. Unfolding Strengths. Corporate Report 2017. Available at https://www.symrise.com/investors/, accessed 13 April 2018.

Symrise AG (2017b). Sharing Values. Unfolding Strengths. Financial Report 2017. Available at https://www.symrise.com/investors/, accessed 13 April 2018.

Thoma, G. (2014). Composite value index of patent indicators: Factor analysis combining bibliographic and survey datasets. *World Patent Information*, **38**: 19–26.

Tijssen, R. J. W. (2001). Global and domestic utilization of industrial relevant science: Patent citation analysis of science-technology interactions and knowledge flows. *Research Policy*, **30**, 1: 35–54.

Wilson, R. M. (1987a). Patent analysis using online databases–I. Technological trend analysis. *World Patent Information*, **9**, 1: 18–26.

Wilson, R. M. (1987b). Patent analysis using online databases–II. Competitor activity monitoring. *World Patent Information*, **9**, 2: 73–78.

Yoon, B. and Lee, S. (2012). Applicability of patent information in technological forecasting: A sector-specific approach. *Journal of Intellectual Property Rights*, **17**, 1: 37–45.

Yoon, B. and Park, Y. (2004). A text-mining-based patent network: Analytical tool for high-technology trend. *The Journal of High Technology Management Research*, **15**, 1: 37–50.

Yoon, J. and Kim, K. (2012). TrendPerceptor: A property-function based technology intelligence system for identifying technology trends from patents. *Expert Systems with Applications*, **39**, 3: 2927–2938.

Biography

Carsten C. Guderian is Data Analyst/Data Scientist at PatentSight GmbH in Bonn, Germany. He holds degrees in Economics and Business Administration from the University of Kiel, Germany. Carsten joined the WHU-Otto Beisheim School of Management in Vallendar, Germany, and subsequently also became Visiting Pre-Doctoral Fellow at the Center for Research in Technology and Innovation at the Kellogg School of Management at Northwestern University in Evanston, USA. His research focuses on patent analytics, patent management, and patent indicator development for competitive intelligence.

Chapter 10

Evaluating the Agile-Stage-Gate Hybrid Model: Experiences From Three SME Manufacturing Firms

Kasper Edwards*,§, Robert G. Cooper†,¶, Tomas Vedsmand‡,∥
and Giulia Nardelli*,**

*DTU Management, Technical University of Denmark, Denmark

†McMaster University, Canada

‡GEMBA Innovation, Denmark
§kaed@dtu.dk
¶robertcooper@cogeco.ca
∥tv@gemba.dk
**ginar@dtu.dk

Agile-Stage-Gate is a hybrid product development model that integrates elements of both Agile and Stage-Gate to help companies realize the strengths of both. Recent studies show positive results in manufacturing companies, although SMEs are notably absent despite being the majority. This paper reports results of a test of the model in three deliberately chosen manufacturing SMEs. Results were improved: time to market, overall new product process, higher success rate. Agile required adaptations, and novel solutions were found by the test firms. The positive results suggest that Agile-Stage-Gate must be considered as a recommended product development approach in SME manufacturers.

Keywords: Agile-Stage-Gate hybrid model; evaluation; manufacturing; small- and mid-sized enterprises.

1. Introduction

Manufacturers have traditionally relied on a gated process, such as Stage-Gate,[1] to drive their new product projects from idea through to commercialization. When Agile Development was introduced by IT-software developers in the mid-late 1990s, strong positive performance results were reported [Begel and Nagappan (2007)].

---

*Corresponding author.

This chapter was originally published in *International Journal of Innovation and Technology Management*, Vol. 16, No. 8, August 2019, published by World Scientific Publishing, Singapore. Reprinted with permission.

[1] Stage-Gate® is a legally registered trademark of R.G. Cooper (and Associates Inc.) in the EU and Canada and of Stage-Gate International in the USA.

Thus, a handful of leading manufacturing firms began to experiment with this new development methodology by creating a hybrid model, namely Agile-Stage-Gate, starting about 2013 [Millward *et al.* (2006); Walters *et al.* (2006); Begel and Nagappan (2007); Tura *et al.* (2017)]. Initial results were exceptionally encouraging [Sommer *et al.* (2015)], and consequently more manufacturers adopted the new method, typically building Agile into their existing gating processes. Recent studies continue to show positive results for manufacturers [Invention Center (2018); Schmidt *et al.* (2018)].

One noticeable void, however, is that all the reported cases and studies done on manufacturers and their use of Agile Development since 2013 are for large, often multinational corporations, such as GE, Honeywell, Volvo, and LEGO. Noticeably absent are any mentions of small- and mid-sized enterprises (SMEs) in the manufacturing sector and their experiences and results with this new Agile Development approach. This void is particularly evident when one realizes that SMEs represent the great majority of firms in a modern economy; that they provide most of the new job creation; and further that SMEs are responsible for much of product innovation.

This paper reports the results of a test of this new methodology, notably the Agile-Stage-Gate model Agile-Stage-Gate in three SME manufacturing firms. This test or experiment was sponsored by the Danish employers' organization, The Confederation of Danish Industry (DI), and funded by the Danish Industry Foundation, as a way to probe whether or not this new approach was suitable for SME manufacturers in that country. The new model was carefully introduced to the three firms with considerable training and coaching, and then their experiences, challenges, and performance results were observed for a test development project done over a six-month period. In particular, the unique approaches and "fixes" that these firms evolved when dealing with the issues and challenges of this *new way of working* provide a useful guide to other SME manufacturers that may wish to adopt this faster and more responsive approach to new-product development (NPD).

2. Background

2.1. *Agile development in the software world*

Agile software development is an umbrella term for a set of frameworks and practices based on the values and principles expressed in the Manifesto for Agile Software Development and its 12 Principles [Agile Alliance (2019); Beck *et al.* (2001)]. Ultimately, Agile is a mindset based on the values contained in the Agile Manifesto and values and principles that provide guidance on how to create and respond to change during software development and how to deal with uncertainty. Agile software development methodologies rely on iterative and incremental processes in which product requirements and technical solutions evolve through collaboration between self-organizing and cross-functional teams [Agile Alliance (2019); Gonzalez (2014); Tura *et al.* (2017); Birgün and Çerkezoğlu (2018)].

When Agile emerged in the mid-late 1990s, its methods were seen as the solution to many problems in software development that traditional "waterfall" development processes could not deal with. These traditional processes focus on a big, long-term goal: a final product and its major features. But requirements change rapidly in software projects: The product features defined when the project was initially planned were often no longer valid by the end of a 12- to 18-month development cycle [Tura *et al.* (2017)]. And, as Reagan [2012] puts it, "it's hard to alter course when you're being swept down a large waterfall ... Too much up-front planning means too much change management downstream."

Agile was introduced to deal with these issues through adaptive planning, evolutionary delivery, a time-boxed iterative approach, and flexible response to change. Beck *et al.* [2001] coined the term Agile in their Agile Manifesto, which elaborated a set of 12 supporting principles, including (1) working software to be delivered quickly and iterated frequently (in cycles of weeks rather than months) and (2) working software to be the principal measure of progress.

2.2. *Separate Agile from development basics*

Agile, specifically the Scrum version, is a set of software development methodologies that breaks the development process into a series of short, iterative, incremental sprints, each sprint being typically one to four weeks long [Beck *et al.* (2001); Schwaber (2004); ScrumInc (2017)]. The main components of the process are as follows [Hannola *et al.* (2012); Cooper and Sommer (2018)]:

- *Sprint planning meeting*: At the beginning of each sprint, the development team meets to agree on what it can accomplish in the sprint and creates a task plan.
- *Daily stand-up meetings*: During the sprint, the team meets every morning to ensure that work is on course to accomplish the sprint goals, review what has been accomplished in the last 24 hours and what should be done in the next 24, and resolve problems; these meetings are also sometimes called scrums.
- *Demo*: Toward the end of each sprint, product increments or new features developed in the sprint are demonstrated and validated with stakeholders, including both management and customers.
- *Retrospective meeting*: At the end of each sprint, the team meets to review how team members worked together and how the team can improve.

The development team then plans and begins the next sprint based on customer and management feedback on what needs improving and what needs to be developed next. Product requirements and technical solutions, and even the project plan, thus evolve over the development cycle.

There is no traditional project leader or project manager in Agile. Rather, the process relies on a new set of defined roles:

- *The scrum master*, a servant-leader for the team, ensures that the team adheres to Agile theory, practices, and rules.
- *The product owner*, a member of management, often a senior marketing person, represents the product's stakeholders and the voice of the customer and guides the team (for example, meets with the team at sprint planning meetings).
- *The development team*, a dedicated project team that does the development work; the development team is usually physically co-located.

The development team's work is visible to all, tracked, and monitored via a set of visual scheduling and tracking tools that are displayed in the team room:

- The *product backlog* displays a list of features to be built, and the *sprint backlog* lists those features to be completed in the current sprint.
- The *Kanban board* (also sometimes called the *scrum board*) organizes sprint tasks in three categories: to do, doing (underway), and done.
- The *burndown chart* is a two-dimensional graph that shows progress versus the plan; the sprint time period is on the x-axis and the sprint task times are on the y-axis.

2.3. *The classic gating system used by manufacturers*

Traditionally, many manufacturers of physical products have relied on a gating or Stage-Gate® system to drive ideas through development and into market [Cooper and Sommer (2016b)]. Such gating models have been widely adopted by manufacturers in both B2B and B2C sectors [Griffin (1997); Ettlie and Elsenbach (2007); Grönlund *et al.* (2010); Cooper (2017); Tesch *et al.* (2017)]. As Sommer *et al.* [2013] explain: "The sequential model is the most broadly used model within PD [product development] project management [Griffin (1997); Grönlund *et al.* (2010); Ovesen (2012)]. It is often referred to as a stage-gate model, inspired by the Stage-Gate® model introduced by Cooper in 1983 [Cooper (1983); Griffin (1997)]. Here, project tasks are divided into a number of sequentially dependent stages with well-defined gates in between [Nicholas and Steyn (2012)]".

In practice, a stage-gating system breaks the idea-to-launch process into a series of five or six discrete stages or phases, beginning with "Discovery" or "Idea Generation" and moving through to "Product Launch" and beyond (Fig. 1). Each stage costs more than the preceding stage, so that the process is very much an incremental commitment one, much like buying a series of options on a property — thus risk is mitigated. Each stage contains a set of known success-drivers and tasks, such as voice-of-customer studies, fact-based product definition, and robust front-end homework, so that best practices are built into every development project by design.

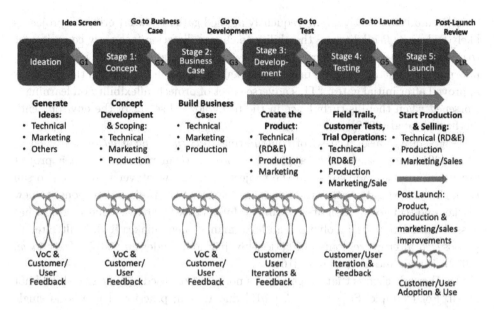

Fig. 1. The integrated Agile-Stage-Gate hybrid model — a typical 5-stage, 5-gate Stage-Gate idea-to-launch system, with Agile sprints (green) and feedback loops to customers (red) built into each of the stages.

Preceding each stage is a gate, where Go/Kill and investment decisions are made: Are we doing the right project, and are we doing this project right? At gates, poor projects are culled out, so that resources are funneled to the best projects as their potential becomes clearer. Stage-Gate is also cross-functional (that is, involves people from marketing, sales, and operations alongside technical personnel). Gating models, in general, are considered to be plan-based approaches.

While gating methods have proved very effective in most development applications, there have been criticisms as well [Becker (2006); Lenfle and Loch (2010); Cooper (2014)]. Such models are seen as being too *linear, too rigid, and too planned* to deal with today's fast-paced and often quickly changing world and to handle more innovative or dynamic projects: Simply stated, Stage-Gate is *not adaptive enough* and does *not encourage experimentation* — product definitions and project plans tend to be locked in too early [Sætre and Brun (2013)]. Jetter *et al.* [2016] expand on this concern about introducing *too much rigidity* into organizational routines and cultures: "To obtain approval, product development teams may commit to precise project parameters and freeze product specifications early in the development process, even against their better judgment." Committing early to features and a schedule means that compromises will be needed late in the project; early commitments to major design features, long schedules, long feedback loops, and the re-planning inherent in traditional product development processes create inefficiencies and slow the development cycle. Sethi and Iqbal [2008] similarly note that with a strictly enforced objective, and frequently applied gate review criteria, the project is likely to *lose its flexibility* and the ability to change direction (too early commitment to design and specs). And there is also *loss of learning* and a failure to integrate new information gained during the project and make changes in plans when the project is approved after initial gates. "This adverse effect of project inflexibility on learning is worsened when there is turbulence in the technological sector of the environment" [Sethi and Iqbal (2008)].

Stage-Gate is also accused of contributing to a *rigid and fixed mindset*. Jetter *et al.* [2016] note that "after approval, a project team may engage in a project execution mind-set and focus on the project plan and whatever is required to sail through the next gate, rather than making changes to the project in response to new market and technology insights" [Sethi and Iqbal (2008)]. The fact that a project has passed formal reviews involving high-level management makes it difficult later to propose an alternative course of action [Svejvig and Andersen (2015); Daly *et al.* (2012); Budak and Ustundag (2016)].

Another criticism is that Stage-Gate is not context-based — one size should not fit all. For example, Salerno *et al.* [2015] find that in practice "there is no single innovation process that fits all types of innovation projects" and that there are different processes that better deal with contingencies of a project, and "different ways of treating uncertainties in innovation processes." Almost two decades ago, Ajamian and Koen [2002] proposed a special version of stage-gate to handle technology development (new science) projects.

Yet another critique is that the gates in the process are thought to be too structured or too financially based, and the system is too controlling and bureaucratic, loaded with paperwork, checklists, and too much non-value-added work [Becker (2006); Lenfle and Loch (2010)]. Sethi and Iqbal [2008] also note that Stage-Gate is too time-consuming, has time-wasting activities and bureaucratic procedures, and restricts learning opportunities.

Some experts have taken issue with these criticisms, arguing that most are due to faulty implementation [Becker (2006)], whereas some deficiencies have been corrected in more recent evolutions of Stage-Gate [Cooper (2010)]. For example, now there are multiple versions of Stage-Gate to handle projects of different sizes, complexity, and risk; and iterative experimentation loops have been built into Stage-Gate to enable team to learn and alter the project's direction or product's design [Cooper (2008)]. But issues do remain, and thus a handful of leading firms are rethinking and re-inventing their idea-to-launch gating system.

Traditional *project management methods* have been typically employed within the stages of new-product gating models and have been similarly criticized. Svejvig and Andersen [2015] note that classical project management needs to be rethought in light of new realities. Atkinson *et al.* [2006], who identified a range of sources of uncertainty, assert that: "More sophisticated efforts to recognize and manage important sources of uncertainty are needed." Similarly, Thomas and Mengel [2008] argue that complexity, uncertainty, and chaos play an increasingly important role in projects and project environments. To deal with complexity, alternative perspectives such as *evolutionary management* and *self-organization*, much as what is found in Agile development, are proposed [Saynisch (2010); Sætre and Brun (2013); Svejvig and Andersen (2015); Lee *et al.* (2018)]. Finally, Kreiner [1995] points out that people involved in projects must recognize that the originally intended outcomes will not necessarily remain relevant over time since the environment often drifts. The project manager must thus remain flexible and be prepared to adapt the plan; otherwise the project manager risks "taking the plans literally" [Kreiner (2012)].

3. Moving to the Agile for Manufacturers

3.1. *The Agile-Stage-Gate hybrid model*

As Agile took root in the software industry, some larger software firms with existing gating systems built Agile into their development processes, thereby creating hybrid models. Their experience revealed that Agile and Stage-Gate can be used together to advantage: Karlstrom and Runeson [2005, 2006] note that, "Agile methods give the Stage-Gate model powerful tools for microplanning, day-to-day work control, and progress reporting." Gating models are generally "plan-driven models," whereas Agile is more "plan and build on the fly." Boehm and Turner [2004] argue the two are complementary: Stage-Gate is a comprehensive idea-to-launch system and a macro-planning process, whereas Agile is a microplanning project management methodology.

Agile-Stage-Gate has recently begun to interest developers of physical products, some as early as 2013 [Cooper (2016); Kortelainen and Lättilä (2013)]. Conforto *et al.* [2014] revealed that some Brazilian manufacturers are experiencing the use of some Agile management practices even though they do not belong to the software industry sector. Project management practitioners are successfully adapting Agile practices because they were struggling with their current and formalized project management processes when undertaking innovative projects [Bers and Dismukes (2012); Jahanshahi and Brem (2017); Svejvig and Andersen (2015)]. Approaches that combine macro- with micro-management tools, methods and processes for NPD are, for example, design thinking [Ben Mahmoud-Jouini *et al.* (2016)], lean-startup [Gudem *et al.* (2014); Yordanova (2018)], and real options reasoning [Jahanshahi and Brem (2017)]. Sommer *et al.* [2015] report the successful use of Agile in five Danish manufacturing firms, who simply utilize Agile methods within their existing stage-and-gate system; performance results were positive. In hardware firms, Agile was often first adopted by IT groups, whose initial results encouraged R&D groups working on hardware development to experiment with Agile [Cooper and Sommer (2016b)].

A hybrid model that integrates elements of both Agile and Stage-Gate can help manufacturing companies capitalize on the strengths of both. The *agility construct* in the context of product development in a manufacturing firm is defined as "the capacity to change the project plan and the active involvement of customer in the development process" [Conforto et al. (2016)], thereby enabling verifying or adjusting the product's design as the development proceeds. Such a hybrid Agile and gating model for manufacturers has been described in some detail [Cooper (2014, 2016); Cooper et al. (2019); Cooper and Sommer (2016a, 2016b, 2018); Sommer et al. (2015)]. The term "Agile-Stage-Gate" hybrid model was coined by Sommer et al. [2015].

3.2. How Agile-Stage-Gate works

In practice, an Agile-Stage-Gate hybrid model for manufacturers embeds the Agile way of working within the stages of Stage-Gate as in Fig. 1, replacing traditional project management tools and approaches, such as Gantt charts, milestones, and critical path planning, with Agile project management tools and processes. The project's stages — Development, for example — are broken into short time-boxed increments called sprints or iterations, each about 3–4 weeks long (the small green circles in Fig. 1), but often longer [Cooper et al. (2019)]. For example, Honeywell uses eight-week iterations for hardware development (versus two-week sprints for software), whereas Corning employs 60–90-day planning cycles or iterations [Cooper and Sommer (2018); Cooper (2014)]. This longer time allows the team to realistically produce something that they can demo.

As in Agile-Scrum for software development, in Agile-Stage-Gate for manufacturers, each sprint is preceded by a sprint planning meeting: The project team agrees on a sprint goal (what they can accomplish in that sprint) and identifies the tasks needed — see the sprint circle in Fig. 2. Teams meet regularly in stand-up or

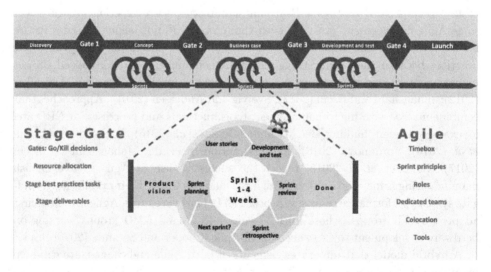

Fig. 2.   The SME adapted Agile Stage-Gate used in the test projects [Adopted from Vedsmand et al. (2017a)].

scrum meetings to discuss progress, synchronize their project and tasks, and resolve issues, but less frequently than in the software-Agile system, typically 2–3 times per week rather than daily [Cooper (2016); Cooper *et al.* (2019)].

At the end of each sprint, the project team produces "something tangible" that can be demonstrated to stakeholders, including management. In the case of some, but not all, iterations, the demo is to customers or users, again to seek feedback and validation, and to identify corrections needed, notably to the product's design, features, and functionality. For example, a study of 138 manufacturers using Agile plus gating found that the median interval between prototypes demo'd to customers was 17–24 weeks; that is, much less frequently than at the end of each sprint iteration [Invention Center (2018)]. Each sprint is followed by a retrospective meeting at which progress is reviewed and lessons for the next sprint are identified, including feedback from the customer.

3.3. *Where Agile-Stage-Gate is employed*

Initially, Agile was employed mainly in the technical stages, namely, Development and Testing, in a firm's Stage-Gate system, Stages 4 and 5 in Fig. 1. With maturity, manufacturing firms used Agile-Stage-Gate for more than just these two technical stages, namely, in the pre-development stages, for example to develop the concept and to assess feasibility [Vedsmand *et al.* (2016)]. Further, these manufacturing firms do not use the new method for all projects: Indeed, the Invention Center [2018] in Germany reports that the great majority of manufacturing firms using Agile Development (62%) do less than 25% of their projects with Agile. Agile is usually reserved for larger projects that are more ambiguous (higher uncertainty) and risky.

3.4. *Positive performance results for manufacturers*

The results from the early adopters of Agile-Stage-Gate have been quite positive [Cooper (2016); Cooper and Sommer (2016a, 2016b)]. The study of Danish manufacturing firms that implemented Agile-Stage-Gate identified major benefits [Sommer *et al.* (2015)]. In hybrid model, the study found:

- Increased design flexibility;
- Improved productivity, communication, and coordination among project team members;
- Drove better focus on projects, resulting in better prioritization of time and effort;
- Raised team morale.

Since then, a number of manufacturers have adopted Agile or facets of it, and results continue to be very positive [Gonzalez (2014); Sætre and Brun (2012); Tura *et al.* (2017)]. A large sample study of 228 German manufacturing firms using Agile [Schmidt *et al.* (2018)] revealed that the new model increased development productivity, yielded higher success rates, and resulted in shorter development times. However, for all six key performance metrics used, the expectations on these metrics were higher than the results achieved: That is, *the hype exceeded results* for this new Agile method. Nor were the performance metrics used "hard metrics: They were all qualitative (the opinions of participants in the user firms). A second large-sample study of 130 European manufacturing firms revealed positive results as well [Invention Center (2018)]: higher team morale, improved ability to handle uncertainties and changing situations, and better customer orientation. All the studies and results cited above, however, were for large manufacturing firms. ... which begs the question, does Agile-Stage-Gate work as well for smaller manufacturers? And what modifications must smaller firms make to the new model work?"

3.5. *Agile-Stage-Gate challenges and issues in practice*

Despite its preliminary positive results, Agile-Stage-Gate also poses challenges. Agile-Stage-Gate combines macro-project management tools with micro-activities to perform on a daily basis. While the combination can enhance knowledge transfer and strengthening of tacit knowledge [Hannola *et al.* (2012)], it also introduces new procedures in already burdened innovation systems. Adding new methods and tools to pre-existing innovation management systems can saturate employees' ability to be flexible and thus be counterproductive. Furthermore, gating methods are not always adopted, especially within the context of SMEs [Salerno *et al.* (2015)]. In these cases, Agile-Stage-Gate might prove even harder to adopt and use, as it introduces two different sets of tools, methods, and processes for innovation management.

The flexibility that Agile-Stage-Gate offers can only be obtained if relevant technical and managerial skills are available to support the innovation project [Judi and Beach (2010)]. In fact, and especially within SMEs, the implementation of an effective NPD process is the main distinguishing factor between the best and worst performing companies [Millward *et al.* (2006)]. Without support from management, employees would have issues adapting to Agile-Stage-Gate, which combines two competing performance management systems [Hannola *et al.* (2012); Svejvig and Andersen (2015)]. Therefore, the methods, tools, and processes offered by Agile-Stage-Gate will have most impact if the employees and managers understand and commit to its grounding principles [Walters *et al.* (2006)].

Considering that manufacturing firms only recently begun to work with this development method, it is not surprising that there are only few empirical studies on Agile-Stage-Gate. The available studies, however, confirm that in practice implementing Agile-Stage-Gate in the manufacturing sector has not been easy, and many challenges and apparent conflicts and inconsistencies have been identified. The early Danish study revealed some immediate negatives, namely, delays due to the difficulty of finding dedicated team members, difficulties in linking project teams to the rest of the organization, mismatches between the requirements of Agile and the company's reward system, and a sense that the system was still too bureaucratic [Sommer *et al.* (2015)]. The Brazilian study also identified potential barriers, issues and challenges faced in Agile implementation in more "traditional industries" [Conforto *et al.* (2014)]. These issues include the need to assign full-time dedicated project teams; the challenge of co-locating all project team members; the difficulty in creating large multidisciplinary teams (with all project competences involved); the challenge of involving customers with a high degree of influence in project development; and the superficial involvement of suppliers [Bhatia *et al.* (2017)]. Still other challenges for manufacturers adopting Agile practices have been identified, including a lack of scalability (to larger, more complex programs with multiple sub-projects; or to global projects), a proliferation of meetings, and a lack of management buy-in due to the differences from familiar gating systems [Cooper and Sommer (2016b)].

The more recent and large-sample German study also voiced some words of warning [Schmidt *et al.* (2018)] and major difficulties were encountered, however, in:

- embedding Agile teams into the classic organizational structure,
- interpreting Agile practices for physical products, and
- modularizing the product or project (breaking the project into increments that could be undertaken within a single sprint).

4. The Test Methodology

4.1. *Declaration of roles*

In this project, the authors have assumed different roles in implementation and data collection. All authors have contributed to developing the tailored Agile-Stage-Gate model that was tested. The first and fourth author interviewed developers and administered the surveys. The second author provided training and advice to the study participants. The third author was funded as part of the project to teach and coach the participating development teams. Two observers from DI participated during teaching and coaching session with the purpose of learning the method. The first, third, and fourth author and two observers from DI participated in the final evaluation workshops with managers.

4.2. *The three SME firms*

To test and evaluate the Agile-Stage-Gate system for smaller manufacturing firms, a longitudinal in-depth multi-case approach was elected. Three Danish SMEs that were about to begin an innovation project and also who were willing to test Agile-Stage-Gate were identified by DI and selected as test companies; the study was funded by the Danish Industry Foundation. DI selected the companies from their network based on the following criteria: (1) manufacturing and development was done in-house, (2) the

Table 1.   Characteristics of the three companies participating in the Agile-Stage-Gate test.

Characteristics	Company A	Company B	Company C
Industry	B2B convenience food	B2B audio equipment	B2B radar systems
Founded (year)	2000	1992	1977
Number of employees	142	155	98
Annual sales (million Euro)	35	28	NA
Annual profits (million Euro)	2.0	3.3	1.5

company was about to initiate a product development project, (3) the company did not use Agile in their current development practice, and (4) the company was willing to use Agile-Stage-Gate in their project. Characteristics of the three firms are in Table 1.

Prior to the test, the Agile-Stage-Gate system was tailored for SMEs using a participatory approach: bringing together experienced innovation managers from four large manufacturing firms and an SME which were already experienced in the use of Agile-Stage-Gate (LEGO, Danfoss, Grundfos, Coloplast, and the SME ForeNAV), together with Agile-Stage-Gate experts (consultants and coaches) [Nardelli and Edwards (2018)]. The tailored Agile-Stage-Gate system was published as a 20-page manual describing Agile-Stage-Gate and as a supplement manual containing descriptions of relevant tools [Vedsmand et al. (2017a, 2017b)].

4.3. Implementing Agile-Stage-Gate in the three firms

The Agile-Stage-Gate system was tested over a period of six months in 2017. The test project's development teams participated in a joint Agile-Stage-Gate workshop; here the teams were instructed on the Agile-Stage-Gate model and on the most important methods in both Stage-Gate and Agile. Training was provided by the second author and facilitated by the third author, and based on the developed manual and tools [Vedsmand et al. (2017a, 2017b)].

Following this training session, the three project teams were then asked to prepare an overall sprint plan: that is, a map showing the approximate number of sprints, an expected timeline for major product releases or deliverables, and a rough estimate of resources (including a map with allocation rates of different competencies and people required for each sprint). Additionally, the teams defined roles: the product owner, scrum master, development team, and stakeholders. And they also outlined for which stages and gates they would use the hybrid model for their project (for example, for Stages 1–3 and Gates 1–3 in Fig. 1). In order to foster commitment and accountability, each team presented their project and sprint plan at this first workshop.

Project team members in each firm were subsequently trained on location by the third author on more of the details of the Agile-Scrum methods and approach, including:

- the Agile mindset;
- the scrum process and roles;

- events and artifacts, such as daily scrum, demos or reviews, retrospectives, product backlog, sprint backlog, and the definition-of-done; and
- tools such as user stories, the scrum board, and the burndown chart.

Training on Stage-Gate front-end methods, such as design thinking (personas, user-research, and visual prototyping), was also undertaken. All companies received initial coaching on how to apply these new methods and roles, while product owners and scrum masters received intense coaching during the first two sprints with decreasing amount of coaching throughout the rest of the project.

4.4. *Data collection*

Prior to starting their Agile-Stage-Gate projects, project managers from the test projects were interviewed about their existing product development practices and general information about the company and products by the first author. The project managers were asked to explain the process of the last product they had developed and to map the sequence of events on a whiteboard. The interviews were recorded, and the drawings of the development processes photographed.

A questionnaire was distributed to all development team members of the three projects ($N = 15$) before project start (baseline) and after project's end (follow-up). The questionnaire covered Agile development practices such as co-location, sprints with clear goals and deadlines, etc. (15 practices and behaviors were gauged via 5-point Likert scaled questions, strongly agree/strongly disagree, shown in Fig. 3). The baseline questionnaire was distributed just before the start of the Agile-Stage-Gate project and captures the normal development practice. The follow-up questionnaire specifically asked about the Agile-Stage-Gate project. This allows an estimate of the effect of the project on Agile practices. Following the six-month test period with their test projects, the test participants were interviewed. Two evaluation sessions were conducted in each company:

(1) an evaluation workshop with management and
(2) a group interview with project team members.

The evaluation workshops with senior management focussed on estimating the effect of Agile-Stage-Gate assessed from *a management perspective*. Despite efforts to use hard metrics, none of the three companies had metrics in place to precisely track and evaluate development projects. Difficulties in getting hard metrics is not unique to this project or SMEs; for example, in the Cooper and Sommer [2018] study, "only one of the six case-study firms had implemented formal metrics". The large-sample German study [Schmidt *et al.* (2018)] also had to rely on qualitative data. As Brem [2016] notes: "...there are no predefined measures existing — on the contrary: defining success always depends on a subjective view...." Thus, effect measures are

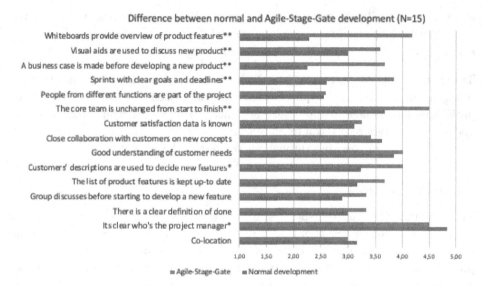

Fig. 3.   Effect of Agile-Stage-Gate in the three companies. Measured using a 5-point Likert scale, 1 = strongly disagree, 5 = strongly agree.

Note: *$P < 0.1$; **$P < 0.05$, two-tailed *T*-text

managers' estimates, which consisted of three elements: First, senior managers shared their experiences and the results of the project. Secondly, the results were discussed with the researcher (first author), DI observers, and the Agile coach (third author). Thirdly, senior managers were asked to evaluate the effect of Agile-Stage-Gate by comparing "your [test] project to similar projects in your company". It was explained that "similar" meant similar in size, scope, complexity. Two managers per firm participated in each of these workshops, and they were asked individually to score their experiences using the following four questions:

(1) Was development time slower, same, or faster (as a percent).
(2) Was development cost higher, same, or lower (as a percent).
(3) Overview of the innovation process (worse, same, better).
(4) Success rate (success probability) for the project (worse, same, better).

Care was taken to avoid unfounded claims as a consequence of social desirability bias of scoring the effect higher. From the first contact with companies, it was highlighted that the project was a test to evaluate whether Agile-Stage-Gate was useful to manufacturing SMEs. Managers were asked to explain and exemplify their reasons for their answers to each question in detail. The evaluation workshops were recorded, company presentations collected, and responses recorded. The group interviews with development team members focussed on their experiences during the test project using the Effect Modifier Assessment (EMA) method [Edwards and Winkel (2018)]. The EMA method captures changes in work practices and organization during the

Agile-Stage-Gate project period and assesses whether the changes are a result of the Agile-Stage-Gate method or other contextual factors. By focussing on changes in work practice — simply identifying and explaining how work has changed in the project and not evaluating Agile-Stage-Gate — social desirability bias is minimized. Respondents were asked to elaborate and explain the changes to provide a rich detailed account of the work-practice changes.

5. Results in the Three Companies

The three participating companies completed the test on one project each using the Agile-Stage-Gate hybrid model. The companies had existing development processes resembling Stage-Gate; however, the processes were used more like guidelines rather than as a disciplined process. As with most manufacturers, the test companies *did not adopt the software version of Agile as is*; rather, they were trained in the tailored Agile-Stage-Gate model, which each firm then slightly adopted to suit their own unique situation — see Table 2.

Table 2. Adoption and use of the tailored Agile-Stage-Gate model in the three companies.

Agile Stage-Gate Elements	Company A	Company B	Company C
Project type/scope	Convenience snack	Audio headset	Modular power supply
Team size	6	4	5
Stage start	Discovery	Discovery	Scoping
Stage end	Development	Development and testing	Concept/business case
Agile and innovation methods	Adopted scrum	Adopted scrum	Adopted scrum
	Design-thinking	User-stories	Integrated product development
	Daily scrum two times a week	Daily scrum 0–1 times a week	Daily scrum
	Personas	Product backlog	2-week sprint + 1-week development moratorium
	Prototyping	Prototyping	
Stage-Gate elements used	Early stages	Full Stage-Gate model, detailed front-end	Early stages
	Scorecards, criteria Gate meetings		Scorecards, criteria Gate meetings
Adoption after project end	Adapted scrum	Full Stage-Gate model (as before project)	Fencing R&D resources
	Sprint reviews as gates	Agile front-end model adopted	Scrum for R&D projects Scorecards with criteria Stage-Gate under development

5.1. *Performance results achieved*

Performance results measured at the senior management workshop are generally positive on four important metrics — see Table 3. Senior management believed that each of the test projects was *executed about* 20% *faster* than previously done comparable projects, a consistent result across all three companies. There were few or no perceived development cost reductions or faster spending rates of development budgets, however. Company B actually saw an increase in development spending, but only because they added a new activity to the process, namely, overseas end-user interviews.

In two of the three firms, senior management believed that the *innovation process overall had been improved.* Previously, project planning had been *ad-hoc* and idiosyncratic and based on the lead developer's own experience. In the test projects, the sprint planning meetings provided a common understanding of what was needed, goals, and next steps for both management and the development team. The third firm already had a tried-and-proven development process that they followed and which was understood by all.

In all three firms, management concluded that there was *a higher probability of success* for the test project than for previous comparable projects. This higher success probability was judged to be because, unlike previous projects, the test projects had included *user insight via customer interviews*, the result being that both management and developers believed the product had a potential customer base and clear market. The end-user interviews also *changed the directions* of the test projects; for example, in one firm, end-user insights resulted in one product line of accessories being completely canceled because end-users already had a cheap off-the-shelf solution for the envisioned accessory products.

5.2. *Impact on practices and behavior*

The use of Agile-Stage-Gate for the test projects generally had a positive impact on the development teams' behavior and practices. There are improvements in 13 of 15 items, measured before and after the test project, as shown in Fig. 3.

Table 3. Summary of senior managers' evaluation of the Agile-Stage-Gate compared with comparable innovation projects.

Performance metric	Company A	Company B	Company C
Development time	−20%	−20%	−20%
Development cost	Same	+10%	Same
Overall innovation process	Better	Better	Same
Estimated probability of success	Higher	Higher	Higher

The behavioral changes in Fig. 3 demonstrate that the three companies were generally compliant and actually put Agile-Stage-Gate into practice in their test projects. And development teams appeared to have adopted some Agile best practices. Of the 13 significant improvements noted in Fig. 3, the greatest in descending order of impact are:

- The use of visual displays of product features to be built (e.g. on a whiteboard).
- The development of a strong business case.
- Breaking each stage into defined time periods, each with clear goals and deadlines, namely, *time-boxed sprints*.
- Having a core project team with the same people from the start of project to its end.
- Employing customers' descriptions of product-use situations (for example, through user stories).
- Use of visual descriptions, such as drawings, to facilitate team discussion.
- Having an up-to-date product feature list (for example, the product or sprint backlog).
- Having a team meeting to discuss a new feature before beginning its development on the sprint planning meeting.

But understanding when a product feature or sprint task was completed (the definition of done) improved only marginally. In some areas, the new Agile-Stage-Gate model had surprisingly little or no impact (Fig. 3), such as *understanding of customer needs* and *knowledge of customer satisfaction data* (complaints, quality issues, etc.). The greatest negative surprise that the survey of development team members showed is that there was a decrease in *collaboration with customers on new concepts* (even though two of the firms began their projects with customer interviews). The latter may be related to the wording of the question that focusses on "new concepts" (no new concepts had been developed at the time the follow-up questionnaire was administered).

In terms of organization, there were also few or no improvements. Development teams minimally had a better understanding of who the project manager was (note: the test projects employed a *scrum master* to lead the daily scrums, whereas normal projects used a more traditional *project manager* role). Further, there was no change in the team cross-functionality or team composition (for example, the inclusion of team members from other departments in the project). Finally, there was no higher propensity for the team to co-locate, one of the key features of Agile (in fact, there was a slight decrease in co-location).

Finding dedicated resources to work on the projects, a requirement when using Agile-Stage-Gate, also proved problematic. Company C was the best here, with 60% of development team members spending more than 50% of their work-time on the test project — see Table 4. In contrast, two-thirds of the team members in

Table 4.   Amount of work-time spent on the project in the three development teams.

Work-time spent on project (%)	% of development team		
	Company A (%)	Company B (%)	Company C (%)
1–9	17	0	0
10–19	50	75	0
20–29	0	0	40
30–49	17	25	0
50–74	17	0	20
75–100	0	0	40

Company A spent 19% or less of their work-time on the project; whereas in company B, 75% of team members spent only 19% or less of their work-time on the project.

A year after the project ended, both Companies A and B have introduced their new products to the marketplace. Initial sales in both companies are promising, and Company B has received critical acclaim for their product [Clark (2018)].

6. Issues, Learnings, and Solutions in Agile-Stage-Gate Implementation

The three SME firms faced a number of challenges and issues as they employed Agile-Stage-Gate for their test projects. Modifications, work-arounds, and fixes, some quite clever and novel, were found, however, and provide a guide to other SME firms which are planning to adopt this new Agile-Stage-Gate approach.

6.1. *Sprints or iterations*

To implement Agile-Stage-Gate for their test projects, the three companies generally kept their existing and familiar stages in their current new-product process, but broke the stages into *time-boxed sprints*. These sprints were often longer than the two-weeks common in software Agile, often 3–4 weeks. And they were of variable length, sometimes lasting as long as eight weeks.

The longer and variable definition of the length of sprints or iterations is at odds with the tenets of software Agile, where a *consistent sprint time* helps to create a rhythm or heartbeat, and a *short two-week sprint* puts some time pressure on team members. However, it is somewhat similar to the practices found in larger manufacturing firms [Cooper *et al.* (2019)], in which sprints typically are indeed longer, for example, 3–4 weeks or longer, but still consistent in length (that is, non-variable) in order to achieve a rhythm.

6.2. *Daily scrums*

The stand-up or scrum meetings proved to be *a key element in achieving positive results* in the three test companies. Only one of the three firms held these scrum meetings every day, however, as prescribed in software Agile. The two other companies held scrum meetings at a lower and also a varying frequency: from twice a week to sometimes even skipping the scrum for an entire week. This lower and variable frequency was somewhat surprising, since the daily scrums were expected to be instrumental in maintaining project momentum; but this practice is partially consistent with practices in larger manufacturing firms, which typically employ 2–3 scrums per week firms [Cooper *et al.* (2019)].

The scrum meetings served a very important function, ensuring that project members were synchronized with regard to project progress. Synchronization means a common understanding of the project and its current direction: Team members in sync have heard, understood, and accepted the decisions made, allowing the team to keep moving forward without having to revisit past discussions. Synchronization thus requires all team members to be present, and if a meeting is missed, that team member must accept the decisions made and not bring up past discussions and slow the project.

In company A, the project team decided that members not actively participating in development could be excused from the scrum meetings. This proved to be quite negative: These absentee team members had important insights to offer, so when they returned to the daily scrums, past decisions were revisited. The end result was that the team failed to synchronize and continued to discuss and change past decisions, thereby slowing project progress significantly. A further negative effect was that the team never converged on a common understanding of the product, and so kept diverging in idiosyncratic perceptions of the product vision; the design freeze thus came very late.

The strong impact of frequent scrum meetings in the three SMEs highlights the importance of *having all team members present at all scrum meetings*. Further, the team may be different for each sprint, but during a sprint, team membership *must remain constant* in order to ensure synchronization.

6.3. *Dedicated teams and resource allocation*

Dedicated teams are a prerequisite for effective Agile development, and the participating companies had all agreed that they would have dedicated teams for their test projects. However, as noted above and in Table 4, none of the three SMEs had team members 100% devoted to the test project, nor even close to 100%. Larger manufacturers in general tend not to have dedicated teams either when using Agile-Stage-Gate, but their team members certainly are more focused (typically 65–70% of their time) than what was observed in the three SME firms [Cooper and Sommer (2016b, 2018); Cooper *et al.* (2019)]. Indeed, the test projects saw some team members with less than 10% time commitment in a sprint, and thus they only participated in the daily scrums. Still, even though they did not commit much time to the project, these team members had special knowledge necessary for the project; thus, their participation in scrums kept the team in sync and allowed these team members to provide their valuable input.

In the test companies, the scrum meetings also inadvertently became a *mechanism for resource commitment*. Most team members had many other obligations besides the test project, and so they had to navigate and plan their time to try to accommodate the situation. But this multi-tasking posed a significant challenge for resource commitment to the project. In addition to syncing projects, the scrum meetings had an added benefit in that they ensured that team members prioritized the project and kept the project at top of mind. Team members typically manage their own time, which makes their commitments made at scrum meetings very important. Commitments are like a promise, a social contract between the team and the team member; and any team member that does not honor their time commitment will feel shame at the next scrum meeting. As such, the scrum meeting was *an effective informal resource allocation mechanism* for these SMEs.

6.4. *Dealing with "other tasks"*

In the three SMEs, as noted above, team members had other responsibilities and tasks in their companies besides the test project, thus making the dedicated team requirement of software Agile a challenge. These "other tasks" typically included providing engineering support for production or undertaking customer support work. SMEs in general have less employee specialization and thus must spread tasks across the staff available. To accommodate these other tasks, for example, Company C modified the normal sprint rhythm: They used two-week sprints but introduced *a one-week project moratorium after each sprint* with no work done on the project for that week. This moratorium allowed team members to catch up on their other responsibilities and tasks and also put a cap or limit on such "other work" and requests. An added benefit was increased respect for the time allocated for development work on the test project, because management had now pushed all non-critical requests into the development moratorium period.

The moratorium at the end of a sprint allows the team to *maintain a fixed rhythm*, yet still provides resources for other necessary activities. The use of a moratorium may be particularly useful in companies that cannot dedicate 100% of project team members' times to a project, which is likely true for most SMEs. This concept of an adjusted fixed rhythm, which is understood by everyone in the company, ensures that expectations can be adjusted and met, thereby reducing the potential for conflict.

The development moratorium also allows project team members to *work on more than one project* at the same time. For example, when a team member completes a sprint on Project X, during its development moratorium, he or she can then do work on a sprint in Project Y. The use of a moratorium is particularly relevant in hardware development: Developing physical samples or prototypes or undertaking product testing can be time-consuming and often have waiting times, and thus there is a need for a team member to be working on several projects at the same time, which this moratorium enables.

6.5. *Co-location of team members*

Co-location is also a facet of software Agile. Co-location improves speed and productivity, because team members can immediately resolve any development problems face to face. None of the test companies implemented co-location, moving team members to the same room, however. And none reported that there was a frequent need to discuss development issues that warranted team members to be in the same room. One company used collocation for some specific development tasks that required considerable interaction, such as interface design and changes.

This lack of co-location may be a unique facet of using Agile methods for hardware development. Team members have distinct competences: For example, one engineer is an electronics specialist, another is an aluminum casing specialist, and a third a power supply engineer. The competence overlap is small if any, and therefore getting immediate help for a problem is not enabled by co-locating the team.

Co-location served a specific purpose in Company C, in which interface issues, such as the redesign of one component, required changes to other components and the structure of the product. This was solved by co-locating the entire team for an afternoon to discuss interfaces. The team used this approach only three times during the project, however.

6.6. *The product backlog and an evolving product design*

One of Agile's tenets is allowing and even encouraging *evolving product designs* as development proceeds. The *sprint or product backlog* thus becomes an important visual tool for the team in software Agile. It is a *flexible document* that lists the features to be developed during the sprint (or for the project), and the backlog changes as the product's design evolves over the development period. Note that in software, discrete product features can easily be added to or removed by simply writing or deleting lines of code. Typically, these changes do not impact the rest of the software product, and so the software product's design can indeed be readily changed and evolve in response to customer feedback.

An evolving product design and the use of the backlog tool proved to be difficult for physical product development in the three test projects, however. In contrast to software development, in most physical products, *features are not discrete*, but are intertwined and tied to the overall product design. As an example, in Company C, a change in the power supply PCB would require changes to the exterior casing and also to the placement of connectors through this casing: Small product changes in one area have ripple effects throughout the entire product's design.

In hardware development, the initial design and feature set thus limit the adding and removing of features later. Design changes are possible of course, but only at the expense of making changes to related components and potentially to the entire product design. Because functions and features are difficult to add later, the product backlog becomes *relatively inflexible.* Instead, in the test projects, the product backlog turned into a *project backlog*, which showed not just product features to be built, but listed *all activities and tasks*, both large and small, that needed to be done in a sprint (or in the project).

One solution is a modular product design, whereby the product itself is broken into relatively independent modules; this permits modules to be changed within limits without impacting other modules. A modular design thus accommodates an evolving product design and so allows the product backlog to be effectively used. The product backlog would be organized around modules that had minimal core functionality and interface specifications. This would allow modules to change functionality in response to customer feedback and so evolve the product's design. However, none of the SMEs adopted a modular design as a possible solution to their inflexible backlog challenge in their three test projects.

6.7. *User input and creating a customer-based design document*

The most important change in the overall development process was in the front-end of the project, where Companies A and B made significant changes and *included voice-of-customer work.* One of the clear requirements of Stage-Gate is a strong customer orientation and a customer-based product definition [Cooper (2017), chapters 2 and 4]. In contrast, Company B's normal mode of development was driven by classic engineering goals, such as increased miniaturization and improved frequency response. New features in the product were often included because of emotion or assumptions: team members' personal desires; the interest level of the engineers (for example, an "interesting technical challenge"); or assumptions about customer needs and market trends. Engineering interest may be particularly detrimental to market fit, as the assumption is that technology interest aligns with user needs; often there is no obvious user need, however, making the product difficult to sell. Note that a lack of market inputs and direct customer knowledge is the number one reason for new product failure [Cooper (2017)].

Company A transformed their customer experience into *personas* [Miaskiewicz and Kozar (2011)], whose needs became the target for product development. These personas are in effect characterizations of target customers, particularly in terms of values sought, needs, and wants. In Company B, the voice-of-customer experience, captured in a design document specifying user needs, vision, and business case, became an important facet of the project. This fact-based design document in the test project eliminated the speculation and assumptions typically found in Company B's normal projects: Each time there was a design choice to be made, the design document would be referred to and formed the basis of their discussion and decision. Company C's project was a "build to order" product under contract, and once the bid or order was won, the development team did not have any further direct customer contact. The head of development assumed the role of the customer at demo and review meetings.

6.8. *The definition of "done"*

All three project teams were focussed on the *definition of done or DoD*, namely, the deliverable to be presented at the end of a sprint and at the next demo meeting. Because the demo presents the results of each completed sprint, what must be completed, namely the DoD, thus served as a clear and *visible short-term objective* for the team during a sprint.

Results for demos were not always a product version or prototype, as in software Agile, however. Indeed, the *results of work done* appeared in many forms, including results of a market analysis; a competitor assessment; visual description of personas on a large cardboard display; a user study; as well as more physical items such as early models of the product: a product concept built from LEGO, or a simple wire prototype.

The requirement to make a demo presentation is an *important driver for reaching a milestone* and puts great pressure on the team to deliver on time. Project team members in the three firms reported, however, that this was an exhaustive way of working, as there was a tendency to promise too much for each sprint. This over-promising parallels experiences in the software world; over time, teams learn to be more realistic about lower promises, consistent with their ability to deliver.

6.9. *Incorporating Stage-Gate into the development method*

The Stage-Gate facet of Agile-Stage-Gate was not strongly evident in the three test companies, although some elements of Stage-Gate were employed for the test projects, as noted in Table 2. All companies had elements of a gating process in place prior to the project; but it was unclear to what extent they were followed. In the three firms, gate meetings were held to evaluate test project progress and involved the managing director and the development team. However, the gate meetings focussed only on the Agile-Stage-Gate project and did not include other major projects competing for the same resources (looking at other projects normally strengthens the competition between project teams and deals with resourcing issues). The three companies only had one development team each, thus no other large and competing projects underway.

Gate meetings differed from those prescribed in a Stage-Gate process. In the test projects, for example, gates were not investment decision meetings and *did not yield a Go/Kill decision* as is the norm in a standard Stage-Gate system [Cooper (2017), chapters 8 and 9]. Rather, the decision was usually Go, or a change of direction for the project, or mothballing the project (putting it on hold) because something more important arose.

The demo meetings presented the sprint's results at the end of each sprint were somewhat like "mini-gates". All companies completed at least four sprints and held proper demos with the product owner and managing director. The demo meetings often presented more than one solution. For instance, in Company A, eight personas were presented at a demo and four selected for further development. The demo meetings thus become in effect *strategy meetings*, where the result of the demo was reviewed against the strategy using scorecards; solutions not in line with strategy were discarded.

7. Discussion, Implications, and Limitations

The study revealed that Agile combined with Stage-Gate could indeed be used by SME manufacturing firms for their NPD projects, and generally gave positive results, for example, faster to market. The various stages of Stage-Gate can indeed be subdivided into time-boxed sprints and run much like sprints as done in Agile in the software domain, although with somewhat longer sprints than used in software development, namely 3–4 weeks. The regular stand-up meetings or scrums were found to be vital to making the system work. Here, all the team members met for a quick update to share knowledge, sync their tasks, and discuss problems. Typically, these scrums were held about 2–3 times per week, but not daily as in software Agile. Where it goes wrong is when all-team members are not at the stand-up meetings; thus all-team attendance is mandatory.

The study revealed that the greatest challenge was finding the dedicated team members that the Agile method demands. The lack of people resources has been identified as a problem for larger manufacturing firms as well [Schmidt *et al.* (2018); Sommer *et al.* (2015); Cooper and Sommer (2016b)]; but for SMEs, where team members often have multiple roles in their companies, the problem is far worse [Millward *et al.* (2006); Walters *et al.* (2006)]. However, it is not realistic to expect companies in general and SMEs in particular to make a firm commitment of dedicated resources and free people from other tasks. Yet, strict adherence to the stand-up meetings — at least two times a week — allows companies to enjoy some major benefits of Agile-Stage-Gate, such as shorter development times and improved quality, the result of having the team assembled when decisions are made.

SME firms may also employ the somewhat unusual solution of a moratorium at the end of each sprint to allow team members to handle their "regular job" tasks for perhaps one week per month. Although not recommended in any of the software Agile literature and guides, the use of a moratorium seemed to work for the one SME in this study and might be considered by others. Finally, although more focussed teams are essential, the study also revealed that co-location as mandated in software Agile was not practical, and indeed in some cases, simply impractical.

A significant challenge was the use of the product backlog and an evolving product definition. The product backlog in hardware is less flexible, and the function the backlog serves in software, supporting the evolution of the product consistent with customer desires, is not always possible in hardware developments. Further work is needed to develop the use of the product (or perhaps project) backlog for hardware development.

All three test firms had a Stage-Gate system in place at the outset, but in some cases it was not working well or there was a lack of discipline. One recommendation is that a functioning Stage-Gate system should be in place before implementing Agile within a manufacturing firm. Note that Agile is not a fix for a poor new product process; Agile creates more transparency and thus simply reveals the flaws in the existing system.

7.1. Implications for management

Management appears to be the most important stakeholder when implementing and using Agile-Stage-Gate. Therefore, commitment to Agile-Stage-Gate by the management is crucial. For each project in which Agile-Stage-Gate methods are to be applied, managers must find the dedicated team. Moreover, managers must make sure that team members have time to fulfill the tasks associated to that specific project at an agile pace, including participating regularly into scrum meetings. In fact, teams working with Agile-Stage-Gate methods should be unchanged throughout each project duration, and all members should always be present at scrum meetings. These aspects are important as they ensure consistency in the work carried out by the team, while avoiding re-negotiations between members. Furthermore, consistency in the timing of sprints is important to achieve a working rhythm, which would be disrupted by obligations to other projects. Consequently, some non-related tasks will need to be solved

Table 5.   Implications for management.

Issue	Management focus
Strong management commitment	Understand and support the agile development process
Dedicated team	Identify dedicated team
	Coordinate resources (team members) with other projects and delegate tasks
	Ensure team members have time for the project
	Keep team consistent during sprint
Daily scrum	Ensure full team is always present during scrum meetings
Dealing with "other tasks"	Negotiate system for dealing with "other tasks"
	Maintain and defend system from immediate requests
Adapting Agile-Stage-Gate	Maintain key principles of Agile-Stage-Gate
Co-location	Use in special situation with interface changes
	May be used for a subset of the team with interoperability issues

by someone else within the organization. Management must either delegate or accept delay for these tasks while the project is running.

In addition, team integrity during sprints is imperative. Therefore, managers cannot change team composition on a whim but must allow the team to complete their sprints. Naturally, major issues in the company can force managers to pull resources or change direction of a team. However, these impromptu decisions must be an exception and not the norm. In SMEs, specifically, respecting team integrity may be a larger issue, as the short distance between manager and project/team member provides ample opportunity to influence project direction. As resources in Agile-Stage-Gate projects need not be fully dedicated, managers can maintain team integrity through proper planning. Used in combination with development moratoria, management should be able to maintain team integrity while also using the resources for other tasks.

Lack of dedicated teams and the fact that team members in SMEs will have other responsibilities and tasks imply that management must setup a system for dealing with these "other tasks." These "other tasks" are not related to the project, and yet that cannot be solved/implemented by employees outside of the Agile-Stage-Gate teams. Management must find and negotiate a suitable system for dealing with these "other tasks." Such methods must satisfy the needs of the other departments. In this project, for example, Company C used a one-week moratorium following each two-week sprint. Management must further maintain and defend the negotiated method against immediate requests to ensure rhythm for the team. The lack of a dedicated team may manifest itself as team members not participating in the daily scrum to the detriment of team performance. Management must vigorously ensure that the full team is always present at the daily scrum meetings.

Moreover, the adaptability of Agile-Stage-Gate should not be seen by managers as an open invitation to make arbitrary change. Agile-Stage-Gate can, and should, be adapted to the practice of the development team while maintaining its fundamental principles. For example, tools such as the inclusion of user input and the definition of done need to be scoped and defined by each team and for each project. However, the adaptation should always be based on Agile-Stage-Gate principles.

Co-location was not a necessary condition for Agile-Stage-Gate in the three companies. However, managers may use this form of collaboration in special situations in which changes in one area require changes to the interfaces and other areas. The central management consideration is to reserve this approach for situations that require all team members for longer time than a daily scrum meeting. Managers may also choose to use co-location for a subset of the team to quickly clarify and resolve interoperability issues between their functional areas.

7.2. *Implications for research*

In existing research, co-location and dedicated teams have been pointed out as key tools to achieve Agile-Stage-Gate. While our three companies did not require co-location, further research should investigate under which circumstances co-location could be beneficial in manufacturing. Newly assembled teams might find an initial short period of co-location beneficial to learn how to work together and interact. As co-locating may be expensive, research should focus on estimating costs and benefits.

Moreover, it was observed that team members in hardware have distinct competences in hardware development. Research should investigate the effects of team composition aspects such as experience and overlap of competences. This could be coupled with studies of how team members exchange tacit and explicit knowledge while working with Agile-Stage-Gate methods and compare varied team composition to develop guidelines.

In this study, on the one hand, the one-week project moratorium solved a resource problem. However, such a break may induce overhead costs associated with employees going back and forth to different projects. A deeper look into the positive and negative effects of the project moratorium, and its length, on overall project progress is needed to make stronger recommendations.

None of the companies, on the other hand, used the product backlog as intended in Agile, instead transforming it into a project backlog. In doing so, the case companies did not use the visual tool that is crucial in Agile methods. Research should investigate if a similar functionality can be developed to support hardware development. This functionality might be achieved either through changed design principles such as a modular product design or rethinking the use and content of the product backlog to fit the needs of hardware development.

Furthermore, sprints are generally longer in manufacturing. Research should thus investigate optimal sprint length in relation to type and complexity of the hardware development task. This work may result in recommendations of how to divide the development task into modules or manageable chunks to fit optimal sprint length.

Similarly, further research should investigate the adaptability of Agile-Stage-Gate methods. Dedicated studies should clarify which aspects can, and should, be adapted to specific contexts, and how manufacturers can implement these changes so as to maximize the potential benefits of Agile-Stage-Gate methods.

None of the companies had metrics to track and evaluate development projects and this is not unique. Research would benefit from developing appropriate metrics and methods to standardize and compare performance data gathered in companies. These new metrics and methods might allow intra company evaluation before and after assessment and even allow intercompany comparison.

Finally, Agile-Stage-Gate prescribes resource allocation as based on a social contract in the team. Indeed, such social pressure can result in key personal withdrawing from projects to avoid the pressure of such social contracts. Further research should investigate possible negative consequences of this mechanism, e.g. bullying and low motivation to participate in teams. Such consequences and indeed the implementation of Agile-Stage-Gate may be influenced by organizational culture. Research should uncover the role of organizational culture on the implementation of Agile-Stage-Gate methods and investigate the most and least supportive contexts and their implications.

7.3. *Limitations*

This study is not without limitations and such a real-life test is open to criticism of compliance and desirability bias. A tailored Agile-Stage-Gate model was developed for the three SMEs, and it was attempted to train the test companies to use Agile-Stage-Gate in the same way in order to allow comparison. The test companies adapted Agile-Stage-Gate to their own contexts, however, and this raises questions about whether the results are indeed caused by Agile-Stage-Gate. The questionnaire shows that the use of Agile practices did in fact increase within the companies, and group interviews with developers did not mention other interventions. Moreover, as the questionnaires were sent out before and after the project, when developers had no contact with the Agile coach; thus the impact of social desirability was minimized. However, social desirability can never be completely avoided and may have influenced respondents.

The selection of test companies may favor companies already interested in Agile-inspired methods, perhaps amplifying the benefits. However, companies not interested in Agile practices are not a relevant target group, thus making these three test companies comparable in motivation to other SMEs looking to adopt Agile practices.

The use of Danish companies is a direct consequence of the focus of the Danish Industrial Foundation. Software Agile has been widely adopted and does not appear to favor specific cultural and country contexts, and so hardware Agile should be no different, suggesting that the results apply to SMEs outside of Denmark.

Hard performance metrics were noticeably missing in all three of the test firms. While the researchers tried to impose metrics, these were largely perceptual. Thus, it would have been more beneficial if the firms had developed, agreed to, and used their own internal metrics, specifically hard metrics to gage performance, such as time-to-market, on-time performance, meetings sales and profit targets, and so on, to permit more reliable, valid, and comparable assessment of performance improvements across the firms. Further, installing metrics at the beginning, as Agile-Stage-Gate is being first implemented, is recommended, so that corrective action can be taken if things do not go well during implementation, thus signaling the need for intervention. Finally, data from such metrics would also help to overcome another potential problem, namely, management skepticism. Still, the use of hard metrics does not guarantee scientific objective and comparable data, as subject and context differ greatly even within the same firms. In this perspective, perceptual measures do offer a telling indication of the effect of Agile-Stage-Gate.

8. Conclusion

Agile methods borrowed from the software world clearly have a role to play in the development of physical products by SMEs. Three SME manufacturers, using a modified version of Agile for physical new product, namely, Agile-Stage-Gate, generally achieved *positive performance results*: faster to market, higher success rates, and a better overall new-product process. But the results were perhaps not as strong as might have been expected, given the very positive results reported from larger manufacturers and software developers alike. Moreover, while some of the elements of Agile were adopted by these SME firms, others were not. Indeed, adopting many of the requirements and methods of Agile as practiced in software development proved to be a major challenge for these SME firms, such as finding dedicated or at least focussed project teams, co-locating teams, evolving the product's design, using the flexible product backlog, and daily scrums. Adaptations of Agile were made, and novel solutions to these challenges were found by the test firms, however, such as building in a moratorium after each sprint, using scrums but less frequently than daily, employing longer and variable-length sprint iterations, and modifying the definition of "done" to include all results of a sprint, not just product versions. Further, some particularly strong and positive aspects of Agile-Stage-Gate that proved highly beneficial to these firms were uncovered; these included the use of regular scrums with the entire project team present to sync projects, enhance team communication, and also to ensure resource commitment among team members; and building a much stronger customer orientation into the project through voice-of-customer work, the use of personas, and developing user stories early in the project. Overall, and in spite of the challenges, the positive results achieved in this study suggest that Agile-Stage-Gate must be considered a recommended product development approach for use in the context of SME manufacturers.

Acknowledgments

We appreciate the support of the Danish Industry Foundation project number 2016-0114. We thank the Implementation and Performance Management group at DTU for helpful comments on earlier drafts. We thank the anonymous reviewers for important comments and suggestions for improving the paper.

References

Agile Alliance (2019). Agile 101. Available at https://www.agilealliance.org/agile101/.

Ajamian, G. and Koen, P. A. (2002). Technology stage gate: A structured process for managing high risk, new technology projects. In *The PDMA Toolbox for New Product Development*, eds. P. Beliveau, A. Griffin and S. Sommermeyer. John Wiley & Sons, New York, pp. 267–295.

Atkinson, R., Crawford, L. and Ward, S. (2006). Fundamental uncertainties in projects and the scope of project management. *International Journal of Project Management,* **24**: 687–698.

Beck, K., Beedle, M., van Bennekum, A., Cockburn, A., Cunningham, W., Fowler, M. *et al.* (2001). Manifesto for Agile Software Development. Available at http://agilemanifesto. org/.

Becker, B. (2006). Rethinking the Stage-Gate process — A reply to the critics. *The Management Roundtable,* July 12.

Begel, A. and Nagappan, N. (2007). Usage and perceptions of agile software development in an industrial context: An exploratory study. In *ESEM '07: First International Symposium on Empirical Software Engineering and Measurement,* Washington, DC, IEEE, pp. 255–264.

Ben Mahmoud-Jouini, S., Midler, C. and Silberzahn, P. (2016). Contributions of design thinking to project management in an innovation context. *Project Management Journal,* **47**, 2: 144–156. https://doi.org/10.1002/pmj.21577.

Bers, J. A. and Dismukes, J. P. (2012). Guerrilla innovation — The accelerated radical innovation model meets the real world. *International Journal of Innovation and Technology Management,* **9**, 01, 1250002. https://doi.org/10.1142/s0219877012500022.

Bhatia, A., Cheng, J., Salek, S., Chokshi, V. and Jetter, A. (2017). Improving the effectiveness of fuzzy front end management: Expanding stage-gate methodologies through agile. In *PICMET 2017 — Portland International Conference on Management of Engineering and Technology: Technology Management for the Interconnected World, Proceedings,* 2017 January, 1–8. https://doi.org/10.23919/PICMET.2017.8125390.

Birgün, S. and Çerkezoğlu, B. T. (2018). A systematic approach for improving the software management process. *International Journal of Innovation and Technology Management,* **16**, 4: 1940006. https://doi.org/10.1142/s0219877019400066.

Boehm, B. and Turner, R. (2004). *Balancing Agility and Discipline: A Guide for the Perplexed.* Addison-Wesley, Boston, MA, pp. 55–57.

Brem, A. (2016). Learning to become better-backward research as a new approach for analyzing organizations' innovation processes. *IEEE Engineering Management Review,* **44**, 4: 26–29. https://doi.org/10.1109/EMR.2016.2623687.

Budak, A. and Ustundag, A. (2016). A risk simulation and optimization model for selection of new product development projects. In *Uncertainty Modelling in Knowledge Engineering and Decision Making,* World Scientific, pp. 1049–1055. https://doi.org/10.1142/ 9789813146976_0162.

Clark, S. (2018). DPA d:screet 6061 & d:fine 6066 headset, Resolutionmag.com, September 2018. Available at https://www.resolutionmag.com/wp-content/uploads/2018/09/DPA-dscreet-6061-dfine-6066-Resolution-V17.6.pdf.

Conforto, E. C., Amaral, D. C., da Silva, S. L., Felippo, A. D. and Kamikawachi, D. S. L. (2016). The agility construct on project management theory. *International Journal of Project Management,* **34**: 660–674.

Conforto, E. C., Salum, F., da Silva, S. L. and de Almeida, L. F. M. (2014). Can Agile project management be adopted by industries other than software development? *Project Management Journal,* **45**, 3: 21–34.

Cooper, R. G. (2008). NexGen Stage-Gate® — What leading companies are doing to reinvent their NPD processes. *PDMA Visions,* **XXXII**, 3: 6–10.

Cooper, R. G. (2010). Stage-Gate idea to launch system. *Wiley International Encyclopedia of Marketing: Product Innovation & Management,* Vol. 5, ed. B. L. Bayus. Wiley, West Sussex, UK.

Cooper, R. G. (1983). A process model for industrial new product development. *IEEE Transactions on Engineering Management*, **EM-30**, 1 Feb 1983: 2–11.

Cooper, R. G. (2014). What's next? After Stage-Gate. *Research-Technology Management*, **157**, 1: Jan–Feb: 20–31.

Cooper, R. G. (2016). Agile-Stage-Gate hybrids: The next stage for product development. *Research-Technology Management*, **159**, 1: 21–29.

Cooper, R. G. (2017). *Winning at New Products: Creating Value Through Innovation*, 5th edition, Basic Books, Perseus Books Group, New York, NY.

Cooper, R. G. and Sommer, A. F. (2016a). The Agile-Stage-Gate hybrid model: A promising new approach and a new research opportunity. *Journal of Product Innovation Management*, **33**, 5: 513–526.

Cooper, R. G. and Sommer, A. F. (2016b). Agile-Stage-Gate: New idea-to-launch method for manufactured new products is faster, more responsive. *Industrial Marketing Management*, **59**, Nov: 167–180.

Cooper, R. G. and Sommer, A. F. (2018). Agile–Stage-Gate for manufacturers — Changing the way new products are developed. *Research-Technology Management*, **61**, 2: 17–26.

Cooper, R. G., Fuerst, P. and Dreher, A. (2019). How Agile development works for manufacturers: Parts 1 & 2. *CIMS Innovation Management Report*, forthcoming.

Daly, J. A., Sætre, A. S. and Brun, E. (2012). Killing mushrooms: The realpolitik of terminating innovation projects. *International Journal of Innovation Management*, **16**, 5: 1–30.

Edwards, K. and Winkel, J. (2018). A method for effect modifier assessment (EMA) in ergonomic intervention research. *Applied Ergonomics*, **72**: 113–120. https://doi.org/10.1016/j.apergo.2018.05.007.

Ettlie, J. and Elsenbach, J. (2007). Modified Stage-Gate regimes in new product development. *Journal of Production Innovation Management*, **24**, 1: 20–33.

Gonzalez, W. (2014). Applying Agile project management to predevelopment stages of innovation. *International Journal of Innovation and Technology Management*, **11**, 4: 1450020. https://doi.org/10.1142/S0219877014500205.

Griffin, A. (1997). *Drivers of NPD Success: The 1997 PDMA Report*. Product Development & Management Association, Chicago, IL.

Grönlund, J., Sjödin, D. and Frishammar, J. (2010). Open innovation and the Stage-gate process: A revised model for new product development. *California Management Review*, **52**, 3: 106–131.

Gudem, M., Steinert, M. and Welo, T. (2014). From lean product development to lean innovation: Searching for a more valid approach for promoting utilitarian and emotional value. *International Journal of Innovation and Technology Management*, **11**, 2: 1450008. https://doi.org/10.1142/S0219877014500084.

Hannola, L., Friman, J. and Niemimuukko, J. (2012). Application of agile methods in the innovation process. *International Journal of Business Innovation and Research*, **7**(1), 84. https://doi.org/10.1504/ijbir.2013.050557.

Invention Center (2018). Rheinisch-Westfälische Technische Hochschule Aachen (RWTH), Consortium Benchmarking 2018 "Agile Invention": Evaluation of the Study Results.

Jahanshahi, A. A. and Brem, A. (2017). Does real options reasoning support or oppose project performance? Empirical evidence from Electronic Commerce Projects. *Project Management Journal*, **48**, 4: 39–54. https://doi.org/10.1177/875697281704800404.

Jetter, A., Albar, F. and Sperry, R. (2016). The practice of project management in product development: Insights from the literature and cases in high-tech. Project Management

Institute Global Operations Center. Available at https://www.pmi.org/learning/academic-research/the-practice-of-project-management-in-product-developmen.

Judi, H. M. and Beach, R. (2010). Achieving manufacturing flexibility: The role of people, technology, innovation and continuous improvement. *International Journal of Innovation and Technology Management*, **7**, 2: 161–181. https://doi.org/10.1142/S0219877010 001891.

Karlstrom, D. and Runeson, P. (2005). Combining Agile methods with Stage-Gate project management. *IEEE Software*, May–June: 43–49.

Karlstrom, D. and Runeson, P. (2006). Integrating Agile software development into Stage-Gate managed product development. *Empirical Software Engineering*, **11**: 203–225.

Kortelainen, S. and Lättilä, L. (2013). Hybrid modeling approach to competitiveness through fast strategy. *International Journal of Innovation and Technology Management*, **10**, 5: 1340016. https://doi.org/10.1142/s0219877013400166.

Kreiner, K. (1995). In search of relevance: Project management in drifting environments. *Scandinavian Journal of Management*, **11**: 335–346.

Kreiner, K. (2012). Comments on challenging the rational project environment: The legacy and impact of Christensen and Kreiner's Projektledning i en ofulständig värld. *International Journal of Managing Projects in Business*, **5**: 714–717.

Lee, Y., John, C. ST., Fong, E. A. and Bao, Y. (2018). Flexible new product development processes and appropriability: Intellectual property and first-mover. *International Journal of Innovation Management*, **22**, 1: 1850002. https://doi.org/10.1142/s13639196185 00020.

Lenfle, S. and Loch, C. (2010). Lost roots: How project management came to emphasize control over flexibility and novelty. *California Management Review*, **53**, 1: 32–55.

Miaskiewicz, T. and Kozar, K. A. (2011). Personas and user-centered design: How can personas benefit product design processes? *Design Studies*, **32**, 5: 17–430. https://doi.org/10.1016/j.destud.2011.03.003.

Millward, H. U. W., Byrne, C., Walters, A. T. and Lewis, A. (2006). New product development within small and medium-sized enterprises: Analysis through technology management maps. *International Journal of Innovation and Technology Management*, **3**, 3: 283–302. https://doi.org/10.1142/s0219877006000806.

Nardelli, G. and Edwards, K. (2018). Co-Developing Agile-Stage-Gate in Danish SMEs. In *Participatory Innovation Conference 2018*, Eskilstuna, Sweden. http://pin-c.sdu.dk/assets/track-5e-nardelli-p360-364.pdf.

Nicholas, J. M. and Steyn, H. (2012). *Project Management for Business, Engineering, and Technology*, 4 edn. Routledge, New York.

Ovesen, N. (2012). The challenges of becoming Agile: Implementing and conducting scrum in integrated product development. Report from Department of Architecture and Design, Aalborg University, Denmark.

Reagan, B. (2012). Going Agile: CA Technologies, Clarity PPM Division's transformative journey. Digital Celerity, San Francisco, CA, Sep 22. http://www.slideshare.net/DCsteve/going-agile-with-ca-clarity-ppm-agile-vision.

Salerno, M. S., Gomes, L. A. D. V., Da Silva, D. O., Bagno, R. B. and Freitas, S. L. T. U. (2015). Innovation processes: Which process for which project? *Technovation*, **35**, 59–70. https://doi.org/10.1016/j.technovation.2014.07.012.

Saynisch, M. (2010). Beyond frontiers of traditional project management: An approach to evolutionary, self-organizational principles and the complexity theory — Results of the research program. *Project Management Journal*, **41**: 21–37.

Schmidt, T. S., Weiss, S. and Paetzold, K. (2018). *Agile Development of Physical Products: An Empirical Study About Motivations, Potentials and Applicability:* Report, University of the German Federal Armed Forces, Munich, Germany. Available at www.unibw.de/produktentwicklung-en.

Schwaber, K. (2004). *Agile Project Management with Scrum.* Microsoft Press, Richmond, WA.

ScrumInc. (2017). *The Scrum Guide.* July. Available at http://www.scrumguides.org/scrum-guide.html.

Sethi, R. and Iqbal, Z. (2008). Stage-gate controls, learning failure, and adverse effect on novel new products. *Journal of Marketing,* January, **72**, 118–134.

Sommer, A. F., Dukovska-Popovska, I. and Steger-Jensen, K. (2013). Barriers towards integrated product development — Challenges from a holistic project management perspective. *International Journal of Project Management,* Available at http://dx.doi.org/10.1016/j.ijproman.2013.10.013.

Sommer, A. F., Hedegaard, C., Dukovska-Popovska, I. and Steger-Jensen, K. (2015). Improved product development performance through Agile/Stage-Gate hybrids — The next-generation Stage-Gate process? *Research-Technology Management,* **158**, 1, Jan–Feb: 1–10.

Svejvig, P. and Andersen, P. (2015). Rethinking project management: A structured literature review with a critical look at the brave new world. *International Journal of Project Management,* **33**: 278–290.

Sætre, A. S. and Brun, E. (2012). Strategic management of innovation: Managing exploration-exploitation by balancing creativity and constraint. *International Journal of Innovation and Technology Management,* **9**, 4: 1250025. https://doi.org/10.1142/S0219877012500253.

Sætre, A. S. and Brun, E. C. (2013). Ambiguity and learning in the innovation process: Managing exploitation-exploitation by balancing creativity and constraint revisited. *International Journal of Innovation and Technology Management,* **10**, 4: 1350014. https://doi.org/10.1142/S0219877013500144.

Tesch, J. F., Brillinger, A.-S. and Bilgeri, D. (2017). Internet of things business model innovation and the Stage-Gate Process: An exploratory analysis. *International Journal of Innovation Management,* **21**, 5: 1740002. https://doi.org/10.1142/S1363919617400023.

Thomas, J. and Mengel, T. (2008). Preparing project managers to deal with complexity — Advanced project management education. *International Journal of Project Management,* **26**: 304–315.

Tura, N., Hannola, L. and Pynnönen, M. (2017). Agile methods for boosting the commercialization process of new technology. *International Journal of Innovation and Technology Management,* **14**, 3: 1750013. https://doi.org/10.1142/S0219877017500134.

Vedsmand, T., Edwards, K., Hvidt, N., Nielsen, M. and Jørgensen, J. K. (2017a). *Agil Stage-Gate®: Ny model for udviklingsprojekter i mellemstore virksomheder.* Dansk Industri. http://dx.doi.org/10.11581/DTU:00000028.

Vedsmand, T., Edwards, K., Hvidt, N., Nielsen, M. and Jørgensen, J. K. (2017b). *Værktøjskasse til Agil Stage-Gate®: Ny model for udviklingsprojekter i mellemstore virksomheder.* Dansk Industri. http://dx.doi.org/10.11581/DTU:00000029.

Vedsmand, T., Kielgast, S. and Cooper, R. G. (2016). Integrating Agile with Stage-Gate® — How new Agile-Scrum methods lead to faster and better innovation. *Innovation Management SE,* August 9: 1–15.

Walters, A. T., Millward, H. U. W. and Lewis, A. (2006). Case studies of advanced manufacturing technology implementation in small companies. *International Journal of*

Innovation and Technology Management, **3**, 2: 149–169. Available at http://search.ebs-cohost.com/login.aspx?direct=true&db=bth&AN=21498066&site=ehost-live.

Yordanova, Z. B. (2018). Lean startup method hampers breakthrough innovations and company's innovativeness. *International Journal of Innovation and Technology Management*, **15**, 2: 1850012. https://doi.org/10.1142/s0219877018500128.

Biography

Kasper Edwards is a senior researcher at the Technical University of Denmark. His research interests are innovation management leadership, sustainable work, the dark side of performance management, organizational social capital and methods for researching organizational interventions. He does consulting focusing on employee driven change and implementation processes. He received his PhD from the Technical University of Denmark in 2004 and in 2009 he received the ALECTIA award for research in healthcare. He is currently the chair of the NOVO-network, a Nordic network for research in health care promoting a triple aim: productivity, quality and wellbeing at work.

Robert G. Cooper Robert Cooper is ISBM Distinguished Research Fellow at Penn State University's Smeal College of Business Administration, USA; Professor Emeritus, DeGroote School of Business, McMaster University, Canada; and a Crawford Fellow of the Product Development & Management Association (PDMA). He is the creator of the *Stage-Gate®* system, widely used by leading firms to drive new products to market. Dr. Cooper holds Bachelors and Masters degrees in Chemical Engineering, and an MBA and PhD in Business. He has written eleven books on new product management, including the best-seller, *Winning at New Products* 5th ed. He is three times winner of the Holland Award from the Industrial Research Institute, Washington; five times winner of the UK award for the best article in the publication *R&D Management*; winner of the Hustad Award for Best Paper in PDMA's *Journal of Product Innovation Management*; and winner of the Lee Rivers Award from the Commercial Development & Marketing Association (U.S.) for his *Stage-Gate®* process.

Tomas Vedsmand is partner in the consulting company GEMBA Innovation in Denmark. Tomas works as an Agile Coach and Management Consultant. His main interest lies in driving organisations to adopt agile-lean ways of working in R&D and product development in HW and HW/SW companies. Tomas is a Certified Scrum Master and Product Owner as well as Certified in Agile Leadership and SAFe 4.5. Tomas has also worked with innovation management and Stage-Gate and received his PhD in 1997.

Giulia Nardelli Giulia Nardelli, PhD, is Associate Professor at DTU Management, Implementation and Performance Management research group. She holds a PhD in Social Sciences. In close collaboration with industry, she researches how organisations innovate and manage change in a variety of contexts, e.g. services, manufacturing, energy providing.

Chapter 11

An Expanded Model of Success Factors for NPD Performance

Tor Guimaraes*

Jesse E. Owen Chair of Excellence
Tennessee Tech University, Cookeville, TN 38505, USA
tguimaraes@tntech.edu

Ketan Paranjape

VP, Diagnostics Information Solutions
9115 Hague Rd, Indianapolis, IN 46256, USA

Mike Walton

Global Head of Manufacturing Industry
Google Enterprise, Cincinnati, OH 45202, USA

Purpose: The literature prescribing important determinants of new product development success can be grouped into six main areas addressing organization culture, strategic leadership, competitive intelligence, management of technology, specific characteristics of the company's NPD process, and the company's absorptive capacity to use available knowledge to produce and commercialize new products. This study expands and tests an expanded model for enhancing the company's new product development success. Design/methodology/approach: A field test using a mailed questionnaire to collect information from 311 manufacturing companies has been used to test the proposed model. To eliminate possible multicollinearity among the independent variables, a multivariate regression analysis was used. Findings: The results provide conclusive evidence about the importance of these success factors individually and in combination to explain the inter-company variance in success performing new product development. Research limitation/implications: Despite the relatively broad scope of the proposed model, other factors may also be important, should be identified, and tested in future studies. Practical implications: The items used for measuring each of the main constructs provide more specific insights regarding how managers should go about developing these success factors within their organizations. Originality/value: While the study is grounded in the literature of what until now have been relatively isolated areas of knowledge, it proposed and empirically tested a unique and increasingly integrated model for these areas considered important to new product development.

*Corresponding author.

This chapter was originally published in *International Journal of Innovation and Technology Management*, Vol. 16, No. 7, December 2019, published by World Scientific Publishing, Singapore. Reprinted with permission.

Keywords: New product development success; competitive intelligence; strategic leadership; management of technology; NPD process; organization absorptive capacity; organization culture.

1. Introduction

Wisegeek [2015], astutely posited that business is all about innovation and change, making it absolutely necessary to change to remain relevant, and any business not realizing the importance of developing new products will not last very long. From a macroeconomic perspective, new products are important for generating employment and economic growth, technological progress, and higher standards of living in general [Bhuiyan (2011)]. From a company perspective, new product development (NPD) is essential to remain competitive, survive, and prosper.

The NPD literature emphasizes the importance of continuously introducing new products to the market for continued business success. NPD's contribution to the growth of companies, its influence on profit performance, and its role as a key factor in business planning have been well documented over time [Cooper (2001); Ulrich and Eppinger (2011)]. The importance of NPD can be dramatically illustrated in the transition from physical books to e-books. Some companies built on the sale of physical books failed to realize the importance of NPD and died out. Other companies embraced NPD wisdoms, anticipated this change and enabled customers to download books from their Web sites, integrated this download with their own personal electronic readers, making it a complete package. Another dramatic illustration of NPD power comes from smart phones where some companies established themselves as market leaders through systematic introduction of new products, carefully managing their products lifecycle. In a study comparing percentage of revenues coming from new products, the results show that half of the revenue for Best-in-Class companies comes from new products, showing a relatively large gap against the 38% for their peers and the industry average [Lopes (2014)]. Therefore Lopes [2014] concluded that "a new product offers an organization the greatest opportunity for increasing revenue and profitability."

However, Lopes [2014] also widely recognized that NPD is a complex process. Its complexity and risks arise from the many phases of the NPD process, its many stakeholders, the intricacy of the product being developed, the changing consumer demands, increased market globalization, extended supply chains and design networks, and regulatory compliance. Managers engaged in improving this complex process must find the right balance between improving execution, efficiency, and timeliness with the excitement of innovation and problem solving. Without great care, it is relatively easy to tip the balance too far in either direction end up with a great product that is late or a poor product that is on time; either case creating a commercial failure [Lopes (2014)].

In the last few decades, as industry increasingly recognized the importance of NPD, the number of new product introductions increased dramatically. On the other hand, managing the NPD process has increasingly also become a challenge requiring good timing, extensive financial and human resources. In practice, as pointed out by Cooper [2001], the majority of new products never make it to market and those that do face a failure rate somewhere between 25% and 45% [Cooper (2001)]. Historically, for every seven new product ideas, about four enter development, one and a half are launched, and only one succeeds [Booz and Hamilton (1982)].

Despite the extensive research on how to achieve success in NPD, firms continue to deliver products that fail and therefore NPD ranks among the riskiest and most confusing tasks for most companies. As the number of dollars invested in NPD goes up, the pressure to maximize the return on those investments also goes up. It becomes worse as an estimated 46% of resources allocated to NPD are spent on products that are canceled or fail to yield an adequate financial return [Bhuiyan (2011)].

In practice, many factors have been recognized as important for NPD success or failure, and the literature reflects the complexity and breadth of the relevant knowledge. Most authors would agree that the change process itself has to bear certain characteristics [Guimaraes and Paranjape (2013)], and many researchers have looked to improvements in strategic leadership as critical to developing an organization environment conducive to innovation [Flatten *et al.* (2015); Lee *et al.* (2014); Sun and Anderson (2011); Waldman *et al.* (2001)]. To help define and prioritize important problems and opportunities to the organization, many have proposed Competitive Intelligence (CI) programs as important to company success [Elbashir *et al.* (2011); Moilanen *et al.* (2014); Vedder and Guynes (2002); du Toit (2003); Tarraf and Molz (2006)]. Further, effective Management of Technology (MOT) is thought to be a critical requirement for successfully implementing most modern business changes [Lee *et al.* (2014); Wang *et al.* (2014); Block (2014); Beattie and Fleck (2005)]. While these propositions are exceedingly important, the existing literature contains little empirical evidence supporting them in the context of NPD.

Another major knowledge deficiency is that while individually the constructs studied here have been addressed by groups of academic researchers in their respective areas, they have been mostly ignored by the researchers in the other areas also important to management of business innovation in general and NPD specifically. For example, despite its clear importance for organization innovativeness, strategic leadership has been substantially ignored by researchers focused on the impact of management of technology for business innovation. Even more surprising academic researchers have neglected of CI as determinant of business innovation success, even though large numbers of CI managers from many companies have formed a professional association publishing a journal to specifically address issues important to this area. Similarly, some researchers of business innovation have addressed special characteristics of the innovation process as an important factor for project implementation success [Guimaraes and Paranjape (2013); Caccia-Bava *et al.* (2005)]. Academic researchers in business innovation management have ignored this construct altogether, especially in the context of NPD. Last, despite the increasing acceptance of organization absorptive capacity as an important influence in identifying the need to innovate, as well as on the entire process for implementing business innovation, relatively little empirical research is available addressing organization absorptive capacity as a factor in business innovation success [Carrillo (2005); Meijboom *et al.* (2007); Nadkarni and Narayanan (2007); Weijermars (2009)]. Thus, it is particularly important to academic researchers and practicing managers alike to propose and test an integrated model, bringing together these major factors potentially important for more successful NPD. That was the primary objective of the field test discussed here.

2. Theoretical Background and Proposed Hypotheses

The theoretical model proposed and tested in this study is graphically shown in Fig. 1, followed by a more detailed description of each construct and how it was measured in this study. Appendix A shows the questions actually used for data collection.

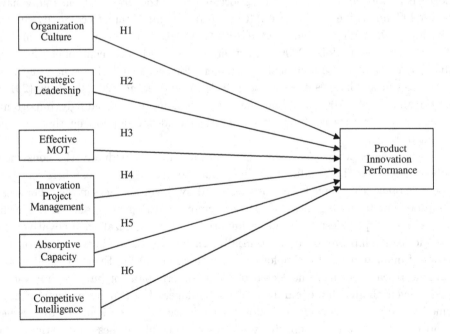

Fig. 1.   A graphical depiction of the theoretical model.

2.1. *Dependent variable — product innovation performance or success*

In the context of this study, NPD encompasses dealing with the implementation of a new product idea including a completely new line of products currently not in the market, or it could be aimed toward significantly upgrading existing products. At the company level, new products are responsible for employment and economic growth, technological progress, and higher standards of living [Bhuiyan (2011)]. NPD's contribution to the growth of the companies, its influence on profit performance, and its key role as a factor in business success have been well documented over time [Booz and Hamilton (1982); Cooper (2001); Ulrich and Eppinger (2011)].

NPD performance or success in this study was measured according to the recommendations by Churchill [1979] and DeVellis [1991]. This measure was validated by Alegre *et al.* [2006] who confirmed product innovation performance as a construct with two dimensions: performance effectiveness and efficiency. Product innovation effectiveness reflects the degree of success of an innovation. Efficiency reflects the amount of effort needed to achieve that degree of success.

As an indication of its importance, NPD has been studied from a very wide variety of perspectives. Enkel *et al.* [2009], among many others, have explored the importance of innovation approaches, which emphasize the inclusion of company outsiders. Johannessen *et al.* [2001] provided some guidelines for categorizing types of innovations in terms of what is being changed, how new, and new to whom. While it is important to understand the great variety of perspectives and factors affecting product innovation, this study has a very specific practical focus as discussed below.

The literature prescribing important determinants of product innovation success falls into six main areas encompassing (1) an appropriate environment for NPD (organization culture), (2) the firm strategic leadership, (3) its competitive intelligence, (4) its ability to manage technology, (5) some specific characteristics of the company's innovation project management process, and (6) the organization's absorptive capacity to translate available knowledge into new products [Elbashir *et al.* (2011); Moilanen *et al.* (2014)]. While these major areas of study may indeed be important to enhance company innovation and competitiveness, the existing literature on each area is not being shared by researchers in the other areas. That has led until now models relatively narrow in scope and primarily focused on the particular research area. A prior study by Guimaraes *et al.* [2018a] proposed a similar but more limited model focused on business innovation in general. This study proposes an expanded model, which tests these constructs as a set of determinants of NPD success. To accomplish that, this study uses a dataset and uses a broad definition of product innovation, without specifically measuring details of the innovation process such as if partners were involved, if it created new markets or new sources of supplies, etc. Each of the six constructs mentioned above is discussed in more detail correspondingly represented by the independent variables, and respective hypothesis to be tested.

2.2. Independent variable — organization culture

Since the early 1980s, company culture has been considered important for company prosperity by many authors [Peters *et al.* (1982); Davis (1984)]. According to Büschgens *et al.* [2013] the literature has been based on two major propositions: first, cultures reflect the values and actions of the senior leaders; second, cultures are important determinants of firm performance. From the beginning while, the importance of organization culture has a strong intuitive appeal as a determinant of company innovativeness and performance, researchers have had difficulties producing conclusive results, let alone being able to make sound recommendations to practitioners about how to improve their company culture to increase success in NPD. Ogbonna and Wilkinson [2003] have recognized some difficulties with the body of research on the organization culture, innovativeness, and performance links. They found that, similar to the organizational behavior literature, some researchers in the human resources area have questioned the importance of the culture concept and the wisdom of planned culture change. More recently, Schneider *et al.* [2013] survey of the literature about organization culture showed little empirical evidence for these assumptions. However, despite academic research confusion, company managers remain highly interested in managing their organization culture.

Similarly, while addressing the organization culture-performance relationship, researchers have encountered many problems such as conceptual difficulties defining culture [Schneider *et al.* (2013)], and several methodological issues due to small sample sizes, construct measurement, and variance created by trying to compare multi-industry assessments [Detert *et al.* (2000)]. To complicate matters, even though the academic research on culture has over time become more sophisticated methodologically, individual researchers have used diverse measures of company culture and performance, making cross studies comparisons more difficult [Sackmann (2011); Hartnell *et al.* (2011)].

Büschgens *et al.* [2013] provided some possible reasons why have researchers not conclusively demonstrated the link between company innovativeness and company culture. First, many firms well known to produce and commercialize new products and services become superficially known for some unique aspect of their corporate culture. For example, 3M explains its innovativeness as being essentially a science-based organization, while Apple's innovativeness supposedly comes from promoting the idea of employees focusing on larger product visions leading to the creation of new major ground-breaking technologies. Similarly, much of Google innovativeness is credited to its employees' individuality and broad freedom. Such superficial analysis of existing cultural traits as determinants of successful innovativeness is misleading because it should be rather obvious by now that company innovativeness will require more than one cultural trait no matter how important. These simple explanations add to the confusion created by the very large number of potentially important culture traits that have been proposed in the literature and found to be mostly empirically irrelevant as determinants for company innovativeness success in general.

Further, as stated by Büschgens *et al.* [2013], "the heterogeneity of culture in practical examples is mirrored by a multitude of cultural values that has been investigated scientifically." In their literature review, they identified more than 40 different cultural traits supposedly related to company innovativeness, comprising a wide range of broad variables such as "innovation culture" [Chandler *et al.* (2000); Gumusluoglu and IIsev (2009)] or "supportive culture" [Abbey and Dickson (1983); Berson *et al.* (2008); Wei and Morgan (2004)] to very specific cultural traits like tolerance for failure [Danneels (2008)] or participative decision-making [Hurley and Hult (1998)]. If one assumed a positive culture–innovation relationship, some confusion is likely to result from such wide diversity of traits being investigated. Indeed, some studies assuming a positive culture–innovation relationship produced counter intuitive results, showing negative correlations for "supportive culture" [Berson *et al.* (2008)] and culture stability [Jaskyte (2004)]. Given the confusion about the various interpretations, their measurements and relationships to company innovativeness and performance, we must agree with Büschgens *et al.* [2013] that "a compelling theoretical explanation for the relation of organizational culture and innovation is still missing."

In summary, regarding the construct of culture as a determinant of company NPD success, the primary issue seems to be related to construct measurement and validity. Only after this issue is resolved will researchers be able to empirically test such relationship. Specifically, the primary issue now is the face and content validity of a measure of culture, which can explain a substantial percentage of the variance in the better established construct of company NPD success. In an effort to cut through all the conceptual and measurement difficulties, this study used a new measure for company culture hopefully more useful in practice [Guimaraes *et al.* (2018b)]. Thus, we propose hypothesis

H1: *Desirable organization cultural traits have a positive effect on its performance in new product development.*

2.3. *Independent variable — strategic leadership*

Many authors have recognized the importance of effective leadership for successful organization innovation [Zenger and Folkman (2016); Flatten *et al.* (2015); Lee *et al.* (2014); Sun and Anderson (2011); Waldman *et al.* (2001)]. While there are many types of leadership (i.e. formal/informal, based on specific skills, social status, etc.) arising from the circumstances in which leaders/followers find themselves, for the purpose of this study the relevant construct is company strategic leadership [Garcia-Morales *et al.* (2012)].

Transformational or "charismatic" leadership is widely recognized [Avolio and Yammarino (2013); Gebert *et al.* (2016); Garcia-Morales *et al.* (2012)]. Highly uncertain organization environments (requiring major innovations) tend to be perceived as risky, where wrong decisions could be costly and probably generate a high degree of stress. Charismatic leadership is thought to reduce stress and generate confidence, and perhaps transform uncertainty into a vision of opportunity and success [Flatten *et al.* (2015); Lee *et al.* (2014); Sun and Anderson (2011); Bass (1985)]. According to Waldman *et al.* [2001] charismatic leaders articulate a vision, providing a sense of mission, as well as showing determination and communicating high-performance expectations. The followers are expected to respond with confidence in the leader, and with admiration and respect. Further, they are expected to identify with the leader's vision and with the organization itself, thus creating a high-level cohesion. This cohesion and the leader's expressions of confidence in the followers' ability to attain their vision, produce in turn, a heightened sense of self-efficacy [Podsakoff *et al.* (1990)]. Also, past research found that, charismatic leaders are likely to show persistence and enthusiasm in pursuing goals and be demanding of others through the communication of high-performance expectations [Kanter (1983); Trice and Beyer (1993)]. Similarly, there is considerable evidence that charismatic leadership at the top level is important for company innovativeness and performance [Hambrick and Finkelstein (1987); Day and Lord (1988); Yukl (1998)].

The second form of strategic leadership and transactional leadership, has also been studied widely [Garcia-Morales *et al.* (2012); Pawar and Eastman (1997)]. This is operationally important for an organization rather than one trying to make major changes. In this case, the company is attempting to satisfy the current needs of followers by focusing on exchanges and contingent reward behavior. It calls for attention to exceptions or irregularities, and for taking appropriate action to making corrections [Burns (1978); Bass (1985)]. Transactional leadership acts to strengthen existing organization processes, structures, strategies, and culture. It is conceptually similar to the cultural maintenance form of leadership described by Trice and Beyer [1993].

Some authors Katz and Kahn [1978] and Bass [1985] proposed transactional and charismatic leadership as being somewhat complementary in that both could be displayed by the same individual leader. Similarly, Trice and Beyer [1993] also acknowledged that a leader could show both maintenance and innovation-oriented leadership over time. Based on the above discussion, we propose hypothesis

H2: *Company strategic leadership is directly related to its performance in new product development.*

Effective strategic leadership represents the ability of the top management team to lead when the organization environment requires innovation. Since transactional and transformational (charismatic) leadership are both potentially important and thought to be complementary [Bass (1985)], we measure them as proposed by Waldman *et al.* [2001], and as shown in Appendix A.

2.4. *Independent variable — management of technology (MOT) for business innovation*

As competition increases, new technology has become increasingly important to business organizations for NPD, improving business processes, and improving the organization work environment. As an important factor to support business innovation, many authors have proposed a wide variety of technologies [Lee *et al.* (2014); Wang *et al.* (2014); Block (2014); Beattie and Fleck (2005); Khalil and Ezzat (2005); Li-Hua and Khalil (2006); Podoski and Žilionis (2008)]. The effects of computer technology on organization operations, design, intelligence, and decision-making have long been of interest to researchers [Guimaraes and Paranjape (2013); Yoon *et al.* (2013); Hostler *et al.* (2011); Hostler *et al.* (2012)]. More specifically, the use of computers for data mining and warehousing has long been thought as essential for decision support, and Friedenberg and Rice [1994] and Yoon *et al.* [1995b] have proposed Expert Systems as viable implementation vehicles for business change because they are effective in capturing and distributing knowledge and knowledge processing capability across an organization. For business innovations requiring technology, their implementation processes would be severely hindered and in many cases rendered impossible without effective MOT. Thus, the above discussion leads us to propose hypothesis

H3: *Company MOT effectiveness is directly related to its performance in new product development.*

MOT Effectiveness is the extent to which the company's needs for technology while implementing business innovation have been met. This was measured by asking the respondents to rate their company along four specific areas important for the successful implementation of innovation, as previously used by Guimaraes and Armstrong [1998a] and Guimaraes *et al.* [2018a].

2.5. *Independent variable — important characteristics of the innovation process*

The literature on business innovation project management process indicates several pre-requisites for successfully implementing innovation: conformity to company objectives, employee and department participation in the innovation process, customer input, reasonably balancing risk taking with cost benefit analysis, monitoring progress, and communication regarding the innovation process [Rabechini Junior and de Carvalho (2013); Carvalho and Rabechini Junior (2015); Rajablu *et al.* (2015); Alexander (2015)]. In summary, how innovation is implemented is an important determinant for success. Thus, we propose hypotheses

H4: *The extent to which the company innovation process bears the desirable characteristics is directly related to its performance in new product development.*

Characteristics of the Innovation Process are defined as the degree to which companies promote "desirable" innovation process activities. This was measured by asking the respondents to rate the importance that the company places on 10 areas (process characteristics) proposed as important for increasing the likelihood of innovation success, as previously used by Guimaraes and Paranjape [2013] and Caccia-Bava *et al.* [2005].

2.6. *Independent variable — absorptive capacity*

According to the dynamic capabilities theory, firms need to adjust their resource base constantly to cope with the changing environment, thereby generating a competitive advantage [Teece *et al.* (1997)]. Absorptive capacity has been originally defined as "the ability of a firm to recognize the value of new, external information, assimilate it, and apply it to commercial ends" [Cohen and Levinthal (1990, p. 128)]. A relatively new approach to understanding the business innovation process comes from the literature on knowledge management proposing and testing the concept of organization absorptive capacity, and its importance as a requirement for companies to manage and prosper in a business environment heavily dependent on innovation [Noblet *et al.* (2011); Popaitoon and Siengthai (2014); Elbashir *et al.* (2011); Kohlbacher *et al.* (2013)]. In the context of innovation management research, absorptive capacity encompass a wide range of theories including organization learning [e.g. Lane *et al.* (2001)], innovation [e.g. Tsai (2001)], a knowledge-based view of the firm [e.g. Zhao and Anand (2009)] and organization's dynamic capabilities [e.g. Zahra and George (2002)].

Cohen and Levinthal [1990] viewed absorptive capacity as a three-dimensional construct composed of three processes: identifying, assimilation, and exploiting external knowledge. Their original proposal has undergone several modifications and extensions [Lane *et al.* (2001); Lewin *et al.* (2011); Todorova and Durisin (2007); Flatten *et al.* (2011)]. Zahra and George [2002] advanced a four-dimensional construct which has been validated by several studies [Brettel *et al.* (2011); Flatten *et al.* (2011); Jansen *et al.* (2005)]. The four dimensions processes or capabilities are: (1) Acquisition referring to the identification and intake of external knowledge potentially relevant to the firm. (2) Assimilation of the knowledge previously acquired through its analysis, understanding, and interpretation. (3) Transformation, focused on combining prior existing knowledge with newly acquired knowledge to update underlying company processes. (4) Exploitation focused on fostering the commercial application of the new knowledge.

Zahra and George [2002] noted that the first two dimensions of acquisition and assimilation deal with exploring potentially relevant knowledge, (thus they are called potential absorptive capacity), expressing the firm's ability to identify and gather external knowledge. The last two dimensions of transformation and exploitation deal with exploiting relevant knowledge and realizing commercial gains from it, (thus they are called realized absorptive capacity), expressing the firm's ability to employ and leverage absorbed knowledge, and to convert such knowledge into new or improved products and processes [Flatten *et al.* (2011)].

While the necessary infrastructure (equipment, employee recruitment, training, etc.) enabling its potential and realized absorptive capacity can be developed and employed separately, they must exist simultaneously in order for the company to achieve the desired results [Zahra and George (2002)]. Indeed, the work of Todorova and Durisin [2007] extends the theoretical absorptive capacity concept to include feedback loops between the potential and realized absorptive capacity concepts to enhance their effects. Therefore, we should expect that the absorptive capacity construct should be viewed as an important determinant of product innovation success. Thus, we propose hypothesis

H5: *The company's absorptive capacity is directly related to its performance in new product development.*

Company Absorptive Capacity is its ability to recognize the value of new external knowledge, and assimilate and apply it successfully. Over time, its measure has been expanded and modified. For this study, we chose the measure validated by several studies [Brettel *et al.* (2011); Flatten *et al.* (2011)] which include four dimensions or capabilities addressing the identification and intake of external knowledge potentially relevant to the firm, assimilation of the knowledge that has previously been acquired, transformation of this knowledge by combining prior existing knowledge with newly acquired knowledge to update underlying processes, and exploitation of the knowledge to produce new products and processes benefitting the company.

2.7. *Independent variable — competitive intelligence*

To keep in touch with what is going on in their markets, managers are increasingly recognizing the importance of competitive intelligence and knowledge management as a key asset [Elbashir *et al.* (2011); Moilanen *et al.* (2014); Vedder and Guynes (2002); du Toit (2003); Swartz (2005); Tarraf and Molz (2006)]. With the increase in business competition, company survival and success is now determined by its rate of learning. If it is faster than external changes, the organization will experience long-term success [Darling (1996)]. Ironically, even though as much as 68% of U.S. companies have an organized approach to providing information to decision makers [Westervelt (1996)], according to Ettorre [1995], probably less than 10% of American corporations manage the CI process well, and effectively integrate the information into their strategic plans. Managers and researchers are increasingly recognizing the importance of competitive intelligence and related knowledge management for keeping in touch with what is going on in their markets, [du Toit (2015); Witell *et al.* (2014); Elbashir *et al.* (2011); Moilanen *et al.* (2014); Vedder and Guynes (2002); du Toit (2003); Swartz (2005); Tarraf and Molz (2006)]. The antecedents and consequences of competitive intelligence dissemination have been studied earlier by Maltz and Kohli [1996], Competitor Analysis (CA) was proposed by Ghoshal and Westney [1991], and other approaches useful for companies to collect information from competitors were addressed by Heil and Robertson [1991]. The importance of organization intelligence to financial performance has also been demonstrated: companies with well-established CI programs on the average showed earnings per share of $1.24, compared to those without CI programs, which lost 7 cents [King (1997)].

Company benefits derived from CI are many including: improved competitive edge [Moilanen *et al.* (2014); McCune (1996); Sawka (1996); Westervelt (1996); du Toit (2003); Editors (2004)] and improved overall company performance [Davison (2001); Babbar and Rai (1993)], which obviously are two essential company goals. Other specific benefits of CI are numerous including: uncovering business opportunities and problems that will enable proactive strategies [Elbashir *et al.* (2011); Moilanen *et al.* (2014); Westervelt (1996)]; providing the basis for continuous improvement [Babbar and Rai (1993)]; shedding light on competitor strategies [Harkleroad (1993); Westervelt (1996)]; improving speed to markets and supporting rapid globalization [Baatz (1994); Ettorre (1995)]; improving the likelihood of company survival [Westervelt (1996)]; increasing business volume [Darling (1996)]; providing better customer assessment [Darling (1996)]; and aiding in the understanding of external influences [Moilanen *et al.* (2014); Sawka (1996)]. Benefits such as these allow companies to better understand the potential impact of proposed innovations and the means by which they can improve their chances of success. Based on the above discussion, we propose hypothesis

H6: *Company CI effectiveness has a positive effect on its performance in new product development.*

The measure for company effectiveness in competitive intelligence used in this study was proposed and used by Guimaraes and Armstrong [1998a] and Guimaraes and Paranjape [2013]. All the questions used for data collection for all constructs in the proposed model are presented in Appendix A. The overall measure for each construct was the average rating for its component items.

3. Study Methodology

This section provides an overview of the data collection procedure, a brief description of the sample and the data analysis procedures.

3.1. *Data collection procedure*

For addressing the strategic factors regarding NPD, we thought top manufacturing managers are likely to be the most appropriate subjects regarding overall organization activities and results in this area. A national directory of manufacturing professionals was used to randomly select 1000 top manufacturing managers. A usable sample of 311 top manufacturing managers (NPD managers or above) shared their organizations' experience regarding their company experience with NPD. A questionnaire was sent directly to the top manufacturing manager with a cover letter explaining the purpose of the study, asking for participation, and offering to share the results. To avoid time distortions, the respondents were asked to address the questions based on their experience within the last five years. Furthermore, our definition of NPD includes the implementation of a new idea, which may have produced a completely new line of products new to the market, or the upgrading of products already in the market.

A wide variety of organizational settings is represented in the sample, with relatively small and large companies, operating in several manufacturing industry sub-sectors. Participation was voluntary, the cover letter assured complete confidentiality of company and respondent information, and that only summary information from the participants would be published. The survey was accompanied by a published report from a previous study on the topic (as a courtesy to prospective respondents) and by a postage-paid envelope addressed for direct return to the researchers.

3.2. *Sample description*

Through the procedure just described, 1000 questionnaires were sent out and 311 were returned in time for data analysis. A total of 31 questionnaires were thrown out due to missing data. The remaining 256 usable questionnaires provide a response rate, which is acceptable for studies of this type [Teo and King (1996)], and consistent with past experience with mailed surveys [George and Barksdale (1974); Igbaria *et al.* (1991)]. To assess the representativeness of the sample, Chi-square tests were used with a sample of non-respondents to check for the possibility of non-response bias. Based on company size (gross revenues) and manufacturing industry sub-sectors, the companies in the sample are similar to those in the target sample. The actual versus the target sample percentage compositions in terms of manufacturing sub-sectors and company gross revenues are presented in Tables 1 and 2, respectively.

3.3. *Construct validity*

Many of the recommendations by Carmines and Zeller [1979] were followed to ensure the validity of the measures in the context of this study. The constructs addressed in this study and their measures have been used by prior studies. To ensure content validity, a thorough survey of the relevant literature was undertaken to identify the important components of each major variable and to ensure that important dimensions of any variable were not neglected.

A pilot test was used to further reduce the possibility of any non-random error, which is the main source of invalidity [Carmines and Zeller (1979)]. For that, a small group of four practitioners from different companies with extensive experience in

Table 1.   Manufacturing industry sub-sectors.

Manufacturing sub-sectors	No. of companies	Actual sample $(n = 311)$	Target sample $(n = 1000)$
Computer and electronic products	22	7%	9%
Chemical products	19	6%	8%
Food, beverage, and tobacco products	18	6%	7%
Pharmaceuticals	36	12%	10%
Petroleum and coal products	25	8%	7%
Machinery	20	6%	5%
Fabricated metal products	16	5%	6%
Textile mills	23	7%	5%
Paper and wood products	18	6%	6%
Plastics and rubber products	21	7%	7%
Electrical equipment, appliances, and components	20	6%	7%
Motor vehicles, bodies, and trailers	18	6%	6%
Other transportation equipment	22	7%	8%
Miscellaneous manufacturing	33	11%	9%
Total	311	100%	100%

Table 2.   Company gross revenues.

Gross revenues	No. of companies	Actual sample $(n = 311)$	Target sample $(n = 1000)$
Less than $100 M	69	22%	31%
$101 M–$400 M	76	24%	25%
$401 M–$700 M	83	27%	22%
$701 M–$1 B	45	14%	12%
Over $1 B	38	12%	10%
Total	311	100%	100%

managing NPD reviewed the questionnaire for validity measuring the relevant constructs (factors related to NPD), completeness of the measures in the questionnaire (including all relevant items), and readability (making it unlikely that subjects will misinterpret a particular question). Some questions were reworded to improve readability; otherwise, the items composing each major variable remained as derived from the literature.

Carmines and Zeller [1979] proposed that construct validation is to focus on the extent to which a measure performs in accordance with theoretical expectations. To ensure construct validity, the constructs theoretical relationships should have been previously established. Further, these relationships should have been empirically supported by different studies over time. In this study, as discussed earlier, the theoretical underpinnings (constructs and hypotheses tested) are relatively well established, with most of the items in each construct having been addressed before by several authors. Second-order factor analyses on the two types of strategic leadership (transactional and charismatic leadership) indicate that they can be combined into a single factor. Similarly, a second-order factor analysis indicated that the four components measuring absorptive capacity could be combined into a single factor, which has been used in this study. Thus, the subsequent multivariate analyses used the combined factors.

3.4. *Construct reliability*

According to Carmines and Zeller [1979], there are four basic methods to assess a measure's reliability (re-test, alternative-form, split-halves, and the internal consistency methods). The main advantage of the internal consistency method is that it requires a single test, in lieu of splitting or repeating of items, and the most widely used of these reliability estimates is given by Cronbach's Alpha coefficient [Carmines and Zeller (1979)] which generally provides a conservative estimate of a measure's reliability.

Authors have varied opinions about what are acceptable levels for the Alpha reliability coefficient, i.e. Nunnally [1978] suggested a coefficient of 0.50 or higher. Van de Ven and Ferry [1980] stated that for exploratory research even a value of 0.4 or higher would be sufficient. Srinivasan [1985] and Magal *et al.* [1988] agreed that even when using a non-validated data gathering instrument in exploratory research, a reliability coefficient of 0.5 or higher is acceptable. Peterson [1994] proposed that Alpha reliability coefficients should be higher than 0.70 for studies that are more rigorous. Table 3 indicates that the internal consistency reliability coefficients (Cronbach's alpha) for the scales used in this study are all well above the level of 0.70 deemed acceptable for studies of this type.

3.5. *Data analysis procedures*

The items comprising each major variable were subjected to a principal component analysis followed by a varimax (orthogonal) rotation to identify composite factors. To be included in a given factor, the item is expected to load unambiguously (i.e. with one loading of 0.5 and no other loadings greater than 0.4), as suggested by Magal *et al.* [1988]. As suggested by several researchers [i.e. Nunnally (1978)], the minimum eigenvalue for which a factor is to be retained was specified as 1.0. This procedure produced multifactor solutions for the main variables. Company absorptive capacity items loaded unambiguously into the four factors as expected. A second-order factor analysis of these four factors produced a single factor representing overall company absorptive capacity, which is used for this study.

In a similar fashion, as a requirement to compute reliability coefficients for each multi-factor construct measure, second-order factor analyses were done on the extracted factors to ensure that they could be treated as one construct. In all cases, the analyses showed that the extracted factors can be combined (loaded unambiguously) into main single factors corresponding to the main variables in the model tested in this study. According to the stated objectives of this study, further analyses shown in Tables 3 and 4 used the combined sub-factors for all major variables.

Table 3.   Correlations between major variables ($n = 311$).

	Mean	Std Dev	1	2	3	4	5	6	7	8
1. Product Innovation Performance	3.94	1.43	(0.74)							
2. Competitive Intelligence	3.31	1.95	0.52**	(0.79)						
3. Transactional Leadership	4.05	1.17	0.36**	NS	(0.83)					
4. Charismatic Leadership	3.16	1.84	0.40**	0.43**	0.31**	(0.76)				
5. Management of Technology	4.21	1.22	0.35**	0.19*	0.27**	0.25**	(0.88)			
6. Innovation Process Features	3.79	1.41	0.42**	0.28**	0.28**	0.33**	0.17*	(0.82)		
7. Absorptive Capacity	3.66	1.38	0.54**	0.44**	0.39**	0.41**	0.43**	0.45**	(0.90)	
8. Organization Culture	3.17	1.31	0.56**	0.60**	0.41**	0.45**	0.52**	0.59**	0.66**	(0.92)

Notes: (Numbers in parentheses diagonally) are Cronbach's alpha reliability coefficients.
NS means not significant, * means $p < 0.05$, ** means $p < 0.01$

Table 4.   Results of multiple regression using stepwise method.

Dependent variable: Product innovation success	Incremental R squared	Significance level
Independent Variables*:		
1. Organization culture	0.31	0.00
2. Management of Technology	0.15	0.00
3. NPD Process Features	0.13	0.00
4. Competitive Intelligence	0.10	0.01
5. Absorptive Capacity	0.07	0.02
6. Strategic Leadership	0.03	NS
Total Variance Explained	**0.76**	

* In the sequence which they entered the regression equation.

The average and standard deviation for each item in the questionnaire is presented in Table 3. Confirmatory factor analyses for the items in each main variable were conducted as the basis for their validation and as a prerequisite for assessing their internal reliability through the Cronbach's alpha coefficients (presented within parentheses). To test the proposed hypotheses, Pearson's correlation coefficients between the major study variables were computed and presented in Table 3. To detect any possible difference between the two strategic leadership types as determinants of business innovation success, they were processed separately in this analysis. A second-order factor analysis indicated that the four components measuring absorptive capacity could be combined into a single factor, which has been used in this study.

Because of the possibility of collinearity among the independent variables, a stepwise multivariate regression analysis was conducted to assess the extent to which each independent variable incrementally contributes to explaining the variance in the dependent variable. The multivariate regression analysis results are presented in Table 4.

4. Results

Table 3 presents the means and standard deviations for the main research variables in this study. In comparison with their main competitors, the manufacturing companies in the sample as a group are thought to be performing slightly above average in the areas of transactional leadership and management of technology. On the other hand, on average the companies in the sample are performing below average in the areas of charismatic leadership, competitive intelligence, and having the cultural traits needed for greater success in product innovation. Also noteworthy is that the relatively large standard deviations indicate significant differences from company to company along all the major variables studied.

Table 3 also shows the Pearson's correlation coefficients used to test hypotheses H1–H6 confirming that all six major independent variables show direct relationship (significant at the 0.01 level or better) to success in product innovation, as defined in this study. To complement this analysis, under the possibility of collinearity among the independent variables, a stepwise multivariate regression analysis has been conducted to assess the extent to which each independent variable incrementally contributes to explaining the variance in the dependent variable. Table 4 shows the results dependent on the specific sequence in which the independent variables entered the regression equation. The desirable cultural traits company alone explains 31% of the variance in product innovation success, followed by performance in management of technology (explaining an additional 15%), the characteristics of the NPD innovation process (13%), competitive intelligence (10%), and absorptive capacity (7%). In this case, each independent variable makes a contribution significant at the 0.05 level or better toward explaining a total of 76% of the variance in product innovation success.

5. Conclusions

Given the importance of effectively implementing product innovation in these days of hyper competitiveness, the results from this study provide strong evidence regarding the importance of company organization culture, absorptive capacity, strategic leadership, competitive intelligence, management of technology, and specific characteristics of the company's innovation process for improving the success of the exceedingly important activity of product innovation as defined in this study. Based on the results, top managers in general and product managers in particular should do whatever they can to improve their company's organization culture and knowledge absorptive capacity as defined here, as well as company performance in the areas of competitive intelligence, strategic leadership, management of technology, and characteristics of the process used to implement the necessary NPD innovations.

Regarding CI, there are some major implications from this study results. To improve their CI programs, managers need to consider the collection of market intelligence based on the six areas addressed in this study: the traditional industry competitors, emerging competitors, traditional customer needs and wants, nontraditional customer needs and wants, relationships with business partners, and NPD. The importance of any one of these areas may be relatively higher or lower, and in some cases, some of these sources may be irrelevant, depending on the company's specific industry sector, line of business, and new products being considered. Good performance in these areas, whenever applicable to the company's industry sector and lines of business, are likely to lead to more effective NPD. In addition, before embarking in major NPD projects, which are supposedly market driven, the implications for company strategic competitiveness from these changes should be validated with CI information, rather than just any more superficial guesswork by top managers. At the very least, the market reaction must be carefully considered by any team charged with projects involving significant innovations to products. As our sample indicates, on average companies are performing below average in this area widely considered most important to successful business innovation.

In the area of strategic leadership, there are also several implications that can be derived from this study. Charismatic leadership (showing determination while accomplishing goals, inspiring confidence, making people feel good around you, communicating expectations for high performance, generating respect, transmitting a sense of mission, and providing a vision of what lies ahead) is on average and as a whole relatively scarce in industry today, and judging by its nature it should be difficult to develop. Nevertheless, managers must try, particularly in high clockspeed industry sectors [Guimaraes *et al.* (2002)] requiring significant NPD projects for survival and success.

Further, insights into the nature of charismatic leadership can be obtained in the work of Gebert *et al.* [2016], and Avolio and Yammarino [2013]. Also apparently important for successful NPD but less scarce than charismatic leadership, transactional leadership (taking action if mistakes are made, pointing out what people will receive if they do what needs to be done, reinforcing the link between achieving goals and obtaining rewards, focusing attention on deviations from what is expected, and rewarding good work) by its nature should be easier to develop. Historically, Pawar and Eastman [1997] have proposed that transactional leadership is more relevant within an existing organization environment instead of one attempting to implement changes. Complementing that wisdom, Katz and Kahn [1978] have found that charismatic leadership may be more relevant where organizations are engaged in significant changes, but that both types of strategic leadership are potentially important. Indeed, our results indicate that for successful product innovation both types of leadership are important.

To improve technology management supporting NPD, managers must look at company performance in terms of its technology leadership position in its main industry sectors, knowledge of how to get the best technology available, effective use of specific technologies, and benchmarking the use of specific technologies against the company's main competitors or best-in-class target organizations. An important requirement to accomplish these objectives is the clear definition of the more important technologies necessary to support the company's main products. Managers also must recognize that the successful implementation of each of the various technologies important to the organization is dependent on their specific success factors some of which may be different from technology to technology. The success factors for the various technologies have been identified and discussed in detail elsewhere [Guimaraes *et al.* (1992, 2014); Udo and Guimaraes (1994); Yoon *et al.* (1995a, 1995b, 1998); Guimaraes and Igbaria (1997)] and are considered beyond the scope of this paper.

Further, to improve the likelihood of NPD success, top managers in general and NPD managers specifically, must ensure that their company's NPD process bear the desirable characteristics studied here: all significant changes must conform to company objectives, all affected departments participate in the change process, individual employee input is considered important, customers input is considered important, business partners input is considered important, managers ability to balance risk taking with cost/benefit, ensuring that clearly defined measures to monitor progress exist, that innovation objectives and progress are clearly communicated, and that the innovation management teams respond quickly and effectively to required change. These guidelines must be widely disseminated and enforced by NPD managers responsible for significant NPD projects.

The effect of company absorptive capacity on NPD success and its success factors is important for research and practice. The results indicate that the ability of the organization to learn from itself and from its environment, to process the newly acquired knowledge in combination with existing knowledge, and then transforming such combined knowledge into actual products might create a magnifying effect on the other success factors for NPD. In other words, the knowledge from effective competitive intelligence, effective management of technology, and effective innovation project management may be leveraged for companies with higher absorptive capacity. On the other hand, performance on the other success factors may be less productive in terms of NPD success in companies with lower absorptive capacity.

While in the past, researchers and practitioners have considered organization culture as likely to be an important determinant of company innovativeness and business performance because the empirical research results have been controversial at best, and many times confusing, the concept has been less than useful in practice. The relatively new measure for organization culture used here produced by experienced practitioners with a track record of company innovation success has shown better results. On the other hand, organization culture as measured here shows relatively high correlation with absorptive capacity perhaps because of the similar nature of the two constructs; thus, comments relevant to absorptive capacity are also applicable organization culture.

From a Human Resources Management perspective, some interesting insights from this study can be surmised by looking at the specific items comprising our measures of organization culture and company absorptive capacity. They both seem quite dependent on employee skills, abilities, and motivation to acquire, process, and manage knowledge as a group. Employees and managers should be encouraged to use external resources to obtain information (e.g. contact with customer, suppliers, personal networks, consultants, seminars, internet, databases, professional journals, academic publications, market research, laws, and regulations). Ditto for their ability to search for relevant information concerning their industry (including the company, competitors, etc.) which might affect every day and long-term company operations. In addition, worthy of consideration are: (1) Managers motivating employees to use and deal with information sources within and beyond their industry. (2) Establishing a company environment which enables employees to communicate ideas and concepts across departments to solve problems as a group where if a business unit obtains important information it communicates this information promptly to all other business units or departments, where there are periodical cross-departmental meetings to exchange information on new developments, problems, and achievements, where employees have the ability to structure and to use collected knowledge, are used to absorb new knowledge as well as to prepare it and make it available for further purposes, are able to successfully link existing knowledge with new insights, and are able to apply new knowledge in their practical work thus developing product prototypes, regularly reconsidering technologies and adapting them to work more effectively.

Given these requirements, one should expect that to develop a company's culture and absorptive capacity the HRM sub-functions (employee recruiting, retention/ weeding out, development/training, performance evaluation, and rewarding) must be taken significantly more seriously (considered more important strategically, planned and executed more proactively) than it is being done today in most organizations. These HRM sub-functions must be revamped and charged with some long-term objectives designed to give the company the people it needs to perform better along the company absorptive capacity items used in this study. Some policy-making directions should for example include a stronger HR department whose director reports directly to the CEO and is an integral member of the corporate executive team. Essential for effective recruiting would be the development of a desirable working environment where intelligent, knowledgeable people want to come to work, rather than viewing people as a commodity whose cost is to be continuously minimized. Also, helpful would be a work environment where workers are empowered to make decisions, are responsible for their results and with promotion from within preferences.

5.1. *Study limitations and research opportunities*

Based on an extensive survey of the relevant literature, this study empirically tests an extended model combining traditionally widely separated areas of knowledge such as organization culture, company absorptive capacity, strategic leadership, competitive intelligence, management of technology, and specific characteristics of the company's product innovation process as determinants of success in company product innovation. While testing this comprehensive integrative model is important, it is likely that new independent variables may be potentially important to further explain the variance in new product innovation success. Another important area for further research would be the identification and empirical testing of variables mediating or moderating the relationships between the independent variables studied here and success in product innovation.

References

Abbey, A. and Dickson, J. W. (1983). R&D work climate and innovation in semiconductors. *Academy of Management Journal*, **26**, 2: 362–368.

Alegre, J., Lapiedra, R. and Chiva, R. (2006). A measurement scale for product innovation performance. *European Journal of Innovation Management*, **9**, 4: 333–346.

Alexander, M. Planning is key to project management success, CIO, June 10, 2015.

Avolio, B. J. and Yammarino, F. J. (eds.) (2013). Introduction to, and overview of, transformational and charismatic leadership. *Transformational and Charismatic Leadership: The Road Ahead 10th Anniversary Edition*. Emerald Group Publishing Limited, pp. xxvii–xxxiii.

Baatz, E. B. (1994). The quest for corporate smarts. *CIO*, pp. 48–58.

Babbar, S. and Rai, A. (1993). Competitive intelligence for international business. *Long Range Planning*, **263**: 103–113.

Bass, B. M. (1985). *Leadership and Performance Beyond Expectations*, Free Press, New York.

Beattie, J. S. and Fleck, J. (2005). New perspectives on strategic technology management in small high-tech companies. In *Proceedings of 2005 IEEE International Engineering Management Conference*, pp. 313–318.

Berson, Y., Oreg, S. and Dvir, T. (2008). CEO values, organizational culture and firm outcomes. *Journal of Organizational Behavior*, **29**, 5: 615–633.

Bhuiyan, N. (2011). A framework for successful new product development. *Journal of Industrial Engineering and Management*, 4, 4: 746–770.

Block, P. (2014). Technology, culture, and stewardship. *Organization Development Journal*, **32**, 4: 9–13.

Booz, Allen and Hamilton, Inc. (1982). *New Product Management for the 1980's*. New York, NY: Author.

Brettel, M., Greve, G. and Flatten, T. (2011). Giving up linearity: Absorptive capacity and performance. *Journal of Managerial Issues*, **23**, 2: 164–188.

Burns, J. M. (1978). *Leadership*. Harper & Row, New York.

Büschgens, T., Bausch, A. and Balkin, D. B. (2013). Organizational culture and innovation: A meta-analytic review. *Journal of Product Innovation Management*, **30**, 4: 763–781.

Caccia-Bava, M., Guimaraes, V. K. and Guimaraes, T. (2005). Empirically testing determinants of hospital BPR success. *International Journal of Health Care Quality Assurance*, **18**, 7: 552–563.

Carmines, E. and Zeller, R. (1979). *Reliability and Validity Assessment*. Sage, Beverly Hills, CA.

Carrillo, J. (2005). Industry clockspeed and the pace of new product development. *Production and Operations Management*, **14**, 2: 125–142.

Carvalho, M. M. D. and Rabechini Junior, R. (2015). Impact of risk management on project performance: The importance of soft skills. *International Journal of Production Research*, **53**, 2: 321–340.

Chandler, G. N., Keller, C. and Lyon, D. W. (2000). Unraveling the determinants and consequences of an innovation-supportive organizational culture. *Entrepreneurship: Theory and Practice*, **25**, 1: 59.

Churchill, G. A. (1979). A paradigm for developing better measures of marketing constructs. *Journal of Marketing Research*, **17**: 64–73.

Cohen, W. and Levinthal, D. (1990). Absorptive capacity: A new perspective on learning and innovation. *Administrative Science Quarterly*, **35**, 1: 128–152.

Cooper, R. (2001). *Winning at New Products: Accelerating the Process from Idea to Launch*. 3rd edn. Perseus Publishing, Massachusetts.

Danneels, E. (2008). Organizational antecedents of second-order competences. *Strategic Management Journal*, **29**, 5: 519–543.

Darling, M. S. (1996). Building the knowledge organization. *Business Quarterly*, **61**, 2: 61–66.

Davis, S. (1984). *Managing Corporate Culture*. Ballinger, Cambridge, MA.

Davison, L. (2001). Measuring competitive intelligence effectiveness: Insights from the advertising industry. *Competitive Intelligence Review*, **12**, 4: 25–38.

Day, D. V. and Lord, R. G. (1988). Executive leadership and organizational performance: Suggestions for a new theory and methodology. *Journal of Management*, **14**: 453–464.

Detert, J. R., Schroeder, R. G. and Mauriel, J. J. (2000). A framework for linking culture and improvement initiatives in organizations. *Academy of Management Review*, **25**, 4: 850–863.

DeVellis, R. F. (1991). *Scale Development: Theory and Applications*. Sage, Newbury Park, CA.

du Toit, A. (2003). Competitive Intelligence in the knowledge economy: What is in it for South African manufacturing enterprises?. *International Journal of Information Management*, **23**: 111–120.

du Toit, A. S. (2015). Competitive intelligence research: An investigation of trends in the literature. *Journal of Intelligence Studies in Business*, **5**, 2: 14–21.

Editors. (2004). Competitive intelligence and records managers. *The Information Management Journal*, **38**, 2: 4.

Elbashir, M., Collier, P. and Sutton, S. (2011). The role of organizational absorptive capacity in strategic use of business intelligence to support integrated management control systems. *The Accounting Review*, **86**, 1: 155–184.

Enkel, E., Gassmann, O. and Chesbrough, H. (2009). Open R&D and open innovation: Exploring the phenomenon. *R&D Management*, **39**, 4: 311–316.

Ettorre, B. (1995). Managing competitive intelligence. *Management Review*, **84**, 10: 15–19.

Flatten, T., Adams, D. and Brettel, M. (2015). Fostering absorptive capacity through leadership: A cross-cultural analysis. *Journal of World Business*, **50**: 519–534.

Flatten, T., Engelen, A., Zahra, S. and Brettel, M. (2011). A measure of absorptive capacity: Scale development and validation. *European Management Journal*, **29**, 2: 98–116.

Flatten, T., Greve, G. and Brettel, M. (2011). Absorptive capacity and firm performance in SMEs: The mediating influence of strategic alliances. *European Management Review*, **8**, 3: 137–152.

Friedenberg, R. and Rice, A. (1994). Knowledge re-engineering as a BPR strategy, working notes [21–26], AAAI-94, *Workshop on Artificial Intelligence in Business Process Reengineering*, Seattle, WA.

Garcia-Morales, V. J., Jimenex-Barrionuevo, M. M. and Gutierrex-Gutierrez, L. (2012). Transformational leadership influence on organizational performance through organizational learning and innovation. *Journal of Business Research*, **65**: 1040–1050.

Gebert, D., Heinitz, K. and Buengeler, C. (2016). Leaders' charismatic leadership and followers' commitment — The moderating dynamics of value erosion at the societal level. *The Leadership Quarterly*, **27**, 1: 98–108.

George, W. and Barksdale, H. (1974). Marketing activities in the service industries. *Journal of Marketing*, **38**, 4: 65–70.

Ghoshal, S. and Westney, D. E. (1991). Organizing competitor analysis systems. *Strategic Management Journal*, **12**, 1: 17–31.

Guimaraes, T. and Armstrong, C. (1998a). Exploring the relation between competitive intelligence, IS support and business change. *Competitive Intelligence Review*, **9**, 3: 45–54.

Guimaraes, T., Armstrong, C., Neto, J., Riccio, E. and Madeira, G. (2014). Assessing the impact of ERP on end-user jobs. *International Journal of the Academic Business World*, **8**, 2: 37–49.

Guimaraes, T., Cook, D. and Natarajan, N. (2002). Exploring the importance of business clockspeed as a moderator for determinants of supplier network performance. *Decision Sciences*, **33**, 4: 629–644.

Guimaraes, N. and Igbaria, M. (1997). Client/server system success: Exploring the human side. *Decision Sciences*, **28**, 4: 851–876.

Guimaraes, N., Igbaria, M. and Lu, M. (1992). Determinants of DSS success: An integrated model. *Decision Sciences*, **23**, 2: 409–430.

Guimaraes, T. and Paranjape, K. (2013). Testing success factors for manufacturing BPR project phases. *Journal of Advanced Manufacturing Technology*, **68**, 9: 1937–1947.

Guimaraes, T., Paranjape, K. and Cornick, M. (2018a). Empirically testing factors increasing manufacturing product innovation success. *International Journal of Innovation and Technology Management*, **15**, 2: 1850019.

Guimaraes, T., Walton, M. and Armstrong, C. (2018b). A new measure of organizational culture for business innovativeness in practice. *International Journal of the Academic Business World*, **12**, 2: 49–58.

Gumusluoglu, T. and Ilsev, A. (2009). Transformational leadership, creativity and organizational innovation. *Journal of Business Research*, **62**: 461–473.

Hambrick, D. C. and Finkelstein, S. (1987). Managerial discretion: A bridge between polar views on organizations. *Research in Organizational Behavior*, eds. Cummings, L. L. and Staw, B. M., Vol. 9, pp. 369–406. JAI Press, Greenwich, CT.

Harkleroad, D. (1993). Sustainable growth rate analysis: Evaluating worldwide competitors ability to grow profitability. *Competitive Intelligence Review*, 4, 2/3: 36–45.

Hartnell, C. A., Ou, A. Y. and Kinicki, A. (2011). Organizational culture and organizational effectiveness: A meta-analytic investigation of the competing values framework's theoretical suppositions. *Journal of Applied Psychology*, **96**: 677–694.

Heil, O. and Robertson, T. S. (1991). Toward a theory of competitive market signaling: A research agenda. *Strategic Management Journal*, **12**, 6: 403–418.

Hostler, R. E., Yoon, V. Y. and Guimaraes, T. (2012). Recommendation agent impact on consumer online shopping: The Movie Magic case study. *Expert Systems with Applications*, **39**, 3: 2989–2999.

Hostler, R. E., Yoon, V. Y., Guo, Z., Guimaraes, T. and Forgionne, G. (2011). Assessing the impact of recommender agents on on-line consumer unplanned purchase behavior. *Information & Management* 48, 8: 336–343.

Hurley, R. F. and Hult, G. T. M. (1998). Innovation, market orientation, and organizational learning: An integration and empirical examination. *The Journal of Marketing*, **62**: 42–54.

Igbaria, M., Greenhaus, J. H. and Parasuraman, S. (1991). Career orientations of MIS employees: An empirical analysis. *MIS Quarterly*, **15**, 2: 151–169.

Jansen, J., van Den Bosch, F. and Volberda, H. (2005). Managing potential and realized absorptive capacity: How do organizational antecedents matter?. *Academy of Management Journal*, **48**, 6: 999–1015.

Jaskyte, K. (2004). Transformational leadership, organizational culture, and innovativeness in nonprofit organizations. *Nonprofit Management and Leadership*, **15**, 2: 153–168.

Johannessen, J., Olsen, B. and Lumpkin, G. T. (2001). Innovation as newness; what is new, how new, and new to whom?. *European Journal of Innovation Management*, **4**, 1: 20.

Kanter, R. M. (1983). *The Change Masters*. Simon & Schuster, New York.

Katz, D. and Kahn, R. L. (1978). *The Social Psychology of Organizations*. 2nd edn. Wiley, New York, NY.

Khalil, T. M. and Ezzat, H. A. (2005). Management of technology and responsive policies in a new economy. *International Journal of Technology Management*, **32**, 1, 2: 88.

King, M. (1997). Corporations take snooping mainstream. *Indianapolis Business Journal*, **17**, 2: 1–4.

Kohlbacher, M., Weitlaner, D., Hollosi, A., Grunwald, S. and Grahsl, H. (2013). Innovation in clusters: Effects of absorptive capacity and environmental moderators. *Competitiveness Review: An International Business Journal*, **23**, 3: 199–217.

Lane, P., Salk, J. and Lyles, M. (2001). Absorptive capacity, learning, and performance in international joint ventures. *Strategic Management Journal*, **22**, 12: 1139–1161.

Lee, J., Lee, H. and Park, J. (2014). Exploring the impact of empowering leadership on knowledge sharing, absorptive capacity and team performance in IT service. *Information Technology & People*, **27**, 3: 366–386.

Lewin, A., Massini, S. and Peeters, C. (2011). Microfoundations of internal and external absorptive capacity routines. *Organization Science*, **22**, 1: 81–98.

Li-Hua, R. and Khalil, T. M. (2006). Technology management in China: A global perspective and challenging issues. *Journal of Technology Management in China*, **1**, 1: 9–26.

Lopes, M. C. (2014). Why new product development is so important to manufacturers. Aberdeen Group Report.

Magal, S. R., Carr, H. H. and Watson, H. J. (1988). Critical success factors for information center managers. *MIS Quarterly*, **12**, 3: 413–425.

Maltz, E. and Kohli, A. K. (1996). Market intelligence dissemination across functional boundaries. *Journal of Marketing Research*, **33**, 1: 47–61.

McCune, J. C. (1996). Checking out the competition. *Beyond Computing*, **5**, 2: 24–29.

Meijboom, B., Voordijk, H. and Akkermans, H. (2007). The effect of industry clockspeed on supply chain co-ordination: Classical theory to sharpen an emerging concept. *Business Process Management Journal*, **13**, 4: 553.

Moilanen, M., Ostbye, S. and Woll, K. (2014). Non-R&D SMEs: External knowledge, absorptive capacity and product innovation. *Small Business Economics*, **43**: 447–462.

Nadkarni, S. and Narayanan, V. K. (2007). Strategic schemas, strategic flexibility, and firm performance: The moderating role of industry clockspeed. *Strategic Management Journal*, **28**, 3: 243–270.

Noblet, J., Simon, E. and Parent, R. (2011). Absorptive capacity: A proposed operationalization. *Knowledge Management Research & Practice*, **9**, 4: 367–377.

Nunnally, J. C. (1978). *Psychometric Theory*. McGraw-Hill, New York, NY.

Ogbonna, E. and Wilkinson, B. (2003). The false promise of organizational culture change: A case study of middle managers in grocery retailing. *Journal of Management Studies*, **40**, 5: 1151–1178.

Pawar, B. S. and Eastman, K. K. (1997). The nature and implications of contextual influences on transformational leadership: A conceptual examination. *Academy of Management Review*, **22**: 80–109.

Peters, T. J., Waterman, R. H. and Jones, I. (1982). In search of excellence: Lessons from America's best-run companies. Yönetim, Yil: 7, Sayi: 24, Haziran 1996, s. 53–56.

Peterson, R. A. (1994). A meta-analysis of Cronbach's coefficient alpha. *Journal of Consumer Research*, **21**: 381–391.

Podoski, K. B. and Žilionis, V. (2008). Scientific and technological advance: Globalization and impact of national policies. *Global Academic Society Journal: Social Science Insight*, **1**, 3: 15–24.

Podsakoff, P. M., MacKenzie, S. B., Moorman, R. H. and Fetter, R. (1990). Transformational leader behaviors and their effects on followers' trust in leader, satisfaction, and organizational citizenship behaviors. *Leadership Quarterly*, **1**: 107–142.

Popaitoon, S. and Siengthai, S. (2014). The moderating effect of human resource management practices on the relationship between knowledge absorptive capacity and project performance in project-oriented companies. *International Journal of Project Management*, **32**: 908–920.

Rabechini Junior, R. and Monteiro de Carvalho, M. (2013). Understanding the impact of project risk management on project performance: An empirical study. *Journal of Technology Management & Innovation*, **8**: 6.

Rajablu, M., Marthandan, G. and Yusoff, W. F. W. (2015). Managing for stakeholders: The role of stakeholder-based management in project success. *Asian Social Science*, **11**, 3: 111.

Sackmann, S. A. (2011). Culture and performance. In *The Handbook of Organizational Culture and Climate*, 2nd ed., eds. Ashkanasy, N. M., Wilderom, C. P. M. and Peterson, M. F., Sage, Thousand Oaks, CA, pp. 188–224.

Sawka, K. A. (1996). Demystifying business intelligence. *Management Review*, **85**, 10: 47–51.

Schneider, B., Ehrhart, M. G. and Macey, W. H. (2013). Organizational climate and culture. *Annual Review of Psychology*, **64**: 361–388.

Srinivasan, A. (1985). Alternative measures of system effectiveness: Associations and implications. *MIS Quarterly*, **9**, 3: 243–253.

Sun, P. Y. T. and Anderson, M. H. (2011). The combined influence of top and middle management leadership styles on absorptive capacity. *Management Learning*, **43**, 1: 25–51.

Swartz, N. (2005). Competitive intelligence underutilized. *Information Management Journal*, **39**, 3: 10.

Tarraf, P. and Molz, R. (2006). Competitive intelligence at small enterprises. *S.A.M. Advanced Management Journal*, **71**, 4: 24–34.

Teece, D., Pisano, G. and Shuen, A. (1997). Dynamic capabilities and strategic management. *Strategic Management Journal*, **18**, 7: 509–533.

Teo, T. S. H. and King, W. R. (1996). Assessing the impact of integrating business planning and IS planning. *Information and Management*, **30**: 309–321.

Todorova, G. and Durisin, B. (2007). Absorptive capacity: Valuing a reconceptualization. *Academy of Management Review*, **32**, 3: 774–786.

Trice, H. M. and Beyer, J. M. (1993). *The Cultures of Work Organizations*. Prentice-Hall, Englewood Cliffs, JN.

Tsai, W. (2001). Knowledge transfer in intraorganizational networks: Effects of network position and absorptive capacity on business unit innovation and performance. *Academy of Management Journal*, **44**, 5: 996–1004.

Udo, G. and Guimaraes, T. (1994). Empirically assessing factors related to DSS benefits. *European Journal of Information Systems*, **3**, 3: 218–227.

Ulrich, K. T. and Eppinger, S. D. (2011). *Product Design and Development*. McGraw-Hill, New York, NY.

Van de Ven, A. and Ferry, D. (1980). *Measuring and Assessing Organizations*. Wiley, New York, NY.

Vedder, R. G. and Guynes, C. S. (2002). CIOs' perspectives on competitive intelligence. *Information Systems Management*, **19**, 4: 49–56.

Waldman, D. A., Ramirez, G. G., House, R. J. and Puranam, P. (2001). Does leadership matter? CEO leadership attributes and profitability under conditions of perceived environmental uncertainty. *Academy of Management Journal*, **44**, 1: 134–143.

Wang, W., Liu, L., Feng, Y. and Wang, T. (2014). Innovation with IS usage: Individual absorptive capacity as a mediator. *Industrial Management & Data Systems*, **114**, 8: 1110–1130.

Wei, Y. S. and Morgan, N. A. (2004). Supportiveness of organizational climate, market orientation, and new product performance in Chinese firms. *Journal of Product Innovation Management*, **21**, 6: 375–388.

Weijermars, R. (2009). Accelerating the three dimensions of E&P clockspeed — a novel strategy for optimizing utility in the oil & gas industry. *Applied Energy*, **86**, 10: 2222–2243.

Westervelt, R. (1996). Gaining an edge: Competitive intelligence takes off. *Chemical Week*, **158**, 25: 29–31.

Wisegeek.com (2015). What is the importance of new product development. August 2.

Witell, L., Gustafsson, A. and Johnson, M. D. (2014). The effect of customer information during new product development on profits from goods and services [Electronic version]. Retrieved [1/17/2017], from Cornell University, School of Hospitality Administration site: http://scholarship.sha.cornell.edu/articles/707

Yoon, V. Y., Hostler, R. E., Guo, Z. and Guimaraes, T. (2013). Assessing the moderating effect of consumer product knowledge and online shopping experience on using recommendation agents for customer loyalty. *Decision Support Systems*, **55**, 4: 883–893.

Yoon, Y., Guimaraes, T. and Clevenson, A. (1995a). Understanding the factors important to expert systems success. *Technology Management*, **2**, 3: 1–14.

Yoon, Y., Guimaraes, T. and O'Neal, Q. (1995b). Exploring the factors associated with expert systems success. *MIS Quarterly*, **19**, 1: 83–106.

Yoon, Y., Guimaraes, T. and Clevenson, A. (1998). Exploring ES success factors for BPR. *Journal of Engineering and Technology Management*, **15**: 179–199.

Yukl, G. A. (1998). *Leadership in Organizations*, 4th edn. Prentice-Hall, Englewood Cliffs, NJ.

Zahra, S. and George, G. (2002). Absorptive capacity: A review, reconceptualization, and extension. *Academy of Management Review*, **27**, 2: 185–203.

Zenger, J. and Folkman, J. (2016). The trickle-down effect of Good (and Bad) leadership, *Harvard Business Review*. Retrieved from https://hbr.org/2016/01/the-trickle-down-effect-ofgood-and-bad-leadership

Zhao, Z. and Anand, J. (2009). A multilevel perspective on knowledge transfer: Evidence from the Chinese automotive industry. *Strategic Management Journal*, **30**, 9: 959–983.

Appendix A

Measuring Product Innovation Performance: Compared with its main competitors, please rate your company along the items below using the scale (1) much worse, (2) significantly worse, (3) slightly worse, (4) about even, (5) slightly better, (6) significantly better, and (7) much better.

1. Replacement of products being phased out.	1	2	3	4	5	6	7
2. Extension of product range within main product field through technologically new products.	1	2	3	4	5	6	7
3. Extension of product range within main product field through technologically improved products.	1	2	3	4	5	6	7
4. Extension of product range outside main product field.	1	2	3	4	5	6	7
5. Development of environment-friendly products.	1	2	3	4	5	6	7
6. Market share evolution.	1	2	3	4	5	6	7
7. Opening of new markets abroad.	1	2	3	4	5	6	7
8. Opening of new domestic target groups.	1	2	3	4	5	6	7
9. Average innovation project development time (a project refers to the creation of a new product or component).	1	2	3	4	5	6	7
10. Average number of innovation projects working hours.	1	2	3	4	5	6	7
11. Average cost per innovation project.	1	2	3	4	5	6	7
12. Degree of global satisfaction with innovation projects efficiency.	1	2	3	4	5	6	7

Measuring Organization Culture Traits for Business Innovativeness. Please rate the extent to which your company shows the specific culture trait listed below, using the scale: 0 = I don't know, 1 = not at all, 2 = a minor extent, 3 = some extent, 4 = a significant extent, 5 = major extent, and 6 = a great extent.

1. People in this organization have a sense of direction, a vision for its future, with clearly defined goals, objectives, and responsibilities.	1	2	3	4	5	6	7
2. People are tuned in to what is going on in the market place regarding customers, competitors and their products/services, suppliers, etc.	1	2	3	4	5	6	7
3. New ideas are encouraged and seriously evaluated.	1	2	3	4	5	6	7
4. People in this organization have a sense of direction, a vision for its future, with clearly defined goals, objectives, and responsibilities.	1	2	3	4	5	6	7
5. People are tuned in to what is going on in the market place regarding customers, competitors and their products/services, suppliers, etc.	1	2	3	4	5	6	7
6. Goals and tasks assignments are discussed and agreed to by the people involved.	1	2	3	4	5	6	7
7. The goals set are challenging but attainable.	1	2	3	4	5	6	7
8. People are accountable for what they agreed to do.	1	2	3	4	5	6	7
9. People are willing to personally sacrifice a little to accomplish their tasks and goals.	1	2	3	4	5	6	7
10. People are rewarded for good performance toward their goals.	1	2	3	4	5	6	7
11. We use metrics on our creative and development processes to track how much time and money is spent on creating and implementing innovation.	1	2	3	4	5	6	7
12. In this organization, employees trust each other, communicate and cooperate freely.	1	2	3	4	5	6	7
13. There is a good balance between specialization and ability to step in to do someone else's work.	1	2	3	4	5	6	7
14. In this organization, employees trust their superiors.	1	2	3	4	5	6	7

Measuring Effectiveness in Competitive Intelligence: Compared with its main competitors, and using the scale (1) much worse, (2) significantly worse, (3) slightly worse, (4) about even, (5) slightly better, (6) significantly better, and (7) much better, please rate your company effectiveness identifying strategic business opportunities and problems while dealing with:

1. Traditional industry competitors,	1	2	3	4	5	6	7
2. Emerging competitors,	1	2	3	4	5	6	7
3. Traditional customer needs and wants,	1	2	3	4	5	6	7
4. Non-traditional customer needs and wants,	1	2	3	4	5	6	7
5. Relationships with business partners, and	1	2	3	4	5	6	7
6. Product or service development.	1	2	3	4	5	6	7

Measuring Effectiveness in *Strategic Leadership.* Using the same scale above please rate the extent to which your company's top managers in general exhibit the particular behavior listed below when compared to managers of main competing organizations.

Transactional leadership:

1. Takes actions if mistakes are made.	1	2	3	4	5	6	7
2. Points out what people will receive if they do what needs to be done.	1	2	3	4	5	6	7
3. Reinforces the link between achieving goals and obtaining rewards.	1	2	3	4	5	6	7
4. Focuses attention on irregularities, exceptions, or deviations from what is expected.	1	2	3	4	5	6	7
5. Rewards good work.	1	2	3	4	5	6	7

Charismatic leadership:

1. Shows determination when accomplishing goals.	1	2	3	4	5	6	7
2. I have complete confidence in them.	1	2	3	4	5	6	7
3. Makes people feel good to be around them.	1	2	3	4	5	6	7
4. Communicates high-performance expectations.	1	2	3	4	5	6	7
5. Generates respect.	1	2	3	4	5	6	7
6. Transmits a sense of mission.	1	2	3	4	5	6	7
7. Provides a vision of what lies ahead.	1	2	3	4	5	6	7

Measuring The Desirable Characteristics of the NPD Process. Using the same scale above, please rate the extent to which your company project generally shows the following characteristics:

1. All significant innovations must conform to company objectives,	1	2	3	4	5	6	7
2. All affected departments participate in the innovation process,	1	2	3	4	5	6	7
3. Individual employee input is considered important,	1	2	3	4	5	6	7
4. Customers input is considered important,	1	2	3	4	5	6	7
5. Business partners input is considered important,	1	2	3	4	5	6	7
6. We have the ability to balance risk taking with cost/benefit,	1	2	3	4	5	6	7
7. We have clearly defined measures to monitor progress,	1	2	3	4	5	6	7
8. Innovation objectives and progress are clearly communicated,	1	2	3	4	5	6	7
9. We respond quickly to required change.	1	2	3	4	5	6	7
10. We respond effectively to required change.	1	2	3	4	5	6	7

Measuring MOT Effectiveness in Supporting Business Innovation. Using the same scale as above, please rate the extent to which compared to its main competitors your company is considered to have:

1. Technology leadership in the industry.	1	2	3	4	5	6	7
2. Knowledge of how to get the best technology.	1	2	3	4	5	6	7
3. Effectiveness with which technology has been used over the years,	1	2	3	4	5	6	7
4. Effectiveness in using technology in comparison with main competitors.	1	2	3	4	5	6	7

Measuring Organization Absorptive Capacity. Using the scale (1 = strongly disagree to 7 = strongly agree) please rate the 14 items measuring this major variable, the specific groups of questions are:

1. Please specify to what extent your company uses external resources to obtain information (e.g. personal networks, consultants, seminars, internet, databases professional journals, academic publications, market research, laws and regulations).   1 2 3 4 5 6 7
2. The search for relevant information concerning our industry is every-day business in our company.   1 2 3 4 5 6 7
3. Our management motivates the employees to use information sources within our industry.   1 2 3 4 5 6 7
4. Our management expects that the employees deal with information beyond our industry.   1 2 3 4 5 6 7

Please rate to what extent the following statements fit the communication structure in your company.
5. In our company, ideas and concepts are communicated cross-departmental.   1 2 3 4 5 6 7
6. Our management emphasizes cross-departmental support to solve problems.   1 2 3 4 5 6 7
7. In our company, there is a quick information flow, e.g. if a business unit obtains important information it communicates this information promptly to all other business units or departments.   1 2 3 4 5 6 7
8. Our management demands periodical cross-departmental meetings to exchange information on new developments, problems, and achievements.   1 2 3 4 5 6 7

Please specify to what extent the following statements fit the knowledge processing in your company.
9. Our employees have the ability to structure and to use collected knowledge.   1 2 3 4 5 6 7
10. Our employees are used to absorb new knowledge as well as to prepare it for further purposes and to make it available.   1 2 3 4 5 6 7
11. Our employees successfully link existing knowledge with new insights. Our employees are able to apply new knowledge in their practical work.   1 2 3 4 5 6 7

Please specify to what extent the following statements fit the commercial exploitation of new knowledge in your company (Please think about all company divisions such as R&D, production, marketing and accounting).
12. Our management supports the development of prototypes.   1 2 3 4 5 6 7
13. Our company regularly reconsiders technologies and adapts them according to new knowledge.   1 2 3 4 5 6 7
14. Our company has the ability to work more effective by adopting new technologies.   1 2 3 4 5 6 7

Biography

Tor Guimaraes has been rated by several independent sources as one of the top researchers in the world based on publications in the top IS journals. He holds the Jesse E. Owen Chair of Excellence at Tennessee Technological University. He has been the keynote speaker at numerous national and international meetings sponsored by organizations such as the Information Processing Society of Japan, Institute of Industrial Engineers, Sales and Marketing Executives, IEEE, Association for

Systems Management, and the American Society for Quality Control. Tor has consulted with many leading organizations including TRW, American Greetings, AT&T, IBM and the Department of Defense.

Ketan Paranjape is the VP of Diagnostics Information Solutions at Roche and his team is focused on harnessing the power of data, diagnostics, and other critical information to support better clinical decisions. Prior to this role, he was a Managing Director at Health2047 and General Manager of Health and Life Sciences at Intel Corp. He has been a member of the US Health IT committee on Precision Medicine, and part of numerous task forces at AAAS-FBI-UNICRI, ITU, and WHO. He has an MBA and MS and is a certified Paramedic.

Michael Walton is the head of enterprise manufacturing at Google where he collaborates with Fortune 500 manufacturers to introduce game-changing strategies and technologies into their manufacturing operations. Walton joined Google in 2014 after working with industry-leading companies such as Atos, PACCAR, Chrysler, Lexmark, Cameron, Varian Medical and many others where he established a strong reputation for building innovative manufacturing platforms tailored to the opportunities and challenges of a highly competitive and constantly changing global manufacturing marketplace. Walton earned a B.A. in computer science and A.A. in mathematics from Thomas More College. He is a member of the board of MESA International and a Lieutenant Colonel in the Army Reserves with over 25 years of service as a Combat Engineer Officer.

Chapter 12

Internet of Management Artifacts: Internet of Things Architecture for Business Model Renewal

Clarissa Rocha*, Clariana Fernandes Narcizo† and Enrico Gianotti‡

*Pontificia Universidade Catolica do Parana Curitiba,
Paraná Brazil*
*clarissa.rocha@pucpr.edu.br
†clarianaf@hotmail.com
‡en.gianotti@gmail.com

In the information and knowledge era, organizations must find ways to survive and remain up-to-date and competitive to face a dynamic environment. The still dominant paradigm regarding the Internet of Things (IoT) focuses more on tangible things and physical devices and less on management and business environment. There is a lack of studies that clarify how the IoT can help business management to create perceived value for the company. The aim of this study is to propose a framework called the Internet of Management Artifact (IoMA) to understand how the IoT ecosystem can support managerial decision-making. Considering that this field of research lacks the empirical evidence that more transparently narrows the relationship between IoT and organizational management, we opted for a framework based on Design Search Research. The main contribution of this study is the proposition of the IoMA framework, which seeks a paradigm shift, changing from a paradigm centered on "things" and physical devices in the information technology architecture that remains dominant in the literature to a paradigm focused on business management. The study highlights how decision-makers can exploit IoT architecture, which provides them with rich, accurate and relevant information to promote business reconfiguration and thus capitalize on these renewals.

Keywords: IoT ecosystem; technological innovation, strategic management; design science research; IoT architecture.

1. Introduction

Companies are exposed to dynamic business environments, driven by fast developments in digital technologies. One of these technologies is called the Internet of Things or IoT for short, a term coined by Kevin Ashton of MIT in 1999 [Ashton

This chapter was originally published in *International Journal of Innovation and Technology Management*, Vol. 16, No. 8, December 2019, published by World Scientific Publishing, Singapore. Reprinted with permission.

(2009)]. The IoT affects most business sectors [SAP (2015, 2016); Gartner (2015); Deloitte (2015); Ammar *et al.* (2018)]. Since the term IoT was first used, it has been applied to connected devices in consumer, domestic, business and industrial settings [Boyes *et al.* (2018)]. The IoT represents the fusion of two domains: the digital domain, represented by the Internet, and the real domain of "things". This technological revolution represents the future of connectivity and accessibility [Wu *et al.* (2010)].

In the IoT, objects become communication nodes on the Internet, through data communication. This leads companies, inserted in an increasingly connected and dynamic context, to analyze how IoT technology will affect their processes, products and even business models. The IoT is expected to open up numerous economic opportunities and can be considered one of the most promising technologies with a huge disruptive potential [Hofmann and Rüsch (2017)]. Companies need to understand how to adapt in order to remain competitive. The products, services and business models of companies need to evolve, so that they can remain competitive in a world of increasing uncertainty, mainly due to digital disruption. If they think that digital disruption will not happen to their business, companies will be putting themselves at risk. If companies ignore this risk, they may jeopardize their competitiveness [Westerman *et al.* (2016)]. Digital transformation is not just a technological issue, but a strategic one [Rogers (2017)].

The IoT architecture creates a low entry barrier. The affordability of smart sensors, which are the first layer of the IoT architecture, opens up huge business opportunities in an emerging ecosystem of new partnerships. Even small startups can instigate changes not only in large corporations, but also in whole industries [Nordic (2016)]. Several companies have failed to respond to the changing needs and expectations of their stakeholders. By ignoring the importance of technological 'innovations, it is likely that many companies will soon be struggling to survive in the marketplace [Nordic (2016)].

Gartner [2015] predicted that the IoT will include nearly 26 billion devices with a global economic value of 1.9 trillion dollars by 2020. The International Data Corporation (IDC) estimates that devices connected to the Internet will generate almost 9 trillion dollars in annual sales by 2020 [Gartner (2015)]. The Internet has always connected devices, which have tended to be human-mediated computers. People share content, create insights in a collaborative way, create resources via crowdsourcing, and make decisions based on treated and relevant data that made the Internet a dynamic place [Gartner (2015)].

Future developments in the IoT architecture and closer relations with business outcomes can optimize the information flow in industrial and social scenarios and revolutionize business communication. Like other milestones in technology, the IoT enables users to measure what could not be measured before [Uckelmann *et al.* (2011)]. For enterprises, this means additional, relevant, right-time and more accurate information for better decision-making in business management.

Most IoT deployments focus primarily on operational costs and provided risk management but do not address other aspects of the business. An analysis of 80 IoT implementations by the 20 largest companies between 2009 and 2013 revealed that 65% of the cases were focused on cost and efficiency reduction, while 22% focused on risk management, and only 13% on revenue, innovation or transformation into the business model [Deloitte (2015)]. While cost savings and efficiency efforts may be valuable to the company, returns decrease as other competitors implement similar efficiency improvements. The IoT provides an opportunity to consider the value of the business more broadly and look disruptively rather than incrementally at business. The IoT is not directly tied to optimizations only, but also to strategic business transformations [Nordic (2016)].

The strategic research agenda of the Cluster of European Projects on the IoT suggests that the IoT is expected to change business, information, and social processes, and provide many unforeseen possibilities [CERP-IoT (2009)]. According to Kyriazis and Varvarigou [2013], the dynamic and technology-rich digital environment of the IoT enables the provision of added-value applications. These applications exploit a multitude of devices that contribute to the capture of large volumes and diversity of data (Big Data), which once treated can generate relevant information [Kyriazis and Varvarigou (2013)]. These data can deliver business value that goes beyond mere efficiency and optimization in business processes [Westerlund *et al.* (2014)].

Using IoT solutions, companies can explore how the ability to collect and analyze data on the business environment in real time can change or even remodel the business. These solutions can be implemented by companies internally and externally, providing opportunities for sustained value creation and even disruption for those who can imagine possibilities beyond incremental change [Deloitte (2015)]. On the other hand, many companies still find it difficult to capture and exploit the complexity of the IoT ecosystem and they may fall into its traps. In addition, IoT ecosystem features, such as co-creation, are not always contemplated when developing new business models [Wang *et al.* (2017)]. Burkhart *et al.* [2012] identified the absence of formalized means of representations to allow a structured view of the business model as a relevant research gap. These researchers applied methods for business modeling and found that the important characteristics of IoT ecosystems could not be addressed by these traditional business modeling methods.

The benefits of using IoT in business have already been illustrated in literature [Brous and Janssen (2015)]. However, research lacks in-depth studies on how IoT can generate benefits for the business from a strategic standpoint. This paper examines how the IoT can benefit decision makers, helping to provide them with rich, accurate and relevant information to promote business reconfiguration and thus capitalize on these renewals. This study proposes a framework focused on business management called the Internet of Management Artifact (IoMA). The IoMA is intended to structure, in a robust and easy-to-understand way for researchers and business practitioners, how the IoT ecosystem can assist managerial decision-making.

The proper use of the information obtained by the IoT infrastructure, focusing on meeting the current and future business needs, could be seen as a source of competitive advantage. Companies need to revisit their business, making adequate use of intelligent and interconnected sensors, which are part of the IoT architecture [Deloitte (2015)]. These sensors have the ability to collect internal data from the company and from the most diverse partners and market contexts. The integration and sharing of information between a company and its stakeholders can instigate the creation of new business models [Gartner (2016)]. Therefore, the IoMA framework is relevant to organizational practice, since it illustrates the flow from sensors to business models.

This paper is divided into five sections. In Sec. 2, we present a brief theoretical background, focusing on the definition, main aspects and implications of the IoT for organizational practice, as well as some IoT architectures and the first efforts of previous research to relate these architectures to the business strategy. In Sec. 3, we present the Design Science Research method, which will support the construction of the artifact. In Sec. 4, details of the IoMA framework are provided. The final considerations are presented in Sec. 5, outlining the limitations of the study, its contributions to theory and organizational practice, and suggestions for future research.

2. Literature Review

The IoT represents a number of uses and technologies that can lead to both unprecedented opportunities and risks for business [Brous and Janssen (2015)]. The key to managing threats and making full use of opportunities is to establish an IoT architecture strategy [Gartner (2016)]. Many companies are already aware of the potential tangible and intangible gains that the IoT has to offer, but they are not sure how to approach IoT or capitalize on its solutions.

Many companies no longer just sell products to customers, but also provide digital platforms on which users can add value [Chan (2015)]. In this section, a literature review is presented, showing the relevance of the IoT in the organizational context, and how it can benefit companies so that they can compete in complex, digital, collaborative markets with low barriers to new starters. Some of these studies constituted the first efforts to emphasize the relationship between IoT architecture and the renewal of business models.

2.1. *The Internet of Things*

The term IoT is not well defined and has been misused as a buzzword in scientific research, especially with regard to marketing and sales strategies. It is still difficult to clearly define this term [Uckelmann *et al.* (2011)]. One definition argued in this paper is formulated in the Strategic Research Agenda of the Cluster of European Research Projects on the IoT (CERP-IoT) (2009)

"Internet of Things (IoT) is an integrated part of Future Internet and could be defined as a dynamic global network infrastructure with self-configuring capabilities based on standard and interoperable communication protocols where physical and virtual 'things' have identities, physical attributes, and virtual personalities and use intelligent interfaces, and are seamlessly integrated into the information network. In the IoT, 'things' are expected to become active participants in business, information and social processes where they are enabled to interact and communicate among themselves and with the environment by exchanging data and information 'sensed' about the environment, while reacting to the 'physical world' events and influencing it by running processes that trigger actions and create services with or without direct human intervention [...]".

For Uckelmann *et al.* [2011, p. 8] "the IoT links uniquely identifiable "things" to their virtual representations in the Internet linking to additional information on their identity, status, location or any other business, social or privately relevant information at a financial or non-financial pay-off that exceeds the efforts of information provisioning and offers information access to non-predefined participants. The provided accurate and appropriate information may be accessed in the right quantity and condition, at the right time and place at the right price". The IoT also includes smart objects. These objects are not only physical but also digital entities. These entities can perform some relevant tasks and inform end users about what actually happens in a given environment. This is the reason why the IoT is not only a hardware and software paradigm, but also includes interactions, collaborations and other social aspects [Kortuem *et al.* (2010)].

Any object embedded with a communication device can become part of the IoT architecture [Aazam *et al.* (2014)]. With the IoT, everyday physical objects can be incorporated with digital technology, such as software, RFID and other sensors to achieve new functionalities [Guinard *et al.* (2011)]. "The IoT can enable the harvesting of real time information of the objects, the interactions, and the environment, as well as potentially allowing the actuation of such objects" [Ng and Wakenshaw (2017, p. 3)].

In the IoT concept, the virtual world of information technology integrates perfectly with the real and physical world. The real world becomes more accessible through computers and networked devices in business and in everyday scenarios. The IoT is more than a business tool for managing businesses more efficiently and effectively. It is a strategic tool that will allow a more convenient way of life [Uckelmann *et al.* (2011)].

Due to recent advances in miniaturization and lower device costs such as RFID, sensor networks, wireless communication, technologies and applications, the IoT has become relevant to many industries and end-users [Uckelmann *et al.* (2011)]. Detecting the real state of "things" through smart, connected sensors, together with detailed data collection and processing, allows an immediate response to changes in the real world of business. This interactive and responsive network between hardware, software, people and places can generate a potential not only for citizens and consumers, but also for businesses. According to Deloitte [2015, p. 5], "higher speed networks, cloud storage and computing power, the proliferation of inexpensive sensors and devices, advanced analytic capabilities and context awareness to make sense of the data are enabling fast advances (e.g. better and predictive decision-making) that make a range of scenarios put forth for the future of IoT plausible".

Companies tend to adopt a technological solution if the expected tangible benefits to the company's performance outweigh the costs and risks. The IoT can inspire a wealth of new business models, which often involve the contribution of various partners, contributing to emerging ecosystems of interactions between or inter-industries [Deloitte (2015); Gartner (2015, 2016); SAP (2015, 2016)]. Over the past few years, the widespread use of the Internet and rapid development of Internet-based technologies have also resulted in shorter life cycles of product and services, thus requiring faster changing business models [Glova *et al.* (2014)].

A business model is an abstraction of a company's complexity, reducing it to its core elements and interrelations, which facilitates the analysis and description of business activities [Glova *et al.* (2014)]. A business model describes how a company creates, delivers, and captures value and, consequently, makes money [Zott and Amit (2010)]. The description of the business model is an important starting point for business innovation and transformation, so that it can serve as a path for aligning technological development and economic value creation [Chesbrough and Rosen-bloom (2002)]. The business model can be seen as the important element that unites technical developments of the IoT with an economic business perspective.

Solutions based on IoT architecture have changed the way products and services are sold and distributed [Glova *et al.* (2014)]. The use of this architecture has affected traditional business models and led to new types of models. Alt and Zbornik [2002] define a typical business transaction through a physical product, information flow and money. Product flow includes order processing, product production, and product distribution. Information flow includes processes such as order processing, supply chain, and product lifecycle data sharing.

The IoT acts as an approach to align and "feed" these different flows [Glova *et al.* (2014)]. It provides a greater level of significant visibility of the actual business status with monitoring and control mechanisms, through the collection and analysis of a diversity of data sources. In the framework proposed in this study, information becomes a strategic source for the creation and proposition of organizational value.

A challenge for IoT solutions to realize business potential is to integrate various business operations into collaborative environments [Wang *et al.* (2017); Chesbrough (2003)]. It is necessary to focus on the analysis of how the business interacts or wants to interact with its stakeholders to create relationships with and between them, or to analyze the usual and/or desired interfaces between company and users. In the current digital era, organizational success will be measured and evaluated by the ability to provide access to the feedbacks and experiences of users and inform them of the benefits of those feedbacks. Because of this new context, companies, when engaging in collaborations with the most diverse parties related to their business, will have to rethink and change their business models. In order to maintain the high volume, variety, speed, veracity and value of the data obtained in these collaborations, this must be done in a way that guarantees data privacy and security.

IoT solution providers have yet to articulate compelling proposals for how IoT solutions can deliver lasting business value to enterprises. Instead, many vendors focus on selling technology to the CIO and CEO, without a comprehensive view of how it will be converted into returns for the business [Deloitte (2015)]. There are still significant obstacles to be overcome. Executives, concerned about security, privacy, and interoperability, are not sure of the economic rewards for the risks of implementing IoT solutions [Gartner (2016)]. Consumer use cases raise additional privacy and security concerns.

Businesses need to respect customers' privacy by giving them the choice to remain anonymous. Companies must be honest and transparent about what is being tracked and how the data are used [Nordic (2016)]. Customers should give permission for companies to use their data, and as long as the company does not link the data to specific people, the company can take advantage of them in a better way. Companies need to be transparent with customers regarding the use of data that will be used to create better products and services for them [Nordic (2016)].

The IoT is connecting real-world business components such as strategic management, collaboration of different stakeholders, products, services and business processes, to the Internet with a diversity of sensors that are becoming smaller, smarter and cheaper. A series of functional layers is becoming visible in a developing ecosystem (Fig. 1), beginning with data generation and moving to the creation of information, followed by the creation of meaning and, finally, to action-taking. The broader categories are: (i) the hardware sensor platform layer, (ii) the software processing layer, (iii) the human readable information visualization layer and (iv) the action layer for human use [Swan (2012)].

2.2. *Previous Internet of Things architectures*

A key feature in the IoT context environment is that these architectures, based on three, four or five layers (Fig. 2) of scanned modular objects, can be decoupled. Thus, the digitized object represents a combination of elements across these layers, which are interconnected through specified interfaces. Architecture is like the backbone of IoT. If not robust and flexible, deploying and using IoT may take longer and need

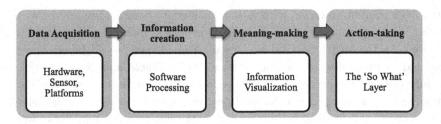

Source: According to Swan [2012, p. 219].

Fig. 1.   The main processes and layers of the IoT ecosystem.

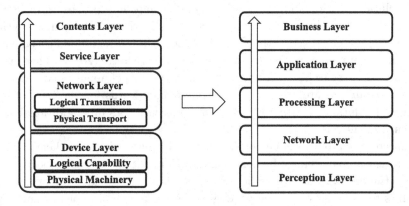

Source: Adapted by the authors based on the research of Aazam *et al.* [2014], Wu *et al.* [2010] and Khan *et al.* [2012].

Fig. 2.   The evolution of IoT architecture frameworks.

reengineering. The IoT architecture is generally considered to be made up of three layers: perception, network, and application. However, some researchers [Wu *et al.* (2010); Khan *et al.* (2012)] added two more layers: processing or middleware and business. This three-layer architecture and its evolution to architecture in five layers are shown in Fig. 2.

The Perception Layer is the lowest layer of the IoT architecture and is where the devices will pick up or pull the data monitored by sensors. As the name suggests, its objective is to perceive the environmental data. The entire data collection occurs in this layer [Aazam *et al.* (2014)]. Bar code labels, RFID tags, GPS, cameras and other sensors, both physical and virtual, are in this layer. Identifying "things" and gathering data are the primary goals of this layer.

The concept of virtual sensor abstraction allows a system developer to specify high-level data requirements [Kabadayi *et al.* (2006)] to be implemented later. The basis of these sensors are algorithms developed to extract a large amount of data that meet previously established parameters. A virtual sensor is a software sensor as opposed to a physical or hardware sensor.

The Network Layer collects the data perceived by the Perception Layer [Aazam *et al.* (2014)]. The Network layer is where communications, through use of the gateways, are put into action. These gateways have the role of translating device data to the cloud or to a local network. This layer collects data from the bottom layer and sends them to the Internet. The Network layer can include a gateway, having one interface connected to the sensor network and one to the Internet. In some scenarios, it may include a network management center or information processing center [Aazam *et al.* (2014)].

The Processing Layer receives data from the bottom layer. Its purposes are data storage and service management. This layer processes information and can make decisions automatically based on results [Khan *et al.* (2012)]. Examples of this layers are cloud storages and data warehouses. This layer then passes its output to the next layer, the Application layer, which performs the final presentation of the data. This layer receives information from the Processing Layer and provides global management of the application that presents the information, based on the information processed by the Processing layer.

Depending on the type of devices and their purpose in the Perception layer, and then on the path through which they were processed by the Processing layer, according to user needs, the Application Layer displays the data in the form of smart city, home, transportation, agriculture, health, or factory, among other types of applications [Khan *et al.* (2012)].

For Aazam *et al.* [2014, p. 415], the "Business Layer is all about making money from the service being provided. Data received at the application layer is molded into a meaningful service and then further services are created from those existing services. Furthermore, information is processed to make it knowledge and further efficient means of usage make it wisdom, which can earn a good amount of money to the service provider". Based on the analysis of results, this layer helps to determine future actions and business strategies [Khan *et al.* (2012)].

The authors referenced in Fig. 2 were the pioneers who related and presented smart sensors in a study, with the business in an IoT architecture. However, these architectures did not focus on the "Business Layer" and did not elaborate on the implications of using the IoT architecture in the business context. In the five layers architecture, although there is a dedicated business layer, it is not explained if and how IoT solutions can be a source of competitive advantage and how the data collected by these sensors can serve as an input to motivate model renewal, processes and products of a business. Therefore, some limitations were identified in this architecture, leading to the development of the framework proposed in this paper.

This paper highlights the need to use the information generated by the monitoring and strategic control mechanisms, together with the emerging IoT concept in the service of companies [SAP (2015, 2016); Gartner (2015)]. Due to the nature of the IoT, sensors are sources for collecting relevant and useful data. Once data on the most diverse organizational environment variables are collected and monitored, companies can develop the capability to analyze and review current business systems, and even identify new opportunities or threats to the business in the near future [Rocha *et al.* (2016)].

For the IoMA, an evolution of the architectures in layers of the IoT was adopted. This evolved architecture is focused on business and its transformation to better structure, organizing the value creation of employees in a digital ecosystem and raising the need to promote adjustments or changes in processes or even business models, revitalizing them.

3. Research Method

For this study, the research delimitation and design are based on the Design Science Research (DSR) method. DSR is a rigorous process of constructing artifacts to solve problems, evaluate what was built or what is working, and communicate or publish the results obtained [Çağdaş and Stubkjær (2011)]. The results should be generalizable for a given class of problems, allowing other researchers and professional to apply the generated knowledge to different situations [Dresch *et al.* (2015)]. The DSR was chosen for its consistency with the need to design an IoT solution that instigates business renewals. DSR seeks to develop and design solutions to improve existing systems, solve problems or create new artifacts, seeking to contribute to better practice [Dresch *et al.* (2015)]. In the case of this research, a framework was proposed that facilitates and improves decision-making in the IoT context. Better decision-making seeks to generate perceived value by using IoT solutions. The created framework aims to outline how technological solutions based on IoT can help in business management and renewal.

The IoMA framework developed with the DSR rationale is expected to provide researchers and practitioners with a model for promptly and continuously analyzing businesses embedded in complex ecosystems. The model aims to facilitate the understanding of how strategy management can be motivated by information stemming from both physical and virtual sensors. With the creation of this framework, it is expected that managers can observe and use an understandable and consistent model to analyze not only their current business, but also to help in the development of new business models more adequately adjusted to future scenarios, respecting the complexity of the IoT ecosystem.

The comprehensive DSR research process was guided by the method described by Manson [2006], Çağdaş and Stubkjær [2011] and Dresch *et al.* [2015], which includes five iterative steps. For the purposes of this study, the first three were applied: (i) Awareness — the initial step of the method when the researcher identifies a problem and seeks to solve it. In the case of this study, it was presented and explained in the Introduction as a research gap (Step 1 output). For this, it is necessary to understand the nature of the problem, context, potentialities and limitations, seeking to understand the environment in which the problem is inserted; (ii) Suggestion — the step of analyzing previous research in the literature to gain insights and define the requirements for solving the problem. In the case of this study, the careful analysis of previous research was conducted in the Literature Review (Stage 2 output), which presented aspects and limitations of previous frameworks that attempted to relate the business with the IoT. In this stage, the researcher uses creativity and previous knowledge to propose solutions that can be used to improve the current situation; and (iii) Development or Prototype of the Artifact — the effective construction of the artifact by the researcher based on the deductive method. In this study, the developed artifact is presented in Sec. 4 (Step 3 output).

It is important to emphasize that this research will not include the last two DSR stages, which are: (i) Evaluation — where the artifact is critically tested and analyzed by external experts from the market or academia in order to validate and improve the proposed artifact; and (ii) Conclusion — where the suggestions and criticisms of the experts are interpreted and can be accepted or rejected for the framework to be consolidated.

4. The IOMA Artifact

The IoMA emphasizes the importance of making and strengthening external collaborations, as well as internal collaborations, for the company. The IoT architecture and the information generated by it are of little value if they do not drive decisions. These actions usually require hardware, software, people, and their collaborative and learning capabilities from generating new and relevant information. The goal is not the application itself but to empower organization to coordinate better their innovative efforts. This means more optimized work, or innovative work to empower business managers to make more assertive decisions based on relevant information generated by sensors. These would have the property of continuously capturing variations in the organizational environment, enabling managers to process data, transforming them into information that could be used as inputs for better decision-making.

Applications can give people the right data at the right time, so they can do the right thing at the right time. The IoMA is part of the IoT architecture, aiming to add value to the business architecture. The IoMA expands the concept of the IoT in the organizational context. Within the IoT ecosystem, the IoMA leverages the IoT architecture to provide companies with tools for optimizing its business processes, transforming its business models and creating new ones.

Information from sensors can provide insights and help develop new capabilities related to a better understanding of how companies acquire or develop customers, products and services. Rather than optimizing a simple transaction such as a sale to a consumer, this information can contribute to how the business should think in terms of using this perspective to increase value [Deloitte (2015)]. Companies could understand the value chain in an integrated way with the help of the IoT.

It is important to emphasize that the IoMA is the focus of this paper, represented by the steps of "Analyze" and "Act", with implications for the business. This is how the proposal of this paper is directed to business management and data sharing by employees, rather than focusing on IT or sensor development. As presented in the Literature Review, this focus on tangible things is still the main goal of most recent research on the IoT.

Previous IoT frameworks mostly focus on IT architecture, leaving Business Architecture in the background, along with the most diverse stakeholders and the implications of their collaborations for the business. The IoMA outlines how companies can use sensors, whether physical or virtual, to impact the business layer. In this way, the paper aims to break one of the current and still dominant paradigms in IoT studies.

Figure 3, developed in this study, shows that the IoT is a new paradigm that visualizes all the "objects" around us connected to the network, providing access to information for organizational users at any time and place [Westerlund et al. (2014)]. The IoT architecture describes the interconnection of smart sensors that will monitor and collect the internal and external contingencies of the company. These contingency data are collected by devices responsible for communicating and translating to a local network or to the cloud where the data will be recorded, accumulated and integrated. Following this phase, a great analysis of data and its most diverse applications can be made. Using this architecture, organizational users benefit from insights gained through Big Data Analytics, and can make better decisions by acting more accurately, assertively, and in a timely manner.

With the IoMA proposition, this paper redirects attention to the business and its necessary transformations to explore how the analysis and use of the information obtained through sensors in the IoT architecture can renew business models. This transformation of the business model affects business processes, products and services. With this redirection, the paper promotes a first effort to explain how the IoT architecture can arouse the need to make changes that are adaptive and timely, such as optimizations in processes or products of the business, or of a disruptive nature, such as the transformational change of the business model. The need to make these changes may eventually trigger the need to develop new organizational capabilities or reconfigure existing ones to address new business models. In this study, it is suggested that this is how the IoT can generate business value.

The essence of the IoT architecture concept is centered on three interrelated and interdependent steps: (i) Monitoring — where tracking of the environment and its oscillations occurs, where the data are sensed and collected in order to permeate the variables of the environment, such as performance of any given equipment or user logins; (ii) Analysis — where the most diverse types of treatment occur for a large amount and diversity of data collected in the previous stage. In this step, analytics tools are used to mine data in order to transform it into information that can indicate, for example, market tendencies or internal alerts. This information can be applied and visualized in a variety of ways by end users, directing positive changes in

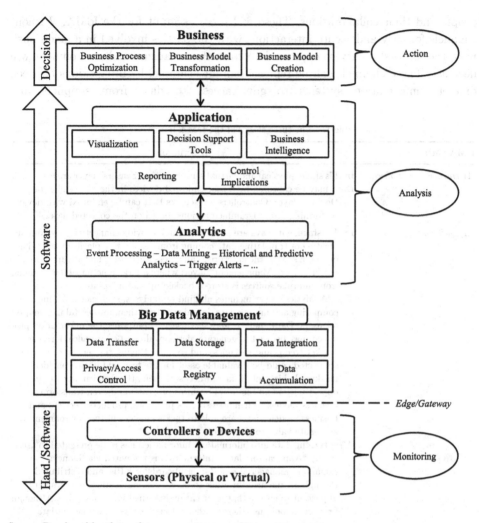

Source: Developed by the authors.

Fig. 3.   The IoMA concept — How the IoT can reconfigure and manage the business.

business behavior; and (iii) Action — where the information collected through sensors can effectively assist better decision-making based on timely, reliable and relevant information. From the transformation of data from the business environment to information, decision-makers are urged to make changes. These business changes are intended to address identified internal problems or anticipate the emergence of these problems, and to address the environmental uncertainties, opportunities, and threats that may hinder current strategy.

Additionally, as shown in Fig. 3, the Action step enables the appearance of the business layer. In this layer, the IoMA framework emphasizes that the IoT includes people and their collaborations. These will serve as input for the IoMA. Without channels for easy and secure interactions with the parties involved in a given business, the sensors' ability to capture data from the organizational environment will decrease. These channels can be represented, for example, by integrations between different information systems to gain access to data from suppliers and

Table 1.   The three stages of the IoMA framework.

IoMA parts	Description
(I) *Hardware & Software*	In this stage, physical and virtual sensors in the "Sensors" layer are activated. Data may be captured by sensor-endowed devices in the "Controller or Devices" layer. Controllers are sensors that can be endowed with devices performing pre-programmed actions, based on the collected data.
(II) *Software*	In this stage, gateways are activated. They provide connectivity by communicating or translating data coming from devices to a platform, a local net or cloud, so that the enterprise can access the data. The data are stored in the "Big Data Management" layer, where a large amount of data coming from multiple sources is stored, backed up and integrated.
	The "Analytics" layer includes all kind of analyses, such as combining, comparing and mining data, in order to turn them into useful information for users. Data analysis may serve several purposes: the information produced may be used to generate alerts, evaluate performance, forecast market trends and revenues, and so on... Having the service or product connected could be a valuable asset for the firm and its stakeholders: by tracking habits, interests and needs of users, the firm can seize new opportunities and renew its business processes and even transform its business models. When assessing its processes, products, services and business models, firms are able to tackle changes in the environment and aggregate value to their offer.
	After turning data into information, information has to be presented to users. In the "Application" layer, information is presented via financial, operational and managerial reports, dashboards or KPIs, and distributed throughout the firm. In order to do so, communication becomes very important to ensure that information is turned into knowledge. Although firms commonly use these methods, the diversity of sources of data requires special attention to analysis and applications.
(III) *Decision*	In this stage, the IoMA triggers innovation by transforming product, services, business processes and even business models. By adjusting and transforming, the firm maintains conditions to compete and fulfil financial and non-financial goals.
	As the world becomes increasingly connected, firms cannot lose interaction with their markets, and employees need to make sure their connections are safe and unbiased. Customers demand increased aggregate value from companies. The IoMA architecture makes it easier to understand the environment by monitoring, analyzing and presenting relevant data on the external and internal environment. The IoMA framework highlights the importance of using monitoring mechanisms to control environmental variables, such as internal processes, performance, competences, needs and requirements of stakeholders, regulation, and competitive forces.

Source: Developed by the authors.

customers. These suppliers and customers, once their data are accessed, can become business partners and thus serve as sources of innovation through crowdsensing [Brown (2017)].

New information can be transformed into business knowledge and allow insights for various evaluations within the Action step, as this information is disseminated and shared across the enterprise. This new information can cause the company to develop new knowledge (e.g. new ways of offering a product or service). This learning process can trigger the need to make incremental or transformational changes. Examples of incremental changes could be continuous improvements or business adaptation to deal with new market information. The most significant changes may imply the transformation of the existing business model, or even the creation of new business models.

The creation of new business models can transform the economy and the way consumers experience their purchases in the near future. IoT architecture, rooted in mobility, collaboration, strong monitoring, virtual sensors, Big Data and Analytics is challenging traditional business models [Gartner (2018)]. Data captured in the environment can allow insights that the emergence of a new process, product or business model is necessary and can enable the company to get ahead in its marketplace and anticipate the movements of its competitors. To allow better organization and structuring, the IoMA framework was also separated into three parts, as shown in Table 1.

5. Discussion

IoT architecture helps to identify problems, threats and opportunities, thus allowing better decision-making when it comes to seizing opportunities or mitigating threats detected by sensors. Therefore, companies may become aware of the need for change, whether it is optimizing the return of existing products or renewing the business model. In the long run, companies may develop the capabilities and flexibility required for constant innovation, which is the ultimate purpose of the IoMA framework. Companies that do not develop these capabilities may not be capable of competing in global markets. Competitiveness and connectivity encourage enterprises to capitalize on opportunities, which can be exploited by using the IoMA framework.

It is important to highlight that some risks arise when implementing IoT architectures, such as cost underestimation, poor planning, lack of security or privacy, regulation change and benefit overestimation [Brous and Janssen (2015)]. Companies need to be aware of these risks and decide how to mitigate them. They can incur troubling issues when ignoring the question of the rights and security of their own customers, resulting in a decline in sales and putting their brands in jeopardy, not forgetting civil lawsuits, fines and operational losses [Nordic (2016)].

From the strategic management perspective, the IoMA can be defined as a framework that emphasizes the importance of measuring and analyzing internal and external environment, so that management can foresee future competitive opportunities. The IoMA may help firms to diagnose business needs and renew them. IoT solutions are expected not only to improve optimization and efficiency, but also to foster the creation of novel business models by raising the consciousness of decision-makers.

Strategic management can be triggered by the appropriate use of the intelligent sensors in the IoT architecture. By collecting data, firms can take more reasoned, appropriate and assertive decisions. The IoMA proposition aims to articulate, in a structured manner, the logic of relationships among layers underlying the IoT architecture, such as hardware and software, in order to empower these decisions to transform businesses, aggregate value and ultimately gain a competitive advantage. The uniqueness of the IoMA lies in the concern over business model creation and transformation, unlike other models that focus on the technological layers.

The IoMA framework specifies the reciprocal relationship between the business and the sensor layers. Users can adjust sensor networks according to the desired competitive strategy, as well as current business needs. Firms must be confident in their desired value proposal and evaluate strengths and weaknesses in terms of resources and capabilities before planning IoT architectures. Having done so, IT managers should design IoT architectures together with business managers, focusing solely on how to obtain business value.

6. Conclusion

The aim of this paper was to present a theoretical framework for managerial decision-making within the IoT ecosystem, which can assist companies when making decisions about renewing their business model. In order to tackle the lack of studies connecting sensors in the IoT ecosystem with managerial decision-making, a change of paradigm was needed. This work extends the IoT vision from things and devices to the business environment. The result is the IoMA framework, which features value creation within the IoT ecosystem and the importance of the internal and external environment, which is also consistent with the device-centered vision.

Unlike other IoT papers relating IoT to business, the IoMA emphasizes the implications of each layer of the IoT architecture for decision-making, which in turn may trigger the need to transform the business, either incrementally or radically. Decisions may address internal issues, market opportunities and external threats. In the IoMA, data collected from sensors are handled to extract real-time information on organizational and market tendencies, useful for decision-making in those settings. Therefore, this paper argues that using IoT architecture can lead to even greater competitive advantage in rapidly changing and highly digitized environments, as firms may manage their businesses with greater agility and ease.

The main contributions of the framework presented address strategic management research in the IoT context, which is an emerging theme, and companies must understand how to use IoT technologies to compete. Researchers may use this framework to analyze how IoT architecture can be structured in layers to aggregate value to businesses and clarify the relationship between IoT solutions and business renewal.

This work also highlighted how DSR can be applied to develop a framework that interfaces with several theoretical themes: strategic management, business models, information systems and monitoring and controlling mechanisms. Although DSR has been a common choice in information systems research, a lack of its use has been noticed in organizational studies [Hevner *et al.* (2008)]. For practitioners, IoMA constitutes a tool to describe, analyze and envision strategic management within the IoT ecosystem, and can support development or transformation of businesses throughout complexities.

6.1. *Limitations and suggestions for further research*

The main limitation of this paper is its theoretical form, since the objective was not to test and evaluate the framework in practice. This study represents a seminal effort to create a transparent framework that explores how IoT solutions can contribute to businesses from a strategic standpoint. Although using the first three steps of the DSR method ensures that the framework relates theory to practice, the authors highlight that applying the IoMA in enterprises and validating the framework with IoT specialists will have to be addressed in future studies. Hence, it is suggested that future research apply steps 4 and 5 of DSR in order to test the framework empirically and extract criticisms, evaluations and suggestions for improvement from scholars, practitioners and specialists.

The full potential of business opportunities has not yet been attained by using IoT architecture alone. Future research may verify the applicability of the IoMA's layers by: (i) validating it with practitioners, managers and IT specialists; (ii) applying it in order to adapt the framework to practice; (iii) exploring further the relationship between the IoMA's layers and consolidated concepts in the strategic management literature. The emerging context of IoT is a fertile environment for further management research, which may include deepening the discussion on transforming existing businesses and creating new ones. Generating insights for new business models will be paramount for companies addressing the needs of ever-changing environments. This paper could not aim to exhaust this complex theme but has instead laid the foundations for further discussion. Future research may explore the possibilities offered by this framework in terms of innovation management, competitive advantage and dynamic capabilities within the context of enterprises.

References

Aazam, M., Khan, I., Alsaffar, A. A. and Huh, E. N. (2014). Cloud of things: Integrating internet of things and cloud computing and the issues involved. In *2014 11th International Bhurban Conference Applied Sciences and Technology (IBCAST)*, IEEE, pp. 414–419. doi: 10.1109/IBCAST.2014.6778179.

Alt, R. and Zbornik, S. (2002). Integrierte Geschäftsabwicklung mit electronic bill present-ment and payment. *Proceedings zur Teilkonferenz der Multikonferenz Wirtschaftsinfor-matik*, **2002**. doi: 10.1007/978-3-642-57487-0_12.

Ammar, M., Russello, G. and Crispo, B. (2018). Internet of things: A survey on the security of IoT frameworks. *Journal of Information Security and Applications*, **38**: 8–27. doi: 10.1016/j.jisa.2017.11.002.

Ashton, K. (2009). That 'Internet of things' thing. *RFID Journal*, **22**(7): 97–114. Available at http://www.rfidjournal.com/articles/pdf?4986.

Boyes, H., Hallaq, B., Cunningham, J. and Watson, T. (2018). The industrial internet of things (IIoT): An analysis framework. *Computers in Industry*, **101**: 1–12. doi: 10.1016/j.compind.2018.04.015.

Brown, T. E. (2017). Sensor-based entrepreneurship: A framework for developing new pro-ducts and services. *Business Horizons*, **60**(6): 819–830. doi: 10.1016/j.bushor.2017.07.008.

Brous, P. and Janssen, M. (2015). Effects of the internet of things (IoT): A systematic review of the benefits and risks. In *International Conference on Electronic Business*, December 2015, Hong Kong. Available at https://www.researchgate.net/publication/306380073_effects_of_the_Internet_of_things_iot_a_systematic_review_of_the_benefits_and_risks.

Burkhart, T., Wolter, S., Schief, M. and Vanderhaeghen, D. (2012). A comprehensive approach towards the structural description of business models. In *Proceedings of the International Conference on Management of Emergent Digital EcoSystems*, ACM, New York, pp. 88–102. doi: 10.1145/2457276.2457294.

Çağdaş, V. and Stubkjær, E. (2011). Design research for cadastral systems. *Computers, En-vironment and Urban Systems*, **35**(1): 77–87. doi: 10.1016/j.compenvurbsys.2010.07.003.

CERP-IoT — Cluster of European Projects on Internet of Things (2009). Internet of things strategic research roadmap. Available at http://www.Internet-of-things-research.eu/pdf/IoT_Cluster_Strategic_Research_Agenda_2009.pdf.

Chan, H. C. (2015). Internet of things business models. *Journal of Service Science and Management*, **8**(4): 552–568. doi: 10.4236/jssm.2015.84056.

Chesbrough, H. (2003). *Open Innovation: The New Imperative for Creating and Profiting from Technology*. Harvard Business School Press.

Chesbrough, H. and Rosenbloom, R. S. (2002). The role of the business model in capturing value from innovation: Evidence from Xerox Corporation's technology spin-off companies. *Industrial and Corporate Change*, **11**(3): 529–555. doi: 10.1093/icc/11.3.529.

Deloitte (2015). The internet of things ecosystem: Unlocking the business value of connected devices. Available at https://www2.deloitte.com/ug/en/pages/technology-media-and-telecommunications/articles/Internet-of-things-ecosystem.html.

Dresch, A., Lacerda, D. P. and Júnior, J. A. V. A. (2015). *Design Science Research: Método de Pesquisa Para Avanço da Ciência e Tecnologia*. Bookman Editora. doi: 10.13140/2.1.2264.2885.

Gartner (2015). Top 10 strategic predictions for 2016 and beyond: The future is a digital thing. Available at https://www.gartner.com/doc/3142020/top-strategic-predictions-future-digital.

Gartner (2016). Gartner's top 10 security predictions 2016 — How to prepare for these new and known threats to enterprise security over the next two to four years. Available at http://www.gartner.com/smarterwithgartner/top-10-security-predictions-2016/.

Gartner (2018). O Poder da Conexão: Liderança, Parceria e Tecnologia, 2018. Available at https://www.gartner.com/binaries/content/assets/events/keywords/data-center/bdcl8/evt_la_2018_bdcl8_brochure_online_v3.pdf.

Glova, J., Sabol, T. and Vajda, V. (2014). Business models for the internet of things environment. *Procedia Economics and Finance*, **15**: 1122–1129. doi: 10.1016/S2212-5671(14)00566-8.

Guinard, D., Trifa, V., Mattern, F. and Wilde, E. (2011). From the internet of things to the web of things: Resource-oriented architecture and best practices. In *Architecting the Internet of things* (pp. 97–129). Springer, Berlin: Heidelberg. doi: 10.1007/978-3-642-19157-2_5.

Hevner, A. R., March, S. T., Park, J. and Ram, S. (2008). Design science in information systems research. *MIS Quarterly*, **28**(1): 75–105. doi: 10.2307/25148625.

Hofmann, E. and Rüsch, M. (2017). Industry 4.0 and the current status as well as future prospects on logistics. *Computers in Industry*, **89**: 23–34. doi: 10.1016/j.compind.2017.04.002.

Kabadayi, S., Pridgen, A. and Julien, C. (2006). Virtual sensors: Abstracting data from physical sensors. *Edge — The University of Texas at Austin*. doi: 10.1109/WOWMOM.2006.115.

Khan, R., Khan, S. U., Zaheer, R. and Khan, S. (2012). Future Internet: The Internet of things architecture, possible applications and key challenges. In *2012 10th International Conference on Frontiers of Information Technology (FIT)*, IEEE, pp. 257–260. doi: 10.1109/FIT.2012.53.

Kortuem, G., Kawsar, F., Sundramoorthy, V. and Fitton, D. (2010). Smart objects as building blocks for the internet of things. *Internet Computing*, **14**(1): 44–51. IEEE. doi: 10.1109/MIC.2009.143.

Kyriazis, D. and Varvarigou, T. (2013). Smart, autonomous and reliable internet of things. *Procedia Computer Science*, **21**: 442–448. doi: 10.1016/j.procs.2013.09.059.

Manson, N. J. (2006). Is operations research really research? *Orion*, **22**(2): 155–180. doi: 10.5784/22-2-40.

Ng, I. C. and Wakenshaw, S. Y. (2017). The internet-of-things: Review and research directions. *International Journal of Research in Marketing*, **34**(1): 3–21. doi: 10.1016/j.ijresmar.2016.11.003.

Nordic Semiconductor (2016). Entering the internet of things: Opportunity, risks & strategy. Available at http://response.nordicsemi.com/download-entering-the-Internet-of-things-opportunity-risks-strategy.

Rocha, C., Duclos, L. C., Veiga, C. P., Bischof, C. and Neves, N. (2016). The control mechanisms on the performance of the strategic initiatives management: Analysis of critical sales process in a metallurgical business. *International Business Management*, **10**: 357–369. doi: 10.3923/ibm.2016.357.369.

Rogers, D. L. (2017). *Transformação Digital: Repensando o Seu Negócio Para a Era Digital*. São Paulo: Autêntica Business Editora.

SAP (2015). Internet of things (IoT) for the enterprise — the big picture. Available at https://blogs.saphana.com/2015/05/29/Internet-of-things-iot-for-the-enterprise-the-big-picture/.

SAP (2016). SAP internet of things (Iot) in a connected world. Available at: https://blogs.sap.com/2016/12/15/sap-Internet-of-things-iot-in-a-connected-world/.

Swan, M. (2012). Sensor mania! the Internet of things, wearable computing, objective metrics, and the quantified self 2.0. *Journal of Sensor and Actuator Networks*, **1**(3): 217–253. doi: 10.3390/jsan1030217.

Uckelmann, D., Harrison, M. and Michahelles, F. (2011). *Architecting the Internet of Things*, 1st edn., New York: Springer.

Wang, F., Zhao, J., Chi, M. and Li, Y. (2017). Collaborative innovation capability in IT-enabled inter-firm collaboration. *Industrial Management & Data Systems*, **117**(10): 2364–2380. doi: 10.1108/IMDS-09-2016-0392.

Westerlund, M., Leminen, S. and Rajahonka, M. (2014). Designing business models for the Internet of things. *Technology Innovation Management Review*, 4(7), 5. doi: 10.22215/timreview/807.

Westerman, G., Bonnet, D. and McAfee, A. (2016). *Liderando na Era Digital: Como utilizar tecnologia para transformação de Seus Negócios*. M. Books Editora, São Paulo.

Wu, M., Lu, T. J., Ling, F. Y., Sun, J. and Du, H. Y. (2010). Research on the architecture of Internet of things. In *Advanced Computer Theory and Engineering (ICACTE), 2010 3rd International Conference*, IEEE, Vol. 5, pp. V5–484. doi: 10.1109/ICACTE.2010.5579493.

Zott, C. and Amit, R. (2010). Business model design: An activity system perspective. *Long Range Planning*, **43**(2–3): 216–226. doi: 10.1016/j.lrp.2009.07.004.

Biography

Clarissa Rocha Master in Business Administration and Ph.D. Researcher from the Business School on R&D Collaborations in the context of Industry 4.0, and a member of the Strategy Research Group at Pontifical Catholic University of Parana.

Clariana Fernandez Narcizo Master in Business Administration from the Business School at the Pontifical Catholic University of Parana.

Enrico Gianotti Master in Mathematics from the Università degli Studi di Torino and Ph.D. Researcher from the Business School on innovation of business models through the use of the Internet of Things, and member of the Strategy Research Group in the Pontificia Catholic University of Parana.

Chapter 13

Building Blocks of Successful Digital Transformation: Complementing Technology and Market Issues

Ulrich Lichtenthaler

International School of Management
Cologne, Germany
lichtenthaler@web.de

Strategic transformation is the primary reason why digitalization, artificial intelligence and related changes are on the top of most corporate agendas. Currently, many firms have completed the stage of strategy formulation for their digital transformation and are in the phase of strategy implementation. Here, many firms face major difficulties, which often result from an emphasis on technology issues at the expense of market-related issues. Following the innovation-based view and a conceptual framework of technology push and market pull effects, this conceptual paper presents important building blocks of successful digital transformation. On this basis, it illustrates the typical focus of most firms at present and highlights the limitations of these approaches. To overcome these limitations, several implementation steps are presented. As such, this paper contributes to research into digital transformation and artificial intelligence as well as into managing strategic renewal in light of technological change.

Keywords: Digital innovation; digital transformation; digitalization; market pull; strategic renewal; technology push.

1. Introduction

Digitalization, artificial intelligence and related changes are on the top of most corporate agendas at present [Agrawal *et al.* (2018a); Al-Ansaari *et al.* (2014); Davenport and Ronanki (2018); Iansiti and Lakhani (2014); Lichtenthaler (2020)]. Many firms' executives are actively trying to find suitable strategic alternatives in light of these changes which have the potential to fundamentally transform entire industries [Ahn (2014); Andriole (2017); Westerman and Bonnet (2015)]. This potential transformation is the primary reason for the immense attention that digitalization currently receives from the highest strategic management levels to

This chapter was originally published in *International Journal of Innovation and Technology Management*, Vol. 17, No. 1, February 2020, published by World Scientific Publishing, Singapore. Reprinted with permission.

lower operational levels in organizations. This enormous attention to digitalization can be observed in a variety of industrial sectors, including automotive, chemicals, construction, consumer products, electronics, financial services, machinery and pharmaceuticals [Do (2014); Gupta *et al.* (2017); Loebbecke and Picot (2015)]. Many firms' executives in these industries have acknowledged that the response to the digitalization challenges will determine the future success or failure of their firms [Bughin (2017); Harland and Yörür (2015); Klein (2014); Oshri and Weeber (2006)].

Whether digitalization will affect a firm's performance in the short, medium or long-term depends strongly on the particular industry and its product life cycle. Some industries, such as information technology and electronics are leading in the evolution towards digitalization, and the short lifecycles in these industries favor a relatively rapid business transformation [Kane *et al.* (2015); Sarkkinen and Kässi (2015); Tura *et al.* (2017); Verganti and Buganza (2005)]. Other industries, such as machinery or construction may be lagging behind to some degree which gives the players in these industries more time to prepare for the changes that will definitely affect them sooner or later. In a similar vein, service industries, such as financial services and consulting, are affected by digitalization [Amit and Han (2017); Huang and Rust (2018)]. Accordingly, it is not the question whether to act or to react, but rather how to move on.

As such, many executive boards have already completed the initial stage of strategic analyses with respect to digitalization and artificial intelligence. Currently, they are in the stage of strategy formulation and strategy implementation. On this basis, many firms face substantial difficulties [Andriole (2017)]. A major reason for the difficulties is the variety of these changes, which comprise new technological developments as well as new market evolutions. On the one hand, firms face a multitude of technological possibilities, such as intelligent robotics, various connectivity technologies and advanced data analytics [Ili and Lichtenthaler (2017); McAfee and Brynjolfsson (2012)]. Besides the multitude of different technological evolutions, many of these developments converge, and this convergence further complicates strategic technology planning. On the other hand, firms need to cope with a variety of market transformations, such as digital health, autonomous driving and smart home. This variety of market changes in different industries further complicates market planning [Aversa *et al.* (2017); Ng (2016)].

Jointly, these technology and market transformations lead to important push effects and pull effects with regard to digitalization [Di Domenico *et al.* (2014); Lichtenthaler (2017)]. New technologies motivate firms to consider and to develop new market solutions, whereas new customer requirements on the markets call for further developing critical technologies in order to be able to deliver convincing digital products and services. These technology push and market pull effects result in a multitude of new management challenges in firms from all industries [Nambisan (2017); Tripsas (2009)]. With regard to strategic challenges, for example, executives need to develop convincing strategic responses to new entrants [Ross *et al.* (2017)]. Concerning organizational challenges, many firms have created the position of a Chief Digital Officer as the key responsible person for all digitalization efforts [Rometty (2016)]. Regarding process challenges, many firms have begun to transform their traditional systematic innovation processes in order to be able to dynamically respond to environmental changes [Doz and Kosonen (2010)].

Based on the push and pull trends, the new managerial challenges of digitalization will have fundamental consequences in many industries [Adner (2002); Kolbjornsrud *et al.* (2016)]. Many firms intensely prepare for these changes and try to actively influence the industry transformations in order to protect their core businesses and to generate new growth opportunities [Chao and Kavadias (2008); Kavadias *et al.* (2016)]. Beyond strategic, organizational and process transformations, such as assigning a Chief Digital Officer, many firms from distinct industries, such as automotive, electronics and many more, have started specific digitalization initiatives [Phan *et al.* (2017); Plastino and Purdy (2018)]. These initiatives constitute detailed programs which are directed at proactively shaping and/or reactively addressing the particular digitalization challenges in a firm's specific situation, such as smart home solutions in the construction industry or autonomous driving in the automotive industry. These digitalization initiatives are usually strategic programs, which comprise several building blocks [Agrawal *et al.* (2017); Wilson *et al.* (2017)].

However, many of these strategic initiatives have not yet met their initial objectives. In fact, many firms claim that their digital transformation initiatives have failed so far [Andriole (2017); Bughin (2017); Ili and Lichtenthaler (2017)]. Therefore, it is particularly important to address the relevant building blocks of digital transformation initiatives in order to deepen our understanding of successful transformation processes towards digitalization and artificial intelligence. In this regard, Sec. 2 of this conceptual paper first presents a framework which addresses several building blocks. Section 3 then explicates the theoretical implications, avenues for future research as well as the managerial implications, pointing out major implementation steps to avoid the typical pitfalls in digital transformation. Finally, Sec. 4 presents a brief conclusion and outlook.

2. Conceptual Framework

2.1. *Building blocks*

A key feature of digitalization is the evolution of traditional products towards smart connected products, which encompass smart components, such as sensors, and connectivity components, such as communications protocols [Porter and Heppelmann (2014)]. Besides making products smart and connected, digitalization often leads to a transformation of products towards integrated solutions. Accordingly, the separation and the boundaries between products, services and related digital applications are blurred [Chesbrough (2011); Huang and Rust (2018)]. As such, manufacturing firms increasingly offer solutions that involve a physical product, immaterial services and potentially further digital applications. These different parts are bundled, and they provide an integrated solution based on smart and connected product components [Porter and Heppelmann (2015)].

In many cases, these solutions cannot be developed exclusively in-house because hardly any firm has all relevant expertise internally [Amit and Han (2017)]. Instead, firms often need to collaborate with external partners to co-create these integrated solutions [Adegbesan and Higgins (2011); Araújo Burcharth *et al.* (2014); Brem and Bilgram (2015); Grosse-Kathoefer and Leker (2012); Herzog and Leker (2010); Knudsen (2007)]. Beyond collaborations in the development of digital solutions, a single firm usually depends on external players in the commercialization and use of its products. In particular, the benefits and value of many integrated digital solutions depend on a network, which includes a firm and multiple external players [Nambisan and Sawhney (2007)]. Thus, the success of a firm's products is not determined exclusively by the firm and the market, but also by further partners and their complementary solutions [Adner (2006); Daim *et al.* (2006)].

In particular, the partner networks for digital solutions often do not go along with traditional industry boundaries. Instead, they often involve partners from distinct industries [Adner and Kapoor (2010); Rohrbeck *et al.* (2009)]. On this basis, firms can cope with the variety of these integrated solutions, which provide the basis for the success of their digitalization initiatives. In this regard, firms usually need to consider the following four building blocks to make their digitalization initiatives successful [Bughin (2017); Ili and Lichtenthaler (2017); Loebbecke and Picot (2015); Rometty (2016); Tripsas and Gavetti (2000); Yoo *et al.* (2012)]: smart solution, integrated communication, value generation and value appropriation (Fig. 1).

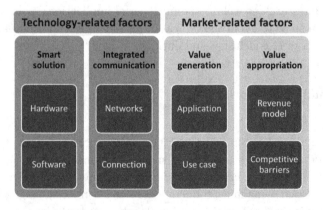

Fig. 1.   Building blocks of successful digitalization initiatives.

Because of the conceptual nature of this paper, the four building blocks in Fig. 1 have been newly identified in an overview of the management literature addressing digital transformation, artificial intelligence and related evolutions [Agrawal *et al.* (2018b); Brem and Bilgram (2015); Davenport (2018); Dubé *et al.* (2018); Giones and Brem (2017); Huang and Rust (2018); Lewrick *et al.* (2018); Lichtenthaler (2020); Neubert (2018); Richter *et al.* (2017)]. This overview has drawn on the innovation-based view and the well-known distinction of technology push and market pull as a conceptual foundation [Lichtenthaler (2016); Meyer (1999); Rodrigues-Alves (2018); Schmoch (2007); Spaeth *et al.* (2010)]. Basically, each of the four building blocks needs to be covered although firms will often collaborate with external partners in the development and management of some of these building blocks. However, neglecting one of these buildings blocks usually puts the success of an entire digitalization initiative at risk.

2.2. *Technology-related factors*

The first building block is the smart solution, and it includes the hardware and software of the smart connected solutions [Loebbecke and Picot (2015); Motohashi and Yuan (2010)]. As such, this part goes beyond the traditional product, which often lacked an electronic component. For example, a traditional car key was a purely mechanical device. Beyond these traditional products, smart connected products include hardware, such as sensors for gathering data. In addition, software applications are needed to make use of the particular hardware components. Because of these electronic components that extend the functionality of a traditional product, this product becomes smart — but this does not mean that the product is connected to any other components or systems [Porter and Heppelmann (2014)].

The second building block is, therefore, the integrated communication [Ili and Lichtenthaler (2017); Loebbecke and Picot (2015)]. It includes the networks and connections to establish linkages between a smart component and any other components. Here, it is important to note that only connectivity makes a product actually intelligent [Porter and Heppelmann (2015)]. Although many people talk about the benefits of smart products, the value of a smart product component itself is very limited. Only by establishing the communication between a smart product and some other components, a product actually becomes intelligent — meaning that it has some enhanced functionality that a traditional product lacked. To successfully establish this integrated communication, firms need to consider suitable networks as well as the specific connections to send and receive data for the particular application [McAfee and Brynjolfsson (2012)].

In this regard, the digitalization initiatives of most firms have a relatively clear focus. Most manufacturing firms strongly emphasize technology issues in their digital transformation efforts [Andriole (2017); Ili and Lichtenthaler (2017)]. While nearly all of these digitalization initiatives are strategic programs that have been launched by senior executives, the focus on technology issues often is not a deliberate and planned strategic move. Instead, it often is the outcome of emergent planning processes for the digital transformation agenda [Kane *et al.* (2015); Ross *et al.* (2017)]. At first glance, this particular focus of most manufacturing firms from the machinery, electronics, automotive and related sectors appears to be suitable. Digital transformation is strongly driven by new digital technologies. Consequently, a focus on technological opportunities and challenges might be beneficial. However, most firms concentrate excessively on the technology issues, and they neglect a broader strategic perspective.

In fact, most firms' primary attention to technology issues comes at the expense of market-related opportunities and challenges [Iansiti and Lakhani (2014); Westerman and Bonnet (2015)]. The underlying strategic logic behind many digitalization initiatives is technology push. These initiatives start with the identification of new digital opportunities, and this initial stage is immediately followed by the selection of technology suppliers and the implementation of specific technological solutions [Amit and Han (2017); Ili and Lichtenthaler (2017)]. As such, the firms do not achieve sufficient balance between technology push and market pull approaches. Because of the transformation process of digitalization, firms need to conduct thorough strategic analyses that comprise both — the technology and the market domain. Thus, the market-related building blocks of value generation and value appropriation deserve as much attention as the smart solution and integrated communication, especially in the early stages of digitalization initiatives.

2.3. *Market-related factors*

The third building block is value generation, and it refers to the particular application and to the specific use case in which a digital solution is applied [Bettis (2017); Perr *et al.* (2010)]. This application perspective is essential because without a practical purpose and user story, the first two building blocks are relatively useless. Smart solutions and integrated communication are only valuable when they fulfill a particular function whose value depends on the specific application [Loebbecke and Picot (2015); Porter and Heppelmann (2014)]. In the example of the car key, the smart solution and integrated communication enable the application of a remote locking of a vehicle. While this is a standard functionality today, it was considered as an innovative solution some decades ago, and customers were willing to pay a premium for this functionality.

The fourth building block is value appropriation, and it includes the revenue model as well as competitive barriers [Iansiti and Lakhani (2017); Zott *et al.* (2011)]. While the application of a digital solution provides the context for generating value, it does not ensure that a firm is able to capture a noteworthy portion of the value that is created. In this respect, the revenue model is essential because it helps to understand how firms may profit from a specific digital solution [Demil and Lecocq

(2010); Zott and Amit (2008)]. Beyond establishing a suitable revenue model, executives need to pay particular attention to potential competitive barriers in order to protect their integrated solutions from attacks of established or new competitors. Here, it is particularly important to carefully examine the industry boundaries in future digital markets because established firms and start-ups from completely different industries may invade a firm's fields of business [Chesbrough (2003); Jacobides and Billinger (2006)].

In this respect, it is key to consider in detail the impact of digitalization on a firm's business model. In a nutshell, digitalization is often so challenging because the variety of technology and market transformations lead to the need for a completely new strategic positioning of a firm. The solutions and services of a firm with respect to its customers may change. On this basis, completely new business models may be required with new revenue streams and with a new value generation architecture. In particular, many manufacturing firms need to complement their traditional product business with additional services, such as smartphone applications for remote data transfer and management [Porter and Heppelmann (2014)]. Partly, these services are free to customers in order to increase the value of the products, whereas some other services may be stand-alone services that are billed. On this basis, there are plentiful opportunities and needs for revising a firm's business model [Amit and Han (2017); Westerman and Bonnet (2015)].

3. Discussion

3.1. *Theoretical implications*

The conceptual framework that has been developed in the previous section has several theoretical implications. With regard to strategic renewal in light of digitalization [Agarwal and Helfat (2009); Ben-Menahem *et al.* (2013)], many firms seem to have an intuitive tendency towards emphasizing technology issues in their digitalization initiatives. While convincing technology solutions are important, an overemphasis on technology, especially information technology issues, is detrimental [Kane *et al.* (2015); Kavadias *et al.* (2016)]. In fact, this tendency strongly limits the potential benefits of most transformation initiatives because it narrows the strategy space for digitalization and leads firms to exclude potentially promising avenues upfront. For example, an immediate discussion of technological challenges of further developing a firm's product range towards smart connected products may lead to neglecting the great opportunities of developing completely new product solutions based on the new digital possibilities [Porter and Heppelmann (2015)].

In fact, the great opportunities primarily derive from the development of new markets even if digital transformation initiatives are facilitated by the recent advances in digital technology. In a similar vein, many managerial challenges that emerge in the context of digitalization are strongly related to a firm's markets. Here, a clear understanding of the strategic levers and interdependencies is needed in the early stages of digitalization initiatives. The technology challenges are important, but the key decisions in terms of digital solutions and external service providers need to be taken on the basis of convincing strategic plans for digital transformation with regard to the business model. Usually, transformations in these fields will also lead to a growing importance of partner networks, where competition is increasingly based on broader solutions for the customers rather than on individual products or components of a single firm [Adner and Kapoor (2010); Li (2009)]. Accordingly, an overemphasis on technology issues is often detrimental, especially in the early stages of digital transformation initiatives.

In addition, a strong focus on technology issues will often lead to an unclear understanding of suitable revenue streams that derive from the digital solutions. Accordingly, a profitable business model may only emerge over time, and firms are unable to design the entire solution to fulfill the requirements of the most promising business model [Di Domenico *et al.* (2014); Ross *et al.* (2017)]. Thus, successful strategic renewal involves additional challenges in the context of digital transformation. Specifically, it is important to consider in detail the market-related challenges before starting with the actual implementation of technological solutions. This strong relevance of market-related challenges in light of major changes in the firms' technology domains provides new insights into managing strategic renewal [Capron and Mitchell (2009); Kwee *et al.* (2011)]. While technology intelligence activities are helpful in identifying relevant technological changes, they are insufficient for managing strategic renewal because successful implementation strongly depends on market-related factors [Azzone and Manzini (2008); Lee *et al.* (2010)].

3.2. *Managerial implications*

Despite the negative impact of a strong technology focus, this strategic emphasis can be observed in many firms' digitalization initiatives [Davenport and Ronanki (2018); Plastino and Purdy (2018)]. Interestingly, the focus on technology issues is often particularly pronounced among experts that lack a strong information technology background [Berman (2012); Kane *et al.* (2015)]. Often, software experts clearly see the technological opportunities and challenges, and they are aware of the suitable business models for profiting from the digital technologies. In contrast, executives with limited software expertise often want to get things done based on an immediate move towards technology implementation [Bughin (2017); Kane *et al.* (2015)]. The required business models then only emerge when the solutions are already in the market, and these procedures usually limit the profitability of the new digital products and services[Ili and Lichtenthaler (2017); Kolbjornsrud *et al.* (2016)].

To avoid this overemphasis on technology issues, the extant literature suggests that executives need to move along an implementation process that may appear somewhat counterintuitive at the beginning [Kane *et al.* (2015); Ross *et al.* (2017)].

Nonetheless, this procedure is a key success factor for digitalization initiatives. First, executives should focus on the market-related issues. In particular, they may want to start with the application and carefully understand the benefits of a particular solution along with relevant use cases and user scenarios [Kleber (2018); Trabucchi *et al.* (2017)]. Second, the importance of addressing the value issues can hardly be overemphasized. A careful design and choice of the business model along with establishing potential competitive barriers is the key cornerstone of profitable outcomes of digitalization initiatives [Dellermann *et al.* (2017); Helfat and Raubitschek (2018)]. In particular, this issue is so important because digital transformation substantially changes the established business models in many industries. Consequently, new opportunities arise, and a thorough analysis of suitable business models is key in order to profit from this evolution.

Third, executives need to consider the smart solution challenges [Ili and Lichtenthaler (2017); Schrage (2017)]. Only after addressing the market-related issues, the technology issues deserve full attention. The market-related issues may initially appear somewhat non-digital, and this may be one major reason why they are often addressed only in a superficial way. However, firms will neither be able to identify the most suitable hardware components or the most promising software suppliers if they have neglected a careful analysis of the market-related issues in the first place. Fourth, executives have to establish the integrated communication with respect to the networks and actual connections in order to enable the full range of smart and connected functionalities of their integrated solutions [Kane *et al.* (2015); Porter and Heppelmann (2014)].

Fifth and finally, executives need to regularly revisit, realign and transform their digital solutions. In light of the fundamental character of the changes that digital transformation brings to many industries, executives need to be aware that experimentation is important in the early phases of digital initiatives [Iansiti and Lakhani (2014); Ross *et al.* (2017)]. On the one hand, the digital applications and markets continue to develop with customers continuously demanding new features. On the other hand, digital technology, such as sensors and connectivity solutions, are improved so regularly that they offer new opportunities in shorter periods than the typical cycle times of many established products, especially with respect to machinery in business-to-business markets. As such, executives need to balance the development of holistic long-term solutions and the pragmatic implementation of short-term to medium-term solutions with reduced functionality levels in order to achieve the full potential of digital transformation — now and in the future [Nambisan (2017); Rometty (2016)].

3.3. *Limitations and future research*

In light of the conceptual nature of this paper, there are several interesting avenues for further research, especially for qualitative and quantitative empirical studies.

First, concerning strategic renewal, future studies may examine the link between technology and market issues in transformation processes beyond digitalization [Harryson *et al.* (2008); Kim and Pennings (2009)]. Second, regarding digital transformation, there is a need for better understanding the relationship between smart solutions and integrated communication because the benefits of digital solutions often depend on seamless connectivity [Porter and Heppelmann (2014); Shukla *et al.* (2017)]. Third, concerning artificial intelligence, the interplay of hardware and software including various human–machine interfaces, especially voice recognition, deserves particular attention [Hirsch (2018); Teece (2018)], including the effect on leadership [Berman (2012); Muethel (2013)]. Fourth, regarding business model innovation, the choice of multiple business models for commercializing a single technology in the context of a variety of use cases needs further detailed studies [Berman (2012); Remane *et al.* (2017)].

4. Conclusion and Outlook

By now, nearly all firms have acknowledged the relevance of digital transformation and the strategic challenges that are associated with it. On this basis, many firms, especially from the manufacturing sector, have launched digitalization initiatives. So far, however, most of these initiatives have not achieved the initial objectives [Amit and Han (2017); Kane *et al.* (2015)]. For instance, firms are slow in implementing digital solutions, or new applications do not achieve the projected revenue streams. As a consequence, many firms have already redirected their digitalization initiatives — with limited success rates. Some of these managerial challenges are normal in light of the major transformations of digitalization [Andriole (2017); Iansiti and Lakhani (2014)]. Many other challenges, however, seem to derive from an inappropriate strategic emphasis of the digitalization initiatives, which tend to strongly focus on technology issues at the expense of market-related issues.

To avoid this lack of balance in managing digitalization, executives need to thoroughly consider the market-related challenges in the early stages of their firms' digitalization initiatives. Following the implementation steps that are suggested in this paper will ensure a sufficient emphasis on the core challenges related to finding the appropriate business model for digital products and services. Often, these digital products and services will be bundled in integrated solutions, and the different building blocks are jointly addressed with external partners [Porter and Heppelmann (2014)]. To succeed in digital transformation, firms will need to address the non-technological challenges first to arrive at concepts for profitable digital solutions [Kane *et al.* (2015)]. On this basis, the critical technology issues can be emphasized in order to facilitate smooth technology implementation. Only by complementing technology and market issues, firms will succeed in digital transformation — today and in the future.

References

Adegbesan, J. A. and Higgins, M. J. (2011). The intra-alliance division of value created through collaboration. *Strategic Management Journal*, **32**: 187–211.

Adner, R. and Kapoor, R. (2010). Value creation in innovation ecosystems: How the structure of technological interdependence affects firm performance in new technology generations. *Strategic Management Journal*, **31**: 306–333.

Adner, R. (2002). When are technologies disruptive? A demand-based view of the emergence of competition. *Strategic Management Journal*, **23**: 667–688.

Adner, R. (2006). Match your innovation strategy to your innovation ecosystem. *Harvard Business Review*, **84**: 98–107.

Agarwal, R. and Helfat, C. E. (2009). Strategic renewal of organizations. *Organization Science*, **20**: 281–293.

Agrawal, A. K., Gans, J. S. and Goldfarb, A. (2017). What to expect from artificial intelligence. *MIT Sloan Management Review*, **58**, 3: 23–26.

Agrawal, A., Gans, J. and Goldfarb, A. (2018a). Is your company's data actually valuable in the AI era? *Harvard Business Review Digital Articles*, 2–4.

Agrawal, A., Gans, J. and Goldfarb, A. (2018b). *Prediction Machines: The Simple Economics of Artificial Intelligence*, Harvard Business Review Press, Boston.

Ahn, M. J. (2014). Enhancing corporate governance in high-growth entrepreneurial firms. *International Journal of Innovation and Technology Management*, **11**: 1–16.

Al-Ansaari, Y., Pervan, S. and Xu, J. (2014). Exploiting innovation in Dubai SMEs: The effect of strategic orientation on organizational determinants. *International Journal of Innovation and Technology Management*, **11**, 1–22.

Amit, R. and Han, X. (2017). Value creation through novel resource configurations in a digitally enabled world. *Strategic Entrepreneurship Journal*, **11**: 228–248.

Andriole, S. J. (2017). Five myths about digital transformation. *MIT Sloan Management Review*, **58**, 3: 20–22.

Araújo Burcharth, A. L. de, Knudsen, M. P. and Sondergaard, H. A. (2014). Neither invented nor shared here: The impact and management of attitudes for the adoption of open innovation practices. *Technovation*, **34**: 149–161.

Aversa, P., Haefliger, S. and Reza, D. G. (2017). Building a winning business model portfolio. *MIT Sloan Management Review*, **58**: 49–54.

Azzone, G. and Manzini, R. (2008). Quick and dirty technology assessment: The case of an Italian Research Centre. *Technological Forecasting & Social Change*, **75**: 1324–1338.

Ben-Menahem, S. M., Kwee, Z., Volberda, H. W. and van den Bosch, F. A. J. (2013). Strategic renewal over time: The enabling role of potential absorptive capacity in aligning internal and external rates of change. *Long Range Planning*, **46**: 216–235.

Berman, S. J. (2012). Digital transformation: Opportunities to create new business models. *Strategy & Leadership*, **40**, 2: 16–24.

Bettis, R. A. (2017). Organizationally intractable decision problems and the intellectual virtues of heuristics. *Journal of Management*, **43**: 2620–2637.

Brem, A. and Bilgram, V. (2015). The search for innovative partners in co-creation: Identifying lead users in social media through netnography and crowdsourcing. *Journal of Engineering & Technology Management*, **37**: 40–51.

Bughin, J. (2017). The best response to digital disruption. *MIT Sloan Management Review*, **58**, 4: 80–86.

Capron, L. and Mitchell, W. (2009). Selection capability: How capability gaps and internal social frictions affect internal and external strategic renewal. *Organization Science*, **20**: 294–312.

Chao, R. O. and Kavadias, S. (2008). A theoretical framework for managing the new product development portfolio: When and how to use strategic buckets. *Management Science*, **54**: 907–921.

Chesbrough, H. (2003). *Open Innovation: The New Imperative for Creating and Profiting from Technology*, Harvard Business School Press, Boston.

Chesbrough, H. (2011). Bringing open innovation to services. *MIT Sloan Management Review*, **52**: 85–90.

Daim, T. U., Rueda, G., Martin, H. and Gerdsri, P. (2006). Forecasting emerging technologies: Use of bibliometrics and patent analysis. *Technological Forecasting & Social Change*, **73**: 981–1012.

Davenport, T. H. and Ronanki, R. (2018). Artificial intelligence for the real world. *Harvard Business Review*, **96**: 108–116.

Davenport, T. H. (2018). *AI Advantage: How to Put the Artificial Intelligence Revolution to Work*, MIT Press, Cambridge.

Dellermann, D., Fliaster, A. and Kolloch, M. (2017). Innovation risk in digital business models: The German energy sector. *Journal of Business Strategy*, **38**, 5: 35–43.

Demil, B. and Lecocq, X. (2010). Business model evolution: In search of dynamic consistency. *Long Range Planning*, **43**: 227–246.

Di Domenico, M., Daniel, E. and Nunan, D. (2014). 'Mental mobility' in the digital age: Entrepreneurs and the online home-based business. *New Technology, Work and Employment*, **29**: 266–281.

Do, T. H. (2014). Determinants of innovation commercialization management and anticipated returns: An exploratory typology of SMEs. *International Journal of Innovation and Technology Management*, **11**: 1–20.

Doz, Y. L. and Kosonen, M. (2010). Embedding strategic agility: A leadership agenda for accelerating business model renewal. *Long Range Planning*, **43**: 370–382.

Dubé, L., Du, P., McRae, C., Sharma, N., Jayaraman, S. and Nie, J.-Y. (2018). Convergent innovation in food through big data and artificial intelligence for societal-scale inclusive growth. *Technology Innovation Management Review*, **8**, 2: 49–65.

Giones, F. and Brem, A. (2017). Digital technology entrepreneurship: A definition and research agenda. *Technology Innovation Management Review*, **7**: 44–51.

Grosse-Kathoefer, D. and Leker, J. (2012). Knowledge transfer in academia: An exploratory study on the Not-Invented-Here Syndrome. *Journal of Technology Transfer*, **37**: 658–675.

Gupta, D., Gupta, R., Jain, K. and Monaya, K. S. (2017). Innovations in mobile value-added services: Findings from cases in India. *International Journal of Innovation and Technology Management*, **14**, 6: 1–27.

Harland, P. E. and Yörür, H. (2015). Decisions in product platform development projects. *International Journal of Innovation and Technology Management*, **12**: 1–24.

Harryson, S. J., Dudkowski, R. and Stern, A. (2008). Transformation networks in innovation alliances — the development of Volvo C70. *Journal of Management Studies*, **45**: 745–773.

Helfat, C. E. and Raubitschek, R. S. (2018). Dynamic and integrative capabilities for profiting from innovation in digital platform-based ecosystems. *Research Policy*, **47**, 8: 1391–1399.

Herzog, P. and Leker, J. (2010). Open and closed innovation — different innovation cultures for different strategies. *International Journal of Technology Management*, **52**: 322–343.

Hirsch, P. B. (2018). Tie me to the mast: Artificial intelligence & reputation risk management. *Journal of Business Strategy*, **39**, 1: 61–64.

Huang, M. H. and Rust, R. T. (2018). Artificial intelligence in service. *Journal of Service Research*, **21**, 2: 155–172.

Iansiti, M. and Lakhani, K. R. (2014). Digital ubiquity: How connections, sensors, and data are revolutionizing business. *Harvard Business Review*, **92**: 90–99.

Iansiti, M. and Lakhani, K. R. (2017). The truth about blockchain. *Harvard Business Review*, **95**: 118–127.

Ili, S. and Lichtenthaler, U. (2017). *FAQ Digital Transformation and Artificial Intelligence: 101 Questions - 101 Answers*, Ili Consulting, Karlsruhe.

Jacobides, M. G. and Billinger, S. (2006). Designing the boundaries of the firm: From "make, buy or ally" to the dynamic benefits of vertical architecture. *Organization Science*, **17**: 249–261.

Kane, G. C., Palmer, D., Phillips, A. H., Kiron, D. and Buckley, N. (2015). Strategy, not technology, drives digital transformation. *MIT Sloan Management Review*, Online.

Kavadias, S., Ladas, K. and Loch, C. (2016). Artificial intelligence is almost ready for business. *Harvard Business Review*, **94**: 91–98.

Kim, H. E. and Pennings, J. M. (2009). Innovation and strategic renewal in mature markets: A study of the tennis racket industry. *Organization Science*, **20**: 368–383.

Kleber, S. (2018). As AI meets the reputation economy, we're all being silently judged. *Harvard Business Review Digital Articles*, 1–5.

Klein, G. (2014). Evaluation of core and symbolic capabilities during due-diligence processes in new biotechnology firms. *International Journal of Innovation and Technology Management*, **11**: 1–20.

Knudsen, M. P. (2007). The relative importance of interfirm relationships and knowledge transfer for new product development success. *Journal of Product Innovation Management*, **24**: 117–138.

Kolbjornsrud, V., Amico, R. and Thomas, R. J. (2016). How artificial intelligence will redefine management. *Harvard Business Review Digital Articles*, 2–6.

Kwee, Z., van den Bosch, F. A. J. and Volberda, H. W. (2011). The influence of top management team's corporate governance orientation on strategic renewal trajectories: A longitudinal analysis of Royal Dutch Shell plc, 1907–2004. *Journal of Management Studies*, **48**: 984–1014.

Lee, A. H. I., Wang, W.-M. and Lin, T.-Y. (2010). An evaluation framework for technology transfer of new equipment in high technology industry. *Technological Forecasting and Social Change*, **77**: 135–150.

Lewrick, M., Link, P. and Leifer, L. (2018). *The Design Thinking Playbook: Mindful Digital Transformation of Teams, Products, Services, Businesses and Ecosystems*, Wiley, New York.

Li, Y.-R. (2009). The technological roadmap of Cisco's business ecosystem. *Technovation*, **29**: 379–386.

Lichtenthaler, U. (2016). Toward an innovation-based perspective on company performance. *Management Decision*, **54**: 66–87.

Lichtenthaler, U. (2017). Shared value innovation: Linking competitiveness and societal goals in the context of digital transformation. *International Journal of Innovation and Technology Management*, **14**: 1–14.

Lichtenthaler, U. (2020). Integrated intelligence: Combining human and artificial intelligence for competitive advantage. Campus: Frankfurt.

Loebbecke, C. and Picot, A. (2015). Reflections on societal and business model transformation arising from digitization and big data analytics: A research agenda. *Journal of Strategic Information Systems*, **24**: 149–157.

McAfee, A. and Brynjolfsson, E. (2012). Big data: The management revolution. *Harvard Business Review*, **90**: 60–68.

Meyer, M. (1999). Does science push technology? Patent citing scientific literature. *Research Policy*, **29**: 409–435.

Motohashi, K. and Yuan, Y. (2010). Productivity impact of technology spillover from multinationals to local firms: Comparing China's automobile and electronics industries. *Research Policy*, **39**: 790–798.

Muethel, M. (2013). Accepting global leadership responsibility: How leaders react to corporate social irresponsibility. *Organizational Dynamics*, **42**: 209–216.

Nambisan, S. and Sawhney, M. (2007). A buyer's guide to the innovation bazaar. *Harvard Business Review*, **85**: 109–118.

Nambisan, S. (2017). Digital entrepreneurship: Toward a digital technology perspective of entrepreneurship. *Entrepreneurship Theory & Practice*, **41**: 1029–1055.

Neubert, M. (2018). The impact of digitalization on the speed of internationalization of lean global startups. *Technology Innovation Management Review*, **8**: 5, 44–54.

Ng, A. (2016). What artificial intelligence can and can't do right now. *Harvard Business Review Digital Articles*, 2–4.

Oshri, I. and Weeber, C. (2006). Cooperation and competition standards-setting activities in the digitization era: The case of wireless information devices. *Technology Analysis & Strategic Management*, **18**: 265–283.

Perr, J., Appleyard, M. M. and Sullivan, P. (2010). Open for business: Emerging business models in open source software. *International Journal of Technology Management*, **52**: 432–456.

Phan, P., Wright, M. and Lee, S. H. (2017). Of robots, artificial intelligence, and work. *Academy of Management Perspectives*, **31**: 253–255.

Plastino, E. and Purdy, M. (2018). Game changing value from Artificial Intelligence: Eight strategies. *Strategy & Leadership*, **46**: 16–22.

Porter, M. E. and Heppelmann, J. E. (2014). How smart, connected products are transforming competition. *Harvard Business Review*, **92**: 64–88.

Porter, M. E. and Heppelmann, J. E. (2015). How smart, connected products are transforming companies. *Harvard Business Review*, **93**: 96–114.

Remane, G., Hanelt, A., Nickerson, R. C. and Kolbe, L. M. (2017). Discovering digital business models in traditional industries. *Journal of Business Strategy*, **38**, 2: 41–51.

Richter, C., Kraus, S., Brem, A., Durst, S. and Giselbrecht, C. (2017). Digital entrepreneurship: Innovative business models for the sharing economy. *Creativity and Innovation Management*, **26**: 300–310.

Rodrigues-Alves, M. F. (2018). Literature on organizational innovation: Past and future. *Innovation & Management Review*, **15**, 1: 2–19.

Rohrbeck, R., Hölzle, K. and Gemünden, H. G. (2009). Opening up for competitive advantage — How Deutsche Telekom creates an open innovation ecosystem. *R&D Management*, **39**: 420–430.

Rometty, G. (2016). Digital today, cognitive tomorrow. *MIT Sloan Management Review*, **58**, 1: 168–171.

Ross, J. W., Beath, C. M. and Sebastian, I. M. (2017). How to develop a great digital strategy. *MIT Sloan Management Review*, **58**, 2: 7–9.

Sarkkinen, M. and Kässi, T. (2015). Predictive modeling of innovation capability in a regional context. *International Journal of Innovation and Technology Management*, **12**: 1–25.

Schmoch, U. (2007). Double-boom cycles and the comeback of science-push and market-pull. *Research Policy*, **36**: 1000–1015.

Schrage, M. (2017). 4 models for using AI to make decisions. *Harvard Business Review Digital Articles*, 1–6.

Shukla, P., Wilson, H. J., Alter, A. and Lavieri, D. (2017). Machine reengineering: Robots and people working smarter together. *Strategy & Leadership*, **45**, 6: 50–54.

Spaeth, S., Stuermer, M. and Krogh, G. von (2010). Enabling knowledge creation through outsiders: Towards a push model of open innovation. *International Journal of Technology Management*, **52**: 411–431.

Teece, D. J. (2018). Profiting from innovation in the digital economy: Enabling technologies, standards, and licensing models in the wireless world. *Research Policy*, **47**, 8: 1367–1387.

Trabucchi, D., Buganza, T. and Pellizzoni, E. (2017). Give away your digital services. *Research Technology Management*, **60**, 2: 43–52.

Tripsas, M. and Gavetti, G. (2000). Capabilities, cognition, and inertia: Evidence from digital imaging. *Strategic Management Journal*, **21**: 1147–1162.

Tripsas, M. (2009). Technology, identity, and inertia through the lens of "The Digital Photography Company". *Organization Science*, **20**: 441–460.

Tura, N., Hannola, L. and Pynnönen, M. (2017). Agile methods for boosting the commercialization process of new technology. *International Journal of Innovation and Technology Management*, **14**, 3: 1–23.

Verganti, R. and Buganza, T. (2005). Design inertia: Designing for life-cycle flexibility in internet-based services. *Journal of Product Innovation Management*, **22**: 223–237.

Westerman, G. and Bonnet, D. (2015). Revamping your business through digital transformation. *MIT Sloan Management Review*, **56**: 10–13.

Wilson, H. J., Daugherty, P. and Bianzino, N. (2017). The jobs that artificial intelligence will create. *MIT Sloan Management Review*, **58**, 4: 14–16.

Yoo, Y., Boland Jr. R. J., Lyytinen, K. and Majchrzak, A. (2012). Organizing for innovation in the digitized world. *Organization Science*, **23**: 1398–1408.

Zott, C. and Amit, R. (2008). The fit between product market strategy and business model: Implications for firm performance. *Strategic Management Journal*, **29**: 1–26.

Zott, C., Amit, R. and Massa, L. (2011). The business model: Recent developments and future research. *Journal of Management*, **37**: 1019–1042.

Biography

Ulrich Lichtenthaler is a Professor of Management and Entrepreneurship at International School of Management (ISM) in Cologne, Germany. He holds a Ph.D. degree in technology management and further is an executive consultant, who has successfully completed over 20 digital transformation and AI projects in recent years. He has taught executive education courses at leading business schools, and he has written multiple books and articles for journals and newspapers. He further is author of the recent book 'Integrated Intelligence: Combining Human and Artificial Intelligence for Competitive Advantage'.

Chapter 14

Global Diffusion of Innovation during the Fourth Industrial Revolution: The Case of Additive Manufacturing or 3D Printing

Harm-Jan Steenhuis*, Xin Fang† and Tolga Ulusemre‡

Hawaii Pacific University
College of Business 900 Fort St. Mall
Suite 600, Honolulu, HI 96813, USA
*hsteenhuis@hpu.edu
†xfang@hpu.edu
‡tulusemre@hpu.edu

Additive manufacturing can be considered an innovative and high-technology and one of its characteristics is that it has limited dependency on the location. The purpose of this study is to examine this aspect by investigation how additive manufacturing is spreading globally. The focus is on established manufacturers of industrial additive manufacturing machines. It was found that the early-stage diffusion of this technology is primarily in advanced economies. Furthermore, many of the currently established companies that manufacture industrial 3D printers come from already existing companies that expanded into AM or that led to spin-off companies. The complexity of AM which requires expert knowledge across a range of fields may be the key reason for this finding. Recommendations for further research are provided.

Keywords: Additive manufacturing; 3D printing; industrialization; technological development; innovation.

1. Introduction

After the first industrial revolution based on steam power from roughly 1790 until 1840, a second industrial revolution based on electricity from roughly 1890 to 1930, and a third industrial revolution based on informatics which started around 1970 [von Tunzelmann (1997)], the world is currently experiencing a fourth industrial revolution that started at the turn of the century [Schwab (2016)]. This fourth revolution is

---

*Corresponding author.

This chapter was originally published in *International Journal of Innovation and Technology Management*, Vol. 17, No. 1, February 2020, published by World Scientific Publishing, Singapore. Reprinted with permission.

fundamentally different from the previous three as it is based not on a technology but on the fusion of technologies and their interactions across the physical, digital and biological domains [Schwab (2016)]. One of the drivers of this revolution is additive manufacturing (AM), also known as 3D printing [Schwab (2016)].

Although AM is not just one technology, i.e. there are seven process categories [Redwood *et al.* (2017)], these seven categories share a commonality namely that AM involves a process of additively building up a part one layer at a time [Redwood *et al.* (2017)]. The AM industry in 2016 had a size of roughly $6 billion [Wohlers Associates (2017)] and it is expected to grow to almost $24 billion by 2025 [Grand View Research (2018)]. Manufacturing with AM provides several advantages such as cost benefits and simpler processes to produce complex products [Atzeni *et al.* (2010)] and these characteristics have a range of implications across many industries [Steenhuis and Pretorius (2017); Caviggioli and Ughetto (2019)].

AM has been the topic of academic studies related to business, for instance, through special issues in 2016 (Technological Forecasting and Social Change [Ford *et al.* (2016)] and the Journal of Manufacturing Technology Management [Ortt (2016)]) as well as in 2017 (the International Journal of Physical Distribution & Logistics Management [Rogers *et al.* (2017)] and the Journal of Manufacturing Technology Management [Ortt (2017)]) and also in 2018 (the International Journal of Manufacturing Technology and Management [Rayna and Striukova (2018)]. Since AM is not just one technology but a bundle, and because it has a variety of aspects, studies have looked at AM from many different perspectives. Some studies have looked at the economics of AM, e.g. Atzeni and Salmi [2012] and Niaki *et al.* [2019], improvements in production [Marzi *et al.* (2018)] and many studies have looked at AM in the context of the supply chain, e.g. Oettmeier and Hofmann [2016], Chan *et al.* [2018], Martinsuo and Luomaranta [2018] and Fratocchi [2018] and related to the business models, e.g. Öberg *et al.* [2018], Woodson *et al.* [2019], as well as how AM can be disruptive, e.g. Rayna and Striukova [2016] and Beltagui *et al.* [2020]. Other areas that have received attention are the consumer or prosumer side of things, e.g. de Jong and de Bruijn [2013], Fox [2014], Matias and Rao [2015], Steenhuis and Pretorius [2016], Halbinger [2018], Kleer and Piller [2019] and law and intellectual property [Ballardini *et al.* (2018); Kannattukunnel (2016)] or society related issues, e.g. Smith [2017], Matos and Jacinto [2019]. What has received less attention is the geography of the AM innovation, i.e. how it has spread. This geography aspect is the topic of this paper. Next, in Sec. 2 the literature on innovation will be covered and the research questions are developed. This is followed by an explanation of the methodology used in Sec. 3, the findings in Sec. 4 are followed by a discussion in Sec. 5. The conclusion is provided in Sec. 6.

2. Innovation

Innovation is important for society and is often considered a key factor in economic development [Porter (2003); Artz *et al.* (2010)]. As such, policies on innovation, e.g. Wydra [2015], Morgan and Nauwelaers [2003] as well as the processes of innovation diffusion, e.g. Ortt and Schoormans [2004] and Rogers [1995] and innovation adoption, e.g. Hossain *et al.* [2016], Adams *et al.* [2017]; Ebrahimi Sarcheshmeh *et al.* [2018] and Baiyegunhi *et al.* [2019], have received significant academic attention. High technology has received specialized attention as the adoption of high technology adds several complications to the adoption process, see e.g. Chiesa and Frattini [2011], Moore [2014] and Aarikka-Stenroos and Lehtimäki [2014]. Although the definition of high technology is far from straight forward [Hooton (2018)], AM can be considered high technology due to the newness, novelty and complexity.

Additive manufacturing provides a fairly unique (high) technology situation to study in the context of innovation and geography. This is because 3D printers are used in the production process, that is, can be considered machine tools. The machine tool industry is often considered an important industry for industrial and economic development [Kaplan (1987); Saxena and Sharma (2014)]. This explains why locations with less developed machine tool industries are less economically developed. However, AM has a very low dependency on location [Gress and Kalafsky (2015); Hannibal and Knight (2018)] and can be applied in virtually any location. For instance, AM has been used in a rural location in Nepal that was struck by an earthquake [Scott and Simple (2015)], it has been used in the Sahara desert [Nikolov (2017)], and even in space [Goldstein (2018)]. Furthermore, regions that are challenged by a limited spread of manufacturing can benefit from do-it-yourself (DIY) [Fox (2014)] which is enhanced by AM. For instance, in the US AM has led to maker societies [Anderson (2012)]. Another peculiarity of AM is that it can replicate itself, i.e. a 3D printer can be used to print additional 3D printers [Jones *et al.* (2011)].

With a goal to examine the spread of the AM innovation, this study, therefore, deals with elements of innovation and diffusion. Academic research on innovation and its diffusion can be separated in a few main research streams that have been developed historically. One research stream is that of the origin of innovation. This can be seen as the supply side of innovation. Main theoretical views on the origin or the process of innovation include the linear model, see Fig. 1, with its origins traced back to the first half of the 20th century [Godin (2006)] and the chain-linked model [Kline and Rosenberg (1986)]. Subsequent studies have reassessed the validity of these theoretical models, e.g. Balconi *et al.* [2010] or suggested modifications such as the cyclic innovation model [Berkhout *et al.* (2006)] and the multi-channel interactive learning model [Caraça *et al.* (2009)]. Studies have also focused on specific actors in the innovation process such as the importance of lead users [Von Hippel

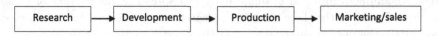

Fig. 1.   Linear model of innovation.

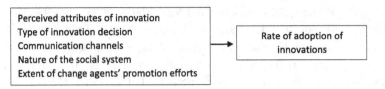

Fig. 2.   Innovation diffusion variables, adopted from Rogers [1995].

(1986)] and the role of universities [Jaffe (1989)]. Research continues in each of these aspects of the innovation process which have led to refinements in understanding, see for example on the lead user aspect [Von Hippel (2005); Hienerth *et al.* (2014); Kankanhalli *et al.* (2015); Brem *et al.* (2018)] and on the role of universities [Cowan and Zinovyeva (2013); Chen *et al.* (2019)].

Another important research stream is that of the diffusion of innovation. This can be viewed as the demand side of innovation. A comprehensive view is provided by Rogers [1995], see Fig. 2. This stream of research examines the process by which users adopt an innovation. Some studies relate to narrower models compared to Rogers [1995] such as the Technology Acceptance Model which is specific to the acceptance by users of information technology [Davis (1989)]. Research on innovation diffusion is extensive and has many different angles. Recent studies cover for instance diffusion of innovations with specific characteristics such as frugal innovation [Hossain *et al.* (2016)] or energy technologies [Hyysalo *et al.* (2017)], diffusion in a particular industry such as automotive [Schulze *et al.* (2015)], and decision maker characteristics for example relating to the not-invented-here syndrome [Hannen *et al.* (2019)]. Research into the diffusion of innovation related to technology platforms [Fichman (2004); Cenamor *et al.* (2013)] provides an overlap with studies on the origin of innovation as in particular open-source platforms provide insight into both the creation as well as the diffusion of technology [Foster and Heeks (2013); Kwak *et al.* (2018); Oh and Hong (2018)].

A third related stream of research into innovation and its diffusion is that of commercialization of the innovation in the context of business which relates to entrepreneurship and intrapreneurship. Examples of topics that are investigated in this research area are academic entrepreneurs and what makes them start companies [Krabel and Mueller (2009)], how universities can help [Fini *et al.* (2011)] and the type of companies created [Pirnay *et al.* (2003); Minshall and Wicksteed (2005); O'Shea *et al.* (2005)]. Similar studies exist for other types of research organization [Clarysse *et al.* (2005); Khanagha *et al.* (2018)] as well as for corporate spin-off companies [Yeganegi *et al.* (2016)].

The purpose of this study is to look at a recent high-technology innovation, i.e. additive manufacturing, and examine its global spread in the context of business situations. Based on the three identified research streams related to the diffusion of innovations, the current study relates to the overlap of these three areas as illustrated in Fig. 3.

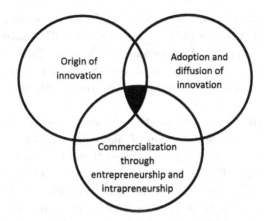

Fig. 3.   Identification of the research area.

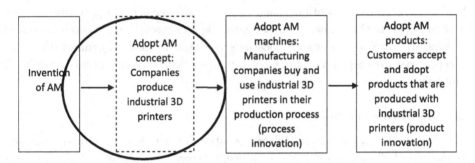

Fig. 4.   Focus of the research.

The focus is on the location of innovative companies that produce and sell these new, industrial type, AM machines. Specifically, the central research question is: where are the successful companies that develop and sell industrial AM machines located? The emphasis is on exploring where and how these companies were formed. This is illustrated in Fig. 4.

Figure 4 illustrates that there are different stages of adoption of AM. After the invention of AM, the first stage of adoption is that of companies that adopt the idea or concept of AM and use it to produce industrial 3D printers. This is indicated with a dotted line box in Fig. 4 to emphasize the unusual nature of this step. This is because AM machines are created which are then used to produce products rather than immediately creating final products. The next stage is where companies accept and adopt AM by acquiring an industrial 3D printer for their production process, see e.g. Schniederjans [2017], Candi and Beltagui [2019], Marak *et al.* [2019]. This adoption of AM is going slowly and can be viewed as dealing with the chasm that occurs with diffusion of high technology [Moore (2014)]. The communication efforts of the companies that produce industrial 3D printers typically relate to explaining how AM can be (financially) beneficial for manufacturing companies. The last stage of adoption is that of customers who adopt or accept a 3D printed product [Norman *et al.* (2017); Lyu *et al.* (2018); Anastasiadou and Vettese (2019)]. This adoption also faces difficulties, for instance, the acceptance of 3D printed houses is faced with challenges because of uncertainties related to the safety, durability, etc. of 3D printed construction.

It is important to stress that the study is not focused on the adoption of 3D printed products, nor on the adoption of industrial 3D printers. The connection between Figs. 3 and 4 is that typical studies that focus on the "creation" of an innovation are on the left side of Fig. 4. Studies that focus on the diffusion of innovation are typically dealing with the right two blocks of Fig. 4. Studies that focus on commercialization through entrepreneurship or intrapreneurship typically focus on the first and third blocks in Fig. 4. The goal of the study is to determine the location of the production of industrial 3D printers and to subsequently investigate the reason behind this location which relates to the second and partially the first block in Fig. 4. In the following sub-sections, the four research questions and related theories are covered: innovative locations (covered in Sec. 2.1), innovation and entrepreneurship (Sec. 2.2), spin-off companies (Sec. 2.3) and academic spin-off companies (Sec. 2.4).

2.1. *Innovative locations*

It has long been recognized that different locations have different innovative outputs [Feldman and Florida (1994)]. For instance, a typical example of a location that is considered very innovative is Silicon Valley. It has also been established that higher innovation rates, in terms of patents, are linked to higher productivity levels that support higher wages [Porter (2003)]. What has been a focus in academic studies is to find out why these differences occur which has led to numerous studies in the field, see e.g. de la Mothe and Paquet [1998], Feldman [1994], Audretsch and Feldman [1996], Audretsch [1998], Kuchiki and Tsuji [2010] and Zanello *et al.* [2016]. Porter and Stern [2001] sum up the main conclusion: "the vitality of innovation in a location is shaped by national innovative capacity". This national innovative capacity relates to three broad elements: the common innovation infrastructure, the cluster-specific environment for innovation and the quality of linkages [Porter and Stern (2001)]. What this means is that for example the presence of research universities [Mowery and Ziedonis (2014)] but also the agglomeration and proximity of companies, see Kuchiki and Tsuji [2010] and Balland *et al.* [2015], and people, see Orlando and Verba [2005], play a role in creating innovations and related to this economic development for instance through higher income levels. Note that for instance Varga [1998] found for the US that there are four tiers of Metropolitan Statistical Areas (MSA) and that while a $0.5 million university research spending can be expected to yield 20 innovations in an average top MSA, this value is only 2 in the fourth tier MSA. Based on the above, when looking at the national level it can be expected that most innovations take place in already developed nations and/or nations that have well-developed technologies. Consequently, it can be expected that innovative companies that operate in the AM industries are located in those countries. However, developed nations may, due to for example outsourcing of certain activities have eroded their industrial commons and consequently may have lost the critical mass of work, skills and scientific knowledge [Pisano and Shih (2009)]. Also, AM may have less dependency on location. Thus, AM may not fit the general pattern. The first research question deals with this issue and is formulated as follows: in what type of countries are AM companies located?

2.2. *Age of companies*

Aside from the issue of the type of country where innovation occurs or is diffused/adopted, another issue is the type of firm that exhibits innovative behavior. This relates to the size or age of the firm. These two variables are connected, i.e. companies less than 10 years old tend to be smaller while companies over 10 years old tend to be larger [Breitzman and Hicks (2008)]. Entrepreneurs, in the sense of new firms, are often viewed as a main source for innovation, see e.g. Miller and Garnsey [2000], and young firms rather than small firms make the largest contribution to job creation [Coad *et al.* (2016)]. However, data for instance for the US reveals that roughly 60% of private-sector innovations originate in large businesses, i.e. more than 500 employees, and only 16% in firms with fewer than 25 employees [Breitzman and Hicks (2008); Information Technology & Innovation Foundation (2016)]. Also, young firms are less persistent in their innovative behavior [García-Quevedo *et al.* (2014)]. However, younger [Balasubramanian and Lee (2008)] and smaller [Breitzman and Hicks (2008); Shane (2016)] firms tend to be more productive in terms of innovations. This leads to the second research question: what types of companies are active in the industrial AM industry, in particular in terms of age?

2.3. *Origin of companies*

As discussed in Sec. 2.2, while some industrial AM companies may have already been established, i.e. larger and older, some companies in this new and innovative field may be new, i.e. a start-up situation. Establishment of new firms is an important mechanism through which entrepreneurs use technology to bring new products into existence [Shane (2001)]. There are different types of start-up companies such as university- and company spinoffs, see e.g. Lindhold Dahlstrand [1997] and Wennberg *et al.* [2011]. Schramm [2018] identified three types of start-up companies and provides the following rough estimation in terms of percentages of start-up firms: 5% of entrepreneurs are what many people think of as start-ups, that is, companies created by young high-tech wizards such as Bill Gates (Microsoft), Steve Jobs (Apple) and Mark Zukerberg (Facebook). 15% of the entrepreneurs are company employees in spin-out situations either because the existing company decides to dispose that line of business or because the employees decide to strike out on their own due to lack of support in the company for a new idea, product or service. 80% of startups are replicative, i.e. copy an already existing idea. Half of those are created as franchises, the other half are unaffiliated retail businesses. While this last category of firms is unlikely to occur in the AM industry, the first two categories, i.e. high tech entrepreneurs and spin-out situations are more likely to occur [Goehrke (2019)]. Entrepreneurs seem to particularly have a role in the formation of entirely new industries around technological innovation [Miller and Garnsey (2000)]. This could apply to the AM industry. In terms of spin-off start-ups, previous research from Sweden on technology-based firms concluded that as many as two-thirds of the spin-offs had originated in private firms, and only one-sixth from universities [Lindhold Dahlstrand (1997)]. However, another study indicated that about 55% of new technology-based firms were academic spin-offs while 45% were corporate spin-offs [Löfsten and Lindelöf (2005)]. This leads to the third research question: for those AM companies that were start-ups, what type of startup situation do they represent?

2.4. *Academic spin-off companies*

A specific type of start-up situation is the academic spin-off company. With the basic idea of knowledge economies, universities are considered an important source of innovative activity [Miyata (2000)] and component of regional economic development [Steenhuis and Gray (2006); Trani and Holsworth (2010)]. Universities play a role in firm creation, e.g. through academic spin-off companies [Steffensen *et al.* (1999); Fini *et al.* (2011); Ferretti *et al.* (2019)] but also in other forms of knowledge spillovers [Khanagha *et al.* (2018); Mowery and Ziedonis (2014); Hsu and Yuan (2013)]. For instance, one study found that the number of graduates of a university is the main source of university spillovers that explains new business location near universities [Acosta *et al.* (2011)]. Another study found that local pools of graduates in biophysical sciences did not have a significant impact on the location choice of academic entrepreneurs [Kolympiris *et al.* (2015)]. Also, new knowledge and technology-based firms in general, i.e. not necessarily academic spin-off companies, have a high propensity to locate close to universities [Audretsch *et al.* (2005)]. There are different definitions for academic spin-off companies, mostly relating to whether technology and/or people related to a university are at the core of the new company [Carayannis *et al.* (1998); Pirnay *et al.* (2003)]. In this study, the people connection is used and therefore academic spin-offs are those where people connected to a university start a new company.

It has previously been established that universities with higher quality research tend to be more innovative [Miyata (2000); Zahringer *et al.* (2017)]. Similarly, academic spin-offs are more likely to occur for more eminent universities [Di Gregorio and Shane (2003)]. Research has also shown that many academic entrepreneurs locate spin-off companies close to the university but that academic entrepreneurs at later stages of their career are considerably more likely to start their firm away from their academic homes. This leads to the fourth research question: from what type (level) of university did the academic spin-off companies originate? And, related to this, is the spin-off located in the university's vicinity?

3. Methodology

The research questions posed, and thus the study in general, are exploratory in nature. The purpose is to look at a recent high technology innovation, i.e. additive manufacturing, and look at its global spread in the context of established innovative companies that develop, produce and sell industrial type AM machines. In this regard, four research questions were formulated related to: in what types of countries the companies are located, their age, for new companies the type of start-up, and for academic start-ups the type of university it relates to and whether it is located in the vicinity of the university.

There are five main research strategies, i.e. survey, experiment, case study, grounded theory approach and desk research [Verschuren and Doorewaard (2005)]. Since the data that is sought is mostly secondary data, the desk research strategy was selected.

The focus in the study is on established companies that produce industrial AM machines. This means, there has to be some recognition of their established position. To determine the sample for the study, a main industry source [Wohlers Associates (2017)] was used which identifies the important globally established companies. A total of 33 companies are recognized in Wohlers Associates [2017]; however, three of these have become subsidiaries of other companies. Arcam and Concept Laser were both acquired by GE Additive [Anderson Goehrke (2016)] while Solidscape was acquired by Stratasys [Andorka (2011)]. Therefore, the sample for the study contains 30 companies, as shown in Table 1.

Data were mainly collected from company websites. Most of the established companies that produce industrial 3D printers have websites that include a section on their location, start-up history, etc. Where necessary, additional information was sought by searching online. Stories, for example interviews with company founders, frequently appeared in industry newsletters such as: 3dprint (https://3dprint.com), 3dprintingindustry (www.3dprintingindustry.com/), All3DP (https://all3dp.com), Fabbaloo (www.fabbaloo.com) and Sculpteo (www.sculpteo.com/en/).

To determine the type of country, three sources were used. The World Bank provides a classification of economies based on the income level, i.e. Gross National Income (GNI) per capita. Four types of economies are distinguished in terms of GNI/capita: Low-income countries ($1025 or less), lower middle income ($1026–$4035), upper middle income ($4036–$12 475), and high income ($12 476 or more)

Table 1.   Sample of established industrial AM companies.

North American companies	European companies	Other
Carbon	Additive Industries	Aspect
Cincinnatti	AddUp	Carima
Envision TEC	DWS Systems	Farsoon
ExONE	EOS	Stratasys
Formlabs	Lithoz	Tiertime
GE Additive	Mcor	Xery
HP	Prodways	
Markforged	ReaLizer	
Optomec	Renishaw	
Skiaky	Sisma	
3D Systems	SLM Solutions	
	Trumpf	
	Voxeljet	

[World Bank (2017)]. Therefore, the World Bank's World Development Indicators [World Bank (2017)] is used as one source to classify countries. Another type of classification is provided by Porter [1990] who classifies economies based on the sources in an economy that cause its industries to be internationally competitive. The World Economic Forum (WEF) applies this distinction of factor-driven, efficiency-driven and innovation-driven economies and, therefore, the WEF's Global Competitiveness Report [World Economic Forum (2017)] is used for determining this classification. Since the topic, AM, can be considered high-technology, another source used for country classification is the high-technology indicators [Porter *et al.* (2008)]. This source provides country rankings in terms of high technology.

For the universities, two world rankings were used: the QS World University Ranking 2018[a] and the Times Higher Education World University Rankings 2018.[b] Both of these are established rankings that provide insight into the (perceived) quality and eminence of the universities. Additional variables such as age, and the type of start-up were determined from the available data, i.e. company websites, and thus these were not related to one main source. Based on the above description and data presented below, there is a high reliability of the study, i.e. the findings can easily be checked and the study repeated with the same result.

4. Findings

The four research questions are answered below, i.e. country of companies (Sec. 4.1), age of companies (Sec. 4.2), type of start-up (Sec. 4.3), universities for academic

---

[a] https://www.topuniversities.com/university-rankings/world-university-rankings/2018.

[b] https://www.timeshighereducation.com/world-university-rankings/2018/world-ranking#!/page/0/length/25/sort_by/rank/sort_order/asc/cols/stats.

start-ups (Sec. 4.4). In each of these sections, the findings are presented and discussed in the context of the literature.

4.1. *Location of the companies*

The location of the main industrial 3D printer companies is shown in Fig. 5. This illustrates that there is a concentration in Europe and in the US. Additionally, there are some companies located in Asia. In the analysis, one company, i.e. Stratasys, was determined to be located in Israel. This is somewhat debatable. Stratasys was initially founded in the US. In 2012, Stratasys merged with Israel-based Object and the new headquarters were determined to be in Israel. That is why, in Table 1 and Fig. 5, Stratasys was classified as a company that is located in Israel. There is no prominent 3D printer company in Latin America, Africa or Australia. Companies in the US are mostly on the east side of the country.

Table 2 shows the number of companies per country and the classification of the country. This shows that in terms of country location, established AM companies are mostly in advanced countries. The one exception is China which has a lower income level, and is also at the efficiency-driven stage instead of the innovation-driven stage. There is some linkage of the Chinese companies and other countries, see also Fig. 6. For instance, Farsoon is a company that operates in the field of powder bed fusion, more specifically selective laser sintering. Farsoon's founder Xu Xiaoshu is a Chinese

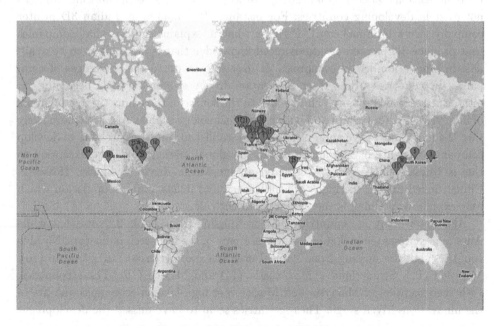

Fig. 5.   Location of established industrial AM companies.

Table 2.   Countries in which established industrial AM companies are located.

Country	Number of companies	Stage of development based on GNI	Stage of development based on source	High technology ranking
USA	11	High income	Innovation-driven	2
Germany	5	High income	Innovation-driven	3
China	3	Upper-middle income	Efficiency-driven	1
Italy	2	High income	Innovation-driven	17
France	2	High income	Innovation-driven	5
Ireland	1	High income	Innovation-driven	14
Israel	1	High income	Innovation-driven	18
Austria	1	High income	Innovation-driven	n.a.
Netherlands	1	High income	Innovation-driven	9
South Korea	1	High income	Innovation-driven	6
UK	1	High income	Innovation-driven	7
Japan	1	High income	Innovation-driven	4

American who worked as technology director for several American leading laser sintering manufacturing companies before founding Farsoon.[c]

The comparison with the high-tech indicators ranking in Table 2 shows that many of the companies are based in countries that have top high-technology standing ranking.

These findings show that although AM has less dependence on location [Gress and Kalafsky (2015); Hannibal and Knight (2018), the established companies are still confirming theories that explain that advanced economies are more likely to have innovations [Zanello et al. (2016)]. However, this does not mean that AM does not exist in developing countries. For instance, Brahma3 is an Indian 3D printer company (www.brahma3.com). Perhaps what it explains more is that companies that produce 3D printers need advanced knowledge that is more likely to be available in innovation-driven economies. It may also relate to the challenges of companies in countries other than innovation-driven economies with becoming an established global company. This relates to the source of the competitive advantage of industries [Porter (1990)] and with a high technology such as AM, it is more likely that the most innovative and economically established countries are able to develop companies that are main competitors in the global marketplace. The exception to this is China, which is not considered an innovation-driven economy. However, China ranked first in the high-tech indicators, and it has a large population which may explain why China is the exception to the rule.

Also noteworthy are countries that are missing from Table 2. Note that while Austria is represented in Table 2, it was not part of the high-tech indicators. Notable countries that are missing from Table 2 are: Singapore (ranked 8th), Taiwan (10), Malaysia (11), Switzerland (12), Canada (15) and Mexico (16). These countries, with the exception of Malaysia and Mexico, are high-income economies and are in the innovation-driven stage. These countries seem to have missed the development

---

[c] https://www.crunchbase.com/person/xiaoshu-xu.

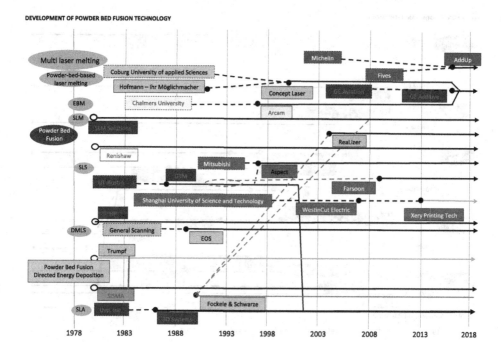

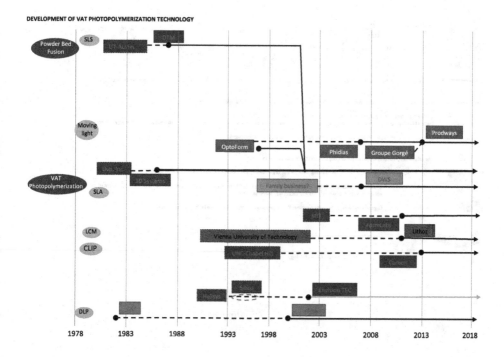

Fig. 6. Historical development of industrial 3D printer companies in different AM technologies.

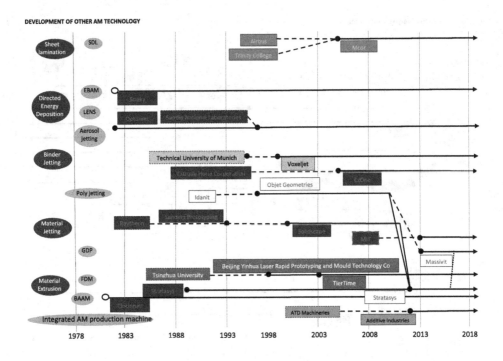

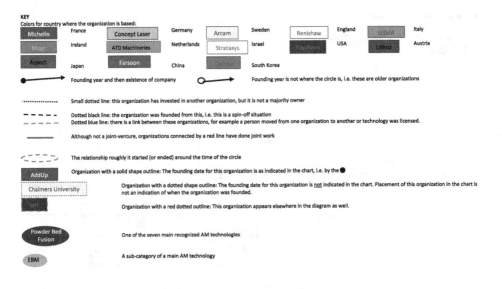

Fig. 6.   (*Continued*)

of this new industry. Part of the explanation for this might be the sample selection, i.e. the main companies that produce industrial 3D printers. There are additional companies that are in an early life stage and/or have not yet established themselves. Some of these companies are located in Singapore, Taiwan and Switzerland [Wohlers Associates (2017)]. Nevertheless, Malaysia, Canada and Mexico are among the countries that are underrepresented in terms of companies that produce industrial 3D printers. Another part of the explanation may be the reasoning behind the high-technology indicators ranking. This high technology ranking is that of technological standing which is defined as an indicator of a country's recent overall success in exporting high technology products [Porter *et al.* (2008)]. This measure has an emphasis on electronics as this is assumed to be a vital contributor to much of the high-technology development in recent years [Porter *et al.* (2008)]. However, it is not clear whether there is a correlation between success in electronics and success in additive manufacturing equipment. Hence, the ranking of high-technology countries may not be that applicable to the design, development and production of industrial 3D printers.

It is also noteworthy that within the US, the companies are mostly oriented in the north-east region and the number of companies in for example the Silicon Valley area is limited.

4.2. *Age of the companies*

The second research question focuses on the age of companies. It is important to provide a little context about "the age" of additive manufacturing. There is some controversy over the initial AM invention. For example, the laser curing approach actually originated in Japan in 1980 by Dr. Kodama from the Nagoya Municipal Industrial Research Institute who initially applied for a patent in 1980 but the full application was not submitted on time and there were also French inventors who had earlier ideas but did not accomplish a patent [Fabbaloo (2018)]. The result is that the initial three main patents that were granted in the area of additive manufacturing were established about 30–35 years ago. Vat Photopolymerization technology, US Patent 4575330 for Chuck Hill founder of 3D systems, is from 1984. The initial material extrusion technology, US Patent 5121329 for Scott Crump co-founder of Stratasys, is from 1989. And, the initial powder bed fusion technology, US Patent 4863538, is from 1989 for Carl Deckard who was at the University of Texas at Austin. In this context, Table 3 shows the age of established AM companies. This table shows for companies that were 20 years or younger age groups based on five-year intervals. An additional category was added for the companies that were 20–30 years old. Companies that were older than that were grouped together. In addition to Table 3, Fig. 6 provides an overview of the history of the companies by the AM process in which they are active.

Table 3 shows that 70% of the companies are 10 or more years old, 40% of the companies are 20 or more years old, while 30% of the companies are 30 or more years

Table 3.   Age of established industrial AM companies.

Age group	Companies
Founded 2013 or later	5
Founded 2008–2012	4
Founded 2003–2007	6
Founded 1998–2002	3
Founded 1988–1997	3
Founded 1987 or earlier	9

old. Only 17% of the companies are five or less years old. This confirms the innovative behavior of older firms [García-Quevedo *et al.* (2014)]. Since the sample is based on established companies, this is not necessarily surprising. However, what is noteworthy is that there are several companies that are relatively old but that are active in this innovative and high technology industry. The nine companies that were established before 1987 are: Cincinnatti (established 1890), HP (1939), Optomec (1982), Renishaw (1973), Skiaky (1939), Sisma (1961), SLM Solutions (1863), Trumpf (1923) and 3D Systems (1986). As discussed above, 3D Systems was an initial patent holder and started by Chuck Hill. The other eight companies all existed before the first AM patent was granted. They were operating in different industries and all demonstrate innovative behavior that led them to enter the new AM industry.

4.3. *Origin of the companies*

As discussed in Sec. 2.3, five types of origins of companies can be distinguished: existing companies that expanded into AM, the traditional start-up company, a start-up company that is the result of a corporate spin-off, and a start-up company that is the result of an academic spin-off company. Companies can also be founded as the result of a merger or acquisition. It should be noted that in a few instances, it is challenging to classify a company because it could be categorized in different ways. For example, GE Additive was categorized under corporate spin-off because it was founded in 2007 as a new business which resulted from a spin-off from GE Aviation. However, it could be argued that this is an existing business because GE has existed for a considerable time. It could also be argued that this can be categorized under the merger and acquisition category because GE Additive more or less immediately acquired two existing 3D printer companies. The reason that it was classified as a corporate spin-off and not an existing business is because it was established as a separate entity. The reason that it was not classified as a merger/acquisition is because the acquisitions were done by GE Additive and did not lead to a new entity. Another example is Stratasys. This company was categorized as a "traditional" start-up company. This is because the founder of Stratasys was basically working

Table 4.   Origin of the established industrial AM companies.

Company origin source	Number of companies
Existing company that expanded into AM	8
Merger/acquisition	2
"Traditional" start-up	1
Corporate spin-off company	13
Academic spin-off company	6

from his garage when he invented one of the key 3D printing technologies and as a result founded the company in 1989. In 2012, Stratasys and Objet merged. However, since the merged company continued under the same name and since it was essentially the combination of two existing businesses and not the creation of an entirely new business, it was decided not to include Stratasys in the merger/acquisition category. The resulting classification is illustrated in Table 4.

First, as was mentioned in Sec. 4.2, eight of the companies already existed before the invention of 3D printing, i.e. the patents. These companies had expertise in a related area, for example operating in the machine tool or printing industry, and 3D printing was a logical extension of their business. An example is US-based HP. Second, two companies were founded as the result of a merger or acquisition of existing businesses which were operating in related fields and where knowledge or awareness of 3D printing existed. The merger or acquisition led to a new company that was dedicated to 3D printing. An example is France-based AddUp which is a new joint venture company created by Michelin and Fives. Third, one company, Stratasys, was started as a traditional entrepreneurial start-up. That means, it is not a corporate or academic spin-off company. Fourth, 13 of the companies can be considered as corporate spin-offs. That means, the founder(s) of these companies were already working in industry and due to this work experience had become exposed to 3D printing or the idea of 3D printing which led to the founding of the 3D printer company. An example of this is Japanese-based Aspect, the founder worked at Mitsubishi before founding the company. Fifth, six of the companies can be considered as academic spin-offs. That means, the founder(s) of these companies were studying or working at a university during or immediately prior to founding the company. An example is US-based Carbon which was founded by professors who were working at the University of North-Carolina in Chapel Hill.

For virtually all of these main industrial 3D printer companies, the founding was based on a product orientation, i.e. development of 3D printers, and for virtually all of these companies, this was related to specific knowledge and expertise in 3D printing processes. More specifically, the founders had a process innovation, which had intellectual property such as a trademark or patent connected to it, which was utilized to develop (a range of) 3D printers. In some situations, this related to expertise in printing specific materials such as ceramics or carbon or a mix of materials.

Table 5.   Break-down of start-up situation of established industrial AM companies.

Type of start-up	Percentage of companies
Traditional start-up	5%
Corporate spin-off	65%
Academic spin-off	30%

Overall, 20 of the companies are based on a start-up situation with a break-down as shown in Table 5.

This confirms Schramm [2018] in the sense that the percentage of pure start-ups is low and that many more start-ups originate from spin-off situations. These figures also provide insight to other studies discussed in Sec. 2.3. First, not all studies use the same breakdown of start-up situations. For example, most do not include the replicative option. This may be because in high technology situations, such as AM, this option is not (yet) available. The traditional start-up is also not always separately considered. Second, similar to the AM data, some studies find that the percentage of technology-based spin-offs from corporations is higher than from academic institutions, e.g. Lindhold Dahlstrand [1997], while others find the reverse, e.g. Löfsten and Lindelöf [2005].

4.4. Academic spin-offs

In this section, the academic spin-offs and their related universities will be analyzed. In Sec. 4.3, it was shown that 6 of the 30 established industrial 3D printer companies were founded as academic spin-offs. The list of six has been expanded by three companies for the improvement of the analysis: Arcam, Concept Laser and Mcor. Arcam and Concept Laser were added to the list because these were academic spin-off companies, and prior to 2016, when they were acquired by GE Additive, these were considered established companies in their own right [Wohlers Associates (2017)]. Mcor was added because even though in the analysis in Sec. 4.3 it was listed as a corporate spin-off in Table 4, this is an example of a company where the founding can be considered as a mix of a corporate spin-off and an academic spin-off. The issue is how the spin-off is defined. Often a company is considered an academic spin-off if a core technology is transferred but it might also be considered as a spin-off if it involves personnel transfer but not technology transfer [Pirnay et al. (2003)].

These resulting nine academic spin-off companies were started out of eight universities as two of them originated from the same university, that is, MIT. Table 6 illustrates the ranking of the eight universities based on the QS World University Ranking 2018, this includes 959 ranked universities, as well as the Times Higher Education World University Rankings 2018 which includes 1000 universities. As 3D printing is a technical area, the rankings of these eight universities in the field of

Table 6. Academic spin-offs and university rankings.

Academic spin-off	University	QS world university ranking 2018 (out of 959)	Times higher education world university rankings 2018 (out of 1000)
Formlabs & Markforged	MIT	1 (1)	5 (4)
Tiertime	Tsinghua University	25 (10)	30 (22)
Voxeljet	Technical University of Munich	64 (24)	41 (20)
Carbon	University of North Carolina-Chapel Hill	80 (196)	56 (not ranked)
Mcor	Trinity College	88 (155)	117 (101–135)
Arcam	Chalmers University of Technology	133 (98)	201–250 (79)
Lithoz	Vienna University of Technology	182 (115)	301–350 (126–150)
Concept Laser	Coburg University of Applied Sciences	Not ranked	Not ranked

engineering and technology are also stated (between brackets). Both rankings include 501 universities in this category.

The following provides additional background on some of the academic spin-off companies as well as some of the complexities in categorizing the founding of these companies.

- Mcor: In the early 2000s, Conor McCormack, one of the founders of the family firm Mcor was working with Airbus as an engineer on the A380 and was exposed to a lot of 3D CAD packages and 3D printing. While working on his PhD at Trinity College, he realized that, due to the high cost of the materials, only one of the students had an opportunity to print a model at the end of the year — just one – defeating the whole purpose of a 3D printer. Conor and his brother Fintan saw that while machine prices were coming down, the price of consumables kept going in the opposite direction. That was the seed of an idea that started with, "Could we make a super low cost machine that is also very eco-friendly for everyone to use?" Mcor was set up in 2005 and Conor and Fintan worked on developing the technology and from this the Mcor Matrix was born [3D Printing Industry (2013)].
- Concept Laser: Frank and Kerstin Herzog met at Coburg University. During the mid-1990s, Frank joined a nearby prototyping shop owned by Kerstin's uncle. The machines in the shop included one of Germany's first stereolithography machines, which "printed" 3D models from successive layers of resin and solidified them with ultraviolet light. Frank wondered if the same could be done with metals. He registered the idea as his master's thesis at Coburg University and built a small prototype. This was improved with a laser that Kerstin had purchased for her master's project and eventually led to the incorporation of the company in 2000 [GE reports (2018)].

- Lithoz: Many years of research at the Vienna University of Technology equipped Dr. Johannes Homa and Dr. Johannes Benedikt with extensive technical knowledge of additive manufacturing of high-performance ceramics. In 2011 they founded Lithoz GmbH as a spin-off from the TU Vienna [Lithoz (2019)].
- Voxeljet: Voxeljet's roots reach back to the year 1995 with the first successful dosing of UV-resins. In the context of a "hidden" project, initial 3D-printing tests are performed at the Technical University of Munich. In 1996, the project participates in the 1st Munich Business plan contest and in 1998 the first patent is granted. The first sand molds are printed at the University in 1998. The company was established in 1999 with the goal of developing new generative processes for the production of casting and plastics components using 3D printing. In the beginning, operations were launched with four employees at the Technical University of Munich. Shortly afterwards the headquarters in Augsburg were established [Voxeljet (2019)].

Seven of the eight universities are ranked amongst the top universities in the world. The exception is the Coburg University of Applied Sciences. Since this is a University of Applied Sciences, with less emphasis on research, it is not surprising that this university is not ranked.

The performance of universities in terms of start-ups, commercialization of technology and for instance income generated from developed technology has previously been identified as being very much skewed [Di Gregorio and Shane (2003); Scherer and Harhoff (2000); Pressman et al. (1995)], so it is to be expected that not all of the 501 universities have spin-off companies in the field of AM. However, it is noteworthy that out of the main industrial 3D printer companies that were formed as academic spin-offs, only two universities from the top-10 of the universities in technology and engineering were involved, see Table 7.

As previously noted, there are additional AM companies that are in an early life stage and/or have not yet established themselves and therefore these companies may also include academic spin-off companies. Nevertheless, notable top-10 technology-oriented universities in the world that are not represented in Table 7 include for

Table 7.   University rankings in engineering and technology.

Rank	QS world university ranking	Times higher education world university rankings
1	Massachusetts Institute of Technology	Stanford University
2	Stanford University	California Institute of Technology
3	University of Cambridge	University of Oxford
4	ETH — Zurich	Massachusetts Institute of Technology
5	Nanyang Technological University	University of Cambridge
6	Imperial College London	Princeton University
7	National University of Singapore	Peking University
8	University of Tokyo University of Oxford	National University of Singapore
9		ETH Zurich
10	Tsinghua University	Imperial College London

example Stanford University and the University of Cambridge, both of these are known for having relatively successful academic spin-off experiences.

It should be noted, however, that these types of descriptive quantitative data do not always cover the "full story". For instance, the University of Texas — Austin is neither mentioned in Table 6, nor in Table 7. Yet, it seems to have played an important role in AM development, in particular for selective laser sintering. Carl Deckard, initially an undergraduate student at the UT-Austin and later graduate and PhD student played an important role. By the end of his senior year in 1984, Deckard had come up with the idea of using a directed energy beam (such as a laser or electron beam) to melt particles of powder together to make a part. This turned into a graduate school project and led to the formation of a company Nova Automation which became DTM [University of Texas at Austin (2012)]. Dr. Xu, the founder of the Chinese company Farsoon is one of the people who worked at DTM in the mid-1990s and when Farsoon established a US subsidiary in 2017, it did so in the Austin area [University of Texas at Austin (2012)]. Thus, Farsoon can be linked to the University of Texas — Austin. Another company that can be linked is the Japanese company Aspect. Seiji Hayano worked at the Mitsubishi Corporation where he learned about stereolithography. He left Mitsubishi in 1996 to start Aspect and soon acquired exclusive rights to distribute equipment and materials developed by DTM [Farsoon Technologies (2017)]. DTM merged with 3D systems in 2001.

Table 8 shows the current headquarters of the academic spin-off companies and the distance to the academic institution to which it is linked. Determining whether an academic spin-off locates near a university is a bit fuzzy because not all geographical areas are comparable. For instance, in terms of size of a region, Tiertime is in the Beijing area and thus in the same geographic area as Tsinghua University

Table 8. Academic spin-offs and distance from academic institution.

Academic spin-off	Headquarter location	University	Main campus location	Approximate distance in miles
Formlabs	Somerville, MA	MIT	Cambridge, MA	2
Markforged	Watertown, MA	MIT	Cambridge, MA	7
Tiertime	Near Beijing	Tsinghua University	Near Beijing	37
Voxeljet	Friedberg	Technical University of Munich	Munich	37
Carbon	Redwood, CA	University of North Carolina-Chapel Hill	Chapel Hill, NC	2827
Mcor	Dunleer	Trinity College	Dublin	37
Arcam	Mölndal	Chalmers University of Technology	Gothenburg	4
Lithoz	Vienna	Vienna University of Technology	Vienna	2
Concept Laser	Lichtenfeld	Coburg University of Applied Sciences	Coburg	11

which is also Beijing but nevertheless they are 37 miles apart. While Mcor and Trinity College are also 37 miles apart but in this situation they seem to be in different parts of the country.

Table 8 shows that most of the academic start-ups are relatively close to the academic institution. The one exception is Carbon. Carbon's CLIP technology was invented at UNC-Chapel-Hill in North Carolina. A main founder of Carbon is Joe DeSimone, a serial entrepreneur and professor at UNC. The reason for the founding of the company in California rather than in North Carolina, may well have to do with DeSimone's experience as entrepreneur and the ability to raise money. Venture Capital is highly concentrated in a few areas in the US which does not include North Carolina but does include California. In particular, the San Francisco area is the top location in the US [Aspect (2019)]. This is exactly where Carbon is located. Furthermore, the series A round of financing for Carbon was led by Sequoia Capital in Menlo Park [Citylab (2017)] which is approximately four miles from Redwood City where Carbon is located. A series B round of financing for Carbon was led by Silver Lake Krafwerk which is also located in Menlo Park [Recode (2015)].

5. Discussion

In this study, the focus was on looking at how a high technology, i.e. additive manufacturing, is spreading globally. A choice was made to look at the established companies in AM that produce industrial 3D printers and determine where they are located and how they were formed. The result is that the technology that was considered for this study has very specific characteristics:

(1) The technology can be considered high-technology in terms of its newness, novelty and complexity.
(2) The diffusion that is examined is in a way the idea or concept of AM. In the current study, the companies have adopted the idea behind AM and based on this they have used and further developed this to produce machines (3D printers). This focus differs from many previous studies that distinguish between product, process, organization and positioning innovation [Boer and During (2001); Francis and Bessant (2005)] and generally focus on the customer, e.g. consumer adoption of electric vehicles [Egbue and Long (2012)] or on the process improvement, e.g. adoption of a new healthcare process [Cho et al. (2009)]. In the context of AM, these latter studies are more comparable to next stages of adoption of AM such as the adoption of industrial 3D printers by companies for use in the production process or the subsequent adoption by customers of the 3D printed products.
(3) The technology is a break-through technology. Although the AM technology already exists for 34 years, this technology is expected to have a huge impact on society in general and is considered a key part of the fourth industrial revolution

technologies. In a broader sense, it is comparable to the development of the home computer. There are many parts of the development of AM, such as different technologies, developments in materials, aspects such as recycling machines, etc.

The overall pattern for the diffusion of the concept of AM, which is closely related to the creation of AM technologies for the development of the industrial 3D printers, leads to several conclusions:

First, the diffusion is mostly taking place in advanced, i.e. innovation-driven nations. Although in theory AM has less connection to a location, the established companies are almost all located in high-income and innovation-driven countries. What this indicates is that while adoption of 3D printers by companies for use in their production process or the adoption by customers of 3D printed products (the two blocks on the right in Fig. 4) may be less dependent upon location, the creation and the diffusion of the concept of AM seems very much dependent upon the location. The reason for this is in line with what was discussed in Sec. 2.1, that is, the vitality of innovation relates to national innovative capacity. What this also indicates is that while advanced nations such as the US may have been faced with erosion of its industrial commons due to outsourcing [Pisano and Shih (2009)], it still has considerable capabilities that are more upstream in the supply chain.

Second, the creation and subsequent initial diffusion of AM is overwhelmingly (77%) through existing companies that show a history that involved development of AM knowledge. For 57% of these (43% of the total group of companies), it led to a new company via a corporate spin-off. This type of start-up situation already often receives attention in the literature. However, for another 43% of these already existing companies (33% of the total number of companies) the companies expanded their business into the AM field. This highlights the importance of existing businesses as a source for innovation, see for example Breitzman and Hicks [2008] and Information Technology & Innovation Foundation [2016]. Among the companies studied, traditional start-ups are rare. The reason for this is that AM is a complex technology that goes beyond the simple idea of producing in layers. The capability to produce 3D printers requires expert knowledge of several other fields such as material science, machine coding, and also expert knowledge of processes such as photopolymerization or binder jetting. Companies that are already operating in related fields and that already possess expert knowledge have the potential to expand into AM. A traditional start-up by a young high-tech wizard is unlikely because of the level of expertise in a variety of fields that is required to make this successful.

Third, an additional 20% of the companies were formed through an academic spin-off situation. This confirms the previous conclusion in terms of the requirement of expert knowledge to start a company to manufacture industrial 3D printers. It also confirms previous studies such as Lindhold Dahlstrand [1997] about the importance of corporate spin-offs compared to academic spin-offs, that is, in this

Table 9.   Overall findings.

Topic	Finding
Location of company that produces industrial 3D printers	90%: Innovation-driven, high-income country 10%: Efficiency-driven, upper-middle income country
Origin of the company	77% existing companies
	− 43% via corporate spin-off
	− 33% via expansion into AM
	− 20% academic spin-off companies
Academic spin-offs	88% from a worldwide top-20% ranked university Only 20% of worldwide top-10 universities 89% of academic spin-offs locate within 40 miles of the university

study there were roughly twice as many corporate spin-offs than academic spin-offs. The reason for this may be similar to the previously drawn conclusion: expert knowledge is required across several areas. While companies that are already competing in related areas may already possess expertise in a variety of areas, academics are typically narrow in their focus. Therefore, unless very specific expertise is developed at a university that provides exceptional value and where additional expertise can somehow be acquired it seems more likely that an existing company is able to capitalize on the situation. Note for example that for the academic spin-offs Carbon founders already had experience with start-up companies which helped commercialization, Mcor founders already possessed design and 3D printing knowledge due to industry experience, and Concept Laser already possessed expertise with stereolithography. It was also found that academic spin-off companies generally located fairly close to the university, i.e. within 40 miles, confirming Audretsch et al. [2005].

The findings discussed above are summarized in Table 9.

6. Conclusion

This study focused on the geography of the diffusion of AM technology through established companies that manufacture industrial 3D printers. This focus deviates from most diffusion studies as it deals with the early-stage adoption of the AM concept into the production of machines. Most diffusion studies are more focused on the diffusion and adoption of process innovation (which would be equivalent to the adoption of 3D printers in a manufacturing company) or the adoption of a product innovation (which would be equivalent to the adoption of 3D printed products). The study combines elements of the creation of innovation, the diffusion of innovation and the commercialization of innovation.

It was found that in this situation of early-stage adoption the majority of companies are located in innovation-driven economies and that most of the companies

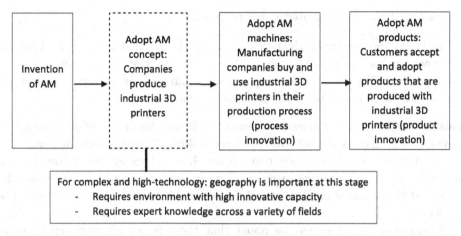

Fig. 7. Link of early-stage adoption of complex and high technology and location.

were existing companies that expanded into AM as a related area or that were corporate spin-offs. The reason for this is probably that AM technology for industrial 3D printers requires expert knowledge in a variety of fields and existing companies that operate in related fields have the best opportunity to capitalize on this, this is illustrated in Fig. 7.

6.1. *Theoretical implications*

This study, while acknowledging its very specific scope as illustrated in Fig. 3, created some important insights that have theoretical implications.

Technology/innovation: It seems that the creation and diffusion of technology has something to do with the particular technology characteristics. The study focused on AM which can be considered high technology although the definition of high technology is unclear [Hooton (2018)]. There are many studies on the nature of technology or innovation such as for instance the distinction of island or integrated technologies based on the dependence upon the environment [Steenhuis and de Bruijn (2004)] and another distinction is the classification by Berkhout *et al.* [2006]. They distinguish five classes of innovation from class 1, i.e. innovation as a result of new developments in a single node in their cyclic innovation model, to class 5 where all cycles of change are linked. Based on the study, it is proposed:

- The higher the number of advanced technological areas that are integrated into an innovation, the higher the likelihood that the initial creation and diffusion of the innovation will be in advanced nations.

This is because these nations present a higher likelihood of possessing the knowledge in the variety of advanced technological areas which allows for the integration to take place.

Start-up: Related to the above, it is proposed:

- The higher the number of advanced technological areas that are integrated into an innovation, the higher the likelihood that the initial creation and diffusion of the innovation will come from the expansion or spin-off from existing corporations that already compete in related fields rather than universities.

This is because these corporations present a higher likelihood of possessing the knowledge in the variety of advanced technological areas which increases the probability that the integration takes place. Researchers at universities have a higher likelihood of operating in more narrowly defined areas which decreases the likelihood of the initial creation and diffusion of the innovation to come from the academic side.

Entrepreneurial: It should be noted that there is considerable vagueness in terminology. For instance, when employees of an existing company work on an academic degree and subsequently start their own company it could potentially be classified as a corporate spin-off, an academic spin-off or even a traditional start-up. This type of complexity or overlap is usually reasoned away for the sake of simplicity but to benefit the development of theory it may be more beneficial to leave some of this in place. Based on the study, it is proposed:

- The higher the number of advanced technological areas that are integrated into an innovation, the higher the likelihood that there may not be a clear distinction and that the entrepreneur possesses a varied background that includes (a variety of) industrial as well as academic experience and knowledge.

6.2. *Practical implications*

Due to the narrow focus of the study, it is not possible to develop strong practical implications that have generalizability. Nevertheless, a few thoughts are presented on implications for companies, universities as well as for governments or public administrators.

Companies: There are two important implication for companies. First, while many companies have outsourced production to low labor-cost countries because advanced economies have become too expensive, the results indicate that companies can still benefit from locating in advanced nations as these locations provide innovation potential. Second, existing companies in related fields have the highest probability to capitalize on AM. Companies should therefore continuously scan the environment and be aware of technological developments that may create new markets. In particular, technologies that require expertise across a variety of fields may present great opportunities as the number of competitors with sufficient expertise across these various areas may be limited. Engagement in university-industry cooperative research such as through NSF's IUCRC program (https://www.nsf.gov/eng/iip/iucrc/home.jsp) is a concrete example of how companies can increase their awareness of technological progress.

Universities are often considered a key part of the knowledge economy and as a source of innovative activity. Nevertheless, this study found that corporations play a more important role. This may be due to the need to have expertise in a variety of fields. Successful universities often already provide an infrastructure that guides the commercialization of university research. This in itself may not be enough and it is recommended to set-up mechanisms that focus on bringing together expertise across a variety of fields and with a focus on the market. Two concrete examples of such mechanisms are the already mentioned university-industry cooperative research and also faculty internships inside corporations. These types of engagements can allow faculty to broaden their perspective and in particular to learn about implications of their research, potential market applications and with this the insight into what kind of changes are necessary in technology to increase the potential.

Public administrators: A few recommendations can be made for countries or governments. First, while advanced nations may have been faced with an erosion of industrial commons, the study illustrates that advanced nations may very well have a competitive edge in the creation and early-stage diffusion of complex (high) technology that requires extensive R&D and innovation capacity. For long-term competitiveness and prosperity, this should remain a focus. Furthermore, while universities play a role in knowledge development, the importance of the expertise of existing companies and the opportunities to capitalize on this expertise should not be underestimated. Policies that encourage companies to continue to do (fundamental) research can lead to opportunities in new fields. Additionally, policies that encourage corporate spin-offs may be beneficial. For countries that are not yet in the innovation-driven stage, it may be most beneficial to build up general innovative capabilities in order to enter the innovation-driven stage.

6.3. *Limitations and suggestions for further research*

A main limitation of this study is that it took place in a narrowly defined area. Due to this context, the study provides limited insight into more general diffusion patterns.

Related to this, some recommendations can be made for further research. First, not all of the innovation-driven economies have established companies that manufacture industrial 3D printers. It would be interesting to find out why some countries do while others do not, as at least in theory they are in a similar stage of innovation. Perhaps, some countries due to their industry portfolio are more likely to be successful in AM. Another area for potential research is to study AM in countries that are not in the innovation-stage. The adoption and diffusion of AM may still occur in these countries but may be related more to the adoption of industrial 3D printers or the products that are made with these 3D printers. It might also be worthwhile to study differences between consumer and industrial 3D printer adoption and whether the stage of economic development of a nation has any influence as the cost of these 3D printers is quite different. A last area for future research is that for academic start-ups. Many of the prominent universities do not have academic spin-offs related to industrial 3D printing while Concept Laser related to Coburg University of Applied Sciences is successful. Studies with a focus on academic spin-off related to applied universities can help to improve understanding under which conditions these universities can play a bigger role in company formation in high technology. Delving deeper into other prominent research universities and what they do in terms of AM can help clarify why not all of the best engineering and technology-oriented universities have been able to spin off AM-oriented companies.

References

3D Printing Industry (2013). Executive interview — Conor MacCormack. https://3dprintingindustry.com/news/executive-interview-series-conor-maccormick-5490/, February 12, 2013 [accessed 12 February 2019].

Aarikka-Stenroos, L. and Lehtimäki, T. (2014). Commercializing a radical innovation: Probing the way to the market. *Industrial Marketing Management*, **43**: 1372–1384.

Acosta, M., Coronado, D. and Flores, E. (2011). University spillovers and new business location in high-technology sectors: Spanish evidence. *Small Business Economics*, **36**: 365–376.

Adams, P., Farrell, M., Dalgarno, B. and Oczkowski, E. (2017). Household adoption of technology: The case of high-speed broadband adoption in Australia. *Technology in Society*, **49**: 37–47.

Anastasiadou, C. and Vettese, S. (2019). "From souvenirs to 3D printed souvenirs". Exploring the capabilities of additive manufacturing technologies in (re)-framing tourist souvenirs. *Tourism Management*, **71**: 428–442.

Anderson, C. (2012). *Makers, The New Industrial Revolution*. Crown Business, New York.

Anderson Goehrke, S. (2016). GE Announces $1.4 Billion Investment: Acquisition of Arcam AB and SLM Solutions. 3DPrint.com. https://3dprint.com/148290/ge-acquires-arcam-slm-solutions/, September 6, 2016 [accessed 12 March 2019].

Andorka, F. (2011). Stratasys Acquires 3-D Printer Solidscape For $38 Million. Industry Week. https://www.industryweek.com/information-technology/stratasys-acquires-3-d-printer-solidscape-38-million, May 4, 2011 [accessed 12 March 2019].

Artz, K. W., Norman, P. M., Hatfield, D. E. and Cardinal, L. B. (2010). A longitudinal study on the impact of R&D, patents, and product innovation on firm performance. *Journal of Product Innovation Management*, **27**: 725–740.

Aspect (2019). Opening up a new future with AM (3D printing). http://aspect.jpn.com/english/company/index.html. n.d. [accessed 12 February 2019].

Atzeni, E., Iuliano, L., Minetola, P. and Salmi, A. (2010). Redesign and cost estimation of rapid manufactured plastic parts. *Rapid Prototyping Journal*, **16**, 5: 308–317.

Atzeni, E. and Salmi, A. (2012). Economics of additive manufacturing for end-usable metal parts. *International Journal of Advanced Manufacturing Technology*, **62**: 1147–1155.

Audretsch, D. B. (1998). Agglomeration and the location of innovative activity. *Oxford Review of Economic Policy*, **14**, 2: 18–29.

Audretsch, D. B. and Feldman, M. P. (1996). R&D spillovers and the geography of innovation and production. *The American Economic Review*, **86**, 3: 630–640.

Audretsch, D. B., Lehmann, E. E. and Warning, S. (2005). University spillovers and new firm location. *Research Policy*, **34**: 1113–1122.

Baiyegunhi, L. J. S., Hassan, M. B., Danso-Abbeam, G. and Ortmann, G. F. (2019). Diffusion and adoption of integrated Striga management (ISM) technologies among smalholder maize farmers in rural northern Nigeria. *Technology in Society*, **56**: 109–115.

Balasubramanian, N. and Lee, J. (2008). Firm age and innovation. *Industrial and Corporate Change*, **17**, 5: 1019–1047.

Balconi, M., Brusoni, S. and Orsenigo, L. (2010). In defence of the linear model: An essay. *Research Policy*, **39**: 1–13.

Balland, P. A., Boschma, R. and Frenken, K. (2015). Proximity and innovation: From statistics to dynamics. *Regional Studies*, **49**, 6: 907–920.

Ballardini, R. M., Flores Ituarte, I. and Pei, E. (2018). Printing spare parts through additive manufacturing: Legal and digital business challenges. *Journal of Manufacturing Technology Management*, **29**, 6: 958–982.

Beltagui, A., Rosli, A. and Candi, M. (2020). Exaptation in a digital innovation ecosystem: The disruptive impacts of 3D printing. *Research Policy*, **49**, https://www.sciencedirect.com/science/article/pii/S0048733319301532.

Berkhout, A. J., Hartmann, D., van der Duin, P. and Ortt, R. (2006). Innovating the innovation process. *International Journal of Technology Management*, **34**, 3/4: 390–404.

Boer, H. and During, W. E. (2001). Innovation, what innovation? A comparison between product, process and organizational innovation. *International Journal of Technology Management*, **22**, 1/2/3: 83–107.

Breitzman, A. and Hicks, D. (2008). An analysis of small business patents by industry and firm size, Small Business Administration, Office of Advocacy.

Brem, A., Bilgram, V. and Gutstein, A. (2018). Involving lead users in innovation: A structured summary of research on the lead user method. *International Journal of Innovation and Technology Management*, **15**, 3, https://www.worldscientific.com/doi/abs/10.1142/S0219877018500220.

Candi, M. and Beltagui, A. (2019). Effective use of 3D printing in the innovation process. *Technovation*, **80–81**: 63–73.

Caraça, J., Lundvall, B. A. and Mendonça, S. (2009). The changing role of science in the innovation process: From queen to Cinderella? *Technological Forecasting & Social Change*, **76**: 861–867.

Carayannis, E. G., Rogers, E. M., Kurihara, K. and Allbritton, M. M. (1998). High-technology spin-offs from government R&D laboratories and research universities. *Technovation*, **18**, 1: 1–11.

Caviggioli, F. and Ughetto, E. (2019). A bibliometric analysis of the research dealing with the impact of additive manufacturing on industry, business and society. *International Journal of Production Economics*, **208**: 254–268.

Cenamor, J., Usero, B. and Fernández, Z. (2013). The role of complementary products on platform adoption: Evidence from the video console market. *Technovation*, **33**: 405–416.

Chan, H. K., Griffin, J., Lim, J. J., Zeng, F. and Chiu, A. S. F. (2018). The impact of 3D printing technology on the supply chain: Manufacturing and legal perspectives. *International Journal of Production Economics*, **205**: 156–162.

Chen, G. Yang, G., He, F. and Chen, K. (2019). Exploring the effect of political borders on university-industry collaborative research performance: Evidence from China's Guangdong province. *Technovation*, **82–83**: 58–69.

Chiesa, V. and Frattini, F. (2011). Commercializing technological innovation: Learning from failures in high-tech markets. *Journal of Product Innovation Management*, **28**: 437–454.

Cho, S., Mathiassen, L. and Gallivan, M. (2009). Crossing the diffusion chasm: From invention to penetration of a telehealth innovation. *Innovation Technology & People*, **22**, 4: 351–366.

Citylab (2017). Venture capital remains highly concentrated in just a few cities. https://www.citylab.com/life/2017/10/venture-capital-concentration/539775/, October 3 2017 [accessed 12 February 2019].

Clarysse, B., Wright, M., Lockett, A., van de Velde, E. and Vohora, A. (2005). Spinning out new ventures: A typology of incubation strategies from European research institutions. *Journal of Business Venturing*, **20**: 183–216.

Coad, A., Segarra, A. and Teruel, M. (2016). Innovation and firm growth: Does firm age play a role?*Research Policy*, **45**: 387–400.

Cowan, R. and Zinovyeva, N. (2013). University effects on regional innovation. *Research Policy*, **42**: 788–800.

Davis, F. D. (1989). Perceived usefulness, perceived ease of use, and user acceptance of information technology. *MIS Quarterly*, **13**, 3: 319–340.

de la Mothe, J. and Paquet, G. (eds.) (1998). *Local and Regional Systems of Innovation*. Kluwer Academic Publishers, Boston.

De Jong, J. P. J. and de Bruijn, E. (2013). Innovation lessons from 3-D printing. *MIS Sloan Management Review*, **54**, 2: 43–52.

Di Gregorio, D. and Shane, S. (2003). Why do some universities generate more start-ups than others? *Research Policy*, **32**: 209–227.

Ebrahimi Sarcheshmeh, E., Bijani, M. and Sadighi, H. (2018). Adoption behavior towards the use of nuclear technology in agriculture: A causal analysis. *Technology in Society*, **55**: 175–182.

Egbue, O. and Long, S. (2012). Barriers to widespread adoption of electric vehicles: An analysis of consumer attitudes and perceptions. *Energy Policy*, **48**: 717–729.

Fabbaloo (2018). The final word: The first 3D printer. https://www.fabbaloo.com/blog/2018/10/25/final-word-the-first-3d-printer? 25 October 2018 [accessed 30 January 2019].

Farsoon Technologies (2017). Farsoon Technologies Expands Global Strategy with Establishment of Americas Subsidiary. http://en.farsoon.com/news_detail/newsId=34.html. September 21 2017 [accessed 12 February 2019].

Feldman, M. P. (1994). *The Geography of Innovation*. Kluwer Academic Publishers, Dordrecht.

Feldman, M. P. and Florida, R. (1994). The geographic sources of innovation: Technological infrastructure and product innovation in the United States. *Annals of the Association of American Geographers*, **84**, 2: 210–229.

Ferretti, M., Ferri, S., Fiorentino, R., Parmentola, A. and Sapio, A. (2019). Neither absent nor too present: The effects of the engagement of parent universities on the performance of academic spin-offs. *Small Business Economics*, **52**: 153–173.

Fichman, R. G. (2004). Real options and IT platform adoption: Implications for theory and practice. *Information Systems Research*, **15**, 2: 132–154.

Fini, R., Grimaldi, R., Santoni, S. and Sobrero, M. (2011). Complements or substitutes? The role of universities and local context in supporting the creation of academic spin-offs. *Research Policy*, **40**: 1113–1127.

Ford, S., Mortara, L. and Minshall, T. (2016). The emergence of additive manufacturing: Introduction to the special issue. *Technological Forecasting & Social Change*, **102**: 156–159.

Foster, C. and Heeks, R. (2013). Conceptualising inclusive innovation: Modifying systems of innovation frameworks to understand diffusion of new technology to low-income consumers. *European Journal of Development Research*, **25**, 3: 333–355.

Fox, S. (2014). Third wave do-it-yourself (DIY): Potential for presumption, innovation, and entrepreneurship by local populations in regions without industrial manufacturing infrastructure. *Technology in Society*, **39**: 18–30.

Francis, D. and Bessant, J. (2005). Targeting innovation and implications for capability development. *Technovation*, **25**: 171–183.

Fratocchi, L. (2018). Additive manufacturing technologies as a reshoring enabler: A why, where and how approach. *World Review of Intermodal Transportation Research*, **7**, 3: 264–293.

García-Quevedo, J., Pellegrino, G. and Vivarelli, M. (2014). R&D drivers and age: Are young firms different? *Research Policy*, **43**: 1544–1556.

GE reports (2018). The Metal Head: How A High School Dropout Built A Pioneering 3D Printing Business. https://www.ge.com/reports/metal-head-high-school-dropout-built-pioneering-3d-printing-business/, April 30, 2018 [accessed 12 February 2019].

Godin, B. (2006). The liner model of innovation, the historical construction of an analytical framework. *Science, Technology & Human Values*, **31**, 6: 639–667.

Goehrke, S. (2019). The 3D printing startup within a major company. https://www.fabbaloo.com/blog/2019/1/15/the-3d-printing-startup-within-a-major-company, January 15, 2019 [accessed 29 January 2019].

Goldstein, P. (2018). NASA Turns to 3D Printing to Help Astronauts Aboard the International Space Station. https://fedtechmagazine.com/article/2018/10/nasa-turns-3d-printing-help-astronauts-aboard-international-space-station, October 24, 2018 [accessed 11 January 2019].

Grand View Research (2018). 3D Printing (3DP) Market Worth $23.79 Billion By 2025 — CAGR: 16.5%. https://www.grandviewresearch.com/press-release/global-3d-printing-market, October 2018 [accessed 11 January 2019].

Gress, D. R. and Kalafsky, R. V. (2015). Geographies of production in 3D: Theoretical and research implications stemming from additive manufacturing. *Geoforum*, **60**: 43–52.

Halbinger, M. A. (2018). The role of makerspaces in supporting consumer innovation and diffusion: An empirical analysis. *Research Policy*, **47**: 2028–2036.

Hannen, J., Antons, D., Pillar, F., Salge, T. O., Coltman, T. and Devinney, T. M. (2019). Containing the not-invented-here syndrome in external knowledge absorption and open innovation: The role of indirect countermeasures. *Research Policy*, **48**, https://www.sciencedirect.com/science/article/pii/S0048733319301428?via%3Dihub.

Hannibal, M. and Knight, G. (2018). Additive manufacturing and the global factory: Disruptive technologies and the location of international business. *International Business Review*, **27**: 1116–1127.

Hienerth, C., von Hippel, E. and Jensen, M. B. (2014). User community vs. producer innovation development efficiency: A first empirical study. *Research Policy*, **43**: 190–201.

Hooton, C. A. (2018). Defining tech: An examination of how the 'technology' economy is measured. *Journal of NBICT*, **1**: 101–120.

Hossain, M., Simula, H. and Halme, M. (2016). Can frugal go global? Diffusion patterns of frugal innovations. *Technology in Society*, **46**: 132–139.

Hsu, D. W. L. and Yuan, B. J. C. (2013). Knowledge creation and diffusion of Taiwan's universities: Knowledge trajectory from patent data. *Technology in Society*, **35**: 172–181.

Hyysalo, S., Johnson, M. and Juntunen, J. K. (2017). The diffusion of consumer innovation in sustainable energy technologies. *Journal of Cleaner Production*, **162**: S70–S82.

Information Technology & Innovation Foundation (2016). https://itif.org/publications/2016/02/24/demographics-innovation-united-states, February 24, 2016 [accessed 25 January 2019].

Jaffe, A. B. (1989). Real effects of academic research. *The American Economic Review*, **79**, 5: 957–970.

Jones, R., Haufe, P., Sells, E., Iravani, P., Olliver, V., Palmer, C. and Bowyer, A. (2011). RepRap — The replicating rapid prototype. *Robotica*, **29**: 177–191.

Kankanhalli, A., Ye, H. and Teo, H. H. (2015). Comparing potential and actual innovators: An empirical study of mobile data services innovation. *MIS Quarterly*, **39**, 3: 667–682.

Kannattukunnel, R. S. (2016). Global patents on 3D printing: Revelations based on vector autoregression analysis for three decades. *International Journal of Innovation Technology Management*, **13**, 6, https://www.worldscientific.com/doi/10.1142/S0219877017500043.

Kaplan, D. (1987). Machinery and industry: The causes and consequences of constrained development of the South African machine tool industry. *Social Dynamics, A Journal of African Studies*, **13**, 1: 60–67.

Khanagha, A., Mobnini Dehkordi, A., Zali, M. R. and Reza Hejazi, S. (2018). Measuring the entrepreneurial orientation of public research centers. *International Journal of Innovation and Technology Management*, **15**, 3, https://www.worldscientific.com/doi/10.1142/S0219877018500281.

Kleer, R. and Piller, F. T. (2019). Local manufacturing and structural shifts in competition: Market dynamics of additive manufacturing. *International Journal of Production Economics*, **216**: 23–34.

Kline, S. J. and Rosenberg, N. (1986). An overview of innovation. *The Positive Sum Strategy: Harnessing Technology for Economic Growth*, eds. R. Landau and N. Rosenberg. National Academy Press, Washington DC, pp. 275–305.

Kolympiris, C., Kalaitzandonakes, N. and Miller, D. (2015). Location choice of academic entrepreneurs: Evidence from the US biotechnology industry. *Journal of Business Venturing*, **30**: 227–254.

Krabel, S. and Mueller, P. (2009). What drives scientists to start their own company? An empirical investigation of Max Planck Society scientists. *Research Policy*, **38**: 947–956.

Kuchiki, A. and Tsuji, M. (eds.) (2010). *From Agglomeration to Innovation*. Palgrave Macmillan, Houndmills.

Kwak, K., Kim, W. and Park, K. (2018). Complementary multiplatforms in the growing innovation ecosystem: Evidence from 3D printing technology. *Technological Forecasting & Social Change*, **136**: 192–207.

Lindhold Dahlstrand, A. (1997). Growth and inventiveness in technology-based spin-off firms. *Research Policy*, **26**: 331–344.

Lithoz (2019). Company overview. http://www.lithoz.com/en/company/company-overview [accessed 12 February 2019].

Löfsten, H. and Lindelöf, P. (2005). R&D networks and product innovation patterns — academic and non-academic new technology-based firms in Science Parks. *Technovation*, **25**: 1025–1037.

Lyu, J., Hahn, K. and Sadachar, A. (2018). Understanding millennial consumer's adoption of 3D printed fashion products by exploring personal values and innovativeness. *Fashion and Textiles*, **5**: 11–35.

Marak, Z. R., Tiwari, A. and Tiwari, S. (2019). Adoption of 3D printing technology: An innovation diffusion theory perspective. *International Journal of Innovation*, **7**, 1: 87–103.

Martinsuo, M. and Luomaranta, T. (2018). Adopting additive manufacturing in SMEs: Exploring the challenges and solutions. *Journal of Manufacturing Technology Management*, **29**, 6: 937–957.

Marzi, G., Zollo, L., Boccardi, A. and Ciappei, C. (2018). Additive manufacturing in SMEs: Empirical evidences from Italy. *International Journal of Innovation and Technology Management*, **15**, 1, https://www.worldscientific.com/doi/10.1142/S0219877018500074.

Matias, E. and Rao, B. (2015). 3D printing: On its historical evolution and the implications for business. In *2015 Proceedings of PICMET '15: Management of the Technology Age*, pp. 551–558.

Matos, F. and Jacinto, C. (2019). Additive manufacturing technology: Mapping social impacts. *Journal of Manufacturing Technology Management*, **30**, 1: 70–97.

Minshall, T. and Wicksteed, B. (2005). *University Spin-out Companies: Starting to Fill the Evidence Gap, A Report on a Pilot Research Project Commissioned by the Gatsby Charitable Foundation.* St. John's Innovation Centre Ltd., Cambridge.

Miller, D. and Garnsey, E. (2000). Entrepreneurs and technology diffusion, How diffusion research can benefit from a greater understanding of entrepreneurship. *Technology in Society*, **22**: 445–465.

Miyata, Y. (2000). An empirical analysis of innovative activity of universities in the United States. *Technovation*, **20**: 413–425.

Moore, G. A. (2014). *Crossing the Chasm*, 3rd edn., HarperCollins Publishers, New York.

Morgan, K. and Nauwelaers, C. (2003). *Regional Innovation Strategies, The Challenge for Less-favoured Regions.* Routledge, London.

Mowery, D. C. and Ziedonis, A. A. (2014). Markets versus spillovers in outflows of university research. *Research Policy*, **44**: 50–66.

Niaki, M. K., Nonino, F., Palombi, G. and Torabi. S. A. (2019). Economic sustainability of additive manufacturing. *Journal of Manufacturing Technology Management*, **30**, 2: 353–365.

Nikolov, N. (2017). Solar-powered 3D printer uses light and sand to sculpt glass objects. https://mashable.com/2017/03/29/solar-powered-3d-printer-sahara-desert/#kfbq6y-PytmqH, March 29, 2017 [accessed 11 January 2019].

Norman, J., Madurawe, R. D., Moore, C. M. V., Khan, M. A. and Khairuzzaman, A. (2017). A new chapter in pharmaceutical manufacturing: 3D-printed drug products. *Advanced Drug Delivery Reviews*, **108**: 39–50.

O'Shea, R. P., Allen, T. J., Chevalier, A. and Roche, F. (2005). Entrepreneurial orientation, technology transfer and spinoff performance of U. S. universities. *Research Policy*, **34**: 994–1009.

Öberg, C., Shams, T. and Asnafi, N. (2018). Additive manufacturing and business models: Current knowledge and missing perspectives. *Technology Innovation Management Review*, **8**, 6: 15–33.

Oettmeier, K. and Hofmann, E. (2016). Impact of additive manufacturing technology adoption on supply chain management processes and components. *Journal of Manufacturing Technology Management*, **27**, 7: 944–968.

Oh, G. and Hong, Y. S. (2018). The impact of platform update interval on platform diffusion in a cooperative mobile ecosystem. *Journal of Intelligent Manufacturing*, **29**: 549–558.

Orlando, M. J. and Verba, M. (2005). Do only big cities innovate? Technological maturity and the location of innovation. *Economic Review — Federal Reserve Bank of Kansas City,* Second Quarter 2005, pp. 31–57.

Ortt, R. (2016). Guest editorial. *Journal of Manufacturing Technology Management,* **27**, 7: 890–897.

Ortt, R. (2017). Guest editorial. *Journal of Manufacturing Technology Management,* **28**, 1: 2–9.

Ortt, J. R. and Schoormans, J. P. L. (2004). The pattern of development and diffusion of breakthrough communication technologies. *European Journal of Innovation Management,* **7**, 4: 292–302.

Pirnay, F., Surlemont, B. and Nlemvo, F. (2003). Toward a typology of university spin-offs. *Small Business Economics,* **21**: 355–369.

Pisano, G. P. and Shih, W. C. (2009). Restoring American competitiveness. *Harvard Business Review,* **87**, 7/8: 114–125.

Porter, A. L., Newman, N. C., Jin, X. Y., Johnson, D. M. and Roessner, J. D. (2008). High tech indicators, technology-based competitiveness based on 33 countries, 2007 report. Report to the Science Indicators Unit, Division of Science Resources Statistics, National Science Foundation under Contract # NSFDACS07P1121. Atlanta, GA: Georgia Institute of Technology, Technology Policy and Assessment Center, January 22, 2008.

Porter, M. E. (1990). *The Competitive Advantage of Nations.* The Free Press, New York.

Porter, M. E. (2003). The economic performance of regions. *Regional Studies,* **36**, 6/7: 549–578.

Porter, M. E. and Stern, S. (2001). Innovation: location matters. *MIT Sloan Management Review,* **42**, 4: 28–36.

Pressman, L., Guterman, S., Abrams, I., Geist, D. E. and Nelsen, L. L. (1995). Pre-production investment and jobs induced by MIT exclusive patent licenses: A preliminary model to measure the economic impact of licensing. *Journal of the Association of University Technology Managers,* **7**: 49–82.

Rayna, T. and Striukova, L. (2016). From rapid prototyping to home fabrication: How 3D printing is changing business model innovation. *Technological Forecasting & Social Change,* **102**: 214–224.

Rayna, T. and Striukova, L. (2018). Editorial. *International Journal of Manufacturing Technology and Management,* **32**, 1: 1–4.

Recode (2015). Startup says new 3-D printing technique could shift use from prototype to production. https://www.recode.net/2015/3/16/11560306/startup-says-new-3-d-printing-technique-could-shift-use-from, March 16, 2015 [accessed 12 February 2019].

Redwood, B., Schöffer, F. and Garret, B. (2017). *The 3D Printing Handbook.* 3D Hubs B. V., Amsterdam.

Rogers, E. M. (1995). *Diffusion of Innovations.* 4th edn., The Free Press, New York.

Rogers, H., Braziotis, C. and Pawar, K. S. (2017). Guest editorial. *International Journal of Physical Distribution & Logistics Management,* **47**, 10: 950–953.

Saxena, P. K. and Sharma, A. (2014). Role of machine tools industry in economic development. *International Journal of Enhanced Research in Science Technology & Engineering,* **3**, 5: 188–193.

Scherer, F. M. and Harhoff, D. (2000). Technology policy for a world of skew-distributed outcomes. *Research Policy,* **29**: 559–566.

Schniederjans, D. G. (2017). Adoption of 3D-printing technologies in manufacturing: A survey analysis. *International Journal of Production Economics,* **183**: 287–298.

Schramm, C. J. (2018). *Burn the Business Plan, What Great Entrepreneurs Really Do.* Simon & Schuster, New York.

Schulze, A., MacDuffie, J. P. and Täube, F. A. (2015). Introduction: Knowledge generation and innovation diffusion in the global automotive industry — change and stability during turbulent times. *Industrial and Corporate Change*, 24, 3: 603–611.

Schwab, K. (2016). *The Fourth Industrial Revolution.* World Economic Forum, Geneva.

Scott. C. and Simple, A. (2015). 3D Printed Pipe Fitting Has Huge Implications for Disaster Relief. https://3dprint.com/113155/field-ready-nepal-earthquake/, December 30, 2015 [accessed 11 January 2019].

Shane, S. (2001). Technological opportunities and firm creation. *Management Science*, 47, 2: 205–220.

Shane, S. (2016). Patents Granted to Small Entities in Decline, Small Business Trends. https://smallbiztrends.com/2010/07/how-smart-is-the-average-entrepreneur.html, January 20, 2016 [accessed 29 January 2019].

Smith, A. (2017). From IP goals to 3D holes: Does intellectual property law provide a map or gap in the era of 3D printing? *Journal of Intellectual Property Law*, 25, 1: 85–107.

Steenhuis, H. J. and de Bruijn, E. J. (2004). Assessing manufacturing location. *Production Planning & Control*, 15, 8: 786–795.

Steenhuis, H. J. and Gray, D. O. (2006). The university as the engine of growth: An analysis of how universities can contribute to the economy. *International Journal of Technology Transfer and Commercialization*, 5, 4: 421–432.

Steenhuis, H. J. and Pretorius, L. (2016). Consumer additive manufacturing or 3D printing adoption: An exploratory study. *Journal of Manufacturing Technology Management*, 27, 7: 990–1012.

Steenhuis, H. J. and Pretorius, L. (2017). The additive manufacturing innovation: A range of implications. *Journal of Manufacturing Technology Management*, 28, 1: 122–143.

Steffensen, M., Rogers, E. M. and Speakman, K. (1999). Spin-offs from research centers at a research university. *Journal of Business Venturing*, 15: 93–111.

Trani, E. P. and Holsworth, R. D. (2010). *The Indispensible University, Higher Education, Economic Development, and the Knowledge Economy.* Rowman & Littlefield Publishers, Lanham.

University of Texas at Austin (2012). Selective Laser Sintering, Birth of an Industry. http://www.me.utexas.edu/news/news/selective-laser-sintering-birth-of-an-industry, December 6, 2012 [accessed 12 February 2019].

Varga, A. (1998). *University Research and Regional Innovation, A Spatial Econometric Analysis of Academic Technology Transfer.* Kluwer Academic Publishers, Boston.

Verschuren, P. and Doorewaard, H. (2005). *Designing a Research Project.* Lemma, Utrecht.

Von Hippel, E. (1986). Lead users: A source of novel product concepts. *Management Science*, 32, 7: 791–805.

Von Hippel, E. (2005). Democratizing innovation: The evolving phenomenon of user innovation. *Journal für Betriebswirtschaft*, 55, 1: 63–78.

von Tunzelmann, G. N. (1997). Innovation and industrialization: A long-term comparison. *Technological Forecasting and Social Change*, 56: 1–23.

Voxeljet (2019). The Voxeljet company history. https://www.voxeljet.com/unternehmen/unternehmensgeschichte/ [accessed 12 February 2019].

Wennberg, K., Wiklund, J. and Wright, M. (2011). The effectiveness of university knowledge spillovers: Performance differences between university spinoffs and corporate spinoffs. *Research Policy*, 40: 1128–1143.

Wohlers Associates (2017). *Wohlers Report 2017, 3D Printing and Additive Manufacturing State of the Industry*, Annual worldwide progress report, Wohlers Associates Inc., Fort Collins.

Woodson, T., Torres Alcantara, J. and Silva do Nascimento, M. (2019). Is 3D printing an inclusive innovation? An examination of 3D printing in Brazil. *Technovation*, **80–81**: 54–62.

World Bank (2017). *World Development Indicators 2017*. Washington, DC. https://open-knowledge.worldbank.org/handle/10986/26447, 2017 [accessed 30 January 2019].

World Economic Forum (2017). *The Global Competitiveness Report 2017–2018*. https://www.weforum.org/reports/the-global-competitiveness-report-2017-2018, 2017 [accessed 30 January 2019].

Wydra, S. (2015). Challenges for technology diffusion policy to achieve socio-economic goals. *Technology in Society*, **41**: 76–90.

Yeganegi, S., Laplume, A. O., Dass, P. and Huynh, C.-L. (2016). Where do spinouts come from? The role of technology relatedness and institutional context. *Research Policy*, **45**: 1103–1112.

Zahringer, K., Kolympiris, C. and Kalaitzandonakes, N. (2017). Academic knowledge quality differentials and the quality of firm innovation. *Industrial and Corporate Change*, **26**, 5: 821–844.

Zanello, G., Fu, X., Mohnen, P. and Ventresca, M. (2016). The creation and diffusion of innovation in developing countries: A systematic literature review. *Journal of Economic Surveys*, **30**, 5: 884–912.

Biography

Harm-Jan Steenhuis is Associate Dean and Professor of Management, International Business in the College of Business at Hawai'i Pacific University. He previously worked at Eastern Washington University, North Carolina State University, and the University of Twente in Enschede, the Netherlands. He received his MSc in Industrial Engineering and Management and his PhD in International Technology Transfer from the University of Twente. His research areas relate to technological development and economic development related issues such as clusters, technology transfer and diffusion, and innovative technologies.

Xin Fang joined Hawai'i Pacific University in Fall 2011. Prior to that, she was a visiting assistant professor of economics at the University of Illinois at Chicago. She holds a M.A. in economics from Tufts University and a Ph.D. in Economics from University of Illinois at Chicago. Her major research fields are industrial organization, applied microeconomics and applied econometrics.

Tolga Ulusemre is an Assistant Professor at the College of Business, Hawaii Pacific University, where he teaches and researches in the areas of international business and strategy. Before joining Hawaii Pacific University, he was a Visiting Instructor at the Parker College of Business, Georgia Southern University. He holds a PhD in International Business from the University of South Carolina, and a Master of Science in Marketing from the University of Bath, UK.

Chapter 15

Barriers to Information Technology Adoption Within Small and Medium Enterprises: A Systematic Literature Review

Marieme Chouki[*,‡], Mohamed Talea[*], Chafik Okar[†] and Razane Chroqui[†]

*LTI Lab, Faculty of Science Ben M'sik
Hassan II University, Casablanca, Morocco

†LAMSAD, National School of Applied Sciences Berrechid
Hassan I University, Settat, Morocco
‡Chouki.ma@gmail.com

While information technology (IT) has grown rapidly in enterprises, scholars have emphasized the importance of IT factors and aspects, while limited attention has been paid to the barriers and challenges facing the adoption of IT. In light of this, we stress the importance of barriers inhibiting IT adoption within Small and Medium Enterprises (SME). For this purpose, this paper aims to create a systematic literature review in order to provide a better understanding of barriers to IT adoption within SME. On the basis of 132 selected studies, we identify 18 barriers categorized according to internal and external parameters. Finally, we underline a synthesis and avenues for future research, and provide scientific and managerial implications and guidance for the adoption of IT in SME.

Keywords: Information technology adoption; barriers; small and medium enterprises (SME); systematic literature review; information systems.

1. Introduction

Today, the economy is ruled over by hyper-competition, globalization, and information investment. As a result, the economic environment, governmental and legal forms, infrastructure and telecommunications services are more and more scalable. In addition, the needs of companies in technology are constantly evolving [Gurbaxani and Whang (1991)]. As a result of these advances, Information Systems (IS) or Information Technologies (IT) have become a very important driving force for organizations, offering them many opportunities [Agarwal and Brem (2015); Elia *et al.*

---

‡Corresponding author.

This chapter was originally published in *International Journal of Innovation and Technology Management*, Vol. 17, No. 1, February 2020, published by World Scientific Publishing, Singapore. Reprinted with permission.

(2007)]. Their adoption has grown quickly, from traditional systems to automated processes and eventually to complex and revolutionary systems [Li *et al.* (2014)]. These systems shape business structures and give them a new competitive edge [Elia *et al.* (2007); Matharu *et al.* (2015)].

Before discussing the aims and results of our study, it seems first and foremost necessary to define the different concepts used: IS, IT, and adoption. Information systems and information technologies are closely similar, yet, slightly different. IT is a subset of the IS, "IS is defined by a formal and organized system designed to collect, process, store, and distribute information, IS includes technology, machines, users, processes, etc. [Angell and Smithson (2012)]". In our research, we focus on the technological concept of IS which hereinafter will be referred to as IT, "IT is defined by the use of technologies and computers to store, transmit, and manipulate data or information as referring to new technologies that ease work conditions in a company, such as: Internet, Intranets, computer networks, etc. [Angell and Smithson (2012)]". On the other hand, the concept of adoption has been defined as "a process that allows the introduction and use of what is new to an organization [Abdul Hameed *et al.* (2012)]". Regarding IT, it represents the means of resolving problems and developing businesses [Fei and Chung (2015)]. The IT adoption includes all the phases of software and/or hardware adoption (from the decision-making to the use) [Nguyen *et al.* (2013)].

Contrary to traditional systems, IT provides multiple benefits and opportunities for enterprises, including to Small and Medium Enterprises (SME), notably the rise of customer/supplier interactions, fast and satisfactory delivery of products and services, cost cutting, effectiveness of management, business performance improvement and solving communication issues, etc. [Fink (1998); Johnston and Wright (2004); Maldonado-guzmán *et al.* (2014)]. A number of researchers have argued that IT plays an extremely important role in business success [Rangone (1999); MacGregor and Vrazalic (2005); Wiklund *et al.* (2009); Nguyen (2009); Chan *et al.* (2012); Ullah and Lai (2013); Maduku *et al.* (2016); Jernström *et al.* (2016)]. In this regard, Ghobakhloo *et al.* [2012] add that SME must acquire benefits of IT investment (it can offer the competitive advantage, improve its productivity and integrate inter-organization functions and functions with partners). However, despite these IT advantages and despite the important contribution of SME to gross domestic product (GDP) and job creation, several studies conducted in different countries have shown that SME are less likely to adopt IT than large firms, as IT adoption seems to be a challenge for SME, as they appear reluctant to adopt it [Fink (1998); Southern and Tilley (2000); Johnston and Wright (2004); Dibrell *et al.* (2008); Qureshi and York (2008); Bhattacharya (2015); Hsu and Lin (2016); Hamdan and Yahaya (2016)]. By deepening the research on causes and barriers that prevent the IT adoption in SME, some specific organizational, individual, technological, financial, and environmental characteristics are highlighted [Hjorth and Brem (2016); Howard *et al.* (2003); Ghobakhloo *et al.* (2012); Rose *et al.* (2016); Aloini *et al.*

(2016); Barkhordari *et al.* (2017)]. In recent decades, this problem has become the paramount concern of IT specialists, professionals, and researchers [Stockdale and Standing (2004); Kapurubandara and Lawson (2006); Harland *et al.* (2007); Soon Ern (2015); Hamdan and Yahaya (2016); Barkhordari *et al.* (2017); Aloini *et al.* (2016); Gutmann *et al.* (2016)]. In order for these barriers to be better understood, we conduct a "Systematic Literature Review (SLR)" of barriers preventing the IT adoption in SME, to provide a guide on the role of each IT stakeholder, the precautions to take, and the factors to be taken into account to facilitate and ensure IT adoption by SME.

The aim of our research is to better understand IT adoption in SME and define the barriers that obstruct this adoption. For that, we firstly describe in Sec. 2 our plan and methodology used to perform the SLR, based on the guidelines of Kitchenham; Kitchenham [2004; 2007] and Kitchenham *et al.* [2009]. Through this SLR, we examined the previous research presented in the literature, while focusing on the issues related to the IT adoption barriers within SME (detailed in Sec. 3). Secondly, we present in Sec. 3 the results of our research, which proposes the categorization of these barriers. Then, in Sec. 4 we summarize the results found and respond to the research issues in a discussion (Sec. 4). Finally, we conclude in Sec. 5 by a review of the implications and directions for future research in IT adoption.

2. Review Planning and Methodology

In order to give an insight into the previous research work and to provide pointers for future research work, we present in this paper an SLR of barriers to IT adoption in SME. To perform this review, we follow the systematic guidelines of Kitchenham; Kitchenham [2004; 2007] and Kitchenham *et al.* [2009] to assess the maximum available appropriate research to our study. In this section, we define our study's scope and plan, research objectives and aims, research methodology in distinct stages. In order to achieve our research objective of an in-depth study of barriers to IT adoption in SMEs, we examine and classify the barriers which may cause the failure of IT adoption in SME, for the purpose of overcoming them and facilitating the IT adoption success, by reviewing the results of the previous studies. The review method represents a sequence of strategies and procedures used to analyze the objective of the study, to select relevant studies and finally to extract, analyze and synthesize the data. According to Kitchenham's method, an SLR consists of different steps.

The first step is to develop a review protocol; which is a critical step for any SLR. The second step is to identify inclusion and exclusion criteria, which should be based on the aims of research to correctly classify studies. The third step is to perform a search strategy, which is a multistage process to select and identify studies, followed by critical evaluation and finally data extraction and synthesis of findings. The following sub-sections itemize all these previous steps.

2.1. *Review protocol*

To undertake a particular SLR, the first step is to develop and pre-define protocol for next steps. We developed our review protocol (Appendix B), in accordance with recommendations, policies, and guidelines of the Cochrane's Hand Book for Systematic Reviews of Intervention [Higgins and Green (2008)]. The review protocol defines the main research question that guides all the next steps (next sub-sections). So, this SLR was guided by the following research question: What are the barriers that might explain the lack of IT adoption in SME? We identified the stakeholders, the fields, the relevant studies, and materials by focusing on this research question.

2.2. *Inclusion and exclusion criteria*

The selection stage is important for a correct classification of studies and validity of our review. Then, we defined some inclusion and exclusion criteria during the protocol development based on research question, and applied them to our selections. Studies were admissible for inclusion if they first were targeted on general or some specific IT, applied in different lines of business. Studies were selected by date "from 1992 to 2018," which is as long as the IT exists for a length of time in enterprises. Only research studies published in academic publishing were included in the SLR, such as conference proceedings, journal articles, some scientific books, and published Ph.D. dissertations. In contrast, in-progress studies and papers that were not written in English were excluded from this SLR. Finally, since our study was on the IT within SME, we included the meta-analysis, theoretical, qualitative, quantitative, and case studies.

2.3. *Data sources and search strategy*

To select studies and collect data, generating and following a search strategy is necessary (Fig. 1). So the first stage of our search strategy was to form search. To do this we targeted and combined our keywords based on the previous research question. We included the wildcard characters and excluded the stop word in order to reduce the search strings number and speed up the search time. The search strings used two different steps using multiple queries. The first step is the combination of the three following sets of keywords: ["barriers" OR "obstacles" OR "difficulties" OR "challenges"] AND ["information technology adoption" OR "information systems adoption" OR "innovation adoption" OR "IT" OR "IS" OR "ICT"] AND ["small businesses" OR "small enterprises" OR "small and medium businesses" OR "small and medium enterprises" OR "SME" OR "SMB" OR "SB"]. The second step was to target some specific barriers, using the combination of the three following sets of keywords: ["information technology adoption" OR "information systems adoption" OR "innovation adoption" OR "IT" OR "IS" OR "ICT"] AND ["internal barriers" OR "external barriers" OR "top management" OR "CEO" OR "manager"

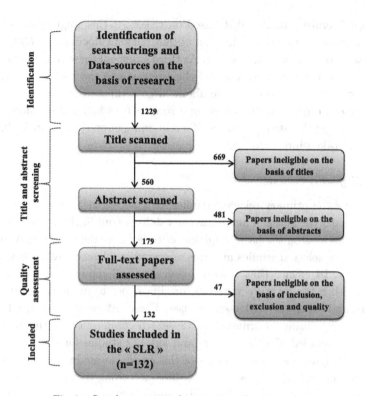

Fig. 1.   Search strategy and systematic selection studies.

OR "owner" OR "users" OR "resources" OR "organization" OR "culture" OR "competences" OR "expertise" OR "acceptance" OR "management" OR "user changes" OR "consultants" OR "partners" OR "satisfaction"] AND ["small businesses" OR "small enterprises" OR "small and medium businesses" OR "small and medium enterprises" OR "SME" OR "SMB" OR "SB"].

The second stage of our search strategy was to identify keywords within titles, abstracts, and keywords of the papers. Electronic sources (databases, Journals, books, reviews, etc.) were included in the search strategy. The selected sources are the following: Science Direct (Elsevier), Springer, the digital library ACM, IEEE Xplore, JSTOR, Emerald insight, Taylor & Francis online, Inderscience online, Wiley Online Library, Journal of small business Management, European Journal of Business and Management, Information Journal, and Management Science Journal. To complement our study, we also searched in search engine and social networking sites for scientists and researchers, such as Google scholar and researchgate.

Our systematic literature review was carried out between December 2016 and November 2018. During first stage, we identified 1229 papers using keywords previously mentioned in different search engines, databases, journals, and books, and listed them in the reference management Mendeley. At second stage, we determined the relevant literature to the SLR based on titles. At this stage, papers that were clearly not about IT were excluded. To obtain relevant documents, 560 documents were selected from among 1229 papers. At third stage, all these remained documents were assessed in term of abstracts and their relation to the research issues we had defined. However, some studies were about large companies, some were lacking information about our research subject, and some others had a disconnected content with their title. At this stage, from the 560 remaining papers, 179 were included to be analyzed and taken into account.

2.4. *Quality assessment*

After selecting the primary relevant studies, it is necessary to assess the quality, in order to minimize the bias and maximize the validity of our SLR. So the 179 remaining papers were assessed on the basis of quality criteria (more details are in Appendix B). We assessed the selected studies in terms of scientific diligence, reliability, accuracy, and propriety, to ensure that research concepts and methods are respected. We assessed whether results were targeted, originals, pertinent, and useful for future researchers, and experts as well as enterprises. These criteria were essential to provide valuable and significant contributions to research community. In this section of assessment, we excluded 47 other papers and left 132 studies for the next step "data extraction and synthesis" (more details of this exclusion are in Appendix B, Quality Assessment). These last studies were classified according to its main research aims, methods, contributions, and results. This categorization has enabled us to identify, extract, classify and synthesis data responding to research issues.

2.5. *Data extraction and synthesis*

In order to extract relevant data and synthesize results, an in-depth analysis was conducted. All of these papers were independently examined and findings of each study were initially identified, analyzed, and synthesized. These findings were classified in order to extract and list all barriers from each study and compare them, using the original terms of the authors. Then, we conducted an analysis on the basis of main stakeholders and categorized this list into preliminary categories (internal and external barriers). Thereafter, we grouped barriers within a number of sub-categories. This list of barriers and its categories was iteratively modified and compared to the previous list in order to give a valuable contribution to research. A final categorization of barriers was concluded by the research team, as well as a classification of available evidence was identified for each barrier to have more credibility of findings.

3. Results

In this systematic literature review, we have identified the main barriers to IT adoption in SME. A multitude of different theoretical approaches are stated to classify and categorize IT adoption influencers, on the basis of prior scientific research and theories [Arroyo *et al.* (2007); Brem and Viardot (2015); Caldeira and Ward (2003); Hamdan and Yahaya (2016); Nguyen (2009); Sarosa and Zowghi (2003); Southern and Tilley (2000); Venkatesh and Brown (2001)]. We categorized them into two principal clusters, which include the most stakeholders influencing IT adoption: Internal and external barriers. This paper reveals 18 barriers to IT adoption in SME (see Table A.1 in Appendix A). Internal barriers are defined as barriers within the organizational, cultural, and financial context of SME and external barriers are defined as barriers within the environmental context of SME. These barriers and categories are some of most important hierarchical and interconnected challenges for SME, defined by sub-categories to grasp the studies' research focus more thoroughly.

3.1. *Top management*

In SME, IT adoption process is directly linked to the top management [Lybaert (1998); Fink (1998)]; they have in particular simple and centralized structures governed by Chief Executive Officer (CEO) [Ghobakhloo *et al.* (2012)]. The role of the top management is more weighing in the SME than in large companies, as it usually takes the most important decisions including those concerning the IT [Holmes and Nicholls (1989); Holmes *et al.* (1991); Thong *et al.* (1993)]. As a result, many researchers and experts saw a more outstanding interest in IT projects in SME than in large enterprises [Brem *et al.* (2008); Raymond and Magnenat-Thalmann (1982); Jarvenpaa and Ives (1991); Fuller-love (2006); Bhattacharya (2015); Dubravac and Bevanda (2015)]. On the one hand, many CEO have a little IT knowledge, and on the other hand, IT executives know very little about the company and often does not understand the real needs in IT of the company, which leads to a bad management and prevent the IT adoption in the company [Igbaria *et al.* (1997); Anderson and Huang (2006)]. According to [Howard *et al.* (2003)], barriers to IT adoption come from the top management, where CEO can be the most powerful driving forces of IT adoption projects success or the most important barrier blocking this change. Several barriers in keeping with top management are blocking IT adoption in SME, in particular:

3.1.1. *Lack of commitment and engagement of top management*

Several studies underline that top management's support and commitment are significantly influencing the success of IT projects [Thong *et al.* (1993); Chesher and Skok (2000); Abdul Hameed *et al.* (2012); Upadhyay *et al.* (2011); Ghobakhloo *et al.* (2012); Bharati and Chaudhury (2012)]. In the context of SME, majority of enterprises have a flat organizational structure managed by CEO [Thong *et al.* (1993)], which is why some studies of the top management support are concentrated on the CEO [El-Gohary (2012); Ghobakhloo and Tang (2013)]. If the CEO is committed to the practices of IT adoption in the whole the company, a heightened awareness and commitment will become a part of the organizational culture for all the staff [Järveläinen (2013)]. In this respect, Liu and Arnett [2000]; Sabherwal *et al.* [2006] have pointed out that the commitment to IT project is a question, which can differentiate between the success and failure of IT adoption within a small enterprise. And Bharati and Chaudhury [2015] have noted that the CEO must be engaged in several responsibilities during the IT adoption in SME to encourage positive attitudes within staff, given that he is the most important user of IT. For example, if the CEO is not enthusiastic about the use of IT and its importance to supporting the company and if the CEO is willing to support IT, it is unlikely that other stakeholders of the company are it. So the project execution often suffers from a bad management and IT adoption fails [Bull (2003); Schniederjans and Yadav (2013)]. This evidence explains how the lack of support and commitment of top management can limit and be a barrier to IT adoption within SME.

3.1.2. *Top management's lack of IT knowledge, competences, capacities, and expertise*

Nowadays, capacity, competence, knowledge, and the expertise of the top management are very important throughout the IT adoption process in SME; in effect the exploitation of relevant opportunities, obtaining the resources necessary for the management, and development of the organization are the responsibilities of the CEO. Otherwise, the SME will be faced with many barriers to IT adoption [Igbaria *et al.* (1997); Hashim (2015)]. Indeed, there are reasons to believe that the SME growth is based on the personal capacities of CEO. According to Wiklund and Shepherd [2003]; Lee [2004], the innovative capacity of the CEO is considered as one of the key capabilities for the success or not of each business project. In this respect, Fink [1998]; Thong and Yap [1995] have noted that changes toward the IT adoption in the SME with innovative managers are more likely to succeed. And Al-Qirim [2007] has reported in his study on the adoption of electronic commerce in small and medium-sized businesses in New Zealand, that the IT adoption in SME is positively influenced by CEO innovation (the innovative SME take the risk and apply solutions of distinct IT by targeting the enterprise's needs). Consequently, we believe that due to the lack of IT expertise, knowledge and innovation of the CEO, the IT adoption will be postponed or even may fail after its implementation unless that those barriers are lowered or bypassed.

3.1.3. *Lack of CEO's interest, motivation, and desire of growth*

Nowadays, IT is regarded as an integral part of the company but closely adopted by SME; SME don't invest or are afraid to invest in the IT adoption in their businesses.

There is no recognition of information's importance in the achievement of business strategies. According to Cragg *et al.* [2002] and Levy *et al.* [1998], CEO's of SME do not have the necessary resources to adopt and use IT; they lack expertise in new technologies and time, therefore they lack attention and interest in respect of IT. And Mehrtens *et al.* [2001] and Wiklund and Shepherd [2003] have argued that the lack of motivation of the decision-maker and CEO limits the ability of SME to conceive a computerized strategy and develop IT adoption strategies within the enterprise. However, the relationship between the interest, motivation, and the SME growth appears to be more complex than expected. It depends on the level of education and experience of CEO as well as the dynamism of the environment in which the company operates; the superficial IT knowledge of CEO makes them non-enthusiastic with regard to informatics and in reluctant to accept changes to IT, although they know that it will help them to increase their productivity [Harland *et al.* (2007)]. A study made by Qureshi and York [2008] has shown that the styles of programming preferred by the owners of small businesses are likely to affect the IT adoption, while this variable seems more important: the learning style of a CEO is among the most important features that decide its interest to adopt IT within SME. Thus one can consider the CEO's lack of interest and motivation with respect to the IT as a barrier to its adoption.

3.1.4. *Top management's lack of confidence and perception of IT benefits*

According to the Theory of Planned Behavior of Ajzen [1988], an individual will have the intention to carry out a certain behavior (such as the belief in adoption of IT) when he or she positively assesses it, then the belief and confidence (positive assessment) of CEO seems to have an impact on the decision to adopt IT. On the other hand, the model Technology Acceptance Model (TAM) designed by Davis *et al.* [1989] have suggested that perceived usefulness of a system is one of the causal histories adoption and behavior of use of IT. Consequently, confidence and perception of IT advantages by top management are some of most defining characteristics influencing IT adoption decision in the enterprise. The literature of IT provides significant evidence of the direct relationship between the confidence and perception of IT benefit by top management with the IT adoption or non-adoption in the SME [Kapurubandara and Lawson (2006); Sutanonpaiboon and Pearson (2006); Al-Qirim (2007); Harland *et al.* (2007); Schniederjans and Yadav (2013); Jussila *et al.* (2014)]. In effect, CEO of SME are very concerned with the question of confidence in security and benefits of new technologies in their organizations, because of the spread of technological fraud [Damaskopoulos and Evgeniou (2003); Schniederjans and Yadav (2013); Aloini *et al.* (2016)]. In this respect, Kapurubandara and Lawson [2006] have indicated that within SME of developing countries, a CEO who is not aware of benefits of e-commerce applications are doubtful and are reluctant to adopt these technologies. Similarly, Hamdan and Yahaya [2016] have confirmed in their studies that the CEO's lack of knowledge in IT benefits or the lack of understanding the way which IT can bring benefits influence the CEO confidence in IT adoption, therefore such concerns may restrict the IT adoption in SME. Finally Pavlou [2003], Love *et al.* [2005], and Tan *et al.* [2009] have affirmed that the perception of a lack of IT advantages are preventing IT adoption within SME.

3.2. *End users*

The SME have an informal attitude toward IT management "lack of training, missed planning and management IT practices". Indeed, the top management must employ a person or a group of individuals to assume the IT responsibility. This person must have a vast knowledge, expertise in IT and the time appropriate to its planning and control. However, most of the SME' staff (supposed to be users of IT) are classified as non-knowing in informatics, which carries out companies to rely on external expertise [Cragg and Zinatelli (1995)]. In this context, we are trying to further research about users/staff as barriers to IT adoption. Some of these barriers are listed below.

3.2.1. *Users' dissatisfaction and resistance to change*

Users' motivation and satisfaction regarding IT within SME are strongly linked to the success of its use within the companies [Fink (1998); Bandow *et al.* (2005); Terziovski (2010)]. However in most SME, staff do not accept changes and are resistant to IT adoption, due to several internal and external reasons: (1) Previous negative experiences with technologies; (2) The pre-judgment of lack of IT needs; (3) Influence of colleagues and supervisors of IT management; (4) Fear of need for additional time for IT management and implementation; (5) Fear of difficulty of IT conceptualizing, of failure or loss of IT control; (6) Lack of perception of IT benefits; (7) Lack of top management and organizational support and encouragement; Insufficiency of IT resources existing in the SME; (8) Lack of IT expertise and qualification of users; (9) Fear of losing their jobs [Mahmood *et al.* (2000); Howard *et al.* (2003); Staples and Niazi (2010); Cragg *et al.* (2011)]. Several researchers have pointed that satisfaction of staff (being users of new technologies) is an essential characteristic of IT adoption within SME [Mahmood *et al.* (2000); Dalcher and Shine (2003); Liu *et al.* (2006); Schniederjans and Yadav (2013)], the users' acceptance may be excessively a benefit related to the IT project's success, as its absence (users' resistance) may be excessively a determinant of its failure [Chau (1995); Malhotra and Temponi (2010); Kakar (2017)]. Nevertheless, more than half of IT is under-used or not used in SME because of users belief positive changes brought by IT [Bull (2003)]. To overcome this barrier, top management must think to encourage and support users during all stages of planning and adoption of IT [Ghobakhloo and

Tang (2013)] and proceed to practical training, motivation, imagination, and creation, (considering that users often resist to social changes that technical changes [Howard *et al.* (2003)]) or even engage new employees that form the current staff [Bruque and Moyano (2007)].

3.2.2. *Lack of users' participation and engagement*

According to Fink [1998], SME with users that have competences and capacities to analyze their needs in technology, to participate and use IT, are more likely to adopt IT. And Thong [2001] has reported in his model that the participation of users in IT adoption projects is regarded as an important tool leading to their success. To bear the staff's worry about IT effects and ensure their participation, Shin [2006] have suggested that top management must make its staff aware of any changes brought by IT and hold them conscious of assets and resources, which they will draw from IT. In this framework, it is necessary to involve them in new IT projects by specifying times for IT projects and include it in their responsibilities, and persuade them that every individual of the team is responsible to translate a high level of IT projects success [Amoako-Gyampah (2007)]. This participation must be done during all the cycle of project (project planning, design and implementation, monitoring, performance test, etc.).

3.2.3. *Lack of users' knowledge and training on IT benefits*

The lack of knowledge of technologies forms an important barrier to IT adoption within SME. In spite of their belief and acceptance, the lack of knowledge of some users prevents them from benefiting from the potential provided by IT. Because of this, they do not perceive demanding reasons for adopting IT; they consider only the complexity of the system which requires a mass of qualified staff in IT and therefore a threat of losing their positions within the company or even their jobs [Damasko-poulos and Evgeniou (2003); Schniederjans and Yadav (2013)]. To increase the level of users' knowledge of IT, it is necessary to provide training to staff (IT users) [Thong (2001); Sarosa and Zowghi (2003)]. Users' awareness of IT benefits influences positively on any stage of IT adoption process, which can be deepened by teaching and training (the greater the level and volume of users' training before IT adoption are raised, the more the visibility of usefulness, ease of use and familiarization with IT are raised too) [Ghobakhloo *et al.* (2012)]. A study done by Qureshi and York [2008] has shown that companies adopting the less successful IT have declared that they haven't ensured to users training necessary to maintain the use of their systems. However, users who have succeeded are those likely to be comfortable with technology at the outset of the project and even before its departure, because they seem to have an idea of its importance for the development of the company's activity [Abdul Hameed *et al.* (2012)]. For these reasons, user's knowledge is one of barriers to IT adoption within SME.

3.2.4. *Lack of users' technical expertise and skills*

Staff is an important asset seriously affecting the success and the survival of companies [Nguyen (2009)]; being IT users within SME, they are an invaluable resource that must be developed to contribute to company success [Zhou *et al.* (2009)]. However, El-Gohary [2012] has reported that due to their small size, SME don't have IT service or Information Systems Department (ISD) or even responsible IT full-time with a formal training. The IT responsible is often a simple employee with simple previous experience with computers and Internet, poorly placed to lead the ISD. According to Hamdan and Yahaya [2016], 52.1% of SME does not have a qualified staff in informatics and able to manage IT, which many CEO estimates that training is useless since the software is easy to use. As well, the lack of internal technical expertise causes a low IT adoption and failure of harvesting its benefits [Abdul Hameed *et al.* (2012)]. Consequently, a serious impediment to IT use and adoption in SME appears to be, given that the successful adoption of IT requires users' knowledge sharing, training and skills [Egbu *et al.* (2005)]. In this respect, a study done by Cragg and Zinatelli [1995], noted that only 20% of employees use IT actively. In fact, in most SME, the internal expertise (users/staff) is limited, which can also be strengthened by developing their own skills, by the practice during employment, by IT courses and free seminars [Cragg and Zinatelli (1995); Ghobakhloo and Tang (2013)]. And Sarosa and Zowghi [2003] have noted that the best technologic and informatic knowledge of IT users requires a positive impact not only on the acceptance, commitment, and use of IT, but also its level of adoption and implementation.

In summary, the lack of internal expertise (IT users) is one of the barriers more influencing IT adoption within SME. To overcome this problem, it is necessary either to strengthen the competences of staff by formation and practice, by specifying in advance the specific need of training, or by seeking assistance from external sources (consultants, IT suppliers...) [Upadhyay *et al.* (2011)].

3.3. *Resources*

SME are known by their limited access and availability to some specific resources compared to large enterprises [Igbaria and Tan (1997); Nieto and Fernández (2005); El-Gohary (2012); Madrid-Guijarro *et al.* (2016)]. Consequently, SME does not adopt IT under the pretext of the lack of resources in the enterprise [Carson and Gilmore (2000); Bhagwat and Sharma (2007); Nguyen and Waring (2013)]. So, resources of SME may strongly affect positively or negatively the process of IT adoption [Cragg and Zinatelli (1995); Dutta and Evrard (1999); Southern and Tilley (2000); Thong (2001); Wiklund and Shepherd (2003); Caldeira and Ward (2003); Harland *et al.* (2007); Ghobakhloo and Tang (2013)]. In this respect, Abdul Hameed *et al.* [2012] have exhibited that the relation between resources and IT adoption is insignificant in the large enterprise than in SME. Some resources lack influencing IT adoption are listed below.

3.3.1. *Lack of financial resources*

Financial/Economic resources are known for years among the most decisive and critical resources to companies' performance and success [Rangone (1999); Madrid-Guijarro *et al.* (2016); Gutmann *et al.* (2016)], particularly in SME, which suffer from the lack of financial resources to invest in new projects (most SME owners invest their own personal capital) [Fuller-love (2006); García Pérez de Lema and Duréndez (2007); Nguyen and Waring (2013); Laufs *et al.* (2016)]. Furthermore, Premkumar [2003]; Hamdan and Yahaya [2016] have approved that the high costs of IT is one of issues hindering IT adoption and use within SME. SME cannot support these raised costs, which have become a common anxiety for CEOs. And the statistics done by Damaskopoulos and Evgeniou [2003] have shown that an estimate of 48% of CEO in Polish SME assert that IT costs are very high. To study this thorny economic question that disturbs and slows IT adoption in SME, it is necessary to study resources as barriers in two respects: Costs assimilated for IT adoption are major constraint that hampers this adoption in SME [Ghobakhloo and Tang (2013); Kurnia *et al.* (2015)]; and Paltry budget of SME requires CEO to be cautious about their spending and investment in IT [Thong and Yap (1995); Ghobakhloo *et al.* (2011); Nguyen (2009)]. However, there are some divergent opinions about this issue. Dibrell *et al.* [2008] have suggested that there is a considerable decrease over the years with regard to the hardware and software prices, which leads to reduced costs of IT adoption.

3.3.2. *Lack of technological resources*

Technological/computing resources are a critical priority for an enterprise, which influences on the assessment of its products and services [Sledgianowski *et al.* (2008); Lee *et al.* (2012)]. Several studies affirm that the lack of technological resources (Infrastructure and adequate hardware and software) may constitute a major barrier that prevents SME to adopt and implement IT [Wang and Cheung (2004); Decker *et al.* (2006); Cheng *et al.* (2002); Schniederjans and Yadav (2013); Hahn *et al.* (2016)]. Abdul Hameed *et al.* [2012] have denoted in their meta-analysis that nine countries out of twelve affirm that infrastructure has a significant influence on IT adoption (in particular for implementation stage) and they finally concluded that 95% of results (calculated by the correlation method) presented a significant relationship between the IT infrastructure and its implementation. Also, Cragg and Zinatelli [1995] have marked in their research that in most small businesses, the main service with computers is that of accounting, while other critical areas (production, marketing, etc.) have not been equipped with computers and software. Consequently, a low level of computerization and IT adoption appear in different functional areas essential for the growth of SME [Ghobakhloo and Tang (2013)]. In addition, the size of IT department can also have an impact on IT adoption, with a larger department often making a more successful adoption process [Abdul Hameed *et al.* (2012)].

3.3.3. *Lack of human resources*

Human resources within enterprises mean staff capacity, skills (technical and managerial) knowledge, experiences, planning and internal organization, and strategy. These elements create more IT adoption success within SME [Carbonara (2005); De Búrca *et al.* (2005); Ghobakhloo *et al.* (2011a); Kmieciak *et al.* (2012)]. Nevertheless, SME suffer from lack of internal IT knowledge and expertise, comparing with large companies [Ghobakhloo *et al.* (2012)]. And Caldeira and Ward [2003] and Buonanno *et al.* [2005] have insisted on the internal expertise power (executives, CEO, employees, supervisors...) as determinants of IT adoption the SME, to provide a high level of IT adoption and the SME satisfaction, it is necessary to: (1) Develop internal human and managerial resources of companies (staff knowledge and skills in IT) [DeLone and McLean (2016)]. (2) Ensure the permanent presence of an individual expert in IT within [Fink (1998); Black and Lynch (2001)]. This individual influences any involved person in the SME, as he convinces top management to adopt IT, and he facilitates the acceptance and commitment of IT users by providing seminars and training [Teo and Ranganathan (2004)]. Mumtaz Abdul Hameed *et al.* [2012] have insisted on the importance of this person for IT success in SME and assigned him the name "Innovation Champion or technology leader."

3.4. *Organization*

To adopt IT, organizations must ensure information and knowledge sharing between managers and users, since all IT adoption processes (preparation, planning, implementation, test...) requires a formal work and acceptance of change from all teams and departments [Kazhamiakin *et al.* (2006); Stam (2010)]. In effect, organizational characteristics are related to IT adoption, IT implementation and IT/strategy alignment [Gray (2006); Hansen and Hamilton (2011); Ullah and Lai (2013)]. Accordingly, previous studies have revealed a number of potential organizational barriers that threaten IT adoption process in SME, in particular.

3.4.1. *Informalization (lack of IT planning, preparation, and strategy)*

Formalization in the context of IT is considered as a technological strategy within the company, which includes organizational planning and preparation [Cragg *et al.* (2002)]. It is also called Strategy of IT or Information Technology planning (ITP) [Tan *et al.* (2007)]. ITP means determining how, why and what improvements and benefits this technology will bring to the company, and then analyzing needs and objectives in computing and conceiving a strategy for long-term [Rojas-Méndez *et al.* (2017)]. It is a very essential factor leading to success and rapid spread of IT adoption within SME [Spinelli *et al.* (2013); Maduku *et al.* (2016)].

Some SME' owners have demonstrated the importance of ITP, as they have confirmed having specific IT according to their specific needs, less costly and fewer complexes than those standards overloaded by unnecessary and irrelevant improvements [Qureshi and York (2008)]. Nevertheless, several previous research [Lefebvre *et al.* (1992); Levy and Powell (2003); Ramayah *et al.* (2005); Mutula and Brakel (2006); Fathian *et al.* (2008); Chan *et al.* (2012)] have mentioned that IT in SME are not as strategically planned as in large enterprises. This is due to the lack of awareness and strategic training; many SME adopt and use IT just to follow other enterprises [Nguyen (2009)]. That is generating barriers to IT adoption such as: Accidental and unplanned competitive advantages, SME influenced by the strategy "Cost Reduction" than the strategy "added value" and an evil delivery or failure of IT projects [Ghobakhloo *et al.* (2012)]. And [Blili and Raymond (1993); Dufour and Son (2015)] emphasize that the main barrier to IT adoption within SME is the informalization and strategic decision-making in short-term (lack of ITP) and notes that IT project barriers may be the cause of other barriers.

3.4.2. *Business type*

Several studies in different countries have considered that business type and sector of activity are among the factors influencing IT adoption within SME [Seyal *et al.* (2000); Love *et al.* (2005); Ghobakhloo *et al.* (2011b); Chan *et al.* (2012); Nguyen and Waring (2013)]. Since years, business type also plays a great part to decide the structure and architecture of IT "companies of similar activity tend to adopt similar IT thanks to similarity of needs, users, attitudes, intensity of information, and requirements of information" [Salmeron and Bueno (2006)]. Therefore, barriers influencing IT adoption in production companies are different than those of services companies [Cheng *et al.* (2002); Damaskopoulos and Evgeniou (2003)]. In this respect, Thong and Yap [1995] have noted that the sectors of activities with great intensity of information have a tendency to adopt IT more than those less intense. In accordance with this, Damaskopoulos and Evgeniou [2003] have affirmed that IT affect the marketing and sales sectors more than the production sector. And [Gaith *et al.* (2009)] have confirmed that Malaysian companies of services use integrated IT more than those of manufacturing and distribution. Finally, Ghobakhloo *et al.* [2012] have considered the business type as a barrier to IT adoption, in the case where the type of IT is not aligned with the activity of SME.

3.4.3. *Business size*

Businesses differ from other in some characteristics, among those, the business size [Brocard and Gandois (1978)]. Business size (index defined by the turnover and number of employees) is a fundamental factor directly influencing IT [Premkumar and Roberts (1999)]. Indeed SME are the most businesses dependent on external interactions for IT adoption than other organizations because of their critical sizes [Gnyawali and Park (2009)]. Previous research has emphasized that business size is the most important discriminant for adoption or non-adoption of IT [Thong and Yap (1995); Harland *et al.* (2007); Zahay and Peltier (2008); Michaelidou *et al.* (2011); Abdul Hameed *et al.* (2012)]. Buonanno *et al.* [2005] have asserted that business size is significantly correlated with ERP adoption within SME. Consequently, we can say that SME tend to integrate IT less effectively and less rapidly than large businesses because of its smallness.

3.4.4. *Organizational culture*

Organizational culture is an important feature for company development and growth [Bruque and Moyano (2007)]. Furthermore, organizational change and growth are the driving forces imposing SME to adopt effective and integrated IT [Drew (2003)]. Consequently, organizational culture has an influence on IT adoption. In this respect, Riolli and Savicki [2003]; Shan and Kumar [2012]; Nguyen and Waring [2013] have suggested that culture is the important element influencing any organizational change including IT project success. And Riduan [2017] have affirmed that the SME with less flexible cultures are more disadvantageous and less likely to adopt and use IT. In effect, organizational culture may influence positively or negatively any behavior in SME [Carmeli *et al.* (2008)], in particular: (1) The openness to changes "SME with flexible organizational culture are more open to changes related to IT [Messersmith *et al.* (2009)], if organizational culture is not favorable, top management, and users attitudes to IT is negative and consequently they resist to changes and IT preparation [Jones *et al.* (2005); Arroyo *et al.* (2007)]"; (2) Organizational Learning "The interrelationship between learning and SME culture is important for improvement of competitiveness of SME, IT adoption in SME requires internal and external knowledge [Graham and Nafukho (2007)]. However, it is difficult to adopt IT with an unwavering staff'; (3) Family Company/Family participation "Involvement and participation of family in business management are higher in SME; managers are characterized by reduced levels of schooling compared to large companies [Venkatesh and Brown (2001)]. The disqualification of family may lead to inefficient management of IT Projects [Harland *et al.* (2007); Solaymani *et al.* (2012)]"; (4) Organization's centralization "In most SME, the decision-making is centralized, with only the CEO makes all the decisions of projects, including IT projects [Kanamori and Motohashi (2006)]. A study made by Abdul Hameed *et al.* [2012] has noted a negative relation between centralization with IT acceptance and initiation, but positive relation between centralization and IT implementation. Then, centralization may be a barrier to IT acceptance and adoption."

3.5. *External barriers*

In some SME, the hiring of internal IT specialists is difficult; they rely on external expertise either to IT planning or IT implementation. Therefore, regardless of all barriers that we have previously mentioned, the quality of external expertise "consultants, technical specialists, suppliers and developers of IT, legal specialist, etc." has a significant impact on IT adoption and effectiveness and can be more critical than internal factors [Qureshi and York (2008); Bianchi *et al.* (2017)]. Previous studies have revealed a certain number of external barriers that impede the IT adoption process in SME, in particular.

3.5.1. *Regulatory form inadequacy and lack of government support*

Importance of national policies, the government support for the IT adoption have been studied by several authors [Yap *et al.* (1994); Southern and Tilley (2000); Tan *et al.* (2009); Kennedy and Basu (2013); Lloyd (2014); Nawaz and Gunapalan (2015); Soon Ern (2015)] and by the Economic and Social Council of the United Nations in the article "legal and regulatory framework for the knowledge economy" published by Vere [2009] indicating that all rules previously developed for traditional commerce and real environment are inappropriate for e-commerce and virtual environment, so this inadequacy can cause a lot of barriers to IT adoption, especially within SME. SME depend on government support more than large companies, because of their size and lack of resources, and government support promotes and facilitates the sharing and transfer of information [Ghobakhloo *et al.* (2011b)]. Consequently, the lack of government support discriminates against the adoption of IT in SME. Vere [2009] has emphasized that in Africa, in about 50 countries in the continent, only about five countries have enacted an IT law[a] to regulate the activities IT. And, Damaskopoulos and Evgeniou [2003] have indicated that in spite of the favorable legal framework for e-commerce, SME of Slovenia, Poland and Romania remain in a much less broad and far from a satisfactory regulation. Consequently, the environment or the regulatory reform can also be considered as a barrier to IT adoption in SME, especially when government support is not enough in terms of infrastructure [Hamdan and Yahaya (2016)], when IT law changes slowly and inadequately and does not take into account the rapid pace of development IT [Damaskopoulos and Evgeniou (2003)] or even when SME does not engage in formulation of IT policies.

---

[a]IT law consists of law which governs the digital dissemination of both information and software, and legal aspects of IT. IT law covers the digital information (including information security and e-commerce) aspects [Lloyd (2014)].

3.5.2. *Lack of adequate external expertise*

Given that the majority of SME seek to survive in today's competitive environment and are not able financially to hire their own internal IT specialists, they use the assistance of professional external IT consultants and suppliers [Haddara and Zach (2011); Jernström *et al.* (2016)]. Consequently, regarding IT adoption within SME, the lack of external expertise may be more crucial than the lack of internal expertise [Qureshi and York (2008); Upadhyay *et al.* (2011); Bianchi *et al.* (2017)].

In effect, IT consultants and suppliers offset IT knowledge among SME; they analyze and respond to business needs, recommend appropriate hardware and software equipment, encourage IT users to accept changes and overcome their fears, train IT users and finally manage IT implementation [Bessant and Rush (1995); Ferneley and Bell (2006); Ghobakhloo *et al.* (2012)]. Therefore SME engaging external consultants have a successful IT adoption, use, integration, and satisfaction of users [Soh *et al.* (1992); Morgan *et al.* (2006); Ismail and King (2014)]. However, engagement of IT consultants and suppliers may cause barriers and negative effects regarding user's satisfaction [Kapurubandara and Lawson (2006); Qureshi and York (2008); Ghobakhloo *et al.* (2012)], such as: (1) Inadequacy between consultants and IT users in SME, (2) IT suppliers conceive their solutions for large organizations without taking the specific needs of SME into consideration, (3) limited contact of SME and external experts (when there is a problem to solve or at the time of the software update), (4) lack of users' understanding of IT solution conceived by consultant/supplier.

3.5.3. *Competitive and environmental pressure*

Previous literature has shown that some SME have adopted IT by customers pressure [Fan (2016)], while others have adopted it for changes and trends of the economic market and also there are those who have adopted it to cope with the competitive requirements [Doherty *et al.* (2016)]. According to Fink [1998], the role of environmental pressures (competition and competitiveness) is not yet clearly determined as barrier (or not) to IT adoption within SME, given the multiple benefits that IT offers to businesses. Some previous researches [Damaskopoulos and Evgeniou (2003); Singh *et al.* (2007, 2008); Ghobakhloo *et al.* (2012); Hamdan and Yahaya (2016) indicate that the need to stay competitive seems an important requirement for IT adoption within SME; SME distinguish themselves from their competitors by adopting IT. Then, ISD must think not only about the internal reasons for IT project adoption but also be concerned with the needs of information of their suppliers and customers [Mehrtens *et al.* (2001); Damaskopoulos and Evgeniou (2003); Bharati and Chaudhury (2015)]. In this sense, Fan [2016] has suggested that the pressure of customers and suppliers is one of the most important external pressures behind IT adoption projects success in SME. Customers are becoming more and more demanding, and being able to respond to their needs means being able to survive and compete in the market [Marinescu *et al.* (2007)]. And according to Dutta and Evrard [1999], the majority of SME rely on IT to provide better services and fluid communication with partners.

Consequently, the lack of desire to survive, to innovate and remain competitive is considered as a barrier to IT adoption and implementation [Ghobakhloo *et al.* (2011b)]; SME of low rate of innovation and intense competitive challenge are less likely to adopt IT [Neirotti and Raguseo (2017)]. In other words, SME adopt IT to outperform their competitors and have a "competitive advantage" [Ghobakhloo *et al.* (2011)]. Nevertheless, the competitive advantage always remains a difficulty for SME, seen as their smallness and lack of resources, which made of competitive pressures a barrier instead of IT adoption advantage.

4. Discussion

Organization for Economic Cooperation and Development (OECD) has noticed that SME have an important part in all countries, including developing countries. However, they are less likely to adopt IT than large companies. In the SLR discussed in this paper, we attempted to understand the IT adoption in SME and reasons that make IT adoption less likely within SME. Indeed, because of multiple characteristics, laws, and conditions those differ SME from large companies. Several barriers, as previously mentioned, might explain the lack of IT adoption, particularly in SME. In summary, far from the complexity and inappropriateness between IT and SME, this review has shown that there is no single explanatory barrier for the lack or failure of IT adoption within SME. In our SLR, on the basis of literature [Arroyo *et al.* (2007); Brem and Viardot (2015); Caldeira and Ward (2003); Hamdan and Yahaya (2016); Nguyen (2009); Sarosa and Zowghi (2003); Southern and Tilley (2000); Venkatesh and Brown (2001)], we have categorized barriers into two principal clusters: internal and external barriers. This paper reveals a number of internal barriers to IT adoption (internal barriers are defined as barriers within the organizational, cultural, and financial context of SME). And it also reveals some external barriers to IT adoption (external barriers are defined as barriers within the environmental context of SME).

Previous research has provided a number of different characteristics and parameters as barriers to IT adoption in SME, which we have classified. Table A.1 in Appendix A provides the evidence of barriers approved by every internal or external stakeholder. Prior research on IT adoption within SME have shown and revealed a number of CEO, users, organizational, and cultural characteristic as barriers to IT adoption which include the lack of CEO and users commitment, engagement, awareness, support, perception of benefits, skills, knowledge and also IT acceptance, in term of organizational characteristics, the business size and type, IT planning and strategies, organizational culture of IT stakeholders and users, IT management. These barriers go hand in hand with the lack of internal human, technical and financial resources "Human resources: lack of skills, competences, knowledge, etc. Technical resources: lack of IT infrastructures, lack of equipment, etc. Financial resources: business size, business department, high costs of IT adoption, implementation, maintenance, etc." In addition, because many SME do not have internal expertise, the external barriers are also greatly affects the IT adoption in SME, such as the lack of external skills and support (consultants, government, suppliers, partners, etc.), external pressure and competition.

Additionally, since the selected studies explores IT adoption barriers within SME for different kinds of IT, and to grasp our systematic literature review focus more thoroughly, we did a more detailed analysis where the classification of identified studies is related to the kind of IT adoption (Fig. 2). As Fig. 2 reveals, 76.74% of all studies selected are related to papers studying IT in general, showing the highest ratio, and thus highlighting the relevance of selected studies. Meanwhile, only 23.26% are shown studying different kinds of IT adoption (ERP, CRM, SCM, etc.).

In accordance with our analysis, Fig. 3 takes up the main findings of SLR. As Fig. 3 shows, we identify sufficient evidence for a link between internal parameters and the lack of IT adoption within SME. With regard to internal barriers, 81.32% of all papers selected cite some internal barriers of IT adoption, where organization and

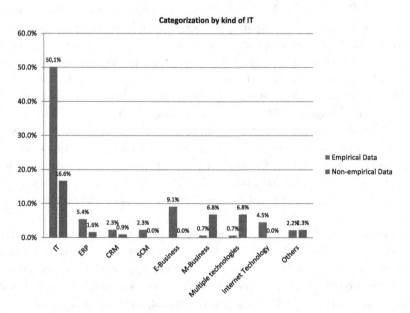

ERP: Enterprise Resource Planning, CRM: Customer Relationship Management, SCM: Supply Chain Management, E-Business: "E-marketing + E-commerce, etc.", M-Business: Mobile services, Multiple technologies: papers studying different kinds of IT, Internet technology: Internet adoption, social media, etc., Others: IoT (Internet of things), CMMI (Capability Maturity Model Integration).

Fig. 2.   Classification of studies related to the kind of IT adoption.

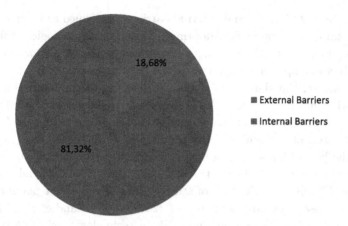

Fig. 3. Distribution of IT barriers among the selected studies.

Table 1. Distribution of selected studies.

		Empirical	Non-empirical
Internal barriers	Top management	16.66%	3.54%
	End users	13.65%	4.54%
	Resources	13.13%	4.04%
	Organization	19.20%	6.56%
External barriers		14.14%	4.54%

top management are the most identified categories (Organization = 25.76% and Top management = 20.2%). In term of these papers, the majority of them are empirical studies (62.64%), while only 37.36 are non-empirical. Not surprisingly, only 18.68% of the retained studies approve the relationship between external factors and the lack of IT adoption.

Additionally, we analyzed findings in greater detail, taking into account sub-categories of internal barriers (Top management, End users, Resources, and Organization) in Table 1.

4.1. *Summary of the findings*

IT adoption has become a paramount concern of IT researchers. Many previous researches have included various barriers influencing and preventing IT adoption in SME. But they did not classify the barriers to IT adoption according to the various stakeholders.

In our SLR, we have categorized the barriers into two principal clusters, which include the most stakeholders influencing IT adoption "subcategories": Internal and external barriers. This paper reveals a number of internal barriers to IT adoption; (1) internal barriers are defined as barriers within the organizational, cultural, and financial context of SME (2) and external barriers are defined as barriers within the environmental context of SME. Adopting information technologies within SME is not an easy task; in particular, there are some challenges, factors, and barriers theoretically and empirically explored by the prior research.

In this context, Hamdan and Yahaya [2016] noticed some internal and external characteristics that may prevent the IT adoption in Malaysian SME. They empirically proved that these characteristics can be considered as barriers to IT adoption, such as the lack of awareness/understanding of IT potential and perception of IT value, the lack of knowledge in financial capacities, the lack of knowledge in IT benefits, the lack of technical expertise and skills, the lack of financial resources, the confusion in IT selection, the lack of strategy and management planning, and the lack of human resources. Ghobakhloo et al. [2012] and Harland et al. [2007] noted in their empirical research based on supply chain technologies within SME some internal and external barriers, specifically barriers related to (1) firm size, (2) owner/manager capability/characteristics, (3) firm awareness of benefits, (4) resources, (5) employee capability, (6) ability to raise finance for eBusiness projects, (7) organizational characteristics and behaviors, (8) external competitive and pressure, (9) difference between sectors, (10) regional/national factors, (11) regulation and government, and (12) IT consultants.

In addition, El-Gohary [2012] affirm that internal factors such as owner skills, available resources, adoption costs, organization size, perceived compatibility and perceived ease of use are the most significant factors affecting positively or negatively the adoption of technologies by small Egyptian organizations. External factors have a very weak influence. These results are in line with Nguyen and Waring [2013] that the SME's likelihood of adopting IT applications depends on various factors; these factors include (1) the top management characteristics, (2) involvement of the employees in the adoption process, (3) IT resources adequacy, and (4) the organizational characteristics (size, industry, etc.). These results are also consistent with Ghobakhloo and Tang [2013]. Ghobakhloo and Tang studied the top management or CEO, considering it the most significant determinant to IT adoption within the developing small businesses. According to Ghobakhloo and Tang, (1) the perceived benefits is the main discriminator between adopter and non-adopters, (2) the managers' perception of compatibility between IT and their business (existing organizational culture and values, preferred work practices, and infrastructure) is another determinant to IT adoption success or failure, (3) lack of confidence and manager's perception of risk is a major barrier to IT adoption, small businesses who are non-adopters of IT perceive these technologies to be risky to adopt and use, (4) the lack of IT adoption is significantly and negatively affected by its costs. Small businesses are often suffer from the lack of financial resources, (5) IT adoption within small businesses is significantly affected by manager's innovativeness, and less affected by their computer knowledge and expertise.

These studies contradict the results of Riduan [2017] suggesting that in addition to some internal factors (Organizational characteristics including the support, communication, culture and collaboration of users, database management system, management participation, organizational relationships, creativity and innovation, etc.), there are also some external factors that affect the IT adoption in Indonesian SMEs such as; the necessary business partner's vigilance, the external influences and environmental characteristics, the understanding of consumer tastes, the external pressure and competitiveness as a form of entrepreneurial orientation. And Ghobakhloo *et al.* [2011], they indicate that the main determinant of IT adoption within Iranian SME is the external support, expertise, and assistance. They notice that the lack of resources such as skills, financial, IT experts, difficulty in recruiting and retaining IT professionals and providing IT training for employees impose a major problem in IT adoption within these companies. In such circumstances, the professional skills of external expertise, and the external assistance are the significant factor of IT adoption. In contradiction to the Nguyen and Waring [2013] and El-Gohary [2012] results, Riduan [2017] and Ghobakhloo *et al.* [2011] confirmed in his study a high relationship between external and environmental characteristics with the innovation adoption within SME.

4.2. *Synthesis*

Synthesizing the outcome of this SLR, we note that previous research has studied and examined many different topics related to our field and aim of our research. While this may be significant for professionals and research community, for some selected studies we are left behind with poor indications that need to be approved by other future research.

By synthesizing the findings of this SLR, it reveals a number of internal barriers to IT adoption. The main stakeholders of these barriers are: (1) Top management. As previously highlighted, the top management (CEO/manager/owner) has a central and important role to the decision-making in SME's projects and activities (including IT adoption projects), so the CEO can be the most powerful driving force of the success of IT adoption projects or the most blocking barrier this change. (2) End users. In SME, along with the role of CEO, employees are considered as important assets seriously affecting the success or failure of IT adoption. SME must develop these precious assets to overcome some important barriers to IT adoption. (3) Resources. Although top management and IT users are strongly considered the driving forces of IT adoption within the SME, the lack of resources is a significant barrier that prevent IT adoption in SME. In effect, SME are distinguished by suffering from their inability to access to some resources compared with large companies. (4) Organization. A number of potential organizational barriers that threaten the IT adoption process in SME are mentioned in Sec. 3; in effect, organizational characteristics are strongly affecting the IT adoption in SME, such as the organizational culture, organizational relationship, IT management, etc. This paper reveals also some external barriers to IT adoption; external barriers are defined as barriers within the environmental context of SME. The main stakeholders of these barriers are: Government, consultants, external technical specialists, suppliers and developers of IT, legal specialist, competitors, and partners. So, the ISD must think not only about the internal barriers of an IT project adoption, but both the internal and external barriers to IT adoption in SME.

In a few words, previous literature suggests that some of the most internal influencers of IT adoption are the top management and end users, the analysis of these results shows that the human factor is the most prominent barrier inhibiting IT adoption, which includes human culture and behavior, human disqualification, human lack of expertise and knowledge, etc. Similar barriers can be observed for organizational barriers which include organizational culture and informalization, which tend to stress the importance of human factor too. With regard to external barriers, one of the most important barriers is "external expertise," which also tends towards human factors.

To our surprise, we can see in previous literature that only handful of studies is specified on human relationship with IT adoption and take a further examination of some human characteristics and their relationship with IT. The majority of studies stress the importance on some specific IT kind (such as ERP, E-commerce, etc.); this impairs the quality of research. Future research has to rely on studies, although they are anything except generalizable, because all of these studies rely on a similar sample.

On the other hand, to succeed an IT adoption project and overcome these barriers, professionals in SME must ensure a formal work of all stakeholders of IT adoption and make sure the acceptance to change of all the organization. SME must ensure the diffusion of information, IT knowledge and skills between users, managers, external consultants and partners throughout all the IT adoption process (preparation, planning, implementation, tests, maintenance, etc.). SME must also define the real IT needs, costs, and budgets of SME to succeed the IT adoption projects.

4.3. *Guidelines to adopt information technology in SME*

Information technologies are indispensable and crucial for organizations. As previously mentioned, SME are now unlikely to adopt these technologies, compared with large companies. Our SLR has exposed several barriers causing this, failure and dissatisfaction of its adoption. To prevent these barriers:

- IT stakeholders must understand the inherent differences between IT in SME and IT in large organizations. The concept of IT adoption is different in the context of

SME. First of all, decision makers must adopt IT in a formalized way; making IT planning and strategies are necessary before implementing IT.

- SME have simple and extremely centralized structures with the top managers (mostly they are the owners); their decision, and involvement influences all firm's activities, attitudes, satisfaction, and involvement toward IT. Then managers must ensure their support, engagement, participation, and involvement in all the stages of IT adoption (initial adoption stage, which include the decision and strategies making, implementation stage, and post adoption stage, which include the use and maintain of the solution).

- SME generally have a limited access to some technical, financial, and human resources. The IT adoption stakeholders and decision makers must target the particular needs of SME in IT, target the budget of these needs, and target the adequate IT solution for the company. To decide the adequate solution for the company, decision makers must take into account the relationship needs/ resources. In this step, a financial strategy must be done.

- Contrary to large companies, SME are influenced by organizational character- istics. The most important characteristics which influence every decision and ac- tivity in SME are cultures; especially national culture which differs from one country to another. The adopters of IT must take into account this critical fact; strategies must have a stage in accordance with users' attitudes, behaviors, and culture. Some training is necessary to learn users' IT benefits, technical use, and expertise of IT. This is necessary to ensure (1) acceptance and satisfaction of users toward IT adoption, (2) users' competences, expertise, and skill on IT. Also managers must engage users in all steps IT adoption from decision making to its use.

- In the term of regulatory, every activity has its regulatory forms and laws. SME should take into account their national IT laws and regulatory forms to avoid legal problems. Also, they must do their research to benefit from governmental support of their country.

- SME have to chose to explore the solutions and IT applications of their compe- titors, choose the adequate external experts, consultants and IT supplier in the national market taking into account the service quality, IT needs and the firm's resources.

5. Conclusion

Our SLR sought to understand barriers that prevent IT adoption in SME. We analyzed the initial search results that returned 179 papers, and then we selected the papers more targeted to our objectives "132 articles". These selected papers were used to explore research on IT adoption barriers within SME for different types of IT, in different lines of business, and in different countries. Finally we classified them according to various parameters. Then, all the data explored in this SLR was used to finally construct categorization of barriers to IT adoption according to different stakeholders and parameters.

5.1. *Research limitations*

Readers of this SLR should consider the following limitations because they probably influenced the results. First, we have conceived this review in the broadest sense of IT, so it is not targeted and does not present an in-depth SLR of certain type of IT or specific parameter. Second, as one of our research objectives was to consider the general field of IT, our research was adapted accordingly. As well the used parameters and the categorization proposed were based on results provided in the previous research. Our study also has considered in particular the barriers products in two or more separate papers. Third, considering the activity and speed of research these last years, the reader should take into the consideration that the data collect process of our study was carried out between December 2016 and November 2018. Therefore the references used are dated before November 2018. Fourth, due to multiple characteristics and conditions of IT adoption for each company, it is not contended that the results are applied to all SME. Therefore, these results require empirical examinations to validate their compliance in the practical framework.

5.2. *Review results and implications*

Despite these previous minor limitations, the SLR discussed in this article has a number of major implications. As previously highlighted, our study has proposed a SLR on barriers to IT adoption in SME. Results from this study greatly expend the understanding of IT adoption within companies and especially within SME, and help managers, SME owners, experts, researchers, and IT adopters in general to build a better knowledge and understanding of barriers preventing IT adoption within SME, for both IT professionals and IT researchers, in both developing and developed countries. First, understanding barriers mentioned in our SLR can enable professionals in SME to overcome them and minimize risks inherent in IT adoption by planning IT adoption strategies. Second, our paper contributes to develop a theoretical review that includes barriers previously validated by different researchers, so we believe that our SLR will be useful to the research community. This paper will serves as a guideline for researchers, who will continue their study and application in IT adoption within SME. Third, these results may be used to structure IT adoption policies, laws, strategies, and procedures in SME.

5.3. *Future work*

Given the objectives, limitation and results of our research, several directions can trace the path of other future research. The research can be extended by including more recent publications in the field and combine these results for the realization of a meta-analysis. The categorization proposed in this paper can be a basis to contrast to reality and validate it empirically in other future research. In addition this SLR can also be a basic study in order to conduct a targeted search for each parameter used (internal and external parameters) to provide more detailed and more reliable results (done for organizational culture as an internal parameter [Chouki *et al.* (2018)]). Also, a model of IT adoption can be proposed in future studies on the basis of these targeted barriers, with a list of preventive measures and guidelines in order to overcome or avoid these barriers. And empirically validate this model as well as these guidelines. Finally, similar research studies must always be done, because barriers, drivers and factors change over time and SME must perfect and refine the information technology adoption planning and strategizing.

Appendix A.   Evidence for Barriers to Information Technology Adoption within Small and Medium Enterprises

Table A.1.   Evidence for barriers to IT adoption within SME.

Category	Barrier		Empirical data	Non-Empirical data
Internal barriers				
Top management	1	Lack of commitment and engagement of top management	Thong et al. (1993); Chesher and Skok (2000); Liu and Arnett (2000); Bull (2003); Upadhyay et al. (2011); Bharati and Chaudhury (2012); El-Gohary (2012); Ghobakhloo and Tang (2013); Järveläinen (2013); Schniederjans and Yadav (2013)	Sabherwal et al. (2006); Abdul Hameed et al. (2012); Ghobakhloo et al. (2012); Bharati and Chaudhury (2015)
	2	Top management's lack of IT knowledge, competences, capacities and expertise	Thong and Yap (1995); Igbaria et al. (1997); Fink (1998); Wiklund and Shepherd (2003); Lee (2004); Al-Qirim (2007); Hashim (2015)	
	3	Lack of CEO's interest, motivation and desire of growth	Levy et al. (1998); Mehrtens et al. (2001); Cragg et al. (2002); Wiklund and Shepherd (2003); Harland et al. (2007)	Qureshi and York (2008)
	4	Top management's lack of confidence and perception of IT benefits	Davis et al. (1989); Damaskopoulos and Evgeniou (2003); Kapurubandara and Lawson (2006); Sutanonpaiboon and Pearson (2006); Pavlou (2003); Al-Qirim (2007); Harland et al. (2007); Tan et al. (2009); Schniederjans and Yadav (2013); Jussila et al. (2014); Hamdan and Yahaya (2016)	Love et al. (2005); Aloini et al. (2016)
End users	5	User's dissatisfaction and resistance to change	Fink (1998); Bull (2003); Bruque and Moyano (2007); Liu et al. (2006); Terziovski (2010); Malhotra and Temponi (2010); Staples and Niazi (2010); Cragg et al. (2011); Schniederjans and Yadav (2013); Ghobakhloo and Tang (2013); Kakar (2017)	Chau (1995); Mahmood et al. (2000); Howard et al. (2003); Dalcher and Shine (2003); Bandow et al. (2005)
	6	Lack of user's participation and engagement	Fink (1998); Shin (2006); Amoako-Gyampah (2007); Thong (2001)	
	7	Lack of user's knowledge and training on IT benefits	Thong (2001); Damaskopoulos and Evgeniou (2003); Sarosa and Zowghi (2003); Schniederjans and Yadav (2013)	Qureshi and York (2008); Ghobakhloo et al. (2012)

Table A.1. (*Continued*)

Category	Barrier	Empirical data	Non-Empirical data
	8 Lack of user's technical expertise and skills	Cragg and Zinatelli (1995); Sarosa and Zowghi (2003); Egbu et al. (2005); Zhou et al. (2009); Upadhyay et al. (2011); El-Gohary (2012); Ghobakhloo and Tang (2013); Hamdan and Yahaya (2016)	Nguyen (2009); Abdul Hameed et al. (2012)
Resources	9 Lack of financial resources	Thong and Yap (1995); Rangone (1999); Premkumar (2003); Damaskopoulos and Evgeniou (2003); Garcia Pérez de Lema and Duréndez (2007); Dibrell et al. (2008); Ghobakhloo et al. (2011); Nguyen and Waring (2013); Ghobakhloo and Tang (2013); Hamdan and Yahaya (2016); Madrid-Guijarro et al. (2016); Laufs et al. (2016)	Fuller-love (2006); Nguyen (2009)
	10 Lack of technological resources	Cragg and Zinatelli (1995); Wang and Cheung (2004); Sledgianowski et al. (2008); Chan et al. (2012); Lee et al. (2012); Ghobakhloo and Tang (2013); Schmiederjans and Yadav (2013); Halm et al. (2016)	Decker et al. (2006); Abdul Hameed et al. (2012)
	11 Lack of human resources	Fink (1998); Black and Lynch (2001); Caldeira and Ward (2003); Teo and Ranganathan (2004); Buonanno et al. (2005); Carbonara (2005); De Búrca et al. (2005); Kmieciak et al. (2012)	Ghobakhloo et al. (2011a); Abdul Hameed et al. (2012); Ghobakhloo et al. (2012); DeLone and McLean (2016)
Organization	12 Informalization (Lack of IT planning, preparation and strategy)	Lefebvre et al. (1992); Cragg et al. (2002); Levy and Powell (2003); Ramayah et al. (2005); Mutula and Brakel (2006); Tan et al. (2007); Fathian et al. (2008); Chan et al. (2012); Spinelli et al. (2013); Dufour and Son (2015); Rojas-Méndez et al. (2017)	Blili and Raymond (1993); Qureshi and York (2008); Ghobakhloo et al. (2012); Ullah and Lai (2013); Nguyen (2009)
	13 Business type	Thong and Yap (1995); Seyal et al. (2000); Cheng et al. (2002); Damaskopoulos and Evgeniou (2003); Salmeron and Bueno (2006); Gaith et al. (2009); Ghobakhloo et al. (2011b); Chan et al. (2012); Nguyen and Waring (2013)	Love et al. (2005); Ghobakhloo et al. (2012)

Table A.1.   *(Continued)*

Category	Barrier	Empirical data	Non-Empirical data
	14 Business size	Thong and Yap (1995); Premkumar and Roberts (1999); Buonanno et al. (2005); Harland et al. (2007); Zahay and Peltier (2008); Michaelidou et al. (2011)	Gnyawali and Park (2009); Abdul Hameed et al. (2012)
	15 Organizational culture	Venkatesh and Brown (2001); Drew (2003); Kanamori and Motohashi (2006); Graham and Nafukho (2007); Arroyo et al. (2007); Harland et al. (2007); Bruque and Moyano (2007); Carmeli et al. (2008); Messersmith et al. (2009); Solaymani et al. (2012); Nguyen and Waring (2013)	Riolli and Savicki (2003); Jones et al. (2005); Abdul Hameed et al. (2012); Shan and Kumar (2012); Riduan (2017)
External barriers			
	16 Regulatory forms inadequacy and lack of government support	Yap et al. (1994); Southern and Tilley (2000); Damaskopoulos and Evgeniou (2003); Tan et al. (2009); Ghobakhloo et al. (2011b); Kennedy and Basu (2013); Nawaz and Gunapalan (2015); Soon Ern (2015); Hamdan and Yahaya (2016)	Lloyd (2014)
	17 Lack of adequate external expertise (IT Consultants/Suppliers)	Soh et al. (1992); Kapurubandara and Lawson (2006); Ferneley and Bell (2006); Morgan et al. (2006); Upadhyay et al. (2011); Ismail and King (2014); Jernström et al. (2016); Bianchi et al. (2017)	Bessant and Rush (1995); Qureshi and York (2008); Haddara and Zach (2011); Ghobakhloo et al. (2012)
	18 Competitive and environmental pressure	Fink (1998); Dutta and Evrard (1999); Damaskopoulos and Evgeniou (2003); Singh et al. (2007); Ghobakhloo et al. (2011b); Hamdan and Yahaya (2016); Doherty et al. (2016); Fan (2016); Neirotti and Raguseo (2017)	Marinescu et al. (2007); Singh et al. (2008); Ghobakhloo et al. (2012); Bharati and Chaudhury (2015)
Number of unique documents = 132 (% of total)		102 (77.2 %)	30 (22.8%)

Appendix B. Review Protocol Developed for the Systematic Literature Review

B.1. *Background*

As many researchers and experts have argued, Information Technologies (IT) plays a very important role in business success in SME, and provides multiple benefits [Rangone (1999); MacGregor and Vrazalic (2005); Wiklund *et al.* (2009); Nguyen (2009); Chan *et al.* (2012); Ullah and Lai (2013); Maduku *et al.* (2016); Jernström *et al.* (2016)]. Therefore, several studies conducted in different countries have shown that SME are less likely to adopt IT than large firms, IT adoption seems to be a challenge for SME [Fink (1998); Southern and Tilley (2000); Johnston and Wright (2004); Dibrell *et al.* (2008); Qureshi and York (2008); Bhattacharya (2015); Hsu and Lin (2016); Hamdan and Yahaya (2016)].

The purpose of the review described in this protocol is to study the current evidence of "Barriers to IT adoption within SME" in both developing and developed countries, using a systematic study to review previous scientific articles from 1992 to 2018 related to IT adoption, in particular the field of our SLR.

In this context and according to systematic guidelines of Kitchenham; Kitchenham [2004; 2007] and Kitchenham *et al.* [2009], SLR is the main method to analysis and synthesis of best quality studies on a specific area or research question. Following these studies, we proposed a systematic literature review (SLR) to better understand IT adoption and barriers that obstruct this adoption.

Systematic Literature reviews were initially developed for medicine research, but it is now being implemented for different other fields e.g. Economics, social policies, Software engineering. Based on Cochrane's Hand book for Systematic Reviews of Intervention [Higgins and Green (2008)] in medicine, the goals of our SLR are:

- To provide a useful guide for professionals, on role of each IT stakeholders, precautions and factors to be taken into account and ensure a successful IT adoption.
- To develop a theoretical review that includes barriers previously validated by different researchers.
- To serves as a guideline for researchers who will continue their studies and applications in IT adoption.

B.2. *Research question*

What are the barriers that might explain the lack of IT adoption in SME?

B.3. *Search process*

The search process is a manual search of some specific books, proceedings and journal papers of our field. Some nominated databases, conferences and journals are shown in the following table (Table B.1).

Table B.1.   Sources to be searched.

Electronic sources	Selected sources	Researchers' search engine and social networking sites
Databases, Journals Books, Reviews.	Science Direct (Elsevier), Springer, the digital library ACM, IEEE Xplore, JSTOR, Emerald insight, Taylor & Francis online, Inderscience online, Wiley Online Library, Journal of small business Management, European Journal of Business and Management, Information Journal and Management Science Journal	Google scholar Researchgate

B.4. *Inclusion criteria*

Papers on the following issues, published between 1992 and 2018 are included:

- Targeted on general or some specific IT.
- Applied on different lines of Business.
- Published in academic publishing (Journal, databse...).
- Only published Ph.D. dissertations.
- Written in English.
- Empirical, qualitative, quantitative and case studies.
- Theoretical, Systematic Literature reviews and Meta-Analyses.

B.5. *Exclusion criteria*

The following forms of papers are excluded:

- Papers that are not written in English
- Unpublished papers.
- Informal literature survey and reviews (No defined a research question, no methodology and search protocol, no defined Data collection and process).

When a review is published in more than one academic publisher, the most complete one is used.

B.6. *Primary study selection*

Results are classified as follows:

- Number of papers per empirical or non empirical data.
- Number of paper per kind of IT studied.
- Number of paper per each barrier per each class (category).

B.7. *Quality assessment*

Our SLR is evaluated by quality assessment checklists and procedures to assess the selected studies (Tables B.2 and B.3), for that:

- Data was collected and extracted in the basis on inclusion and exclusion criteria by one researcher.

Table B.2.   Template of assessment checklist (first researcher).

| Source: | Study title: |
| Authors: | Year of study: |

Publication type:	- Journal Article
	- Abstract
	- Proceeding
	- Other (Specify: Book, Ph.D. dissertation...)
IT kind:	- General
	- ERP
	- SCM
	- CRM
	- Other (specify)
Data extracted:	Details:

Table B.3.   Template of assessment checklist (second researcher).

- Are systematic literature review's inclusion and exclusion criteria defined and appropriate? Y or N	Details:
- Does the data collection and study design meet the criteria for inclusion and exclusion? Y or N	Details:
- Is the SLR search likely to have covered all and only relevant papers? Y or N	Details:
- Did researcher assess the quality/validity of the included papers? Y or N	Details:
- Were the extracted data adequately used and described? Y or N	Details:
Validity:	Include or Exclude

- And checked in the basis on quality criteria by another one.

The development of quality checklists and quality criteria are based on the following questions:

- Are systematic literature review's inclusion and exclusion criteria defined and appropriate?
- Does the data collection and study design meet the criteria for inclusion and exclusion?
- Is the SLR search likely to have covered all and only relevant papers?
- Did researcher assess the quality/validity of the included papers?
- Were the extracted data adequately used and described?

After analyzing the outcome measure in the basis of these questions, developing the quality checklists, and analyzing results of checklists. The scoring analysis is: $\sim 74\%$: (Y) Yes (Papers to be included 132) and $\sim 26\%$ (N) No (Papers to be excluded 74).

B.8. *Data extraction and synthesis*

The data extracted from each paper are:

- Source and Publication type (Journal article, proceeding, book...).

- Study title.
- Authors and affiliation.
- Year of publication, if the paper was published in several different sources both dates and sources are recorded and the more completed one is used in the analysis.
- IT kind and topic area.
- Research question/issue.
- Summary of paper.
- Data extracted (Barriers extracted, type of classification, theory and methodology used).
- Quality score for this study (By quality assessment checklist).

Using these steps, the data are collected, analyzed and extracted by one researcher and checked by another. Validated studies are classified and analyzed to have the last synthesis of our SLR.

References

Abdul Hameed, M., Counsell, S. and Swift, S. (2012). A meta-analysis of relationships between organizational characteristics and IT innovation adoption in organizations. *Information & Management*, **49**: 218–232.

Agarwal, N. and Brem, A. (2015). Strategic business transformation through technology convergence: Implications from General Electric's industrial internet initiative. *International Journal of Technology Management*, **67**: 2/3/4.

Ajzen, I. (1988). *Attitude, Personality and Behavior*, 2nd edn., Open University Press, Berkshire.

Aloini, D., Dulmin, R., Mininno, V. and Spagnesi, A. (2016). Benefits and barriers of social/ collaborative ERP systems: A state of the art and research agenda. *Strengthening Information and Control Systems*, eds. Mancini, D., Dameri, R. and Bonollo, E., Lecture Notes in Information Systems and Organisation, Vol. 14, Springer, Cham, pp. 171–184.

Al-Qirim, N. (2007). The adoption of eCommerce communications and applications technologies in small businesses in New Zealand. *Electronic Commerce Research and Applications*, **6**: 462–473.

Amoako-Gyampah, K. (2007). Perceived usefulness, user involvement and behavioral intention: An empirical study of ERP implementation. *Computers in Human Behavior*, **23**: 1232–1248.

Anderson, R. E. and Huang, W. (2006). Empowering salespeople: Personal, managerial, and organizational perspectives. *Psychology & Marketing*, **23**: 139–159.

Angell, I. O. and Smithson, S. (2012). Information technology and information systems. *Information Systems Management*, **5**: 55–67.

Arroyo, P. E., Ramirez, J. A. and Erosa, V. E. (2007). The elaboration of a model to explain the adoption of information technologies for supply chain. In *PICMET '07 - 2007 Portland International Conference on Management of Engineering and Technology*, Ortland, Oregon, United States, pp. 5–9.

Bandow, D., Suite, N., Batchelor, G., Howard, C., Winter, C. B. and Clark, C. (2005). Redesigning human resources for IT?: Meeting organizational needs in a changing environment. In *Proceedings of 2005 ACM SIGMIS CPR Conference on Computers and People Research*, Atlanta, Georgia, USA, pp. 81–82.

Barkhordari, M., Nourollah, A., Mashayekhi, H., Mashayekhi, Y. and Ahangar, M. S. (2017). Factors influencing adoption of e payment systems: An empirical study on Iranian customers. *Information Systems and e-Business Management*, **15**: 89–116.

Bessant, J. and Rush, H. (1995). Building bridges for innovation: The role of consultants in technology transfer. *Research Policy*, **24**: 97–114.

Bhagwat, R. and Sharma, M. K. (2007). Information system architecture: A framework for a cluster of small- and medium-sized enterprises (SMEs). *Production Planning & Control*, **18**: 283–296.

Bharati, P. and Chaudhury, A. (2012). Technology assimilation across the value chain: An empirical study of small and medium-sized enterprises. *Information Resources Management Journal*, **25**: 38–60.

Bharati, P. and Chaudhury, A. (2015). SMEs and competitiveness: The role of information systems. *International Journal of E-Business Research*, **5**: i–ix.

Bhattacharya, D. (2015). Evolution of cybersecurity issues in small businesses. In *Proceedings of the 4th Annual ACM Conference on Research in Information Technology*. ACM, New York, NY, p. 11.

Bianchi, C., Glavas, C. and Mathews, S. (2017). SME international performance in Latin America: The role of entrepreneurial and technological capabilities. *Journal of Small Business and Enterprise Development*, **24**: 176–195.

Black, S. E. and Lynch, L. M. (2001). How to compete: The impact of workplace practices and information technology on productivity. *Review of Economics and Statistics*, **83**: 434–445.

Blili, S. and Raymond, L. (1993). Information technology: Threats and opportunities for small and medium-sized enterprises. *International Journal of Information Management*, **13**: 439–448.

Brem, A., Kreusel, N. and Neusser, C. (2008). Performance measurement in SMEs: Literature review and results from a German case study. *International Journal of Globalisation and Small Business*, **2**: 4.

Brem, A. and Viardot, É. (2015). Adoption of innovation: Balancing internal and external stakeholders in the marketing of innovation. In *Adoption of Innovation*, Brem, A. and Viardot, É. (eds.). Springer, Cham, pp. 1–10.

Brocard, R. and Gandois, J. (1978). Grandes entreprises et PME. *Economie et Statistique*, **96**: 25–41.

Bull, C. (2003). Strategic issues in customer relationship management (CRM) implementation. *Business Process Management Journal*, **9**: 592–602.

Buonanno, G., Faverio, P., Pigni, F., Ravarini, A., Sciuto, D. and Tagliavini, M. (2005). Factors affecting ERP system adoption: A comparative analysis between SMEs and large companies. *Journal of Enterprise Information Management*, **18**: 384–426.

Bruque, S. and Moyano, J. (2007). Organisational determinants of information technology adoption and implementation in SMEs: The case of family and cooperative firms. *Technovation*, **27**: 241–253.

Caldeira, M. M. and Ward, J. M. (2003). Using resource-based theory to interpret the successful adoption and use of information systems and technology in manufacturing small and medium-sized enterprises. *European Journal of Information Systems*, **12**: 127–141.

Carmeli, A., Sternberg, A. and Elizur, D. (2008). Organizational culture, creative behavior, and information and communication technology (ICT) usage: A facet analysis. *CyberPsychology Behaviour*, **11**: 175–180.

Cheng, C. H., Cheung, W. and Chang, M. K. (2002). The use of the Internet in Hong Kong: Manufacturing vs. service. *International Journal of Production Economics*, **75**: 33–45.

Carbonara, N. (2005). Information and communication technology and geographical clusters: Opportunities and spread. *Technovation*, **25**: 213–222.

Carson, D. and Gilmore, A. (2000). SME marketing management competencies. *International Business Review*, **9**: 363–382.

Chan, F. T. S., Chong, A. Y. L. and Zhou, L. (2012). An empirical investigation of factors affecting e-collaboration diffusion in SMEs. *International Journal of Production Economics*, **138**: 329–344.

Chau, P. Y. K. (1995). Factors used in the selection of packaged software in small businesses: Views of owners and managers. *Information & Management*, **29**: 71–78.

Chesher, M. and Skok, W. (2000). Roadmap for successful information technology transfer for small businesses. In *Proceedings of the 2000 ACM SIGCPR Conference on Computer Personnel Research*. ACM, New York, NY, pp. 16–22.

Chouki, M., Khadrouf, O., Talea, M. and Okar, C. (2018). Organizational culture as a barrier of information technology adoption: The case of Moroccan Small and Medium Enterprises. *2018 IEEE International Conference on Technology Management, Operations and Decisions (ICTMOD)*. IEE, Morocco. doi:10.1109/ITMC.2018.8691130.

Cragg, P. and Zinatelli, N. (1995). The evolution of information systems in small firms. *Information & Management*, **29**: 1–8.

Cragg, P., Caldeira, M. and Ward, J. (2011). Organizational information systems competences in small and medium-sized enterprises. *Information & Management*, **48**: 353–363.

Cragg, P., King, M. and Hussin, H. (2002). IT alignment and firm performance in small manufacturing firms. *Journal of Strategic Information Systems*, **11**: 109–132.

Dalcher, I. and Shine, J. (2003). Extending the new technology acceptance model to measure the end user information systems satisfaction in a mandatory environment: A bank's treasury. *Technology Analysis & Strategic Management*, **15**: 441–455.

Damaskopoulos, P. and Evgeniou, T. (2003). Adoption of new economy practices by SMEs in Eastern Europe. *European Management Journal*, **21**: 133–145.

Davis, F. D., Bagozzi, R. P. and Warshaw, P. R. (1989). User acceptance of computer technology: A comparison of two theoretical models. *Management Science*, **35**: 982–1003.

De Búrca, S., Fynes, B. and Marshall, D. (2005). Strategic technology adoption: Extending ERP across the supply chain. *Journal of Enterprise Information Management*, **18**: 427–440.

Decker, M., Schiefer, G. and Bulander, R. (2006). Specific challenges for Small and Medium-sized Enterprises (SME) in m-business — A SME-suitable framework for mobile services. *ICEB 2006 Proceedings of the International Conference on Ebus*, Setúbal, Portugal, pp. 169–174.

DeLone, W. H. and McLean, E. R. (2016). Information systems success measurement. *Foundations and Trends R in Information Systems*, **2**: 1–116.

Dibrell, C., Davis, P. S. and Craig, J. (2008). Fueling innovation through information technology in SMEs. *Journal of Small Business Management*, **46**: 203–218.

Doherty, E., Ramsey, E., Harrigan, P. and Ibbotson, P. (2016). Impact of broadband internet technologies on business performance of Irish SMEs. *Wiley Online Library*, **25**: 693–716.

Drew, S. (2003). Strategic uses of e-commerce by SMEs in the east of England. *European Management Journal*, **21**: 79–88.

Dubravac, I. and Bevanda, V. (2015). Mobile business intelligence adoption (case of Croatian SMEs). In *Proceedings of the 16th International Conference on Computer Systems and Technologies*. ACM, New York, NY, pp. 136–143.

Dufour, J. and Son, P.-E. (2015). Open innovation in SMEs: Towards formalization of openness. *Journal of Innovation Management*, **3**: 90–117.

Dutta, S. and Evrard, P. (1999). Information technology and organisation within European small enterprises. *European Management Journal*, **17**: 239–251.

Egbu, C. O., Hari, S. and Renukappa, S. H. (2005). Knowledge management for sustainable competitiveness in small and medium surveying practices. *Structural Survey*, **23**: 7–21.

El-Gohary, H. (2012). Factors affecting E-Marketing adoption and implementation in tourism firms: An empiric al investigation of Egyptian small tourism organisations. *Tourism Management*, **33**: 1256–1269.

Elia, A., Lefebvre, L.-A. and Lefebvre, É. (2007). Focus of B-to-B e-commerce initiatives and related benefits in manufacturing small- and medium-sized enterprises. *Information Systems and e-Business Management*, **5**: 1–23.

Fan, Q. (2016). Factors affecting adoption of digital business: Evidence from Australia. *Global Journal of Business Research*, **10**: 79–84.

Fathian, M., Akhavan, P. and Hoorali, M. (2008). E-readiness assessment of non-profit ICT SMEs in a developing country: The case of Iran. *Technovation*, **28**: 578–590.

Fei, X. and Chung, J. Y. (2015). IT for future e-business management. *Information Systems and e-Business Management*, **13**: 191–192.

Ferneley, E. and Bell, F. (2006). Using bricolage to integrate business and information technology innovation in SMEs. *Technovation*, **26**: 232–241.

Fink, D. (1998). Guidelines for the successful adoption of information technology in small and medium enterprises. *International Journal of Information Management*, **18**: 243–253.

Fuller-love, N. (2006). Management development in small firms. *International Journal of Management Reviews*, **8**: 175–190.

Gaith, F. H., Khalim, A. R. and Ismail, A. (2009). Usage of information technology in construction firms: Malaysian construction industry. *European Journal of Scientific Research*, **28**: 412–421.

García Pérez de Lema, D. and Duréndez, A. (2007). Managerial behaviour of small and medium-sized family businesses: An empirical study. *International Journal of Entrepreneurial Behaviour & Research*, **13**: 151–172.

Ghobakhloo, M., Aranda, D. A. and Amado, J. B. (2011). Information technology implementation success within SME in developing coountries: An interactive model. In *POMS 22nd Annual Conference: Operation Management: The Enabling Link*. Reno, Nevada, USA, pp. 1–63.

Ghobakhloo, M., Sadegh Sabouri, M., Tang, S. H. and Zulkifli, N. (2011a). Information technology adoption in small and medium-sized enterprises: An appraisal of two decades literature. *Interdisciplinary Journal of Research in Business*, **1**: 53–80.

Ghobakhloo, M., Benitez-Amado, J. and Arias-Aranda, D. (2011b). Reasons for information technology adoption and sophistication within manufacturing SMEs. In *POMS 22nd Annu. Conf. Oper. Manag.*, Reno, Nevada, U.S.A., pp. 1–40.

Ghobakhloo, M., Tang, S. H., Sabouri, M. S. and Zulkifli, N. (2012). Strategies for successful information technology adoption in small and medium-sized enterprises. *Information*, **3**: 36–67.

Ghobakhloo, M. and Tang, S. H. (2013). The role of owner/manager in adoption of electronic commerce in small businesses: The case of developing countries. *Journal of Small Business and Enterprise Development*, **20**: 754–787.

Gnyawali, D. R. and Park, B. R. (2009). Co-opetition and technological innovation in small and medium-sized enterprises: A multilevel conceptual model. *Journal of Small Business Management*, **47**: 308–330.

Graham, C. M. and Nafukho, F. M. (2007). Culture, organizational learning and selected employee background variables in small-size business enterprises. *Journal of European Industrial Training*, **31**: 127–144.

Gray, C. (2006). Absorptive capacity, knowledge management and innovation in entrepreneurial small firms. *International Journal of Entrepreneurial Behavior & Research*, **12**: 345–360.

Gurbaxani, V. and Whang, S. (1991). The impact of information systems on organizations and markets. *Communications of the ACM*, **34**: 59–73.

Gutmann, B. A., Cosimano, A. J. and O'Sullivan, C. T. (2016). Breaking through the economic barriers of anesthesia information management systems. *AANA Journal*, **84**: 316–321.

Haddara, M. and Zach, O. (2011). ERP Systems in SMEs?: A literature review. In *Proceedings of the 44th Hawaii International Conference on System Sciences*. IEEE, pp. 1–10.

Hahn, S. B., Kwon, S. and Yun, J. (2016). The effects of policy funds on the financing constraints of small- and medium-sized enterprises in South Korea. *Applied Economics Letters*, **24**: 699–702.

Hamdan, A. R. and Yahaya, J. H. (2016). The success factors and barriers of information technology implementation in small and medium enterprises: An empirical study in Malaysia. *International Journal of Business Information Systems*, **21**: 477–494.

Hansen, B. and Hamilton, R. T. (2011). Factors distinguishing small firm growers and non-growers. *International Small Business Journal*, **29**: 278–294.

Harland, C. M., Caldwell, N. D., Powell, P. and Zheng, J. (2007). Barriers to supply chain information integration: SMEs adrift of eLands. *Journal of Operations Management*, **25**: 1234–1254.

Hashim, J. (2015). Information Communication Technology (ICT) Adoption among SME owners in Malaysia. *International Journal of Business and Information*, **2**: 221–240.

Higgins, J. P. T. and Green, S. (Eds.) (2008). *Cochrane Handbook for Systematic Reviews of Interventions*. Chichester: John Wiley & Sons, Ltd.

Hjorth, S. S. and Brem, A. M. (2016). How to assess market readiness for an innovative solution: The case of heat recovery technologies for SMEs. *Sustainability*, **8**: 1–16. DOI: 10.3390/su8111152.

Holmes, S. and Nicholls, D. (1989). Modelling the accounting information requirements of small businesses. *Accounting and Business Research*, **19**: 143–150.

Holmes, S., Kelly, G. and Cunningham, R. (1991). The small firm information cycle: A re-appraisal. *International Small Business Journal*, **4**: 41–53.

Howard, M., Vidgen, R. and Powell, P. (2003). Overcoming stakeholder barriers in the automotive industry: Building to order with extra organizational systems. *Journal of Information Technology*, **18**: 27–43.

Hsu, C. L. and Lin, J. C. C. (2016). Factors affecting the adoption of cloud services in enterprises. *Information Systems and e-Business Management*, **14**: 791–822.

Igbaria, M. and Tan, M. (1997). The consequences of information technology acceptance on subsequent individual performance. *Information & Management*, **32**: 113–121.

Igbaria, M., Zinatelli, N., Cragg, P. and Cavaye, A. L. M. (1997). Personal computing acceptance factors in small firms: A structural equation model. *MIS Quarterly*, **21**: 279–305.

Ismail, N. A. and King, M. (2014). Factors influencing the alignment of accounting information systems in small and medium sized Malaysian manufacturing firms. *Journal of Information Systems and Small Business*, **1**: 1–20.

Järveläinen, J. (2013). IT incidents and business impacts: Validating a framework for continuity management in information systems. *International Journal of Information Management*, **33**: 583–590.

Jarvenpaa, S. L. and Ives, B. (1991). Executive involvement and participation in the management of information technology. *MIS Quarterly*, **15**: 205–227.

Jernström, E., Karvonen, V., Kässi, T., Kraslawski, A. and Hallikas, J. (2016). The main factors affecting the entry of SMEs into bio-based industry. *Journal of Cleaner Production*, **141**: 1–10.

Johnston, D. A. and Wright, L. (2004). The e-business capability of small and medium sized firms in international supply chains. *Information Systems and e-Business Management*, **2**: 223–240.

Jones, R. A., Jimmieson, N. L. and Griffiths, A. (2005). The impact of organizational culture and reshaping capabilities on change implementation success: The mediating role of readiness for change. *Journal of Management Studies*, **42**: 361–386.

Jussila, J. J., Kärkkäinen, H. and Aramo-Immonen, H. (2014). Social media utilization in business-to-business relationships of technology industry firms. *Computers in Human Behavior*, **30**: 606–613.

Kakar, A. K. (2017). Investigating the relationships between the use contexts, user perceived values, and loyalty to a software product. *ACM Transactions on Management Information Systems*, **8**: 1–23.

Kanamori, T. and Motohashi, K. (2006). Centralization or decentralization of decision rights? Impact on IT performance of firms. *Research Center for Advanced Science and Technology, University of Tokyo*. RIETI Discussion Paper Series 06-E-032.

Kapurubandara, M. and Lawson, R. (2006). Barriers to adopting ICT and e-commerce with SMEs in developing countries: An exploratory study in Sri Lanka. Ph.D. Dissertation. School of Computing and Mathematics University of Western Sydney, Australia.

Kazhamiakin, R., Pistore, M. and Santuari, L. (2006). Analysis of communication models in web service. In *Proc. 15th Int. Conf. World Wide Web*. ACM, pp. 267–276.

Kennedy, M. and Basu, B. (2013). Overcoming barriers to low carbon technology transfer and deployment: An exploration of the impact of projects in developing and emerging economies. *Renewable and Sustainable Energy Reviews*, **26**: 685–693.

Kmieciak, R., Michna, A. and Meczynska, A. (2012). Innovativeness, empowerment and IT capability: Evidence from SMEs. *Industrial Management & Data Systems*, **112**: 707–728.

Kitchenham, B. A. (2004). Procedures for performing systematic reviews. Tech. Rep. TR/SE-0401, *Software Engineering Group, Department of Computer Science, Keele University, UK*.

Kitchenham, B. A. (2007). Guidelines for performing systematic literature reviews in software engineering version 2.3, *Keele University and University of Durham, EBSE technical report*.

Kitchenham, B. A., Brereton, O. P., Budgen, D., Turner, M., Bailey, J. and Linkman, S. (2009). Systematic literature reviews in software engineering — A systematic literature review. *Information and Software Technology*, **51**: 7–15.

Kurnia, S., Choudrie, J., Md Mahbubur, R. and Alzougool, B. (2015). E-commerce technology adoption: A Malaysian grocery SME retail sector study. *Journal of Business Research*, **68**: 1906–1918.

Laufs, K., Bembom, M. and Schwens, C. (2016). CEO characteristics and SME foreign market entry mode choice: The moderating effect of firm's geographic experience and host-country political risk. *International Marketing Review*, **33**: 1–42.

Lee, H., Kelley, D., Lee, J. and Lee, S. (2012). SME survival: The impact of internationalization, technology resources, and alliances. *Journal of Small Business Management*, **50**: 1–19.

Lee, J. (2004). Discriminant analysis of technology adoption behavior: A case of Internet technologies in small businesses. *Journal of Computer Information Systems*, **44**: 57–66.

Lefebvre, L.-A., Langley, A., Harvey, J. and Lefebvre, É. (1992). Exploring the strategy technology connection in small manufacturing firms. *Production and Operations Management*, **1**: 269–285.

Levy, M., Powell, P. and Yetton, P. (1998). SMEs and the gains from IS: From cost reduction to value added. In *Proceedings IFIP, Working Conference, Information Systems: Current Issues and Future Changes*, Helsinki, Finland, pp. 377–392.

Levy, M. and Powell, P. (2003). Exploring SME internet adoption: Towards a contingent model. *Electronic Markets*, **13**: 173–181.

Liu, C. and Arnett, K. P. (2000). Exploring the factors associated with Web site success in the context of electronic commerce. *Information & Management*, **38**: 23–33.

Liu, Y., Chen, Y. and Zhou, C. (2006). Determinants affecting end-user satisfaction of information technology service. In *Proceeding of the 2006 International Conference on Service Systems and Service Management*. IEEE, Troyes, France.

Li, X., Kauffman, R. J., Yu, F. and Zhang, Y. (2014). Externalities, incentives and strategic complementarities: Understanding herd behavior in IT adoption. *Information Systems and e-Business Management*, **12**: 443–464.

Lloyd, I. J. (2014). *Information Technology Law*, 7th edn., Oxford University Press, Oxford, UK.

Love, P. E. D., Irani, Z., Standing, C., Lin, C. and Burn, J. M. (2005). The enigma of evaluation: Benefits, costs and risks of IT in Australian small–medium-sized enterprises. *Information & Management*, **42**: 947–964.

Lybaert, N. (1998). The information use in a SME: Its importance and some elements of influence. *Small Business Economics*, **10**: 171–191.

MacGregor, R. C. and Vrazalic, L. (2005). A basic model of electronic commerce adoption barriers. *Journal of Small Business and Enterprise Development*, **12**: 510–527.

Madrid-Guijarro, A., García-Pérez-de-Lema, D. and Auken, H. V. (2016). Financing constraints and SME innovation during economic crises. *Academia Revista Latinoamerica de Administracion*, **29**: 84–106.

Maduku, D. K., Mpinganjira, M. and Duh, H. (2016). Understanding mobile marketing adoption intention by South African SMEs: A multi-perspective framework. *International Journal of Information Management*, **36**: 711–723.

Mahmood, M. A., Burn, J. M., Gemoets, L. A. and Jacquez, C. (2000). Variables affecting information technology end-user satisfaction: A meta-analysis of the empirical literature. *International Journal of Human-Computer Studies*, **52**: 751–771.

Maldonado-guzmán, G., Citlallilópez-torres, G., Martínez-serna, M. C. and Ramírez, R. G. (2014). Information technology and collaboration in Mexican small business. *International Journal of Engineering Innovation & Research*, **3**: 871–876.

Malhotra, R. and Temponi, C. (2010). Critical decisions for ERP integration: Small business issues. *International Journal of Information Management*, **30**: 28–37.

Marinescu, M. M., Mihaescu, C. and Niculescu-Aron, G. (2007). Why should SME adopt IT enabled CRM strategy? *Information Economics*, **1**: 109–112.

Matharu, G. S., Mishra, A., Singh, H. and Upadhyay, P. (2015). Empirical study of agile software development methodologies. *ACM SIGSOFT Software Engineering Notes*, **40**: 1–6.

Mehrtens, J., Cragg, P. B. and Mills, A. M. (2001). A model of Internet adoption by SMEs. *Information Management*, **39**: 165–176.

Messersmith, A. S., Keyton, J. and Bisel, R. S. (2009). Teaching organizational culture. *Communication Teacher*, **23**: 81–86.

Michaelidou, N., Siamagka, N. T. and Christodoulides, G. (2011). Usage, barriers and measurement of social media marketing: An exploratory investigation of small and medium B2B brands. *Industrial Marketing Management*, **40**: 1153–1159.

Morgan, A., Colebourne, D. and Thomas, B. (2006). The development of ICT advisors for SME businesses: An innovative approach. *Technovation*, **26**: 980–987.

Mutula, S. M. and van Brakel, P. (2006). E-readiness of SMEs in the ICT sector in Botswana with respect to information access. *Electronic Library*, **24**: 402–417.

Nawaz, S. S. and Gunapalan, S. (2015). Evaluating the adoption of enterprise applications by small and medium enterprises in Sri Lanka. *European Journal of Business and Management*, **7**: 324–335.

Neirotti, P. and Raguseo, E. (2017). On the contingent value of IT-based capabilities for the competitive advantage of SMEs: Mechanisms and empirical evidence. *Information Management*, **54**: 139–153.

Nguyen, T. H. (2009). Information technology adoption in SMEs: An integrated framework. *International Journal of Entrepreneurial Behavior & Research*, **15**: 162–186.

Nguyen, T. H. and Waring, T. S. (2013). The adoption of customer relationship management (CRM) technology in SMEs. *Journal of Small Business and Enterprise Development*, **20**: 824–848.

Nguyen, T. H., Newby, M. and Macaulay, M. J. (2013). Information technology adoption in small business: Confirmation of a proposed framework. *Journal of Small Business Management*, **53**: 207–227.

Nieto, M. J. and Fernández, Z. (2005). The role of information technology in corporate strategy of small and medium enterprises. *Journal of International Entrepreneurship*, **3**: 251–262.

Pavlou, P. A. (2003). Consumer acceptance of electronic commerce: Integrating trust and risk with the technology acceptance model. *International Journal of Electronic Commerce*, **7**: 101–134.

Premkumar, G. and Roberts, M. (1999). Adoption of new information technologies in rural small businesses. *Omega*, **27**: 467–484.

Premkumar, G. (2003). A meta-analysis of research on information technology implementation in small business. *Journal of Organizational Computing and Electronic Commerce*, **13**: 91–121.

Qureshi, S. and York, A. S. (2008). Information technology adoption by small businesses in minority and ethnic communities. In *Proceedings of the 41st Hawaii International Conference on System Sciences*. IEEE, pp. 1–10.

Ramayah, T., Yan, L. C. and Sulaiman, M. (2005). SME e-readiness in Malaysia: Implications for planning and implementation. *Sasin Journal of Management*, **11**: 103–120.

Rangone, A. (1999). A resource-based approach to strategy analysis in small-medium sized enterprises. *Small Business Economics*, **12**: 233–248.

Raymond, L. and Magnenat-Thalmann, N. (1982). Information systems in small business: Are they used in managerial decisions? *American Journal of Small Business*, **6**: 20–23.

Riduan, R. (2017). Reconciliation of high-tech and high-touch for SME innovation performance in Indonesia. *Russian Journal of Agriculture and social-Economics Sciences2004*, **1**: 224–230.

Riolli, L. and Savicki, V. (2003). Information system organizational resilience. *Omega International Journal of Management Science*, **31**: 227–233.

Rojas-Méndez, J. I., Parasuraman, A. and Papadopoulos, N. (2017). Demographics, attitudes, and technology readiness: A cross-cultural analysis and model validation. *Marketing Intelligence and Planning*, **35**: 18–39.

Rose, J., Jones, M. and Furneaux, B. (2016). An integrated model of innovation drivers for smaller software firms. *Information Management*, **53**: 307–323.

Sabherwal, R., Jeyaraj, A. and Chowa, C. (2006). Information system success: Individual and organizational determinants. *Management Science*, **52**: 1849–1864.

Salmeron, J. L. and Bueno, S. (2006). An information technologies and information systems industry-based classification in small and medium-sized enterprises: An institutional view. *European Journal of Operational Research*, **173**: 1012–1025.

Sarosa, S. and Zowghi, D. (2003). Strategy for adopting information technology for SMEs: Experience in adopting email within an Indonesian furniture company. *Electronic Journal of Information Systems Evaluation*, **6**: 165–176.

Schniederjans, D. and Yadav, S. (2013). Successful ERP implementation: An integrative model. *Business Process Management Journal*, **19**: 364–398.

Seyal, A. H., Rahim, M. M. and Rahman, M. N. A. (2000). An empirical investigation of use of information technology among small and medium business organizations?: A Bruneian Scenario. *Electronic Journal of Information Systems in Developing Countries*, **2**: 1–17.

Shan, Z. and Kumar, A. (2012). Optimal adapter creation for process composition in synchronous vs. asynchronous communication. *ACM Transactions on Management Information Systems*, **3**: 1–33.

Shin, I. (2006). Adoption of enterprise application software and firm performance. *Small Business Economics*, **26**: 241–256.

Singh, R. K., Garg, S. K. and Deshmukh, S. G. (2007). Strategy development for competitiveness: A study on Indian auto component sector. *International Journal of Productivity and Performance Management*, **56**: 285–304.

Singh, R. K., Garg, S. K. and Deshmukh, S. G. (2008). Strategy development by SMEs for competitiveness: A review. *Benchmarking*, **15**: 525–547.

Sledgianowski, D., Tafti, M. H. A. and Kierstead, J. (2008). SME ERP system sourcing strategies: A case study. *Industrial Management & Data Systems*, **108**: 421–436.

Soh, C. P. P., Yap, C. S. and Raman, K. S. (1992). Impact of consultants on computerization success in small businesses. *Information & Management*, **22**: 309–319.

Solaymani, S., Sohaili, K. and Yazdinejad, E. A. (2012). Adoption and use of e-commerce in SMEs: A case study. *Electronic Commerce Research*, **12**: 249–263.

Soon Ern, P. A. (2015). Barrier-driver model for enhancement of ICT implementation in IBS production process management in construction industry. Ph.D. Dissertation. Faculty of Technology Management and Business Universiti Tun Hussein Onn Malaysia.

Southern, A. and Tilley, F. (2000). Small firms and information and communication technologies (ICTs): Toward a typology of ICTs usage. *New Technology, Work and Employment*, **15**: 138–154.

Spinelli, R., Dyerson, R. and Harindranath, G. (2013). IT readiness in small firms. *Journal of Small Business and Enterprise Development*, **20**: 807–823.

Stam, E. (2010). Growth beyond Gibrat: Firm growth processes and strategies. *Small Business Economics*, **35**: 129–135.

Staples, M. and Niazi, M. (2010). Two case studies on small enterprise motivation and readiness for CMMI. In *Proc. 11th Int. Conf. Prod. Focus. Softw.* ACM, New York, NY, pp. 63–66.

Stockdale, R. and Standing, C. (2004). Benefits and barriers of electronic marketplace participation: An SME perspective. *Journal of Enterprise Information Management*, **17**: 301–311.

Sutanonpaiboon, J. and Pearson, A. M. (2006). E-commerce adoption: Perceptions of managers/owners of small- and medium-sized enterprises (SMEs) in Thailand. *Journal of Internet Commerce*, **5**: 53–82.

Tan, J., Tyler K. and Manica, A. (2007). Business-to-business adoption of eCommerce in China. *Information Management*, **44**: 332–351.

Tan, K. S., Chong, S. C., Lin, B. and Eze, U. C. (2009). Internet-based ICT adoption: Evidence from Malaysian SMEs. *Industrial Management & Data Systems*, **109**: 224–244.

Teo, T. S. H. and Ranganathan, C. (2004). Adopters and non-adopters of business-to-business electronic commerce in Singapore. *Information Management*, **42**: 89–102.

Terziovski, M. (2010). Innovation practice and its performance implications in small and medium enterprises (SMEs) in the manufacturing sector: A resource-based view. *Strategic Management Journal*, **31**: 892–902.

Thong, J. Y. L., Yap, C. and Raman, K. S. (1993). Top management support in small business information systems implementation: How important is it? In *Proceedings of the 1993 Conference on Computer Personnel Research*. ACM, New York, NY, pp. 416–425.

Thong, J. Y. L. and Yap, C. S. (1995). CEO characteristics, organizational characteristics and information technology adoption in small businesses. *Omega International Journal of Management Science*, **23**: 429–442.

Thong, J. Y. L. (2001). Resource constraints and information systems implementation in Singaporean small businesses. *Omega International Journal of Management Science*, **29**: 143–156.

Ullah, A. and Lai, R. (2013). A systematic review of business and information technology alignment. *ACM Transactions on Management Information Systems*, **4**, 1: Article 4. doi:10.1145/2445560.2445564.

Upadhyay, P., Jahanyan, S. and Dan, P. K. (2011). Factors influencing ERP implementation in Indian manufacturing organisations: A study of micro, small and medium-scale enterprises. *Journal of Enterprise Information Management*, **24**: 130–145.

Venkatesh, V. and Brown, S. A. (2001). A longitudinal investigation of personal computers in homes: Adoption determinants and emerging challenges. *MIS Quarterly*, **25**: 71–102.

Vere, A. (2009). Cadre juridique et réglementaire pour l'économie du savoir: Note conceptuelle. Première session du Comité de l'information, de la science et de la technologie pour le développement (CODIST I). *Conseil économique et social Nations unies*, pp. 1–15.

Wang, S. and Cheung, W. (2004). E-business adoption by travel agencies: Prime candidates for mobile e-business. *International Journal of Electronic Commerce*, **8**: 43–63.

Wiklund, J. and Shepherd, D. (2003). Aspiring for, and achieving growth: The moderating role of resources and opportunities. *Journal of Management Studies*, **40**: 1919–1941.

Wiklund, J., Patzelt, H. and Shepherd, D. A. (2009). Building an integrative model of small business growth. *Small Business Economics*, **32**: 351–374.

Yap, C. S., Thong, J. Y. L. and Raman, K. S. (1994). Effect of government incentives on computerisation in small business. *European Journal of Information Systems*, **3**: 191–206.

Zahay, D. L. and Peltier, J. (2008). Interactive strategy formation: Organizational and entrepreneurial factors related to effective customer information systems practices in B2B firms. *Industrial Marketing Management*, **37**: 191–205.

Zhou, Z., Li, G. and Lam, T. (2009). The role of task-fit in employees' adoption of IT in Chinese hotels. *Journal of Human Resources in Hospitality & Tourism*, **8**: 96–105.

Biography

Marieme Chouki is a researcher at the Faculty of Science Ben M'sik, Hassan II University. She obtained her MASTER degree in information processing from Faculty of Science Ben M'sik, Hassan II University Casablanca, Morocco in 2013. She has participated in many conferences and published articles in scientific journals. Her research field is Information Technology.

Mohamed Talea is a Professor of Higher Education at the Faculty of Sciences Ben M'Sik, University HASSAN II MOROCCO CASABLANCA. He obtained his PhD in collaboration with the LMP laboratory in Poitiers University, FRANCE in 2001. He obtained a Doctorate of High Graduate Studies degree at the University Hassan II-Mohammedia in 1994. Actually he is the Director of Information Treatment Laboratory. He has published twenty papers in conferences and national and international journals. His search major field is on Systems engineering and in security of system information.

Chafik Okar is a Professor at National School of Applied Sciences, Hassan 1st University, Morocco. He got three Master in Mathematic, supply chain and Information System. After a long experience as a Manager in information system department of many companies, he obtained his PhD in supply chain management in 2011 and began his career as professor in 2011. He has published fifty papers in conferences and national and international journals. His search major fields are: Data science, Information System Management, supply chain management and Performance management.

Razane Chroqui is a Professor, in charge with the Management Techniques Major in the National School of Applied Science of Berrechid–Hassan the 1st University–Morocco. She has a B.A. in Accountancy, an M.A. in Finance from the University of Sfax (Tunisia), an M.A. in Management Control and Information Systems from Hassan the 1st University (Morocco), and a PhD from Reims Champagne Ardennes University (France), awarded in 2009. She has participated in many conferences, has published many artciles in scientific journals and has taught abroad. Her research area is Performance Management.

Chapter 16

Innovating with Strangers; Managing Knowledge Barriers Across Distances in Cross-Industry Innovation

Hilda Bø Lyng

Faculty of Health Sciences
University of Stavanger, Norway
hilda.b.lyng@uis.no

Eric Christian Brun*

Faculty of Science and Technology
University of Stavanger, Norway
eric.brun@uis.no

We explore the types of knowledge barriers that are encountered at organizational level in cross-industry innovation, what influences them and how they can be overcome. Eleven cross-industry projects were qualitatively analyzed at the individual level of activity. Innovation collaboration occurred at three levels; intra-organizational, inter-organizational, and inter-institutional. Each level exhibited added relational distances as well as semantic and pragmatic barriers, of which the latter type was the most challenging. Effort necessary to overcome knowledge barriers accumulated at each level. Knowledge barriers were increased by legitimacy differences and communicational deficiencies, and lowered by reduction of interdependencies, use of knowledge brokers, and previous cross-industry experience.

Keywords: Cross-industry innovation; knowledge barriers; relational distances; boundary spanning.

"Most of the work still to be done in science and the useful arts is precisely that which needs knowledge and cooperation of many scientists and disciplines.

That is why it is necessary for scientists and technologists in different disciplines to meet and work together, even those in branches

---

*Corresponding author.

This chapter was originally published in *International Journal of Innovation and Technology Management*, Vol. 17, No. 1, February 2020, published by World Scientific Publishing, Singapore. Reprinted with permission.

of knowledge which seem to have least relation and connection with one another" [Antoine Lavoisier, in Elfner *et al.* (2011, p. 2)].

1. Introduction

The act of innovation in today's society is becoming more demanding. Firms can no longer rely solely on their internal resources, and therefore have to look beyond their own organizational boundaries to gain access to crucial knowledge. However, as the quote above demonstrates, the need for combining highly different knowledge domains in order to innovate is not a new thought. A vast amount of literature emphasizes the potential for combining and reusing knowledge originally developed in different industries, in order to achieve novelty and radical innovation [e.g. Enkel and Gassmann (2010); Hacklin and Wallin (2013); Leonard (1995)].

Literature of *cross-industry innovation* (CII) has provided valuable insights into how knowledge from different industries can be combined to achieve innovation. However, the attention of this literature has mostly been given to the *discovery* of useful knowledge in foreign industries [Brunswicker and Hutschek (2010); Enkel and Gassmann (2010); Gassmann and Zeschky (2008); Herstatt and Kalogerakis (2005); Kalogerakis *et al.* (2010)], as well as *antecedents* for CII [Enkel and Bader (2016); Enkel *et al.* (2017); Enkel and Heil (2014); Enkel *et al.* (2017); Heil and Enkel (2015)].

A related literature stream has addressed the concept of *recombinant innovation* (RI). In RI, knowledge that has been developed in one field is transferred and combined to knowledge in another field [e.g. Bessant and Trifilova (2017); Griffith *et al.* (2017); Subramanian and Soh (2017)]. Subramanian and Soh [2017] argue that in order to combine new ideas from diverse technological domains, innovating firms form portfolios of alliances. The technological diversity of a firm's alliance portfolio, they claim, positively influences the firm's breadth of RI. As argued by Bessant and Trifilova [2017, p. 1100], RI "... reduces learning costs since much of the original development of an innovation has been undertaken in a different context."

Yet, collaborations between actors from highly different work communities is also known to be associated with knowledge barriers based on differences in knowledge domains, experiences, professional languages, perspectives, organizational cultures, and interests [Bechky (2003); Carlile (2002, 2004); Dingler and Enkel (2016); Dougherty (1992); Rau *et al.* (2016)]. On a related note, Griffith *et al.* [2017] argue that market frictions hamper the transfer of ideas between firms, leading to higher costs of discovering and utilizing ideas from another firm than one's own.

So far however, research literature has not been able to fully provide us an understanding of the nature of such knowledge barriers between the actors collaborating in CII. Truly, literature on *boundary spanning* has contributed with valuable understanding of knowledge barriers between actors working together across organizational boundaries [Berends *et al.* (2011); Carlile (2002, 2004); Edenius *et al.* (2010); Edmondson and Harvey (2018); Majchrzak *et al.* (2004, 2012); Rau *et al.* (2016)]. A particular useful contribution is the framework by Carlile [2004], which categorizes knowledge barriers into syntactic, semantic, and pragmatic boundaries.

However, the contributions within the boundary spanning literature are empirically based on the crossing of occupational communities *within* a firm or an industry branch [Bechky (2003); Carlile (2002, 2004); Dougherty (1992); Dougherty and Dunne (2012)]. Furthermore, these contributions implicitly assume fairly stable and well-bounded teams, while teams that form across knowledge boundaries in order to innovate are often of a temporary and informal nature [Edmondson and Harvey (2018)]. Some recent research contributions discuss boundary spanning with heterogeneous teams [Somech and Khalaili (2014); Wilson and Ettlie (2018)], but not in a cross-industry context.

As such, the findings from current research do not immediately provide understanding of knowledge barriers in CII, as cross-industry collaborations introduce new and other levels of differences between the collaborating actors than the crossing of occupational boundaries within the confines of firms or industry branches. In the empirical foundation in Rau *et al.*'s [2016] qualitative study, some of the cases can be classified as cross-industrial cases. Still, the focus within their study is concentrated towards newly emerging interfaces and not towards cross-industry actors working together in shared innovation collaborations over some time. There is therefore a gap in the understanding of knowledge boundaries at the continuum between initiation and completion of a CII process.

On a separate account, a useful stream of literature is the research literature studying the role of relational *proximities* [Balland (2012); Boschma (2005), Fitjar *et al.* (2016); Knoben and Oerlemans (2006)] — or its inverse — *distances* [Parjanen *et al.* (2011)] between collaborating actors. However, this stream of literature has its main focus at the regional geographic level. To our knowledge, the role of different relational distances has so far not been studied in terms of their influence for knowledge barriers at organizational levels in cross-industry contexts.

Hence, there exists a theoretical gap between these streams of literature. Boundary spanning literature does not address the challenges of knowledge barriers in cross-industry collaborations. Literature on relational distances in innovation does not address knowledge barriers at the organizational level. And finally, there is a lack of research literature describing the nature and management of knowledge barriers within CII. In order to contribute to fill the void between these streams of literature the research questions we pursue is this study are;

What type of barriers are encountered at the organizational level when new distances are introduced by moving into inter-organizational collaborations in cross-industry innovation? Furthermore, what influences these barriers and how can they be overcome?

Our paper is structured as follows; In Sec. 2, the literature review will expand on contributions and theoretical gaps for the phenomenon under study. In Sec. 3, empirical cases and methodology will be explained. In Sec. 4, findings from the multiple case study will be presented and discussed concerning their influence for cross-industry collaborations. In Sec. 5, we will conclude by discussing theoretical and practical implications.

2. Literature Review

Actors in cross-industry collaborations are faced with a variety of barriers to the transfer of knowledge across organizational boundaries, due to differences among the involved actors. Different streams of literature provide different understandings and implications of how to manage such differences between actors.

2.1. *Literature on boundary spanning*

Carlile and Rebentisch [2003] relate knowledge barriers to increasing levels of three types of knowledge properties; *differences, novelty, and dependency*. These properties of knowledge cause knowledge barriers by increasing the level of complexity at boundaries between individuals and organizations. *Differences* refer to knowledge barriers caused by actors possessing different *levels* of accumulated knowledge, or different *types* of knowledge, meaning that the knowledge possessed by each actor is from different knowledge domains. Strong knowledge specialization therefore increases the level of differences and accordingly increases the effort needed to develop a common ground between the actors.

The dimension of *dependencies* will always be present to some extent in collaborations. Carlile and Rebentisch [2003] argue that dependencies relate to complexity; the more interdependencies between actors, the higher the level of complexity. If there are no dependencies between actors, present differences between actors would be of no impact [Carlile (2004)]. A high level of interdependencies between actors will lead to a need for negotiations of different interests in order to develop a common ground between the actors. In cross-industry collaborations, where actors from different industries work together towards a shared solution, interdependencies are present, meaning that their inherent differences will be of consequence for the collaboration.

Novelty alludes to an additional dimension of knowledge barriers. Novelty may be present in terms of new knowledge, new technology or new context, leading to an absence of common ground between the actors. According to Carlile [2004]; "When novelty is present, both the *capacity* of the common knowledge to represent the differences and dependencies now of consequence and the *ability* of the actors involved to use it become important issues" (p. 557 italic in original). Hence, stored and invested knowledge needs to be translated, transformed and adapted to the new problem context in order to be useful. Cross-industry collaborations will be highly influenced by novelty, in that the involved actors will meet new partners, new terms of knowledge, new industry contexts, and new organizational cultures, leading to an increase in complexity of knowledge barriers.

These properties of knowledge: differences, dependencies and novelty, determine the hierarchical level of knowledge boundaries between collaborative actors. At the *syntactic* boundary, actors share a common lexicon, which allows for a specification and understanding of present differences and dependencies between the actors. Knowledge can then be transferred across the boundary in a "straightforward" manner. As novelty increases, the common lexicon between the actors no longer facilitates a shared understanding of differences and dependencies, and the *semantic* boundary is entered. When working together in occupational communities, people develop their own professional language and "thought worlds" [Bechky (2003); Dougherty (1992)]. The aim at the semantic boundary is thus to develop a *shared meaning*, i.e. alignment of different thought worlds and languages of the actors through translation processes [Carlile (2004)].

If novelty further increases, the pragmatic boundary is entered. At the *pragmatic* boundary high levels of novelty affect the interests of the involved actors. As knowledge becomes invested in practice, actors are reluctant to change the way they work, and their situated knowledge easily becomes at stake, leading to different interests and incentives among the actors. As Carlile [2004] argues; "When actors have different interests, the dependencies between them are not indifferent" (p. 559). The aim at the pragmatic boundary is thus to develop a *shared context* [Carlile and Rebentisch (2003)], i.e. align the different interests and incentives of the actors through a process of knowledge transformation [Carlile (2004)].

Rau *et al.* [2012] argue that knowledge transfer and knowledge management have primarily been studied based on the conditions of the syntactic boundary. Having the syntactic perspective in focus, knowledge is viewed as a tangible resource that can be transferred, stored and managed as a commodity [Haider and Mariotti (2010); Rau *et al.* (2016)]. Hence, Rau *et al.* [2016] call for future research to explore the role of semantic and pragmatic boundaries in collaborations where innovation is desired.

The framework provided by Carlile [2004], illustrated in Fig. 1, describes such knowledge barriers based on differences, dependencies, and novelty in knowledge across organizational communities *within a firm*. The boundaries to be crossed between occupational communities within a firm take place within some contextual conditions that are stable, in that the collaborative actors possess shared relational properties such as common organizational, institutional and geographical dimensions. When collaboration for innovation is extended — as in this study — to also involve for cross-industry actors, the collaboration will be affected by new differences in relational properties. It is therefore necessary to involve other streams of literature

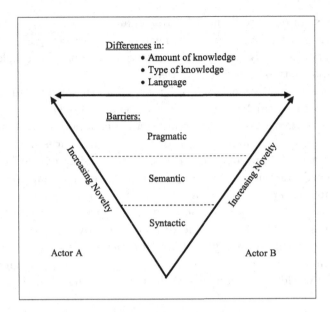

Fig. 1.   Framework for the management of knowledge across boundaries within an organization [Adapted from Carlile (2004)].

to develop understanding of how these extended relational properties affect knowledge transfer in CII.

2.2. *Literature on relational distances*

In a literature review of innovation practices and boundary crossing mechanisms by Rau *et al.* [2012], they request future research into deeper descriptions of inherent differences between actors in collaborations. A contribution to this end has been provided by a stream of literature studying the effects of different *relational proximities* on knowledge transfer for innovation [Boschma (2005); Fitjar *et al.* (2016); Knoben and Oerlemans (2006); Parjanen *et al.* (2011); Torre (2008)]. The empirical focus for this literature is however at a regional geographical level, with an orientation towards economic geography, with little attention given to the organizational level. However, in order to understand important dimensions of cultural, organizational, institutional differences taking place in cross-industry collaborations between organizations, it is of value to make use of contributions from the literature on relational distances. This literature partly uses the term *relational proximity*, partly its inverse; *relational distance*, i.e. low proximity implies high distance and vice versa. In the following, we will mainly use the *distance* term, as we believe it compares easier with similar terms used in boundary-spanning literature and CII literature.

Based on its application to regional economic geography studies, the most commonly used dimension in this literature is *geographical distance*. Boschma [2005] expanded this literature by including *cognitive, social, organizational, and institutional distance*. Later on, Parjanen *et al.* [2011] discussed a separate *communicational* dimension, as opposed to Boschma [2005] who considered communicational distance to be a subcategory of cognitive distance. *Cultural distance* is additionally a dimension often included in proximity studies [Knoben and Oerlemans (2006)], as a way of differentiating organizational cultures [Parjanen *et al.* (2011)]. As a consequence of increased mobility of individuals, Torre [2008] included *temporal distance* into the framework. And finally, Guan and Yan [2016] emphasized a dimension named *technological distance*, which Parjanen *et al.* [2011] designate as *functional distance*, i.e. differences in expertise and competences.

A critique of the literature on relational distances is the lack of consistency in their definitions of the different distance dimensions. Knoben and Oerlemans [2006] found definitions and their operationalization to be both overlapping and ambiguous. As a means to help clarify, Knoben and Oerlemans [2006] have presented a framework where they consider the dimensions of cultural, social, institutional, and organizational distance to account for most overlapping aspects. The authors argue that these dimensions should all be grouped together under the category *organizational distance*, referred to as; "the set of routines — explicit or implicit — which allows coordination without having to define beforehand how to do so" [Knoben and Oerlemans (2006, p. 80)]. Even if Knoben and Oerlemans [2006] provided valuable insights of relations and overlap between the different dimensions, they did not suggest new, unambiguous definitions, but still rest on the original contributors' definitions. Hence, the overlap and ambiguity of relational distance dimensions still prevails.

For the purpose of our study, we will in the following make use of the categories *cognitive, communicational, functional, cultural, social, organizational, institutional and geographical* dimensions of distance, and their operationalization will be described further in the Method section.

2.3. *Distances and barriers to develop shared meaning*

Shared common meaning builds on having shared "thought worlds" and a shared language. A shared language is the basis for the conveyance of information and understanding, and thus represents a communicative dimension, whereas shared thoughts worlds is the basis of interpretation and represents a cognitive dimension.

2.3.1. *Shared thought worlds*

"When all think alike, then no one is thinking" *Walter Lippman* (*American political reporter*).

Having different thought worlds make actors interpret new and unfamiliar knowledge differently, based on their situated mental frames. This provides opportunities for new ideas, but also causes knowledge barriers to rise [Dougherty (1992); Rau et al. (2012)]. A result of not handling such different thought worlds properly is that; "pitfalls will be overlooked, meaning lost and communication curtailed" [Dougherty (1992, p. 195)]. Boundary spanning literature [Bechky (2003); Carlile (2002, 2004)] argues for the development of a common ground, through means of translation and transformation, in order to deal with cognitive differences. Thus, the boundary spanning literature perspective emphasizes the development of homogeneity in thought worlds.

Rau et al. [2016] classify the lack of shared thought worlds at the semantic boundary into two subcategories; the *fuzziness* boundary and the *unbalanced mental model* boundary. The fuzziness boundary refers to settings where actors are found unable to make use of familiar objects to convey their knowledge. The unbalanced mental model boundary refers to barriers caused by actors failing to acknowledge the perspective of their counterpart, and thereby misinterpret underlying assumptions. Both sub-boundaries result in actors communicating in a "cross-purpose" manner [Rau et al., (2016, p. 345)].

According to the literature on relational distances, cognitive proximity is defined as "similarities in the way actors perceive, interpret, understand and evaluate the world" [Knoben and Oerlemans (2006, p. 77)]. The aspect of having different knowledge domains is covered by the term functional proximity, defined as "shared technological experiences and knowledge bases" [Knoben and Oerlemans (2006, p. 77)]. Cognitive distance thus refers to the ways of thinking and understanding new knowledge, while functional distance reflects your operational background.

Fitjar et al. [2016] argue that the breadth and width of searches for external knowledge follow the so-called "Goldilocks" principle, where too narrow searches will increase the possibility of missing opportunities, while too wide searches will increase the possibility of information overload and lack of understanding [Boschma (2005); Enkel and Heil (2014)]. Nooteboom et al. [2007] accordingly found an inverted u-shaped relationship between cognitive distance and innovative performance, where too low cognitive distance resulted in knowledge redundancy and too high distance resulted in a lack of understanding.

The CII literature [Brunswicker and Hutschek (2010); Enkel and Bader (2016); Enkel and Gassmann (2010); Enkel and Heil (2014); Gassmann et al. (2011); Gassmann and Zeschky (2008)] emphasizes high cognitive and technological diversity between actors in order to increase innovation novelty. Enkel and Bader [2016] argued that cognitive distance should not be seen as a barrier for the participation in cross-industry collaborations, as long as the actors are motivated and perceive the knowledge boundary to be manageable.

The cross-industry concept itself, of combining and reusing knowledge from different industry sectors, relies on high functional distance. However, even if there may be a high functional distance between collaborating actors from separate industries, the cognitive distance between them may still be fairly low if they hold comparable levels of higher education. Actors having high levels of education are usually trained in abstract thinking, facilitating development of abstractions and analogies [Lyng and Brun (2018)], which has been found to play an important role in cross-industry knowledge transfer [Enkel and Gassmann (2010); Gassmann and Zeschky (2008); Herstatt and Kalogerakis (2005); Kalogerakis *et al.* (2010)]. Prior knowledge and experience of cross-industry collaborations has also been found to increase the ability to develop abstractions and analogies, as well as to enhance motivation for future cross-industry collaboration [Enkel and Bader (2016)].

2.3.2. *Shared language*

"*language cannot be understood, much less translated, without reference to a great deal of knowledge about the world*" [Holland and Quinn (1987, p. 5)].

Communication involves both the process of *transmission*, where knowledge is prepared, transferred and received through some sort of media, and information *processing*, which includes the attribution of meaning to the information. Information processing relies on the individuals' own mental models, like prior knowledge and experiences, as well as contextual factors [Dennis *et al.* (2008)]. While Boschma [2005] includes communicational distance as a subcategory within the cognitive distance dimension, Parjanen *et al.* [2011, p. 930] describes communicative distance as a separate dimension and defines it as "*differences in concept and professional languages.*" Interaction through language is a crucial part of innovation and accordingly, communicative proximity holds a natural place in innovation studies at the micro level. We will therefore treat communicational distance as a separate category in this study.

The objective for successful communication is the development of shared understanding. Shared understanding does not only depend on the actors' *own* understanding of the meaning, but additionally that the actors understand how knowledge is interpreted by *other* actors in the team [Dennis *et al.* (2008)]. Shared understanding among highly different actors will therefore require familiarity with the counterpart's language and capability of *perspective taking* [Boland and Tenkasi (1995)]. Rau *et al.* [2016] describe the lack of shared language as the *terminology boundary*, which is further a sub-boundary under the semantic boundary. They found actors not able to transcend this boundary to be impeded by cross-purpose communication and a behavior they call "playing hide-and-seek," where actors avoid clarification due to embarrassment of lacking knowledge of the topic under discussion.

Daft *et al.* [1987] split lack of shared understanding into whether it is based on uncertainty or equivocality. In their account, uncertainty in communication occurs in situations where the task at hand requires more information than what is offered, while equivocality occurs in situations where the actors holds multiple and conflicting interpretations about the task and increases as actors' mental frames differ. Daft *et al.* [1987] further argue that by using rich media, like face-to-face communication, equivocality between actors will be reduced, and especially if the communication concerns negotiations and conflicts. Having a low geographical distance enables face-to-face communication, which is also found beneficial for the transfer of tacit knowledge [Antonio Messeni *et al.* (2007); Boschma (2005); Fitjar *et al.* (2016)].

In the theory of media synchronicity, Dennis *et al.* [2008] categorized the two steps of communication (transmission of information and processing of information) as information *conveyance* and information *convergence*. Information conveyance includes the transfer of a sufficient amount of new and raw information from one actor to another, while information convergence includes the two actors agreeing on a shared understanding of the information. Resting on the framework by Daft *et al.* [1987], conveyance will reduce communication uncertainty. The receiving actor is later on required to make sense of the new knowledge through cognitive processes. Information convergence depends on the different interpretations held by the actors, and includes processes of developing shared understanding and agreements [Dennis *et al.* (2008)]. According to Dennis *et al.* [2008]; "Convergence typically needs rapid, back and forth information transmission of small quantities of preprocessed information" (p. 580), a process which typically will be easiest to conduct through face-to-face communication.

2.4. *Distances and barriers to develop shared context*

"People are reluctant to change their hard-won outcomes, because it is costly and difficult to achieve knowledge and skills" [Edenius *et al.* (2010, p. 137)].

Both differences in thought worlds and languages involve contextual aspects of cultural, social, institutional and organizational differences. Differences in organizational contexts influence the actors' practices, methodologies, incentives, and interests. Carlile [2004] describes these differences as pragmatic barriers. At the pragmatic boundary one actor's invested knowledge becomes influential for the perceived value of another actor's knowledge [Rau *et al.* (2012)], making experts feel they are "juniors" in a new knowledge domain. In order to develop a common ground at the pragmatic boundary, actors need to negotiate shared interests and work processes [Carlile (2004); Edenius *et al.* (2010)]. Combining actors from foreign industries will lead to contextual differences, and thereby divergent perspectives, interests, and incentives, making it necessary to include processes for alignment of these issues.

Rau *et al.* [2016] describe two sub-boundaries at the pragmatic level; the *trajectory* boundary and the *everybody-is-an-innovator* boundary. The former refers to situations where the actor needs to gain or transform their situated knowledge, causing behaviors where actors engage in active resistance or they end up going solo.

The latter sub-boundary refers to situations where there is ambiguity of responsibility and roles, causing behaviors where actors refrain from engagement, in Rau *et al.*'s words; "playing possum" [2016, p. 349].

Included in Knoben and Oerlemans's [2006] definition of organizational distance are the dimensions of social, cultural and institutional distance. Social distance refers to "social relationships, and the amount of trust included in them" [Parjanen *et al.* (2011, p. 930)]. Social distance is hence related to the concepts of ties [Hansen (1999)], embeddedness [Granovetter (1985)], socialization [Dingler and Enkel (2016); Jansen *et al.* (2005); Volberda *et al.* (2010)], and communities of practice [Wenger (1998)]. Low social distance, from its definition, facilitates the development of trust between actors, which is found beneficial for the transfer of tacit knowledge [Boschma (2005); Parjanen *et al.* (2011)], and thus innovation [Bruneel *et al.* (2010); Bunduchi (2017)]. Trust is defined as firm beliefs that "something is safe and reliable" [Cambridge Dictionary (2018)], and holds an important role in collaborations that involve uncertainty. In a cross-industrial setting, where collaborating actors lack prior relations about their counterpart's knowledge, technology, and industry, the development of trust will not be as straightforward as between more similar actors [Gassmann *et al.* (2010)]. When an unfamiliar actor is perceived to be both safe and reliable, the actor will be considered as a legitimate partner for the collaboration. *Legitimacy* is found to increase the willingness for providing resources into the collaboration [Bunduchi (2017)]. Suchman [1995] defines legitimacy as "a generalized perception or assumption that the actions of an entity are desirable, proper, or appropriate within some socially constructed system of norms, values, beliefs, and definitions" (p. 574). He further argues that legitimacy is based on alignment in terms of a "collective audience," and not by individual observers as may be the case in trust. Hence, when the considered entity is a single actor within a collaboration, the terms of trust and legitimacy can have similar meaning.

Organizational distance refers to organizational practices involved in interactive learning, like how organizations share, integrate and coordinate knowledge. Knoben and Oerlemans [2006] have shown how organizational distance has been ambiguously defined over various accounts of the term, based on similarities to social, cultural, and institutional distances. Studies of organizational distance are performed at two different levels; the structural and the dyadic level [Knoben and Oerlemans (2006)]. The structural level focuses on whether firms are positioned in the same network, where the dyadic relationship between two firms is excluded. Dyadic studies of organizational proximity, on the other hand, focus on interactions between firms and focus on similarities and differences in organizational context.

Organizational culture influences the way knowledge is transferred, valued, and created in organizations. The importance of organizational culture is described by McDermott and O'dell [(2001), p. 77]; "however strong your commitment and approach to knowledge management, your culture is stronger." An organization's culture consists of the organization's explicit values as well as implicit levels of how actors act and understand each other's knowledge, language and practice [McDermott and O'dell (2001)]. Consequently, when actors are confronted with actors from foreign organizational cultures, they interpret their counterparts based on "their respective cognitive scheme" [Rau et al. (2012, p. 183)]. Cultural distance is defined as "differences in organizational cultures, values etc" [Parjanen et al. (2011, p. 930)], and Knoben and Oerlemans [2006] argue that low cultural distance eases interactions between actors, due to the alignment in interpretations and routines.

The dimension of institutional distance has been operationalized through a variety of measures in literature, leading to ambiguity of the term [Fitjar et al. (2016)]. An often used operationalization, which we have applied in our study, is to classify organizations as to whether they belong to commercial or non-commercial sectors [Balland (2012); Fitjar et al. (2016); Ponds et al. (2007)]. Accordingly, much research of institutional distance has a focus on Triple-Helix collaborations [Etzkowitz (2008); Etzkowitz and Leydesdorff (2000)] and university-industry linkages [Bloedon and Stokes (1994); Bruneel et al. (2010); Gomes et al. (2005)]. Collaborations encompassing university and industry are known to be hampered with uncertainty [Bruneel et al. (2010)]. The barriers caused by institutional gaps can be differentiated into whether they are based on differences in *orientation*, or based in *transaction-related* differences (e.g. IP). Bruneel et al. [2010] found that prior experience of collaborative research helped transcend orientation-related barriers, while trust acted as an enabler to transcend both orientation and transaction-related barriers. Low institutional distance has been found to "provide stable conditions for interactive learning to take place effectively," and thus beneficial for innovation [Boschma (2005, p. 68)]. High institutional distance, on the other hand, is known to increase divergent perspectives in objectives, interests, and time horizons [Bjerregaard (2010)]. In the words of Ponds et al. [2007, p. 427]; "in academia actors want to maximize the diffusion of their knowledge, while companies want to minimize such diffusion." Institutional gaps lead to different institutional logics, which alter the focus of collaborative researchers away from the scientific and technological issues, and instead towards the institutional gap [Bjerregaard (2010)]. The importance of institutional distance is also emphasized by Gertler [2003] who argues that having low organizational and social distance is not sufficient for the facilitation of efficient interactive learning, when institutional distance is high. If the actors hold fundamentally different incentive systems, developing shared objectives will be difficult. Even if these aspects have been widely studied, few studies have investigated the role and nature of barriers and mechanisms that help actors transcend them [Bruneel et al. (2010)], and even less so in terms of cross-industry collaborations.

2.5. *Summary*

The above literature review reveals contributions from different streams of literature for understanding how relational differences between actors affect knowledge barriers in CII. The combination of boundary spanning literature and literature on relational distances provides valuable instruments to describe differences between actors and their consequences for knowledge barriers in cross-industry collaborations.

The boundary spanning framework has been widely used in research to describe knowledge barriers affecting interacting actors; however this literature does not provide a structure to consider the impact of relational differences that occur between actors in CII. By integrating boundary spanning literature and literature on relational distances, for exploring a phenomenon not previously investigated within the CII literature, this study will contribute to each of these streams of literature. Boundary spanning literature will be empirically extended to account for knowledge boundaries in cross-industry settings. Literature on relational distances will be extended to address micro-level interactions — research that has been called for [Fitjar *et al.* (2016)]. Furthermore, CII literature will be extended to include micro-level interactions taking place between knowledge discovery and the innovation outcome. Important to note is that "knowledge diversity in itself does not produce performance benefits; in the face of a creative and complex task, knowledge diversity spurs team interaction through which diversity can be put to good use" [Edmondson and Harvey (2018, p. 351)]. Meaning that it is not the differences itself that allow for novel innovations, but how actors are able to cross knowledge boundaries and take advantage of the present differences.

3. Empirical Cases and Method

3.1. *Research design*

Due to the nature of the research objective, were we sought to provide understanding of a phenomenon not previously well described in existing literature, a qualitative research strategy was found to be the most appropriate. New understanding developed through this research is according to Gregor [2006] of an explanatory theory type, providing understanding of *how* a phenomenon takes place in a particular context. The phenomenon under study here is knowledge boundaries, and the particular context is cross-industry collaborations. Following the social science tradition, this explanatory research builds on the notion of relationships, rather than causality [Gregor (2006)]. A case study design was chosen, as this approach is appropriate to study *how* phenomena take place [Yin (1994)]. Unlike surveys, whose purpose is statistical generalization to a larger population (and hence require samples representative to the larger population), a case study aims to generalize empirical findings to theory [Yin (1994)]. In a theory-building case study then, rather than necessarily representing a larger population, it is more important that the selected cases are representative of the particular phenomenon under study, for which one seeks to build theory.

Accordingly, the empirical data for this research was collected through a multiple case study of 11 individual collaborations encompassing actors from highly different industries. The choice of cases was based on theoretical sampling, i.e. selecting cases in which one expects to find a richness of data for the phenomenon under study [Eisenhardt (1989)]. Seven of the cases were individual collaborations funded by a network organization named "Pumps & Pipes Norway" (PP, see Table 1), established for the purpose of achieving innovation from knowledge transfer across the petroleum industry and the medical sector. The PP cases were hence all joint collaborations of medical and petroleum actors. The informants from the PP cases, with the exception for PP#7, having a later start, were interviewed at two different points in time. Interviews in the first round lasted for 30–58 min, and between 15 and 72 min in the second round (time interval relied on the level of progress present).

The next four cases were member firms in a cluster named "Norway Health Tech" (NHT, see Table 1). All of the cases had made use of cross-industry collaborations in order to develop their respective innovation within medical technology. However, the collaboration partners of the NHT actors were not restricted to the petroleum industry. The informants from the NHT cases were all founders or CEOs, and the interviews lasted between 23 and 40 min.

The use of multiple cases allows for cross-case comparison, which is relevant for obtaining a deeper and more multifaceted understanding of the phenomenon under

Table 1.   Description of the empirical cases.

PP#1 Project manager interview twice (March 2017 + January 2018) Participated at seminar 14.10.2016.	This collaboration encompassed a research center, a university, and a hospital. The project used a mathematical flow model developed for oil reservoirs to simulate and visualize forces involved in tumor spread and growth. The objective was to increase the understanding of physical forces involved in cancer. Involved petroleum researchers and medical doctors.
PP#2 1–2 project managers interviewed twice (March 2017 (1) + November 2017 (2)). Participated at seminar 16.12.2016	This case was a startup firm that used a petroleum technology for picking up fragile items to make an automated mattress for preventing bedsores for patients with low-mobility issues. The firm consisted of former students who collaborated with a petroleum engineering company and the public health care sector.
PP#3 Project manager interviewed twice (March 2017 + November 2017). Participated at seminar 28.10.2016	This case was a collaboration between a research center, a university and a hospital. The project used mathematical models for the modelling of porous media of fractured oil reservoirs to increase interpretation of dynamic MRI. The collaboration encompassed petroleum mathematical researchers, medical doctors and researchers within imaging.
PP#4 1–2 project managers interviewed twice (March 2017 (2) + January 2018 (1). Participated at seminar 24.03.2017	This project was a collaboration between a private technology firm and a hospital. The petroleum industry has been in the forefront in using VR technology for safety training and subsea operations (ROV). These experiences were used to develop VR-software for treatment of elderly people with dementia and chronic diseases.

Table 1. (*Continued*)

PP#5 Project manager interviewed twice (May 2017 + October 2017). Project advisor interviewed May 2017. Participated at seminar 16.09.2018. Radio-interview 09.01.2018 transcribed and coded	The objective for this collaboration was to develop a non-invasive method for the determination of the severity of stenosis, based on a computer model of oils and water in reservoir rocks. The collaboration was a combination of petroleum researchers at a research center and medical doctors at a hospital. The research objective was put forward to the petroleum researchers by a cardiologist at the first Norwegian Pumps & Pipes conference (01.10.2015).
PP#6 1–2 project managers interviewed twice (April 2017 (2) + November 2017 (1)) Participated at seminar 10.03.2017.	This project used knowledge and technology for visualization of offshore installations in order to develop visualization software for communication and decision-making for use in planning of a new hospital. The collaboration consisted of a technology company specialized in petroleum solution, and an internal project group for planning of the new hospital. The hospital project manager at the hospital had a background as a nurse, leaving the collaboration as a mixture of petroleum engineers and health workers.
PP#7 Project Manager interviewed September 2017. Participated at seminar 21.04.2017.	This case concerned a start-up medical device firm, which was developing a product for paramedics for clearing patients' airways. The project under study here was the collaboration between the start-up firm and petroleum researchers at a university. The project sought to develop a technology for demobilization of liquids in a chamber, which would facilitate use of the device in all directions.
NHT#1 Medical manager interviewed June 2018	NHT#1 was a Med Tech firm, which had developed software that allowed for remote care of elderly and chronically sick patients. In order to develop the product the firm had collaborated cross-industry with firms specialized in radar technology, sensors, ICT, bluetooth technology, as well as with the health care sector.
NHT#2 Interview of Founder/CEO May 2018.	The innovation product developed by this med tech firm was an automated disinfection robot. The development needed collaborations cross-industry with partners specialized in process control, automation, sensors, communication, as well as with the health care sector. The product was used in nursing homes and the firm was at the time of study entering the food production industry.
NHT#3 CEO interviewed June 2018	NHT#3 specialized in developing products for maintenance treatment of dental implants. Through the product development, NHT#3 collaborated cross-industry with different partners in e.g. material technology, academia, sterilization, and clinical research.
NHT#4 Founder and CEO interviewed September 2018	NHT#4's medical innovation was a technology for hand disinfection in a more efficient, safer, comfortable way. The founder of NHT#4 was an educated economist previously working, among other things, in real estate, who had to collaborate with actors from the health sector in order to develop the technology.

study. All of the cases had high technological, social, cultural, communicational, and organizational distance. With respect to institutional distance, the seven PP cases possessed a high proportion of non-profit actors (universities, research centers, and hospitals), and the inclusion of four private NHT firms made the data more balanced in terms of institutional distance. Having a balanced sample of different distances made it easier to compare their influence across all the 11 cases. In addition to interviewing informants from the 11 cases, the managers of each network (PP and NHT) were interviewed, thus providing an overarching perspective of the phenomenon we studied.

The data from the 11 cases were collected through;

- Interviews with project managers and key participants in each of the 11 cases.
- Archival sources (webpages, publications in newspapers and journals and radio-interviews)
- Participant observation at a Norway Pumps and Pipes seminar series, two Norway Pumps and Pipes conferences (01.10.2015 and 04.11.2015), and two Norway Health Tech conferences (2016 and 2017).
- Media-files from one Norwegian Pumps and Pipes conference (01.10.2015).
- Interviews of managers in the Norwegian Pumps and Pipes association and the Norway Health Tech cluster.

All interviews followed a semi-structured approach, where the interviewees were asked broad questions from an interview guide. The interviewees were all given the following questions;

(1) Describe the project from the ideation phase to the present.
(2) How often did the involved actors meet?
(3) What is the educational backgrounds and work experiences of the involved actors?
(4) Explain differences between the involved actors/industries that affected the collaboration.
(5) How do you communicate across industry domains?
(6) What type of barriers affected the collaboration?
(7) Describe factors leading to these barriers.
(8) How, if ever, were the barriers overcome?

3.2. Data analysis

All interviews, in total 23, were audio-recorded and transcribed. The following data analysis was performed using the NVivo 11 software tool to structure and document the analysis process. To guide the analysis the following questions were used;

AQ1: What type of knowledge barriers were found, and what were the characteristics of these knowledge barriers?

AQ2: What type of relational distances were found in the cases?
AQ3: How did knowledge barriers relate to relational distances?
AQ4: What factors influenced knowledge barriers in a positive or negative direction?

The empirical data were analyzed according to grounded theory methodology as described by Gioia *et al.* [2013], from 1st order concepts, to 2nd order themes and 3rd order aggregated dimensions, see Fig. 2. The initial coding was based on both preset categories from informing literature (different relational distances, legitimacy, information conveyance, information convergence), and on induction of emerging themes. These initial codes constituted the 1st order concepts. Further, the 1st order concepts were aggregated into 2nd order themes and 3rd order dimensions following the framework by Gioia *et al.* [2013]. Both authors met on a regular basis to discuss coding and aggregations of codes.

The analysis was performed in the following steps: Firstly, addressing AQ1, the presence of semantic and pragmatic knowledge barriers were identified on the bases of Carlile's [2004] definitions of the terms. Secondly, addressing AQ2, the presence of high relational distances was identified based on their definitions in Table 2. Thirdly, to address AQ3, findings from the first and second step were cross-tabulated against each other. Fourth, influencing factors were identified by AQ4, and further categorized as to whether they influenced the knowledge transfer process in a positive or a negative manner. Finally, the findings from step 4 were cross-tabulated against identified barriers from step 1 and identified distances in step 2.

4. Findings and Discussion

The data analysis described in steps 1, 2, and 4 in Sec. 3.2 addressing analytical questions AQ1, AQ2, and AQ4 resulted in categories summarized in the data model shown in Fig. 2.

The results of the cross-tabulations performed in steps 3 and 5 are shown in Tables 3, 4, and 5. The figure in each cell indicates the number of occurrences that were found in the data that were coded as both the category stated in the row and the category stated in the column.

4.1. *Semantic and pragmatic barriers*

Semantic barriers included barriers emerging from a lack of shared meaning between cross-industry actors.

> *"They are unable to concretize what this means to us. What does this provides for us? We are failing to see the benefit gained for us here"*. (Medical actor describing lack of understanding about the project objective).

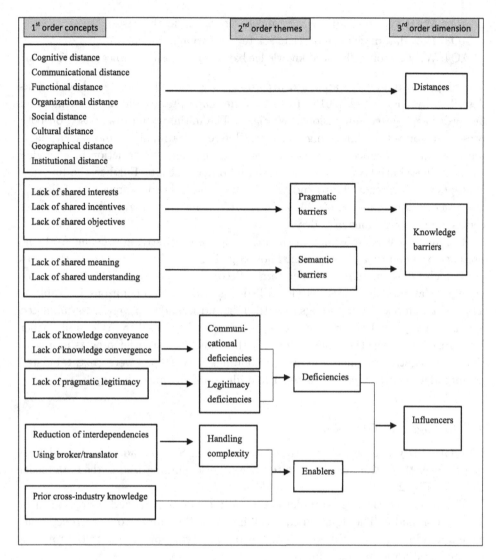

Fig. 2.   Data model. Results from the data analysis relative to the analytical questions.

The quote is in line with the semantic fuzziness boundary described by Rau *et al.* [2016], where actors are impeded by a lack of shared thought worlds.

Pragmatic barriers included barriers emerging from diverging interests, perspectives, and incentives and thus leading to a lack of shared consensus of the development process and project objectives among the involved actors.

Table 2.   Code descriptions of relational distances.

Distances	Defined in coding as
Cognitive distance	Differences in accumulated knowledge, like level of education
Communicational distance	Differences in professional languages
Functional distance	Differences in experiences and knowledge bases
Geographical distance	Physical distance between collaborative actors
Social distance	Lacking degree of social relationships and the amount of trust between actors.
Cultural distance	Differences in organizational cultures, like values and norms.
Organizational distance	Differences in organizational routines, practices and coordination of knowledge
Institutional distance	Whether organizations are commercial or non-commercial actors

Table 3.   Presence of relational distances versus knowledge barriers.

Distances versus knowledge barriers		
Relational distances	Pragmatic barriers	Semantic barriers
High cognitive distance	44	21
High communicational distance	20	22
High cultural distance	55	14
High functional distance	65	15
High geographical distance	4	0
High institutional distance	65	18
High organizational distance	28	3
High social distance	31	7

Table 4.   Presence of deficiencies versus knowledge barriers.

Deficiencies versus barriers		
Deficiencies	Pragmatic barriers	Semantic barriers
Lack of knowledge conveyance	34	36
Lack of knowledge convergence	81	23
Lack of Legitimacy	54	11

"*There are many (firms) that want to test their gadgets. They're not interested in finding out what people need. . . . And that's where we stand very differently. They have a gadget, and they want some justification for it, so they can sell it. While we have put it very high that we will first find out what people actually need*". (Medical actor about different interests leading to a lack of agreement of the development process).

This quote is associated with the pragmatic trajectory boundary, as described by Rau *et al.* [2016]. However, where trajectory boundaries within the study of Rau

Table 5.   Presence of deficiencies versus relational distances.

Distances	Distances versus deficiencies		
	Lack of knowledge conveyance	Lack of knowledge convergence	Lack of legitimacy
High cognitive distance	22	36	27
High communicational distance	20	18	7
High cultural distance	17	35	23
High functional distance	25	38	28
High geographical distance	0	2	2
High institutional distance	23	58	53
High organizational distance	7	15	13
High social distance	12	28	32

et al. [2016] were referred to as taking place at the intersection between traditional and new approaches, a trajectory boundary within a cross-industrial context would, as we see it, refer to the crossing of highly different methodological approaches and contextualized practices.

We found pragmatic barriers to account for the majority of knowledge barriers in cross-industry collaborations. Pragmatic barriers accounted for 157 instances in total, while semantic barriers accounted for 55 instances. As we know cross-industry actors to possess different professional languages, like medical and petroleum actors in the PP cases, we do not interpret the lower count of semantic barriers as an indication of shared language between the actors. From our understanding of the interviewees, we rather believe this finding indicates that semantic barriers were considered less influential for the joint collaboration, or were found easier to overcome by the actors. It is worthwhile to mention at this point, that all of the informants in this study held a high level of education, and hence could be expected to have good capabilities for developing abstractions and analogies. Abstractions and analogies have in previous research been found to be crucial for the transfer of knowledge between cross-industry actors [Gassmann and Zeschky (2008); Herstatt and Kalogerakis (2005); Kalogerakis *et al.* (2010)]. As exemplified by a manager in a PP case company using knowledge from the petroleum industry in order to develop an absorbent for medical suction devices:

> *"An oil reservoir is nothing more than a sponge that has absorbed oil"*.

4.2. *The influence of distances for knowledge barriers*

The second and third analytical questions concern the presence of relational distances within the cases and their influence for knowledge barriers.

As can be seen from Table 3, semantic barriers were mainly associated with high cognitive and communicational distances. From the definition of communicational distance in Table 2, its association to semantic barriers is apparent. The presence of high cognitive distance refers to a dissimilar way of interpreting new knowledge between the actors. Low levels of cognitive distance allow actors to communicate across knowledge domains, through the use of concepts, abstractions, and analogies understood by each other [Lyng and Brun (2018)]. In situations of high cognitive distance though, the results may be a loss of shared understanding, which can explain the association to semantic barriers.

Pragmatic barriers were found to be more affected by increased levels of relational distances, than what was the case for semantic barriers. As Table 3 shows, high institutional distance and high functional distance were found to be the distances most commonly associated with pragmatic knowledge barriers, followed by cultural distance. Both cultural and institutional distance affect organizational practices, interests, and incentives and can therefore explain their influence on pragmatic barriers. Functional distance was high in all cases. However, high functional distance constitutes a necessary precondition of CII. If there is no functional distance, the collaboration is not cross-industry. In our analysis we have therefore considered functional distance as an underlying precondition rather than a variable, and have therefore excluded it from our further analysis.

Cross-industry collaborations are exposed to increased levels of relational distances between actors. Increased levels of functional distance, which refers to differences in knowledge bases and present in all of our cross-industry cases, will introduce differences in thought worlds (cognitive distance) and in professional languages (communicational distance). Both cognitive and communicational distance are influential for the development of shared understanding among actors and are thus associated with sematic barriers. As argued before, cognitive distance between cross-industry actors may still be low, even in cross-industry settings, based on equivalent levels of education, providing similar ways of understanding new knowledge.

Differences in thought worlds and languages are based on contextual dimensions of social, cultural and organizational character. By working together people develop contextual practices, relationships and organizational cultures in order to establish a sense of belonging and the allowance of efficient coordination. As knowledge becomes internalized into practices and relationships, differences in these contextual dimensions will result in pragmatic barriers. Hence, cross-industry collaborations introduce an increased level in relational distances, where both semantic and pragmatic barriers are encountered.

From our findings, we propose a framework for the management of knowledge across boundaries in CII, shown in Fig. 3. In the following, we will use the framework to guide the discussion of our findings.

The lowest level in Fig. 3, the intra-organizational level, corresponds to the framework proposed by Carlile [2004] shown in Fig. 1, where actors work together and transfer knowledge for innovation across occupational communities *within an organization*. Organizational, social, functional, and cultural distances will be low

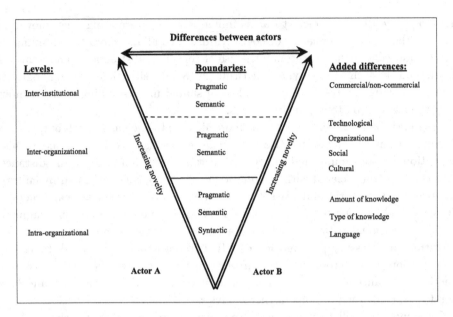

Fig. 3.   Framework for the management of knowledge across boundaries in CII.

among actors collaborating within a firm. The area of the model above the horizontal solid line represents the contextual setting where knowledge transfer takes place *across company and industry borders*. The portion between the solid and the dotted horizontal lines represents innovation collaborations across organizations from different knowledge domains, but within the same institutional category, i.e. either between non-commercial or between commercial actors. The differences present among the actors *accumulates* as the novelty increases, meaning that at the inter-institutional level (i.e. the area above the dotted horizontal line in Fig. 3) the actors are influenced by commercial/non-commercial differences in addition to the differences taking place at the level below (cognitive, communicational, cultural, organizational, functional, social). Hence, when collaborations takes place at a higher level within the model, actors are affected by accumulated levels of differences due to increasing relational distances.

4.2.1. *Inter-organizational level*

Moving from the intra-organizational level up to the inter-organizational level, where actors from foreign industries collaborate for innovation, new distances will be introduced and become influential for the collaboration.

Organizational distance refers to differences in practices, routines, and the co-ordination of knowledge. Between actors from for instance petroleum and medicine, there will be many organizational differences in practices, methodology, and routines. An element influenced by organizational distance is the way actors make and accept simplifications and assumptions. Petroleum actors tended to hold a system perspective (e.g. focus at forces taking place at the system level), while the medical actors based their perspective at the micro-level (e.g. focus on organ level, or patient cases). These different perspectives led to a lack of consensus in terms of inherent simplifications and assumptions among the actors, as explained in this quote by a petroleum researcher;

> "*They are living systems, and they can fit into equations, but they never fit 100%. So one has to make some assumptions, which is something many biologists are reluctant to accept. There will always be some simplifications. However, they (the biologists) accept all the simplifications they do at the lab. For instance when they grow cancer cells separately, it may not necessarily provide precise understanding of how the cancer cells will behave in the body*".

As people work together, they form organizational cultures, which will influence the way actors act and understand new knowledge, practice and methodologies. Actors in foreign industries will — based on different organizational cultures — have different values and norms concerning the development process and the project objectives. The gap in organizational cultures was found to hamper the collaboration in terms of the understanding of roles, risk and responsibilities, as the quote beneath exemplifies.

> "*We met an industry which is controlled by a lot of fixed borders, one way of thinking, and the fact that one hour is worth XX Norwegian kroner, no matter what*". (Medical PP case company about their collaborative petroleum industry partner).

Unfamiliarity with the actors, knowledge, and industry leads to high social distance. As both counterparts were experts within their own knowledge domain but novices in their counterparts' knowledge, the issue of being considered legitimate was crucial for social ties to develop. We will return to a further discussion on the issue of legitimacy in Sec. 4.4.2.

Organizational, cultural, and social distances are additional differences coming into play when extending the crossing of boundaries to include foreign industries, and were found strongly associated with pragmatic barriers, see Table 3. Even if geographical distance is found beneficial for knowledge transfer in other studies, the geographical dimension was not found to be associated with knowledge barriers in this context. Geographical distance is not a specific characteristic of CII. In these cases some actors from the two collaborating industries were located relatively nearby each other, like in the same city, while others were located in different cities. Hence, the spatial aspect did not — in this study — reflect cross-industry differences between actors.

Our findings align with those of Liu and Ma [2019], who found the process of RI to be facilitated in settings of low geographical distance but high technological distance between interacting firms.

Cognitive and communicational distances are described in the framework by Carlile [2004] and thus present even at the intra-organizational levels. However, when moving up to the inter-organizational level, both cognitive and communicational distances will be enlarged as novelty and differences increase when moving upwards within in Fig. 3.

4.2.2. *Inter-institutional level*

Moving further up to the inter-institutional level of the model, actors are exposed to high institutional distance in addition to the relational distances encountered at the lower levels. Crossing borders between commercial and non-commercial actors introduces additional barriers. This additional burden of high institutional distance for cross-industry collaborations, already having many knowledge barriers to deal with, where reflected in a particularly high occurrence of pragmatic barriers, as can be seen from Table 3. Infusing high institutional distance into an already strained collaboration, having high communicational, social, organizational, and cultural distances between actors, was difficult to handle simultaneously for the cases involved in this situation. Literature of university-industry collaborations reports high levels of uncertainty to be characteristic for these types of collaborations. Similarly, the cases working at inter-institutional level within this study were affected by high levels of uncertainty from many sources, as actors were new to each other, new to the knowledge domain, and new to the organizational industrial context of their counterpart. The extra uncertainty infused by high institutional distance therefore resulted in difficulties in the development of shared interests and the motivation for engagement.

> "*There are huge differences in culture between different industries. Especially when it comes to academia and industry. This is because the incentives are so very different, which means that the motivation is also very different*". (Commercial actor about collaborating with academia).

Gomes *et al.* [2005] argue that the gap of institutional logic between commercial and non-commercial organizations is difficult to manage in the development process. In their words: "Because the aims differ, the means to achieve them are also different" (p. 89). Consequently, high institutional distance may result in diverging interests and incentives between the actors, which further results in divergent perspectives for reaching the goal. Diverging methodology and processes are closely related to pragmatic barriers [Carlile (2004)] and can therefore explain the prominent role of high institutional distance in our findings. As illustrated in two quotes

from medical non-commercial researchers about challenges taking place in collaborations with commercial petroleum industry counterparts;

> *"A research process is not just like sitting in a meeting saying
> 'Great, let's do this — when can we come to the nursing home and
> do the testing? That's not how it works — it's something about
> understanding the process we need to go through"* (Medical actor
> about different understanding of the developing process with their
> industry partner).

> *"To me, we are not developing something together. It's not based on
> an order from me like; I need this and this. It's more as if they have
> some competences and an idea, and that they want to enter a
> market. So they will develop a solution, and then provide it to us"*...
> (Medical actor about the collaboration with their industry partner).

The non-commercial medical actors in our cases expressed a high emphasis on
fulfilling a user's (often a patient's) need. Their way of organizing projects followed a
bottom-up approach, in contrast to the industry actors who focused on system
compatibility and world-wide solutions. This micro and macro-level approach
affected these cases to a great extend in terms of methodology, time perspectives,
and the overall project objectives. Described in this quote by a petroleum actor;

> *"Our challenge as a company is that when we are coming up with
> ideas and new concepts; then we are thinking; this is for everyone.
> Later we look at the individual level. Things are often produced for
> the entire world. But they (the medical actors) are doing it the
> opposite way. They start at the individual level, which is not always
> easy for us to do if we are working with a concept or a part of
> technology. We can't always work like that, as it may lead us to
> distortion from the first step"*

Knowledge barriers arising from high institutional distance were considered to be
difficult to cross for both commercial firms collaborating with non-commercial
actors, and oppositely, non-commercial actors found it difficult to collaborate with
commercial firms.

4.3. Interdependencies of distances

Although we defined our categories of relational distances to be as distinct and
separable as possible, we still saw in our findings that a situation representing one
type of distance would also represent another type of distance, and lead to both
semantic and pragmatic barriers. Accordingly, many of the exemplary quotes we
have displayed in the discussion above refer to more than one single distance category. For example, in the quotes given above from informants in cases with high

institutional distance, we also see indications of differences in culture and norms (implying cultural distance), differences in process understanding (i.e. different routines and practices, implying organizational distance), and differences in thinking (implying cognitive differences).

This overlapping characteristic of relational distances in the context of inter-organizational collaboration is discussed comprehensively by Knoben and Oerlemans [2006]. Thus, although a specific type of distance will influence the knowledge transfer process and give rise to a knowledge barrier, it may also contribute to another type of distance, which in turn also affects the knowledge transfer process. The types of relational distances are thus interdependent. Hence as one moves upwards towards increasing novelty along the axes in our model in Fig. 3, the increase in the various types of relational distances between the cross-industry actors leads to a compounded complexity and an increase in the required effort of collaboration, in accordance with Carlile's [2004] argument at the intra-organizational level.

4.4. *Deficiencies*

Knowledge barriers in cross-industry collaborations were found to be negatively affected by two categories of antagonists: communication deficiencies (lack of knowledge conveyance and lack of knowledge convergence), and legitimacy deficiencies.

4.4.1. *Communication deficiencies*

Lack of knowledge conveyance was found to be associated with both semantic and pragmatic barriers, see Table 4. However, for semantic barriers, lack of knowledge conveyance was seen more frequently. In particular, we found that most semantic barriers were associated with the lack of knowledge conveyance about the project objective (e.g. product) and the project application (e.g. who will use it, and for what?). Thus, in cross-industry collaborations, actors need to develop a shared understanding of the outcome of the project and its application in order to overcome semantic barriers.

Lack of knowledge convergence clearly displays, from Table 4, an association to pragmatic barriers. The strong relatedness with pragmatic barriers displays obstacles involved when attempting to converge different knowledge in situations of diverging dimensions of interests, practices, and incentives.

Concerning the association between different relational distances and deficiencies, shown in Table 5, the findings again display how high institutional distance in settings of cross-industrial innovation is highly associated with lack of convergence and lack of legitimacy. Lack of convergence and lack of legitimacy may thus be mutually reinforcing dimensions for these contexts. If there is lack of legitimacy between the actors, the actors are less likely to converge new knowledge from their "non-legitimate" counterpart with their own situated knowledge. In settings of high institutional distance this is especially clear when medical actors view their commercial actor's commercial incentives as non-legitimate for their focus of fulfilling the patient's needs. Their interests for engagement into the collaboration would thus end up divergent.

4.4.2. *Legitimacy deficiencies*

Legitimacy deficiencies, as a category of antagonists, emerged from the *in-vivo* coding, and was found to be associated with pragmatic barriers. Our analysis rests on Suchman's [1995] concept of pragmatic legitimacy, which "rests on the self-interested calculations of an organization's most immediate audiences" [Suchman (1995, p. 578)]. It implies that an actor will only perceive their collaboration partner as legitimate if they consider the other actor as a useful contributor to meet the actor's own strategic self-interests.

The process of transforming knowledge into practice is time and resource intensive, making people reluctant to change their skills and practical competence. In order for actors to change their hard-won competences and be "novices" in a new knowledge domain, their "teachers" needed to be perceived as legitimate. As expressed by an interviewee:

> "...because the collaboration can't turn into a relationship if you all the time need to convince your counterpart that you are good enough".

Further, the quotes in Sec. 4.2.2 exemplify situations where the actors expressed concerns that their collaboration partners did not share their strategic interests in terms of objectives or processes to be followed, hence considered them less useful as knowledge contributors, i.e. as less legitimate partners. Legitimacy is thus an important dimension in CII in order to get access to knowledge resources and for the development of engagement among actors.

4.5. *Enablers*

According to the fourth analytical question, we found three factors to be facilitative.

4.5.1. *Reducing interdependencies*

Carlile [2004] states that by reducing the level of dependencies between the involved actors, present differences will be of less consequence. Accordingly, the act of reducing interdependencies between the actors was found in our study to be a way of transcending knowledge barriers in the cross-industry collaborations. As the CEO of a med-tech firm in our sample expressed:

> *"You do not involve economic issues into academia. You do not burden researchers with time and cost. You just allow every group to contribute with the part that they're best at."*

By separating divergent interests and incentives caused by institutional gaps, cross-industry actors were able to provide pieces of the puzzle without the need for developing full consensus among everyone involved. This way of coordinating CII collaborations is especially useful in temporary settings, as the act of developing consensus takes time. However, by reducing the dependencies, one also reduces the level of learning, which would be important for engagement in future collaborations.

4.5.2. *The use of knowledge brokers*

A second way of knowledge transfer facilitation that was found, was the engaging of a knowledge broker, who could understand both parties and be responsible for communication across boundaries.

> *"We are lucky to have a good mixture of resources in the company. So, we use academic resources against academic resources. To make sure they speak the same language and to eliminate some friction".* (CEO of Med Tech firm explains how they communicate across low institutional distance).

Some of the cases already included employees with knowledge about both industries, as the quote above explains, other cases decided to hire new employees with knowledge broker competence, to ensure more efficient transfer of knowledge between the parties.

As discussed earlier, complexity increases with increasing amount of differences between the actors involved in CII. The two enablers described above coincide well with the two responses that Zack [2001] recommends to manage complexity; either (1) reduce the level of complexity by decomposition, thus reducing inter-dependencies, or (2) increase the organization's capacity to process the complexity.

Bessant and Trifilova's [2017] study on RI has also cited examples of innovations in the medical field through application of ideas from unrelated fields (e.g. from fast food to cataract care and from printer technology to electrocardiography). They too, highlight the importance of brokers acting as translators between the interacting fields, arguing that they hold an important boundary-spanning role.

4.5.3. *Prior knowledge*

Prior knowledge and experiences of cross-industry collaborations are found in previous literature to be favorable for future collaborations. Enkel and Bader [2016] found prior knowledge and experiences with cross-industry collaborations to raise experts' intentions for engaging in future settings of similar type. Similarly,

Edmondson and Harvey [2018] found actors with experience in collaborating with cross-disciplinary and cross-functional teams "to be more capable of transferring, translating and transforming knowledge across syntactic, semantic, or pragmatic boundaries" (pp. 353–354). Hence, participation within cross-disciplinary/functional teams provides learning of boundary crossing. In the context of RI, Subramanian and Soh [2017] found that the relationship between technological diversity and breadth of RI was strengthened by the presence of explorative experience among partners in alliance portfolios.

On a different account, the communities of practice literature highlights the importance of prior knowledge as it increases the level of shared meanings among the involved individuals, by engaging in similar activities [Brown and Duguid (1991); Carlile (2004); Lave and Wenger (1991)].

Prior cross-industry experience was found in our data to be important for future willingness to engage in cross-industry collaborations. Possessing cross-industry knowledge and experience makes the actors aware of likely barriers, which are usually easier to handle if known in advance, and most important, if the actors are aware of the innovation potential.

> *"I don't think it depends on the specific industry, but rather if they have been participating in different arenas before. Then they are more accommodating, because they have seen it before. It's not so much the work experience or the education. It's more about the (cross-industry) experiences they have. Have they worked with a lot of projects and discovered the opportunities out there?"* (Medical actor about the process of finding collaborative partners in different industry domains).

5. Conclusion

This study was undertaken in order to provide a deeper understanding of knowledge barriers in CII. In particular we wanted to develop a better understanding of knowledge barriers when relational distances of various types between collaborative partners increase.

The informants in our study referred more frequently to the presence of pragmatic barriers than semantic barriers in their cross-industry collaborations. Semantic barriers can be transcended by non-traversing techniques [Lyng and Brun (2018)] like analogies and scaffolds [Enkel and Gassmann (2010); Gassmann and Zeschky (2008); Kalogerakis *et al.* (2010); Majchrzak *et al.* (2012)], techniques that can be systemized and learned. Pragmatic barriers encountered in CII are however more challenging to overcome, since they are compounded by a multitude of social, organizational and institutional factors resulting from a variety of interacting distances, leading to more difficult negotiations of different interests, perspectives, and incentives. The development of shared consensus is resource demanding, and relies on the actors' willingness to engage their efforts into the negotiations. Effort increases when moving towards increased novelty and increasing relational distances. Hence moving from intra-organizational to inter-organizational collaborations requires more effort and becomes more challenging for the actors, and even more so when moving further to the inter-institutional level.

Two categories of factors were found to hamper knowledge transfer at inter-organizational and inter-institutional levels; legitimacy deficiencies and communicational deficiencies. In terms of overcoming knowledge barriers in CII the analysis revealed three types of enablers; reduction of interdependencies (decomposition of complexity), increasing the organization's capacity to handle complexity by the use of knowledge brokers, and presence of prior cross-industry knowledge.

A more profound understanding of knowledge barriers in CII is an important step for succeeding with cross-industrial collaborations. The results from this study provide contributions of both theoretical and practical nature.

5.1. *Theoretical contributions*

This research contributes to a deeper understanding of knowledge barriers in cross-industry collaborations.

Firstly, our findings expand the framework by Carlile [2004] and the boundary spanning literature to include innovation collaborations of a cross-industry character. Our study also provides a better understanding of types and roles of relational distances that occur in CII. We found the majority of knowledge barriers in CII to be of a pragmatic nature, which Carlile [2004] argue is caused by raised levels of novelty, differences and dependences between actors. Most of the literature describing knowledge barriers in terms of knowledge sharing do so with a focus at the syntactic boundary, and research addressing semantic and pragmatic barriers have been called for [Rau et al. (2012, 2016)]. This research contributes to that end, by exploring semantic and pragmatic barriers and their relatedness to relational distances. We have also expanded the understanding of the concept of "differences" in knowledge management across boundaries, which in Carlile's [2004] framework refers to differences in the amount or the type of knowledge between collaborating actors. This research shows that differences of many other types (organizational, cultural, social, and institutional) become prominent in CII and lead to pragmatic and semantic barriers as well as increased complexity for the collaboration.

Secondly, our research also extends CII literature to include understanding of different knowledge barriers at the micro-level in CII collaborations. So far, CII literature has mainly studied the early phases of innovation. Our research points to barriers that need to be transcended so one can proceed in the innovation process.

Thirdly, our findings contribute to the literature on relational distances in innovation, by expanding its predominant regional geographic focus to also show the relevance of relational distances on innovation at organizational level.

And finally, our finding that high institutional distance leads to particularly challenging pragmatic barriers in cross-industry collaborations, expands current understanding in literature on university-industry innovation collaboration.

5.2. *Practical implications*

Our research also provides practical implications for managers who arrange or facilitate cross-industry collaborations for innovation.

As the majority of knowledge barriers in cross-industry collaborations are found to be pragmatic barriers, managers should hold a focus on converging and negotiating different and conflicting interests and incentives between actors.

Legitimacy was found to be a highly influential dimension for pragmatic barriers. Managers should therefore seek to develop legitimacy between cross-industry actors, by consciously selecting project participants who are highly capable of understanding and accommodating their collaboration partners' strategic needs.

As high institutional distance is highly associated with pragmatic barriers in cross-industry collaborations, managers need to carefully manage the complexity introduced in this setting, so that the total sum of barriers is not overwhelming. One strategy for doing is to reduce interdependencies with actors of high institutional distance, for example by assembling mainly non-commercial actors in a precommercial research phase, and then involve commercial actors only later in a commercial phase. A second strategy is to make use of knowledge brokers.

As prior cross-industry knowledge and experience is found to facilitate willingness for engagement, managers should increase their employees' level of prior knowledge by engaging them in cross-industry conferences, workshops, and collaborations.

5.3. *Limitations and future research*

The limitations of this exploratory study are based on weaknesses of qualitative research concerning generalizability and validity. Our empirical cases are focused on cross-industry transfer between actors coming from foreign industries, and includes medical actors in all of the cases. In order to increase the generalizability the findings from this study, the phenomenon should be studied in other cross-industry contexts. Also, the use of multiple case study methodology does not provide direct cause-and-effect relationships. Consequently, we encourage further studies to undertake a quantitative approach containing large-N surveys to study cause-effect relations and increase the generalizability of our findings.

Due to the importance of high institutional distance for knowledge barriers in cross-industry collaborations we also claim a need for further studies of knowledge barriers in settings of high institutional distances. Finally, as the different relational distance definitions are overlapping, future efforts should be made to develop more unambiguous definitions better suited for studies at different levels and for different methodologies.

References

Antonio Messeni, P., Vito, A. and Nunzia, C. (2007). Technology districts: Proximity and knowledge access. *Journal of Knowledge Management*, **11**, 5: 98–114. doi: 10.1108/13673270710819834.

Balland, P. A. (2012). Proximity and the evolution of collaboration networks: Evidence from research and development projects within the global navigation satellite system (GNSS) industry. *Regional Studies*, **46**, 6: 741–756.

Bechky, B. A. (2003). Sharing meaning across occupational communities: The transformation of understanding on a production floor. *Organization Science*, **14**, 3: 312–330. doi: 10.1287/orsc.14.3.312.15162.

Berends, H., Garud, R., Debackere, K. and Weggeman, M. (2011). Thinking along: A process for tapping into knowledge across boundaries. *International Journal of Technology Management*, **53**, 1: 69–88.

Bessant, J. and Trifilova, A. (2017). Developing absorptive capacity for recombinant innovation. *Business Process Management Journal*, **23**, 6: 1094–1107.

Bjerregaard, T. (2010). Industry and academia in convergence: Micro-institutional dimensions of R&D collaboration. *Technovation*, **30**, 2: 100–108.

Bloedon, R. V. and Stokes, D. R. (1994). Making university/industry collaborative research succeed. *J Research-Technology Management*, **37**, 2: 44–48.

Boland, R. J. and Tenkasi, R. V. (1995). Perspective making and perspective taking in communities of knowing. *Organization Science*, **6**, 4: 350–372.

Boschma, R. (2005). Proximity and innovation: A critical assessment. *Regional Studies*, **39**, 1: 61–74. doi: 10.1080/0034340052000320887.

Brown, J. S. and Duguid, P. (1991). Organizational learning and communities-of-practice: Toward a unified view of working, learning, and innovation. *Organization Science*, **2**, 1: 40–57.

Bruneel, J., d'Este, P. and Salter, A. (2010). Investigating the factors that diminish the barriers to university–industry collaboration. *Research Policy*, **39**, 7: 858–868.

Brunswicker, S. and Hutschek, U. (2010). Crossing horizons: Leveraging cross-industry innovation search in the front-end of the innovation process. *International Journal of Innovation Management*, **14**, 4: 683–702. doi: 10.1142/S1363919610002829.

Bunduchi, R. (2017). Legitimacy-seeking mechanisms in product innovation: A qualitative study. *Journal of Product Innovation Management*, **34**, 3: 315–342.

Cambridge Dictionary (2018). Available at https://dictionary.cambridge.org/dictionary/english/. Accessed date: 16.10.2019.

Carlile, P. R. (2002). A pragmatic view of knowledge and boundaries: Boundary objects in new product development. *Organization Science*, **13**, 4: 442–455.

Carlile, P. R. (2004). Transferring, translating, and transforming: An integrative framework for managing knowledge across boundaries. *Organization Science*, **15**, 5: 555–568.

Carlile, P. R. and Rebentisch, E. S. (2003). Into the black box: The knowledge transformation cycle. *Management Science*, **49**, 9: 1180–1195.

Daft, R. L., Lengel, R. H. and Trevino, L. K. (1987). Message equivocality, media selection, and manager performance: Implications for information systems. *MIS Quarterly*, **11**, 355–366.

Dennis, A. R., Fuller, R. M. and Valacich, J. S. (2008). Media, tasks, and communication processes: A theory of media synchronicity. *MIS Quarterly*, **32**, 3: 575–600.

Dingler, A. and Enkel, E. (2016). Socialization and innovation: Insights from collaboration across industry boundaries. *Technological Forecasting & Social Change*, **109**, 50–60.

Dougherty, D. (1992). Interpretive barriers to successful product innovation in large firms. *Organization Science*, **3**, 2: 179–202.

Dougherty, D. and Dunne, D. D. (2012). Digital science and knowledge boundaries in complex innovation. *Organization Science*, **23**, 5: 1467–1484. doi: 10.1287/orsc.1110.0700.

Edenius, M., Keller, C. and Lindblad, S. (2010). Managing knowledge across boundaries in healthcare when innovation is desired. *Knowlwdge Management & E-learning. An International Journal*, **2**, 2: 134–153.

Edmondson, A. C. and Harvey, J.-F. (2018). Cross-boundary teaming for innovation: Integrating research on teams and knowledge in organizations. *Human Resource Management Review*, **28**, 4: 347–360.

Eisenhardt, K. M. (1989). Building theories from case study research. *The Academy of Management Review*, **14**, 4: 532–550.

Elfner, L. E., Falk-Krzesinski, H. J., Sullivan, K. O., Velkey, A., Illman, D. L., Baker, J. and Pita-Szczesniewski, A. (2011). Heaving walls & melding silos. *American Scientist*, **99**, 6: 1–8.

Enkel, E. and Bader, K. (2016). Why do experts contribute in cross-industry innovation? A structural model of motivational factors, intention and behavior. *R&D Management*, **46**, S1: 207–226. doi: 10.1111/radm.12132.

Enkel, E. and Gassmann, O. (2010). Creative imitation: Exploring the case of cross-industry innovation. *R&D Management*, **40**, 3: 256–270.

Enkel, E., Groemminger, A. and Heil, S. (2017). Managing technological distance in internal and external collaborations: Absorptive capacity routines and social integration for innovation. *The Journal of Technology Transfer*, **43**: 1257–1290.

Enkel, E. and Heil, S. (2014). Preparing for distant collaboration: Antecedents to potential absorptive capacity in cross-industry innovation. *Technovation*, **34**, 4: 242–260. doi: 10.1016/j.technovation.2014.01.010.

Enkel, E., Heil, S., Hengstler, M. and Wirth, H. (2017). Exploratory and exploitative innovation: To what extent do the dimensions of individual level absorptive capacity contribute? *Technovation*, **60**: 29–38.

Etzkowitz, H. (2008). *The Triple Helix: University-Industry-Government Innovation in Action*. Routledge, New York, NY.

Etzkowitz, H. and Leydesdorff, L. (2000). The dynamics of innovation: From National Systems and "Mode 2" to a Triple Helix of university–industry–government relations. *Research Policy*, **29**, 2: 109–123.

Fitjar, R. D., Huber, F. and Rodríguez-Pose, A. (2016). Not too close, not too far: Testing the Goldilocks principle of 'optimal' distance in innovation networks. *Industry and Innovation*, **23**, 6: 465–487. doi: 10.1080/13662716.2016.1184562.

Gassmann, O., Daiber, M. and Enkel, E. (2011). The role of intermediaries in cross-industry innovation processes. *R&D Management*, **41**, 5: 457–469. doi: 10.1111/j.1467-9310.2011.00651.x.

Gassmann, O. and Zeschky, M. (2008). Opening up the solution space: The role of analogical thinking for breakthrough product innovation. *Creativity and Innovation Management*, **17**, 2: 97–106.

Gassmann, O., Zeschky, M., Wolff, T. and Stahl, M. (2010). Crossing the industry-line: Breakthrough innovation through cross-industry alliances with 'non-suppliers'. *Long Range Planning*, **43**, 5–6: 639–654.

Gertler, M. S. (2003). Tacit knowledge and the economic geography of context, or the undefinable tacitness of being (there). *Journal of Economic Geography*, **3**, 1: 75–99.

Gioia, D. A., Corley, K. G. and Hamilton, A. L. (2013). Seeking qualitative rigor in inductive research. *Organizational Research Methods*, **16**, 1: 15–31. doi: 10.1177/1094428112452151.

Gomes, J. F., Hurmelinna, P., Amaral, V. and Blomqvist, K. (2005). Managing relationships of the republic of science and the kingdom of industry. *Journal of Workplace Learning*, **17**, 1/2: 88–98.

Granovetter, M. (1985). Economic action and social structure: The problem of embeddedness. *American Journal of Sociology*, **91**, 3: 481–510.

Gregor, S. (2006). The nature of theory in information systems. *MIS Quarterly*, **30**, 3: 611–642.

Griffith, R., Lee, S. and Straathof, B. (2017). Recombinant innovation and the boundaries of the firm. *International Journal of Industrial Organization*, **50**: 34–56. doi: 10.1016/j.ijindorg.2016.10.005.

Guan, J. C. and Yan, Y. (2016). Technological proximity and recombinative innovation in the alternative energy field. *Research Policy*, **45**, 7: 1460–1473. doi: 10.1016/j.respol.2016.05.002.

Hacklin, F. and Wallin, M. W. (2013). Convergence and interdisciplinarity in innovation management: A review, critique, and future directions. *The Service Industries Journal*, **33**, 7–8: 774–788.

Haider, S. and Mariotti, F. (2010). Filling knowledge gaps: Knowledge sharing across inter-firm boundaries and occupational communities. *International Journal of Knowledge Management Studies*, **4**, 1: 1.

Hansen, M. T. (1999). The search-transfer problem: The role of weak ties in sharing knowledge across organization subunits. *Administrative Science Quarterly*, **44**, 1: 82–111. doi: 10.2307/2667032.

Heil, S. and Enkel, E. (2015). Exercising opportunities for cross-industry innovation: How to support absorptive capacity in distant knowledge processing. *International Journal of Innovation Management*, **19**, 5: 1550048.

Herstatt, C. and Kalogerakis, K. (2005). How to use analogies for breakthrough innovations. *International Journal of Innovation and Technology Management*, **2**, 3: 331–347. doi: 10.1142/S0219877005000538.

Holland, D. and Quinn, N. (1987). *Cultural Models in Language and Thought*, Cambridge University Press, Cambridge.

Jansen, J. J., Van Den Bosch, F. A. and Volberda, H. W. (2005). Managing potential and realized absorptive capacity: How do organizational antecedents matter? *Academy of Managament Journal*, **48**, 6: 999–1015.

Kalogerakis, K., Lüthje, C. and Herstatt, C. (2010). Developing innovations based on analogies: Experience from design and engineering consultants. *Journal of Product Innovation Management*, **27**, 3: 418–436. doi: 10.1111/j.1540-5885.2010.00725.x.

Knoben, J. and Oerlemans, L. (2006). Proximity and inter-organizational collaboration: A literature review. *International Journal of Management Reviews*, **8**: 71–89.

Lave, J. and Wenger, E. (1991). *Situated Learning: Legitimate Peripheral Participation*, Cambridge University Press, Cambridge.

Leonard, D. (1995). *Wellsprings of Knowledge: Building and Sustaining the Sources of Innovation*, Harvard Business School Press, Boston.

Liu, J. and Ma, T. (2019). Innovative performance with interactions between technological proximity and geographic proximity: Evidence from China electronics patents. *Technology Analysis & Strategic Management*, **31**, 6: 667–679. doi: 10.1080/09537325.2018.1542672.

Lyng, H. B. and Brun, E. C. (2018). Knowledge transition: A conceptual model of knowledge transfer for cross-industry innovation. *International Journal of Innovation and Technology Management*, **15**, 5: 23. doi: 10.1142/S0219877018500438.

Majchrzak, A., Cooper, L. P. and Neece, O. E. (2004). Knowledge reuse for innovation. *Management Science*, **50**, 2: 174–188. doi: 10.1287/mnsc.1030.0116.

Majchrzak, A., More, P. and Faraj, S. (2012). Transcending knowledge differences in cross-functional teams. *Organization Science*, **23**, 4: 951–970.

McDermott, R. and O'dell, C. (2001). Overcoming cultural barriers to sharing knowledge. *Journal of Knowledge Management*, **5**, 1: 76–85.

Nooteboom, B., Van Haverbeke, W., Duysters, G., Gilsing, V. and van den Oord, A. (2007). Optimal cognitive distance and absorptive capacity. *Research Policy*, **36**, 7: 1016–1034. doi: 10.1016/j.respol.2007.04.003.

Parjanen, S., Melkas, H. and Outila, T. (2011). Distances, knowledge brokerage and absorptive capacity in enhancing regional innovativeness: A qualitative case study of Lahti Region, Finland. *European Planning Studies*, **19**, 6: 29.

Ponds, R., Van Oort, F. and Frenken, K. (2007). The geographical and institutional proximity of research collaboration. *Papers in Regional Science*, **86**, 3: 423–443.

Rau, C., Möslein, K. M. and Neyer, A.-K. (2016). Playing possum, hide-and-seek, and other behavioral patterns: Knowledge boundaries at newly emerging interfaces. *R&D Management*, **46**, 2: 341–353. doi: 10.1111/radm.12185.

Rau, C., Neyer, A.-K. and Möslein, K. M. (2012). Innovation practices and their boundary-crossing mechanisms: A review and proposals for the future. *Technology Analysis & Strategic Management*, **24**, 2: 181–217. doi: 10.1080/09537325.2012.647647.

Somech, A. and Khalaili, A. (2014). Team boundary activity: Its mediating role in the relationship between structural conditions and team innovation. *Group & Organization Management*, **39**, 3: 274–299. doi: 10.1177/1059601114525437.

Subramanian, A. M. and Soh, P.-H. (2017). Linking alliance portfolios to recombinant innovation: The combined effects of diversity and alliance experience. *Long Range Planning*, **50**, 5: 636–652. doi: 10.1016/j.lrp.2016.11.001.

Suchman, M. C. (1995). Managing legitimacy: Strategic and institutional approaches. *Academy of Management Review*, **20**, 3: 571–610. doi: 10.5465/AMR.1995.9508080331.

Torre, A. (2008). On the role played by temporary geographical proximity in knowledge transmission. *Regional Studies*, **42**, 6: 869–889. doi: 10.1080/00343400801922814.

Volberda, H. W., Foss, N. J. and Lyles, M. A. (2010). Absorbing the concept of absorptive capacity: How to realize its potential in the organization field. *Organization Science*, **21**, 4: 931–951.

Wenger, E. (1998). *Communities of Practice: Learning, Meaning, and Identity*, Cambridge University Press, Cambridge.

Wilson, D. O. and Ettlie, J. E. (2018). Boundary spanning, group heterogeneity and engineering project performance. *International Journal of Innovation and Technology Management*, **15**, 6: 35.

Yin, R. K. (1994). *Case Study Research: Design and Methods* (2nd ed.), Sage Publications, Newbury Park, CA.

Zack, M. H. (2001). If managing knowledge is the solution, then what's the problem? *Knowledge Management and Business Model Innovation*, ed. Y.Malhotra. Idea Group Publishing, London, pp. 16–36.

Biography

Hilda Bø Lyng is a postdoctoral researcher at the Department of Quality and Health Technology, Faculty of Health Sciences at the University of Stavanger (UiS). She holds an MSc and a PhD in Industrial Economics from the University of

Stavanger. Her PhD thesis focuses on enabling mechanisms and barriers for knowledge transfer in cross-industry innovation.

Eric Christian Brun is a Professor of Innovation Management at the Department of Safety, Economics and Planning, Faculty of Science and Technology at the University of Stavanger (UiS). He holds an MSc in Medical Technology and a PhD in Innovation Management, both from NTNU — the Norwegian University of Science and Technology. Prior to joining UiS, he has worked both in the petroleum industry and in the medical device industry.

Printed in the United States
by Baker & Taylor Publisher Services